THE TRANSFORMATION OF THE CLASSICAL HERITAGE
Peter Brown, General Editor

GUARDIANS OF LANGUAGE:
THE GRAMMARIAN AND SOCIETY IN LATE ANTIQUITY

ROBERT A. KASTER

Guardians of Language: The Grammarian and Society in Late Antiquity

UNIVERSITY OF CALIFORNIA PRESS
Berkeley • Los Angeles • London

The publication of this book was made possible in part by a grant from the National Endowment for the Humanities.

University of California Press
Berkeley and Los Angeles, California
University of California Press, Ltd.
London, England

© 1988 by
The Regents of the University of California

Library of Congress Cataloging-in-Publication Data

Kaster, Robert A.
  Guardians of language.

    Bibliography: p.
    Includes index.
    1. Classical languages—Grammar—Study and teaching—Rome—History. 2. Education, Ancient 3. Education—Rome—History. 4. Language teachers—Rome. 5. Sociolinguistics—Rome. I. Title. II. Series.
PA53.K37 1986   870'.07   85-8593
ISBN 0-520-05535-7 (alk. paper)

Printed in the United States of America

1 2 3 4 5 6 7 8 9

PARENTIBVS OPTIMIS CONIVGIQVE CARISSIMAE

CONTENTS

PREFACE

The ideas that shape this book came together gradually over some seven years; but they found their initial stimulus in two specific sources. There was, first, the commonly observed truth that the late-antique schools of grammar and rhetoric were soundproof against the outside world, their methods and their status largely untouched by the profound political and religious changes that had taken place around them. There was also the simple question, What did it mean to be a professional teacher in these schools? It soon became apparent that the observation and the question were inseparably joined, and that to answer the question I needed to ask another, which the observation inevitably raised: Why did these schools and their prestige remain so impressively unchanged? This in turn pointed me toward the social role of the schools, as places that not only transmitted knowledge but also gave their students standing in a narrowly defined elite. Finally, to focus my investigations, I chose to concentrate on the *grammaticus*: a pivotal figure, about whom we know a good deal, but who has often been overshadowed in modern studies (as he was in antiquity) by his more conspicuous colleague, the rhetorician. Thus the book came to describe the role of the grammarian as a guarantor of social as well as cultural continuity and, more generally, to analyze the notion and practice of a profession in a traditional society.

The book is concerned mainly with the fourth and fifth centuries and consists of a series of studies on the grammarian and his profession (Part I) and a prosopography of the late-antique grammarians and the other teachers of letters below the level of rhetorician (Part II). The scope and purpose of the prosopography are described at length in the introduction to Part II.

In constructing Part I, I have not attempted to argue a single thesis but have tried to follow the leads suggested by one broad topic—the interplay of social status, individual skill, and social relations. After a brief prologue, the first segment, "Letters in the World" (Chapters 1 and 2), sets the terms of the discussion, emphasizing the importance of the grammarian's profession and drawing attention to some of its anomalies or ambiguities. Chapter 1, "The Guardian and His Burden," places the grammarian in the context of the late Roman Empire and describes his part in preserving the linguistic, geographic, and social boundaries that ordered the life of the urban elite. Providing the one experience that all members of the elite would share, his school was a source of continuity and stability, and was not least important as such in the empire restored and renewed after the troubles of the third century. Chapter 2, "*Professio Litterarum*," then examines the grammarian's role as a professional in this context and compares that role with the modern notion of a profession.

There are some evident similarities; but we are here concerned more with the differences between the ancient profession and the modern conception, which stresses the authority and autonomy that the professional gains by mastering a body of specialized knowledge and skills, and which assumes that the professional's skills contribute to the common good. These differences are examined in three sections. In the first, "Some Variable Definitions: Literacy, Letters, and the Grammarian's Profession," we can see two effects of the limited literacy of the empire: it increased the prestige of the grammarian's profession, and it caused the profession to be defined not simply by the specialized skills it comprised but also by the privileged clientele it served. In the next section, "Independence and Constraint: Good and Bad Grammarians and the Power of Convention," we can consider how the profession's authority was fostered from its early history by the grammarian's development and control of a system of rules based on the rational analysis of language—and how the profession was yet limited in its autonomy, domesticated, because it remained firmly embedded in a social milieu that valued personal relations and the qualities conventionally associated with good character as highly as the skills and intellectual abilities specific to the profession. In the third section, "Polished Speech, the Common Good, and Christianity," we come to the assumption that the grammarian's profession—and the high literary culture in general—contributed to the common good: here we can see how that assumption was brought under debate with the rise of Christianity, and how the debate was resolved differently in the East and the West.

The remaining chapters of Part I then take up in some detail the social world of the grammarians and their texts. Chapter 3, "The Social Status of the Grammarians," examines the late-antique grammarians' personal circumstances in a survey of their origins, wealth, and mobility. The survey allows us to place them at the threshold of good society, where they were ambiguous figures. Their generally honorable origins, their properties and professional incomes, and the respect in which they were held for their skills placed them far above the population at large. Yet on the social pyramid of the elite they stood far closer to the base than to the pinnacle: one token of their "social poverty" is their notable lack of social mobility, especially their limited success in winning the careers in the imperial service that were open to many other literary men in the period. The grammarians were thus characterized by a combination of high and low status: this ambiguity in turn anticipates the differing images of the grammarian that emerge first in the following segment, "A Place to Stand" (Chapters 4 and 5), where the grammarians speak for themselves, and then in Chapter 6, "The Social Relations of the Grammarians," which investigates the grammarians' subordination to their patrons.

Chapters 4 and 5 are given over to two major grammatical texts, Pompeius's commentary on the handbook of Donatus and Servius's commentary on the poetry of Vergil. In each work we can clearly hear the voice of a late-antique teacher; each vividly reveals the self-image of a man immersed in his expertise and the sense of authority he draws from his skill. The grammarian in these texts is the master, buoyed up by his profession's tradition, refining it, laying down the laws of language with a confidence verging on complacence—and concerned to protect the integrity of his inherited doctrine.

In Chapter 6, by contrast, we see the grammarian as a dependent. The grammarians' patrons sustain them in their professional lives and affect for good or ill most other areas of their lives beyond the strictly pro-fessional. Here personal relations are paramount: the patron is concerned especially that his client be a good man, and emphasis is given to such personal qualities as modesty, industry, and diligence, the virtues suited to preserving the stable world of the learned elite. (No more than the grammarians would their patrons want to see the inherited doctrine overthrown, though for slightly different reasons.) Nor does it make any fundamental difference whether the power of one's patron is official or informal, whether the patron is a private citizen, a local dignitary, or a representative of the imperial government: the view that the state's control of teachers and education grows broader and more systematic in late antiquity can be shown to be mistaken; and in any case the basic patterns and ethical criteria of personal relations remain the same, regardless of the source of the patron's influence.

In Chapters 3 through 6, then, the external history of the profession surrounds the grammarians and their texts; the facts of social place and social relations press in on either side. This organization, I hope, will make it plain that the grammarian's profession was not only the basic literary profession, but perhaps also the one most constricted by its circumstances.

As this sketch suggests, the aims of the book are limited. It is not a history of grammar or of grammatical instruction in late antiquity. Yet limited as its intentions are, and long though it is, there are still topics I could well have included but have chosen to leave to one side for now. The study of Greek in the West and of Latin in the East is one example. Literary exegesis—especially in the service of ethical instruction—is another: although this part of the grammarian's task is less available for study in the surviving grammatical literature, and although the men of late antiquity emphasized it less than linguistic expertise, there are still interesting things to be found. Readers will think of other topics or issues deserving inclusion: that is both inevitable and all to the good; for the subject is rich, and there is much work to be done.

*   *   *

The basic research for the book was completed by 1981, and a draft was finished by 1984; a slightly different version of Chapter 5 appeared in *Classical Philology* (75 [1980]: 216–41) under the title "The Grammarian's Authority." Although I attempted to take into account the most important secondary literature published from 1981 through 1983, there are doubtless regrettable omissions. It has been possible to include very little that has reached me since November 1983.

I have been extraordinarily fortunate in the support that I have received from institutions and individuals alike. I therefore wish to thank the National Endowment for the Humanities for an Independent Study and Research Fellowship (1980-81) that provided me a year in which to read, think, and write free from my ordinary duties; the Division of the Humanities in the University of Chicago and Karl J. Weintraub, formerly Dean of the Division, for the leave of absence that allowed me to take up the fellowship and for the funds that later helped me put the draft of the book on computer for revision; the Joseph Regenstein Library for its splendid resources, and particularly—when even those gave out—the staff of Interlibrary Loan, who handled any number of odd requests with unfailing speed and courtesy; the University of California Press, for undertaking to publish a big book on a subject outside the mainstream of current classical scholarship; and the people at the Press who have had a hand in the project: Doris Kretschmer for her long patience and good advice, Mary Lamprech for her efficient supervision of the production, and Paul Psoinos for the marvelous precision and intelligence of his editing. My gratitude to all these is all the more deeply felt when I reflect that each represents a form of support unavailable to the men who are the subject of this book.

From the work of other scholars I have profited immensely: this will, I hope, be evident from the notes, where I have tried to record my debts rather than pursue disagreements. My great personal thanks must go to Peter Brown, who has long followed and encouraged the progress of the book and who, as editor of this series, swiftly put his finger on the places that needed improvement in the completed draft; and to Arnaldo Momigliano, whose invitation to speak about the grammarians and their audience to his seminar in November 1976 brought my thoughts into focus at an early, critical stage, and who has always been ready to talk about my work with the range and authority that is uniquely his. In addition, Alan D. Booth, Alan Cameron, C. P. Jones, Charles E. Murgia, and James E. G. Zetzel have all reviewed either the entire manuscript or large portions of it, some of them more than once. I am very grateful to each of them for reassurance or improvement, and I hope that none of them will take it amiss if I single out for special thanks my colleague Peter White, editor *nonpareil*, who for ten years now has shown himself to be the best and toughest critic of my work. That the book is not better for all this attention is to be attributed to my stubbornness, my weariness, and, no doubt, to other shortcomings of which I am less keenly aware.

Finally, there is my wife, Laura, who not only lived with what must too often have seemed an obsession but also found the time, amid the demands of motherhood and of her own profession, to pass her stern attorney's eye over my guilty prose. Only she can know what her help has meant to me. To her and to the two others to whom I owe the greatest debt this book is dedicated.

R. A. K.
Hyde Park
6 February 1985

ABBREVIATIONS

Abbreviations of journal titles are those found in *L'année philologique*, with a few small and familiar variations. Papyrological collections, series, and the like are denoted by the abbreviations found in J. F. Oates et al., *Checklist of Editions of Greek Papyri and Ostraca*, 2d ed., Bulletin of the American Society of Papyrologists, supplement 1 (Missoula, Mont., 1978). Beyond the abbreviations noted below, and except in the case of very common texts, editions of primary sources are noted in the citations, usually by the editor's name. The bibliography provides full references for the books and articles cited in the notes and in the prosopography.

ACO   E. Schwartz, ed., *Acta conciliorum oecumenicorum*, 4 vols. in 14 (Berlin and Leipzig, 1914–82)

AE   *L'année épigraphique: Revue des publications épigraphiques relatives à l'antiquité romaine* (Paris, 1888–)

AIJ   V. Hoffiller and B. Saria, eds., *Antike Inschriften aus Jugoslavien* 1 (Zagreb, 1938)

Anecd. Helv.   H. Hagen, ed., *Anecdota Helvetica* (Leipzig, 1870)

Anecd. Mared.   G. Morin, *Anecdota Maredsolana*, 4 vols. (Maredsoli, in Monasterio S. Benedicti, 1893–1932)

ANRW   H. Temporini and W. Haase, eds., *Aufstieg und Niedergang der römischen Welt* (Berlin, 1972–)

ASS   *Acta sanctorum quotquot toto orbe coluntur*, 68 vols. (Paris, 1863–1940)

Bekker, Anecd.   I. Bekker, ed., *Anecdota Graeca*, 3 vols. (Berlin, 1814–21)

BHG   F. Halkin, ed., *Bibliotheca hagiographica Graeca*, 3d ed., 3 vols., Subsidia hagiographica, 8a (Brussels, 1957)

Bibliotheca sanctorum   *Bibliotheca sanctorum*, 13 vols. (Rome, 1961–70)

Bull. ép.   J. Robert and L. Robert, *Bulletin épigraphique* [appearing in the annual issues of *REG*; cited by the year and the number of the entry within the survey]

Bury, *LRE*   J. B. Bury, *History of the Later Roman Empire from the Death of Theodosius I to the Death of Justinian (A.D. 395 to A.D. 565)*, 2 vols. (London, 1923)

CAG   *Commentaria in Aristotelem Graeca*, 23 vols. in 46 (Berlin, 1882–1909)

CC CM   *Corpus Christianorum*, Continuatio mediaevalis (Turnhout, 1966–)

CC SG   *Corpus Christianorum*, series Graeca (Turnhout, 1977–)

CC SL   *Corpus Christianorum*, series Latina (Turnhout, 1953–)

CGL   G. Goetz, ed., *Corpus glossariorum Latinorum*, 7 vols. (Leipzig, 1888–1923)

Chron. min.   T. Mommsen, ed., *Chronica minora saec. IV. V. VI. VII.*, 3 vols. *MGH* AA, vols. 9, 11, 13 (Berlin, 1892–98)

Chr.-Sch.-St.   W. von Christ, *Geschichte der griechischen Literatur*, Handbuch der Altertumswissenschaft, 7, 2. Teil, *Die nachklassische Periode der griechischen Literatur*, 2. Hälfte, *Von 100 bis 530 nach Christus*, umgearbeitet von W. Schmid und O. Stählin (Munich, 1924)

CIG   A. Boeckh, ed., *Corpus inscriptionum Graecarum*, 4 vols. (Berlin, 1828–77)

CIL   *Corpus inscriptionum Latinarum*, 16 vols. (Berlin, 1863–)

CJ   P. Krueger, ed., *Codex Iustinianus*, Corpus iuris civilis, 2 (Berlin, 1929)

CLA   E. A. Lowe, *Codices Latini antiquiores*, 11 vols., with supplement (Oxford, 1934–71)

CLCAG   *Corpus Latinum commentariorum in Aristotelem Graecorum* (Louvain, 1957–)

CMG   *Corpus medicorum Graecorum* (Berlin, 1915–)

Corp. ét.   B. Boyaval, ed., *Corpus des étiquettes de momies grecques* (Lille, 1976)

Cramer, *Anecd. Oxon.*   J. A. Cramer, ed., *Anecdota Graeca e codicibus manuscriptis bibliothecarum Oxoniensium*, 4 vols. (Oxford, 1835–37)

Cramer, *Anecd. Paris.*   J. A. Cramer, ed., *Anecdota Graeca e codicibus manuscriptis bibliothecae regiae Parisiensis*, 4 vols. (Oxford, 1839–41)

CSCO Scr. Syr.   *Corpus scriptorum Christianorum Orientalium*, Scriptores Syri (Paris, 1903–)

CSEL   *Corpus scriptorum ecclesiasticorum Latinorum* (Vienna, 1866–)

CSHB   *Corpus scriptorum historiae Byzantinae*, 50 vols. (Bonn, 1828–97)

CTh T. Mommsen, ed., *Theodosiani libri XVI cum Constitutionibus Sirmondianis* (Berlin, 1905)

Dig. T. Mommsen, ed., *Digesta*, Corpus iuris civilis, 1 (Berlin, 1893)

FD *Fouilles de Delphes* (Paris, 1908–)

Festschr. Berl. *Festschrift zum 150jährig. Bestehen des Berliner ägyptischen*
ägypt. Mus. *Museums*, Staatliches Museum zu Berlin, Mitteilungen aus der ägyptischen Sammlung, 8 (Berlin, 1974)

FGrH F. Jacoby, ed., *Die Fragmente der griechischen Historiker* (Berlin and Leiden, 1923–)

FHG K. Müller, ed., *Fragmenta historicorum Graecorum*, 5 vols. (Paris, 1851–85)

Forsch. Eph. *Forschungen in Ephesos* (Vienna, 1906–)

FX *Fouilles de Xanthos*, Institut français d'archéologie, Istanbul, and Institut français d'études anatoliennes d'Istanbul (Paris, 1958–)

Geerard, Clavis M. Geerard, ed., *Clavis patrum Graecorum*, Corpus Christianorum (Turnhout, 1974–)

GG *Grammatici Graeci* (Leipzig, 1867–)

GL H. Keil, ed., *Grammatici Latini*, 7 vols. (Leipzig, 1855–80)

Gloss. Lat. W. M. Lindsay et al., eds., *Glossaria Latina*, 5 vols. (Paris, 1926–31)

GVI W. Peek, ed., *Griechische Vers-Inschriften* 1 (Berlin, 1955)

Hist. Gr. min. L. A. Dindorf, ed., *Historici Graeci minores*, 2 vols. (Leipzig, 1870–71)

Hunger H. Hunger, *Die hochsprachliche profane Literatur der Byzantiner*, 2 vols., Handbuch der Altertumswissenschaft, 12:5.1 and 2 (Munich, 1978)

IAEpidaur. W. Peek, ed., *Inschriften aus dem Asklepieion von Epidauros*, Abhandlungen der Sächsischen Akademie der Wissenschaften zu Leipzig, philologisch-historische Klasse, 60:2 (Berlin, 1969)

IANice-Cimiez G. Laguerre, ed., *Inscriptions antiques de Nice-Cimiez (Cemenelum, Ager Cemenelensis)*, Fouilles de Cemenelum, 2 (Paris, 1975)

IAOSPE V. Latyshev, ed., *Inscriptiones antiquae orae septentrionalis Ponti Euxini Graecae et Latinae*, vols. 1, 2, 4 (St. Petersburg, 1885–1901); vol. 1, 2d ed. (St. Petersburg, 1916)

IBubon F. Schindler, ed., *Die Inschriften von Bubon (Nord-Lykien)*, Sitzungsberichte der Österreichischen Akademie der Wissenschaften, philosophisch-historische Klasse, 278:3 (Vienna, 1972)

ICVR   G. B. de Rossi, ed., *Inscriptiones Christianae urbis Romae septimo saeculo antiquiores*, 2 vols. (Rome, 1857–88)

ICVR, n.s.   G. B. de Rossi et al., eds., *Inscriptiones Christianae urbis Romae septimo saeculo antiquiores*, nova series (Rome, 1922–)

IDelos   F. Durrbach et al., eds., *Inscriptions de Délos* (Paris, 1926–)

IDR   *Inscriptiile Daciei Romane* (Bucharest, 1975–)

IEPD   *Inscriptiones extra fines Pannoniae Daciaeque repertae ad res earundem provinciarum pertinentes*, 4th ed. (Amsterdam, 1975)

IG   *Inscriptiones Graecae* (Berlin, 1873–)

IGBulg.   G. Mikhailov, ed., *Inscriptiones Graecae in Bulgaria repertae*, Academia litterarum Bulgarica, Institutum archaeologicum, series epigraphica (Serdica, 1956–)

IGLS   L. Jalabert, R. Mouterde, et al., eds., *Inscriptions grecques et latines de la Syrie*, Service des antiquités et des beaux arts, Bibliothèque archéologique et historique (Paris, 1929–)

IGLTyr   J.-P. Rey-Coquais, ed., *Inscriptions grecques et latines découvertes dans les fouilles de Tyr (1963–1974)*, vol. 1, *Inscriptions de la nécropole*, Bulletin du Musée de Beyrouth, 29 (Paris, 1977)

IGR   R. Cagnat et al., eds., *Inscriptiones Graecae ad res Romanas pertinentes*, 4 vols. (Paris, 1901–27)

IGSK   *Inschriften griechischen Städte aus Kleinasien* (Bonn, 1972–)

IGVR   L. Moretti, ed., *Inscriptiones Graecae urbis Romae* 1–3, Studi pubblicati dall'Istituto italiano per la storia antica, 17, 22, 28 (Rome, 1968–79)

IKyzik.   E. Schwertheim, ed., *Die Inschriften von Kyzikos und Umgebung*, vol. 1, *Grabtexte* (Bonn, 1983 [*IGSK* 18])

ILAfr.   R. Cagnat and A. Merlin, eds., *Inscriptions latines d'Afrique (Tripolitaine, Tunisie, Maroc)* (Paris, 1923)

ILAlg.   S. Gsell et al., eds., *Inscriptions latines de l'Algérie*, 2 vols. (Paris, 1922, 1957)

ILCV   E. Diehl, ed., *Inscriptiones Latinae Christianae veteres*, 3 vols. (Berlin, 1925–31)

ILER   J. Vives, ed., *Inscripciones latinas de la España romana: Antología de 6800 textos*, 2 vols. (Barcelona, 1971–72)

ILS   H. Dessau, ed., *Inscriptiones Latinae selectae*, 3 vols. (Berlin, 1892–1916)

IMEGR   A. Bernand, ed., *Inscriptions métriques de l'Égypte gréco-romaine: Recherches sur la poésie épigrammatique des Grecs en Égypte*, Annales littéraires de l'Université de Besançon, 98 (Paris, 1969)

Inschr. Eph.   H. Wankel, C. Börker, R. Merkelbach, et al., eds., *Die Inschriften von Ephesos* 1–7 (Bonn, 1979–81 [*IGSK* 11–17])

Inscr. Ital.   *Inscriptiones Italiae* (Rome, 1931–)

IPriene   F. Hiller von Gaertringen, ed., *Die Inschriften von Priene* (Berlin, 1906)

Jones, CERP²   A. H. M. Jones, *The Cities of the Eastern Roman Provinces*, 2d ed. (Oxford, 1971)

Jones, LRE   A. H. M. Jones, *The Later Roman Empire 284–602: A Social, Economic, and Administrative Survey*, 2 vols. (Norman, Okla., 1964)

Kaibel   G. Kaibel, *Epigrammata Graeca ex lapidibus conlecta* (Berlin, 1878)

Labraunda 3:2   J. Crampa, ed., *Labraunda*, vol. 3, parts 1, 2, *The Greek Inscriptions*, Skrifter utgivna av Svenska institutet i Athen, 4°, vol. 5, ser. 1, part 3, nos. 1, 2 (Stockholm, 1969–72)

LSJ   H. G. Liddell and R. Scott, *A Greek-English Lexicon*, 9th ed., revised and augmented by H. S. Jones, with a supplement edited by E. A. Barber (Oxford, 1968)

LThK   M. Buchberger et al., eds., *Lexikon für Theologie und Kirche*, 2d ed. (Freiburg, 1957–)

Magie, RRAM   D. Magie, *Roman Rule in Asia Minor to the End of the Third Century after Christ*, 2 vols. (Princeton, 1950)

MAMA   W. M. Calder et al., eds., *Monumenta Asiae Minoris antiqua*, 8 vols. (Manchester, 1928–62)

Mansi   G. D. Mansi et al., eds., *Sacrorum Conciliorum nova et amplissima collectio*, vols. 1–31a (Florence and Venice, 1759–98); vols. 31b–53 (Paris–Arnhem–Leipzig, 1901–27)

MGH AA   *Monumenta Germaniae historica*, Auctores antiquissimi, 15 vols. (Berlin, 1877–1919)

MGH SS rer. Langob.   *Monumenta Germaniae historica*, Scriptores rerum Langobardicarum et Italicarum saec. VI–IX. (Hanover, 1878)

Nov. "App."   R. Schöll and W. Kroll, eds., *Novellae*, Corpus iuris civilis, 3 (Berlin, 1928)

Nov. "Val."   P. M. Meyer and T. Mommsen, eds., *Leges Novellae ad Theodosianum pertinentes* (Berlin, 1905)

OLD   P. G. W. Glare, ed., *Oxford Latin Dictionary* (Oxford, 1968–82)

Olympia   W. Dittenberger and K. Purgold, eds., *Olympia*, vol. 5, *Die Inschriften von Olympia* (Berlin, 1896)

Pack²   R. A. Pack, ed., *The Greek and Latin Literary Texts from Greco-Roman Egypt*, 2d ed. (Ann Arbor, 1965)

PECS   R. Stillwell, ed., *The Princeton Encyclopedia of Classical Sites* (Princeton, 1976)

PG   J. P. Migne et al., eds., *Patrologiae cursus completus*, series Graeca, 161 vols. (Paris, 1857–66)

PIR²   E. Groag, A. Stein, et al., *Prosopographia imperii Romani saec. I. II. III.*, 2d ed. (Berlin and Leipzig, 1933–)

PL   J. P. Migne et al., eds., *Patrologiae cursus completus*, series Latina, 221 vols. (Paris, 1844–1900)

PLG⁴   T. Bergk, ed., *Poetae lyrici Graeci*, 4th ed., 3 vols. (Leipzig, 1914)

PLRE I   A. H. M. Jones, J. R. Martindale, and J. Morris, *The Prosopography of the Later Roman Empire*, vol. 1, *A.D. 260–395* (Cambridge, 1971)

PLRE II   J. R. Martindale, *The Prosopography of the Later Roman Empire*, vol. 2, *A.D. 395–527* (Cambridge, 1980)

PO   *Patrologia Orientalis* (Paris, 1907–)

Preisigke, WB   F. Preisigke et al., *Wörterbuch der griechischen Papyrusurkunden* (Berlin, 1925–)

Prosop. chrét. I   A. Mandouze, *Prosopographie chrétienne du Bas-Empire*, vol. 1, *Prosopographie de l'Afrique chrétienne (303–533)* (Paris, 1982)

RE   A. F. von Pauly, G. Wissowa, et al., eds., *Real-Encyclopädie der classischen Altertumswissenschaft* (Stuttgart, 1894–1972)

RE Suppl.   G. Wissowa et al., eds., *Paulys Real-Encyclopädie der classischen Altertumswissenschaft*, Supplementbände, 15 vols. (Stuttgart, 1903–78)

Rhet. Lat. min.   K. Halm, ed., *Rhetores Latini minores* (Leipzig, 1863)

RICM   D. Feissel, ed., *Recueil des inscriptions chrétiennes de Macédoine du IIIᵉ au VIᵉ siècle*, Bulletin de Correspondence Hellénique supplément 8 (Paris, 1983)

RIGCAM   H. Grégoire, ed., *Recueil des inscriptions grecques chrétiennes d'Asie Mineure* (Paris, 1922)

RIGCE   G. Lefebvre, ed., *Recueil des inscriptions grecques chrétiennes d'Égypte* (Cairo, 1907)

RIT   G. Alföldy, ed., *Die römische Inschriften von Tarraco* (Berlin, 1975)

RIU   L. Barkóczi and A. Mócsy, eds., *Die römische Inschriften Ungarns* (Amsterdam, 1972–)

RLAC   F.-J. Dölger et al., eds., *Reallexikon für Antike und Christentum* (Leipzig, 1941–)

Sch.-Hos.   M. Schanz, *Geschichte der römischen Literatur bis zum Gesetzgebungswerk des Kaisers Justinian*, Handbuch der Altertumswissenschaft, 8:2–4: 2. Teil, C. Hosius, *Die römische Literatur in der Zeit der Monarchie bis auf Hadrian*, 4th ed. (Munich, 1935); 3. Teil, M. Schanz, *Die Zeit von Hadrian*

(117) bis auf Constantin (324), 3d ed., rev. C. Hosius and G. Krüger (Munich, 1922); 4. Teil, 1. Band, M. Schanz, *Die Literatur des vierten Jahrhunderts*, 2d ed. (Munich, 1914); 4. Teil, 2. Hälfte, M. Schanz, C. Hosius, and G. Krüger, *Die Literatur des fünften und sechsten Jahrhunderts* (Munich, 1920)

SEG   *Supplementum epigraphicum Graecum* (Leiden, 1923–)

Spengel, *Rhet. Gr.*   L. Spengel et al., eds., *Rhetores Graeci* (Leipzig, 1892–1936)

Syll.[3]   W. Dittenberger, ed., *Sylloge inscriptionum Graecarum*, 3d ed., 4 vols. (Leipzig, 1915–21)

TAM   E. Kalinka et al., eds., *Tituli Asiae Minoris* (Vienna, 1901–)

Teuffel   W. S. Teuffel, *Geschichte der römischen Literatur*, 3. Band, *Die Literatur von 96 nach Chr. bis zum Ausgange des Altertums*, 6th ed., rev. W. Kroll, F. Skutsch, et al. (Leipzig and Berlin, 1913)

TLL   *Thesaurus linguae Latinae* (Leipzig, 1900–)

Walz, *Rhet. Gr.*   C. Walz, ed., *Rhetores Graeci*, 9 vols. in 10 (Stuttgart and Tübingen, 1832–36)

PART I

Anazarbus

In the southeast corner of Asia Minor lies the great plain left behind as the Taurus Mountains drop away from the coast before turning back to meet the Amanus range, which rises from the south. The pocket of land thus formed was called by the Greeks Cilicia Pedias (Cilicia of the Plain) and provided the conditions for a prosperity unknown to the neighboring wilderness of Cilicia Tracheia (Rough Cilicia): soil that was—and still is—among the richest on the Anatolian Peninsula, especially favorable for grain and cotton; three major rivers that drained the territory from north to south and linked the inland regions to the coast; and the important trade routes that ran overland from the Syrian Gates in the Amanus Mountains to the Cilician Gates in the Taurus, funneling goods and men through the region. Such conditions made for a robust urbanization. Gradually detached from the control of local kings and brought under Roman rule, the plain showed some seventeen cities by the end of the first century A.D., both very old and very new foundations, set along the coast or on one of the three rivers, with Tarsus enjoying pride of place.[1]

Originally among the cities of second rank was Anazarbus, located on a tributary of the Pyramus, the easternmost of the major rivers, about forty kilometers as the crow flies from the nearest point on the coast. Probably ruled with the rest of the upper Pyramus by the native Tarcondimotid dynasty until A.D. 17, Anazarbus was issuing imperial coinage at least by the reign of Claudius (A.D. 41–54). From the late first century onward it is shown by its coins and inscriptions to have entered into the

---

1. See Jones, *CERP*[2] 191ff. For general accounts of Anazarbus (following paragraph), see ibid. 204ff.; Magie, *RRAM* 275, 408; Verzone, "Città"; and esp. Gough, "Anazarbus."

patterns of civic life and the inevitable intercity competition typical in the eastern provinces of the empire.[2]

With seeming suddenness, however, Anazarbus came at the very end of the second century to claim a new position of prestige, rivaling Tarsus as first city of the region in political and religious importance. Its inscriptions from the Severan era proclaim Anazarbus both μητρόπολις, a title long worn by Tarsus, and νεωκόρος, or temple warden of the provincial cult of the emperor.[3] How Anazarbus won these honors is not precisely known, but its prominence was apparently neither short-lived nor of purely local interest. The rivalry with Tarsus was finally resolved two centuries later, when the province of Cilicia was reorganized: Tarsus was made the metropolis of Cilicia Prima; Anazarbus, of Cilicia Secunda.[4] Probably about the same time, an account of the local history and antiquities (πάτρια) of Anazarbus was composed, a distinction usually enjoyed by cities that could be said to have arrived.[5]

But already in the early third century the new prestige of Anazarbus was recorded as far away as Delphi, where all the city's titles were duly mentioned in an inscription raised to one of its native sons. The publicist on this occasion was a grammarian, here honored in much the same way as a long line of literary men from other cities: "The Delphians made me a Delphian, a much-lettered[?] poet and grammarian, Naevianus, who have as my home Anazarbus, twice temple warden, ally of the Westerners, metropolis of the Cilicians."[6] The epigram nicely balances the man's cultural status with his city's political status, and the circumstances hint at a reciprocal relation: the prosperous city of the provinces has

2. Dedications to Domitian (including a temple, as Διόνυσος Καλλίκαρπος) and Hadrian, as well as to the local tutelary gods, Zeus, Hera Gamelia, and Ares: Gough, "Anazarbus" 95f. Priest of Roma: Mellor, ΘΕΑ 88f., 226 no. 220. Competition, esp. in the form of agonistic festivals: Jones, CERP² 205f.

3. Metropolitan status and neocorate: the milestone published by Ramsay, "Inscriptions" 157 no. 18, with Gough, "Anazarbus" 96f., 138, 143, and Dagron and Marcillet-Jaubert, "Inscriptions" 383f. no. 8; and (for νεωκόρος) Woodward, "Neocorate" 7ff., Ziegler, "Münzen" 36ff., Weiss, "Abkürzungen" 550f. Cf. also Jones, CERP² 207.

4. Under Theodosius I or II: see Jones, LRE 1460–61.

5. Anth. Gr. 9.195, Κωνσταντινιάδης Ἀσκληπιὸς ἄστυ γεραίρων / γράψεν Ἀναζαρβοῦ πάτρια κυδαλίμης; not before s.IV med., in view of Asclepius's patronymic (cf. PLRE I s.v. Asclepius 5, p. 116), and probably not later than 517, when the city's name was officially changed to Justinopolis (later Justinianopolis; cf. Gough, "Anazarbus" 98; Verzone, "Città" 10).

6. FD 3:1.206: [πο]ιητὴν καὶ γραμματικὸν πολυ[γράμματον ὄντα] / Ναιουιανὸν Δελφοὶ Δελφὸν ἔθεντο [νόμῳ], / πατρίδα Ἀναζαρβὸν δὶς νηοκόρον με ἔχοντα, / σύμμαχον Αὐσονίων, μητρόπολιν Κιλίκων. On the titles and date, see (in addition to n. 3) Kaster, "Date." For other grammarians similarly honored at Delphi, see ibid. 132 n. 7.

nourished the individual, whose talents carry him to the center of the old Greek world, to an honor that reflects his city's glory.[7]

Just over a century later another grammarian appears in one of the few detailed glimpses of Anazarbene life that our sources afford.[8] The incident is set around the year 332; its main actor is Aetius. Later an important theologian of the Arian sect and the teacher of Eunomius, leader of its most radical wing, the young Aetius who appeared at Anazarbus was already marked as a talented and troubling figure. Impoverished by his father's death, he had worked as a goldsmith in his native Antioch to support his mother and himself. At the same time "the strength of his nature" drew him to "the lessons of argument" as auditor of the bishop Paulinus, to whom he devoted himself when his mother died. He became a skilled and combative debater—perhaps too skilled and combative for his own good, since after the death of his protector, Paulinus, the ill will he had accumulated caused Paulinus's successor to drive him from the city. Taking up his goldsmith's craft again, Aetius traveled north from Antioch, no doubt following the trade routes through the Syrian Gates, until he came to Anazarbus.

Approaching from the south, Aetius would first have spied a face of the great limestone tor that rises from the plain to shelter the city; then, rounding the foot of the crag, he would have passed through the city's main gate, where an ambitious arch from the Severan period still stood as a monument of the city's earlier surge of prosperity. Indeed, although burned by the Persians in 260, the city must still have been known to be prosperous, else the goldsmith would not have chosen it as a promising site for his expensive skills.[9] It had of course changed as well, in a way that Aetius could have anticipated; for the city that had boasted the title of temple warden several generations earlier could now claim its own Christian martyrs and a regular ecclesiastical hierarchy, overseen by the Arian bishop Athanasius.[10]

---

7. The mutual honor would have been brought out all the more if, as commonly in such circumstances, a copy of the formal decree was sent by the host city to be set up in the honorand's native town: cf., for example, *Labraunda* 3:2.66, on the grammarian Ti. Claudius Anteros, pp. 135f.; and *IGBulg.* 3:2.1573; *MAMA* 8.418; *IG* 12 Supp. 248C; C. P. Jones, *Roman World* 60 n. 26.

8. For the following two paragraphs, see Philostorg. *HE* 3.15, with Part II no. 167.

9. Arch: Gough, "Anazarbus" 110ff.; L. Robert, "Épigraphie" 487–89, dating the arch to the reign of Caracalla; differently Verzone, "Città" 15ff., dating to s.II 3/4. Persians: Magie, *RRAM* 708.

10. Martyrs: *Acta SS. Tarachi, Probi et Andronici MM.*, cc. 3–4 (*ASS* Oct. V, 575ff.), and the version now in Halkin, *Inédits byzantins* no. 13, cc. 14ff.; cf. Gough, "Anazarbus" 97; Halkin, *Inédits byzantins* 211f. For Athanasius's Arian activity before the Council of Nicaea, see Athanas. Alex. *De synod.* 17 (*PG* 26.172); and cf.

Both the old and the new were joined in the local grammarian, a teacher in the line of Naevianus and a Christian, to whom Aetius came to owe most at Anazarbus and whom he repaid least well. Spotting Aetius's talent, the teacher took him into his household: in return for Aetius's domestic services, the grammarian shared his expertise, bridging the ancient division between the banausic and liberal skills.[11] But as a Christian, the grammarian knew the sacred texts as well as the classical and used to discuss Scripture with his pupil. It was at one such discussion that Aetius, disagreeing with the teacher's interpretation, "publicly heaped much shame upon him for his ignorance." The grammarian took Aetius's insult to be inappropriate repayment "to the household that was his benefactor" and drove him from his home. Not for the last time, Aetius landed on his feet: taken in by Bishop Athanasius at Anazarbus, he was soon in Tarsus and then in Alexandria, continuing to circulate easily among the cities of the East. Of Aetius's grammarian we know nothing more, not even his name.

*   *   *

Anazarbus was not one of the great cities of the empire, and it has not figured in modern accounts of ancient education. In just such cities, however, most of the history of ancient education was made, by fairly ordinary men like Naevianus or Aetius's anonymous teacher; and the lines of the sketch above will be redrawn with varying definition and shading in the following chapters, as we try to achieve a detailed picture of the grammarian's place in late antiquity. Like the two we have already glimpsed, the grammarians in the pages below will share a number of traits with many of their contemporaries, as creatures of the city, driven by a desire for honor and a loathing of shame, consciously or unwittingly participating in the play of continuity and change. Like the Anazarbenes, too, they will have a role that is very much the grammarian's, as social and cultural mediator.

---

the letter of Athanasius to Eusebius of Nicomedia, Epiphan. *Panar. haeres.* 69.6, and Theodoret. *HE* 1.4.

11. Note that while the social distinction would have been real enough, it need not in this case imply a great economic distinction. A goldsmith would ordinarily stand among the upper range of artisans in a town (cf. Norman, "Gradations" 80); this is implicitly acknowledged by Gregory of Nyssa, in whose highly polemical account Aetius's status is lowered to that of a mere smith or tinker, καμινευτής: *C. Eunom.* 1.38f. But the description of the grammarian's circumstances suggests he had a modest household and could not afford the pure beneficence of offering his services without salary or fee, as is recorded, e.g., of a physician of Lesbos, *IG* 12:2.484.28ff. For the waiver of fees, see further Chap. 3 pp. 122–23.

The grammarian was one of antiquity's great middlemen. He might turn his talents outward, like Naevianus, to link his city with the world; more often, as with Aetius's teacher, his attentions would be circumscribed by the city walls, his skills poised between town and country, between distinct levels in urban society, between the family and the community, or between the two cultures of prestige, classical and Christian. But unlike other important middlemen with whom we are familiar—rhetoricians and bishops, for example—the grammarian found that his distinctive role was also his greatest weakness: the man whose function set him amid many vital spheres of activity most often was without a place at the center of any of them.

Many students of antiquity today are only peripherally aware of the grammarian. In this they are like the ancients themselves. To his contemporaries, the grammarian was commonly a shape spied out of the corner of the eye, a recurrent figure in the margins of a series of great murals: although the central subjects of the tableaux might change, the marginal figure persisted, in different attitudes serving different structural ends in the compositions. To understand the attitudes and the ends, we must first come to terms with their varied contexts.

Letters in the World

κύριε, ἀγαθὸν νοῦν χάρισαί μοι, ἵνα μάθω τὰ γράμματα καὶ νικῶ
τοὺς ἑταίρους μου.

Lord, give me the grace of good understanding, that I might
learn letters and gain the upper hand over my fellows.

—*A child's prayer at baptism. Eustratius,* Vita Eutychii 8

If the grammarian often slipped beyond his contemporaries' notice, that
was no doubt in part because his contribution to their way of life was so
familiar. For the classes that held the upper hand in late antiquity, entry
into the grammarian's school was the first step beyond the confines of
the family. A child's identity as a member of the elite and so his future
power and prestige were to a great extent determined by that passage
and by the schooling that followed.

Typically that schooling was purely literary. From about age seven or
eight (although the age was variable), the student's experience was
governed by three goals, pursued first in the grammarian's school, then
in the rhetorician's: mastery of correct language, command of a fairly
small number of classical texts, and an ability to turn the knowledge of
language and literature to a facility in composition and speech. Set in a
form already centuries old, the grammarian's main contribution to those
ends consisted of the "knowledge of speaking correctly" and the "explication of the poets."[1]

1. Quintil. *Inst.* 1.4.2: *recte loquendi scientiam et poetarum enarrationem* (cf. ἡ ἐπὶ
ποιητῶν ἐξηγήσει καὶ διορθώσει τῆς Ἑλληνικῆς λέξεως καθημένη τέχνη, Damasc.
V. Isid. epit. Phot. 60 = frg. 111 Zintzen).

11

Knowledge of correct speech the grammarian conveyed as a set of rules governing phonology, morphology, and the behavior of the individual parts of speech; though syntax had been brought into the ambit of grammar in Greek before the end of the second century, it did not for the most part concern Latin grammarians until the work of Priscian, in the early sixth century. Explication of the poets combined study of the language, as its larger part, with historical and ethical instruction. In line-by-line and word-by-word progress through the text, the poet's language was explained and used as a tool to confirm the grammarian's rules. Persons, events, and other *Realien* and the swatches of philosophical or religious doctrine with which the author was supposed to have draped his verse were glossed as they occurred. The actions of men and gods were explained and judged in terms of accepted *mores* and so were used to confirm them.[2]

The grammarian's instruction and the effects of the literary education are to modern eyes appalling. Indictments are common. The scope was intolerably narrow, excluding most studies now associated with a liberal education. Within its own domain, moreover, the education was suffocating. Merely pedantic (it is said) where not superficial, it first choked the spirit of literature with its rules, then hid the body under a rigid formalism. Worst of all, it fragmented the student's understanding while doing little to provide the governing classes with the specific skills or conceptual habits they needed to govern competently.

Far from understanding his culture, the man emerging from the schools of grammar and rhetoric would have no overall view of history, only a memory of disjointed but edifying vignettes; no systematic knowledge of philosophy or of any philosophic school, but a collection of ethical commonplaces; no organic sense even of the language he had so painstakingly acquired, but rules and categories, divided and subdivided, or rare lexical tidbits to display like precious jewels. The items amassed over years of schooling, like slips filed away in a vast rank of pigeonholes, could be summoned up individually and combined to meet the needs of the moment, but no unifying relationship among them was perceived.[3]

---

2. For the best and most recent accounts of grammatical instruction, see Marrou, *Histoire*[6] 243ff., 400ff.; Clarke, *Higher Education* 11ff.; Bonner, *Education* 189ff.; and cf. Barwick, *Remmius* 215ff.; Quacquarelli, *Scuola* 40ff. On ethical utility as an aim of the grammarian's *enarratio*, see esp. Dahlmann, *Kleine Schriften* 257ff., and, e.g., Aug. *De catech. rud.* 6.10, Greg. Naz. *Or.* 4 *C. Iulian.* 1.118 (on allegorical interpretation used to remove ethical problems in Homer). On scholastic structure in general, see below Chap. 1 pp. 24–26.

3. On this fragmentation, or *atomisme psychologique*, see esp. Marrou, *Saint Augustin* 1–157.

Because of such narrow, fragmented schooling, a man could seriously misjudge the needs of the moment if he came to comment on or participate in the workings of the empire. Since literary analysis consisted of weighing individual words, phrases, and verses, the one false note in a passage would be recognized more quickly than the place of the passage in the work as a whole; similarly, imperial laws tend to analyze and treat problems *ad hoc*, apparently with no recognition of their structural causes and consequences. Since good literary style was elaborate, variegated, and allusive, the imperial laws of late antiquity, composed in a kindred style, lack the simplicity and clarity that consistent, precise technical language could have provided. Where literature was judged ethically, it is unsurprising that contemporary events were sooner interpreted morally and personally than analyzed in impersonal and institutional terms. The schools of literary study at best did nothing to prepare their students to understand change; at worst, they blinded them to the fact of change.[4]

These grim observations, the product of a warm humanist ideal or the practical good sense of a technological and democratic society, are all the more piercing because they come from the outside. Their accuracy is rather confirmed than negated by the likelihood that most educated men of late antiquity would have shrugged off such criticisms, if they could have understood them at all; one might add only that the cultural situation thus described was not peculiar to late antiquity, or to antiquity in general.[5] But those views also offer us a starting point; for though the fox knows many things, the hedgehog knows one big thing. To place the grammarian's school in its context, it is necessary to begin with a feature of the school that explains both the criticisms and the reason why they would have been opaque to the ancients. The grammarian's instruction was shaped at least as much by social as by intellectual considerations, and the grammarian himself was embedded in a social system where what mattered were wealth, distinction, and eloquence amid a population vastly poor, anonymous, and illiterate; where among the wealthy, distinguished, and eloquent, fine hierarchical discriminations came as

4. On the general question of competence and "the usefulness of their education to the elite of government," see MacMullen, *Crisis* 48ff.; on the character of "Roman bureaucratese," see his so-titled study in *Traditio* 18 (1962) 364ff. On the "blindness" of the educated classes, see Alföldi, *Conflict* 96ff., esp. 106ff.; but Alföldi's thesis leads him seriously to overstate how peculiar the attitudes described were to the fourth century and to the Roman senatorial aristocracy. For a less charged judgment of the literary education in the fourth century, see Downey, "Education."

5. See esp. Finley, *Use* 193ff.; and the "Retractationes" in Marrou, *Saint Augustin* 672ff.

naturally as breathing and were every bit as important; where competence was defined largely by personal and social, not technical, criteria,
and one's conception of *humanitas* was so circumscribed as to embrace
only those who shared one's own attainments. Whatever its other shortcomings, the grammarian's school did one thing superbly, providing the
language and *mores* through which a social and political elite recognized
its members.

The first two chapters, then, will survey the social context in which
the grammarian must be set; their burden can be described simply. During the first five centuries of our era, the grammarian's school was the
single most important institution, outside the family, through which the
governing classes of the empire perpetuated and extended themselves.
Offering those classes the one thing that approached a common experience, it only increased in importance as other, competing institutions—
for example, the old Greek gymnasium—withered away, while its position was not seriously challenged by the rise of Christianity.[6] Persever-
ing in the East, it was undermined only gradually in the West by the
contraction of the imperial government and the Church's concomitant
development of new paths of leadership for the elite to follow. The
chapters below will elaborate these points and so will consider the different angles from which the grammarian's profession must be viewed.

6. End of the gymnasia: Claude, *Byzantinische Stadt* 76; Liebeschuetz, *Antioch*
156ff.; and note Sijpesteijn, *Liste*, with the supplement at *PJulTheon.* appendix
A—a total of 55 individual gymnasiarchs known from fourth-century Egypt,
with all but 7 of the datable examples falling before 350, the latest (*Liste* nos.
469–72) occurring in 370 at Oxyrhynchus.

CHAPTER 1

The Guardian and His Burden

One of our earliest witnesses to the grammarian's role is an inscription from the Ionian city of Priene honoring a local benefactor, dating to sometime after 84 B.C. Among the man's services is noted his subsidy for a grammarian to instruct the youth of Priene in language and literature (φιλολογία), "through which souls progress toward excellence [ἀρετή] and the condition proper to humanity [πάθος ἀνθρώπινον]."[1] Itself a commonplace, a token of shared assumptions, the statement reflects the belief that excellence and humanity not only could be derived from the literary education but could even be defined by it. If the soul thus tutored knew the "condition proper to humanity," one not so educated was less than human, like uneducated Fortune (ἀπαίδευτος Τύχη)—irrational, brute, and cruel.[2] Having made himself human, the educated man belonged to a breed apart.[3]

This enduring belief in the separateness belonging to and created by the literary culture found expression in several persistent metaphors. Most notably, an idea of sacredness attached to the instruction and to its texts. In the late first century A.D. one grammarian claimed on his epitaph, "I began the holy instruction [ἱερὴ ... διδασκαλίη] of well-born children";[4] another not long after praised his profession as the "study of sacred letters":[5] the sentiments reecho down to the fifth century, and

1. *IPriene* 112.73ff.
2. *CIG* 2722.4.
3. Cf. Snell, *Discovery* 247ff.; Marrou, ΜΟΥΣΙΚΟΣ 209ff.
4. The epitaph of Didius Taxiarches, *CIL* 6.16843 = *IG* 14.1587 = *GVI* 136 = *IGVR* 3.1189.8f.; cf. the description of the grammarian Damocharis (Part II no. 42) as γραμματικῆς ἱερὴ βάσις, *Anth. Gr.* 7.588 (Paulus Silentiarius).
5. Florus *Verg. or.* 3.8, *praecipientem bonos mores et sacrarum studia litterarum*, with Dahlmann, *Kleine Schriften* 256f., emphasizing the connection between the aims of ethical instruction (*boni mores*)—and so, good order—and the sacredness

15

the praise of Vergil's work as a sacred poem.[6] Such voices spoke with the knowledge that they possessed something set apart and enduring, something fundamental to the scheme of right order: the sacred exercised a powerful centripetal pull on a select group of men, to whom it afforded a special, shared, coherent way of life.

Consequently, the question of how one could gain access to the sacred also arose, to be elaborated in two common but antithetical metaphors. In one, the literary culture was a mystery, of the Muses or the ancients; its acquisition was an initiation, by which "the things not to be spoken" were revealed.[7] The metaphor well conveys the sense of distinction shared by an elect. But insofar as initiation in a mystery implies a transfiguring revelation, a passive experience, an irreversible change, the recurrent cast of thought does little to convey the reality of the literary education;[8] its true character is more accurately captured by the second metaphor, at once more common and more consequential. The school of literature is "the gymnasium of wisdom, where is shown the path to the blessed life."[9] The literary education is the "gymnastic of the soul";[10] the

---

attributed to the *litterae*. In addition to the authors cited by Dahlmann, ibid. 257 n. 6 *ad fin.*, contemporary with Florus and speaking of the sacredness of literary pursuits, see also Quintil. *Inst.* 1.4.6, *interiora velut sacri huius adeuntibus apparebit multa rerum subtilitas*, in his encomiastic defense of grammar.

6. Phocas *V. Verg.* praef. 24: *carmen sacrum*. Macrob. *Sat.* 1.24.13: *sacrum poema*.

7. Cf. Gell. *NA* praef. 20–21, borrowing Aristoph. *Frogs* 354ff.; *SB* 5.7567 (s.III), [ἂν] γὰρ ἐπ' ἀγαθοῖς πρότερον τῶν Μ[ο]υσῶν τὰ μυστήρια τελε[σθῶσι], reading thus with Wilcken, "Urkunden-Referat" 305; Lib. *Or.* 15.27, on the ἀπόρρητα of Homer and the poets (cf. Part II no. 106 *ad fin.*; Greg. Naz. *Or.* 4 C. *Iulian.* 1.118); the description of the initiatory rites (τὰ τελούμενα) to which novices in the sophists' schools at Athens were subjected, Greg. Naz. *Or.* 43.16, Olympiod. frg. 28 (*FHG* 4.63f. = Phot. *Bibl.* cod. 80, 1.177f. Henry); Theodoret's use of the phrase παιδείας ἀμύητος (*vel sim.*) at *Hist. phil.* 8.2 and 13.8 Canivet, and at *De cur. Graec. affect.* 8.3ff. (p. 196.4f., 22f. Raeder); Choric. *Or. fun. Procop.* 5 (p. 111.8f. Foerster-Richtsteig), οἱ τὰ ῥητόρων τελούμενοι (= the students of rhetoric), and ibid. 7 (p. 111.22f.), τὸ τοὺς νέους μυσταγωγεῖν τοῖς τῶν ἀρχαίων ὀργίοις (= the task of the sophist).

8. Rejection of the idea of "mystery": Macrob. *Sat.* 1.7.5ff. and 1.24.12f., with Kaster, "Macrobius" 253f. (the recesses [*penetralia*] of the sacred poem are to be thrown open; the poetry, demystified and made accessible through *diligentia*). Cf. Choric. *Or. fun. Procop.* 7 (p. 112.7ff.), ὁ δὲ φύσεώς τε ῥώμη καὶ πόνων ἐπιμελείᾳ καθάπερ ἑκάστῳ συνεσκεμμένος ὅσα πεποίηκεν ἕκαστος, οὕτω σὺν ἀκριβείᾳ τὰ πάντων ἦγεν εἰς φῶς, on Procopius as exegete of the ancients, contrasted with the "mystagogues."

9. Phocas *GL* 5.411.2ff.

10. Galen Περὶ ἐθῶν 4 (2.25.13 Marquardt-Mueller-Helmreich); cf. Chap. 2 pp. 77f., on St. Basil.

literary culture, a matter of training (ἄσκησις), achieved through "the sweat of the Muses."[11]

The process was gradual, painstaking—and painful. Like the athlete trained in the old gymnasium, the student of literature slowly acquired his knowledge and skills by replacing unrefined habits with good habits until these (ideally) became second nature; lapses into the bad, old habits were repaid with a beating.[12] Unlike the initiate, the gymnast was not separated decisively from his past but had to struggle constantly against it, using his virtues—memory, diligence, discipline—to fight free of the old ways and so rise above himself. Unremitting and austere, the effort offered correspondingly great rewards. Through "tenacious memory" and "toil," the grammarian Diomedes writes, we achieve "the square-set soundness of speech and its polished brilliance produced by skill." We are then as superior to the uneducated as they are to cattle.[13] The comparison was the oldest article of faith in the literary culture, extending back to Isocrates, repeated later through the Renaissance and beyond. The eloquent man was nothing less than a distinct and artificial species: he had created himself, and was for that reason enormously proud of his achievement.

At the threshold of that achievement stood the grammarian, controlling the access to eloquence with his texts in one hand and his cane in the other. The grammarian's position here is captured in another recurrent metaphor, that of the *custos*, or guardian.[14] The grammarian was, first, the guardian of the language, *custos Latini sermonis*, in a phrase of Seneca, or "guardian of articulate utterance," in the description of Augustine.[15] He was to protect the language against corruption, to preserve its coherence, and to act as an agent of control: thus, early in his

11. ἀσκεῖν in connection with the literary culture: e.g., *IG* 5.1186 = *GVI* 2003 Gytheion; *IG* 14.932 = *GVI* 1111 Ostia; Ramsay, *Cities* no. 232 = *IGR* 4.743 Eumeneia (Emirjik); *IBubon* 9, with *Bull. ép.* 1973, 455, citing other examples; Justinian *ap.* Ioan. Lyd. *De mag.* 3.29; Cyril Scythop. *V. Euthym.* 4, on two lectors πρὸς τῇ θείᾳ γραφῇ καὶ τὴν ἔξω παιδείαν ἀκριβῶς ἠσκημένοι; the ostracon published by Henrichs, "Zwei Fragmente," esp. 48ff. *Sudor musicus*: Priscian *De laud. Anast.* 249, and, e.g., Jerome *C. Rufin.* 1.17, *litterae . . . sudoris comites sunt et laboris;* John Cassian *Conlat.* 5.21, the *sudor multus longaque doctrina* of those possessing *saecularis eruditio* vs. the wisdom arrived at naturally (i.e., through the ascesis of fasting) by the Christian; cf. also Lib. *Or.* 1.12 and *passim*, on his πόνοι and "sweating over" his compositions.

12. Overcoming bad habits the function of the school: see esp. John Chrysost. *Ad pop. Ant.* hom. 8.5 (*PG* 49.97); and cf. Chap. 5 pp. 187–89.

13. Diomedes *GL* 1.299.18ff.; cf. Gell. *NA* 13.17 (liberal education = *humanitas* = *cura et disciplina*, setting men apart from beasts), and Chap. 2 n. 301.

14. Cf. Kaster, "Macrobius" 219f.

15. Sen. *Ep.* 95.65. Aug. *Solil.* 2.19: *vocis articulatae custos*.

history we find the grammarian claiming the right to limit the grant of citizenship (*civitas*) to new usages.[16] But by virtue of his command of the poetic texts, the grammarian's guardianship extended to another, more general area, as guardian of tradition (*historiae custos*).[17] The grammarian was the conservator of all the discrete pieces of tradition embedded in his texts, from matters of prosody (to which Augustine refers in his characterization), to the persons, events, and beliefs that marked the limits of vice and virtue.

The two realms of the guardianship thus answered to the two divisions of the grammarian's task, the knowledge of speaking correctly and the explication of the poets, and the task imposed a formidable burden upon him. As guardian of language and tradition, the grammarian joined those who preserved the boundaries between order and chaos. The weight of the burden can be gauged by comparing the grammarian with other *custodes*: the military commander on the frontier (*limes*) of the empire,[18] or the provincial governor in his role as judge, the "guardian of the laws."[19] Each was a pivotal figure. The soldier preserved the geographic distinction between the insider and the outsider; the governor, placed between the local population and the central government, maintained the hierarchical distinctions that shaped the empire's political structure and its system of laws, wherein legal status depended on social status. The grammarian was similarly pivotal in his own sphere, standing where linguistic, geographic, and social distinctions converged. Although those distinctions are essentially inseparable, it is useful to consider them one by one.

The grammarian's linguistic guardianship, the most important and most complex element of his profession, will be discussed in later chap-

---

16. Suet. *Gramm.* 22, the grammarian M. Pomponius Marcellus criticizing a usage of Tiberius: *tu enim, Caesar, civitatem dare potes hominibus, verbo non potes.* For the anecdote, cf. also Cassius Dio 57.17.1–3, with the comment that Tiberius did not punish Marcellus καίπερ ἀκρατῶς παρρησιασάμενον. Cf. Sen. *Ep.* 120.4, and Chap. 2 n. 113.

17. Aug. *De mus.* 2.1.1.

18. *CIL* 3.6660 = *ILCV* 798 = *IGLS* 5.2704, on Silvinus, *limitis . . . fortissime custos*. For his rank, *comes et dux Phoenices*(?), cf. *PLRE* I s.v., p. 842.

19. *CIL* 6.1722, in honor of Fl. Honoratianus, *v.c., custodi iuris ac legum, parenti totius humanitatis, amico civilitatis et iustitiae*. Despite *PLRE* I s.v. 3, p. 438 ("he might have been *consularis* of Numidia, but the phraseology suggests rather that he was an *advocatus* at the Numidian bar"), Honoratianus's relation to *leges* and *iustitia* (cf. Lib. *Ep.* 5, ἡ τῶν νόμων φυλακή, with Robert, *Hellenica* 4.13ff., 24ff., 62ff., 99ff., and Ševčenko, "Late Antique Epigram" 30f., for other examples, mostly Eastern), his possession of the clarissimate and the Flaviate, and the dedication of the statue with inscription by the staff (*officium*) of the *sedes consularitatis* to their *patronus*, all combine to make it more likely that Honoratianus was a governor, sometime after 324.

ters; for the moment it is sufficient to sketch its salient features. In essence, the grammarian presented himself as an arbiter of the claims of three competing forces:[20] the habit of contemporary usage (*consuetudo; usus*), the authority (*auctoritas*) of the classical literary models, and nature (*natura*), that is, the natural properties of the language, determined by reasoned or systematic analysis (*ratio*) and set down as rules (*regulae*) in the grammarian's handbook (*ars*). In practice, the grammarian spent much of his time protecting the nature of the language (and so his own *ars*) against the influences of habit and authority.

The consequences were twofold. First, the grammarian, as a man of regular speech, was fundamentally a man of distinctions. Grammar defines and separates: *grammatica dividit.*[21] As a distillation of the grammarian's expertise the phrase could not be bettered, and the definition applies both to the effects of grammar on the language and to its social consequences, distinguishing the educated man from the masses.[22] Second, by a paradox suited to the self-created species, the language the grammarian taught was simultaneously artificial and natural, a product of human skill that claimed objective validity and permanence. The grammarian created for himself and for his students a stable place to stand, the square-set soundness of articulate utterance, which laid the foundation for a coherent way of life. As a result, the grammarian's rules offered a liberation: the young man educated in his school could be said to have "embraced the restraints of grammatical instruction, and those rule-bound confines of speech, for the sake of freedom."[23] The paradox, although intended by the comment's author, would have been less remarkable to his contemporaries or his ancestors than it is today. The young man in question had gained freedom through discipline, finding a small spot of coherence in a sea of noise. Close at hand the vulgar language murmured—for example, the Greek and Latin of Scripture, which many of the educated had found repellent[24]—and not much farther off he could hear the hiss of the vernacular, which existed everywhere in the empire.[25]

20. See Chap. 5 pp. 176ff.
21. Sidon. Apoll. *Ep.* 5.2.1.
22. For *leges grammaticorum* and *Latinitas* vs. *intellectus populi* and *quod vulgo dicitur* (*vel sim.*), see, e.g., Rufinus *Transl. Orig. in Cant.* 3 (p. 180.3ff. Baehrens); Jer. *Comm. Ezech.* 12.40, 14.47 (cf. *Comm. Ion.* 4; *Comm. Ephes.* 3.6); Aug. *Serm.* 37.14, *En. in Ps. 36* serm. 3.6, *En. in Ps. 123* 8, *En. in Ps. 138* 20. Cf. also Olympiod. *Comm. Alcib. 1* 95.17ff. Westerink, οἱ πολλοί vs. οἱ γραμματικοί.
23. Ennod. *Epist.* 1.5.10.
24. See, e.g., Lactant. *Inst.* 5.1; Arnob. *Adv. nat.* 1.59; Jer. *Comm. Is. proph.* prol., *Comm. Ion.* 3; Cyril. Alex. *C. Iulian.* 7 (*PG* 76.853); Isid. Pel. *Ep.* 4.28, 67, 91.
25. Vernacular languages: see Bardy, *Question;* Jones, *LRE* 991ff.; MacMullen, "Provincial Languages"; Millar, "Local Culture"; Brunt, "Romanization" 170ff.

The center of coherence was the town. A rough measure of that fact is provided by the following detail: of the hundred-odd grammarians we can identify and place from the mid-third through the mid-sixth centuries, all taught in spots that emerged as episcopal sees at some time during this period.[26] To be sure, we should not assume that every see had a grammarian's school; nor were all bishops' towns grand places (the grammarians in fact are mostly found in the larger sees). Such places did, however, tend to be the centers of gravity in the secular as well as the spiritual lives of their regions, and they therefore presume at least a minimal urban organization and urban life. To that extent—and because he was not concerned, like the bishop, to extend his message and his influence into the hinterland—the grammarian in late antiquity still participated in the ancient division between town and country.

Entering the grammarian's school meant that one was safely past an important geographic hurdle, that one had joined the small minority of the population who shared the life of the towns. It also meant that one would be drawn willy-nilly into a town-bound vision of the world, a

---

Hiss: cf. Jerome's regular use of *stridor* and *stridulus* to characterize the sound of the various Semitic languages (*Ep.* 130.5, 125.12; *Comm. Galat.* 3 prol.; *V. Hilarion.* 22; *Comm. Is. proph.* 4.11; *Comm. Tit.* 3), and Maxim. Taurin. *Serm.* 50 (*PL* 57.635). For one's speech to change suddenly from the vernacular to a language of culture was the sign of a miracle: Mark the Deacon, *Vie de Saint Porphyre* 66–67 Gregoire-Kugener; *Apophth. Patr.*, "De abbate Poemene" 183 (*PG* 65.365f.). The opposite change was a mark of demonic possession: Jer. *V. Hilarion.* 22. Predictably, in a controversy with Augustine, the pagan grammarian Maximus of Madaurus picks as one line of attack the barbarous names of local African martyrs: Aug. *Ep.* 16.2; cf. Augustine's rebuke, *Ep.* 17.2. See also Lib. *Ep.* 369.9.

26. For the known geographic distribution of the grammarians, see Appendix 5. To my knowledge, a comparable distinction could be made for the earlier empire: thus, in the East, a grammarian from Tarsus, P. Tattius Rufus, taught at Zela in Helenopontus (Anderson et al., *Studia Pontica* 3.248 no. 276 Tchaï-Keuï, in the region of Zile), and another grammarian, Maximus, taught at Sebastopolis in Armenia I (Kaibel 402 = *IGR* 3.118 = *GVI* 1184 Soulou-Seraï), both places later episcopal centers. Compare also the grammarian Chrestus from Nicomedia at the old Greek city of Philippopolis in the interior of Thrace: *IGBulg.* 3:1.1021 = *GVI* 614 Plovdiv, where Ἀστακίδου δὲ Χρηστοῦ should be printed, the latter as the man's name, the former as designation of his origin (on Ἀστακία [-κίδης] = Nicomedia[n], see Robert, "Hellenica" 166f. [with *Hellenica* 2.65 n. 2; *Bull. ép.* 1950, 195; "Documents" 424]; Helly and Marcillet-Jaubert, "Remarques" 253; Moretti, "Nuovi epigrammi" 81ff. no. 11). The case of such a man as Rufus of course remains important evidence for the penetration of the Hellenic literary culture "aux villageois barbares des montagnes" (Cumont in Anderson et al., *Studia Pontica* 3.249; cf. 159). On the distribution of the schools see also Marrou, *Histoire*[6] 427ff.; Jones, *LRE* 997f.; Étienne, *Bordeaux* 253, for fourth-century Gaul; Riché, *Education* 23ff.; and Chap. 3 pp. 106f. For small-town teachers (not grammarians) see, e.g., Part II nos. 120, 158, 178, and perhaps also no. 263.

vision so fixed that the "natural ignorance" of the rustic might casually be used to explain a verse of Vergil[27] and so powerful that the Christian preacher would need to emphasize that the grace of God is everywhere, and does not reach only the educated city-dweller like the favors bestowed by men.[28] People could easily assume that the classically educated man of the town had nothing to learn from the man of the country,[29] and that assumption was reinforced by the linguistic gulf between the two. The countryman might well not speak the language of culture at all; if he did, he would probably speak a version of it so uncouth as to require apology lest it offend "urban ears."[30]

The grammarian's school could bridge the divide between town and country—although that is not to say it regularly did so. We know, for example, of the young Hilarion, sent for his entire education to Alexandria from the hamlet (vicus) of Tabatha, in the hinterland of Gaza;[31] one would be hard put, however, to cite many such dramatic transitions from hamlet to metropolis. More common was the movement found in the educational careers of Jerome and Augustine: Augustine certainly (and Jerome possibly) received some preliminary education in his modest home town before being sent to a larger center for further instruction.[32] For reasons described below, even this sort of movement was subject to notable constraints. It does, however, point to two important characteristics of the literary education, a marked geographic mobility and a close conformity to the patterns of upper-class life.

It is necessary to imagine the educational geography of the empire, not in terms of the great land masses ringing the Mediterranean but as an archipelago of cities where schools of liberal letters were to be found. This distribution encouraged a good deal of island hopping. To an outsider, like the desert father St. Anthony, the spectacle of the would-be

27. *Naturalis inperitia*: Ti. Claudius Donatus *Interp. Vergil., ad Aen.* 7.482 (2.72.5ff. Georgii).

28. Cyril of Jerusalem *Catech.* 17 *De spir. sanct.* 2.35.

29. *Apophth. Patr.*, "De abbate Arsenio" 6 (*PG* 65.89): when Arsenius consults an old Egyptian peasant, ἕτερος ἰδὼν αὐτὸν εἶπεν· "Ἀββᾶ Ἀρσένιε, πῶς τοσαύτην παίδευσιν Ῥωμαϊκὴν καὶ Ἑλληνικὴν ἐπιστάμενος τοῦτον τὸν ἀγροῖκον περὶ τῶν σῶν λογισμῶν ἐρωτᾶς."

30. John Chrysost. *De sanct. mart.* hom. 1 (*PG* 50.646), on the enmity between πόλις and χώρα at Antioch, with remarks on the Syriac speakers of the hinterland: cf. *Ad pop. Ant.* hom. 19.1 (*PG* 49.188f.); *In cap. 1 Genes.* hom. 4.4 (*PG* 53.43); *In Matth.* hom. 7.2 (*PG* 57.74). *Urbanae aures*: Sulp. Sev. *Dial.* 1.27.2–4 (cf. at Chap. 2 n. 204). For even illiterate townsmen feeling themselves superior in their speech to the *rustici*, see Aug. *De doct. Christ.* 4.3.5. Cf. n. 25 above.

31. Jer. *V. Hilarion.* 2.

32. For Augustine, see Part II no. 20. For Jerome, see *C. Rufin.* 1.30, with n. 46 below.

educated "leaving home and crossing the sea, that they might learn letters," appeared frenetic and fragmented when compared with "us who have no need to leave home for the sake of the Kingdom of Heaven, or to cross the sea for the sake of excellence."[33] The vision has the same strength and weakness as many an outsider's view, seeing only a part of the truth but seeing it clearly. The world of letters was fluid, with effects that were often fragmenting. After leaving home and crossing the sea, many did not return. Some died while studying abroad.[34] Others died away from home after beginning the careers their education had brought them.[35] Some never came home, having discovered wisdom of one variety or another;[36] others found a secular career to relieve them of curial obligations in their native cities.[37]

Yet amid the movement there was pattern and stability. As far as the literary education is concerned, only the upper levels of the population were geographically mobile. Hence traditional boundaries—for example, between town and country—were preserved far more often than vio-

33. Athanas. Alex. *V. Anton.* 20, purportedly from a sermon delivered by Anthony τῇ Αἰγυπτικῇ φωνῇ, quoting Luke 17.21, ἡ βασιλεία τῶν οὐρανῶν ἐντὸς ὑμῶν ἐστιν.

34. See Lib. *Or.* 1.151; Symm. *Ep.* 4.56, 9.54; with some epitaphs, mostly earlier, of students who died away from home: *SEG* 2.461 = *GVI* 1519 = *Bull. ép.* 1958, 336 (cf. Robert, *Hellenica* 1.154); *GVI* 1081; Kaibel 228 = *GVI* 970 = *Inschr. Eph.* 6 (*IGSK* 16) 2101 (with the corrigenda at *Inschr. Eph.* 7.1, p. 28; cf. also *Inschr. Eph.* 6.2202, 2211); *ILAlg.* 1363; *CIL* 8.12152; *IG* 14.1436 = *IGR* 1.208 = *GVI* 1025 = *IGVR* 3.1165; *IG* 14.1728 = *IGR* 1.279 = *GVI* 745 = *IGVR* 2.1243; *ILCV* 740 = *IEPD* 672.

35. E.g., Aur. Harpocration from Panopolis (*PKöln* inv. 4533ᵛ = Browne, "Panegyrist" and "Harpocration"), a panegyrist wandering "from Greece to Rome, and from Rome to Constantinople, and from one city to another, going about practically the entire earth," and apparently garnering the offices of *procurator* and *curator civitatis* in the process; Conon, from Ayasofya (anc. Colybrassus?) in eastern Pamphylia (Bean and Mitford, *Journeys* no. 49, with important corrections by J. and L. Robert, *Bull. ép.* 1972, 504, by Gilliam, "Student," esp. for the date, s.IV, and by Lebek, "Begräbnis"), who died young after studying Latin and law at Berytus, finding some legal employment in Palestine, moving on to Antioch and Nicomedia, then serving until his death as *assessor* of the *praeses Thebaidos* (with Conon's career, cf. Dörner, *Bericht* no. 154, the epitaph of one Zeno, who was returned home for burial after dying abroad at twenty ἤδη νομικῷ ἐνδόξῳ); the career of Caesarius, brother of Gregory Nazianzen, *Or.* 7.6ff. (with *PLRE* I s.v. Caesarius 2, pp. 169f.).

36. Compare Marin. *V. Procli* 8 (Proclus's early education, his father's ambitions for his career, and his own desire for philosophy; sim. Eunap. *V. phil.* 6.1.1 [Aedesius]) with Zach. Schol. *Vie de Sévère* 54ff. (the education of Evagrius of Samosata, his father's ambitions for his career, and his own desire for philosophy, i.e., the monastic life).

37. Cf. Petit, *Étudiants* 170ff., with the qualifications of Liebeschuetz, *Antioch* 174ff. (esp. 180f.), and 245f., on *CTh* 14.9.1 (an. 370).

lated; and the movement of students, like that of the teachers, was determined by the personal relationships between leading men in the cities who commended and received them.[38] Most important, when the literary education combined with geographic mobility to produce social mobility, it did so above an already existing and clearly definable threshold of privilege. Broadly speaking, social mobility occurred only among the portions of the urban upper classes that still maintained their eminence and its traditions, or in those segments of the imperial service that absorbed members of the urban aristocracy and their values.

The statement that one's cousins had "suffered not even a grammarian"[39] revealed as much about their social standing as it did about their linguistic and literary attainments. To make such a statement without blush or reproach, as Augustine did, signaled that one was stepping outside the culture of secular prestige. It was a step few of his educated contemporaries were wholeheartedly prepared to take. Anyone who reached the age at which Augustine wrote those words would have had a quarter-century of conditioning, forming assumptions of prestige and privilege that would have become second nature. Such assumptions are found everywhere, from letters of recommendation—a central document of the age, to which we will return repeatedly—to more unexpected or oblique forms: the knowledge that one could appropriately refer to his education as grounds for special consideration in a legal appeal,[40] or the casual assumption that even pagan literary men could by virtue of their cultural authority and social standing competently judge a religious debate between Mani and a Christian bishop,[41] or even the distinctions that produced what can be called a socially stratified sense of humor. Walking along the streets of Cyrene, a man could see the graffito, "Question: Who was the father of Priam's children?" and smile, recognizing a schoolboy's parody of the grammarian's catechism, perhaps recalling the jokes of his own school days.[42] Just so, the recipient of one of Symmachus's letters would have smiled knowingly to see him apply the obliquely obscene Vergilian tag *huic aliud mercedis erit* to an enemy.[43]

---

38. See esp. Petit, *Étudiants* 112ff., 122ff., on Libanius's recruiting students from the provinces; on teachers' movement, see Chaps. 3 and 6.

39. Aug. *De beat. vit.* 1.6.

40. Cf. *PSI* 13.1337.21–23 (s. III, prov. unknown: a petition to the prefect), with a like note struck in similar documents of the fourth century (*PKöln* inv. 4533^{r}56–57 and 4533^{v}9–10 [an. 348, Panopolis], quoted by Browne, "Harpocration" 192f.) and the fifth (*PCairMasp.* 3.67295, with Part II no. 78).

41. See *Acta Archelai* 12 = Epiphan. *Panar. haeres.* 66.10ff., with Part II nos. 179, 236. The doubtful historicity of the account does not detract from the point made here.

42. *ASIA* 1961–62, 219ff. no. 192, with Kaster, "Schoolboy's Burlesque."

43. Symm. *Ep.* 6.22.1 and Verg. *Ecl.* 6.26, with Kaster, "Echo."

These comforting assumptions were produced by schools not only sparse in geographic distribution but markedly exclusive in social organization. It is necessary here to think not of a single, integrated track of primary and secondary schools, like the system known to (and produced in) the twentieth century, but of different types of schools serving different segments of the population.[44] The population at large, massively illiterate, was served (however ill) by the "schools of letters" (γραμματο-διδασκαλεῖα, *ludi litterarii*), institutions of low prestige that provided general, utilitarian literacy. But others, those who had access to the liberal schools of grammar and rhetoric, would receive the rudiments of instruction at home or from teachers assigned to impart the first elements in the grammarian's school; they thus would meet the grammarian as their first teacher. The typical product of the school of liberal letters was therefore insulated from the lower orders, just as the teachers of liberal letters were distinguished by their higher fees and their legal privileges from the common teacher of letters.

Two points should be stressed concerning this arrangement. First, it is not in itself peculiar to late antiquity, the product of a sudden aristocratization of the literary culture, but stands revealed in sources ranging from the first through the sixth centuries. If any change is visible, it is not in how the schools were structured but in how the structure was maintained and in the clientele it served: the authority and the burden were perhaps increasingly shared by the imperial government,[45] and sons of some imperial functionaries perhaps took places that sons of the depressed segment of the curial order had vacated. Second, there was some movement from one type of school to the other, especially when a student was fortunate enough to move from an outlying town that had no grammarian to a larger center that did. But passage from a school of letters to a liberal school was irregular, a trickle, not a steady stream. Of the three men noted above—Hilarion, Jerome, and Augustine—only the last clearly began in a school of letters.[46] While there were surely other

44. For the following, which differs somewhat from the usual account of the institutional configuration of the schools, see Kaster, "Notes"; Booth, "Schooling" and "Elementary Education"; cf. also Jones, *LRE* 997f. For further nuance, see Chap. 2 "Some Variable Definitions."

45. See Chap. 6 pp. 216ff.

46. Augustine: cf. Kaster, "Notes" 326, 341. For Hilarion, Jerome (*V. Hilarion.* 2) mentions no preliminary schooling before he was sent to the grammarian's school at Alexandria; he was probably among those who had the grammarian as their first teacher (see Kaster, "Notes" 329ff.). Jerome: Booth ("Date," esp. 351ff.) has argued plausibly that Jerome began his education under a grammarian (the *Orbilius saeviens* of C. *Rufin.* 1.30) at Rome. Note that even if his arguments are rejected in favor of the standard view, that Jerome received some education at Stridon before going to Rome, the nature of that education is not immediately clear; cf. Kaster, "Notes" 342ff.

such instances,[47] specific examples do not thrust themselves forward: one must not generalize from the familiar but perhaps exceptionally brilliant (and fortunate) case of Augustine.

The higher fees the teachers of grammar and rhetoric charged, the additional largesse they traditionally received on special occasions, and the allowances young men would need if they traveled to major centers of study all required surplus wealth.[48] As Lactantius remarked, instead of giving thanks for being born human, male, Greek, Athenian, and a contemporary of Socrates, Plato should have given thanks that he was born talented, teachable, "and with the resources to be liberally educated."[49] The social origins of the sophist Libanius's students show that few categories in the population had resources on the necessary scale: government functionaries, teachers of liberal letters, members of other liberal professions (for the most part, advocates), some gentlemen of no visible occupation, and *curiales*.[50] To these can be added some Christian bishops and presbyters,[51] and of course the old senatorial aristocracy in the West.[52]

While some from among these categories—teachers, imperial bureaucrats, advocates—could count on salaries, fees, or *douceurs* (paid in the stable currencies of gold and silver, no small advantage),[53] the common denominator was still land: thus, Jerome presumes that a man unable to pay a teacher's fee in a pinch would give a landowner's excuses—crops damaged by hail or drought, profits eaten up by taxes.[54] The excuses, especially the latter, are ominous. By no means could all landowners—or *curiales*—manage easily: although his father was a town councilor of middling means with an estate,[55] Augustine's education was a close thing, begun in the lower-status school of letters and continued only through the extraordinary efforts of his father and the timely beneficence of a family connection.[56]

47. See esp. Symeon of Mesopotamia *Hom.* 15.42, quoted and discussed by Kaster, "Notes" 326.

48. On fees and largesse, see Chap. 3; on allowances, see Liebeschuetz, *Antioch* 84 with nn. 8, 9; and on living conditions generally, see Petit, *Étudiants* 144ff.

49. Lactant. *Inst.* 3.19. Cf. ibid. 3.25; Hesychius 1.1.15ff. Latte, the interpretation of the title of Diogenianus's Περιεργοπένητες.

50. Petit, *Étudiants* 172, 194f.

51. Jer. *Comm. Ephes.* 3.6 (PL 26.574A).

52. On social origins and access to schools in the West, see also Nellen, *Viri* 98ff.

53. Liebeschuetz, *Antioch* 86.

54. *Comm. Galat.* 3.6 (PL 26.459B). Jerome's education was probably made possible by his family's landholdings, for which see *Ep.* 66.14.

55. *Conf.* 2.3.5; *Ep.* 126.7.

56. See Part II no. 20.

The outlook for the lower orders was still less promising. Few students from lower levels of society than those already mentioned are known to have entered the grammarian's school: Aetius, patronized by the anonymous grammarian of Anazarbus;[57] or Eustathius, the son of a clothes factor, educated (according to the hagiographic tradition) by a grammarian at Nicomedia;[58] or the three freedmen's sons who taught as grammarians at Bordeaux.[59] In addition, there was probably a significant dropout rate. Of fifty-seven students whose length of study in Libanius's school is known, thirty-five followed the course of rhetoric for only one or two years, twelve for only three or four years, and the other ten for five or six years.[60] Evidence suggests that the pyramid of enrollments should be projected farther downward,[61] that there was also attrition between the schools of grammar and rhetoric and within the grammarian's school—hence the earlier statement that the grammarian's school would be the only thing approaching a common experience for the elite. Yet in some respects it was enough: in language and manners, the man who had never attended the grammarian's school was more marked than the man who had attended the grammarian's school but had not gone on to rhetoric; the latter, moreover, was not necessarily shut off from a career open to a man of liberal education.[62] If nothing else, he

57. Philostorg. *HE* 3.15, with "Prologue" above.
58. See Part II no. 234 for comment also on the historicity of the account.
59. See Part II nos. 40, 146, 165. Note that these are the only grammarians of this social standing known in the period: see Chap. 3. Among other liberally educated men of humble origins who achieved some eminence, one might mention, e.g., Festus of Tridentum (= *PLRE* I s.v. Festus 3, pp. 334f.), described as *ultimi sanguinis et ignoti* at Amm. Marc. 29.2.22; Pamprepius the grammarian and political adventurer, said to have begun life as a poor man (Part II no. 114); and perhaps Fl. Mallius Theodorus, whose antecedents are passed over in Claudian's panegyric (cf. *PLRE* I s.v. Theodorus 27, p. 902). But "low birth" and "poverty" are notably relative terms; there is no reason to suppose that Festus, for instance, was in his origins the social inferior of, say, Jerome: see Matthews, *Western Aristocracies* 47; cf. Part II no. 46 *ad fin.* It is unlikely that any of these men was comparable in his origins to the figures mentioned in this and the preceding two notes.
60. Petit, *Étudiants* 62ff., with pp. 95–96, 155f., 170ff. Note the most common reasons for withdrawal after one or two years: family circumstances, e.g., replacement of a deceased father in the local *curia* (cf. Kopaček, "Curial Displacements" 327ff., for the career of Firminus); or the pursuit of careers in advocacy and the law. For three years as the "indispensable minimum" for a thorough grounding in rhetoric, at least in the opinion of Libanius, see Petit, *Étudiants* 65.
61. See esp. *Vie d'Alexandre l'Acémète* 5 (*PO* 6.660f.): Alexander proceeds to serve as *praefectianus* directly from education in grammar. Cf. also the career imagined by Symeon of Mesopotamia (above n. 47) and, e.g., the case of Eustathius (above n. 58).
62. Cf. *Vie d'Alexandre* (preceding note) and Symeon of Mesopotamia (above n. 47).

could claim the "letters" (that is, liberal letters) or the "gifts of the Muses" sufficient for purely personal distinction.

The exclusiveness of the literary culture had two evident consequences. First, "letters" or the like recurred as one of the three or four most important marks of status—what Paulinus of Nola meant when he referred to *honos, litterae, domus* as the "tokens of prestige in the world," or what Jerome had in mind when he spoke of the "noble man, fluent of speech, wealthy," a vivid figure flanked by an "accompaniment of the powerful," set off against the backdrop of the "mob."[63] At one extreme, literary attainments would provide eminence at the tomb, if nowhere else, a fact that accounts for the frequent mention of such attainments on the epitaphs of children or youths, pathetic reminders of dignity achieved and promise cut short.[64] At the other extreme, literary culture followed one through life, to be noted regularly, for example, among the virtues of men who had gone on to hold the highest offices of state.[65] The phrase "among the virtues" is used advisedly here: the literary culture in itself guaranteed virtue; its acquisition signaled that one possessed discipline, an appetite for toil, and the other ethical qualities that marked a man fit to share the burden of government.[66] *Doctrina* presumed *mores*; to be a scholar presumed that one was the right sort, a gentleman. That fact must engross the attention, however irrelevant to competent rule the literary education might seem to modern eyes.[67]

63. Paulin. Nol. *Carm.* 24.481f.; Jer. *Ep.* 66.6; cf. id. *Comm. Ion.* 3 (*PL* 25.1143B).

64. The tiniest selection, chosen for geographic spread: *ILAlg.* 1363, 1364 (Thubursicum Numidarum); *CIL* 8.646 (Mactar); *CIL* 8.8500 = *ILS* 7761 (Sitifis); *CIL* 8.23243 (Henchir Divana); *CIL* 2.4465 = *ILER* 1706 (Aeso [Tarracon.]); *CIL* 13.1910 (Lugdunum); *ILCV* 727, 738; *CIL* 11.2839 (Volsinii), 3194 (Falerii), 6435 (Pisaurum), 7856 (Carsulae); *AE* 1971, 322 = *RIU* 557 (Pannonia); *Bull. ép.* 1976, 289 (Megara); *IG* 4² 288 = *IAEpidaur.* 36; Verilhac, "Déesse" (Salamis [Cyprus]; N.B. a would-be liberally educated, but prematurely dead, child μέλλων τὰ Μουσῶν δ[ῶ]ρα βαστάζειν; *Bull. ép.* 1974, 573 no. 29 (Nicomedia); *IGR* 3.463 = *IBubon* 14; *IGLS* 4.1350 (Apamea); *IGLTyr* 1.149A, B, 150; Kaibel 415 = *GVI* 1089 = *IMEGR* 74 (Lycopolis); and Marrou, ΜΟΥΣΙΚΟΣ 197ff.; Robert, *Hellenica* 13.47ff.; n. 34 above; n. 83 below. Cf. also, e.g., Paulin. Nol. *Carm.* 31.23ff.; Greg. Naz. *Epitaph.* 29ff. = *Anth. Gr.* 8.122ff.

65. E.g., *eloquentia* (*litterarum lumen*, etc.) included with *iustitia, integritas, auctoritas, nobilitas* (*vel sim.*) in honorific inscriptions dedicated to L. Aurelius Avianius Symmachus *signo* Phosphorius (*CIL* 6.1698), Iulius Agrius Tarrutenius Marcianus (*CIL* 6.1735), Petronius Probus (*CIL* 6.1751), L. Turcius Secundus *signo* Asterius (*CIL* 6.1772). Cf. *CIL* 5.7917 = *IANice-Cimiez* p. 94, epitaph of C. Subrius Secundinus, *flamen et patronus provinciae, pietatis eloquentiae morum magister*.

66. For the learned = the good, and the uneducated = the crude and slothful (*inertes*), cf. Aur. Vict. *De Caes.* 9.12. For the place of such virtues as discipline and diligence in the ideology of letters, see above on the gymnastic of the soul and below, Chap. 2 "Independence and Constraint."

67. Cf. Marrou, *Histoire*⁶ 444f.

Letters validated claims to status, both moral and social—although the two were hardly separate to the liberally educated man.

The fusion helps to explain the second consequence of the literary culture's exclusiveness, the importance of liberal studies in upward social mobility. If in theory the man of letters could be presumed to be the right sort, in practice the presumption provided entry into the network of personal relationships and patronage that could lead to wealth, offices, and good marriages. The general observation of Augustine and John Chrysostom, that liberal letters furthered temporal ambitions,[68] is amply borne out by specific cases: Augustine himself, Ausonius and other teachers at Bordeaux,[69] Libanius's students,[70] rhetoricians and advocates who became governors,[71] wandering panegyrists,[72] and even a few fairly obscure grammarians.[73]

When we face this picture, it is important to remember several points. First, the man thus prized for his education fundamentally embodied continuity. This is true in the obvious sense that literary attainments formed part of the foundation for success in the imperial service already in the high empire.[74] It is, however, also true in another sense, which touches more directly on the coexistence of continuity and change. The literary men—for example, the sophists of the Greek East—who were drawn into the imperial upper class from the local elites of their towns in the second and early third centuries shared the responsibility for

68. Aug. *De discipl. Christ.* 12; John Chrysost. *Adv. oppugn. vit. monast.* 3.5.

69. Hopkins, "Social Mobility"; and below, Chap. 3.

70. Petit, *Étudiants* 166, 185.

71. See Chap. 3 nn. 133, 178.

72. E.g., Aur. Harpocration of Panopolis (above n. 35); the sinecure as *tribunus et notarius* gained by Claudian, *CIL* 6.1710 = *ILS* 2949 = *IGVR* 1.63, with Alan Cameron, *Claudian* 390ff.

73. On the social mobility of the grammarians, see Chap. 3. On the general phenomenon of "gebildetes Beamtentum" in the West in s.IV, see the material collected by Nellen, *Viri*.

74. See MacMullen, "Roman Bureaucratese" 368 n. 16; Bowersock, *Greek Sophists* 43ff. (with the qualifications of Bowie, "Importance"); Millar, *Emperor* 83ff., 101ff. (cf. also 491ff.); Champlin, *Fronto, passim*. For continuity within a single family, see the case of M. Postumius Festus, an African orator, acquaintance of Fronto (cf. *Ad am.* 2.11.1 van den Hout), participant in a vignette of Gellius (*NA* 19.13.1ff.), senator, and suffect consul in 160 (Alföldy, *Konsulat* 174), whose memory as an *orator* is kept alive through two of his *pronepotes*: T. Flavius Postumius Varus, himself a suffect consul and *PVR* in 271, an *orator . . . beatus diis, amicis, literis* (*CIL* 6.1417 = *ILS* 2940) and *sectator* of Festus (*CIL* 6.1416 = *ILS* 2929); and T. Flavius Postumius Titianus, consul II in 301 and *PVR* in 305–6, and an *orator, pronepos, et sectator M. Postumi Festi orat(oris)* (*CIL* 6.1418 = *ILS* 2941). For Titianus and Varus, see *PLRE* I s.vv. Titianus 9 (pp. 919f.), Varus 2 (pp. 946f.); for the nuance of *sectator*, see further Chap. 2 "Independence and Constraint" at nn. 84, 107.

cracking the shell of provincial life and showing new horizons to their peers.[75] If the pressures of the third century enlarged that crack beyond repair, they also guaranteed that the new horizons would remain permanently in view, providing a new measure of ambition and a new setting for old forms of homage. The man of the second and early third century who could anticipate (and take it as his due) that his townsmen would praise and remember him for his education and other ἀρεταί[76] has as his epigonus the governor of the third through sixth centuries, honored by the city for his wisdom, his literary attainments, and his other virtues.[77] The change marks part of the shift in the empire's center of gravity; insofar as the schools participated in that change, they did so by providing reassurance that nothing basic had shifted, that the right, honorable men were still conspicuously present and accounted for.

Redistribution of land after the disturbances in third-century Gaul,[78] the rift that began to open between superior and inferior town councilors in the second century[79] and produced a crisis by the early fourth century, the expansion of the imperial bureaucracy under Diocletian (A.D. 284–305) and the increased opportunity for wealth it brought to some of its members—all were elements of the third century's "loosening of society."[80] The schools thereafter had to consolidate the effects of that loosening by continuing their old job of sorting out and identifying the elite.[81] They would not only provide the basis of a career but also add the traditional adornment to a gentleman's life.[82] They would confirm status already held more frequently than they would serve as the springboard to higher status. And they would contribute to mobility,

75. See Bowersock, *Greek Sophists* 28f.

76. E.g., *IG* 5.466, 563, 1168, 1369; *Olympia* 5.470; *SEG* 11.321 (Argos); *Inschr. Eph.* 3 (*IGSK* 13) 710; Miltner and Miltner, "Epigraphische Nachlese" 10ff. no. 2 (Ancyra); *SEG* 6.57 (Ancyra); *AE* 1971, 305 (Dassare [Dalmatia]).

77. See Robert, *Hellenica* 4.24ff. and, for σοφία, 4.61, 66, 91, with Charneux, "Inscriptions" 616f., Miltner, "Vorläufiger Bericht" 347, Ševčenko, "Late Antique Epigram" 30ff.

78. See Wightman, "Peasants" 111.

79. See Garnsey, "Aspects."

80. MacMullen, *Enemies* 246.

81. Cf. Marrou, *Christiana tempora* 49ff.

82. I would add this to balance the general and, I believe, one-sided emphasis on the purely careerist motives associated with late-antique education: our sources by their nature more often reveal the public man than the one who "knows that the calm of retirement is appropriate to those raised in philosophy and literature" (*PKöln* inv. 4533v9–10 at Browne, "Harpocration" 193: the words of Aur. Ammon, brother of the wandering panegyrist Aur. Harpocration; cf. n. 35 above) and who has "escaped our knowledge, simply by having escaped distinction" (Brown, *Religion* 186, on the members of the senatorial order at Rome).

where they did so, by validating the aspirant's claim to standing and prestige and ushering him into predictable channels of influence, in effect acting as a brake on sudden, unstructured mobility. The sorting might take two or three generations:[83] so much the better reason for believing that virtue was safe in the order—the *disciplina*—Diocletian and his successors restored. Affronts to that order by jumped-up litterateurs—cases of spectacular mobility built on letters, cutting disturbingly across class lines—would not often come from the schools of liberal studies.

With its emphasis on order, discipline, and regularity, the sketch above might be read as an elaboration of Salvian.[84] Writing after the fragmentation of the imperial government in much of the West, Salvian used Carthage as an example of the impurity of Africa under Roman rule, because that city "contained virtually all those things by which the order of the commonwealth [*disciplina rei publicae*] is maintained or guided in the world as a whole." He listed the institutions responsible: the military forces, the governor's office and the other tools of administration, and the "schools of liberal arts"—grammar and rhetoric—which with the "philosophers' workshops" made up "all the gymnasia of language or *mores*." Salvian's hostile vision brings us back to our starting point: the grammarian as guardian, ranged alongside the military commander and provincial governor, maintaining the language and tradition of the special man produced by the gymnastic of the soul and thus preserving the *disciplina* and social coherence of at least one segment of the commonwealth. So deeply rooted and enduring is this conception of the grammarian's role that it persists even when—or perhaps especially when—the comparable roles of commander and governor have been submerged or radically transformed. Although at first glance surprising, it seems on reflection predictable that a grammarian in Milan should have been called guardian of the empire (*imperii custos*) at the start of the sixth century under the Ostrogothic kingdom.[85]

83. Cf. the case of Victor, grammarian at Cirta / Constantina by 303 (Part II no. 161), of Moorish descent, whose father had been a *decurio* at Cirta and whose grandfather had been a soldier in the *comitatus*. For a possible glimpse of the process cut short, cf. the epitaph published by Mitchell, "R.E.C.A.M. Notes" 84 no. 18 (s.III init., Ancyra), set up by Nicetes, a veteran of *leg. I Parthica*, and his wife to their son Kastresios (= Castrensis), dead aged 13, πάσῃ χάριτι κὲ παιδείᾳ κεκοσμημένον. A similar span separates the dislocation and impoverishment of Ausonius's grandfather and the spectacular success of Ausonius himself (cf. Matthews, *Western Aristocracies* 81ff.)—the family starting out higher on the social ladder than Victor's but, after reverses, also reaching higher.

84. *Gub. Dei* 7.16.67–68.

85. Ennod. *Carm.* 2.90.1; cf. *Dict.* 9.5, *libertatis index, boni testimonium sanguinis;* all applied to Deuterius, for whom see Part II no. 44.

Yet our sketch, spare and selective as it is, is also artificially distinct. Drawn largely from the point of view of the literary culture, the picture tends to credit the classical elite's view of itself as living the only coherent and worthy life. That was, of course, a delusion. Moreover, the sketch cumulatively attributes to the grammarian a more important place than many of his contemporaries within and without the literary culture would have been willing to grant him. As a guardian the grammarian was also a threshold figure, exposed and ambiguous; his position of strength was vulnerable, capable of being chipped away on several sides. The next chapter accordingly is intended to blur some of the distinctions and give further nuance to the picture above by drawing in some of the forces that impinged upon the grammarian and his profession.

CHAPTER 2

Professio Litterarum

On 13 December 320 the grammarian Victor of Cirta / Constantina was brought before Zenophilus, governor of Numidia, for questioning. The interrogation began as follows:

> Zenophilus . . . said, "What is your name?" He answered, "Victor." Zenophilus . . . said, "What is your personal condition [*condicio*]?" Victor said, "I am a professor of Roman letters [*professor sum Romanarum litterarum*], a Latin grammarian." Zenophilus . . . said, "What is your social status [*dignitas*]?" Victor said, "My father was a decurion of the people of Constantina; my grandfather, a soldier. He had served in the *comitatus*, for our origin derives from Moorish blood."[1]

Several points in the exchange should be noted. First, when asked his condition, Victor specifies his livelihood, his profession of letters.[2] Moreover, in the context of the exchange, personal condition implies (or effectively means) *dignitas*—social status and prestige.[3] Finally, condition and social status are inextricably associated with legal status: as a member of a liberal profession and the son of a *curialis*, Victor would have possessed a fairly lofty position (*honestas*, the state of being a gentleman)[4]

---

1. *Gesta apud Zenophilum*, CSEL 26.185.7ff. (cf. Chap. 1 n. 83).
2. Cf. ibid. 193.5f., *Zenophilus . . . dixit: cuius condicionis es? Saturninus respondit: fossor*; ibid. 11f., *Zenophilus . . . dixit: cuius condicionis es? Victor* [another man of the same name, not the grammarian] *dixit: artifex sum*.
3. Note that when Saturninus and Victor (n. 2) have stated their *condiciones*, no further inquiry is made concerning their *dignitas*. Cf. also ibid. 195.14f., *Zenophilus . . . dixit: cuius condicionis es? Castus dixit: nullam dignitatem habeo*; and Garnsey, *Social Status* 225ff.
4. Cf. ibid. 185.14, Zenophilus to Victor: *memor fidei et honestatis tuae simpliciter designa*.

and so certain legal privileges—for example, exemption from torture—
that those of lowlier status (*humiliores*) did not have.

These points touch on two of the themes of this chapter. First, the
concept of a profession in Victor's world evidently involved some attributes different from those of modern professions: for example, the professional man—a physician, say, or an architect—who gives testimony
before an American bench cannot expect his professional standing to
affect his treatment under the law should he show contempt of court, or
to distinguish him juridically from a day laborer or tradesman in similar
circumstances. Second, theory and practice do not always coincide: thus
Victor, when reluctant to testify, found himself threatened with torture,
from which his *honestas* supposedly protected him.[5]

We can better understand the grammarians' position by comparing
their profession with the modern concept of a profession. The comparison is suggested not only by the etymological link *professio litterarum*
provides[6] but also by important substantive similarities.

For the contemporary notion of a profession, consider the physician or
attorney.[7] First, and most obvious, the profession of each is based on a
conceptually distinct system of knowledge and practice that is recognized
as such by society and is reflected in the structural differentiation of
society's institutions. For instance, the law in the United States today is
a system of thought separate from, say, religion: the attorney does not
think of himself (or, of course, herself) as a priest, nor do his fellow
citizens; and the institutions of the law have their own well-defined
place in the structure of American life. Because of this differentiation,
the would-be physician or attorney expects to gain his expertise in a
specialized institution—a professional school, where he is trained by
members of the profession—and he expects his training to be subject to
testing and certification, which will be determined, again, by members of
the profession. He assumes that his success at this and later stages will
depend above all on objective evaluation of his skills. (How often this
meritocratic assumption will prove false is a different matter; we are
concerned here with professional ideology.) In his practice he is expected
to act autonomously and impersonally; the procedures he follows should
be those defined by his expertise and its techniques and should be
unaffected by personal relations or outside authority. The physician

5. Ibid. 186.13ff.: *Zenophilus . . . Victori dixit: simpliciter confitere, ne strictius
interrogeris.*

6. On the phrase, cf. Dahlmann, *Kleine Schriften* 255ff.

7. On the definition of a profession sketched in this and the following paragraph, see Parsons, "Professions" 536; Bledstein, *Culture*, chap. 3, esp. pp. 86–87
and the literature there cited in n. 12.

should in each case prescribe the treatment dictated by his best professional judgment, irrespective of differences in the social status of his patients or his personal ties to them; the attorney should handle a case according to the methods laid down by his training, without regard for the climate of opinion, his personal feelings toward his client, or external pressures. If either man acts otherwise, he behaves unprofessionally, in the most common sense of the word. The physician or attorney is also expected to put his expertise to socially responsible use and is specifically encouraged to do so by institutions—for example, boards of ethics—that his profession has developed.

Contemporary professionalism has several other important characteristics. Since the profession is commonly a full-time occupation that provides a livelihood, it gives its practitioner a distinct place in the economic system of his society; the profession usually has a specialized or technical language (jargon), a restricted code that allows shorthand communication among its members while excluding laymen; and the profession confers (de facto, if not de jure) a distinct and usually respected social status. In general, the emphasis falls on the professionals' individual and collective authority, objectivity, self-determination, and self-regulation, with those characteristics contributing ultimately to the well-being of society.

The grammarian's profession resembled the modern notion in several obvious ways. His expertise was conceptually distinct, with a cultural tradition of its own—embodied, for example, in the technical handbook (ars, τέχνη), which is his most characteristic document. The grammarian was at home in the structurally differentiated institution of his school, which was distinguished horizontally from other institutions (for example, the family) in the society around it and vertically from other institutions (for example, the school of rhetoric) in the literary culture.[8] In addition, his expertise and his institutional niche gave the grammarian a sense of autonomy and authority, which found various forms of expression: the Roman grammarian derived the word *ars* itself from either ἀρετή (excellence) or *artus* (close, firm, tight); the grammarian treated language objectively and impersonally, as a phenomenon subject to the analytical methods of his tradition, and he imagined himself the arbiter of language.[9] Finally, from this position of professional competence and authority he could be thought to contribute to the ordered well-being of society in his role as guardian.

8. For the concept of structural differentiation applied to institutions in the Roman world, see esp. Hopkins, "Structural Differentiation," "Elite Mobility" 108ff., and *Conquerors* 74ff.

9. On these and other consequences of the grammarian's professional niche, see Chaps. 4 and 5.

Yet in other, equally important ways the grammarian's ancient profession stands apart from the modern. Most obvious, there did not exist any specialized training comparable to modern professional education; and in its absence the grammarian was permanently linked to a tradition-minded, aristocratic amateurism, with consequences difficult to overstate. Our purpose in this chapter, then, is to survey how the grammarian's position corresponds to or differs from a modern professional's, in order to view that position and its inherent tensions more closely. We will consider, in turn, how the distinctiveness of the grammarian's profession—its conceptual and institutional differentiation—was affected by its place on the boundary between mere letters and liberal letters, how the profession's differentiation and autonomy were influenced by the social milieu of the high literary culture, and how the grammarian's contribution to the common good was regarded by the second great tradition of late antiquity, Christianity.

SOME VARIABLE DEFINITIONS: LITERACY, LETTERS, AND THE GRAMMARIAN'S PROFESSION

We can begin with two propositions. First, grammar's intellectual and social distinction owed much to its role in a segment of society that had a fairly fixed idea of what literacy involved—a knowledge of letters gained in the *scholae liberales*—and that placed a high premium on acquiring and using this literacy. Second, that segment of society was at all times and on any estimation very small: for the mass of the population, letters of any kind were marginal in daily life. In the following few pages I would like to consider these propositions and their consequences. Specifically, I want to suggest that the marginal place of literacy made the idea of letters more flexible and that this flexibility had the simultaneous (if contradictory) effects of partially emphasizing and partially blurring the distinctiveness of the grammarian's profession.

It is necessary first to gauge the proportions of literacy and illiteracy in the empire—an inevitably imprecise business in the absence of direct and statistically reliable evidence. The overall impression, certainly, is one of massive illiteracy. R. P. Duncan-Jones has provided the clearest indications in a recent comparative study of age rounding (the practice of giving ages in multiples of five) on tombstones from the western half of the empire in the first three centuries of our era.[10] The importance of

10. Duncan-Jones, "Age-Rounding, Illiteracy," superseding the similar study by Mócsy, "Unkenntnis," esp. in the statistical method used. Cf. also Duncan-Jones, "Age-Rounding in Greco-Roman Egypt."

the study lies in the correlation it notes between age rounding and illiteracy in contemporary underdeveloped societies: rounding cumulatively betokens ignorance of exact age, which cumulatively betokens circumstances wherein illiteracy is also common. The index of rounding deducible from ancient inscriptions is very high, and that in turn should imply a high rate of illiteracy. As Duncan-Jones remarked, "it is very striking that in modern cases where rounding exceeds [a level much lower than that implied by the Roman evidence], illiteracy of 70% or more is also found."[11] The observation appears all the more suggestive when one considers that a survey of inscriptions can only include those able to afford a tombstone, omitting the economically (and so, presumably, culturally) submerged portion of the population,[12] and cannot take into account the substantial number whose only language was the local vernacular.[13]

Evidence from other parts of the empire, although even patchier than the inscriptions, also points toward pervasive illiteracy. For example, contracts, deeds, and loans, largely preserved in Egypt but appearing here and there in other areas, commonly reveal that the parties (that is, persons participating in the formal economic life of their society at a fairly high level) were illiterate.[14] Or, perhaps still more notable, illiteracy appears among men whose standing or function would seem to favor a knowledge of letters, if not presuppose it; these range from illiterate local officials (including a town secretary) in Egypt of the second, third, and fourth centuries[15] to illiterate abbots, and at least one illiterate

11. Duncan-Jones, "Age-Rounding, Illiteracy" 347.

12. Ibid. 345.

13. On the vernaculars, see Chap. 1 n. 25. There was probably a large overlap between the poorest and the non-Romanized segments of the population, although we need not think it was complete. It is also possible that a person whose everyday language was the local vernacular would have his tombstone inscribed in the language of culture; cf. Brunt, "Romanization" 171.

14. On the ἀγράμματοι in the Egyptian papyri, see Majer-Leonhard, ΑΓΡΑΜ-ΜΑΤΟΙ; Calderini, "Gli ἀγράμματοι"; and esp. Youtie, "Pétaus" (= Scriptiunculae 2.677ff.), "Βραδέως γράφων" (= Scriptiunculae 2.629ff.), "ΑΓΡΑΜΜΑΤΟΣ" (= Scriptiunculae 2.611ff.), "ΥΠΟΓΡΑΦΕΥΣ," and "Because They Do Not Know." Note also IDR 1.40–42, 3 contracts on wax tablets, the first 2 dated to A.D. 163 and 164, all with the formula quia se litteras scire negavit; Courtois, Tablettes Albertini pp. 206f., 34 instruments of sale (A.D. 493–96) from Tuletianus, ca. 260 km south of Hippo Regius, showing at least 31 illiterates; and cf. PItal. 1 p. 271 n. 2: of 51 subscriptions from s.V–s.VII, 18 were in the subscriber's own hand, 26 were made with a signum. (Of the remaining 7, 1 complains of gout, 2 of inbecillitas oculorum [cf. n. 16, on the abbots], and 4 subscribe in Gothic.)

15. See Youtie, "Pétaus" and "Βραδέως γράφων," on the illiterate κωμογραμ-ματεύς Petaus (A.D. 184–87); and cf. PFay. 23(a), 1f. (s.II), literacy and illiteracy among persons qualified for office; POxy. 44.3184 (A.D. 296), some illiterate village

bishop, in the fifth and sixth centuries.[16] At the least, there is reason for "a more pessimistic view of the state of literacy in the mass of Roman society than the one usually adopted."[17] It is hardly going too far to say that the great majority of the empire's inhabitants were illiterate in the classical languages.

Questions naturally arise about this limited literacy: When? Where? Among whom? The first is much the most difficult to answer. Are we, for example, to think of a general decline in literacy, aggravated if not brought on by the "political chaos of the 200's" and simply linear in its direction, with "fewer every year [knowing] how to read and write"?[18]

---

chiefs; *PAmh.* 82 (s.III / s.IV), a former high priest of Arsinoe, evidently not among the γραμμάτων ἐπιστήμονες (see lines 2ff.), appeals his selection by the town council to serve the prefect's tribunal as official recorder. Cf. Majer-Leonhard, ΑΓΡΑΜΜΑΤΟΙ 75ff.; Calderini, "Gli ἀγράμματοι" 25f.; and Youtie, "ΑΓΡΑΜΜΑΤΟΣ" 172f. (= *Scriptiunculae* 2.622f.), with n. 40, on Aur. Isidorus.

16. Bishop: *Gesta Conlat. Carthag.*, an. 411 (CC SL 149A), "Gesta" 1.133.82ff., in a subscription (*qui supra* [= *Trifolius episcopus plebis Aborensis*] *pro Paulino Zurensi praesente, litteras nesciente*); cf. *Collect. Hispan.* can. 1 (*Conc. Afr.*, CC SL 149) = *Statuta Eccl. Ant.* prol. 1ff. (*Conc. Gall.*, CC SL 148.164.1f.): the condition *si litteratus* was included—evidently not without reason—among the requirements for the ordination of a bishop; the condition must refer to the simple ability to read and write (not to a higher literacy, as is sometimes thought), as surely as does the complaint of Aurelius, bishop of Carthage, concerning the difficulty of African churches in finding *unus quidem diaconus, vel inliteratus* (*Reg. Eccl. Carthag.* excerpt. 6, "Notitia de gestis concilii Carthagiensis 16 Iunii 401" [*Conc. Afr.*, CC SL 149.194.421ff.]).

Abbots: see *ACO* 3, "Collect. Sabbait." 5.12, 5.14, 5.26, 5.68 (of 386 subscriptions overall, 42 note the agency of another: in 14 cases, limited or absent literacy is stated as the reason; in 11, physical debilitation of one sort of another; no reason is stated in the remaining 17). On these subscriptions see now Merkelbach, "Analphabetische Klostervorsteher," but note that it is probably hasty to assume illiteracy when no reason is given for reliance on another's hand, since other causes (e.g., enfeeblement by old age or ill health) may be responsible; note also that the formula used in a few cases, διὰ τὸ ἐμὲ μὴ εἰδέναι Ἑλληνιστί, may imply that some were literate in a language other than Greek: cf. the episcopal subscriptions in Syriac at "Collect. Sabbait." 5.131 (pp. 184.3, 185.32), and cf. the lector Aur. Ammonius (*POxy.* 33.2673 [an. 304]), who describes himself as illiterate—i.e., he probably knew Coptic, although ignorant of Greek; cf. Youtie, "ΑΓΡΑΜΜΑΤΟΣ" 163 (= *Scriptiunculae* 2.613) and "Because They Do Not Know"; differently Wipszycka, "Lecteur."

17. Duncan-Jones, "Age-Rounding, Illiteracy" 335, referring to Cipolla, *Literacy*, and to Marrou, *Histoire*[6] (sim., e.g., Picard, "D'Autun à Mactar" 15f.; Riché, *Education* 21f.). See now also Harris, "Literacy," for varied and powerful arguments against optimistic estimates of literacy's diffusion under the principate: unhappily, this valuable paper came to my attention only as the final touches were being put to this book.

18. So recently MacMullen, *Crisis* 58ff.; and cf. Turner, *Greek Papyri* 83.

That is the common opinion, and it is probably correct—in part, and for some areas more than for others.[19] But it is also surely true that—in a manner and to a degree that the current state of our knowledge prevents us from specifying—the common opinion must be modified to take account of likely regional differentiation, of varying periods of resilience and depression within a given region, and especially of the modest bench-mark against which any decline must be measured. For unless the evidence is completely misleading, the general level of literacy at even the best of times must have been very low.[20]

The case of Oxyrhynchus is instructive here.[21] Over the course of the third century the city gives evidence of alternating depression and pros-perity; in particular, complaints of ruin in the century's second quarter are replaced by signs of economic exuberance in the third quarter, when one finds public works in progress, ambitious games, an expensive corn dole, and municipal concern for education, in the person of a publicly appointed grammarian. Yet toward the end of the third quarter, over two-thirds of the known applicants for the corn dole—themselves members of a privileged segment of the town's citizenry—are illiterate. Allow for the possibility that some of these were illiterate because of an earlier economic depression and decline: the proportion found among a select group of citizens toward the end of a period of prosperity must still point to fundamental illiteracy in the population at large, enduring through good times and bad.

19. Note, e.g., MacMullen's general statement (*Crisis* 59, based on Mócsy, "Unkenntnis") that age awareness in the western provinces decreases from the earlier to the later principate and that "in the latter period cities gradually sink toward the level of the rural areas." In fact, the chronological distinctions in Mócsy's work—based in turn on the tabulations of J. Szilágyi (see Mócsy, p. 388 n. 3; on the limited validity of these distinctions and tabulations, see Duncan-Jones, "Age-Rounding, Illiteracy" 350f.)—yield very mixed results: of the 65 towns and cities surveyed, 20 show age awareness remaining at roughly the same level, i.e., fluctuating by less than 5%, between the earlier (s.I–s.II) and later (s.III–s.VII) periods; 22 show a rise in age awareness of 5% or more between the two periods; and 23 show a fall of 5% or more. Of the provinces overall, 6 show age awareness remaining at roughly the same level (Dalmatia stays the same; Africa, which contributes 40% of the data, shows a rise of 3%; Gaul, Italy, Spain, and Moesia show a fall of 4%, 4%, 3%, and 2%, respectively); 7 show rates of age awareness increasing by 5% or more; but none shows a comparable decrease.

20. Concerning periodic and regional fluctuations in prosperity, as against a generalized and steady decline, see the recent, suggestive survey by Whittaker, "Inflation."

21. For the following, see Parsons, *PCollYoutie* 2 pp. 438ff., with Part II no. 90; Rea, *POxy.* 40, pp. 2ff., on qualifications for the dole at Oxyrhynchus (see also Lewis, "Recipients"); and J. D. Thomas's review of Rea, in *CR* 26 (1976) 111, drawing attention to illiteracy among the applicants for the dole.

The other questions permit more straightforward answers. As could be expected, the tendency toward age rounding—and so, probably, illiteracy—increases the farther one goes from a major city[22] and the farther down one goes on the economic ladder. Thus the index of rounding for town councilors in Italy and Africa is only one-third that for the citizens at large in those two areas,[23] and illiterates in the papyri tend to belong to the lower economic levels of society.[24]

But it would be wrong to think that higher economic status guaranteed literacy at all times and in every area. The index of rounding for Italian and African *curiales* in the first three centuries A.D., though much lower than that for the humbler orders, is not insignificant; possibly we find here a hint that Diocletian's ruling of 293, that illiteracy was no bar to curial status, did not so much mark a sudden shift as clarify and legitimize a situation that had existed for some time, especially in smaller towns, where the curial order was a heterogeneous mixture of occupations and backgrounds.[25] Similarly, the members of the gymnasial class in Egypt might predictably be literate, but they were not uniformly so: letters were as a rule taught outside the gymnasium, were learned desultorily, and if learned were sometimes forgotten.[26] Conversely, literacy could reach down to humble levels, to slaves trained as secretaries.[27]

What general formulation is possible, then? First, we must imagine a state of very sparse literacy at best, subject to fluctuation from time to time and place to place. Though we may suppose that literacy declined in the later empire (with the erosion affecting the margins of the upper classes most), perceptions of a broad decline should probably be tempered by a more sober view of literacy in the early empire.[28] Second, we should imagine that literacy ranged across the spectrum of classes in a way that

22. Duncan-Jones, "Age-Rounding, Illiteracy" 341ff., on the evidence of Africa.

23. Ibid. 338: the sharpness of the cleavage is especially noteworthy, suggesting a rapid drop in the rate of literacy below the curial order.

24. Cf. Majer-Leonhard, ΑΓΡΑΜΜΑΤΟΙ; Calderini, "Gli ἀγράμματοι."

25. *CJ* 10.31.6; on the evidence concerning illiteracy and curial status in Egypt, see Youtie, "ΑΓΡΑΜΜΑΤΟΣ" 175 (= *Scriptiunculae* 2.625) n. 49.

26. See Nilsson, *Hellenistische Schule* 94f.; Youtie, "ΑΓΡΑΜΜΑΤΟΣ" 174f. (= *Scriptiunculae* 2.624f.), esp. on *PTebt.* 2.316 (A.D. 99). Cf. also Bingen, "Note," and Sijpesteijn, "Some Remarks" 142f., on μανθάνειν γράμματα (probably = "literature": so Bingen, and see further n. 40 below) as a distinguishing feature of youths in *SB* 5.7561 and *POxy.* 22.2345.

27. E.g., the notary manumitted in the will of Gregory Nazianzen, *PG* 37.392.

28. To put it another way, the general properties of the curve suggested below would probably have remained fairly constant, with chronological differences dependent on changes in the pitch of the pyramid (whether, and to what degree, and with what fluctuations it became more steep) in a given place at different times.

combined the traits of both horizontal and vertical segmentation. For example, the knowledge of *litterae* (that is, of Latin) in the Western Middle Ages, or the classical (as opposed to the modern) secondary education in nineteenth-century Germany, tended to be engrossed by groups not defined or united simply by common economic standing;[29] in contrast, basic literacy under the empire was probably first and foremost a function of one's place on the economic pyramid. Yet the evidence suggests that the distinction was not purely vertical, that the presence or absence of literacy was not simply marked by a single class line. We should probably think of a curve superimposed on the economic pyramid, starting near the bottom and including greater proportions of each class as it approaches the top:

Another curve with similar properties could be added higher on the pyramid to mark off those who were literate in liberal studies:

The characteristics of these curves are of course purely hypothetical. The picture might nonetheless serve crudely to represent the distribution of literacy and its relation to the different types of schools:[30] above the second curve are those taught in the *scholae liberales*; between the two curves are those educated only in the school of letters. The bulk of the pyramid represents those innocent of formal schooling.

Such a picture has social and political implications that have only begun to be explored, prompting different, equally valid responses when viewed

29. The clergy in the one case; the liberal professions, the gentry, high civil servants, and officers in the other. Cf. Grundmann, "Litteratus" 14; Ringer, *Education* 76. In both cases there was significant horizontal segmentation: e.g., the sons of German merchants tended to receive an education different from the sons of high civil servants, although the means of the two groups might place them on an economic par.

30. See Chap. 1 pp. 24ff.

from different perspectives. Writing with an ideal of administrative efficiency in mind, one historian can rightly question the quality of the information that would reach the central government from a world pervaded by illiteracy.[31] Another, considering the humbler mechanics of a society that necessarily "made a large place for illiteracy," can rightly emphasize that letters were a peripheral concern, occasionally useful, not necessary in the daily lives of most men, and that far more than is imaginable today the ordinary illiterate was able to live a sound and productive life with no apparent economic or social disability, "to function in a broad variety of occupations, to be recognized as a respectable member of his class, to attain financial success, to hold public office, to associate on equal terms with his literate neighbor."[32] Our concern with the grammarian's position suggests still another point of view, determined by two evident and related facts: first, literacy was not simple in definition or possession; second, different notions of literacy existed in the different groups represented on either side of the upper curve in my second figure. I want to propose that these two facts in combination not only gave the grammarian's profession some of its distinctiveness (as could be expected) but at the same time helped to blur that distinctiveness at its edges.

Despite the tendency of modern states to standardize education on a scale unknown in antiquity, our notion of literacy is still fluid. The literate person, in the most basic sense of the term, can read and write his society's standard language (in societies that recognize a standard language) with minimal competence. But university teachers in the United States today increasingly complain of their students' illiteracy, by which they mean anything from gross deficiency in basic skills to inability to read and write with far more than minimal sophistication. And anyone seeking a university teaching position will score a point if he can be said to be literate, that is, broadly conversant with the higher literary culture, or, simply, cultured. Having so many possible applications of the term is a symptom of situational literacy: the meaning and connotation of "literacy" depend on such variables as geographic or social context and the user's view of his own literacy.

Not surprisingly, similar fluidity was apparent in antiquity.[33] At one extreme were the illiterates who appear in the contracts, deeds, loans,

---

31. Cf. the trenchant comments of MacMullen, *Crisis* 58ff.

32. Youtie, "ΥΠΟΓΡΑΦΕΥΣ" esp. 219ff., on the relations among literate and illiterate members of the same household and on illiteracy as a centripetal force in the family.

33. For a useful survey of *litteratus* and *illiteratus* in Latin literary usage, see Grundmann, "Litteratus" 15ff. Grundmann's primary concern, however, was the Middle Ages; a more thorough study of the classical and late-antique evidence is needed.

and titles from Egypt and elsewhere, the men and women described as "those who do not know letters" (γράμματα μὴ εἰδότες, *litteras nescientes*): "letters" in this case refers to basic skills in reading and writing Greek or Latin, and the phrases are purely descriptive, registering a fact of life that involves no practical disadvantage and implies in itself no social or economic inferiority.[34] At the other extreme is a liberally educated man like Jerome, who reveals his own assumptions and values in the heat of polemic. Clearly, when Jerome taunts Rufinus with the charge that he and his followers "have not learned their letters," or when he calls Rufinus an "illiterate author" (συγγραφεὺς ἀγράμματος) and recommends that he go back to (note well) the grammarian's school to "learn his letters," he primarily means that Rufinus is deficient not in his ABCs but in more advanced literary skills.[35] Equally clearly, the deficiency in itself carries a stigma.[36]

Examples can be collected and located between the two extremes. There is Aurelia Thaisous, who asserts in petitioning for the *ius trium liberorum* (the laws that "give women adorned with the 'right of three children' the ability to act as their own guardian and conduct all their business without a guardian") that the laws gave this ability "especially to women who know letters," and who describes herself as "literate [ἐγγράμματος] and able to write with the greatest of ease."[37] Her claim of literacy is substantively fairly modest, the simple ability to write fluently. But by gilding the basic provisions of the law ("especially . . . ") she shows she is, if not boasting of her attainment,[38] at least aware she possesses a distinction that would buttress her claim to privilege and provide a practical advantage in her dealings without a guardian once the privilege was granted.

34. Cf. Youtie, "ΑΓΡΑΜΜΑΤΟΣ" 168ff. (= *Scriptiunculae* 2.618ff.), "ΥΠΟ-ΓΡΑΦΕΥΣ"; and cf. n. 36 below.

35. *C. Rufin.* 1.17, 3.6; cf. 1.30: *litteras discere* covering everything in Jerome's education from its beginnings through rhetoric. With Jerome's oxymoron συγγραφεὺς ἀγράμματος (3.6), compare the younger Pliny's self-deprecating description of his *inliteratissimae litterae* (*Ep.* 1.10.9), a conceit taken over by Sidonius Apollinaris (*Ep.* 4.3.10). The effect in Pliny and Sidonius is of course the opposite of self-deprecation, since the phrase draws attention to the author's exquisite literacy while denying it.

36. Note in general that *illiteratus* appears to have pejorative connotations in Latin only when (if not always when) the higher sense of *litteratus* is the implied or expressed antithesis; cf. Grundmann, "Litteratus" 16ff. Similarly, Youtie's statement that the illiterate could "associate on equal terms with his literate neighbor" ("ΥΠΟΓΡΑΦΕΥΣ" 201, quoted above) would most commonly be true of the lower forms of literacy.

37. *POxy.* 12.1467 (A.D. 263).

38. Youtie, "ΑΓΡΑΜΜΑΤΟΣ" 166f. (= *Scriptiunculae* 2.616f.), and the second thoughts at "ΥΠΟΓΡΑΦΕΥΣ" 221 n. 62.

Or again, there is the fourteen-year-old boy whose application for membership in the gymnasium includes the statement that he is "learning letters" (μανθάνων γράμματα).[39] Here "letters" probably means literature rather than the simple ability to read and write, and the attainment is mentioned since it "serves to enhance the boy's status."[40] Yet since such an attainment was certainly not required for membership, its absence by itself would scarcely have involved a disability or stigma for other members of the gymnasial class. In these examples the sense of "(il)literacy" and "(not) knowing letters" depends not only upon absolute or substantive criteria but also upon more fluid and less tangible considerations—the context in which the terms are used, the expectations of the circles with which one is familiar, and (clearly in Jerome's case) how far self-esteem and one's claims on the respect of others depend on literary sophistication.[41]

The curves in my second figure above are drawn in dotted lines because the concepts of letters and literacy were so fluid and so much a product of circumstantial—especially social—definition. The boundary between literacy and illiteracy marked by the lower curve was at once real and vague. The "slow writers" and "persons of few letters," who could painstakingly sign legal documents but were otherwise illiterate,[42] or the man who could only read block letters,[43] would all have called themselves literate; they were clearly not "without letters" (ἀγράμματοι, *illiterati*), even if they could not claim such fluency as Aurelia Thaisous. Standing on the boundary of literacy, they could regard themselves, and act, as literate for a set purpose or under certain conditions. So the village secretary Petaus could state that Ischyrion, the secretary of another village, was not illiterate, because he could add the appropriate brief subscription to the documents that came before him.[44] In this case, even

---

39. *POxy.* 22.2345 (A.D. 224), with other, similar documents discussed by Bingen, "Note," and by Sijpesteijn, "Some Remarks."

40. Sijpesteijn, "Some Remarks" 143. That γράμματα here means something more than elementary letters is strongly suggested by, *int. al.*, the age of the boy and the fact that the attainment is mentioned so rarely in documents of this type.

41. Thus, for example, the question whether or not the illiterate village secretaries Petaus and Ischyrion attempted to mask their illiteracy in order to avoid its "stigma" (so Turner, *Greek Papyri* 83; *contra*, Youtie, "ΑΓΡΑΜΜΑΤΟΣ" 172 [= *Scriptiunculae* 2.622]) could be settled finally only with more explicit testimony from Petaus and Ischyrion themselves. I suspect, however, that Turner has the better part of the argument here; see just below and n. 44.

42. Cf. Youtie, "Βραδέως γράφων" (= *Scriptiunculae* 2.629ff.).

43. Petron. *Sat.* 58.7, *lapidarias litteras scio*, with Daniel, "Liberal Education" 157ff.

44. Youtie, "Βραδέως γράφων" 239f. (= *Scriptiunculae* 2.629f.), with the comment on 240 (= *Scriptiunculae* 2.630): "What lends a special tang to Petaus'

the most marginal literacy has evident social repercussions, acquitting Ischyrion of a charge that he was unfit for his position.

It is plain enough that at the lower boundary literacy is often perceived variably and individually, that it is defined both by objective or substantive criteria (how well and how much one can read and write) and by context. The important point is, the upper boundary—between mere letters and liberal letters, between schools of letters and liberal schools, between teachers of letters and grammarians—was also both real and porous; its demarcation was similarly influenced by circumstance and substantive considerations. But whereas at its lower ranges the circumstantial definition of literacy can be approached through variations in individual perception, at its upper range it can be more usefully discussed in terms of larger categories: institutions, class, and geography.

As we saw above, Jerome's idea of knowing letters and his play with the idea of Rufinus's illiteracy bear the stamp of his own upper-class liberal education. Just so, the Gallo-Roman aristocrat Sidonius Apollinaris can say of one of his peers that from birth he drank in letters (*litteras bibere*), without having to specify *liberales*. Even if that sense were not clear from the context, Sidonius could be sure that his audience, men of background and expectations similar to his own, would assume as much for themselves.[45] Such men had a fairly fixed idea of what in substance literacy meant, or at least of the minimum attainments proper to a man who could be called literate: contact with the main classical texts and the correctness and adornment of language to show for it.

This conception of literacy was widely diffused geographically and ancient in its tradition, providing the liberally educated classes with much of their mental furnishings and (however much a Jerome might struggle with it) a sense of their own status and worth.[46] The importance of letters in this regard reinforced the traditional definition of knowing letters. The grammarian was of course a fixture of this tradition, his profession both distinguished and bound by its antiquity and diffusion. His instruction was standardized, but by shared conventions, not by statute. Because of the tradition of his profession and, hence, because of his clientele's expectations, a grammarian's classroom in Bordeaux would probably have looked much like its counterpart in Rome or Carthage, and a grammarian's classroom in Alexandria would probably have looked much like one in Antioch or Nicomedia.

---

refutation of the charge of illiteracy brought against Ischyrion is that . . . he was in effect offering a defence not only of Ischyrion . . . but also of himself," since his own literacy was similarly limited.

45. Sidon. Apoll. *Carm.* 23.204ff.
46. See Chap. 1 above; on Jerome, see pp. 81f. below.

The same is not, however, obviously true of the local teachers of letters, "boys' masters," or the like, who were scattered throughout the empire, teaching beneath the level of grammarians, in less prestigious institutions.[47] Even without any evidence we might predict that such teachers, especially in areas away from the great educational centers, would not be tied to a uniform tradition as broad or strong as the grammarian's and would offer more varied instruction. We might expect to see a more fluid understanding of literacy, depending much more on local needs and the local notion of what constituted letters as well as on the teachers' own attainments and inclinations. But there is no need for conjecture. For example, the teacher of letters Cassianus was evidently responding to one notion of letters and exploiting a particular attainment of his own when he included the useful skill of shorthand in his instruction at Imola, in northern Italy.[48] But the school of letters in Spain where Orosius had the *Aeneid* burned into his memory was evidently run according to a different idea of letters, one that overlapped with the grammarians'.[49]

The presence of Vergil—the poet *par excellence* of the Latin grammarian—in the *ludus litterarius* well suggests how permeable was the boundary between the two spheres and how broad, traditional distinctions could be blurred according to circumstances. This is not to say that Orosius's experience was universal, that classical texts were taught in every school of letters: neither the argument nor the evidence implies this, although there is at the same time no need to think Orosius's experience was unique.[50] Nor was the boundary less real for being porous, any more than the ambiguity of literacy at its lower levels meant there was no real distinction between knowing and not knowing letters. The point, rather, is that the boundary was marked by such intangibles as individual predisposition, locality, or class, as well as by objective criteria. In some cases mere letters and liberal letters, the school of letters and the grammarian's school, might overlap because of a local variation that

47. On the subject of local variation that follows, see Kaster, "Notes" 342ff.

48. Prudent. *Perist.* 9, with Part II no. 26; cf. Protogenes teaching shorthand together with the Psalms and Gospels as another form of letters at Antinoopolis under Valens: Theodoret. *HE* 4.15. For teaching the Psalms and hymns instead of τὰ Ἑλληνικὰ παιδεύματα, see also Part II no. 192.

49. Oros. *Adv. pagan.* 1.18.1, the tale of Aeneas's labors *ludi litterarii disciplina nostrae quoque memoriae inustum est*. Reading Vergil would necessarily also involve, at least incidentally, a fairly sophisticated level of linguistic instruction. For common ground between the *ludus litterarius* and the grammarian's school in linguistic instruction, see Quintil. *Inst.* 1.4.27, with the discussion by Kaster, "Notes" 339.

50. For more evidence, see Kaster, "Notes" 342ff.; and note esp. the boys' master (*magister puerorum*) Clamosus and his son of the same name and profession, both at Parentium: Part II nos. 29, 30.

would raise the substance of mere letters to approach liberal letters. In other cases, perhaps more commonly, a similar overlap would result from factors, primarily social, that would bring the substance of the grammarian's school down to approach mere letters.

Upper-class students who aimed at an education in liberal letters would normally have the grammarian as their first teacher.[51] Some students might have received private tuition in the elements before entering the grammarian's school; some would begin as young as seven. This mixture of ages and backgrounds could be served by a mixed corps of teachers, as we find among the grammarians of Bordeaux, whom we know especially well.[52] Some of these grammarians—including, at one point, Ausonius, who began as a teacher of the youngest students—gave elementary instruction (called *prima elementa* or the like); others taught at a more advanced level. The classrooms of the former, in the age and attainments of their students and the level of their instruction, would not have looked very different from the classroom of a teacher of letters. Yet they were all *grammatici*, by definition teaching liberal letters, however humble the early stages might be:[53] they were defined by their context, as teachers in an important center of literary studies, educating children who belonged for the most part to the best families of Bordeaux, Aquitaine, and Gaul at large. At the outset of his career, Ausonius was no less a grammarian for giving elementary instruction to children he "nurtured in their suckling years."[54] Indeed, it might be said that Ausonius was then a grammarian simply because he gave that instruction in the setting he did to the children he did. In such a case, circumstances outweighed substance, intangibles defined boundaries that objectively might seem violated.

Where literacy and letters were not objectively defined but, being fluid in meaning and connotation, were dependent on the contexts in which they were embedded, it is not surprising that the agents of literacy were similarly dependent. For the grammarian this meant that his profession was marked off both by objectively definable skills (knowledge of correct speech, the explication of the poets) and by nontechnical—what we might regard as nonprofessional—considerations. As we see from the *grammatici* of Bordeaux, the latter were no less important in defining the grammarian's position. The differentiation of his profession coincided with and was determined by the differentiation of his skills; but the differentiation of his profession also coincided with and was determined by the

51. See Chap. 1 n. 44.
52. On the *grammatici Burdigalenses*, see Appendix 4.
53. Cf. above n. 35, on *litterae* at Jer. *C. Rufin.* 1.30.
54. Auson. *Epist.* 22.67f., with which compare Kaster, "Notes" 333, on Augustine as grammarian.

social differentiation of the world around him—with consequences that a modern eye, accustomed to seeing a profession in terms of its technical attributes, might overlook or misjudge.[55] The grammarian was who he was not only because he possessed the traditional skills of his craft but also because he taught in circumstances and served a clientele defined by a traditional structure of prestige and privilege. It is as though a physician's profession today were partly defined by his traditionally serving patients of a certain social status.

Yet, another point of view is possible. Because he stood at the boundary of liberal letters, the grammarian was in an ambiguous position. Although he was easily distinguished from the next figure in the sequence of liberal education, the teacher of rhetoric—there would ordinarily be little opportunity to confuse their classrooms—the same statement cannot be made so flatly concerning the grammarian and the teachers of letters outside the liberal schools. With some grammarians' instruction descending to the level of the latter and the instruction of some of the latter rising to the level of the grammarian, and in view of the fluidity of letters, it is little wonder that the same general style—"agent of letters" (i.e., teacher: γραμματιστής, *litterator*)—is often used of both.[56]

In a world of limited and varied literacy, the grammarian's *professio litterarum* was only one among a number of competing educational forms, each offering its own competence and status, even power. Those who stood outside the literary culture of prestige not only were able to live productive lives but might have a freedom of movement extraordinary in itself and repugnant, if not threatening, to those loyal to traditional structures of privilege.

Among the more familiar examples of such freedom are the stenographers (*notarii*, "notaries") who provide some of the more spectacular instances of social mobility in the fourth century.[57] Practicing a form of literacy distinct from liberal letters and traditionally reserved for men of humble origins, the notaries were increasingly drawn into the imperial service in the first half of the fourth century, meeting the bureaucracy's need for more and more clerks. They thus merged with the new aristocracy of service; and in particular those who worked close to the emperor—

---

55. For example, Jouai, *Magistraat* 32ff., correctly recognized the different functions of the *grammatici* of Bordeaux but had to make the distinction intelligible by singling out one set as "de 'echte' grammatici," against the evidence. The situation is clearly and firmly described by Booth, "Elementary Education" 6ff.

56. See Appendix 2.

57. For the following, on the notaries, their status, and their relation to liberal culture, see Marrou, *Histoire*[6] 448ff., *Christiana tempora* 55ff.; Wolf, *Schulwesen* 53ff.; Petit, *Libanius* 363ff., *Étudiants* 80; A. H. M. Jones, "Social Background" 28f., *LRE* 572ff.; Liebeschuetz, *Antioch* 242f.; Hopkins, "Elite Mobility" 114.

the notaries of the sacred consistory, for example—drew power from the contact, profiting from an access few could match, being entrusted with extraordinary commissions, and enjoying a corresponding mobility as they rose to higher office and wealth. A man like Libanius—who thought of access to power as a commodity reserved for his students or men much like them, emerging from the urban upper classes and passing through the schools into a network of friends—could find the phenomenal rise of such parvenu clerks repellent on several levels. It was, for one thing, a victory of *technicité* over *humanisme* and the traditional culture of letters.[58] To a man whose life was anchored by his daily contact with the ancients, the notary's craft could represent the ultimate plunge of literacy into shapelessness and transience. More galling still was the diminution of his own privilege, which he perceived as following from the notary's circumventing the traditional structure of prestige.[59] Such disgruntlement had a predictable outcome: the upper classes coopted the notary's position.[60] After the mid-fourth century, the elite managed to win for itself the access to the emperor that notaries of humble origins had previously enjoyed. The status stenography could provide made learning notarial skills along with liberal letters in an upper-class education not only desirable but even respectable.[61] By the first half of the fifth century, the title of notary became virtually honorary.[62]

A figure comparable to the notary, if less well known, is the autodidact.[63] Like the notary in his heyday, the successful autodidact appeared to prosper independently of traditional structures and was subject to the disgruntled attacks of men who identified with those structures: talking about a man of humble origins who became an advocate by haunting the tribunals and went on to gain wealth and office, Libanius sounded much the same as he did when heaping contempt on *arriviste* stenographers.[64]

58. Cf. Marrou and Petit as cited in the preceding note.

59. "Perceived" is used here advisedly: since we know that Libanius's complaints are exaggerated (his own students continued to prosper; cf. the remarks of Petit, *Libanius* 368ff., *Étudiants* 83), it was evidently the mere thought of such circumvention that stung, as much as its effects.

60. Cf. Hopkins, "Elite Mobility" 114, comparing the displacement of freedmen by *equites* in the service of the emperor in the early empire.

61. See, e.g., Amm. Marc. 29.1.8, on Theodorus in the West; Hauser-Meury, *Prosopographie* 131, on the education of the sons of Nicobulus in the East. A similar mixture is implied at the beginning of the sixth century by the early career of Ioannes Lydus; see Part II no. 92.

62. The real work of the notaries was done by a smaller number than bore the title, or by other functionaries in the bureaucracy: see Jones, *LRE* 574.

63. I know of no comprehensive study of this interesting type.

64. *Or.* 62.46ff. on Heliodorus; directly comparable with *Or.* 42.23–24, the rogues' gallery of men who rose through stenography.

In the eyes of the expert who had painstakingly acquired his skill within the confines of his cultural tradition, the autodidact was an intruder,[65] an eccentric talent succeeding through mother wit alone,[66] disturbingly unencumbered by the forms through which expertise was customarily attained.

To be thus unencumbered meant one's achievement was intensely personal; at the same time it necessarily meant one's position was isolated and exposed. In this lonely distinction the autodidact was unlike the notary. In place of a prestigious tradition, the notary had his institutional niche and the power it could provide; but from his first appearance, the autodidact commonly found validation in another source. The claim of the bard Phemius, "I am self-taught [αὐτοδίδακτος], and the god has implanted in my wits songs of all kinds,"[67] is echoed in the epitaph of a literary man "whose life was all-pure, whom the Muse made self-taught"[68] and even in the epitaph of a woman "excelling in her devotion to her husband, for Athena herself made her self-taught in her accomplishments."[69] The charismatic claim at once asserts a splendid singularity and draws back from affirming a purely personal achievement, revealing the tendency inherent in αὐτοδίδακτος for the meaning "self-taught" to fall together with "untaught"—owing nothing to human mediators— and hence with "god-taught." The autodidact, in this sense, embodies the claim of natural knowledge, standing outside or above ordinary human culture, like the man who, "mastered by no constraint of human-kind, but educated by the providence of the gods, acquired an incomparable, natural [lit., "self-generated": αὐτοφυής] wisdom."[70] Such a figure

---

65. The implied attitude of Libanius in *Or.* 62.46ff. For other fields, cf. Galen *Thras.* 46 (3.97.16ff. Marquardt-Mueller-Helmreich), the attack on an unnamed αὐτοδίδακτος (probably Theon of Alexandria); and the attacks of Simplicius on Ioannes Philoponus quoted in Part II no. 118.

66. On the dominant nuance of Greek αὐτοδίδακτος as connoting one who knows a thing instinctively or by mother wit (and so approaching "untaught," ἀδίδακτος), see Nock, "Orphism" 306, 309 (= Stewart, ed., *Essays* 1.507f., 510), and further below.

67. Homer *Od.* 22.347f.

68. *Bull. ép.* 1973, 475 no. 1 (Cremna [Pisidia]), lines 5f.

69. *GVI* 791 (s.III / s.IV?, Syracuse), lines 7f.; the subject of the verses was, interestingly, a Christian.

70. *IAOSPE* 1.42 (s.III init., Olbia), lines 11f. Cf. the epithet θεοδίδακτος applied to Ammonius Saccas by Hierocles *ap.* Phot. *Bibl.* cod. 214 (3.126.1ff. Henry), cod. 250 (7.191.30ff. Henry); and *IGVR* 3.1480, where the subject of the epitaph claims [– – –]ην ποιεῖν θείως ἐδιδάχθην. Because of the state of the stone, just what the speaker was divinely taught to do or make (evidently the thing referred to as a singular gift in the next verse, ἐ]μοὶ δὲ μόνῳ τόδε δῶρον) is unknown.

approximates the god who is "natural, untaught";[71] he has knowledge directly and immediately, like Apollonius of Tyana, who "knew all languages, having learned not a one."[72]

The socially mobile notary had joined his skill with an undeniable institutional source of power and prestige and had thus circumvented the traditional route to elite status. The charismatic autodidact vaulted over human institutions and traditions in a triumphant display of spiritual mobility. The one troubled the literary culture of prestige until he was tamed by it; the other was most evidently associated with Christianity, which emerged in the fourth century as the second culture of prestige. When we turn to the two great traditions, we will see how the history of the grammarian's profession in the classical literary culture was marked by tensions and cooptation much like the experience of the notary, and how the charismatic self-taught (untaught, god-taught) man stood near the center of the relations between the grammarian and the Christian culture of the fourth and fifth centuries.

INDEPENDENCE AND CONSTRAINT: GOOD AND BAD GRAMMARIANS AND THE POWER OF CONVENTION

In Book 14, Chapter 5 of his *Attic Nights*, Aulus Gellius presents a curious spectacle. Two eminent Roman grammarians are engaged in a heated public argument, all but coming to blows over the correct vocative form of the adjective *egregius*: first one, then the other presses the claims of his rationalized account (*ratio*) or rule (*definitio*), then back again; no end in sight. With a shrug and a sniff Gellius withdraws: "But since . . . their competition was going on at quite some length, I did not judge it worth my while to listen longer to those same, well-known arguments, and left them yelling and battling." The incident is intended to amuse and appall, as each grammarian clings to his *ratio* as though his life depended on it, in a display of emotion and egotism at once unseemly and boring.

The episode, like so many in Gellius, involves a competition for prestige centering on the literary culture. Explicitly, the contestants are the two

---

71. αὐτοφυής, ἀδίδακτος, ἀμήτωρ, ἀστυφέλικτος: cf. Lactant. *Inst.* 1.7, with the oracle of Oenoanda (Bean, *Journeys* no. 37), and with the comment on the epithets by Robert, "Oracle" 597ff.

72. Philost. *V. Apoll.* 1.19, with Euseb. Caes. *C. Hieroclem* 9; the latter rejects Apollonius's claim of ἡ τῶν φωνῶν ἁπασῶν αὐτοφυὴς καὶ αὐτοδίδακτος ξύνεσις and its implied θεία δύναμις. Cf. Aug. *C. Acad.* 1.16.18ff., the debate on the wisdom of Albicerius, who could quote Vergil "although he had scarcely ever seen a grammarian's school in passing."

grammarians, each with his professional authority invested in his own *ratio*. But Gellius's dismissal implies the larger competition played out in the *Attic Nights* as whole: Gellius and his learned friends versus the *vulgus semidoctum*, "the common run of half-educated men," to which the "half-educated grammarian" (*semidoctus grammaticus*) belongs.[73] In various vignettes the grammarians thrust themselves and their learning forward only to be embarrassed by their betters; they are consistently losers in the competition for a place in the "aristocracy of letters."[74] This competition, its tensions, and its resolutions are perhaps most responsible for shaping the grammarian's relations as a professional teacher with men of culture at large and for defining the image of the grammarian in the literary tradition from the early empire onward.

In this section, then, we will briefly trace the origins and consequences of this competition. Along the way we will see how the early grammarians were able to claim a place in the world of liberal letters through their technical skills; how the social and cultural elite regarded the rise of the profession; how once the profession and its skills were established the elite coopted them; and how as a result the elite's conventional values limited the profession's independence.

Of course for competition there must be competitors. The grammarians were latecomers to the contest, owing their position to the gradual emergence of the Roman schools of liberal letters as institutions distinct from the family, where the education of the upper classes had long been embedded.[75] Appearing at Rome from the late second century B.C., the grammarians over the course of the next century slowly disengaged themselves from the great households to which they were formally tied as slaves and freedmen or on which as men of otherwise humble origin they were wholly dependent. Like the teachers of rhetoric, the grammarians began opening their own schools from about 100 B.C. and gradually became identified as the teachers of children in language

---

73. *Vulgus semidoctum*: NA 1.7.17. *Semidoctus grammaticus*: 15.9.6.

74. For the *grammatici*, apart from the passages cited above and below, see esp. NA 4.1, 5.4, 6.17, 8.10 praef., 13.31, 16.6, 18.6, 19.10, 20.10. For the most important exception, Gellius's teacher Sulpicius Apollinaris, see below, pp. 59–60. The place of letters in the larger competition for prestige and social standing among Gellius's contemporaries is well described by Champlin, *Fronto* 45ff., esp. 49.

75. On the development of the grammarian's school at Rome, see recently Bonner, *Education* 37ff.; and esp. Booth, "Appearance." On competition within the aristocracy as a spur to the emergence of the liberal schools, see the sensible remarks of Wallace-Hadrill, *Suetonius* 30ff. For the idea of structural differentiation applied to education in a systematic account of institutional change, see Hopkins, *Conquerors* 76ff. The present discussion, less concerned with the reasons for the differentiation, takes as its starting point the fact that it did occur.

and literature.[76] In general, we can say that structural differentiation had gone as far as it would go by the beginning of the first century A.D. By that time the grammarian's school was formally separate both from the family and from other educational institutions, the rhetorician's school within the field of liberal studies and the school of letters outside.[77]

These changes did not occur without friction between old and new. In their earliest, most explicit form the tensions of competition had as their focus the new institution that impinged most on public life. In a decree of 92 B.C. the censors attempted to close the schools of Latin rhetoric on the grounds that they contradicted the "habit and custom of the elders" (*consuetudo ac mos maiorum*):[78] the *mos*, we can infer, was the novitiate of the forum (*tirocinium fori*), the traditional form of apprenticeship for public life, through which the prospective man of affairs attached himself as a youth to an established figure, learning how to act and speak as he followed his model and watched him go about his business. By its nature the *tirocinium* was part of a closed and rigid system that monopolized entry to a civic career. Access depended heavily on the ascribed status of the participants and the connections of family and friendship, and its methods were informal, based upon the personal relationship between the younger and the older man. The schools of rhetoric, offering wider access to an important skill, threatened the monopoly and provoked the (fruitless) attempt at repression.

Probably because the grammarian's connection with public life was always less direct than the rhetorician's, similar tensions involving the grammarian's school were less dramatic in their appearance and longer in coming. In fact, the most overt and sustained reactions did not begin until the first century A.D., when the grammarian had already settled into his institutional niche and had begun explicitly to stake out language

76. On the freedmen and slaves as grammarians, see now Christes, *Sklaven*. For dependence and disengagement, see esp. the cases of Antonius Gnipho and Lenaeus (Suet. *Gramm.* 7, 15). On schools of rhetoric, see below, n. 78. On the date, and on the gradual identification with the education of younger children, see esp. Booth, "Appearance" 123f. Suetonius's statement (*Gramm.* 3.3) that at certain times (*temporibus quibusdam*) there were more than twenty schools of grammar at Rome is unfortunately vague in its chronology, but it must refer to a period well into the first century B.C.

77. On the different kinds of schools, see Chap. 1 n. 44; for limitations on the differentiation from the school of letters see "Some Variable Definitions" above.

78. Suet. *Gramm.* 25.2, specifying Latin rhetoricians with their own schools (*ludi*), thus different from the more general *SC de philosophis et de rhetoribus* of 161 B.C. (Suet. *Gramm.* 25.1; Gell. *NA* 15.11.1); on the opening of the schools of rhetoric in the first decade of s.I B.C. and for the interpretation of the edict of 92 B.C. that follows, see Schmidt, "Anfänge."

as his area of expertise: it is possible here to glimpse the causes and effects, as the profession's differentiation fostered and was reinforced by the development of a specialized skill, with repercussions in the literary culture more broadly. A grammarian's claim to stand against Tiberius and control Latinity by limiting words' "citizenship"[79] and, in Nero's reign, Seneca's sarcastic reference to the grammarians as the "guardians of Latin speech"[80] mark out the period when the grammarian became identified in his own mind and in others' eyes as the agent of linguistic control. It is not accidental that the first comprehensive *ars* appears in Latin during this same period, composed by the professional grammarian Remmius Palaemon and providing the model for future handbooks.[81] Intellectual history here catches up with institutional and social history: the *ars* defined and codified the professional's expertise, the systematic analysis and the rules that were his special excellence, and so helped install the grammarian in a cultural system to which he was a newcomer.

In this conservative milieu, the grammarian's rules can still seem novel to Gellius a century later, when he turns an unfriendly gaze on "those who pay homage to the new-fangled conventions [*nova instituta*] of the *grammatici* as though they were the sacred objects of sacred precincts [τεμένων ἱερά]."[82] Yet Gellius's impatient disdain here clearly has a meaning different from what he intended. His characterization really shows how far the grammarians had progressed: it recognizes both the validity the common run of educated men attributed to the new-fangled conventions and the prestige those conventions' makers had come to enjoy.

This common grant of validity and prestige had several results. If two grammarians battling over the fine points of morphology are burlesque figures, the comedy nonetheless has a truth at its core: the rival grammarians cling as if for life each to his own rule because their lives—insofar as these were identified with professional and cultural status—did indeed depend on the rules. At the same time, for literary men who would stand apart from the common run, the *grammatici* became figures with whom they must reckon and from whom they might distinguish them-

79. See Chap. 1 n. 16; cf. n. 113 below.

80. *Ep.* 95.65. See also *Ep.* 108.30ff., Seneca's contempt for the grammarians, as figures concerned only with linguistic detail; and cf. *Ep.* 58.1ff., on "wasting one's time with a grammarian."

81. On the influence of Palaemon's achievement, see Barwick, *Remmius* 146ff., 236ff. On previous *artes* at Rome as early as the Sullan age, and so within a generation of the introduction of the grammarian's school, see Barwick, ibid. 109ff., 229ff., with, e.g., Bonner, *Education* 55.

82. *NA* 17.2.15. Note also Gellius's contempt for *turba grammaticorum novicia* at *NA* 11.1.5; and cf. *NA* 16.7.13, *isti novicii semidocti.*

selves. Writing on the language as a learned amateur in the time of
Nero, the elder Pliny could foresee that his work would provoke the
grammarians, and he registered a combative glee when his prediction
proved correct.[83] A generation later, the literary guru Valerius Probus
self-consciously set himself apart from the ordinary professional grammarian: Probus had followers (rather than pupils), three or four of whom
he would admit to his home of an afternoon (not meet in larger groups,
in a classroom, in the morning), where he would recline (not sit in a
teacher's *cathedra*) and hold conversations (not deliver lectures).[84] It is
the picture of an intimate and elite coterie, gentlemen meeting in an
aristocracy of letters. It is of a piece with this picture that Probus despised
"those rotten rules and cesspools of grammar."[85]

Several factors aggravated the tensions that developed over the course
of the first century and continued into the next. First, there was the
propaedeutic paradox: grammar had become and was to remain the first
stage in a liberal education, the *fundamentum* of eloquence, in the metaphor
repeated from Quintilian through Cassiodorus;[86] as such, it was both
niggling and necessary. At the end of the first century Quintilian still
had to defend grammar against the view that it was "insubstantial and
jejune."[87] The reasons for this view are understandable. Seemingly
removed from the concerns worthy of gentlemen by its immersion in
minutiae, grammar required the mastery of those rotten rules; narrow
and achingly technical, it summoned up the old distinction between the
technician's specialized training and the broad culture of the aristocratic
ideal, and fell decisively on the side of the former.[88] But because of the
institutional norms and cultural expectations that had developed among
the elite, grammar was also unavoidable. The grammarian, as guardian,
controlled access to the language and the education one's peers valued.

83. *NH* praef. 28.

84. Suet. *Gramm.* 24.2, with Grisart, "Valerius" 385. On the connotations of
"follower" (*sectator*) in particular, see below, with n. 107.

85. The phrases appear in the anecdote preserved at Gell. *NA* 13.2.1: *finitiones
illas praerancidas et fetutinas grammaticas.*

86. Quintil. *Inst.* 1.4.5; Cassiod. *Var.* 9.21.3.

87. Quintil. *Inst.* 1.4.5ff.

88. On the distinction, see the recent survey of Christes, *Bildung* 15ff., 196ff.
The narrowness is part of, e.g., Gellius's contempt for the *semidocti*: for the
narrowness of the grammarian vs. the broader culture of the ideal, see esp. *NA*
20.10. Note that Quintilian's review of the grammarian's tasks, *Inst.* 1.4–8, dwells
on his linguistic instruction; the culturally more inclusive task of *enarratio* is
considered only in the latter part of 1.8. Contrast Florus's attempt to put a fair
face on the grammarian's *professio litterarum*, concentrating wholly on the ethical
content of the instruction and, at least as his text is now preserved, ignoring the
linguistic-technical: cf. Chap. 1 n. 5.

His institutional place by itself made the grammarian a consequential figure endowed with power and respectability as a cultural authority, and his mastery of the language gave him a conceptual power that even those who might despise his pedantry were unwilling to abandon themselves.[89]

Yet the grammarians were not obviously or unambiguously gentlemen, worthy of this power: they were by and large stigmatized for taking fees,[90] and—especially at Rome, in the early first century—they were still comparable in their humble social origins to the grammarians of the preceding century. As competitors, they were at once worthy in their cultural standing and unworthy in their persons. Remmius Palaemon is emblematic of such circumstances, a grotesque in the eyes of the upper classes. Born a slave, he originally learned the lowly craft of weaving (the story went), and got his first taste of letters by accompanying his mistress's son to school; he then taught as a freedman at Rome, where his school brought him yearly earnings equivalent to a knight's census, and an estate. All his wealth went to satisfy his taste for luxury and his lusts; because of his vices, Tiberius and Claudius warned students off his school, but without effect. Vergil, he claimed, had used the name "Palaemon" in his work (*Ecl.* 3.50ff.) because he had foreseen that Palaemon himself would one day be the greatest scholar of poetry. Varro—a Roman senator and the greatest scholar of Latin before him— he called a pig.[91]

The sketch is familiar: it is the standard picture of the arrogant and depraved parvenu. With some adjustment, this image of Palaemon could be superimposed on the caricatures of wealthy and powerful freedmen from the first century, especially in the imperial service, or of the suddenly risen *notarii* from the fourth. In each case the picture appears when competition for honor has been aggravated by the inconsistent status of some of the competitors, men who might enjoy prestige in one

89. Thus grammar's *multa rerum subtilitas, quae . . . exercere altissimam quoque eruditionem ac scientiam possit* (*Inst.* 1.4.6), provides Quintilian with the bait to entice those *qui hanc artem ut tenuem atque ieiunam cavillantur*; thus, too, Gellius often uses the grammarian's argument from *ratio*, despite his general disdain for *grammatici*. Compare, from a later period, Syrian. *Comm. in Hermog.* (Spengel, *Rhet. Gr.* 16:2.47.11f. Rabe), partially adapting the grammarian's pedantry, λεπτο-λογία, to the πολυμαθία befitting a rhetorician.

90. Cf. Dahlmann, *Kleine Schriften* 256 (and add Suet. *Gramm.* 3; Dio Chrys. *Or.* 7.114); Hopkins, *Conquerors* 124; Booth, "Image" 5; and below, n. 103. In his comment on Suet. *Gramm.* 24.2, *numquam enim ita docuit* [sc. *Probus*] *ut magistri personam sustineret*, Grisart was probably correct to conclude ("Valerius" 385 n. 26) that "la phrase veut dire que Probus ne fut jamais un *professionel* exerçant son art *moyennant salaire*" (Grisart's emphasis). On change and continuity in attitudes toward payment, see Chap. 3 pp. 122–23.

91. Suet. *Gramm.* 23; cf. most recently Christes, *Sklaven* 98ff.

or more areas (letters and wealth for Palaemon, political office and power for the *notarii*) but have none in others (birth in Palaemon's case, letters and birth in the case of the *notarii*).[92]

Which features of our picture of Palaemon might be caricature it is not my purpose to decide here,[93] nor is it necessary to question individual details. The overall emphasis speaks for itself: it betrays the tendency of a tradition to move in the direction of cliché and to resolve awkward inconsistencies by imposing a single image. An illustration can be found close to hand. One can gather references to teachers of letters in the high literary tradition from Demosthenes to Libanius and emerge with the consistent picture of a thoroughly humble figure with no claims to status in any form, a "gagne-petit universellement méprisé."[94] Nothing learned from these sources will prepare one to find, for example, a teacher of letters offering a substantial dedication to the goddess Leto in the name of the emperor, on equal footing with a rhetorician.[95] This does not mean that the tradition is wholly wrong, still less that the literary references are simply a mindless commonplace. On the contrary, the example points to an important need the commonplace meets, offering the reassuring image of a world where the people one despises are really no better than they ought to be. In Palaemon's case, that reassuring image is preserved, at very least, by the proportions in the tradition Suetonius retails and by the shape it takes in the telling. In the long entry on Palaemon, only three terse clauses are devoted to his cultural achievements;[96] all else is given over to his regrettable *mores*. His main claim to achieved status is thus submerged; his other potential claim, his

92. On inconsistencies in status and their consequences for the imperial freedmen, see Weaver, "Social Mobility." On the *notarii*, see above "Some Variable Definitions" *ad fin.*

93. Note that Suetonius's phrasing at the start of the entry (*Gramm.* 23.1: *Q. Remmius Palaemon Vicetinus mulieris verna primo, ut ferunt, textrinum, deinde . . . litteras didicit;* cf. *ferunt* at ibid. 3 [below, n. 98]) should suggest that the account bears the stamp of gossip, and should therefore recommend greater caution than is usually apparent in its handling.

94. Marrou, *Histoire*[6] 484. For references to teachers of letters, see the collections of Marrou, ibid. 223; Booth, "Image" 2, "Some Suspect Schoolmasters"; and cf. Part II no. 241.

95. *SB* 1.680, reconstruction of the temple wall by the γραμματοδιδάσκαλος Petenephotes, 19 June 108 (prov. unknown); *SB* 5.8815, a dedication of the same type to Isis, 30 Aug. 103 (Coptos), by the rhetorician Didymus son of Theon.

96. Suet. *Gramm.* 23.1f.: *sed capiebat homines cum memoria rerum tum facilitate sermonis: nec non etiam poemata faciebat ex tempore. scripsit vero variis nec vulgaribus metris.* Note that even the phrasing here seems not entirely neutral: *capiebat* = "charmed," "won over," almost "seduced." With the brevity here, contrast the sketch of Valerius Probus, *Gramm.* 24, a much larger proportion of which is devoted to the man's scholarly activity.

wealth, is tainted by association with his inherent vices.[97] In sum, he emerges as a man without weight or substance, ultimately laughable.[98]

We could never gauge Palaemon's contribution to grammar from the tradition that Seutonius passes along to us; the main lines of that tradition aim to put the upstart in his place. He is a bad grammarian, and not in the sense that he is a bad scholar (as we would use the phrase, to mean that he is bad at what he does) but because he is a bad person— morally defective, unworthy of the trust placed in him (recall the warnings of Tiberius and Claudius) and surely unworthy of his spectacular success. Not for the last time, as we shall see, personal and ethical judgments play a significant part in determining how one is to regard the grammarian; insofar as the tale of Palaemon is remarkable, it is so because ethical judgment seems to play the only part. The matter is thereby simplified considerably.

Things would not, however, always be so simple, as the *Attic Nights* shows. The competition informing so much of that work is, to be sure, predictably resolved by the revelation that one's competitors—including many bad grammarians—are laughable and unworthy. But for Gellius, writing in the second half of the second century, the competition is complex: there are no blatant inconsistencies of status; the villains cannot easily be caricatured and dismissed as *arriviste* grotesques, and their claims to learning receive close attention. Thus the portraits of the bad grammarians also become complex as their lapses in learning are drawn in to complement and highlight their lapses in *mores*.

This complexity has much to do with how the social composition of the profession changed, and that change in turn is a measure of how prestigious the grammarian's role had become. From the late first and early second century onward, the profession began to attract members of the respectable classes. This was a familiar process: the elite habitually claimed positions that were worth holding, "pulling the ladder up after themselves."[99] The *grammatici* who appear in Gellius's work as despised rivals for a place in the aristocracy of letters would probably not have had social origins radically different from Gellius's own.[100] The competition takes place more nearly among peers, which probably made it only

97. His wealth is mentioned only to provide a measure for his *luxuria*: *Gramm.* 23.2, *luxuriae ita indulsit ut saepius in die lavaret, nec sufficeret sumptibus, quamquam ex schola quadringena annua caperet, ac non multo minus ex re familiari.*

98. The entry ends (*Gramm.* 23.3) with a joke handed down (*ferunt*) at Palaemon's expense, concerning his *libidines*.

99. Cf. Hopkins, "Elite Mobility."

100. On Gellius's *vita*, to be set in the middle range of good society, see Holford-Strevens, "Towards a Chronology." It is significant that although the *grammatici* are spared little in the *NA*, none is skewered for his social origins. (I

more tense and difficult and no doubt influenced the strategy Gellius chose.

In anecdote after anecdote Gellius shows that whatever their claims or pretensions, most grammarians were nonetheless neither scholars nor gentlemen. Their main claims to cultural standing—their control of the language, and especially their rules—are repeatedly deflated, and their intellectual failure is usually combined with ethical lapse and social catastrophe. The grammarian who misguidedly trusts in his skill and arrogantly claims center stage is reduced to "blushing and sweating" before his betters.[101] Or, as in the anecdote earlier described,[102] the grammarians make an absurd and regrettable spectacle of themselves, not just engaging in an undignified public wrangle (that would be bad enough) but wrangling over something Gellius can dismiss as old hat. Or, in a direct confrontation with Gellius, an unbecomingly boastful fellow (*homo inepte gloriosus*) must finally cover his embarrassed ignorance with a self-important (but self-destructive) defense, "That's no small question you ask; I don't teach that sort of thing for free": his desperate retreat into professional status is simply the finishing touch in a picture of cultural and ethical inferiority.[103] Or, meeting another contentious grammarian, Gellius amuses himself by coolly making up his own rule (*finitio ficta*) on the spur of the moment to suit his argument and sends the grammarian off with a flea in his ear: the rule is false, Gellius says, but you cannot prove it is.[104] The implications are of course disastrous: so far as the grammarian's precious rules are concerned, anyone can play the game, with no authentic claim to validity; and without the claim, there remain only those rotten rules and cesspools of grammar that Probus had denounced, and the grammarian's silly and arrogant pedantry, which Greek epigrammatists had satirized at Rome still earlier in the first century.[105]

Yet such vignettes tell only part of the story. They report easy victories over faceless grammarians, but they do not convey the importance that Gellius attributed to grammar itself. That was a serious business for

---

assume here, as elsewhere in my comments on Gellius, that the details in his vignettes can claim verisimilitude when they are not strictly historical, and that when historical they are subject to the improvement of Gellius's literary art.) On the grammarians' origins in this period, see now also Wallace-Hadrill, *Suetonius* 38f.

101. *NA* 19.10.
102. *NA* 14.5.
103. *NA* 13.3.3; cf. 18.14.1 (the contempt for a *iactator quispiam et venditator Sallustianae lectionis*, who is contrasted with Sulpicius Apollinaris) and n. 90 above.
104. *NA* 15.9.6ff.
105. Cf. esp. *Anth. Gr.* 11.321 (Philippus), with 11.347; 11.138, 140 (Lucilius); cf. also 11.279 (Lucilius).

Gellius, as he demonstrates not only in his insistent attacks on the grammarians—if they were unimportant, he would not attack them—but also in the high proportion of chapters that are devoted to grammatical questions and show Gellius's readiness to use the grammarians' techniques and categories when it serves his purpose. How could he not, when he had been immersed in them through his schooling? The substance of grammar was just too important, in fact, to be left to the common run of grammarians, the bad grammarians. Accordingly, heroes must be summoned up to show how it should be done and to put the villains to rout; and the hero himself can be a grammarian, provided he is the right sort—a good grammarian, like Gellius's teacher, Sulpicius Apollinaris.

Sulpicius is of course shown to be more broadly and more deeply learned than the grammarian of the *vulgus*. More noteworthy, the difference is presented as much in terms of personal attachment and *mores* as in *doctrina*. Gellius first associates with Sulpicius not as a *puer* of the age normal for a grammarian's student but only after assuming the *toga virilis*, when he has gone on his own in search of "more expert teachers":[106] the relations and status of student and teacher are immediately characterized as extraordinary thereby. Gellius is not a common pupil but a "follower";[107] Sulpicius is "our friend Apollinaris," a *familiaris*,[108] contrasted at one point with a vulgar "peddler of Sallust."[109] The bond is different from and more intimate than the exchange of cash for learning, the normal, tainted relationship between student and teacher. Further, the experiences of Gellius and Sulpicius are not set in the classroom but belong to the palace, the booksellers' quarter, or the *bibliotheca Tiberiana*[110] and are thus part of the public or semipublic intellectual life of the city. Their experiences in fact suggest nothing so much as a metamorphosis of the old *tirocinium fori*. Nor is the relationship confined to Gellius's adolescence, since Sulpicius is there to give advice to the more mature Gellius,[111] as he does to men still more eminent.[112]

---

106. *NA* 18.4.1, which of course implies that even at this still-tender age Gellius was able to distinguish the good coin from the base.

107. *Sectari: NA* 7.6.12, 13.18.3, 20.6.1; for *sectator* elsewhere in the *NA*, see, e.g., 3.1.5, *sectatores* of Favorinus. Cf. above, with n. 84, on Valerius Probus. For the connotations of personal loyalty inherent in *sectator*, appropriate to members of succeeding generations within a family, see esp. Chap. 1 n. 74 (on *CIL* 6.1416, 1418); and cf. Anon. *Pan. Lat.* 7.23.2 Galletier, *multi sectatores mei* equated in the preceding sentence with the rhetorician's natural children.

108. *NA* 11.15.8, 13.20.1.

109. Cf. n. 103 above.

110. *NA* 19.13, 18.4, 13.20.

111. *NA* 12.13, when Gellius was a *iudex*.

112. *NA* 13.18, advising Erucius Clarus; cf. 19.13.

Personally, where other grammarians are assertive and combative, Sulpicius is content not to press his authority:[113] mild in rebuke and quietly confident when he knows he is right, he handles pretenders to learning with "the kind of wily irony that Socrates used against the sophists."[114] "A man with a surpassing knowledge of literature," "a man adorned with choice knowledge," "the most learned man I recall,"[115] Sulpicius could be taken for one among the learned amateurs, did not Gellius tell us that he was a *grammaticus* and *magister*.[116] That, of course, is precisely the point: Sulpicius is the grammarian as gentleman. Consistent with this, his writings were belletristic *epistulae*,[117] not an *ars* or other technical tract.

In his portrait of Sulpicius and in his concern with things grammatical, Gellius shows us a stylized, idealized gentrification of the discipline: gentlemen and the grammarian as gentleman together immersed in grammar. If grammar had become established as part of Rome's literary world, much of Gellius can be read as an attempt to show how it should behave accordingly, with manners and learning alike refined and exquisite. The attempt is not unique to Gellius but recurs in the period with which we are centrally concerned.

Two and a half centuries after the *Attic Nights*, another good grammarian is sketched in the pages of one of Gellius's literary descendants—Servius in Macrobius's *Saturnalia*.[118] As in the case of Sulpicius, Servius's excellence is expressed in terms of both *doctrina* and *mores* and is revealed in informal, personal relationships: he is "at once admirable in his learning and attractive in his modesty" (*iuxta doctrina mirabilis et amabilis verecundia*),[119] and both his learning and his *verecundia* are displayed in the symposium held by "nobles and other learned men" in their discussions of Vergil. The most striking feature here is that the virtue attributed to (or imposed on) the grammarian sets the tone of the entire work, which is itself the most profoundly grammatical product of the amateur literary tradition in late antiquity.

One of the cardinal virtues, *verecundia* can be translated as "modesty"; more accurately (if more cumbersomely), it names the sense of propriety deriving from a regard for the opinion of other men and an awareness

---

113. Note esp. *NA* 19.13.3: Sulpicius graciously allows Fronto the authority to give citizenship to words—an evident alteration of the metaphor's original application (cf. Chap. 1 n. 16) that conforms to the ethos of Sulpicius.

114. Mildness: *NA* 13.20.5. Irony: 18.4.1.

115. *NA* 4.17.11, 16.5.5, 13.18.2.

116. *NA* 7.6.12, 18.4.1.

117. *NA* 15.5.3; cf. 13.18.2f.

118. For the points raised in the following paragraphs, see further Kaster, "Macrobius."

119. *Sat.* 1.2.15.

of one's own position (especially one's hierarchical position) relative to others in a given context. It is the quality found, for example, in the deference an inferior owes to a superior (women to men, a young man to an older man, a humble man to an aristocrat), in the sense of shame that restrains a superior from humbling himself before an inferior, or in the awareness of parity that, ideally, checks competition between equals.[120] *Verecundia* is the virtue of knowing one's place, the virtue *par excellence* of the *status quo*, an abundantly social virtue, regulating the behavior of men in groups.

In the ideal world envisioned by Macrobius, *verecundia* is so spontaneous as to seem innate. Thus Servius, who possesses a *naturalis verecundia*,[121] is found now deferring as a young man and a grammarian to his elders and betters, now offering a contribution as an expert, according to the propriety of the situation. So too the other guests as a group spontaneously take their places in a hierarchical rank (*ordo*)[122] and know individually when to yield to others' expertise, when to assert their own, how to combine becomingly the two kinds of behavior. And Vergil himself is presumed to have exhibited precisely the grammarian's qualities in his own sphere, delicately coordinating deference and self-assertion in his treatment of the literary tradition.[123]

This deep sense of propriety gives the *Saturnalia* its core and makes erudition a moral quality. The innate regard for others' opinions, the capacity for gauging how one ought to behave in general, and how in particular one should respect the cultural heritage others value provide the impulse to learning. That impulse is brought to fruition by another virtue, *diligentia*, the scrupulousness that in social relations characterizes the dutiful behavior of friends and in intellectual life maintains and deepens one's contact with one's culture and makes one truly learned.[124] The model of excellence is the scrupulous reader (*diligens lector*), exerting himself out of respect for the text, doing his duty by reciprocating the

120. See Kaster, "Macrobius" 224ff.; with, e.g., Ambros. *De off. min.* 1.17.65ff., on *verecundia* among the *officia adulescentis*; and esp. Jer. *Ep.* 66.6, where *verecundia* denotes the sense of shame produced by consciousness of rank, and the consequent difficulty for a member of the upper classes to descend to the life of the *vulgus*. Cf. *Reg. orient.* 17 (*PL* 103.479D): among the rules governing a *praepositus* of a monastery, the injunction *ne perdat animam suam propter verecundiam*. Cf. also Ambros. *Apol. David altera* 11.56: *non mediocre autem quod Nathan denuntiavit ei* [sc. *David*], *hoc est inferior propheta. gravis enim verecundia pudorque delictum ab inferiore reprehendi*.

121. *Sat.* 7.11.1.

122. *Sat.* 2.2.1ff., 7.4.1ff., with Kaster, "Macrobius" 227ff.

123. *Sat.* 1.16.44, *poeta doctrina ac verecundia nobilis*, with Kaster, "Macrobius" 231ff.

124. See Kaster, "Macrobius" 234ff. With this *diligentia*, compare the union of πόνοι and σωφροσύνη stressed by Libanius at *Or.* 1.12 and *passim*.

poet's *diligentia*; conversely, the ignorant man (most notably, in the *Saturnalia*, the cross-grained aristocrat Evangelus) is such because he lacks *diligentia*, and he fails to be scrupulous because he lacks *verecundia*.

Learning thus follows *mores*: the learned man must first be virtuous; the ignorant man is necessarily depraved. As a result, the grammarians who are criticized in the *Saturnalia*, as in the *Attic Nights*, are vulnerable for more than their failures in learning. The "vulgar troop of *grammatici*" from whom Servius is distinguished, grammarians concerned only with their linguistic expertise, who neglect the *studia potiora*—religion, philosophy, antiquities, and other *Realien*—that Vergil incorporated in his work, are fundamentally moral failures.[125] But a curious twist is involved here as well, one of the features that distinguish the *Saturnalia* from the *Attic Nights*, and Macrobius's Servius from Gellius's Sulpicius. The bad grammarians are among the villains of the piece, but Servius, the good grammarian, is himself apportioned only linguistic matters in the communal discussion of Vergil; the *studia potiora* belong to the noble guests. The grammarian's ethos and expertise stand at the center of the work, but the grammarian himself is at the margins: so thoroughly has grammar been engrossed by the learned amateurs of Macrobius's ideal that the group must even be reminded to include Servius in distributing their roles.[126]

Later on we shall consider the behavior of real grammarians and trace the lines they followed in life between the idealized images just described: the good grammarian of Gellius, moving freely among men of power and standing, and the good grammarian of Macrobius, following in the noblemen's wake, "his eyes upon the ground and looking as though he were trying to hide."[127] But in moving from the time of Gellius to that of Macrobius, one notices a fact that requires preliminary discussion here, since it concerns the development of the grammarian's profession. The grammarians have no lack of competitors and critics in the literary world of the early empire; in the later period the critics' silence is startling by contrast.

The sniping at grammarians in the *Saturnalia* is far less elaborate than in the *Attic Nights* (perhaps partially as a function of genre, and certainly because of Macrobius's greater concern to present a front of unity, compared with the open combativeness of Gellius).[128] Beyond the passing hits in the *Saturnalia* and a similar swipe in Tiberius Claudius Donatus's *Interpretationes Vergilianae* (1.1.5ff. Georgii), criticisms or lampoons fall into three categories: a few scattered and largely sectarian or *ad hominem*

125. See *Sat.* 5.19–22, 1.24.12f., with Kaster, "Macrobius" 235f., 252ff.
126. *Sat.* 1.24.14–20.
127. *Sat.* 1.2.15.
128. Cf. Kaster, "Macrobius" 247f., 259f.

sneers from one or another of the learned professions,[129] a few limp revivals in Latin of the earlier epigrammatic tradition,[130] and the remarkable poems of Palladas in Greek.[131] A grammarian in his own right, Palladas yet turns his general contempt for the world upon himself and his profession, and falls upon the sword of his own satirical epigrams. And that is all—save for a few voices among a new group of potential competitors, the Christian Fathers.[132]

Since from no point of view can the grammarians be said to have become unimportant to the literary culture and therefore too insignificant to be attacked, an explanation for this late-antique calm must be sought elsewhere. It is possible, for example, to point to cultural inertia: the grammarians' conventions were no longer new-fangled but had long since become familiar fixtures in the life of the liberally educated elite and could be valued as such, or at least be taken for granted. It is also possible that some tensions were dissipated by changes in the grammarians' social status as members of the respectable classes took over the profession. The trend visible at the end of the first century is certainly dominant by the fourth; although a few grammarians still emerge from humble levels of society,[133] the other grammarians whose origins and circumstances are observable cluster around the curial order and belong to the landed classes. They are not categorically their students' social and economic inferiors.

Yet these observations are not sufficient to explain the absence of comment and criticism. Cultural inertia evidently involves a *petitio principii*, since it does not address the questions, Why did those conventions settle into such easy familiarity? Why, in fact, did so little change in the substance and especially in the conceptual bases of grammar over the centuries? The familiar conventions of course continued to serve the advantage of the grammarians, who therefore had little incentive to

---

129. For different strains, cf. Syrian. *Comm. in Hermog.* (Spengel, *Rhet. Gr.* 16:2.47.11f. Rabe), above, n. 89; the sneers that are part of Simplicius's *ad hominem* attack on Ioannes Philoponus (above, n. 65); the devaluing of τεχνικά (including grammar and rhetoric, along with Aristotelian philosophy) in favor of τὸ ἔνθεον in Damasc. *V. Isid.* Zintzen, esp. in the case of Isidore himself (epit. Phot. 35), with frg. 41, on Sarapion, and frg. 282, on Severianus. Cf. also Synes. *Dion* 12 (*PG* 66.1152), contrasting φιλόσοφοι and the "blind children" of the γραμματικοί.

130. Cf. *Epigr. Bob.* 46, 47, 61, 64.

131. See Part II no. 113.

132. See "Polished Speech, the Common Good, and Christianity" below.

133. See Chap. 1 n. 59 for the grammarians of libertine birth at Bordeaux. Note that the inconcinnity is still felt by Ausonius, although not as grounds for contempt: thus *Prof.* 21.25–28, on Crispus and Urbicus, *ambo loqui faciles, ambo omnia carmina docti, / callentes mython plasmata et historiam, / liberti ambo genus, sed quos meruisse deceret / nancisci ut cluerent patribus ingenuis.* On the grammarians' social status generally, see Chap. 3.

change.[134] Part of the answer no doubt lies there. But that can still tell
no more than half the story, since it overlooks the grammarians' acqui-
escent audience—the members of the educated classes. Nor can change
in the grammarians' status offer a solution, since, as Gellius shows,
competition need be no less intense when it takes place among men who
are more nearly peers.

It is possible, however, to suggest a broader hypothesis that might
provide, if not a solution, at least a framework for fruitful discussion.
The grammarians' conventions stayed as they were, and the grammarians
ceased to be disturbing competitors, because the profession's social circumstances limited its differentiation and autonomy. Despite their emergence as separate institutions, the schools—and perhaps especially the
grammarian's school—remained partially domesticated: the profession's
horizontal differentiation was limited because the grammarians remained
tied directly to the family, to the representatives of the gentlemanly
amateur tradition, and to the values of both.

Although it is commonly said, for example, that second- or fourth-
century pedantry represents a decadent acquisition of knowledge for its
own sake, one could well suggest a different view of the matter: knowledge was pursued not for its own sake but as a predominantly social
phenomenon, as an appanage of personal relations and a token of accepted
virtues. Knowledge could not usually be pursued, analyzed, pondered for
its own sake. Or to put it another way, the habit of speaking (anachronistically) of ancient universities ought to be avoided, not simply because
it obscures substantive curricular differences but especially because it
obscures the institutional differences and their consequences. Antiquity
lacked the institutional buffer that is raised between the lay and professional worlds by the modern university, which serves as the seedbed
of the learned professions; and as a result antiquity had no place where a
profession could attempt to set its own course and determine its own
values.[135]

In the grammarian's world autonomy and dependence, achieved and
ascribed status, professional skill and the virtuous regard for the opinions
of (nonprofessional) others rubbed shoulders. The distinction—so basic
to the modern notion of a profession—between impersonal evaluation

134. See Chaps. 4 and 5, esp. Chap. 5 pp. 196–97.
135. This does not of course imply that restraints on the institutional and
personal autonomy of the professions cannot be found in the recent past or
today, or that the modern professions are context-free; rather, the embedding
takes different forms in different contexts. For studies of the problem in specific
settings, see Clark, *Prophets*; Keylor, *Academy*; and esp. Ringer, *Decline*, and Weisz,
Emergence. Much light is also thrown on the question by Bledstein, *Culture*. For a
recent general discussion, see Ben-David, "Organization."

of skill and personal favor or antipathy had no central place in the dominant ideology; instead, the distinction was blurred by an ideal that subordinated skill to ethical qualities. Old patterns of behavior persisted long after the profession's formal establishment: the face-to-face relations that characterized the dealings of grammarians with their patrons in the great households of late republican Rome never fundamentally changed, regardless of the different ways those relations came to be articulated, linking the teacher now to one, now to another benefactor— a parent, a town council, a provincial governor, or an emperor.

These relations had their ideological foundation in the union of *doctrina* and *mores*, the combination already found in the heroes and villains of the literary tradition. The centrifugal force of learning, tending toward personal distinction and autonomy, was balanced by the centripetal force of *mores*, urging conformity to established values and behavior. The meeting of the two forces and the resolution of their tensions are differently expressed in different contexts, accordingly as the grammarian is glimpsed in his professional writings or in a social setting.[136] There is, overall, a strong normative urge to resolve the tensions by subordinating *doctrina* to *mores*.

First, good learning and good *mores* are assumed to be inseparable: Gellius's half-learned grammarians are not quite gentlemen; his gentleman grammarian is among the most learned men he ever knew. The union of qualities is part of the line of continuity in the classical tradition from the early to the late empire and between literary and social convention. Macrobius's praise of his idealized grammarian, "at once admirable in his *doctrina* and attractive in his *verecundia*," recapitulates the qualities patrons desired in their dependents and imagines a man capable of finding the middle course between the extremes of professional life described in a fourth-century letter of recommendation: "You know, of course, . . . how rare is the affinity of eloquence and good character [*bonum pectus*]: either *verecundia* diminishes an unassuming talent [*modestum ingenium*] or the eloquent man gets above himself in his success."[137]

136. See Chaps. 4 and 5, and Chap. 6, respectively.
137. Symm. *Ep.* 1.43, recommending an *advocatus* to Ausonius; for *verecundia* in an earlier letter of recommendation, see, e.g., Fronto *Ad Verum imp.* 2.7.7 (p. 128.11f. van den Hout): *nihil isto homine officiosius est, nihil modestius, nihil verecundius.* For other examples of the *mores et doctrina* type in the *commendaticiae* of Symmachus, see esp. *Ep.* 1.15, 79; 2.2, 16, 29, 39; 3.22; 7.58, 91; 9.2, 54. Specimens from other sources are collected by Pedersen, *Late Roman Public Professionalism* 30f. nn. 84, 85. Compare also Auson. *Prof.* 10.37–41, on the grammarian Ammonius, *doctrina exiguus, / moribus implacidis: / proinde ut meritum, / famam habuit tenuem;* and esp. the edifying tale of Marcellus in *Prof.* 18: his talent (*indoles egregia*) brought him success, including a good marriage, but his bad character (*pravum ingenium*) led—inevitably—to his ruin (lines 9–10; cf. Part II no. 94).

The conventions suggest that at least ideologically the grammarian's profession was not a *carrière ouverte aux talents* in any simple sense. *Doctrina* and *mores* might overcome the absence of high birth, but mere talent was not enough—unless "talent" be taken to include the seemingly innate qualities, on the order of *naturalis verecundia*, that predispose one to respectful and scrupulous behavior. Hence the first assumption slides easily into a second: *doctrina* and *mores* are not simply inseparable qualities or opposing forces in equipoise; the former is subordinate to the latter. When the emperor Julian laid it down that teachers "ought to be surpassing in their *mores* first of all, and then in the skills of speech," the novelty probably lay less in the sentiment than in the sectarian use to which it was presently put, in driving the Christian teachers from the schools.[138] The sentiment surely overlaps with the *Saturnalia*'s pervasive belief that virtue is the prerequisite for true learning.[139]

The emphasis on ethical qualities (especially those conducive to stability and hierarchy) as attributes equal or superior in importance to skills, which we take to be the primary qualifications for a profession, resulted from the direct contact between the professional and amateur spheres.[140] It should be added at once, however, that this contact did not produce a broad conflict along lines clearly drawn; we might think more usefully of an interpenetration of the two spheres. In this respect it is symptomatic that, in Macrobius certainly, but already in Gellius, a chief attribute of the professional that we might assume would separate him from the dilettante is taken over by the amateur literary tradition and regarded as a moral trait, one of the attributes of the good man—his scrupulous attention to the details of his cultural tradition (what impatient modern readers of Macrobius and Gellius commonly call their "pedantry"). Conversely, Servius, the grammarian whom Macrobius idealized, can remark in the introduction to one of his technical treatises, "I met with Horace when I was at my leisure in Campania":[141] a work that would seem to be a piece of professional writing is presented as a parergon of the scholarly leisure (*otium*) affected in the West by the amateur litterateurs of the aristocracy.

Nowhere is this interpenetration more apparent than in the value set on the personal bond between teacher and pupil. This urge to intimate attachment, exemplified, as we have seen, by the follower (*sectator*), is

138. *CTh* 13.3.5 (17 June 362), elaborated in the subsequent directive specifically affecting the Christians, *Ep.* 61c Bidez.

139. Cf. also at Chap. 1 n. 13.

140. Passages that seem to base judgment of qualifications primarily or purely on skills are rare: see esp. Auson. *Prof.* 7.9–11, on the grammarian Leontius *signo* Lascivus; and cf. *Prof.* 9, on Leontius's brother, Iucundus.

141. *GL* 4.468.6: *Horatium, cum in Campania otiarer, excepi.*

expressed with special force in the blending of the images of teacher and father, and follows from the father's responsibility for his son's education. Gellius and Macrobius dedicated their works to their sons and in so doing took their places in a long and broad tradition, putting their accumulated wealth of learning and wisdom at their sons' disposal as part of their patrimony.[142] The literary convention, like most conventions, is a compound of actual practice and normative pressure: it reflects both the fact that a father supervised his son's education and the belief that such was the father's proper role.

The supervision might be direct: far from being a quaint and isolated figure, the elder Cato in taking personal charge of his son's lessons[143] is part of a tradition that runs from one of the earliest references we have to ἡ γραμματικὴ τέχνη, in the third century B.C.,[144] to the households of late antiquity.[145] But the father's responsibility is no less emphasized when the supervision is mediated by the professional teacher. Libanius's extensive correspondence with his students' fathers[146] and his shock that one of his enemies would canvass prospective students' mothers[147] belong to the same world where a marriage contract stipulates a father's responsibility for his sons' liberal education,[148] or where a student writes asking his father to visit "so that you might learn whether or not the teacher is paying attention to me"[149] or asking his father to write "so

142. For the dedication of works of literary scholarship to sons in late antiquity, see, e.g., Mart. Cap. *De nupt.* 1.2. and 9.997, 1000; Fl. Mallius Theodorus *De metris, GL* 6.585f.; Nonius Marcellus (cf. Part II no. 237); Ti. Claudius Donatus (date uncertain; cf. Part II no. 209); Vibius Sequester *De fluminibus,* dedicated to his son Virgilianus, who was probably a grammarian (cf. Part II nos. 163, 254); Ioannes Stobaeus (Phot. *Bibl.* cod. 167, 2.149 Henry); and probably Fl. Sosipater Charisius (cf. n. 153 below). For the tradition active in other areas, cf. Basil's dedication of his essay on Greek literature to his nephews; Claudius Marius Victor's dedication of his *Comm. in Gen.* to his son (Gennad. *De vir. ill.* 60); and Eucherius of Lyon's dedication of the *Liber formularum spiritalis intelligentiae* to his son.

143. Plut. *Cat. mai.* 20.

144. *PEnteux.* 25 (221 B.C.), the complaint of a father maltreated by his son in his old age. The complaint begins by enumerating the father's benefactions, including (line 2) [ἐμοῦ γὰρ δι]δάξαντος αὐτὸν τὴν [--- κ]αὶ τὴν γραμ[ματικὴν] (sc. τέχνην).

145. See, e.g., Symm. *Ep.* 4.20.2, 6.61; Eustrat. presb. *V. Eutych.* 8 (*PG* 86:2.2284); Callin. *V. Hypat.* 1. Cf. Paulin. Pell. *Euchar.* 60ff., the *pietatis opus studiumque insigne parentum* associated with his education at home; Greg. Naz. *Or.* 43.12; Aug. *Ep.* 2* 12–13, esp. 13.2–3; Sidon. Apoll. *Ep.* 4.12.1.

146. Cf. Petit, *Étudiants* 18ff., 104f., and esp. 151ff.

147. *Or.* 39.4.

148. *POxy.* 2.265.24 (A.D. 81/95): [τὴν πρέ]πουσαν ἐλευθέροις παισὶ παιδείαν.

149. *SB* 3.6262 (s.III).

that I might pay reverence to your hand, because you have educated me nobly."[150]

Injecting himself into this deeply traditional and highly charged relationship, the teacher in turn was captured by it. In one of the most common images of the teacher in late antiquity, he assumes the role of surrogate father: he "nurtures" his students, his "children"; he is their "father in letters."[151] The literary image—again, not merely a convention—also appears in another form. Though amateur litterateurs dedicated their works to learned friends or sons, no professional grammarian we know in late antiquity dedicated a work to his own son; dedications were to learned friends or patrons, or to pupils.[152] A double impulse can be seen here. The professional's distinguishing mark was his stepping aside from his own role as father,[153] but this withdrawal took the form of a transference, with the dedications to pupils reproducing the traditional pattern of family relationships. The relationship was not one-sided: it was reciprocated, for example, in a former pupil's funeral oration for his teacher or in the inscriptions recording dedications students made to teachers.[154]

150. *BGU* 2.423 (s.II): ἵνα σου προσκυνήσω τὴν χέραν, ὅτι με ἐπαίδευσας καλῶς. Cf. *Coll. Harl.* (*CGL* 3.108.3ff. [= 3.638f.]); and *PRyl.* 4.624 (A.D. 317/24), from Hephaestion and Horigenes, students at Alexandria, to their father, Theophanes, a letter *cum* essay on filial piety "designed principally to demonstrate in expression and sentiment the degree of culture to which they have attained thanks to [Theophanes'] beneficence" (C. H. Roberts *ad loc.*, pp. 113f.).

151. See Petit, *Étudiants* 31ff., on Libanius's use of τρέφω, παῖς, etc.; and, e.g., Anon. *Pan. Lat.* 7.23.2 Galletier; Auson. *Epist.* 22.67–69; Paulin. Nol. *Ep.* 7.3 and 8.1 (on Augustine as the teacher of Licentius; cf. Kaster, "Notes" 333); Dion. Ant. *Ep.* 24; Ennod. *Dict.* 8.8ff.

152. For grammarians' dedications, see Part II nos. 19, 31, 47, 52, 60, 72, 73, 110, 126, 132, 136, 156; cf. nos. 188, 265. For dedications to pupils, see nos. 57, 130, 136; cf. no. 221.

153. Thus the examples are sufficiently numerous, and the distinction sufficiently clear, that Charisius's dedication of his work to his son can add further and perhaps decisive weight to the evidence that he was an amateur and a palatine official rather than a professional grammarian: see Part II no. 200.

154. Funeral oration: Ael. Arist. *Or.* 32, for Alexander of Cotyaeum; cf. Lib. *Or.* 1.105, for Zenobius. Dedications (a selection): *CIL* 8.5228 (an. 211/12, Thibilis), with 5229; *IG* 14.2454 (Massilia); *CIL* 6.9444, 9449, 9827; *ILCV* 721 = *CIL* 6.10008; *IG* 2² 3897, with Raubitschek, "Phaidros" 99f.; *IG* 2² 3793 (s.I); Raubitschek, "Greek Inscriptions" 248f. no. 10; *IG* 2² 3813 (s.III med.); *IDelos* 1801; Robert, *Collection* no. 46 (Madytos, Thracian Chersonese), with ibid. pp. 56ff. for other examples; *Inschr. Eph.* 7:2 (*IGSK* 17:2) 4340; *AE* 1941, 141 (Prusa); *MAMA* 7.358 (Çarbaşli Yaila, eastern Phrygia). See also the comparable expressions of piety in Dracontius *Rom.* 1 and 3, for his teacher Felicianus (cf. Part II no. 59); the poem of Georgius for his teacher Coluthus (cf. Part II nos. 33, 63); and Priscian on his teacher Theoctistus (esp. *GL* 2.238.5f.). Note that the sentiment is not confined to teachers of liberal studies: see Şahin, "Neue Inschriften" 34 no. 103 (with C. P. Jones, "Two Epigrams"), a sepulchral inscription set up by

Such details trace the normative model of relations between teacher and student. They are the concrete tokens of the desire for close attachment and of the belief that, in a favored phrase of Libanius, teachers act on their students' souls.[155] To be sure, it was not the only image of the teacher,[156] and the ideal of personal attachment was often violated in practice. But the ideal was far from inert; it prepared the way for action, to the teacher's benefit: thus Libanius asks a provincial governor to show favor (εὔνοια) to the brother-in-law of the grammarian Calliopius, so that Calliopius and his father, who were then teaching Libanius's son, would in turn be more favorably disposed (εὐνουστέρους) toward their charge.[157]

This cooptation should not be thought of as either dramatic or conspiratorial. The ruling elite did not rise up as a body to crush a nascent professional middle class built on the independence of achieved status and personal skill; it was a case of assimilation, a gradual process leaving room for upward mobility. Nor should we expect the teachers to regard the consequences as pernicious. To refer to the example just cited from Libanius: in comparable circumstances the modern academic presumably would claim to be equally shocked by the suggestion that official favor shown to one of his connections could influence professional dealings with a pupil and by the suggestion that his personal relations could justify manipulating the public administration for the sake of personal privilege. He would be inclined to find the transaction thoroughly corrupt, from the assault on his professional integrity to the undermining of one of the cornerstones of the common good, government without fear or favor. But the ancient academic would find equally shocking the suggestion that any discontinuity existed between professional relations and personal relations, between personal relations and customary privilege, between customary privilege and social good.

The arrangement Libanius sketches was not simply ordinary; it was proper. The outrage lay in its violation.[158] One can diagnose corruption in this sort of transaction only from outside the social system in which the transaction was embedded, and with a different image of community and social good in mind. Historical remove can provide such a vantage point, allowing us to describe as "self-satisfied idiocy" the identification

---

an apprentice weaver to his teacher with the appropriate expressions of regard and gratitude.

155. Cf. *Ep.* 337.1, 398.2, 969.1.

156. For an opposing image, the Christian teacher as father vs. the grammarian with his cane, cf. Aug. *Tract.* 1, p. 449.31ff. Morin.

157. Lib. *Ep.* 678 to Iulianus, *praeses Euphrat.* See further Chap. 6, pp. 209ff.

158. Cf. Lib. *Ep.* 309.5: καὶ γὰρ ἂν εἴη δεινόν, εἰ μὴ τοῖς ἐμοῖς φίλοις αἱ τῶν ἐμῶν ἑταίρων δυνάμεις ὠφελείας φέροιεν.

of the learned with the good and to regret all the consequences that flow
from it.[159] Another such perspective might be found in a contemporary
culture with different roots or a different angle of vision—the culture of
the Christians, to whom we now turn.

POLISHED SPEECH, THE COMMON GOOD,
AND CHRISTIANITY

Visions show men what they want to see; reports of visions tell men
what they want to hear. In the first half of the fifth century, the
grammarian Alypius of Isaurian Seleucia is said to have been stricken
with a wasting illness that brought him and his family to despair.[160]
Taking refuge in the shrine of St. Thecla, Alypius slept, and in his sleep
was visited by the saint, herself "a lover of λόγοι, a lover of the Muses,
ever showing grace to those who speak her praises in learned speech."
When Thecla asked what troubled him, Alypius replied with Achilles'
answer to his mother, Thetis (Il. 1.365): "You know. Why am I to tell
you, who know all these things?" The saint then "smiled, delighted with
both the man and the verse, struck with wonder that he made so suitable
a reply," and began his cure.

At the end of the fifth century, in the metropolis of Arles, the young
Caesarius (bp. 502–42) is said to have come from the monastery of
Lérins and to have been taken into the household of a local magnate,
Firminus.[161] Firminus wanted to provide him with a classical education
"that his monastic simplicity might be polished by the discipline of secular
learning," and so entrusted him to the African Iulianus Pomerius, who
was then teaching as a grammarian in the city. One night, Caesarius
chanced to fall asleep over one of the books his teacher had given him to
read and in a vision saw "the shoulder on which he was lying, and the
arm that had rested on the book, being gnawed by a coiling serpent."
Frightened from his sleep, Caesarius reproved himself bitterly, "because
he wished to join the brilliance of salvation's rule with the foolish wisdom
of the world. He therefore despised these things straightway, knowing
that the adornment of polished speech is not wanting for those in whom
spiritual understanding looms large."

159. MacMullen, *Crisis* 50f. n. 7, reacting to Aur. Vict. *De Caes.* 9.12; cf.
Chap. 1 n. 66.

160. For the following, see [Basil. Sel.] *Vie et miracles de Sainte Thècle* 2.38
Dagron; cf. Part II no. 6.

161. For the following, see *V. Caes.* 1.8–9 (2.279f. Morin), with Part II
no. 124.

The visions of the literate saint or the ravenous serpent, of the traditional culture as a bond of intimacy and health or as a suffocating coil, define the poles the grammarian ranged in the Christian imagination. At the same time, the visions represent different solutions to an old problem in which the grammarian was much involved.[162] Where the literary culture was not simply an elaboration of esthetic principles but a distinguishing possession of a small and extraordinarily influential segment of society, how was one to understand the relation between the polished speech of the few and the grace of God available to all? What did polished speech have to do with spiritual understanding? How did the rules and forms of grammar and rhetoric meet the real needs of men, their good relations with one another in this world and their preparations for life in the next? Such questions challenged at its base the notion that the grammarian's profession and the literary culture served the well-being of the individual and the common good of society.

The questions had their roots both within and without the Christian community. The canonical reminder that Peter and John were "illiterates and laymen" (Acts 4.13) and Paul's claim to be "ignorant in speech, but not in understanding" (2 Cor. 11.6) converged on the powerful model of the illiterate or ill-educated apostle as charismatic teacher, whose truth owed nothing to the conventions and institutions of men. But the classically educated men of the non-Christian world rejected that truth, spurning the uncouth language in which it was transmitted.[163]

In apologetics the Christian could meet that contempt readily enough with the claim that such men saw only surfaces. Not for the first or last time, a group on the defensive would align itself with substance, leaving its opponents mere words: the literary culture was a culture of the tongue, not of the heart; it invested everything in trappings meant to increase prestige among men in a world rotten with false values, and cared nothing for grace, the inner truth that bound a man to God and gave a stable center to his life and his relations with others.[164]

---

162. The following pages, with their narrow focus, do not pretend to offer a full survey of the relation between Christianity and the classical culture. In addition to the works cited in the notes to this section, see esp. Laistner, *Christianity*; Baynes, *Byzantine Studies* 1ff., 24ff.; Gaudemet, *Église* 582ff.; Jaeger, *Early Christianity*; Dodds, *Pagan*; Chadwick, *Early Christian Thought*; Gigon, *Antike Kultur*; Lemerle, *Premier humanisme* 43ff.; Quacquarelli, *Scuola*; Ševčenko, "Shadow Outline"; Kennedy, *Greek Rhetoric* 180ff.; Wilson, *Scholars* 1ff.; Hagendahl, *Von Tertullian zu Cassiodor* esp. 83ff.

163. See Chap. 1 n. 24.

164. E.g., Lactant. *Inst.* 3.13, 5.1; Arnob. *Adv. nat.* 1.59; Zeno Veron. *Tract.* 3.1 (*PL* 11.280); Paulin. Nol. *Carm.* 10.20ff.; "Ambrosiaster" *In 2 Cor.* 11.6 (*CSEL* 81:2.283.4ff.); Quodvultdeus *De acced. ad grat.* 1.1.4ff., *Lib. promiss.* 1.37.54; Vigilius

When directed outward, across boundaries that could simultaneously distinguish non-Christian from Christian and liberally educated from layman, those straightforward claims might provide comfort and reassurance, a sense of old battles fought and won once more: rejecting the classical formalism recreated the apostle's charismatic leap over the written law to the natural law instilled in the heart by the grace of the Holy Spirit; the tongue of the literary culture, with its puffed-up and hollow pretensions, was like the lips of the Jews, who adhered to the shell of the Law.[165] But when, from the late third century onward, those boundaries became ever less distinct, and when more Christian voices came to speak with that tongue, answers to old questions became less clear-cut, less easily generalized. It becomes possible to trace different answers in the two halves of the empire. Beyond their specific circumstances and details, the visions of Alypius and Caesarius bespeak divergent trends in the East and the West concerning the standing and function of the literary culture and its polished speech. In the East, that culture came to be regarded less as a divisive force and was inserted in the hierarchy of values in such a way that old loyalties could blend with new. In the West, the literary culture remained an important symbol of fundamental divisions, defining loyalties more sharply and making certain that old oppositions continued to be felt.

Of course no distinctions are simple and uniform; similarities between the two halves of the empire coexist with the differences.[166] Educated men were assimilated into Christianity in the West as in the East, notably among the Christian academics teaching in the schools of grammar and rhetoric by the mid-fourth century. Julian's vindictive logic, which dictated that a Christian (whether sincere or insincere in his belief) had no place in the traditional schools, was applied and unwelcome in both parts of the empire:[167] claiming an absolute and exclusive congruence between classical literature and pagan belief that even most non-Christians would have thought *outré*, it had short-lived effects.[168] Conversely, one can note

---

Tapsens. *C. Eutych.* 1.15 (*PL* 62.104B); Iulianus Pomerius *De vit. contemp.* 1.24; John Chrysost. *Adv. oppugn. vit. monast.* 3.8 *fin.* (*PG* 47.363), *Expos. in Ps.* 4 2 (*PG* 55.42); Isid. Pel. *Ep.* 4.88, 91 (cf. 1.180); Cyril Alex. *Hom. Pasch.* 4.3 (*PG* 77.460; cf. *Dial. quod unus sit Christus* [*PG* 75.1253f.], with *Comm. in Ioan. Evang.* 5.8.30 [*PG* 73.849f.]); and cf. Mohrmann, *Études* 3.157ff.

165. Cf., e.g., Ambros. *Explan. in Ps.* 36 69 (*CSEL* 64.128.15ff.), with Rom. 2.17–29.

166. For this emphasis, see Marrou, *Histoire*⁶ 456ff.; and for continuing tensions in the East, see recently Alan Cameron, "Empress" 282ff., citing evidence of the fifth-century debate on the value of classicizing paraphrases of Scripture.

167. On Julian's school law, see esp. Hardy, "Emperor"; Brown, *World* 91ff.

168. Note esp. that Libanius, though a committed pagan himself, does not appear to have been much concerned with the religious loyalties of his students:

the rejectionist views expressed within the Christian community. In the East, the *Didascalia Apostolorum* repudiated the "books of the gentiles" and proposed the study of Scripture as a satisfactory alternative.[169] In the West, the *Statuta Ecclesiae Antiqua* forbade ordained bishops to read the classics.[170]

Yet even within these similarities it is possible to discern important differences. Consider, for instance, the men from the mid-third to the end of the fourth century who we know taught in the schools of grammar or rhetoric and (usually later) held some position in the Church hierarchy, who might therefore most conspicuously represent the mingling of the traditionally educated classes and local Christian leaders: in the West, Cyprian at Carthage, Victor, the grammarian and lector at Cirta/Constantina,[171] Marculus, a rhetorician who became a bishop and Donatist martyr,[172] and Augustine; in the East, Malchion, rhetorician and later presbyter at Antioch,[173] the two Apollinarii at Laodicea (the elder a grammarian and presbyter, the son a rhetorician and later a bishop),[174] and other rhetorician-bishops—Gregory of Nyssa, Amphilochius of Iconium,[175] Optimus of Phrygian Agdamia and Pisidian Antioch, and Ablabius, the Novatian bishop of Nicaea.[176] The Easterners are not only more numerous, they show a wider geographic spread; significantly, the Westerners are all from Africa, where Christianity had made its greatest gains in the West in the third century. The clustering is symptomatic of the uneven rate of Christianity's spread in the western provinces, which as a whole lagged behind the East.

Or again, consider the prescriptions of the *Didascalia Apostolorum* and the *Statuta Ecclesiae Antiqua*. The former sets down guidelines meant (in vain) for all "servants and sons of God"; but the latter imposes its restrictions only on the bishop, in effect emphasizing the distinction

---

Petit, *Étudiants* 120f. (cf. 133 n. 210); Liebeschuetz, *Antioch* 226f. Cf. also n. 201 below. Julian's merging of literature and religion—almost treating paganism as a religion of The Book—is so extreme and so unusual for a pagan that we should probably regard it as a legacy of his Christian upbringing.

169. *Didascalia Apostolorum* 1.6.1ff. Connolly (s.III).

170. *Stat. Eccl. Ant.* can. 5 (*Conc. Gall.*, CC SL 148) = *Collect. Hispan.* (Conc. Carthag. IV, an. 398) can. 16 (*Conc. Afr.*, CC SL 149), the *Statuta* compiled ca. 475 by Gennadius of Marseilles.

171. See Part II no. 161.

172. PL 8.760ff. (= *Prosop. chrét.* I s.v., pp. 696f.).

173. Euseb. Caes. *HE* 7.29; Jer. *De vir. ill.* 71.

174. See Part II no. 14.

175. Basil *Ep.* 150.2, 4.

176. For Optimus and Ablabius, see *PLRE* I s.vv, pp. 650 and 2, respectively; for other Novatian bishops with backgrounds as teachers, see Part II nos. 116, 238. Note also, just slightly later, Anatolius (*Vie et miracles de Sainte Thècle* 2.9 Dagron); Silvanus (*PLRE* II s.v. 2, p. 1011).

between the community at large and a single figure specially charged with a burden of holiness. The difference is still more eloquent and reveals a consequential trait of Christianity in the West: a tendency to treat more self-consciously or explicitly the divisions in the community and in the world.

By the early fourth century most Christians of the East were prepared to look out on the world as a place with which they had much in common; the Church in the West, by contrast, was more inward-turning, still regarding itself as a small gathering of the elect, an alien body in an environment of dangerous contradictions and divisions. These divergent positions had underpinnings both intellectual and social. The decisive messages of Tertullian and Origen still reached receptive audiences, but the two men spoke with very different voices. To an educated Christian of the East, the stringent puritanism of Tertullian would have seemed strangely backward. It was at best an unsophisticated notion that classical culture in all its forms was a poison, or that education in the traditional schools, though perhaps necessary for want of an alternative, was nevertheless a regrettable and evil necessity; at worst, the idea revealed a disquieting lack of confidence in Christian intelligence and judgment. The harsh antitheses implicit in Tertullian's question "What has Athens to do with Jerusalem?" could easily be resolved along the lines Origen laid down: Athens was part of Jerusalem's perfection—in itself imperfect or immature, no doubt, with a mixture of truth and falsehood that required discrimination, but an inseparable, in fact desirable, part nonetheless. Origen had banished the choice of either/or by telling the educated Christian that he occupied the enviable position of the connoisseur: with untroubled superiority he could surely and subtly separate the true from the false, the important from the inconsequential.

This sense of easy and sophisticated superiority was further cushioned by the social experience of Christians in the East. Christianity there had not only spread more quickly than in the West, but it stood in a different relation to the organization of urban life. The Christian community closely followed the continuum of social gradations in the towns.[177] The educated bishop who emerged from the local upper classes could justifiably claim a position among his city's social and cultural elite; as the

177. Note esp. *IGLTyr* 1, a Christian necropolis of the late third and the fourth century: the arrangement of the necropolis reflects the social distinctions between free and slave, *honesti* and *humiles*; see the remarks of Rey-Coquais, pp. 162f. An unusually large number of inscriptions reveal the metiers of the deceased, with a range of craftsmen and tradesmen, and one member of a learned profession (a physician, no. 217). There are also epitaphs of the familiar type for liberally educated youths, praising their relations with the Muses (nos. 149A, B, 150); see Chap. 1 n. 64; and cf. Feissel, "Notes (III)" 550ff., with the addendum at "Notes (IV)" 474.

leader of an important group that cut across class lines within the town, he could take his place as a force to be reckoned with, alongside—and in the manner of—the factional leaders of the old town councils.[178]

But in the West the social structure was surmounted by the class of great landowners, especially among the old senatorial aristocracy, a group of men who had no exact counterpart in the East and with whom few Western bishops could associate as social or cultural equals.[179] Seeming to stand aloof in their pursuit of *otium* while devoting themselves to their own interests and those of their dependents, such men were raised up by their wealth, education, and birth, and loomed over the towns. Late in coming into the Church, they provided a continuing reminder of the worldly authority and prestige of the classical culture that lay outside. They were not easily domesticated when they came in;[180] their power required gingerly treatment on the part of the bishop to coax and bend them to his purposes.[181] The status and self-assurance they derived from their wealth and education made them potential competitors of men who had risen through the ranks of the Church. Their desirability as bishops threatened to upset the developing order of ecclesiastical office.[182] The tensions did not quickly dissipate: the right that the learned (and perhaps senatorial) layman Priscillian claimed late in the fourth century, to discuss noncanonical texts as a lay teacher, and the lethal reaction of the more anxious members of the Church hierarchy, sharpened the conflict between two differently constituted elites and splintered Christian opinion.

The components of worldly and spiritual standing were at variance longer in the West, insuring that the distinctive pattern of each would remain conspicuous. At the same time, other lines of division were superimposed. The early development of vernacular Christianity in the East meant that religious boundaries were no longer fundamentally congruent with linguistic boundaries; in the West, where nothing comparable developed, Latin provided the single path of access to the vital texts. Hence,

178. He was also increasingly likely to have his origins in the curial order; see recently Eck, "Einfluss."

179. Cf. Eck, "Einfluss," emphasizing the exceptional status of the aristocratic bishops in Gaul and Italy of the late fourth and the fifth century; and Chadwick, *Priscillian* 11, on the modest social origins and intellectual attainments of the Spanish bishops.

180. Cf. Aug. *De cat. rud.* 8.12, still conscious of the *eruditi catechizandi* as a special set offering special difficulties.

181. Cf. Brown, *Augustine* 192f.

182. See *Canones Osii* 13, with Hess, *Canons* 103ff. The canon insists that, if a wealthy man, an advocate (*scholasticus forensis*), or a civil official be desired as bishop, he must first pass through the ranks of lector, deacon, and presbyter. Cf. n. 319 below.

what kind of Latin one should use remained a sticking point and a center of attention: in many minds, the polished speech of the few continued to be incompatible with the spiritual understanding of the many. In the East, where the question of language was more diffuse, solutions were more numerous. Loyalties could be so expressed as to deflect attention away from polished speech and its conflict with spiritual understanding. A readiness to hear the Truth spoken, for instance, in a Graeco-Syriac patois[183] made it possible to turn aside from one's own highly cultivated speech—to treat it as something detachable, neutral, and so taken for granted—in a way unknown in the West. In part, the Eastern vernaculars added one more cushion against self-consciousness, a way of avoiding the problems framed in the language of either/or.

A further, decisive factor was the persistence of political unity in the East, which both sheltered urban Christianity and kept it in check, drawing it into the structure of civilian life and competing institutions with a web of familial, social, and political relations. But the sudden fragmentation of the western empire in the early fifth century tore apart that structure just when it was being finally and firmly joined with the Catholic Church. As a result the Church was isolated yet endowed with its own hauteur, left to provide the leaders of society with new careers and the institutions on which to base them. Life in the West did not suffer collapse so much as compression. Communities were thrown back on their own resources, which were frequently identical with the resources—the men, money, and culture—that the local episcopacy could mobilize. The problem of leadership, put thus acutely, would be solved differently according to the individual bishops' backgrounds and angles of vision—including the vision of the literary culture.

We can trace the points of divergence noted above in more detail, beginning with how Christians of the East resolved the problem of the traditional education. Most characteristic are the strategies that emphasize differences in value in order to discard unwanted antitheses: opposition is replaced by safe, hierarchical relationships. So, for example, one could draw on typology to adjust the relationship between charismatic teaching and the learning of men. David, the singer inspired by God, and Moses, "educated in all the wisdom of the Egyptians," can embody two acceptable types of holiness, the former "brought up in a hamlet, raised in the hands of peasants, a shepherd from childhood," the latter nurtured "in a city, in the embrace of royalty, a guardian of letters from boyhood." The two types might represent the two poles of class and culture; but the tension between them is eased by the recognition that the holiness

183. See below, p. 79.

of David is ultimately superior, though the external learning of Moses remains nonetheless valued.[184]

Gregory Nazianzen can be seen making a similar adjustment in order to smooth the way for his literary attainments. He dissociates himself from the normative model of St. Peter (with more than a touch of sarcasm for those who would hide behind it), declaring himself unable to match it: "I myself would have embraced the ἀλογία that some see fit to call faith if I were a fisherman . . . and if I had the power of signs as my own form of speech." At the same time Gregory makes a place for his own eloquence, claiming that through the divine λόγοι he has "ennobled" and "sweetened" the "tongue educated in external λόγοι." The problem of the tongue is thus defused by finding one's proper place in the hierarchy of holiness and accommodating—or elevating—one's education to it.[185]

But perhaps the most important variation on this general strategy is found in Basil's influential tract, written for his nephews, on the use of Greek literature.[186] The work is neither an encomium of the classics (as some used to think) nor a recommendation that their form be approved but their content be rejected, with a warning, in the manner of Tertullian, against the danger of things evil in themselves (as others have recently claimed). Instead it is an exhortation and a guide to right choices. Beginning with the principle of utility (ὅσον χρήσιμον)[187] and referring that term to what is good and useful, not in the life of men only, but for the "other life,"[188] Basil makes the classical texts subject to the moral sensibilities and spiritual aims of Christians. Without polemic, without the suggestion that one is reluctantly coming to grips with a necessary evil,[189] the status and function of the classics are simply and firmly redefined: they provide the preliminary exercises in a truly liberal education (ἐλευθερίως παιδεύεσθαι),[190] the new gymnastic of the soul, which will finally raise men up and liberate them from the transient world of crude sensation by steeping the soul in the wisdom of Christian λόγοι. Of course the poets, historians, and orators cannot be sufficient for such

184. For the comparison of David and Moses, see esp. Asterius soph. *Hom.* 23.15–16 (p. 180.25ff. Richard). On Moses (cf. Acts 7.22), see below, p. 78.

185. *Or.* 36.4, where note that Gregory dismisses putative critics of his distinctive literary skills as simply envious. Cf. *Or.* 43.11, where critics of ἡ ἔξωθεν παίδευσις are treated with similar bluntness, as stupid and uneducated levelers.

186. Now available in the critical edition of Wilson, *Saint Basil*.

187. Basil 1.24ff.

188. Basil 2.1ff.

189. Cf. Wilson, *Saint Basil* 10.

190. Cf. Basil 9.86ff.

a job by themselves. Warnings must be issued not to believe what is said of the gods,[191] or to make certain that the actions of bad men are taken as negative examples; but at the same time the actions of good men are there to be imitated, and the texts have a substantive, ethical value that can help in the progress toward the true and final good of the soul.[192]

The external culture (τὰ ἔξω, ἡ θύραθεν σοφία, τὰ ἔξωθεν παιδεύματα) is the first stage in this gymnastic of the soul:[193] thus Moses, Basil says, "having exercised his intelligence [ἐγγυμνασάμενος τὴν διάνοιαν] in the learning of the Egyptians, proceeded to the contemplation of reality."[194] In a different metaphor, Basil compares the external culture to the leaves of a tree that protect the fruit (the Christian Truth growing in the soul) and give it a pleasing appearance.[195] In still another metaphor, the classical texts lend themselves to a sketch or outline (σκιαγραφία) of virtue, which "our λόγοι" will teach more completely.[196] All Basil's metaphors converge on the same point: an obvious difference in value (say, between the fruit and the leaves) can exist without implying a necessary opposition.[197] The external culture and "our λόγοι" are distinct and unequal: each has a function and value in its own sphere, and once the functions are recognized, the hierarchy of values sorted out, the external culture is no longer a threatening force.

Basil does the external culture the favor of allowing it to remain both clearly secular and clearly useful in Christian terms.[198] Its noxious elements remain safely outside (or below); its healthy elements ease one's passage inside (or upward). One can thus enjoy the best of both worlds. From the position Basil sketched, it requires only a short step to redefine the lover of λόγοι as the man who knows both classical and Christian authors.[199] At that point, one is no distance at all from the saint as φιλόλογος in a grammarian's dream, a kindly mother to a new Achilles.

191. Basil 4.19ff.
192. Basil 2.34ff.; cf. 4.5ff., 7.2ff., and the ethical exegesis of Hom. *Od.* 6.135ff. at 5.25ff. Compare Gregory Nazianzen's funeral oration on Basil, *Or.* 43.11, where the essentials of Basil's position are restated and their implicit premise is drawn out: the classical culture, like all the components of the created world, is a mixture of the useful and the harmful, which are to be distinguished by an understanding surrendered to Christ.
193. For the gymnastic, see Basil *passim* and esp. 8.44f. Cf. at Chap. 1 nn. 9–11.
194. Basil 3.13ff. With the thought and metaphor, cf., e.g., *V. Marcell. Archimand. Akoimeton* §2 Dagron, *Anal. Boll.* 86 (1968) 288.
195. Basil 3.6ff.
196. Basil 10.1ff.
197. Just as there is a difference but no necessary opposition between the created and the Creator; cf. n. 192 above.
198. Contrast below, pp. 87–88, on Augustine.
199. See Kuch, "Φιλόλογος" 337ff., on φιλόλογος in Sozomen.

In all these cases, men have found their way around stark choices. The literary culture does not get in the way of what really matters; one can glide from one sphere to the other, since the attainments and behavior traditionally valued by literate, upper-class society are compatible with Christian duties and loyalties. In the fourth century, Gregory Nazianzen could mediate a dispute between two sophists or recommend a pupil to Libanius,[200] and Gregory of Nyssa could hope that the pagan Libanius would review the style of his tract against Eunomius.[201] Neither those dealings nor the careful Atticism that the Cappadocian Fathers cultivated was felt to be inconsistent with their regard for the monastic ideal or with their remarkable efforts in proselytizing (and hellenizing) their rude province.

In the next century Theodoret, bishop of Cyrrhus, sent pupils to the pagan sophist Isocasius[202] or acted as a middleman, receiving letters of recommendation for an Egyptian rhetorician from two presbyters and in his turn recommending the rhetorician to the *comes* Ulpianus.[203] Theodoret's involvement in such transactions does not detract a whit from his deep admiration for the illiterate saints of the Syrian hinterland. The concerns of the tongue and their associated social forms and relations remain comfortably apart from or are dwarfed by the concerns of the heart. As a result, when the cultured townsman encounters the saint in the pages of Theodoret, the meeting is imagined as taking place with remarkable ease and tranquility: the holy man Aphraates appears at Antioch, speaking a mixture of Syriac and Greek, "crying out with the great Paul, 'I am ignorant in speech, but not in understanding'"; and at once all people come running to meet him, the high, educated, and rich together with the humble, ignorant, and poor, "the latter receiving in silence what he offered, the former questioning, learning, proposing topics for discussion."[204]

Or again, in the second quarter of the sixth century, the bishop Marcian of Gaza was among the patrons of the sophist Choricius. The beneficiary of a full literary education,[205] Marcian was interested in the local school of rhetoric and enjoyed (or endured) at least two of

200. Greg. Naz. *Ep.* 192 and 236, respectively.
201. Greg. Nyss. *Ep.* 15, with the remarks of Wilson, *Saint Basil* 11.
202. Theodoret. *Ep.* XVII, XXVIII; cf. XLIV. For Isocasius, see Part II no. 85.
203. Theodoret. *Ep.* 19, 20, 22.
204. Theodoret. *Hist. phil.* 8.2 Canivet. The scene has no true counterpart in the West, nor could it, in view of the linguistic situation there; cf. above, pp. 75f. It is noteworthy that in the closest Western approximation (Sulp. Sev. *Dial.* 1.27.2–4) an apology for the rustic speaker's offense to urban ears must be confected, and the polarities thus emphasized, so that a show can be made of brushing the offense aside.
205. Choric. *Laud. Marc.* 2.7 (p. 29.17ff. Foerster-Richtsteig).

Choricius's encomia, in which he heard recounted his own student days, when he "culled from poetry whatever was useful, while smiling at the myths."[206] Town-bound as it is by the rhetorical tradition in which Choricius was working—his Gaza is completely and impeccably Greek-speaking: no more than Libanius does his epigonus reveal that the country people were largely Semitic speakers, whose language would fill Gaza's streets during the festivals Choricius lovingly describes—the sophist's point of view shows us how the local Christian gentry had merged with the civic life around them. In the Gaza of Choricius the literary culture is still an important mark of status, joined with *mores* ("a reverend way of life") and wealth (in the form of charitable benefactions) to form the triad "that makes men exalted."[207] Marcian's family, too, besides Marcian himself, was involved in public life: one of his brothers was an advocate; another held a provincial governorship or some other imperial office.[208] And as a local benefactor Marcian takes his place alongside the governor Stephanus and the *duces* Aratius and Summus as a subject of Choricius's praise.[209]

Basil allowed Greek λόγοι to remain both external and useful in the new gymnastic of the soul; Gregory Nazianzen claimed to ennoble the literary language; Theodoret imagined a world where the question of language is spontaneously set aside; Choricius kept his eyes fixed on the upper-class life of the town. Each in his own way overcame the problem of the traditional literary culture. The same process of accommodation of course occurred among Christians in the West: Ausonius (sometimes— quite unfairly—said to have been a nominal Christian) could not agree with Paulinus of Nola that "hearts dedicated to Christ are not open to

206. Choric. *Laud. Marc.* 1.6 (p. 4.1ff.).

207. *Or. nupt. in Proc.* 33 (p. 94.20ff.): ἅπαντας αὐτῶν τοὺς γονεῖς σεμνύνει πλεονεκτήματα, παιδεία τε λόγων καὶ βίος σεμνὸς καὶ τὸ λαμπρῶς εὖ ποιεῖν τοὺς ἐνδείᾳ πιεζομένους.

208. Advocate: *Or. funebr. in Mariam* 8 (p. 102.7ff.). Governor(?): ibid. (p. 102.5f.), ὁ μὲν ἐν ἐξουσίᾳ πλεονεξίας δικαιοσύνην ἀσκεῖ (on the presence of justice [for δικαιοσύνη, see Robert, *Hellenica* 4.100] and the absence of greed among the virtues of governors, see esp. Ševčenko, "Late Antique Epigram" 30f.), with ibid. 21–22 (p. 105.18ff.), on τῷ τὴν ἡμετέραν λαχόντι πρυτανεύειν ἀρχήν, to whom his mother (Maria, the mother of Marcian and his brothers) appeared in a dream to heal an abdominal lesion while he was traveling to the emperor. The passage makes it plain that one of the brothers is the official in question; if governor, ἡμετέρα ἀρχή must refer to Palaestina I. A fourth brother, Anastasius, was bishop of Eleutheriopolis: ibid. tit. (p. 99.9f.); cf. ibid. 7 (p. 101.23ff.).

209. *Laud. Arat. et Steph.* (pp. 48ff.), *Laud. Summ.* (pp. 69ff.). Cf. also *Laud. Marc.* 1.7 (p. 4.11ff.), with *Laud. Marc.* 2.16 (p. 32.5ff.); *Laud. Marc.* 1.30–31 (p. 10.11ff.).

Apollo";[210] the two Clamosi, father and son, schoolmasters at Parentium, contributed to the construction of the Christian basilica in their town at the end of the fourth and again in the mid-fifth century;[211] the grammarian Calbulus donated a baptistery to his church and adorned it with his own pious verses at the end of the fifth or the beginning of the sixth century.[212] (We will meet others below.) But influential voices continued to express doubts that fundamental conflicts could be so easily resolved. Would worldly eloquence, for example, simply become antiseptic as the junior partner of faith? Or would it inevitably foster qualities—pride in personal ingenuity and achievement, competitiveness, pretensions to status fixed by ephemeral standards—that were a disease on the soul and divisive in the community? To Jerome and Augustine, the second possibility seemed more likely. To each of them the social good of the grammarian's profession continued to appear questionable, if not illusory; and for each, controlling the effects of his own education was a struggle set between scarcely reconcilable poles.

"You are a Ciceronian, not a Christian; 'where your treasure is, there too is your heart.'" So the Heavenly Judge spoke to Jerome in the dream that terrified him on his way to Bethlehem in 374, as he recounted it to edify Eustochium a decade later.[213] The "old serpent" had mocked him. Beguiled by the style of Plautus, Jerome could not turn back to Scripture without disgust at its uncouth speech; and yet, "I reckoned it the fault not of my eyes but of the sun that I could not see the light in my blindness." Fastidiously confident of his own judgment, the Ciceronian was the captive of his past, its vainglory, and its false values; he could be freed only by the salutary humiliation of the flogging he received in the dream at the Judge's order.

The crosscurrents of eloquence and faith, pride and abasement, that disturbed Jerome's sleep on that occasion continued to drag at him as he attempted to come to terms with his own highly prized literacy:[214] "It is no small thing for a noble man, a man fluent of speech, a wealthy man, to avoid the accompaniment of the powerful in the streets, to mingle with the crowds, to cleave to the poor, to associate with peasants."[215] This praise of Pammachius's descent to the life of the *vulgus* was written by a man with sensibilities in tune with his subject's, aware of the tug of worldly prestige, the difficulty of pulling free (aware, too, of the rare

---

210. Paulin. Nol. *Carm.* 10.22f. On Ausonius, see Étienne, *Bordeaux* 278ff.
211. See Part II nos. 29, 30.
212. See Part II no. 23.
213. Jer. *Ep.* 22.30; see Kelly, *Jerome* 41ff.
214. See esp. Hagendahl, *Latin Fathers* 318ff.
215. Jer. *Ep.* 66.6.

satisfaction of being seen conspicuously to try). "I know that among Christians flaws of speech are not usually criticized, but . . . "[216] Enemies are skewered for their lack of education,[217] and educated men who come to Scripture from liberal letters are mocked for their pretensions: "If they chance to have soothed the ear of the people with an elegant speech, they reckon whatever they have said is the law of God."[218]

The balance was so hard to find. Split by experience and conscience, Jerome worked his conflicts out in his writings. We see him in the contemporary commentaries on Ephesians and Galatians trying to control the problem of Paul's literacy. Some were able simply to imagine Paul among the illiterate[219] or to take his agitated question "See with what big letters I've written to you?" (Gal. 6.11) as evidence that he was marginally literate, a slow writer.[220] Ridiculous, says Jerome. Yes, Paul was a "Hebrew born of Hebrews," learned in his vernacular, unable to shape his deep thoughts in an alien tongue;[221] yet Paul of course knew, for example, the literary trope of allegory, just as we learn about it in school, because he too had had some contact with secular letters.[222] Then again, he does commit solecisms[223]—of course, because his literary education was not perfect.[224] And anyway, "He did not care about the words, as long as he preserved the sense."[225] In these arguments we can sense Jerome's attempt to thread his way between two unacceptable alternatives, a Paul with too little worldly learning, or one with too much. In that respect, the arguments are symptomatic of Jerome's continuing debate on the value of his own worldly learning and of his attempt, never quite successful, to find a safe and stable (and distinctive) place between the "two imperfections" of "holy rusticity" and "sinful eloquence."[226]

216. Jer. C. Rufin. 2.20.

217. Cf. n. 35 above; Hagendahl, Latin Fathers 311 n. 4.

218. Jer. Ep. 53.6f.; cf. C. Rufin. 3.34 and esp. Comm. Ephes. prol.

219. See, emphatically, John Chrysost. In 1 Cor. hom. 3.4 (PG 61.27).

220. Comm. Gal. 3.6 (PL 26.463C), Jerome's scorn for the view of a vir apprime nostris temporibus eruditus. For the slow writer (βραδέως γράφων), able to add his subscription to a document but otherwise illiterate, see n. 42 above.

221. Comm. Gal. 3.6 (PL 26.455A–B); cf. Comm. Ephes. 3.5 (PL 26.553A).

222. Comm. Gal. 2.4 (PL 26.416A–C).

223. Comm. Ephes. 2 prol. (PL 26.509B–D); cf. Tract. de Ps. 81 8.221ff. (CC SL 78.89 = Anecd. Mared. 3:2.80).

224. Comm. Gal. 2.4 (PL 26.416A–C).

225. Comm. Gal. 3.6 (PL 26.455A–B).

226. Jer. Ep. 52.9: nec rusticus et tantum simplex frater ideo se sanctum putet, si nihil noverit, nec peritus et eloquens in lingua aestimet sanctitatem. multoque melius est e duobus imperfectis rusticitatem sanctam habere quam eloquentiam peccatricem. Cf. Ep. 27.1, 53.3f., 57.12; Comm. Ezech. 2.7 (PL 25.61).

The problem with which Jerome wrestled in his own conscience was solved more directly by others, in the broader setting of the Christian community. The solution at once preserved the polarities of eloquence and faith, the learned and the simple, and attempted to mediate between them, *de haut en bas*. "Why does Paul lower himself [*se humiliat*]," Jerome's contemporary "Ambrosiaster" asks, "when he says he is ignorant in speech?"[227] Because he wanted to serve as an example against those who sought approval for their eloquence instead of their faith:[228] he could speak in the manner of the learned of the world, but he did not choose to. Paul's statement, and by extension the blunt and restless spontaneity of his style, thus become part of a self-conscious and self-imposed *humiliatio* growing out of his message.

The idea had been anticipated in the apologetics of Arnobius, whose defense of the uncouthness of the Christians' Latin includes the claim that certain Fathers, although they could speak more ornately and more richly, "not only put off the cultivation of speech but even intentionally pursued a common lowness of speech [*trivialis humilitas*]" lest the weight and rigor of their message be corrupted by sophistic display.[229] Transposed from apologetics to the apostolic duty of the bishop, the idea motivates Peter Chrysologus (bp. of Ravenna; d. 450) when he calls for a "natural language," "popular" and made up of "common speech," to provide a common ground for the learned and the simple;[230] or Augustine, when his preaching plays off the formidable *strepitus* of Cicero against the inviting sound of Scripture[231] or the "grammarian's laws" against the "people's understanding."[232] Put into effect, the idea takes the form of the humble style, *sermo humilis*, the style of the Christian message[233]—humble in its descent from the shimmering, timeless standards of classical correctness and adornment down to a language intent on making the Truth plain and immediate to a heterogeneous congregation. It is the vivid, simple style of Augustine's preaching,[234] fluent talk in plain language. Turning away from the classical canons that matched levels of style to importance of subject (for "everything we say is of great importance"),[235] the speaker feels free to range spontaneously

227. *In 2 Cor.* 11.6 (*CSEL* 81:2.283.4ff.).

228. Ibid.: *hoc ergo dicens non se loqui nescire voluit intellegi, sed propter eos qui non per fidem sed per eloquentiam commendari volebant.*

229. *Adv. nat.* 1.59.

230. *Serm.* 43 (*PL* 52.320A).

231. *En. in Ps. 103* serm. 3.4.

232. *En. in Ps. 36* serm. 3.6, *En. in Ps. 123* 8, *En. in Ps. 138* 20, *Serm.* 37.14.

233. Cf. Auerbach, *Literary Language* 27ff.

234. See van der Meer, *Saint Augustin* 2.212ff.

235. Aug. *De doct. Christ.* 4.18.35.

over the various styles according to the didactic needs and emotional pitch of the moment.[236] Augustine wanted such a style to reach a largely uneducated audience[237] and to extend the "franchise of the Latin language" in a mixed population of Punic and Latin speakers by simultaneously pressing Latin's claim as the only point of entry for full participation and making the entryway as wide as possible.[238]

The style was also a subtle form of episcopal discipline. Implicitly discounting the distinctions and prestige of the traditional literary culture, it was a chastening reminder for the learned that what was important, true, and correct—in language as in substance—could not be defined by external standards. Those standards belonged rather to the arsenal of worldly competition; they divided the community. Augustine had felt their divisiveness in himself: always conscious of the pride and competitive urge of the learned,[239] he knew soon after his ordination that his enduring love of praise required the "medicine" of retirement and study.[240] His style, with its "simplicity achieved at the other side of vast sophistication,"[241] was another, continuing form of self-restraint, a way of working free of the time in his own career when those standards had meant so much. Spoken from the authoritative *cathedra* of the bishop, his language was a unifying force, moving downward to instruct the simple, reaching upward to set the *docti* an example.

This need for compelling, authoritative, yet accessible speech, capable of opening up texts singularly important in their truth but often obscurely deep or seemingly ambiguous in its presentation, motivates the *De doctrina Christiana*, Augustine's formal answer to the claims of the traditional literary culture.[242] Begun in 396 and completed in 427—thus nearly framing his episcopacy—the work sketches for clergy and educated layman the possibility of an alternative literary culture based on Scripture. As a necessary part of its argument, the work divorces communication from the authority of classical grammar and rhetoric.

Augustine shows that the traditional standards of correct speech refer to a man-made order and so strips them of their veneer of permanence. As classical rhetoric's seemingly absolute judgments concerning dignity of subject matter have no meaning in Christian experience,[243] so the

236. Aug. *De doct. Christ.* 4.19.38ff.

237. Cf. MacMullen, "Note."

238. Cf. Brown, *Religion* 287ff.

239. *De bono vid.* 15.19. Cf. *Ep.* 95.4, 266.2; *De Gen. ad litt.* 10.39; *In Ioan. evang. tract.* 57.2, 6; and cf. n. 251 below.

240. See Brown, *Augustine* 205f.

241. Brown, *Augustine* 268.

242. See esp. Marrou, *Saint Augustin* 331ff., 505ff.; Brown, *Augustine* 263ff.

243. See nn. 235, 236 above.

definitions and rules of classical grammar, concerning phonology, morphology, barbarisms, and solecisms,[244] have no absolute validity but are only habitual observances: "What then is soundness of speech [*integritas locutionis*, the traditional province of the grammarian and his rules][245] save the preservation of an alien habit [*aliena consuetudo*] supported by the authority of ancient speakers?"[246]

The grammarian would answer that soundness of speech was definitely no simple matter of habit and authority but was founded on the nature of the language.[247] One said *inter homines*, not *inter hominibus*, because the former expression preserved, and the latter corrupted, the natural force of the preposition and the natural relationship between the components of the phrase—not simply because, as Augustine claimed, it was the manner of "those who, before us, spoke with some authority."[248] But Arnobius had already rejected claims to a permanent validity for rules founded in nature; he began from the position that "no speech is sound by nature" (*nullus sermo natura est integer*) and went on to describe the distinctions of grammar as merely human, hence mutable, conventions.[249] His point is essentially the same as that of Augustine, who elsewhere devalues the artifices of the grammarians as nothing more than the coventional adherence to the authority of the past:[250] the mortmain has nothing to do with us.

At one and the same time Augustine shrugs off the burden of an alien tradition, remote in the past and appealing to criteria of no permanent value, and places the grammarian in a morally untenable position. The strength of his rules—and so his own strength—lies in his weakness and others', their ambitious regard for the good opinion of other men. Where barbarisms, solecisms, or the conventions of classical phonology are concerned, "men are all the more offended by their violation the weaker they are, and all the more weak in proportion to their wish to seem more learned."[251] That weakness could be overcome by submission to the yoke of God,[252] joined with the realization that the only correct speech was speech effective in context, communicating the Truth clearly, whether or not it was correct by extrinsic, formal standards.[253] The *ars*

---

244. *De doct. Christ.* 2.13.19–20, 38.56; 4.10.24.
245. Cf. *De doct. Christ.* 4.3.5: *ipsa arte grammatica, qua discitur locutionis integritas.*
246. *De doct. Christ.* 2.13.19.
247. See Chap. 5 p. 176.
248. *De doct. Christ.* 2.13.19.
249. *Adv. nat.* 1.59.
250. Cf. *De mus.* 2.1.1, *C. Cresc.* 3.79.86.
251. *De doct. Christ.* 2.13.20. For pride and self-consciousness connected with the rules of correct speech, cf. 2.14.21, 41.62; 4.7.14; with *Conf.* 1.18.28–29.
252. *De doct. Christ.* 2.13.20.
253. *De doct. Christ.* 4.10.24.

grammatica could therefore be dispensed with, so long as children could grow up among men who spoke correctly.[254]

"'Here we will not be troubled by fear of the grammarians or be afraid lest our careless use of words be punished by those who have put their goods at our disposal.' When the others had laughed . . . "[255] In the rarified atmosphere of Cassiciacum, the enclave of retirement and study the grammarian Verecundus provided outside Milan, it still seemed possible to integrate the liberal arts smoothly with Christian studies.[256] Augustine could then urbanely joke about fear of the grammarian's authority. But when the idea recurs in a sermon of Augustine the bishop,[257] joking in sheltered surroundings has been replaced by instruction in a community at once the only means of salvation and split by contradictions. Augustine had "come home"[258] and found a place where the grammarians' claims were in equal measure intrusive and irrelevant. The irritating fellows simply would not go away: witness the pagan grammarian who so disapproved of Christianity that he contemned the barbarous names of local African martyrs,[259] or the Donatist layman Cresconius, who paraded his professional expertise as part of his polemics with Augustine.[260] Yet such concerns seemed pointless when the typical newcomer to the Church was an uneducated townsman,[261] when Christians accustomed to the language of Scripture thought the locutions of Latin *auctores* strange,[262] when Augustine's colleagues at Hippo would most often have been like Possidius, "nurtured not by those letters that the slaves of diverse passions call 'liberal' but by the bread of the Lord,"[263] and when not a few of Augustine's fellow bishops were ill-educated by classical standards.[264] (Indeed, it should be remembered that the one illiterate bishop whom we know was Augustine's contemporary and countryman.)[265]

---

254. *De doct. Christ.* 4.3.5. How long men would continue to speak correctly—even by the relativist measure of clarity and effectiveness in context—once the formal criteria were devalued is a question with which Augustine did not concern himself; cf. Brown, *Augustine* 268; Dionisotti, "On Bede" 125–26.

255. Aug. *De beat. vit.* 4.31.

256. Cf. Fuchs, "Frühe christliche Kirche."

257. *Serm.* 37.14: *dum omnes instruantur, grammatici non timeantur.*

258. See Brown, *Augustine* 266f.

259. Maximus of Madaurus *ap.* Aug. *Ep.* 16.2, with Augustine's rebuke, *Ep.* 17.2.

260. Cf. Weissengruber, "Augustins Wertung" 104ff.

261. *De cat. rud.* 16.24.

262. *De doct. Christ.* 2.14.21.

263. *Ep.* 101.1.

264. E.g., *Ep.* 34.6, on the bishops Proculianus and Samsucius.

265. See n. 16 above.

To stand in awe of the grammarian and his definitions in such circumstances was to surrender to the weakness of pride and self-satisfied idiocy.[266] The liberal attitude toward language expressed in the *De doctrina Christiana* was a way of overcoming that weakness. But at the same time, it was liberalism in the service of a scarcely tolerant and stringently exclusive counterculture. To be sure, Augustine takes it for granted that men should be literate[267] and allows that oratory may be learned—quickly, by those who have the time—in the traditional ways.[268] Like Basil he grants, momentarily, that the liberal disciplines have some ethical value in themselves.[269] Yet while he gives with one hand, he takes away massively with the other.[270] One can learn the traditional rules of oratory—but really there is little point, since a student capable of learning such rules to begin with will gain nothing that he could not acquire for himself by listening to eloquent men or by reading ecclesiastical writings.[271] Similarly, correct speech can be learned without the *ars grammatica* and so without the grammarian.[272] And as for the grammarian's skill as exegete, in resolving, say, a perplexity of interpretation by punctuating correctly,[273] that can be learned as well, if not better, from the example of Augustine himself, or from other commentators on Scripture.[274] In short, though Augustine assumes an audience educated like himself, most of what he says debunks that education, or shows how the familiar institutions of the traditional culture, and much of its substance, can be circumvented.

Above all, the substance of the traditional culture is to be retained as useful only insofar as it can contribute directly to understanding and communicating the faith.[275] Thus it happens that when Augustine sounds most like Basil, in offering advice to "industrious and talented youths" on their studies outside the Church,[276] he is least like Basil in fact. Far from even hinting that the utility of the classics could be defined in terms of such immediate and limited relevance, Basil assumes that the

266. To borrow Ramsay MacMullen's phrase; see above, n. 159.
267. *De doct. Christ.* 2.18.28, 25.40; cf. prol. 4.
268. *De doct. Christ.* 4.3.4.
269. *De doct. Christ.* 2.40.60.
270. Cf. *De doct. Christ.* 2.42.63, on the general theme that all that can usefully be learned elsewhere—and more—is found in Scripture.
271. *De doct. Christ.* 4.3.4–5.
272. See above, n. 254.
273. See *De doct. Christ.* 2.2.2ff., for application of the method.
274. Cf. Marrou, *Saint Augustin* 415ff.
275. Cf. *De doct. Christ.* 2.18.28, *utile ad intellegendas sanctas scripturas* and *ad spiritualia capienda*; 2.28.42, *ad libros sanctos intellegendos*; 2.40.60, *usui veritatis aptiores* and *ad usum iustum praedicandi evangelii*.
276. *De doct. Christ.* 2.39.58–42.63.

literary culture would remain a sanitized but unmistakably secular pro-paedeutic: as the first step toward the final good of the soul, Moses' preliminary gymnastics among the Egyptians have a value in themselves and are left, so to speak, *in situ*.[277] But when Augustine speaks of the use of the foreign culture, in the metaphor of despoiling the Egyptians, the emphasis is wholly on passing out of Egypt.[278] The bits and pieces of the literary culture that one can surreptitiously appropriate (*clanculo vindicare*) are valued only to the extent that they do not remain secular; the metaphor of propaedeutic, with its implications of continuity and prog-ress, yields before the metaphor of possessive alienation. For the spiritual *émigrés* envisioned in the *De doctrina Christiana*, rigorous and direct sub-ordination is the only alternative to rejection of the literary culture or surrender to it. If the *De doctrina Christiana* is the "fundamental charter for Christian culture,"[279] then as such it recognizes no middle way, no compromise, in any real sense of those terms; it is thoroughly like its author, neither desiring to break free of the traditional culture[280] nor able to reach a comfortable rapprochement with it.

Augustine's views were not decisively influential until the deep con-fusion of the sixth century, when Cassiodorus could find in the *De doctrina Christiana* part of his formula for stripping the humanities of their vanity and including them as a branch (and nothing more) of divinity.[281] To the aristocracy—Christian and non-Christian alike—along whose edges Augustine had moved at Rome and Milan, the path he followed as bishop would have seemed both wayward and dangerous. The traditions of the literary culture were identifying marks of the natural superiority of their class; both the traditions and the assumptions of superiority largely transcended differences of religion. During the long process by which the senatorial aristocracy in the West came to Christianity,[282] classicism and paganism rarely coalesced to divide the aristocracy—least of all in the late fourth century. Although often attractively mounted,[283] attempts to find in Symmachus a Julian without

277. See above at n. 194 and p. 78.
278. Thus *De doct. Christ.* 2.40.60–61, *exire de Aegypto* (*vel sim.*) repeated four times in two paragraphs.
279. Marrou, *Saint Augustin* 413.
280. On the course and extent of Augustine's classical reading during his episcopacy, see most recently O'Donnell, "Augustine's Classical Readings."
281. On *De doct. Christ.* and *Inst.*, see O'Donnell, *Cassiodorus* 205f., 212f. Cf. Riché, *Education* 130f., on Eugippius's use of *De doct. Christ.*
282. See esp. Chastagnol, "Sénateur"; Brown, *Religion* 161ff.; Matthews, *Western Aristocracies* 101ff. For the period up to and through the reign of Con-stantine, see Eck, "Eindringen"; Novak, "Constantine."
283. Most influentially within the last generation by Bloch, "Pagan Revival." See also, e.g., Klingner, *Römische Geisteswelt*[4] 528ff.; Paschoud, *Roma* 100ff.; Klein, *Symmachus* 67ff.; Markus, "Paganism."

portfolio, the center of a defensive pagan revival that sought to preserve the literary culture as a distinctive possession of a resisting elite, do not survive analysis.[284] It is more accurate and more productive to think of the literary culture as a neutral zone of communication and shared prestige, across which the best families could move, near the turn of the fifth century, toward a "respectable, aristocratic Christianity."[285] Having made the passage, the Christianized aristocracy brought the literary culture with it as naturally as it brought the traditional values and perquisites of family and class. When the fifth-century grammarian Phocas (himself a Christian, or at least writing for a largely Christian public at Rome) spoke of the schools of liberal letters as "the gymnasium of wisdom, where is shown the way to the blessed life,"[286] he would have raised hardly a ripple of disagreement in his audience.

For the Christian aristocracy the blessed life of the schools persisted through the disruptions of the fifth century,[287] which saw a Visigothic court in southern Gaul from 418 and senatorial domination in Italy transmuted by the establishment of an Ostrogothic court in Ravenna at the century's end.[288] In Italy, the change produced a fateful division: the senate and the papacy, intertwined in their connections at Rome, averted their eyes from the Germans and looked to their past or to the East; in the north more flexible figures set about domesticating their new rulers.[289] At the court in Ravenna the Italian Cassiodorus, through the edicts now gathered in the *Variae*, "tried to give Roman *dignitas* to the orders of his barbarian masters," even suggesting that their concern for the schools at Rome showed them to be not barbarians in fact, since "barbarian kings have no use" for grammar, the "mistress of words."[290] He tried,

---

284. For a decisive but, one suspects, unfortunately not final demythologization of the pagan revival and of the role of the circle of Symmachus, see now Alan Cameron, "Paganism." The pagan reaction in politics (commonly linked with the revival in letters and followed to its dramatic resolution at the battle of the Frigidus, in 394) has benefited from a similar but independent inspection, which has qualified the specifically pagan character of the events and has emphasized the essential isolation of Nicomachus Flavianus; see J. Ziegler, *Zur religiösen Haltung* 85ff.; O'Donnell, "Career" 136ff.; Szidat, "Usurpation"; and cf. Matthews, *Western Aristocracies* 241ff.

285. Brown, *Religion* 177.

286. *GL* 5.411.6f., *gymnasium sapientiae, quo ad beatam vitam semita demonstratur*, with Part II no. 121 *ad fin.* Contrast Aug. *De doct. Christ.* 2.39.58: *videtur mihi studiosis et ingeniosis adulescentibus . . . salubriter praecipi ut nullas doctrinas quae praeter ecclesiam Christi exercentur tamquam ad beatam vitam capessendam secure sequi audeant.*

287. See Appendix 5; Riché, *Education* 24ff.

288. Domination: Matthews, *Western Aristocracies* 352ff. Transmutation: Wes, *Ende*.

289. Momigliano, *Secondo contributo* 191ff.

290. *Var.* 9.21.4 (*MGH AA* 12.286.15ff.).

too, to give them the equally important *dignitas* of a past, in his *Getica*.[291] As deacon of the church at Milan, the Gallic nobleman Ennodius could praise the martial Theodoric and the *status rei publicae*, and shepherd his own young relatives and wards into the school of Deuterius, teacher and *custos imperii*.[292]

In southern Gaul, much of fifth-century aristocratic life consisted of a "reversion to type,"[293] a return to the local expression of power characteristic of the Gallic aristocracy in the first and second centuries of the empire. Delicately maintaining their relations with the Visigothic court, less delicately taking over what remained of the imperial structure administered from Arles, and making occasional forays into the government in Italy, the senatorial families turned their attention to their libraries, their munificence to their local communities, and their backs on their German guests, establishing their place as the center of Gallo-Roman society. In this milieu, to be learned was to know that one was still Roman: the man who postponed the eclipse of Latin letters in troubled times was a heroic figure, deserving honor as "a second Demosthenes, a second Cicero."[294] But to be truly learned was to be a Christian scholar as well, and the library worth envying had Augustine next to Varro, Prudentius next to Horace.[295] More critical still, to be Roman and Christian was to be Catholic; that was a distinction the Goths' persistent Arianism did not allow forgetting, whether the persistence was regarded as a regrettable habit in a useful Goth or the noxious motivation of a hostile one.[296] To possess all these characteristics, and to combine one's cultural and religious identity with a social standing that could command local loyalties and orchestrate local resources, was to become a characteristic figure of the period, the senatorial bishop.[297]

Such a man was Sidonius Apollinaris. Sidonius, who passed smoothly from secular to episcopal concerns, is the most conspicuous example of that blending of traditional and Christian culture already noted in the

291. Momigliano, *Secondo contributo* 206; O'Donnell, *Cassiodorus* 43ff., 55ff.

292. Cf. Chap. 1 n. 85 and, on Deuterius, Part II no. 44.

293. Matthews, *Western Aristocracies* 348ff.

294. Sidon. Apoll. *Ep.* 8.2, with Part II no. 80. In a calmer period, Sidonius invites the grammarian Domitius to enjoy his estate at Avitacum, evoking the good old Roman custom of *contubernium* (*Ep.* 2.2.3; cf. Part II no. 50).

295. Sidon. Apoll. *Ep.* 2.9.4. See also *Ep.* 4.3 and 5.2, on the qualities of the *De statu animae* of Claudianus Mamertus; *Ep.* 9.7, on the *declamationes* of Remigius of Reims; cf. Ennod. *Epist.* 2.6.2, 4ff., on the accomplishments of Iulianius Pomerius (Part II no. 124) in *utraque bibliotheca*.

296. Cf. Matthews, *Western Aristocracies* 344f., with Sidon. Apoll. *Ep.* 7.6.6, on Euric; and, a bit differently, Wormald in a review of Matthews, *JRS* 66 (1976) 222f.

297. On the type, see esp. Stroheker, *Senatorische Adel* 72ff.

East. The library Sidonius admired for its stock of secular and Christian classics recalls the definition of the φιλόλογος as the man who knows both classical and Christian authors;[298] the cordial correspondence of Sidonius and other bishops with the teachers of liberal letters recalls the Eastern bishops' involvement in their own literate society. "The jewel of friends and letters," Sidonius calls the young Hesperius, whose education warmly reminded Sidonius of his own; Hesperius one day would teach the son of another highly placed bishop, Ruricius of Limoges.[299] The spiritual leader of a community did not sever the ties of friends and letters that had become the accoutrements and support of his status. Sidonius and other *litterati* among the bishops of the late fifth and early sixth century might say that to continue their secular literary endeavors was inconsistent with their episcopal *professio*, and attempt to adjust their behavior to match their statements.[300] There is, however, little reason to think that such moves represented a fundamental detachment from their own education or a devaluation of its worth.

Far from it. When bishop of Clermont, Sidonius could repeat the ancient assertion that "the educated are as far superior to the uncultured as human beings are to beasts."[301] The belief did not, of course, prevent him from caring for the uncultured by dispensing alms to the poor or defending his town against Gothic attack. It does, however, suggest the perspective he brought to the job, and what he and his fellow townsmen believed his task was: to step in as a great protector, with the authority and sense of duty of his social station.[302] His education and his rhetorical style, exquisite and arabesque, were part of that station. In fulfilling the demands of episcopal office he used that style as naturally as he did his material wealth; and deficiencies of style (at least in an address composed for an audience of other bishops) demanded apology as much as would a failure of charity.[303]

Yet the mixture of classical and Christian that marks the writings and attitudes of Sidonius occurs at a level of lonely eminence unknown to the Cappadocian Fathers, or to Theodoret of Cyrrhus, or to Marcian of

298. See above, n. 199 and at n. 295.

299. See Part II no. 229. Cf. Sidon. Apoll. *Ep.* 8.9, to Lampridius; 8.11, to Lupus.

300. On the variable success of such renunciations by Sidonius, Avitus, and Ennodius, and their probable connection with ecclesiastical pressure (cf. *Stat. Eccl. Ant.* can. 5, n. 170 above), see Riché, *Education* 96ff. For a balanced survey of Sidonius's attitudes and practice, see Gualandri, *Furtiva lectio* 6ff.

301. *Ep.* 4.17.2; cf. Chap. 1 n. 13.

302. Cf. Stevens, *Sidonius* 137f.

303. Regret for the supposed absence of sufficient stylistic elaboration: *Ep.* 7.9.1f.; cf. n. 35 above. His preaching parallel with the dispensation of his personal wealth in charity: *Ep.* 4.2.3, from Claudianus Mamertus.

Gaza; for the same conditions that encouraged the emergence of the senatorial bishops isolated their classical culture and that of their peers among the laity. To flourish, the classical schools had always depended on their students' skills and prestige being acknowledged by an audience of significant others, whether locally or in the imperial administration. But the schools were now hemmed in by circumstance. The arena for display had become narrower: Sidonius speaks of the diminishing scope of letters, now pursued to distinction by few men in a "world already growing old."[304] The elegiac remark acquires force by appearing in the praises of an advocate, the sort of man for whose talents the thriving imperial bureaucracy a century earlier had provided a venue and opportunity for advancement. Such a man, Sidonius implies, is now one of a dying breed. Since advocacy and governorship had survived the German settlements, a fifth-century Gallic family might produce an advocate and a provincial governor as well as bishops in a single generation;[305] but opportunities for such secular careers were ever more rare and became the preserve of a small circle. Constriction of opportunities had a double effect: it made the classical culture a preserve of the high aristocracy to an extent scarcely paralleled since the last days of the republic; and it made a position of local, ecclesiastical leadership an attractive or necessary alternative to an imperial, secular career.[306]

Hence there had to develop a different institutional base for such a position. It has been well remarked that "the nearest successors to Ausonius' 'Professors of Bordeaux' are the monks from the monasteries of the south":[307] one glimpses here how institutions have consequences unintended at their inception. Founded as centers of withdrawal and meditation, where entrants could be taught literacy sufficient for the study of Scripture and where the world at large could point to a reassuring store of holy intercessors before the Heavenly Judge,[308] the monasteries at Lérins, Marseille, and elsewhere came progressively during the fifth century to serve as sources of bishops. Some of these men, like Eucherius of Lyon, had received a classical education before finding refuge in the monastery and had resumed their interest in the literary culture after leaving the monastery behind.[309] But more consequential was the

---

304. *Ep.* 8.6.3.

305. Cf. n. 208 above, on the family of Marcian of Gaza.

306. The constriction is well described by Matthews, *Western Aristocracies* 347f. For the bishoprics of the Gallic aristocracy as alternative careers, see recently Heinzelmann, "Aristocratie"; Mathisen, "Hilarius."

307. Matthews, *Western Aristocracies* 348.

308. Cf. Sidon. Apoll. *Ep.* 7.9.9.

309. Cf. Riché, *Education* 102. Note the fusion of religious and cultural authority that provides the conceit for Agroecius's dedication of his *Orthographia* to Eucherius, *GL* 7.113.1ff.: *libellum Capri de orthographia misisti mihi. haec quoque res*

trend that can be found already in the first half of the fifth century, in the shift from a father who became a bishop after holding the praetorian prefecture to his son, brought up in a monastery before becoming a bishop in his turn.[310] The fact that the father's literary sophistication could distinguish him from his son is symptomatic of the shift and of the emergence among the episcopal aristocracy of a new group, owing none of its prestige and authority to the traditional culture.[311]

The voice of that new elite is heard clearly in the *Vita* of Caesarius of Arles, which recounts his vision of—and triumph over—the serpent of worldly wisdom and polished speech.[312] The vision bears an evident likeness to the anxious dream of Jerome, but more significant are the differences, which emphasize the spiritual muscle of the monastic visionary: no Judge, no need for a flogging to turn the dreamer to humility, and no tears of repentance; Caesarius awoke, reproved himself, and "despised these things straightway"—and that, to all appearances, was that. Far from marking the beginning of a long inner turmoil, as it did for Jerome, the dream conveys an image of instant superiority. The temptation of foolish wisdom and its vainglory is only a moment in an otherwise direct *carrière* that takes Caesarius from Lérins to holy orders at Arles, and from the abbacy of the suburban monastery at Arles to the episcopal throne.[313] The secular culture and its prestige intrude only as a foil for the greater strength, and greater authority, of the monastic culture Caesarius first acquired at Lérins and later recreated for the clerics in the *domus ecclesiae* at Arles.[314]

---

proposito tuo et moribus tuis congrua est, ut, qui nos in huius vitae actibus corrigere vis, etiam in scribendi studiis emendares. nihil ergo quod in nobis est alienum a castigatione tua credis: omnia nostra, et quae dictu parva sunt, sollicita indage rimaris. . . . *hoc est vere summum Dei sacerdotem esse, commissos sibi homines, ut ipsi dicitis, et secundum spiritum imbuere et secundum litteram perdocere.* Cf. Part II no. 181. Contrast the case of Gregory of Nyssa sending his tract against Eunomius to Libanius for vetting, above, n. 201.

310. The Petronii: the father, bishop of Verona; the son, bishop of Bologna. See Gennad. *De vir. ill.* 42, with Mathisen, "Petronius" 108ff.

311. Gennad. *De vir. ill.* 42: *Petronius* . . . , *vir sanctae vitae et monachorum studiis ab adulescentia exercitatus, scripsisse putatur vitas patrum Aegypti monachorum.* . . . *legi sub eius nomine de ordinatione episcopi . . . tractatum, quem lingua elegantior ostendit non ipsius esse sed, ut quidam dicunt, patris eius Petronii, eloquentis et eruditi in saecularibus litteris viri: et credendum, nam et praefectum praetorio fuisse se in ipso tractatu designat.* The distinction, although rejected in the past, has been vindicated by Mathisen, "Petronius."

312. See above, n. 161.

313. *V. Caes.* 1.8–14.

314. This became the prototype of the episcopal schools, the training ground for a professional clergy: Riché, *Education* 124ff. On the "episcopal aggression" that might have motivated some such establishments, see briefly Wormald's review of Matthews, *JRS* 66 (1976) 225.

Whether the account of the vision originated with Caesarius or with his biographers, it seems accurately to suggest the extent of Caesarius's hostility to the classical culture[315] and his limited familiarity with it:[316] certainly Caesarius's style owes more to Scripture than to classical rhetoric[317] and is the idiom of a man "nurtured not by the letters that the slaves of diverse passions call 'liberal' but by the bread of the Lord."[318] But what is equally important, the account eloquently conveys both the tensions and the quiet arrogance of men asserting against the secular prestige of the liberally educated the authority and independence of their own institutions as the framework for a career. If the movement from secular career and classical school to ecclesiastical career and the Church as educator can be thought of as a *translatio imperii*, it was, like all such transfers, a movement accompanied by friction.[319]

The simplicity of speech Caesarius insists upon when he offers his *sermo pedestris* as an example while sharply directing the bishops under his primacy to keep their worldly rhetoric out of their churches,[320] or when he draws attention to his own rusticity in his sermons,[321] is of course suited to the bishop's role as mediator, disciplining the learned while drawing into the congregation people on the margins of Latinity.[322] The role itself was not new—Augustine had molded himself to it at Hippo[323]— nor were the circumstances: it is doubtful that Arles at the beginning of the sixth century was a radically less learned place than Hippo at the beginning of the fifth.[324] The difference lies in Caesarius's blunt and unmodulated certainty, a luxury and a defense his background provided. In place of the tense dialectic through which Augustine took his traditional education for granted even as he distanced himself from it, there is the unalloyed excellence of Caesarius's monastic simplicity, a badge to be worn proudly, an emblem of divine grace[325] and in itself a guarantee

315. See esp. *Serm.* 99.3.

316. Cf. Riché, *Education* 114f.

317. See Bonini, "Stile."

318. To apply Augustine's description (above, n. 263) of Possidius, who like Caesarius passed from the monastery (at Hippo) to the episcopacy (at Calama).

319. For similar tensions appearing elsewhere in slightly different terms, see esp. Sidon. Apoll. *Ep.* 7.9.14, on the objections that Sidonius anticipates should he nominate a bishop from among the laity who have enjoyed a secular career. Sidonius's solution was to propose a man who could point both to bishops and to magistrates in his family's history (ibid. 17) and whose wife could count both bishops and professors among her ancestors (ibid. 24).

320. *Serm.* 1.20; cf. 1.12–13.

321. Cf. *Serm.* 86.1, 114.2.

322. Cf. Auerbach, *Literary Language* 91; Riché, *Education* 93f.

323. See above, p. 84.

324. See above, p. 86.

325. Cf. *V. Caes.* 1.9.

of virtue.[326] His simplicity is ultimately as aggressive and self-satisfied as the sophistication and polished speech of the classical culture it opposes.

In Sidonius and Caesarius one hears two distinct voices of the episcopal aristocracy, each speaking from a different position of strength, each equally removed from the struggles of Jerome and Augustine. Sidonius assumes the episcopacy as an extension of his secular primacy, of which his classical culture was a part—he was not one to suffer from visions. In counterpoise there is the image of Caesarius easily exorcising the demon of classicism, the straw man for his own monastic culture. Where Augustine had needed to think and feel his way to a resolution of his own experience, Sidonius never fully knew the need, and Caesarius never had such experience. In their differences, the two men symbolize the still-conflicting claims of worldly and spiritual sources of authority, and the divided legacy with which continental Europe entered the Middle Ages—a division in which the classical culture continued to figure and across which the men of the following generations would make their way only along such narrow paths as those pointed out by Augustine's *doctrina Christiana*.

In the eyes of friends and critics alike, the grammarian's profession stood for the tenacious maintenance of one kind of order. It fostered and defined, and was fostered and delimited by, a hierarchy of individual status and social relations built on the good opinion of other men. In this way the profession contributed to an idea of permanence that sought to control the instabilities of idiosyncratic achievement and historical change. In the following chapters we will look more closely at the lives and teachings of the grammarians themselves within that hierarchy. As a start, we can examine the places they occupied—the range of their social and economic circumstances, the fact and limits of their social and geographic mobility, their roles as private or public persons—between the humble experience of the common run of men and vertiginous ambition for earthly power or heavenly grace.

326. See esp. the defense of rusticity—in effect, an assertion of moral superiority—at *V. Caes.* praef. 2.

Mediocrity

CHAPTER 3

The Social Status of the Grammarians

ista autem sedes honoris, sella curulis, . . . in cuius me fastigio ex qua mediocritate posuisti, quotiens a me cogitatur, vincor magnitudine et redigor ad silentium, non oneratus beneficiis, sed oppressus.

Whenever I think of the glorious seat of the consulship and of the eminence to which you raised me from a station so ordinary, I am overcome by the greatness of it and reduced to silence, not burdened by your favor, but overwhelmed.

—*Ausonius*, Gratiarum actio 1.32–36

In any attempt to define the grammarian's social and economic circumstances, we are inevitably at the mercy of our sources. Largely anecdotal, subject to distortions, unevenly distributed geographically and over time, the evidence forbids any generalizations that could lay claim to statistical significance.[1] Such limitations, of course, are hardly unique to our subject; but there is a further limitation, perhaps especially severe in the grammarians' case, which can be expressed in terms of the principle, The more one knows, the less one knows. Most grammarians surface briefly in a single source and then sink without a trace. It follows that the more varied our information is concerning a given grammarian (for example, the adventurer Pamprepius), the less justified we are in using that information to sketch a typical case: the fact that we know so much creates the strong presumption that he is somehow extraordinary.

Yet even if we are shut off from some methods of analysis, there is still much to be said; for our evidence, although fragmentary and scattered, is still sufficiently abundant to allow us to sketch the range of

---

1. For one reminder of the limits of our knowledge, see Appendix 5, Macedonia, showing only two (possibly three) grammarians active on the old Greek mainland during the three centuries surveyed.

possibilities systematically and in some detail, and to suggest where the center of that range might lie. We will begin, then, by examining briefly what is perhaps the most familiar group of teachers, the *grammatici* of Bordeaux commemorated by Ausonius. Having drawn what inferences we can concerning the social and economic standing (or standings) of the *Burdigalenses*, we will compare those results with the information from other areas of the empire.

BORDEAUX

Ausonius's loyal record of the grammarians and rhetoricians of his native town was composed sometime after 385, near the end of his long life.[2] Living in retirement as a former praetorian prefect and consul, Ausonius had by then far surpassed the successes of any other teacher of Bordeaux; he had also far outstripped the *mediocritas* of his own origins as the son of a physician of curial status and a woman of good birth but small means.[3] Looking back over more than half a century to the days when he himself had been a grammarian and then a rhetorician, Ausonius may have found that experience somehow remote and difficult to bring into focus: so much at least would account for his inconstancy and ambiguity in characterizing the grammarians' status at Bordeaux, speaking now of the *exilis cathedra*, now of the *nomen grammatici . . . tam nobile*.[4]

Yet this ambiguity is perhaps not inappropriate, for the nineteen grammarians of Bordeaux catalogued by Ausonius seem to have been a notably mixed lot, comprising, at one extreme, men a generation removed from slavery, and, at the other, a descendant of a noble family of old

---

2. The best general treatment of the *Professores* as a social document is by Hopkins, "Social Mobility" 244ff., to which this section owes much; less balanced for the *grammatici* is Étienne, *Bordeaux* 254, 256f. Valuable discussion of prosopographical questions is provided by Booth, "Notes" and "Academic Career"; and by Green, "Prosopographical Notes." For full documentation and discussion of the teachers touched on in this and the following section, the reader is referred to the entries in Part II.

3. The family of Ausonius: Hopkins, "Social Mobility" 240ff. But the suggestion (p. 241), based largely on Ausonius's silence, that Ausonius's paternal grandfather was a freedman should be resisted; cf. Matthews, *Western Aristocracies* 81f.

4. *Exilis cathedra, Prof.* 7.9–12; with *Prof.* 10.41, *fama . . . tenuis* (cf. *Prof.* 12.6); *Prof.* 10.51–52, *gloriolam exilem / et patriae et cathedrae*; cf. *Prof.* 22.17–18, *exili nostrae fucatus honore cathedrae, / libato tenuis nomine grammatici*, of the *subdoctor* Victorius. For *nomen grammatici . . . tam nobile*, see *Prof.* 9.2.5; and cf. *Praef.* 1.18, *nomen grammatici merui; Prof.* 18.8, *grammatici nomen divitiasque*, of Marcellus at Narbo.

Rome.[5] Thus, three were sons of freedmen;[6] another five are grouped by Ausonius under the general rubric "of lowly origin, standing, and deserts."[7] But three others were of not less than curial rank (Ausonius, his nephew Herculanus, and Acilius Glabrio), and similar origins can be conjectured fairly confidently for a fourth.[8] Unfortunately, Ausonius offers no information on the families of the remaining seven. If one is willing to trust his silence concerning these teachers, they presumably fell somewhere between the two extremes, "freeborn, but in general undistinguished"; but this might place some of them too low.[9]

The evidence suggests, then, a middling group of men, with the balance perhaps tipped more obviously toward the lower end of the range than in our evidence from other areas of the empire (see "Beyond"). There is, however, another feature of the grammarians' origins, which we will see

5. Nineteen grammarians: the number includes Ausonius and excludes Marcellus (*Prof.* 18), who only taught at Narbo, and the *subdoctor* Victorius (*Prof.* 22); cf. Appendix 4. *Stemmate nobilium deductum nomen avorum*: *Prof.* 23.3, of Acilius Glabrio.

6. *Prof.* 10.15–16, of Sucuro. *Prof.* 21.27, of Crispus and Urbicus: for Ausonius's sense of the inconsistency of their cultural standing and their birth, see *Prof.* 21.25–28, quoted at Chap. 2 n. 133.

7. *Prof.* 10.5–6, *humili stirpe, loco ac merito*, covering Macrinus, Phoebicius, Concordius, Ammonius, Anastasius, as well as the freedman's son Sucuro; note that all teachers so described were active early in the period covered by the *Professores* (see Part II no. 35). It is of course difficult to say with any precision what Ausonius, writing from the perspective of his own success, might have meant by *humilis* (cf. Chap. 1 n. 59), save that the men were likely of less than curial status. That he takes the trouble specifically to note the *libertina progenies* of Sucuro might suggest a somewhat more honorable origin for the rest, but that does not take us far; neither does the Druid stock claimed by Phoebicius, nor his service as *aedituus* of the temple of Apollo-Belenus at his native Bayeux (*Prof.* 10.24–25; cf. *Prof.* 4.9ff.).

8. Nepotianus (*Prof.* 15), grammarian and subsequently rhetorician and provincial governor. Unless his later career is an example of truly extraordinary mobility, his origins will have resembled those of his friend Ausonius (ibid. 4ff.), whose career was comparable to Nepotianus's; see below. The noble marriage enjoyed by Marcellus at Narbo (*Prof.* 18.5–6) might also presuppose at least respectable antecedents at Bordeaux.

9. Cf. Hopkins, "Social Mobility" 246. Ausonius does not comment at all concerning Iucundus, Leontius, Corinthus, Spercheus, Menestheus, or Citarius (the last four all *grammatici Graeci*), and he states his ignorance in the case of Thalassus (*Prof.* 12). Hopkins' inference from Ausonius's silence might here be justified, but we should remember that Ausonius elsewhere omits information that we would think too significant to pass over: note that we know of Herculanus's relatively high origins from the *Parentalia* (*Par.* 15, on his father, Pomponius Maximus), not from the *Professores*. Cf. Booth, "Notes" 238 n. 12; and below, n. 24, on the social origins of the rhetoricians at Bordeaux.

elsewhere: the noticeable (but by no means exclusive) tendency for recruitment to follow family lines. Thus, besides the Greek *grammatici* Spercheus and Menestheus, father and son, we find the two brothers Iucundus and Leontius, as well as Ausonius and his nephew Herculanus, the son of a *vir primarius* in the curia of Bordeaux. There is also an example of professional mobility from one generation to the next in Phoebicius, a grammarian and the father of a rhetorician, Attius Patera, whose success carried him as far as a chair at Rome.[10]

As for other indications of status, there is little to be found except at the upper level of the group. Acilius Glabrio and Ausonius are the only landholders we know among them. Concerning Glabrio, we are given no specific information;[11] in Ausonius's case, the evidence suggests that by the end of his life he may have owned as many as eight properties.[12] Of

---

10. On Patera at Rome, see Booth, "Notes" 244. For the family's fortunes in the third generation, see the account of the career of Attius Delphidius Tiro— advocate, political adventurer under Procopius, and finally teacher of rhetoric at Bordeaux—in Booth, "Notes" 236f.; cf. Green, "Prosopographical Notes" 23. Besides Phoebicius, only 4 of the *grammatici*, Nepotianus, Acilius Glabrio, Ausonius, and Spercheus, are known to have had children; Citarius married but died before children were born; Herculanus died young, leaving his family without heirs. Of the rest—all three freedmen's sons and the four remaining *humiles* (nn. 6, 7, above), plus Leontius, Iucundus, Thalassus, Menestheus, and Corinthus—we are told nothing. Compare the showing of 19 epitaphs raised to or by grammarians in the earlier empire (i.e., all those from which some inference can be drawn): 9 give evidence of marriage and/or children (*CIL* 3.10805 = *AIJ* 249 Neviodunum; *CIL* 6.9447 = *ILS* 7770, *CIL* 6.9448, *CIL* 9.1654 = *ILS* 6497 Beneventum, *CIL* 10.3961 Capua, *CIL* 13.3702 = *ILS* 7768 Trier, *IGVR* 3.1261, *GVI* 1182 = *IKyzik.* 515 Kirmasti [Hellespontus]); 10 (dedicated by a friend, mother, *libertus, vel sim.*) suggest that the grammarian either had not married or was not survived by wife or children (*CIL* 2.3872 = *ILS* 7765 = *ILER* 5715 Saguntum, *CIL* 2.5079 = *ILER* 5713 Asturica Augusta, *CIL* 3.12702 [with 13822] = *ILS* 7767 Doclea, *CIL* 6.9444, *CIL* 6.9449 = *ILS* 1848, *CIL* 6.9450, *CIL* 6.9454 = *ILS* 7769, *CIL* 6.33859, *CIL* 8.21107 Caesarea, Kaibel 534 = *GVI* 1479 Byzantium). Cf. also *CIL* 5.5278 = *ILS* 6729 Comum, a bequest by the Latin grammarian P. Atilius Septicianus of his *universa substantia* to Comum, probably implying that he had no heirs of his blood.

11. *Prof.* 23.7: *cultor in agris.*

12. For what follows, see esp. Étienne, *Bordeaux* 351ff. (following Loyen, "Bourg-sur-Gironde," with some adjustments), who is certainly correct to insist that Ausonius's *villula* (the *parvum herediolum* of *Dom.* 1) must be distinct from the estate Lucaniacus (see also below, n. 21; differently Hopkins, "Social Mobility" 240f., following Grimal, "Villas"). But Étienne and Loyen may go too far in attributing to Ausonius villas of which he may simply have enjoyed the hospi- tality; cf. the restraint of Green, "Prosopographical Notes" 26 n. 33. For the evidence of Ausonius and the patterns of land tenure in Roman Gaul, see Wightman, "Peasants."

these, one derived from his father (the *parvum herediolum* described in *Dom.* 1), as perhaps did two others (a house in Bordeaux proper and land in the *pagus Novarus*); his wife's dowry certainly brought one property (the estate Lucaniacus), and possibly another in the territory of Saintes. Ausonius tells us most about the *parvum herediolum*, a parcel of 1,050 *iugera* (200 arable, 100 vineyard, 50 pasturage, 700 woodland) tended by his great-grandfather, grandfather, and father before Ausonius inherited it.[13] This *herediolum* was *parvum* only relatively: as Keith Hopkins has remarked, although the estate was a good deal smaller than some known senatorial or even curial holdings, it would have been "very much larger than the average."[14] Ausonius did not come to his teaching career a wealthy man—certainly not by the standards with which he would have become familiar in the orbit of the emperor. But neither did he come to it a pauper in the modern sense.[15] It is worth recalling that Ausonius's father, a physician, could offer his skills without fees to all[16] and that Ausonius evidently completed his literary education up through rhetoric— and thus satisfied one of the central expectations of upper-class life— with none of the financial strains apparent, for example, in Augustine's schooling.[17]

Ausonius's education is significant in another respect: it allowed him, at least early in his career, to divide his time between the classroom and practice as an advocate. Here again he is joined by Acilius Glabrio,

13. Description: *Dom.* 1.21–23. Inheritance: ibid. 1–3, *pace* Hopkins, "Social Mobility" 240f., who argues against a paternal line of succession in the belief that Ausonius's paternal grandfather was a freedman, and who equates the *herediolum* with the *tenuis . . . pecunia* acquired with much effort by his maternal grandfather, Arborius (*Par.* 4.15–16). On the status of his paternal grandfather, cf. above, n. 3; note that Ausonius clearly attributes the *tenuis . . . pecunia* to the efforts of his maternal grandfather only—i.e., it could not have come down from his maternal *proavus*, as *Dom.* 1.1–3 would require.

14. Hopkins, "Social Mobility" 241 n. 3. The value of the property would depend greatly on the quality of the arable (1 *iug.* vineyard = 4 *iug.* 1st-class arable = 8 *iug.* 2d-class = 12 *iug.* 3d-class; so Ausonius's 100 *iug.* of vineyard would have been worth 2–6 times his 200 *iug.* of *ager*). On the relative value of arable, vineyard, and pasture, see A. H. M. Jones, *Roman Economy* 228f.

15. Ausonius characterizes as *pauperes* Aemilia (his maternal grandmother, *Par.* 4.14; compare ibid. 15–16, on his grandfather Arborius) and his paternal aunt Iulia Cataphronia (*Par.* 26.5; contrast the *magna pecunia* attributed to his *patruus* at *Par.* 2.3). In Aemilia's case, at least, this probably indicates nothing worse than reduced circumstances of a not very harrowing sort, a lack of conspicuous wealth (*opes*) that was at odds with the high standing of Aemilia's family (cf. *Prof.* 16.5–8, on her son, Aemilius Magnus Arborius) and with Arborius's earlier high fortune (*Par.* 4.3–8).

16. *Epiced.* 11–12; cf. n. 128 below.

17. *Conf.* 2.35.

whose advocacy Ausonius also recalls.[18] Practice at the bar is another index of social status, implying rhetorical training and so the wherewithal to support it. Advocacy might also be taken as a sign of ambition; for although it was not the route that Ausonius eventually chose, it could provide an entry into the imperial service.[19] There were other opportunities open to grammarians at or from Bordeaux. Ausonius's respectable origins and his literary skills, combined no doubt with other ornaments attributable more to his family than to himself,[20] brought him a noble wife and a substantial dowry, probably at an early date in his career.[21] Again, Ausonius was not alone in this good fortune: the Greek grammarian Citarius also found a rich and noble wife at Bordeaux not long after his arrival from Sicily.[22] But the loftiest prospects seem to have been open only to those who moved beyond their positions as grammarians. We know of two instances of professional mobility among the *grammatici Burdigalenses*: Ausonius and Nepotianus, both of whom began as grammarians but moved upward in the professional hierarchy to teach as rhetoricians.[23] This movement in itself probably accounts for the fact that these two alone among the grammarians made their way into the imperial service, Ausonius initially as tutor to the prince Gratian, Nepotianus as a provincial governor.

Indeed, where such opportunities are concerned, the contrast between the rhetoricians and the grammarians at Bordeaux seems clear; and it is worth noting that the difference between the two groups is less evident in their origins than in their prospects.[24] For example, more rhetoricians

18. Glabrio: *Prof.* 24.7. Ausonius: *Praef.* 1.17f., *nec fora non celebrata mihi, sed cura docendi cultior*; on the interpretation of this remark, see Part II no. 21.

19. Thus the path taken by Attius Delphidius Tiro: see above, n. 10; cf. at n. 133 below.

20. Hopkins, "Social Mobility" 242, well emphasizes the fame at court of his maternal uncle, the rhetorician Aemilius Magnus Arborius, and the local influence of his brother-in-law, Pomponius Maximus.

21. Attusia Lucana Sabina (*Par.* 9.5, *nobilis a proavis et origine clara senatus*), daughter of Attusius Lucanus Talisius (*Par.* 8). The estate Lucaniacus (see *Epist.* 16.36, *villa Lucani—mox potieris—aco*, with *Epist.* 26.1.12, 26.2.43–44, *Epigr.* 48.7; and cf. Paulin. Nol. *Carm.* 10.256, *aut quum Lucani retineris culmine fundi*) is to be associated with this family; cf. n. 12 above.

22. *Prof.* 13.9; and cf. Marcellus, a native of Bordeaux who taught as a grammarian at Narbo, *Prof.* 18.5–6. Note that the grammarians appear to have been not much less successful than the rhetoricians in finding *uxores nobiles*: see *Prof.* 16.9, on Aemilius Magnus Arborius, *Prof.* 7.35–36, on Alethius Minervius; cf. *Prof.* 23.5, on Dynamius, like the grammarian Marcellus a native of Bordeaux who taught in a different city (Ilerda), where he found a wealthy wife.

23. *Prof.* 15 tit. and 10ff., on Nepotianus, *Epist.* 22.73–76 and *Prof.* 24.5–6, on Ausonius, with the comments in Part II nos. 105, 21.

24. On the differences in mobility, see Hopkins, "Social Mobility" 247. Although none of the rhetoricians is said to have had origins as lowly as those of

than grammarians practiced at the bar,[25] though of course public advocacy may have been at least partially a consequence of their profession. More revealing are the instances of professional and social mobility: only two of the grammarians are said to have left positions at Bordeaux to teach elsewhere, one apparently out of financial necessity, another out of ambition.[26] None achieved the success of several of the rhetoricians, whose fame made them sought, or drove them to chairs at Rome or Constantinople, bringing reflected glory to Bordeaux.[27] No doubt such men may have been more talented in their metier than their colleagues among the *grammatici*. Yet one suspects that beneath the language of fame and compulsion lie the workings of patronage (which we will have occasion to examine in a later chapter) and that patronage at the level necessary for such brilliant success was more easily available to the rhetoricians of Bordeaux than to the grammarians. That suspicion is hardly diminished by the other clear distinction between the two groups of teachers, the opportunity for entry into the imperial service: all the *professores* who rose to the governing class had first been rhetoricians.[28]

---

some grammarians (e.g., the sons of freedmen), Ausonius describes only two rhetoricians in terms that show they were of at least curial background (*Prof.* 14.7, Censorius Atticus Agricius; 16.8, Aemilius Magnus Arborius). Yet it is difficult to believe that the majority of the rhetoricians of Bordeaux were of less than curial origin, given the great rarity of such instances elsewhere; Ausonius's silence here may simply pass over something that his audience would take for granted, and may lead us to underestimate the origins of many teachers. It would follow, then, that at least some of the grammarians whose origins are not specified were men of higher standing than we might at first conclude; cf. at n. 9 above. In general, we can think that the social composition of the two groups significantly overlapped, with the lower range of *grammatici* more humbly placed than the corresponding *rhetores*, and perhaps with the upper range of *rhetores* possessing loftier origins than most *grammatici*. Cf. also n. 22 above.

25. *Prof.* 2.17, on Latinus Alcimus Alethius, 3.11, on Luciolus, *Par.* 3.13–14, on Aemilius Magnus Arborius; cf. *Prof.* 23.2, on Dynamius, with n. 10 above, on the career of Attius Tiro Delphidius.

26. Cf. *Prof.* 10.19–21, on Concordius, *qui profugus patria / mutasti sterilem / urbe alia cathedram* (on *patria* here, see Part II no. 35); ibid. 46ff., on Anastasius, whom *transtulit ambitio / Pictonicaeque dedit* (Ausonius notes his failure at Poitiers in vv. 49–53). Cf. below at n. 153.

27. Ti. Victor Minervius (*Prof.* 1.3–4; Jer. *Chron.* s.a. 352), Attius Patera and Censorius Atticus Agricius (*Prof.* 14.9, with Booth, "Notes" 244); and cf. Aemilius Magnus Arborius (*Par.* 3.15), whose *crescens fama* made him *petitus*, and (*Prof.* 16.14) whose *fama* drove him (*pepulit*) to Constantinople.

28. The governorship of Nepotianus (*Prof.* 15.18) has already been mentioned; with the success of Ausonius via his service as imperial tutor, cf. the career of Exuperius, a native of Bordeaux who taught as a rhetorician at Toulouse and Narbo (*Prof.* 17.7ff.; for his governorship in Spain, cf. v. 13). Hopkins ("Social Mobility" 242) and others are probably wrong, however, to attribute a *praesidatus* of Narbo to Aemilius Magnus Arborius on the strength of *Par.* 3.12; the reference

Taken individually, then, the grammarians of Bordeaux show considerable range in their social origins; as a group, they probably enjoyed a middling respectability in the city's elite. Their profession appears to have been a social bridge, sufficiently prestigious to attract the son of the leader of the local senate but not of such high status that it was beyond the reach of some freedmen's sons, for whom it no doubt represented a step up in the world. The position held some opportunity for professional, social, and geographic mobility, but without direct access to the highest prizes mobility could bring. In this respect, the grammarians were overshadowed by the men at the next level of the professional hierarchy, the rhetoricians. In the next section we will attempt to supplement this bare summary by drawing on the more abundant but more fragmentary evidence from other cities of the empire.

BEYOND

As we have already noted, the search for grammarians in the empire leads one to regional centers.[29] Smaller towns, if they were unable to supply a steady stream of pupils or to offer a formal position by funding a chair, probably could not long sustain a teacher even if they had one in their midst: thus Augustine began his career as a private *grammaticus* in his native Thagaste but did not remain long.[30] By contrast, Bordeaux, a provincial capital as well as an episcopal see, could afford municipally funded positions for a teaching corps that (it appears) commonly ran to more than one grammarian.[31] It is impossible to say how many cities were as fortunate. If one looks beyond Rome and Constantinople, the number of attested positions supported by public (that is, municipal or imperial) funds is not large: Oxyrhynchus in the mid-third century; Heliopolis, in Phoenice, the provincial capitals of the northern Gallic diocese, and Alexandria in the fourth century; and Athens in the fifth.[32]

---

is probably to his advocacy. Green, "Prosopographical Notes" 20, is rightly skeptical; cf. also Booth, "Academic Career" 330.

29. See Chap. 1 at n. 26; cf. Appendix 5.

30. Possid. *V. Aug.* 1; Aug. *Conf.* 4.1.1, 2.2, 4.7, with Part II no. 20. Compare Tetradius, teaching (at what level is not clear) in the Gallic backwater of Iculisma: Part II no. 263.

31. Municipal funding: see esp. Ausonius's reference to his *municipalis opera*, *Praef.* 1.24. On the size of the teaching corps, see Appendix 4.

32. Oxyrhynchus: see below, pp. 115f., on Lollianus. Northern Gaul: *CTh* 13.3.11 (an. 376), with Bonner, "Edict" 114ff., and Kaster, "Reconsideration" 100ff. Heliopolis: Lib. *Ep.* 1255, 1256, with Part II no. 4. Alexandria: *Anth. Gr.* 9.175 (Palladas), with 9.171, 11.378, and Part II no. 113. Athens: Damasc. *V. Isid.* epit. Phot. 168 (= frg. 290 Zintzen) and Malch. frg. 20, with Part II no. 114.

This number could, however, easily be expanded—to include at least Narbo, Toulouse, Carthage, and Milan in the West, Nicaea, Nicomedia, Elusa, Caesarea, Tyre, Syrian Chalcis, Apamea, and Antioch in the East— if one were to assume that the presence of a public chair of rhetoric should imply at least one similar endowment for a grammarian.[33] Smaller still is the number of places beyond Rome and Constantinople where more than one grammarian can be found at the same time: in the fourth century one can point with certainty only to the major centers of Milan, Trier, and Antioch (in addition to Bordeaux), although some fairly modest cities—Hermopolis and Gaza—appear to have claimed at least two grammarians in the late fifth or early sixth century.[34] It seems that most *grammatici* were likely to be sole practitioners in their towns; as such they would have been free from competition but at the same time isolated, large fish in small ponds.

If we look, then, at the origins and social standing of our teachers, we see a range similar to that at Bordeaux. The most significant difference occurs at the lower reaches: nowhere but at Bordeaux do we find men as low on the social ladder as freedmen's sons teaching as grammarians, and we can find only one who might resemble in his origins those whom Ausonius describes as *humili stirpe*.[35] The profession must surely have included other such lowly figures, now concealed by the fragmentation of our sources: even among the grammarians we happen to know—well over a hundred—we can specify or legitimately infer the circumstances of only about fifty. Yet we do know enough to conclude—as Ausonius's

33. Narbo and Toulouse: see esp. Auson. *Prof.* 17.7–8. Carthage and Milan: Aug. *Conf.* 6.7.11, 5.13.23; for Carthage in the sixth century, see *CJ* 1.27.1, 42. Nicaea and Nicomedia: Lib. *Or.* 1.48–49. Caesarea: Lib. *Or.* 31.42; Choric. *Or. fun. Procop.* 12 (p. 113.21ff. Foerster-Richtsteig), the latter mentioning Tyre also. Elusa: Lib. *Ep.* 132, with Part II no. 55. Chalcis: Lib. *Or.* 54.48. Apamea: Lib. *Ep.* 1391. Antioch: Lib. *Or.* 31, with Kaster, "Salaries" 54ff. Perhaps also Cyzicus: cf. Lib. *Ep.* 527.1. Many of the cities mentioned in this and the preceding note have been remarked by Jones, whose discussion of the teachers' circumstances, *LRE* 998f., is the best brief survey.

34. Milan: see Part II nos. 159, 172. Trier: Auson. *Epist.* 13, on Ursulus and Harmonius. Antioch: Part II nos. 25, 32, 169, with Petit, *Étudiants* 85f. (The position of these teachers at Antioch is problematic.) Hermopolis: *BGU* 12.2152, Fl. Her . . . , Fl. Pythiodorus. Gaza: Procop. Gaz. *Ep.* 13, the Greek grammarians Alypius and Stephanus, the Latin grammarian Hierius: but all three appear to have left Gaza for Antioch; see below at nn. 140, 147. Note also the grammarians Agathodaemon and Ophelius, joint recipients of Isid. Pel. *Ep.* 5.439, thus presumably active in the same place (unknown, perhaps Egypt; cf. Part II no. 3).

35. Pamprepius of Panopolis, said to have begun as a pauper and to have had a difficult youth, Rhetorius *Catal. cod. astrol. Graec.* 8:4.221.2, 8:4.222.8ff. This characterization might, however, be influenced by a contrast with his later good fortune, beginning with his arrival in Athens: cf. Rhetorius 8:4.221.3, and below at n. 160.

special notice of the freedmen's sons should imply—that men of low birth were out of the ordinary.

The evidence clusters instead at a level closer to Ausonius's own *mediocritas*. Where the data are fairly explicit, we know of seven men certainly or probably of curial status, and one equestrian.[36] In a number of other instances we find reasonably clear indications of respectable origins. The grammarian's own education can offer a hint, as in the case of Marius Plotius Sacerdos, once a fellow pupil and a *contubernalis* of the *vir clarissimus* Gaianus, son of the senator Uranius.[37] Alternatively, family attainments provide the token of honorable standing, as with Dioscorius of Myra, the brother of a distinguished sophist, and Metrodorus of Tralles, who counted an architect, two physicians, and a lawyer among his brothers, sons of the physician Stephanus.[38] Or again, several sources of inference can converge. Calliopius, who had Libanius's son among his pupils during his time at Antioch, belonged to a well-placed family of the city:[39] even without explicit testimony to that effect, we might have been able to conclude as much from Calliopius's full literary education and from his sister's marriage to the influential Seleucus.[40] In view of these social indicators, it is particularly noteworthy that Calliopius's father was also a grammarian:[41] to this pair can be added several other examples of the profession passing through two or (in one case) three generations in the same family.[42]

36. Curial: Augustine (*Conf.* 2.3.5; Possid. *V. Aug.* 1), Eudaemon of Pelusium (Lib. *Ep.* 108.2, γένος εὐγενείᾳ . . . οὐδενὸς ὕστερον), Calliopius of Antioch and his father (Part II nos. 25, 169), Aur. Cyrus of Antaeopolis(?: Part II no. 41), Annius Namptoius of Thuburbo Maius (Part II no. 103), Victor of Cirta / Constantina (*Gesta ap. Zenoph.*, CSEL 26.185.10ff.); cf. also below, on the holders of the Flaviate. Equestrian: L. Terentius Iulianus *signo* Concordius (Part II no. 87). Flavius Sosipater Charisius possessed the perfectissimate but was probably not a professional grammarian; cf. Chap. 2 at n. 153, with Part II no. 200. For the earlier empire, note *CIL* 8.5528–29 (an. 211/12, Thibilis), the teacher Q. Cornelius Rusticus, *equo publico exornatus*.

37. *GL* 6.496.5ff. Note also the grammarian Ophelius, who appears to have had a full rhetorical education: cf. Isid. Pel. *Ep.* 4.162, with Part II no. 109.

38. Dioscorius: Part II no. 48. Metrodorus: Part II no. 101. Compare Ammonianus (Part II no. 8), a relative of the philosopher Syrianus and of Aedesia, the wife of the philosopher Hermias and mother of Ammonius and Heliodorus.

39. Lib. *Ep.* 18.2: πολίτης τ᾽ ἐμὸς καὶ τῆς πόλεως τὰ πρῶτα.

40. Education: pupil of Zenobius, teacher of Libanius, Lib. *Ep.* 625.4, with *Ep.* 18.2. Marriage: Lib. *Ep.* 625.4, 678.2. For Seleucus, see *PLRE* I s.v. Seleucus 1, p. 818, with Part II no. 252.

41. Part II no. 169.

42. Fathers and sons: Danaus and Diphilus, Part II nos. 43, 49; the Clamosi of Parentium, Part II nos. 29, 30; Alypius and Olympius of Isaurian Seleucia, Part II nos. 2, 95. Three generations: Horapollon, who taught at Alexandria and Constantinople, with his son Asclepiades and grandson, Fl. Horapollon, Part II

There are further, explicit indications of the rank some grammarians enjoyed, which take us still higher on the ladder of prestige; this evidence, however, requires a brief separate discussion because it is difficult to evaluate unambiguously and because, unlike the evidence discussed so far, it appears to involve a clear chronological distinction. I refer to the grammarians who are known to have possessed the clarissimate or the Flaviate: that is, respectively, the rank (clarissimus, λαμπρότατος) belonging to members of the lowest grade in the senatorial order; or the name "Flavius," which was derived from the gentilicium of Constantine and served from the second quarter of the fourth century onward "as a kind of status designation," setting those who had served in the imperial military or civil service "apart from the masses of the population who continued to retain the name Aurelius, usage of which may be traced back, in the large majority of instances, to the time of the Constitutio Antoniniana."[43] In both cases, the mark of rank is associated with grammarians only in the second half of the fifth century and beginning of the sixth.

Certainly no grammarian before the year 425 is known to have possessed senatorial status by birth or to have achieved it in consequence of his teaching, although a few reached that rank after leaving their teaching careers and entering the imperial service;[44] and though we know of a few men who were elevated in 425 as a result of their teaching, they belong to the special group of grammatici active at Constantinople.[45] From the late fifth century on, however, we find not only Cledonius, Romanus senator, teaching at Constantinople, but also Rufinus, v.c., at Antioch, Flavius Horapollon, ὁ λαμπρότατος, of Alexandria, and even a vir spectabilis, Deuterius of Milan.[46] Similarly, those teachers of the fourth century

---

nos. 77, 17, 78. For recruitment within the family at Bordeaux, see above, p. 102; with the instance noted there of professional mobility from one generation to the next (Phoebicius and Attius Patera), compare the Apollinarii of Laodicea: the father a grammarian (Part II no. 14); the son, a rhetorician (and later a heresiarch).

43. On the Flaviate, see Keenan, "Names" (1973; quotation from p. 51) and (1974).

44. E.g., Ausonius, Fl. Simplicius; see below, pp. 130f. Consentius, v.c. and author of a grammatical treatise, was probably not a grammarian by profession; see Part II no. 203. On the clarissimate attributed (very dubiously) to Aelius Donatus, see Part II no. 52.

45. Helladius, Syrianus, and Theofilus, who received the comitiva ord. pr. and rank of ex-vicar (= spectabilis) on 15 March 425. See CTh 6.21.1 (with CJ 12.15.1) and Part II nos. 67, 147, 154.

46. Clarissimi: see Part II nos. 31, 78, 130. Spectabilis: see Part II no. 44 (Deuterius, v.s., grammaticus). Note that Deuterius seems to have taught both grammar and rhetoric, although it is not clear whether or how that would have affected his rank.

whose nomenclature shows the Flaviate almost certainly won the distinction through their service, beyond their teaching, as imperial functionaries.[47] By contrast, of the four grammarians who postdate the mid-fifth century and whose full formal names are known from legal documents, three were Flavii, not Aurelii: Flavius Horapollon, who thus possessed both the clarissimate and the Flaviate, and the two grammarians of Hermopolis, Flavius Her[. . .] and Flavius Pythiodorus.[48] Indeed, we have a document suggesting that in this later period a grammarian would normally be assumed to be a Flavius: a formulary concerning the sale of a house, dated 21 September 510. Although the document is merely a model draft, in which the buyer and seller have been given the blank names Φλαύιος ὅδε and Αὐρήλιος ὅδε, respectively, the parties have also had occupations assigned to them: the buyer, Flavius, is styled "the most eloquent grammarian and teacher of liberal Greek literature," in contrast to the seller, who bears the lower-status name "Aurelius" and is made a πραγματευτὴς ὀθονιακός, a trader in linen or sailcloth.[49]

The grammarians' possession of these ranks and titles thus seems to involve a chronological distinction and so presumably an historical development. Yet it is difficult to interpret the change, because we are completely ignorant of how the grammarians acquired these marks of status. We cannot know whether the grammarians who boast the clarissimate inherited their rank, or won it through some unattested mechanism because of their teaching, or received it as an honorary grant for some other reason.[50] The difficulties that the Flaviate presents are greater still, since the mechanics and regularity of its distribution to those outside the imperial bureaucracy are uncertain: the Flaviate of the two grammarians of Hermopolis, for instance, could be due simply to their possession of curial status.[51] In fact, the historical development at issue here

47. See esp. Part II nos. 137, 211, with the comments at Part II no. 105. Cf. also Part II nos. 200, 241. Contrast, e.g., Aurelius Augustinus and Aurelius Theodorus: the latter was γραμματικός and σχολαστικός at Hermopolis in 398 (Part II no. 150); he is the last σχολαστικός (Keenan, "Names" [1973] 60) and one of the last γραμματικοί (cf. n. 48) known to bear the name "Aurelius."

48. See Part II nos. 78, 68, 128, respectively. One could add Fl. Cresconius Corippus, although his possession of the Flaviate may be due to his service as a *palatinus* at Constantinople; see Part II no. 37. Note also Fl. Fortunatus (Part II no. 62), a *magister litterarum* of Aquileia. For the exceptional Aurelius, see Part II no. 41.

49. For the details of the formulary (*SB* 1.5941), see Part II no. 220.

50. E.g., Fl. Horapollon's rank could conceivably have passed down from his grandfather, who taught with distinction at Constantinople under Theodosius II (cf. Part II no. 77) and who may have been honored as a result.

51. Keenan, "Names" (1974) 293, notes "the increasing proportion of Flavii among 5th and 6th century decurions in general." On the Flaviate and the decurions, see ibid. 290ff.; on the mechanics of its distribution, ibid. 297ff.

may concern the grammarians' titles more than their actual standing, for both the clarissimate and the Flaviate suffered a cheapening in the course of the fifth century.[52] It would be imprudent, therefore, to conclude that the grammarians of the late fifth and early sixth centuries suddenly or dramatically rose in status.[53] Still, even the most cautious interpretation of the titles' significance would confirm the picture of respectability our other evidence suggests.

The formulary mentioned above is noteworthy not only because it assigns the higher-status name "Flavius" to a γραμματικός but also because it makes the γραμματικός the buyer; it thus assumes that Flavius the grammarian would have some disposable wealth. The assumption is consistent with the evidence available. Small tokens can be found in the ownership of slaves: for instance, a casual reference in a letter on papyrus shows a grammarian of Hermopolis lending his slave to a local advocate or rhetorician so that the latter could reclaim some books he had lent to a colleague in another town.[54] More impressive are the grammarians' public dedications. In the mid-fourth century, an African *magister studiorum*, Annius Namptoius, restored the baths of his native town.[55] Something over a century later, when the local basilica had become the focus of a town's life, we find the grammarian Calbulus adorning with his own verses a large baptistery he had donated.[56] Similarly, at Parentium, where the basilica was built at the end of the fourth century and rebuilt in the middle of the fifth, the benefactions of two generations of teachers are memorialized in the mosaic floors of the church.[57] Such displays

52. On "whittling down" the prestige and privileges of *clarissimi* and *spectabiles* in the years 450 to 530, precisely the period to which the grammarians noted above belong, see Jones, *LRE* 529 (cf. p. 542): by 530 at the latest, possibly as early as the reign of Zeno, or even of Leo, the title *senator* and most of the privileges attaching to it were reserved to the highest grade, the *illustres*. For an "inflationary" trend possibly affecting the Flaviate as well, see Keenan, "Names" (1974) 293–94, 302.

53. Note, however, that the late fifth and early sixth centuries offer the first instances of the honorific κύριος or *dominus* applied to grammarians: see Part II nos. 24, 173, with Priscian, *GL* 3.231.4. Cf. also at n. 93 below.

54. Maehler, "Menander" 305ff., with Part II no. 173. As Alan Cameron has remarked ("Roman School Fees" 258), even Palladas, who of all the grammarians complains most bitterly about his poverty, could afford a slave (*Anth. Gr.* 10.86). Grammarians' ownership of slaves in the earlier empire is attested by *SB* 1.5808 = *Stud. Pal.* 13, p. 1 (Arsinoe, an. 124); *CIL* 2.3872 = *ILS* 7765 = *ILER* 5715 (Saguntum); *CIL* 6.9454 = *ILS* 7769; *CIL* 6.33859.

55. Part II no. 103.

56. *Anth. Lat.* 1:1.378, with Part II no. 23.

57. *Inscr. Ital.* 10:2.58, 74, with Part II nos. 29, 30. The father and his wife donated 100 feet of pavement, the son and his wife 111 feet. The gifts of the other local worthies recorded in the floors range from as little as 13 feet to as much as 400; the teachers' donations are about average.

imply at least a modest surplus of wealth and a comfortable standard of living. Although none of the grammarians would be likely to rival the ῥήτωρ Evangelus of Caesarea, who purchased a nearby κώμη for three hundredweights of gold,[58] many would have been able to afford such touches of civilized life as the woodcarver's services commended to the sophist Isocasius.[59]

The grammarians' professional income, which we will consider presently, contributed to that style of life; but sometimes we catch glimpses of the landholdings—especially family property—that would have been a firmer foundation.[60] Augustine is probably the most familiar example; his father's holdings (which Augustine as heir later placed at the Church's disposal) were sufficient to provide the beginnings of the saint's education, although the financial difficulties that interrupted his schooling suggest the holdings were modest.[61] At Milan, however, Augustine encountered a grammarian who appears to have been better off, Verecundus, who owned the estate Cassiciacum, outside Milan, and could offer extended hospitality to Augustine and several of his friends and relations.[62] The conversations at Cassiciacum on liberal learning and spirituality conform to an image of aristocratic *otium*, even if the host and his guests were not themselves members of the aristocracy. We have already mentioned a similar reflection or imitation of aristocratic life in the case of Servius, who owned or had access to a retreat in Campania.[63]

Other grammarians, however, put their holdings to different use. We find one grammarian and his heirs acting as landlords, collecting rent on one of his parcels.[64] Others were absentee owners, retaining and presumably drawing income from their property while they taught elsewhere. The family of Flavius Horapollon maintained holdings at Phenebythis, in Egypt, for at least three generations while its members taught at Constantinople or Alexandria.[65] Libanius refers to one Didymus, an Egyptian grammarian who taught at Antioch and Constantinople

58. Procop. Caes. *Anecd.* 30.18–20.

59. Theodoret. *Ep.* XXXVIII. Cf. the wedding gift of a pearl given by the teacher Arethusius of Antinoopolis, Part II no. 187.

60. Cf. pp. 102f. above, on Acilius Glabrio and Ausonius at Bordeaux.

61. See esp. *Conf.* 2.3.5. Contrast Augustine's notice (*Conf.* 6.10.17) of the *rus optimum* in the vicinity of Carthage belonging to the family of his friend Nebridius, who worked (unambitiously and beneath his abilities, *Conf.* 8.6.13) as the *subdoctor* of the grammarian Verecundus at Milan.

62. See esp. *Conf.* 9.3.5, *De ord.* 1.2.5, with *De beat. vit.* 4.31.

63. Implied by *GL* 4.468.6; cf. Chap. 2 at n. 141.

64. Aur. Cyrus: see Part II no. 41. Cf. the κέλλιον that Palladas put out to rent, *Anth. Gr.* 11.351.

65. *PCairMasp.* 3.67295, with Part II nos. 17, 77, 78. Note that we know of this holding because of the attempt by Fl. Horapollon's wife—who was also his

while owning property in his native land.[66] After Didymus's death, when his son, Rhetorius, a former pupil of Libanius, was returning to Egypt to claim his father's estate, Libanius had occasion to remark to the *dux Aegypti* that the estate was small, a mere "solace for a poor man."[67] The characterization is probably meant to place Rhetorius and his father among those of modest means, in the sense that they did not belong to the category of εὔποροι, the truly wealthy.[68] Similar circumstances probably stand behind Libanius's description of Eudaemon, whose family at Pelusium he calls "second to none in birth, although their possessions are not many because of their virtuous restraint" (ἐπιείκεια).[69]

Such evidence of respectability is not surprising—the immunities that grammarians and rhetoricians enjoyed did, after all, presuppose their being landholders. It should not, however, be overestimated. No grammarian can be shown to have been wealthy, in the sense of being able to afford the public expenditures that traditionally established and reinforced claims to social preeminence.[70] Some may have verged on poverty in the absolute economic sense;[71] the line between respectability and disaster could be thin. Libanius comments of one of his own former teachers, the grammarian Cleobulus, that he had sufficient means to avoid ignoble employment, but he adds that those means were insufficient to bear unjust penalties easily.[72] Libanius's comments were prompted by a lawsuit in which Cleobulus found himself embroiled in 359; when the suit

---

first cousin—to appropriate some of his property. Such a marriage was one way of preventing the fragmentation of a family's estate: cf. Libanius's betrothal to his cousin, the daughter of Phasganius, *Or.* 1.95, with Norman, *Autobiography* 174 *ad loc.* For earlier examples of scholars at Alexandria owning land in the χώρα, see Turner, *Greek Papyri* 86f.

66. Part II no. 46.

67. *Ep.* 318.3: πένητι δὲ παραμυθία. Cf. the phrase *solamen fesso* used by Ausonius to characterize the *pecunia* accumulated by his maternal grandfather, Caecilius Argicius Arborius: *Par* 4.16, with n. 15 above.

68. Cf. *Ep.* 318.3: Ῥητόριος δὲ τῶν οὐκ εὐπόρων.

69. *Ep.* 108.2; cf. *Ep.* 164.1.

70. On the idea of social wealth, cf. Patlagean, *Pauvreté* 9ff. The sole exception here may be Annius Namptoius: see above at n. 55; but see also Ausonius's reference to the *grammatici nomen divitiasque* won, only to be lost, by Marcellus at Narbo (*Prof.* 18.8).

71. With Ausonius's characterization of the *tenuis victus*, or the like, of some of the *Burdigalenses* (e.g., *Prof.* 10.44ff.), compare the complaints of Palladas, *Anth. Gr.* 9.174 (cf. 9.168, 171, 173, 175; 10.97; 11.378; with Alan Cameron, "Roman School Fees"; Part II no. 113; and below, pp. 120f.); and of Lollianus, *PCollYoutie* 2.66 = *POxy.* 47.3366, C59f., B28, with p. 115 below.

72. *Ep.* 52.3. That Cleobulus possessed independent means is suggested also by the fact that he accepted few students (because of his frailty, *Ep.* 361.2); cf. below, p. 121. The episode touched on here is discussed in more detail at Chap. 6 pp. 213f.

finally went against him, Cleobulus was forced to pay the insupportable fines Libanius had feared, and he was saved from ruin only by a former pupil's timely subvention. Although Cleobulus may ordinarily have been prosperous, his means were unequal to the sudden extraordinary expenses a run of bad luck might bring. A similar conclusion can be drawn for Diphilus, another grammarian Libanius knew.[73] Already established as a teacher in one of the Palestinian provinces during the late 380s, Diphilus hoped to make his mark as a poet. Encouraged by an influential man who offered to promote a series of performances in Cilicia, Diphilus made the circuit of that province in late 387 or early 388. But the patron reneged, and the trip was a literary and financial disaster: Diphilus returned from Cilicia depressed and seriously out of pocket.[74] In view of the strain this brief episode evidently put on Diphilus's finances, it is not surprising to find that as a wandering poet he played it safe: after the debacle in Cilicia we still find him traveling to further his poetic career, but he clearly did not give himself over wholly to his wanderings; he kept his position in Palestine as a hedge against failure and as a base of operations for his forays.

Diphilus's apparent reliance on his teaching post brings us to the income a grammarian could receive directly or indirectly from his profession. There were three possible sources: salaries from public funds, fees from individual students and their parents, and occasional supplements, including traditional gifts.[75] Since the evidence for all three is not extensive, each can be considered briefly in turn.

Public salaries (*salarium*, σύνταξις) were of two types, municipal and imperial. Municipal salaries were derived from city revenues and were paid (probably in cash, as a rule)[76] to teachers appointed to public chairs by the local town councils. Imperial salaries were drawn from imperial funds and from the fourth century on were regularly paid or calculated in kind; salary in kind, however, could be commuted to cash.[77] The

---

73. For what follows, see Part II no. 49, and Kaster, "'Wandering Poet.'"

74. Lib. *Or.* 54.55.

75. On teachers' incomes, in addition to the studies cited in nn. 76–129 below, see Bergmann, *Geschichte* 34ff.; Marquardt, *Privatleben* 94f.; Friedländer, *Roman Life* 1.156ff.; Forbes, *Teachers' Pay*; Walden, *Universities* 162ff.; Headlam, *Herodas* 122ff.

76. See below, pp. 115–16, on Lollianus of Oxyrhynchus, and at n. 86; cf. Choric. *Or. fun. Procop.* 12 (p. 113.21ff. Foerster-Richtsteig), on the salary offered to Procopius at Caesarea. Cf. perhaps also Antioch: Petit, *Libanius* 299f.; Liebeschuetz, *Antioch* 84 n. 1; but see Kaster, "Salaries" 54 n. 61.

77. On salaries in kind, see Jones, *LRE* 396ff.; and below, p. 116. For commutation to cash (*adaeratio*) of teachers' salaries, see Lib. *Ep.* 132, 800.3, with Petit, *Libanius* 409f., Liebeschuetz, *Antioch* 88f. For payments in kind, cf. also n. 98 below.

geographic range of imperial salaries seems to have expanded in late antiquity, so that even a teacher active at a city as obscure and far removed from the imperial center as semibarbarous Elusa could hope to win a place on the imperial payroll.[78] It is not clear whether any teachers simultaneously drew both municipal and imperial salaries. No man is known to have been so fortunate,[79] but neither does there appear to have been any formal prohibition.

For detailed knowledge of a grammarian's municipal salary, we are limited to a single early example, which gives some idea of the size of such emoluments and of the difficulties that might arise in their payment.[80] The salary belongs to Lollianus, public grammarian (δημόσιος γραμματικός) of Oxyrhynchus in the reign of Valerian and Gallienus; we know of his situation from two drafts of a petition he sent to the emperors (perhaps in 258 or 259) asking them to compel the town council to heed his complaints,[81] and from the draft of a letter seeking a friend's intervention at court for the petition to gain a hearing. From the documents it appears that although Lollianus had been granted a salary of 500 *denarii* (per annum, presumably), the salary was paid only irregularly, and then only in soured wine and spoiled grain.[82] As a result, Lollianus was attempting to convince the council to grant him in place of his salary the use of one of the civic properties of Oxyrhynchus, an orchard he could rent out for 600 *denarii* (again, presumably per annum). The proposal finds a close parallel in *Or.* 31 of Libanius, who tried a century later to persuade the council of Antioch to supplement the irregularly paid civic salaries of his four assistants by granting them the same income from a municipal property that his predecessor, Zenobius, had enjoyed.[83] The similarity of the circumstances is noteworthy, not least for the reminder that a salary ordained need not have been a salary paid. Also noteworthy are the sums in Lollianus's case (500 *den.* [= 2,000

78. Elusa: Lib. *Ep.* 132, with Part II no. 55. *Semibarbarum*: Jer. *V. Hilar.* 25; cf. *Comm. Is. proph.* 5.15. Concerning this trend and the administration of municipal and imperial subsidies, see Chap. 6 pp. 227ff. On the distribution of salaried chairs, see above at nn. 32, 33.

79. Libanius has been thought to provide an instance; but see Kaster, "Salaries" esp. 54ff.; and cf. the comments of Bonner, "Edict" 132f.

80. For what follows, see Part II no. 90, with the excellent discussion of Parsons at *PCollYoutie* 2, pp. 409ff. For an earlier and more obscure example, see below, n. 86.

81. Concerning the questionable premises on which Lollianus bases his petition, see Parsons, *PCollYoutie* 2, pp. 441ff.

82. *PCollYoutie* 2.66 = *POxy.* 47.3366, B29f. (cf. B34, C65).

83. Remarked and elaborated by Parsons, *PCollYoutie* 2, pp. 413f.; see also Kaster, "Salaries" 54ff. Cf. the income drawn from imperial land by Libanius, evidently in addition to his ordinary salary from the emperor, when he was a public teacher in Constantinople: Lib. *Or.* 1.80, with Kaster, "Salaries" 39ff.

dr.], 600 *den.* [= 2,400 *dr.*]), for as P. J. Parsons has observed, they are, "on the face of it, quite substantial":[84] 500 *denarii* could perhaps have purchased as much as 167 *artabae* of wheat at contemporary prices, more than a year's rations for ten men.[85] This should at least have provided subsistence for Lollianus and his wife and children; but again, Lollianus's complaint suggests that his payment in kind amounted to a good deal less.[86]

The evidence for grammarians' imperial salaries comes from a later period, when such salaries were calculated in multiples of the ordinary soldier's yearly ration (*annona*) and fodder (*capitus*).[87] There are two relevant documents, which suggest that the imperial stipends were somewhat more generous than the municipal salaries (than the salary Lollianus received, at least), although they also suggest that the imperial salaries could vary significantly. The first is the edict of 23 May 376 (*CTh* 13.3.11), sometimes known as "Gratian's School Law," by which the emperors set the imperial salaries for teachers in the provincial capitals of the northern Gallic diocese. Under the terms of the edict, rhetoricians were to receive 24 *annonae*, grammarians (Greek or Latin) 12. A higher scale was set for the Latin teachers in Trier (then the imperial residence in the West), where the rhetorician was to receive 30 *annonae*, and the *gram-*

84. *PCollYoutie* 2, p. 413; but cf. below, n. 86 *ad fin.*
85. Calculated according to the prices of wheat attested in Egypt in A.D. 254–56, 12–16 dr./*artaba* (Johnson, *Economic Survey* 2.311), and taking 1 *artaba/* month, e.g., the size of the dole at Oxyrhynchus under Claudius II and Aurelian, as a standard ration (Rea, *POxy.* 40, p. 6). Note, however, that this was about one-third less than the monthly allotment of 5 *modii* (= ca. 1.5 *artabae*) received by the *plebs frumentaria* at Rome (Duncan-Jones, *Economy* 146f.; for the measures, cf. Hopkins and Carter, "Amount," correcting Rea, *loc. cit.*).
86. *PCollYoutie* 2.66 = *POxy.* 47.3366, B28, C59f. For a grammarian's municipal salary from an earlier period, note the epitaph of the Latin grammarian L. Memmius Probus, *CIL* 2.2892 Tritium = *ILER* 5714 (which omits the last line), *CVI RES (PVBLICA) TR(I)T(I)ENSIVM AN(NOS) HABEN(TI) XXV RAIAR* [= *SALAR(IVM)*] *CONSTITVÆ* [= *-IT*] *M·C·LI: CS· EI·L....* The last line may specify the sum, i.e., at least HS1,100 (possibly *M·C·L·IIS* = HS1,150, or *M·C·D·IIS* = HS1,400; hardly anything so odd as HS1,151, as assumed by Szilágyi, "Prices" 329). With Lollianus's 2,000 dr., contrast the 6,000 dr. paid as municipal salary to the rhetorician Apollonius at Athens at the end of s.II, Philost. *V. soph.* 2.20 (p. 600).
87. An imperial salary of HS600,000 was decreed in 299 for the rhetorician Eumenius to enable him to reorganize and teach at the schools of Autun: *Pan. Lat.* 5.14.14 Galletier, *salarium te in sexcentis milibus nummum ex rei publicae viribus consequi volumus, ut intellegas meritis tuis etiam nostram consuluisse clementiam*; cf. ibid. 11.2. The phrase *ex rei publicae viribus* must refer in context to imperial funds, although it has sometimes been thought that the municipal resources of Autun are meant; the sum is twice the amount that Eumenius had lately been receiving as *magister memoriae* with the rank of *trecenarius*. Eumenius's is the latest imperial subsidy for a teacher expressed simply in cash values.

maticus 20; the Greek *grammaticus*, "if any worthy one should be found," was to receive 12 *annonae*, like the *grammatici* of the other cities.[88] The rhetorician's higher salary implies his more favored status.[89] Nonetheless, a grammarian who received even 12 *annonae* would be doing quite respectably; for that would be roughly six and a half times the ration and fodder an ordinary soldier drew at the beginning of his service, and a good deal more than even a veteran would be drawing when his honorable discharge would be advisable "lest he should prove a burden to the state by continuing to receive" his higher salary.[90] To look at the sum from a different perspective: if the grammarian were able to commute his 12 *annonae* to cash, he might realize between 48 and 60 *solidi*, the equivalent of a year's fees from students in a good-sized class. Drawing 20 *annonae*, the Latin grammarian at Trier would of course be still more fortunate.[91]

By comparison with the edict of 376, the other schedule of salaries we possess sets rates more modest but still not niggardly. After Justinian's reconquest of Africa, an edict of 534 laid down the salaries for a wide range of personnel at Carthage, including two grammarians and two rhetoricians. The teachers' pay is expressed both in kind and in cash, with 10 *annonae* and 5 *capita* (= a total of 70 *solidi*) to be shared by the two teachers at each level;[92] each grammarian would thus receive the

88. For the limitation to the provincial capitals of the northern Gallic diocese, see Bonner, "Edict" 113ff., with Kaster, "Reconsideration" 100ff.

89. Although a difference in salaries is not surprising, since rhetoricians traditionally commanded higher fees than grammarians (cf. Juv. 7.217, Diocl. *Ed. pret.* 7.70–71, with Bonner, *Education* 150ff., Alan Cameron, "Roman School Fees" 258), the difference here may be exceptionally great: contrast the ratio of only 5:4 in the rhetorician's favor in the fees set by Diocletian's edict just noted (and below, p. 119); compare the parity of rhetoricians and grammarians established by *CJ* 1.27.1, 42 (an. 534; see below at n. 92). The great difference between the municipal salaries of Apollonius and Lollianus (n. 86) probably has as much to do with where they taught, Athens vs. Oxyrhynchus, as with their different metiers.

90. Six and a half times: the figure takes account of the 1 *capitus* received by the common soldier in addition to the *annona*—the edict of 376 does not include *capitus* as part of the teacher's pay; cf. below, on *CJ* 1.27.1, 42 (an. 534)—and assumes that 1 *capitus* was worth ca. 80% of 1 *annona*, as in the edict of 534 just noted. Veterans: Anon. *De reb. bell.* 5.2 (p. 96.17ff. Thompson, specifying "5 *annonae* or more" and presumably including a certain amount of *capitus* as well, although this is not remarked by the author), cited by Bonner, "Edict" 132. For comparison with salaries of civil servants, see below at n. 94.

91. Assuming a value of 4 (*Nov.* "Val." 13.3 [an. 445]) or 5 (*CJ* 1.27.1, 22 [an. 534]) *sol./annona*. (Equivalents are not available from the fourth century.) On fees and class size, see below, pp. 120–21. For the possession of ca. 50 *solidi* as a threshold for the passage beyond poverty, see Patlagean, *Pauvreté* 380ff.

92. *CJ* 1.27.1, 42; the wording of other provisions (e.g., ibid. 41, for physicians) makes it clear that the sums mentioned are to be divided between the teachers at each level. One *annona* is reckoned as = 5 *sol.*; 1 *capitus*, as 4 *sol.*;

equivalent of 35 *solidi*.[93] Although this is appreciably less than the grammarians of northern Gaul earned in the fourth century and only a tiny fraction of the 100 pounds of gold Justinian ordained for the praetorian prefect at Carthage, it was probably still equivalent to a year's fees from a sizable class and compares favorably with the other civil servants' salaries in the edict.[94]

Grammarians on public salary would have benefited from an indirect subsidy as well. Public appointment would also normally entail release from burdensome and costly *munera*; especially for the grammarian of curial status, these immunities might well represent a long-term financial benefit greater than the direct payment he received from city or emperor.[95] In addition to these subventions, the public teachers would also receive fees (*mercedes*, μισθοί) from their pupils.[96] By contrast, the man who taught without public appointment, as Augustine did at Thagaste, could look forward only to his fees. The two pieces of specific evidence we possess indicate that apart from such special arrangements as Aetius made, paying his γραμματικός at Anazarbus through personal indenture,[97] fees were normally paid in cash. Payment in kind, however, cannot be ruled out.[98]

---

cf. ibid. 22. For *capitus* included in a teacher's imperial salary in the fourth century, see Lib. *Ep.* 28, with Seeck, *Briefe* 241, and Kaster, "Salaries" 51.

93. The parity of rhetoricians and grammarians under the decree may reflect not so much a decline in the rhetoricians' status as a slight increase in the status of grammarians in the late fifth and early sixth centuries: see above at n. 53.

94. Prefect's salary: *CJ* 1.27.1, 21. In the *officia* of the prefecture (ibid. 22–38) only the heads of the financial *scrinia* receive a higher salary (46 *sol.*, ibid. 22–23) than the teachers, whose 35 *sol.* are in turn significantly more than the sums received by the heads of the other *scrinia* and subclerical *scholae*. (For tabulation and comment, see Jones, *LRE* 590f.; and cf. Part II no. 92 *ad fin.*) To put it another way, the amount decreed for the four grammarians and rhetoricians (140 *sol.*) is roughly equivalent to the salaries budgeted for all twelve members of the judicial *scrinium commentariensis* (143 *sol.*, ibid. 25). Note, however, that the teacher's salaries are a good deal less than the amounts ordained for physicians (50–90 *sol.*, according to grade: ibid. 41).

95. On immunities, see Chap. 6 pp. 223ff.

96. Thus Palladas speaks of both a σύνταξις (*Anth. Gr.* 9.175; cf. 9.171, 11.378) and μισθοί (9.174; see below). For rhetoricians collecting both a municipal salary and fees, see Aug. *Conf.* 6.7.11 (*publica schola uterer*, at Carthage), with *Conf.* 5.12.22 (see below, n. 109). See also Lib. *Or.* 31.19, 25–33, with Kaster, "Salaries" 56 n. 68, on Libanius's assistants.

97. Philostorg. *HE* 3.15, with "Prologue" n. 11 above.

98. Note the payment of ¹⁄₁₂ *artaba* of wheat and 1 *artaba* of barley to the γραμματοδιδάσκαλος Sarapion (for an unspecified period, possibly one month: see Part II no. 133) and the six months' payment of 20 *artabae* of wheat to the γραμματικός Heraclammon (Part II no. 69). In neither case, however, do we know the cause or the source of the payment.

The first document, Diocletian's Edict on Maximum Prices, issued in 301, is problematic, being prescriptive rather than descriptive. The rate it fixes for the grammarian's fees, 200 *denarii* per pupil per month (as against 250 *denarii* per pupil per month for a rhetorician),[99] is part of a comprehensive schedule of prices and wages meant to counteract inflation. The amount might therefore be significantly less than the rate or rates paid in practice: so, for example, the edict fixes the prices of wheat and barley at only one-third those in an account on papyrus that must be almost exactly contemporary; and we cannot in any case be sure that the prescribed rate was observed.[100] Nonetheless, the edict is useful for suggesting relative values: thus, the grammarian's fee is four times that of the simple teacher of letters, who stood outside the realm of liberal learning,[101] and a grammarian with a class of twenty fee-paying students (rather small, in a good-sized town)[102] would have had four times the income of a carpenter fortunate enough to find paying work twenty days a month.[103] Similarly, if the grammarian received the set rate, and if wheat were available at the set rate as well, three pupils would suffice for a monthly ration of 5 *modii*, with a bit to spare:[104] indeed, a year's fee from a single pupil, reckoned according to the edict's set price for gold, would be rather more substantial than the year's fee (also reckoned in gold) our other evidence attests.[105] But the precariousness of such calculations has already been suggested.

99. *Ed. pret.* 7.70–71. These figures of course reflect a significant devaluation of the *denarius* since the time of Lollianus, with his annual salary of 500 *den.*, two generations earlier.

100. *Ed. pret.* 1.1a, wheat at 100 *den./modius* = ca. 330 *den./artaba*; ibid. 1.2, barley at 60 *den./modius* = ca. 200 *den./artaba*. But *POxy.* 24.2421 assumes a price of wheat of 984 *den./artaba*; and of barley, 655 *den./artaba* (for the date and details, see Part II no. 133). With the edict's (7.65) set fee of 50 *den./*month*/*child for a pedagogue, compare the pay of 1 talent (= 1,500 *den.*) per month received for eight months by a pedagogue at the beginning of s.IV (*Stud. Pal.* 20.85ʳ, pag. post., 11).

101. *Ed. pret.* 7.66.

102. See below, pp. 120–21.

103. *Ed pret.* 7.3a, 50 *den./*day, plus food. Cf. Lib. *Or.* 31.25, on the craftsmen at Antioch who envy the wealth of the teachers.

104. Cf. n. 85 above.

105. For 1,800 to 2,000 *den.* (a year's fee from one pupil, calculated on the basis of a nine- or ten-month school year, to allow for the summer vacation: cf. Aug. *Conf.* 8.6.13ff.; Lib. *Or.* 1.77, 86, 110; *Ep.* 419.1; with Festugière, *Antioche* 135) one could purchase between $\frac{1}{40}$ and $\frac{1}{36}$ lb. of gold at the price set by the edict (30.1a: 72,000 *den./pondum*; see Naumann and Naumann, *Rundbau* 57; cf. Crawford and Reynolds, "Aezani Copy" 197 [28.1a–2]). This would be a noticeably better rate of pay than 1 *sol.* (= $\frac{1}{72}$ lb. of gold) per student per year, for which see immediately following. But again, it is not clear how the price set by the edict should be regarded: for prices, including gold, in the early fourth

We are on firmer ground with our second piece of specific evidence, provided by Palladas, the Alexandrian poet and grammarian. While complaining of his students' vicious ways, Palladas reveals that his fee was 1 *solidus* a year, payable either in a lump sum or in monthly installments.[106] A scholium to Juvenal's comments on grammarians' income mentions the same fee: *in annum unum solidum accipit.*[107] Although the statement is evidently anachronistic in its application to Juvenal's time, it does represent the assumption of a reader in the late fourth century (the scholium's probable date); it thus provides a roughly contemporary confirmation of Palladas's statement and suggests that such a scale of payment was familiar not only in Palladas's Alexandria but also in the West, where the scholium was presumably written. Neither of these notices, however, is meant to suggest that 1 *solidus* was an especially generous sum, and some grammarians probably commanded a higher fee.[108]

Income from fees might vary wildly, depending on the size of the grammarian's class and on his students' willingness or ability to pay. The latter qualities were not always evident. The grammarian Palladas grumbles about students who deserted his class just before it came time to pay their year's fee. Augustine recalls a similar delinquency among students of rhetoric, in a way that suggests the offense still rankled long after his teaching days. Libanius even suggested something quite unparalleled, a formal contract (συνθήκη) between the student's parent and the teacher, to combat the problem at Antioch.[109] Conversely, Libanius's assistants are said to have taken on some students who simply could not pay, as a kindness and in order to prevent their classrooms from becoming depopulated.[110] Concerning class size we have no direct evidence for the grammarians. A passage from Libanius's autobiography, however, suggests that forty students would have been a very respectable number for either a private or a public teacher of rhetoric at Constantinople, and there is no reason that the information cannot be applied to the gram-

century, see Rémondon, "À propos du papyrus" 146; Bagnall and Sijpesteijn, "Currency" 114ff.

106. *Anth. Gr.* 9.174, with Alan Cameron, "Roman School Fees." For monthly payment of fees, see also Fulg. *Verg. cont.* 86.4–6 Helm.

107. *Schol. vet.* 7.241.2 Wessner. The significance of the note was remarked by Bonner, "Teaching Profession" 30; cf. also Clarke, "Juvenal."

108. Note the 100 *solidi* given by the praetorian prefect Phocas (an. 532) to the Latin teacher Speciosus (Part II no. 138: grammarian or rhetorician?) as an initial payment: Ioan. Lyd. *De mag.* 3.73. But the episode is obscure—no services appear to have been required of Speciosus after the payment—and the sum surely extraordinary.

109. Palladas: *Anth. Gr.* 9.174.9–12. Augustine: *Conf.* 5.12.22. Libanius: *Or.* 43 *passim*; for συνθήκαι, see esp. §§11–13, 16.

110. *Or.* 31.29–32.

marian.[111] But the same source shows how much variation was possible: Libanius boasts that at the height of his success as a private teacher at Constantinople he had a class of more than eighty students; yet a few years later, newly arrived as a private teacher in his native Antioch, he had as few as fifteen,[112] and it has been suggested that even as a public teacher with several assistants at Antioch Libanius probably never accommodated one hundred pupils per year.[113] Evidently, independent means would protect a teacher against the risks of the fee system and allow him to be more selective about his pupils.[114]

Beyond salaries and fees, the grammarian could expect a bit of incidental largesse. This might take the form of occasional gifts or of a benefaction to meet a specific need.[115] There were other forms of largesse, however, tied to the teacher's activity during the school year and sufficiently regular to qualify as expected supplements. Jerome mentions the New Year's *strena*, the *sportula* at the Saturnalia, and the *Minervale munus* as common gifts;[116] it is clear that these particular gifts were of considerable antiquity and of some geographic diffusion.[117] The scale of the gifts is uncertain. Ausonius records that through his intervention (when he was *quaestor sacri palatii*) the grammarian Ursulus of Trier received a New Year's *strena* of 6 *solidi* from the emperor,[118] but the sum must be regarded as exceptional. There were probably other, more localized forms such gifts could take: from Choricius, in the age of Justinian, we learn that it was customary at Gaza for the rhetorician, at least, to receive a gift of 1 *solidus* when one of his students successfully completed a composition.[119]

---

111. *Or.* 1.31, Nicocles' offer to provide Libanius with 40 pupils; such a class would have made Libanius, then still a private teacher, a serious rival of the publicly appointed sophists.

112. Eighty: *Or.* 1.37. Fifteen, most of whom followed Libanius from Constantinople: *Or.* 1.101, with Norman, *Autobiography* 175 *ad loc.*

113. Petit, *Étudiants* 72ff. Étienne, *Bordeaux* 244f., in calculating that the rhetorician Ti. Victor Minervius regularly enrolled 200 students per year, misunderstands the hyperbole of Ausonius's effusive lines, *Prof.* 1.9–10: *mille foro dedit hic iuvenes, bis mille senatus / adiecit numero purpureisque togis.*

114. See above, n. 72, on Cleobulus.

115. For the gifts received by Libanius, see Petit, *Étudiants* 144f.; Liebeschuetz, *Antioch* 84. From an earlier period, cf. the gifts of food to καθηγηταί recorded in *PGiss.* 80 (s.II init.; Hermopolite nome?); *POsl.* 3.156 (s.II; the Fayûm). Note also Apul. *Apol.* 23, provision of dowries for some of his teachers' daughters.

116. Jer. *Comm. Ephes.* 3.6 (PL 26.574A).

117. E.g., the three occasions mentioned by Jerome are also mentioned by Tertullian, plus two others: see *De idol.* 10, with Bonner, *Education* 148f.

118. *Ep.* 13 tit., 1–24.

119. *Apol. mim.* 104 (p. 368.8ff. Foerster-Richtsteig). For compositions by a grammarian's students at Gaza, see Part II no. 83.

All these forms of income could in favorable circumstances add up to a substantial if not lordly sum: a grammarian with a decent public salary and a sizable class of regularly paying students could probably realize more than 100 *solidi* a year, or well over a pound of gold, with little difficulty. Perhaps only an exceptionally fortunate grammarian, however, could have put away 1,500 *solidi* after eight years' teaching, as Libanius appears to have done.[120] Clearly, too, circumstances were not always favorable, nor was the combination of salary and fees always available: we have seen evidence of difficulties with both kinds of payment; in the worst case, a private teacher with no public subsidy and a small class of delinquent students might labor all year for very little indeed.

If the grammarians' receipts could vary considerably, so evidently could their needs: the complaints of Lollianus and Palladas suggest that they depended heavily on their professional incomes, but one can infer a greater freedom for others—Verecundus at Milan, for example, or Cleobulus at Antioch. Notably absent at all levels of the profession, however, is any reluctance to accept payment. In the second century, a distinguished grammarian's receipt of fees had called for explanation and justification in his funeral oration;[121] the examples of such compunction could easily be multiplied.[122] But one must listen hard for any echo in late antiquity—in the euphemism, for instance, that makes a public salary an "encouragement."[123] Far louder are the unembarrassed complaints of Augustine and Palladas[124] or the equally frank good wishes Procopius of Gaza extends to various teachers of his acquaintance, that they might grow wealthy in their profession.[125] Even Libanius, who most shows the traces of the older attitudes, marks the shift. Libanius might have preferred to regard his payments as gifts and to divert his public salary at Antioch to his assistants while stressing his own honorable freedom from the "need to receive";[126] but his orations in behalf of his assistants or against delinquent students, as well as other, incidental comments, reveal that in principle he saw no stigma for the teacher—one of the

120. Implied by *Or.* 1.61, as Jones, *LRE* 1002, remarks.

121. Ael. Aristid. *Or.* 32.16. The subject of the eulogy, Alexander of Cotyaeum, had been one of the tutors of Marcus Aurelius; cf. *PIR*² A.502.

122. See Chap. 2 pp. 55, 58.

123. παραμυθία, Damasc. *V. Isid.* frg. 178 Zintzen, on the salary of Pamprepius at Constantinople; cf. the account in Malch. frg. 20, where the regular term, σύνταξις, is used.

124. See n. 109 above.

125. Procop. Gaz. *Ep.* 13, 86, 89.

126. Payments as gifts: cf. Petit, *Étudiants* 144f.; Liebeschuetz, *Antioch* 84. Refusal of salary: implied by *Or.* 31 (see Kaster, "Salaries" 54ff.), but note that at the same time Libanius was probably receiving an imperial salary; see also below, n. 128.

"better sort of person"—in his professional income.[127] The reasons for the change in attitudes are not at all clear. One can, however, conjecture that for grammarians, at least, the change in the teacher's social status played a part: the stigma earlier associated with the recipient's generally low and often servile standing may gradually have been effaced as the profession came to attract men of more respectable origins. In any case, it would appear that though to refuse payment was still a mark of honor, to accept it, even to insist upon it, was no longer felt to be shameful.[128] No grammarian of late antiquity gives evidence of waiving his salary.[129]

Up to this point, our survey of the main evidence for the grammarians' standing—their origins, family connections, and wealth—has suggested a group of men who might differ considerably in their individual situations but who would on the whole belong to the quality of their towns, respectable if unprepossessing members of the local elite. A few touches can briefly be added to this picture from other, less direct evidence.

Whether as a participant in the *adventus* of the governor in fourth-century Antioch or as a favored guest on the estate of a Gallic magnate in the fifth, the grammarian would be an appropriate ornament in the public or private retinue of the powerful: honorably placed in a proximity few could enjoy, but clearly subordinate, a peripheral figure.[130] A similar favored subordination is apparent in other contexts, when a grammarian steps out of his role as a teacher—for example, trying his hand as an encomiast. It was no simple matter to gain access to an imperial administrator or local *potens* for that purpose: the man's residence would be

127. In addition to *Or.* 31 and *Or.* 43 *passim*, see, e.g., his enthusiastic prophecy of the benefits that Gerontius would receive as a result of his appointment at Apamea, *Ep.* 1391. "Better sort of person": *Or.* 31.19, τοῖς σεμνοτέροις, οἷον εἶναι προσήκει τὸν διδάσκαλον. Cf. *Ep.* 756.1, τέχνη τῶν σεμνοτέρων, of medicine.

128. Waiver of payment in liberal professions—rhetoric: e.g., Lib. *Or.* 36.9, 38.2, 62.19f., *Ep.* 140, 466, 1539 (and cf. n. 126); Eumen. *Pan. Lat.* 5.11.3 Galletier. Medicine: Auson. *Epiced.* 11–12; Greg. Naz. *Or.* 7.10 (*PG* 35.768A), cf. *IG* 12:2.484.28f. (Hiera [Lesbos]); *IGR* 3.733 = *TAM* 2:3.910.17 (Rhodiapolis). Philosophy: Symm. *Rel.* 5.2.3, on the philosopher Celsus.

129. I know of only one instance of a grammarian's refusing payment in any period, and that in special circumstances: the grammarian Menander of Kassopa in Epirus, lecturing at Delphi at the beginning of the first century B.C., presented his learning as an offering to the god and to the city and refused the contribution (ἔρανος) that the city offered him (*FD* 3:3.338 = *Syll.*[3] 739).

130. *Adventus*: Lib. *Ep.* 255.6, to Eudaemon of Pelusium (Part II no. 55), with Liebeschuetz, *Antioch* 208f.; on the teachers' status at Antioch, cf. Norman, "Gradations" 79, 82. Fifth-century Gaul: Sidon. Apoll. *Ep.* 2.2, with Part II no. 50.

crowded with rival poets and others seeking favor; the way would have to be cleared by a timely introduction or letter of commendation from a respected connection.[131] The grammarians could muster the necessary influence, as is demonstrated by their fair showing as encomiasts of regional administrators and even, among those who moved to the capital, of emperors.[132]

Proximity to administrators was possible in another form as well: advocacy. In the fourth century especially, advocacy was a promising path for an ambitious man, not least because provincial governors often chose their own counselors (*assessores*) from among the advocates, and the governors in turn were heavily recruited from among the assessors. In fact, as we shall see below, Simplicius, the only grammarian in our period who became a provincial governor, had earlier been an assessor, and he had possibly combined advocacy with his teaching before that.[133] If so, he would not have been alone: we have already seen that Ausonius early in his career and Acilius Glabrio were active as advocates at Bordeaux, and there are a couple of examples from elsewhere.[134] But if

131. The problem of access is put clearly in Lib. *Ep.* 969.2, to the governor Heraclianus on behalf of the poet Diphilus (Part II no. 49): Δίφιλος δὲ τῶν μὲν εἰς τὴν οἰκίαν σου πολλάκις ἐστὶν ἐλθόντων, τῶν δὲ οὐδ᾽ ἅπαξ ἰδεῖν σε δυνηθέντων. Compare the frankness of *Ep.* 633, advising another poet, Eudaemon of Pelusium, to exploit fully against possible rivals the connection with the prefect of Egypt Gerontius that Libanius has provided; cf. *Ep.* 632, to Gerontius.

132. Besides Diphilus and Eudaemon (n. 131), whose success or failure is not recorded, see Bergk, *PLG*[4] 3.342ff. nos. 2, 3 (with Part II no. 83 [Ioannes of Gaza]); Coripp. *Iohann.* (cf. Part II no. 37); *Anth. Gr.* 16.34 (with Part II no. 264 [Theodoretus]); probably Olympiod. *Comm. in Alc. 1* 2.80ff. Westerink (with Part II no. 12 [Anatolius]); and perhaps Aur. Cyrus (Part II no. 41). Encomia (*vel sim.*) of emperors: Helladius (Part II no. 67); Dioscorius (Part II no. 48); Priscian (Part II no. 126); cf. also Part II nos. 37 (Corippus) and 92 (Ioannes Lydus), and note that no grammarian is attested as imperial encomiast before the reign of Theodosius II.

133. Amm. Marc. 28.1.45, 52, with Part II no. 137. For advocates passing to positions in the imperial administration, largely governorships, in the fourth century, note in *PLRE* I: Ambrosius 3, Domnio 2, Fl. Eusebius 40, Eutherius 2, Gaianus 6, Heraclius 7, Fl. Asclepiades Hesychius 4, Fl. Antonius Hierocles 3, Iovinus 1, Vindaonius Magnus 12, Marcianus 7, Maximinus 7, Nemesius 2, Olympianus 2, Palladius 18, Petronius 2, Priscianus 1, Sabinus 5, Severus 14 (withdrawn from Libanius's school, not at the latter's request, as stated in *PLRE* I, but at his father's, so that he could immediately begin his career as an advocate: *Or.* 57.3), Fl. Severus 24, Theodorus 11, Fl. Mallius Theodorus 27 (cf. his brother Lampadius 3, with *PLRE* II pp. 654f.), Ulpianus 3. See also above at n. 10, on Attius Delphidius Tiro; and Jones, *LRE* 512.

134. Aur. Theodorus of Hermopolis (Part II no. 150); Eudaemon of Pelusium at Elusa (Part II no. 55). Calliopius of Antioch, who also rose to a prominent position (see below at n. 171), appears to have practiced as an advocate only after his teaching: see Lib. *Ep.* 18.2, with Part II no. 25.

Simplicius had practiced as an advocate, he was alone in the success it brought him; no other grammarians gained the promising post of assessor. That position was evidently more accessible to others.

So too was another position, rather different in the ambitions it might satisfy, but perhaps revealing as well as any other the secondary standing of the grammarian in the local elite. From the early fourth century onward we find grammarians occupying or moving into positions in the ecclesiastical hierarchy of their towns; but they appear in the second rank of the clergy, as presbyters. Only once does a grammarian become a bishop; and the singularity of that event is all the more noticeable when it is contrasted with the success of rhetoricians and sophists in getting bishoprics.[135] The fortunes of the two types of teacher in the world of the Church clearly reflect their positions not only in the world of letters but also in the community at large.

It is possible of course to find grammarians of more than usual distinction, men capable of reaching out from their teaching positions to affect events at even the highest levels. Nicocles, for example, in virtue of his having taught the prince Julian at Constantinople, was a person of some consequence during Julian's reign, able to mediate between the population of Constantinople and the city's prefect during a crisis, and a suitable ambassador from the city to the emperor himself.[136] Perhaps still more striking is the fame of Timotheus of Gaza, whose literary efforts were credited with persuading the emperor Anastasius to abolish a hated tax.[137] But these men were exceptional in their connections or in their successes. More commonly, while he remained in the town where he taught, the grammarian would have resembled Lollianus of Oxyrhynchus: claiming personal connections that might extend into the imperial administration, perhaps even running to a friend at court, but attaining only a middling status[138] and satisfied (or, in Lollianus's case, dissatisfied) with his modest local eminence. For the grammarian who wanted more, there was little alternative to stepping out from his town or from his profession.

135. Rhetoricians as bishops: see, besides Augustine, Chap. 2 at nn. 172, 175, 176. Grammarian, *ut vid.*, as bishop: Part II no. 116. Grammarians as presbyters: see Part II nos. 81, 82, 124; and cf. Part II, nos. 5 (μοναχὸς ἀπὸ γραμματικῶν), 161 (grammarian and lector). Note especially the Apollinarii of Laodicea: the father, a grammarian and presbyter (Part II no. 14); the son, a rhetorician and bishop.

136. Lib. *Ep.* 1368.

137. *Suda* T.621; Cedren. 1.627.8f. Bekker. On Nicocles and Timotheus, see Chap. 6 pp. 202f.

138. Beyond the man at court whom he calls "Brother," he refers to an *optio beneficiariorum* and relative of the *corrector Aegypti* Theodorus, and to the brother of a *canaliclarius*: see *PCollYoutie* 2.66 = *POxy*. 47.3366, B26f., 28, 38, with the remarks of Parsons, *PCollYoutie* 2, p. 415.

And step out they did, above all geographically. Of the 140-odd grammarians whose place of teaching is known, a quarter can be seen to have moved from their homelands or otherwise to have changed their place of teaching.[139] As we might expect, such movement was predominantly from smaller or less promising areas to larger, more promising centers: from Thagaste to Carthage, from Aegeae or Gaza to Antioch, or from Gaza to Alexandria.[140]

The capital cities especially were magnets. Augustine's testimony to the lure of the greater profit and higher status that even a private teacher of rhetoric could expect at Rome[141] is more than borne out for the grammarians. For example, all but one of the Africans who moved went to one of the imperial centers: Nicomedia under Diocletian, or Rome and Constantinople in the fourth century and later.[142] Similarly, most of the Egyptians who left their native land went to Constantinople, either directly or by way of Athens or Antioch.[143] But not only Africans and Egyptians felt the tug: in the fourth through sixth centuries we find grammarians from Sparta and the provinces of Lycia, Phrygia, Asia, and Lydia teaching in the new Rome.[144] Already by the mid-fourth century

139. Based on Appendix 5, eliminating those styled διδάσκαλοι (vel sim.; see the preface to Part II) and those grammarians whose location is questionable.

140. Thagaste to Carthage: Aug. Conf. 4.4.7, 4.7.12ff.; cf. Conf. 5.7.13, C. Acad. 2.2.3. Aegeae to Antioch: Isocasius (Part II no. 85). In both cases the change in location was linked with a change in profession from grammarian to rhetorician; see below, p. 129. From Gaza to Antioch and Alexandria: the grammarians Stephanus, Alypius, Hierius (Procop. Gaz. Ep. 13, with Part II nos. 141, 7, 75), and Stephanus (Procop. Gaz. Ep. 57, with Part II no. 142). Note also the movement of Tetradius from Iculisma to Saintes(?), Auson. Epist. 11.21ff., with Part II no. 263; but his metier in either place is uncertain. Compare, from s.II, POxy. 6.930, a teacher forsaking the χώρα for Alexandria and in the process abandoning a pupil in the middle of a book of Homer.

141. Conf. 5.8.14.

142. Nicomedia: Flavius, Jer. De vir. ill. 80. Rome: see Part II no. 170 (Anonymus 4); perhaps also Aelius Donatus and Probus (Part II nos. 52, 127). Constantinople: Chrestus, Jer. Chron. s.a. 358, with Part II no. 27; Priscian (if from Caesarea Mauretania), Part II no. 126; Speciosus, a Latin grammarian or rhetorician from Africa, Part II no. 138. (Corippus also went from Africa to Constantinople, but he is not known to have taught in the latter place: cf. Part II no. 37, and below, pp. 130f.) The exception is Iulianus Pomerius (Part II no. 124), who went from Africa to the metropolis of Arles in the late fifth century: V. Caes. 1.9; [Gennad.] De vir. ill. 99.

143. See Part II nos. 10, 46 (from Egypt via Antioch), 67, 77, 111, 114 (from Panopolis via Athens). Note also Part II no. 226, Harpocration's movement from Egypt via Antioch; but he was more likely a sophist than a grammarian. Two other Egyptians are sometimes thought to have taught at Constantinople, but their movement is questionable: see Part II nos. 79, 110.

144. Sparta: Part II no. 106. Lycia: Part II no. 48. Phrygia Salutaris: Part II no. 56. Asia: Part II no. 101. Lydia: Part II no. 92: Ioannes Lydus, initially drawn

Constantinople's attraction for mobile teachers was sufficiently strong for Libanius to complain that skilled teachers were being drawn from Antioch, where they were needed, to where there was a surplus.[145]

Like many of Libanius's complaints, however, this probably should be taken with its grain of salt: Constantinople's draw was no doubt all that Libanius asserts; but surely Antioch too exerted a considerable pull, attracting teachers from Egypt and from provinces in its own diocese, Oriens. From Libanius's correspondence we know that grammarians from Egypt, Arabia, Phoenice, and Palestine made their way to Antioch.[146] Over a century later, Antioch was still attractive enough to bring the entire corps of grammarians from Gaza to the city's suburb of Daphne, evidently in hopes of greater prosperity.[147] Although the evidence for other great cities—Carthage, Alexandria—is less abundant, it seems probable that like Antioch they too drew teachers from lesser cities in their regions and were a springboard for the leap to Rome or Constantinople.

Compared with the mobility visible elsewhere, the fixity of the grammarians of Bordeaux, especially their apparent failure to move to more brilliant centers,[148] suggests that they were either atypically complacent or unlucky. Yet the mobility and sheer footloose freedom many grammarians seem to have had is remarkable.[149] Teachers had of course long been among the most mobile groups; the late-antique phenomenon is nothing new.[150] But the ease with which such men appear to have

---

to the imperial service, only later becoming a Latin *grammaticus*; on the unusual sequence in his career and the reasons for it, see ibid. Cf. also Part II no. 42: from Cos to Constantinople?

145. *Ep.* 368.1.

146. Egypt: Part II nos. 32, 46. Arabia: Part II no. 155. Phoenice: Part II no. 4. Palestine (Elusa): Part II no. 55. Cf. Lib. *Or.* 31.9: all four of Libanius's assistants ca. 360 were foreigners, drawn from their home towns by reports of the prosperity of Antioch's teachers.

147. See above, n. 140, on Stephanus, Alypius, Hierius, with Procop. Gaz. *Ep.* 13.11ff., indicating that they constituted τὸ κεφάλαιον ὅλον of grammarians at Gaza. For movement to Antioch in the mid-fifth century, see n. 140, on Isocasius.

148. See above, p. 105.

149. Note the movements of Eudaemon of Pelusium that can be traced— from Elusa, where he was teaching, to Egypt, to Antioch, where he also did some teaching, to Constantinople, and back to Egypt—all in little more than a year: Lib. *Ep.* 255, 632, 633, with Part II no. 55.

150. To note only a few earlier examples from inscriptions: Kaibel 534 = *GVI* 1479 Byzantium, Theodorus from Bithynion/Claudiopolis, who won κλέος as a grammarian first at Athens, then at Byzantium; *CIL* 3.12702 = 13822 = *ILS* 7767 Doclea, the Greek *grammaticus* C. Gord(ius) Maximianus (for the name "Gordius," suggestive of Cappadocian origins, see Robert, *Noms* 526, 548f.; Moretti, "Nuovi epigrammi" 69f. = *IGVR* 3.1186); *FD* 3:3.338 (= *Syll.*³ 739), 3:4.61, 3:1.465,

moved is particularly noteworthy at a time when the central government was attempting by force of law to bind its citizens (not least curials) to their places of origin[151] and when—less formal, but perhaps no less important—the force of sentiment might work a similar restraint. Ausonius, for example, much admired the teachers of rhetoric whose fame compelled them to leave their *patria* for posts at Rome or Constantinople and thus brought honor indirectly to Bordeaux.[152] But he appears to have had no special regard for the two grammarians who left their chairs at Bordeaux for other cities less prestigious than the capitals: indeed, he speaks of one of them as though he were guilty, if not of betrayal, then of something very like it.[153] Similar feelings can be deduced from Libanius's comment that it was a happy town that could appoint one of its own citizens to a chair, or from the eulogy of a teacher for having loyally resisted the blandishments of other cities and having remained in his native town.[154] In view of the potential obstacles, the freedom of movement displayed is all the more remarkable, whether in response to an imperial invitation or in hasty retreat from a scene of riot and murder.[155] Such mobility says much about the power of patronage, which we shall examine in a later chapter.

Change of place could bring a dramatic change in fortune, linking geographic and social mobility. As we have already seen in Bordeaux, marriage offered one route.[156] If a man were ambitious, it helped to be unmarried. A wife and children already on hand were an anchor:[157]

3:2.115, 3:1.206, grammarians from diverse cities who were honored at Delphi; *Labraunda* 3:2.66, the γραμματικός Ti. Claudius Anteros, honored at Athens and, *ut vid.*, other cities. Cf. Chap. 1 n. 26, and the itinerary sketched at Flor. *Verg. or.* p. 107.13ff.

151. Cf. MacMullen, "Social Mobility" 49ff. Curials: Jones, *LRE* 740ff.; and, for a regional study of Cappadocian curials, Kopaček, "Curial Displacements."

152. See above at n. 27.

153. Concordius and Anastasius: see n. 26 above; note esp. the motive attributed to Anastasius, characterized by the pejorative *ambitio*, and the emphasis on his failure at Poitiers.

154. Lib. *Ep.* 1366.2, *Or.* 1.92; Choric. *Or. fun. Procop.* 12–14 (p. 113.15ff.); cf. also Aug. *C. Acad.* 2.2.3. For the earlier empire, note especially the implications of Flor. *Verg. or.* p. 108.1ff., the newcomer's characterization of the *populus Tarraconensis* as *tarde quidem, sed iudicio hospitalis*.

155. Invitation: Agath. *Hist.* 5.6.5f. Keydell, on Metrodorus of Tralles, emphasizing his κλέος; Jer. *Chron.* s.a. 358, *De vir. ill.* 80, on Chrestus and Flavius. Riot and murder: Soc. *HE* 5.16.10, 15, with Part II nos. 10, 67.

156. See above, p. 104.

157. Cf. *PCollYoutie* 2.66 = *POxy.* 47.3366, B22f., 28: Lollianus points to his family as the reason he must remain at Oxyrhynchus, unable to visit his friend at court.

some teachers, like Augustine, prudently remained unencumbered;[158] others less scrupulous cut themselves free.[159] The rewards could be significant. Pamprepius's appointment as grammarian at Athens was followed by a good marriage, and appointment and marriage together raised him above the hard life he had previously led.[160]

But Pamprepius may have been as unusual in this good fortune as he was in other elements of his career.[161] Available evidence shows no other grammarian prospering in the same way, beyond the teachers of Bordeaux already noted. Nor do many grammarians appear to have taken another opening that geographic mobility might offer, changing place to step up in the profession. When Augustine went from Thagaste to Carthage, he moved to rhetoric from grammar; a similar shift followed Isocasius's move from his native Aegeae to Antioch.[162] The change was decisive for each man's career. Augustine, of course, was finally carried by rhetoric to Milan, where his conversion canceled the good marriage he had contracted and the hopes he entertained for a governorship.[163] Isocasius's position at Antioch brought him influence with the imperial administration and, eventually, high office in the palatine service.[164] In this respect the careers of Augustine and Isocasius are comparable to those of Nepotianus and Ausonius, the only grammarians of Bordeaux to exchange the grammarian's chair for the rhetorician's and then to prosper in the imperial administration. The comparison, however, extends not only to the rise in profession, expectations, and fortunes of the two pairs, but to their isolation as well. No other grammarians are known to have followed the same path.[165]

---

158. See Brown, *Augustine* 62; cf. Lib. *Or.* 1.12, 53–54, offers of marriage; ibid. 278, Libanius's concubine; *Ep.* 1391, Libanius foresees a γυναῖκα τῶν εὐδαιμόνων καὶ πλῆθος οἰκετῶν καὶ γεωργίας following from Gerontius's appointment at Apamea.

159. Teachers abandoning their families: Procop. Gaz. *Ep.* 57 (with Part II no. 142), *Ep.* 91 (with Part II no. 231; the man's family appears to have rejoined him later: *Ep.* 124).

160. Appointment, marriage, rise in fortune: see Part II no. 114 for the sequence.

161. See below, pp. 130ff.

162. See n. 140 above.

163. *Conf.* 6.13.23 (marriage contracted), 6.11.19 (ambition for governorship).

164. Influence: cf. Theodoret. *Ep.* LII. Position as *QSP* under Leo: Malal. 369.17ff.; *Chron. Pasch.* 595.6ff.; Theoph. *Chron.* p. 115.9ff. de Boor; Cedren. 1.612.21 Bekker; and below, p. 130.

165. Note, however, that at the beginning of the sixth century Deuterius of Milan taught grammar and rhetoric concurrently, the only teacher in the period who can be seen to have done so; see Part II no. 44. Cf. also Part II nos. 124, 140.

Despite their geographic mobility, in fact, the grammarians were otherwise not conspicuously mobile. They tended to remain grammarians; and although as grammarians they might under circumscribed conditions receive significant preferment from the emperors,[166] they do not appear in our period to have had notable success in gaining other, richer rewards. Consider, for example, the informal yet prestigious position of imperial tutor, which not uncommonly led to high honors and office, and for which a grammarian of any distinction might be thought a reasonable candidate by virtue of his profession. We know of a fair number of men from the early fourth century onward who taught the children belonging to the households of reigning emperors; but not until the second half of the fifth century, with Dioscorius of Myra, tutor to the daughters of Leo, do we find the sole instance of a man who came to the job as a grammarian. For the rest, the position appears to have been held by more distinguished men of letters, especially rhetoricians (once again) or those still more highly placed.[167]

If we consider the grammarians' service in the imperial bureaucracy, the evidence tells a similar tale of restricted access. Indeed, one should properly say "ex-grammarians' service," since nearly all those who succeeded here had left their positions as *grammatici* well before, either advancing in the profession or striking out in a different direction. Thus in the palatine service we find[168] Ausonius, *quaestor sacri palatii* in 375–76; Calliopius, *magister epistularum* in 388; Isocasius, *QSP* in 467; Pamprepius, *QSP* with an honorary consulship and the patriciate in early 479 and *magister officiorum* under the rebel Leontius after July 484; and Corippus, who appears to have held some palatine office in the first years of Justin II.[169] Of these five men, with their careers scattered over more than two centuries, only Pamprepius can be said with any confidence to have reached his position still fresh from his profession as a grammarian.[170]

166. See above, n. 45, on the rank awarded some *grammatici* at Constantinople.

167. Dioscorius: *Suda* Δ.1208, with Part II no. 48, and cf. below. For other tutors of imperial offspring, besides the eunuchs Mardonius (Iul. *Misopog.* 352A–B) and Antiochus (= *PLRE* II s.v. 5, pp. 101f.), note Lactantius (Jer. *De vir. ill.* 80, with Eck's review of *PLRE* I in *Zephyrus* 23–24 [1972–73] 330; Barnes, *Constantine* 13); Fl. Optatus (Part II no. 241); Exuperius (Auson. *Prof.* 17.9ff.); Aemilius Magnus Arborius (*Prof.* 16.15, with Booth, "Notes" 244ff.); Marcianus (Part II no. 238); Decimus Magnus Ausonius (Part II no. 21); Themistius (*Or.* 16.204B–C, 213A–B); Arsenius (= *PLRE* I s.v. 4, p. 111). Nicocles' tuition of Julian at Constantinople is a special case; see Part II no. 106 *ad fin.*

168. For the following, see Part II nos. 21, 25, 85, 114, 37, respectively.

169. Note also Fl. Eugenius, *magister scrinii* after 385(?) and later Augustus in the West. But the evidence of his ever having been a *grammaticus* is questionable; see Part II no. 211.

170. See below, p. 132.

The careers of Ausonius and Isocasius, both of whom became teachers of rhetoric (and Ausonius, an imperial tutor) before reaching their offices, have already been remarked. Calliopius, whom we met as the son of a grammarian and member of a well-placed and well-connected family of Antioch,[171] appears to have taught only in his youth, before going on to practice as an advocate; Corippus is only known to have taught in Africa some twenty years before appearing at Constantinople. The showing is even more sparse when we look beyond the central administration: Ausonius, again, who moved from the *palatium* to assume praetorian prefectures in 377–79;[172] Nepotianus, a provincial governor (perhaps of Tripolitania) in the mid-fourth century;[173] Simplicius, assessor to Maximinus during the latter's governorship of Corsica or Sardinia, then governor of Numidia in the late 360s or early 370s, and finally *vicarius urbis Romae* in 374–75;[174] and Dioscorius, described as "ex-prefect of Constantinople" in 467, and later honorary consul.[175] Here again, only one man, Simplicius, might have stepped directly into the imperial service from his grammarian's chair.[176] Nepotianus of Bordeaux, like his friend and colleague Ausonius, had made the transition from grammar to rhetoric; Dioscorius almost certainly was already the tutor of Leo's daughters by 467. Indeed, the rank (ἀπὸ ἐπάρχων πόλεως) he held in that year may well have been honorary (as his later consulship unquestionably was), a distinction bestowed by his pupils' grateful father.[177]

All this is not to diminish the dramatic rise of some of these men. One would not have predicted the praetorian prefect Ausonius from the *grammaticus* of the 330s; still less would Pamprepius's early years as a wandering poet have foreshadowed his later role as an agent of rebellion. As individuals, such figures testify to the social fluidity of the period and the possibilities that were open when ambition, talent, and the right connections met in the same man; but they scarcely combine to suggest a pattern of mobility in the grammarian's profession itself.[178] Since most

171. See above, p. 108.
172. See Part II no. 21.
173. See Part II no. 105.
174. See Part II no. 137; *PLRE* I s.v. 7, p. 844.
175. Note also the career of Ioannes Lydus as *praefectianus*, the greater part of which preceded his activity as a teacher: Part II no. 92.
176. Conceivably Simplicius had been an advocate (see above, p. 124), like his protector Maximinus (Amm. Marc. 28.1.6).
177. On this and other questions concerned with the titles attributed to Dioscorius, see Part II no. 48.
178. Contrast the success of the following men, who passed from their activity as rhetoricians or sophists to a place in the imperial service in the fourth century (in *PLRE* I): Alexander 9, Belaus, Fl. Bonus, Calliopius 2, Celsus 3, Demetrius 2, Eros 2, Eustathius 6, Fl. Antonius Hierocles 3, Ianuarius 6,

of these men left the regular practice of the grammarian's profession before their rise, their careers suggest rather the opposite: that ambition and talent were led to find outlets in different spheres, where the necessary relations of patronage were also more available.

The two apparent exceptions, Simplicius in the fourth century and Pamprepius in the fifth, only support that suggestion. Though the offices of both men appear to have followed close upon their teaching as *grammatici*, their fortunes were made not through a network of patrons gradually assembled but by the favor they received from a single powerful protector.[179] Simplicius began his service in the imperial administration as assessor to Maximinus and reached the vicariate of Rome during the same man's ascendancy. Similarly, Pamprepius gained his chair at Constantinople through the favor of the Isaurian Illus—and then lost the chair when his protector withdrew from the capital not long after. Yet Pamprepius remained attached to Illus as his confidant and agent; and Illus for his part soon gave Pamprepius an office and titles and drew him into the adventure of Leontius. The careers of Simplicius and Pamprepius might also offer a salutary warning of the risks that were run when a spectacular rise was combined with such singular dependency: having tied his fortunes to one patron, each man shared his patron's fall. Simplicius and Maximinus were executed early in the reign of Gratian, and Pamprepius was murdered by Illus and Leontius in desperate anger and suspicion shortly before they themselves were crushed. In their violent deaths no less than in their swift advances the two grammarians are unique.

The grammarians thus show a range of backgrounds and fortunes about as wide as one could imagine, from the sons of freedmen to high ministers of state. Such variety reveals the profession's diverse attractions and the opportunities it could offer, if only exceptionally. But the extremes tell us less than the center, and from the preceding pages we should be able to draw together the elements of the ordinary grammarian's status.

Such a man would be active in one of the larger provincial cities, where—despite the movements of other teachers in his region, and despite whatever ambitions he might nurse himself—he would likely pass all his days. His origins would be among the respectable classes of the city, as the son of a teacher, perhaps, or of a curial family of no great

---

Leontius 9, Marius 1, Musonius 2, Nymphidianus, Palladius 12, Aemilius Quintilius Pyrrhus 3, Quirinus. Cf. also n. 133 for a similar and frequent mobility among the advocates.

179. See Part II nos. 137, 114; on patronage, see Chap. 6.

distinction. If he married, his wife would be from a comparable back-ground and would bring a modest dowry; this dowry, some modest holdings of his own in the city's territory, and his professional income would combine to provide an honorable if not opulent standard of living, unburdened (if he possessed immunities) by liturgical demands, and might even allow a modest benefaction to the community in the course of his life. As an offshoot of his professional activity and general culture, he might dabble in poetry, perhaps gaining a moment in the spotlight for an encomium of a visiting dignitary. If his teaching was distinguished, he would contribute directly to the civic pride of his town—although if the town's educational resources ran to a teacher of rhetoric, the grammarian would probably be accustomed to cooperative subordination, channeling pupils to the rhetorician or sophist and standing in his shadow. Not a *vir primarius* himself, he would know the *primarii* well enough; as their children's teacher he would be respected by them and dependent on them. When with any luck he died at a mature age in his own bed, his loss would be regretted and his work would for a time be remembered.

Our hypothetical ordinary grammarian, in other words, stood as far above the common people in the city and its hinterland as he was below the men who directed the central and provincial administration of the empire. This is perhaps the essence of what Ausonius called his *mediocritas*, as Ausonius and his contemporaries would have understood it: a position within the elite that would appear either undistinguished or insignificant, depending on one's point of view. The combination of high and low standing marked the profession, both in the range of men who practiced it and in the components of the individual grammarian's status. In contrast to the overwhelming mass of the population, his birth, means, and culture placed him in the small circle of those free from ignoble employment. Yet for all that he was a social pauper in the world of the elite. Compared with the imperial aristocracy of birth or service, he was no more than a "mere *grammaticus*."[180]

The grammarian thus was located at the meeting point of several contradictions. So, for example, the teacher's nominal status, especially the honor he derived from his skill, must frequently have been at odds with his economic status. We can recall the conflicting characterizations—the *sterilis cathedra* and the *nomen grammatici tam nobile*—that crop up in Ausonius's *Professores*; the discrepancy is embodied in Lollianus of Oxyrhynchus, who could approach emperors aware that even the world's rulers had traditionally respected men of culture and skill like himself, while yet he scraped along in circumstances that must have seemed

180. Cf. Alan Cameron, "Date" 34 n. 65.

uncomfortably close to vulgar. At the same time, nominal status could extend its support and protection only so far. The *Saturnalia* of Macrobius shows us Servius, carried by his skill into the salons of the high aristocracy, where all the right-minded gentlemen are scholars and the grammarian can consort with them by virtue of his scholarship. Macrobius's portrait sketches a clear hierarchy of birth and learning: the grammarian becomingly assumes his place as the least of the invited.[181] At the same time, the grammarian's vulnerability is no less clear. Servius's willing self-effacement does not save him from—indeed, it provokes—the bullying of the perverse nobleman Evangelus, who sneers at the profession's title and, by implication, at the status it confers.[182] Macrobius's work is of course an idealization, in which only the morose villain of the piece would behave so crudely. In the less than ideal rounds of daily life, the reminders of hierarchy and its barriers, its rebuffs and snubs, would doubtless have been more common and no less vivid.[183]

While making these rounds, the grammarian could hope to be sustained by the knowledge and skills of his profession. In no setting, however, was his hope more certain than in his own classroom: there, if anywhere, he was in his glory. In the next chapters we will look more closely at the grammarian in his professional role and examine his own conception of the cultural authority his expertise provided, before going on to consider in detail the position of genteel obscurity and dependence that he occupied in his relations with patrons and the state.

181. See esp. *Sat.* 2.2.1ff., 7.4.1ff., with Kaster, "Macrobius" 227f.
182. *Sat.* 2.2.12, with Kaster, "Macrobius" 226f.
183. Cf. Lib. *Ep.* 1492, with Chap. 6 at n. 63.

A Place To Stand

ars est rei cuiusque scientia usu vel traditione vel ratione percepta tendens ad usum aliquem vitae necessarium.

A skill is the knowledge of any given matter derived from experience, tradition, or reason and aiming at some advantage essential to life.

—*Diomedes*, Ars grammatica, GL 1.421.4f.

Among the lost works of the ancient grammarians, some no doubt are more to be regretted than others; and no doubt opinions could differ in assessing the losses. For our purposes in this section, we would be especially fortunate to have a work by the grammarian Telephus, onetime teacher of the emperor Lucius Verus, which addressed the question, How much does a grammarian need to know?[1] Telephus's answer, necessarily revealing a grammarian's thoughts about his profession, would have offered us something otherwise hard to come by. Rhetoricians, philosophers, historians, poets—all are given to talking about their craft, their understanding of it, and the claims they would make for it. Not so the grammarians, who among the major participants in the literary culture are the most reticent in staking out their own position. We are for the most part left to draw what inferences we can from the largely impersonal discourse of their technical writings.

Where are we to look, then, to study the grammarian's view of his profession? Time has made the decision easier regarding either side of

1. *Suda* T.495: Τήλεφος, Περγαμηνός, γραμματικός. ἔγραψε καὶ αὐτὸς <Γραμματικὸν βιβλία *vel* Γραμματικά,> ἐν οἷς παρατίθεται πόσα χρὴ εἰδέναι τὸν γραμματικόν. On the lacuna after αὐτός, see Adler's *app. crit.*

the question, the methodical instruction in language or the exegesis of literary texts. Of the latter, only one authentic specimen from the period survives in reasonably complete form, the Vergilian commentary of Servius; and for the former—the side most often mentioned in non-grammatical sources—little in Greek could serve our purpose. To the extent that the efforts of the Greek grammarians survive at all from the fourth, fifth, and early sixth centuries, they survive as scattered excerpts or jejune epitomes. Only one extensive piece has come down to us in its original form, Theodosius's *Introductory Rules of Nominal and Verbal Flexion*, a work that does not provide much scope for the analysis needed here.[2] The remnants of the Latin grammarians offer more promising material.

In the following pages, therefore, we will examine in some detail two major texts. Each is clearly connected with the grammarian's school; each shows a different facet of the grammarian's work and his understanding of it; and each was composed by a man who on any reasonable estimate must be located in the intellectual foothills of the profession. I have resisted the temptation to make for the summit (say, Priscian), in order to gain a more accurate view of the terrain as a contemporary would have seen it. We will begin with Pompeius's commentary on the *Ars* of Donatus, which affords an especially vivid glimpse of the grammarian's mind-set and his sense of continuity or rivalry with his predecessors. We will then turn to Servius's commentary on Vergil, where we will be able to gauge the grammarian's sense of his authority over the language and to observe how he behaves when confronted by the authority of a classical text.

2. For Theodosius, see Part II no. 152; still less useful are the surviving Κανόνες καθολικοὶ περὶ συντάξεως derived from Herodian by Timotheus of Gaza (Part II no. 156) and the spare pamphlet Περὶ τῶν διαφόρως τονουμένων καὶ διάφορα σημαινόντων attributed to Ioannes Philoponus (Part II no. 118). The works of Ioannes Charax likely belong to a later period, as those of Georgius Choeroboscus certainly do (Part II nos. 199, 201, respectively). Extracts and epitomes: see Part II nos. 73, 110, 111, 118, 144, 156, 180. For works known, for the most part, only from their titles, cf. also nos. 16, 55, 56, 67, 72, 77, 79, 91, 114, 188, 207, 265.

CHAPTER 4

Pompeius

Pompeius taught as a grammarian in Africa in the late fifth or perhaps the early sixth century, the countryman and (in rough terms) contemporary of a clutch of African *grammatici* ranging in date from Dracontius's teacher, Felicianus, to the young Corippus.[1] We know Pompeius through his *Commentum Artis Donati*, the most garrulous of grammatical texts and, since its first modern publication by Lindemann in 1820, perhaps the least esteemed.[2] The harsh modern verdict, although overdone, is not entirely undeserved: the commentary's scholarship is flawed, and its sprawling devotion to one of the most elegant Latin handbooks is a stunning paradox.[3] Nonetheless, that devotion can pay generous dividends to the modern reader, for it is expressed in a distinctive, lively voice that strikingly reveals the concerns of a late-antique teacher.

The object of Pompeius's attention was composed by Donatus in the mid-fourth century; by Pompeius's time it was on its way to becoming a central document of Latin studies in the West.[4] Donatus's work consisted of two parts, the *Ars minor* and, in three books, the *Ars maior*. The *Ars*

1. On Pompeius's place and date, see Part II no. 125. On the other African grammarians of this period, see Part II nos. 23 (probably but not certainly African), 24, 37, 58, 59, 124, 126 (if a native of Caesarea Mauretania), and perhaps 138. In this chapter Pompeius and Cledonius are cited by page and line of Keil, *GL* 5; *Explanationes* 1 and Servius's commentary on Donatus are cited by page and line of Keil, *GL* 4.

2. Characterized as a "botch" and a "sham" by Keil, *GL* 5.90; and by Jeep, *Zur Geschichte der Lehre* 43f. The judgment was resumed by Helm, *RE* 21.2313.23f., 2314.63f.

3. Cf. Holtz, "Tradition" 50, who also offers the best concise and general characterization of Pompeius's work.

4. See now the massive study of Holtz, *Donat*, esp. 75ff., on Donatus's relation to the earlier tradition, and 219ff., on the reception of Donatus down through the High Middle Ages.

minor offered a swift introduction to the parts of speech—the heart of the grammarian's doctrine—cast in the form of questions (*partes orationis quot sunt? . . . nomen quid est?*) with the appropriate answers. The *Ars maior* then followed the standard sequence for such handbooks, beginning with brief, introductory definitions (of *vox, littera,* and so on) before taking up the parts of speech in greater detail and concluding with a rapid survey of the *vitia et virtutes orationis.*[5] The work is concise, almost clipped, throughout: drawing on several sources for his doctrine, Donatus evidently tried to pare it down to its essentials. By contrast, Pompeius is brief only in his passing glance at the lesser *Ars,* praising its utility as an introduction and approving its ordering of the *partes.*[6] He then presses on to exhaust the greater *Ars.*[7] To appreciate the value of his comments, we must first try to understand Pompeius's method, his style, and the audience he has in mind. And in turn, to understand his method we must understand his relationship to his main source, Servius's early fifth-century commentary on Donatus.

To speak of Pompeius's "relationship" to Servius is to put the matter delicately, or at least neutrally: some would say that Pompeius shamelessly plagiarized Servius, whom in fact he does not name. Although the charge is inaccurate, as we shall see, the dependence is nonetheless plain—not on the extant, abridged version of Servius, but on a more complete version of his original work. Though that original is now lost, it is represented in different ways and in varying degrees by the surviving epitome (405.2–448.17), by Book 1 of "Sergius's" *Explanationes in Artem Donati* (486.4–534.12), and by Cledonius's commentary on Donatus (9–79).[8] Pompeius drew from Servius much of the substance of his own

5. With the prominence given the *partes orationis* in the *Ars minor* and the modification of the standard sequence thus produced, compare the similar dislocation in Book I of Diomedes; see Jeep, *Zur Geschichte der Lehre* 57.

6. See the full form of the preface published by Holtz, "Tradition" 59–60, with *GL* 5.96.19–98.8.

7. Apparently Pompeius assumes that his audience was already familiar with the *Ars minor;* see 246.32, *legistis illas* [sc. *significationes adverbiorum*] *in prima parte artis,* adverting to Don. 596.1–5 Holtz. Cf. Pomp. 189.27, *quem ad modum legistis in primordiis,* with the apparatus in Holtz's edition of Don. at 587.28; and cf. Keil, *GL* 5.90.

8. On the relationship of Pompeius, Serv. *Comm. Don.,* and *Explan.* 1, see Keil, *GL* 5.92; Helm, *RE* 21.2313.59ff.; and esp. Schindel, *Figurenlehren* 21f., 36f., refining Jeep, *Zur Geschichte der Lehre* 43–53. For clear evidence that Pompeius and *Explan.* 1 draw on a common source, compare, e.g., Pomp. 208.28f. and *Explan.* 502.17f. On Cledonius, see Holtz, "À l'école de Donat" 526, correcting Jeep, *Zur Geschichte der Lehre* 41f.

I should stress that the matter of Pompeius's main source is probably more complex than previously suspected: I use "Servius" in what follows to mean the version of Servius known to Pompeius. That version had very possibly been

comments, including the references to pre-Donatan scholars (Varro, Pliny, Caper, Terentianus, the younger Probus, and others) that pepper the work, and many of the illustrative quotations from *auctores*.[9] The extent of the debt can scarcely be overestimated and can be exemplified by some of the howlers that Pompeius evidently borrowed without blinking an eye,[10] or by a brief passage like the following:

> sed sunt aliquae litterae, quae neque ab "e" inchoant neque in "e" desinunt. hae litterae calumniam patiuntur, ut est "x." idcirco non littera dicitur, sed duplex littera. "k" et "q" neque ab "e" inchoant neque in "e" desinunt. "h" et ista similiter in calumniam venit. (101.18–22)

Pompeius means that the letters *x, k, q,* and *h* were charged with being illegitimate or unnecessary: so much emerges from the parallel passage in the *Explanationes*. But Pompeius has reproduced his source so elliptically— as though forgetting his audience would not have Servius open before them, as he did—that his reference to the letters' *calumnia* becomes

---

interpolated by some intermediary: note, e.g., Pomp. 262.28, where the subject of *dicit* can be neither Donatus nor Servius; or Pomp. 224.32ff., where the nonsensical statements *quam removit* and *"clam" vult remotam esse omnino* may derive from interpolations in Pompeius's source subsequent to Servius; and cf. the appendix to Part II no. 125. It is possible, therefore, that some of Pompeius's departures from Servius discussed below were already present in his main source. It is also conceivable that if Pompeius's version of Servius had already been revised to include non-Servian material, the name of the reviser was Astyagius; see below, nn. 35, 36, and Part II no. 189. (This could, incidentally, account for Pompeius's failure to mention Servius by name: he might not even have known that the work before him was originally Servius's.)

These and other puzzles (e.g., the curious doublet Pomp. 165.19–174.11 vs. 174.12–190.13) need to be considered in a full study of Pompeius (desiderated by Holtz, "Tradition" 50f.), which this chapter does not provide; but such a study must be based on a decent critical edition, a still more pressing need. I have used Keil's text but have tacitly repunctuated in some places.

9. The doubts of Jeep, *Zur Geschichte der Lehre* 44–53, that Pompeius himself ever saw the work, e.g., of Probus were well founded, although Jeep's discussion of some individual passages is vitiated by the belief that Pompeius used the surviving version of Servius's commentary; see, e.g., a garbled version of Probus clearly taken over by Pompeius from Servius: Pomp. 224.30ff., with Jeep, pp. 44f.

10. E.g., Pomp. 215.24f. (cf. Serv. 411.35–37; *Explan.* 504.5f.); and cf. Pomp. 185.33–186.6, the assertion that *mille* in the clause *habeo mille servorum* is in the genitive: the presence of a supporting citation from Cicero suggests that the lesson was already in his source. Note, however, that Pompeius does not reproduce Servius's equally astonishing claim that *vulgus* is attested in the feminine: Serv. 431.27f., citing *in vulgum ambiguam*, evidently a faulty recollection of *Aen.* 2.98f., *spargere voces / in vulgum ambiguas*.

intelligible only when it is compared with the passage in the *Explanationes* derived from the common source.[11]

The way Pompeius mined his Servius can be illustrated from his discussion of the participle, a passage that also exemplifies some of his more peculiar habits. The discussion begins as follows:

> pleraque dicit quae et in superiore arte memoravit, pleraque addit. participium dictum est pars orationis ab eo, quod partem capit nominis, partem verbi, ut siqui dicat "legens" "scribens" "currens": ista participia sunt. nam habent haec quae dixi: "legens" habet et casus et genera et tempora et significationes. quod casus et genera habet, nominis sunt: nam et casus nomini accidit, et genus nomini accidit. quod tempora et significationes habet, haec duo verbi sunt: nam tempus verbo accidit, significatio verbo accidit. ergo participium habet a nomine partes, habet a verbo partes. ideo dicitur participium, quasi particapium. (256.9–17)

The striking feature of the paragraph is Pompeius's cross-reference to an earlier mention of the participle's accidents (256.12, *nam habent haec quae dixi*)—striking because Pompeius has previously said nothing whatever about the specific attributes of the participle and their relation to the attributes of nouns and verbs. But Servius, who worked through both parts of Donatus's text, had earlier reviewed the accidents of the participle in his comments on the *Ars minor*. Pompeius here has simply taken over a cross-reference from Servius: compare *participium est quasi particapium: habet enim a nomine genera et casus, a verbo tempora et significationes, ab utroque numerum et figuram et cetera, quae in superioribus dicta sunt* (440.17–19). This is not an isolated symptom; Pompeius's discussion as a whole is articulated by the introductory statement *pleraque dicit quae et in superiore arte memoravit, pleraque addit* (256.9) and by the transitional statement *hoc est quod legimus etiam in arte superiore. iam addit alia propria et utilia* (260.39). And both the introduction and the transition correspond to Servius's *quae in superioribus dicta sunt. in posterioribus illud adicit* (440.19).

We can see what Pompeius has done with his source in this passage. He starts from the introduction (256.9ff.), with its reference back to Donatus's *Ars minor*, that he found in Servius's discussion of the participle in his commentary on the *Ars maior*; and he offers a preliminary clarification of the difference between the participle and the noun, *antequam tractemus hoc participium, debes scire discretionem participii ipsius a nomine* (256.18f.), which is also derived from Servius's commentary on the *Ars*

11. *Explan.* 520.20–26; cf. also Serv. 422.34ff.

maior.[12] He then makes a new beginning, repeating the definition of the participle (258.6–8 = Don. 644.2–4H.; cf. 597.5–6H.) and the review of its accidents (258.8–10), and discusses the accidents as they occur in Donatus (258.12–260.38 = Don. 644.6–645.3H.). But for this purpose he has turned back to Servius's commentary on the *Ars minor* (416.32ff.), which he follows until the transition *hoc est quod legimus etiam in arte superiore. iam addit . . .* (260.39f.).[13] At this point he resumes Servius's commentary on the *Ars maior*, which he uses until the end of the chapter,[14] garbling its account at one point and disagreeing with it at another.[15] Pompeius's general procedure, flipping back and forth between different sections of his Servius, is especially transparent here, but it is not at all unusual, and requires little comment. To understand the way Pompeius works, however, we must examine his other peculiarities glimpsed above (particularly his tendency toward confusion) and the marks of independence amid his general and profound reliance on his main source.

We can begin with Pompeius's curiously inconstant attitude toward that source. As was noted earlier, Pompeius does not mention Servius by name; but this does not prevent him from occasionally revealing he is aware of his debt. When, for example, Pompeius is about to retail an easy way to distinguish the proper accents of words (127.1ff.), he says, *et hoc traditum est*; he then goes on to present the lesson he found in Servius. Similarly, Pompeius repeats Servius's doctrine that if any part of speech "ceases to be what it is," it becomes an adverb (250.36ff.);[16] when he has occasion farther on to refer to the same lesson, Pompeius says, *legimus enim talem regulam, omnis pars orationis, cum desierit esse quod est, nihil est aliud nisi adverbium* (273.34f.), where *legimus* suggests he was conscious of

---

12. See esp. Pomp. 256.38–258.5, with Serv. 441.16–21; and cf. Don. 646.3–6H. For this sort of preliminary ground-clearing in Pompeius, cf. 112.6ff., 128.15ff.

13. Note that Pompeius omits discussion of *numerus* and *figura*, which occur in Donatus (645.9–12H.) only after the material (645.4–8H.) that provokes his return to Servius on the *Ars maior*.

14. Cf. Pomp. 261.1–264.15, with Serv. 440.19–441.15 and 441.21–27—i.e., all of Servius's discussion except 441.16–21, which had already contributed to Pompeius's preliminary remarks; see n. 12 above.

15. Disagreement: compare Pomp. 262.26–33 and 263.5–9 vs. Serv. 441.4–10; for other examples of Pompeius's independence, see pp. 150ff. below. Garbling: compare Pomp. 261.21–26 and Serv. 440.27–29; similar instances occur, e.g., at Pomp. 101.27ff. (cf. Serv. 421.16ff., *Explan.* 520.27ff., with Keil's apparatus on p. 102), 105.19–29 (cf. *Explan.* 521.21ff., with Don. 604.5–6H.), 231.9f. (cf. Serv. 437.14f.), 286.7ff. (cf. Serv. 445.8–10, with p. 157 below).

16. Cf. Serv. 439.22f. The notion does not appear in Donatus.

having read the lesson in Servius and is in effect citing his source.[17] But Pompeius is far from consistent in this. Discussing *communes praepositiones* Pompeius concludes his series of examples for *in* with the remark *iam de aliis* [sc. *exemplis*] *saepius dixit* (275.28f.); the subject of *dixit* here cannot be Donatus but must be Pompeius's source.[18] A bit earlier, however, in his comments on the prepositions, Pompeius includes the cross-reference *sicut . . . diximus* (275.6). As in the passage on the participle, Pompeius here refers back to the discussion of a topic he has nowhere treated before; like *haec quae dixi* (256.12), the clause *sicut . . . diximus* must have been lifted from his source. In the space of less than a page, then, Pompeius wavers between nonsensically reproducing his source and consciously referring to it as a separate entity. The example is not unique.

Elsewhere, to conclude his explanation of why the nominative is regarded as a *casus* even though *cadit* cannot accurately be said of a noun in the nominative, Pompeius draws an analogy with the positive degree of comparison, so regarded even though the *positivus gradus* does not make comparisons. He introduces the analogy by saying, *habet hoc etiam exemplum de gradibus* (182.15f.). Once again, the subject of the verb (here, *habet*) must be his source; the clause functions as an acknowledgment of a debt, like *et hoc traditum est* (127.1). But when he offered the same analogy a bit earlier, he said, *diximus etiam talem rem de gradu positivo* (171.1ff.)—another cross-reference with no antecedent, which must have been taken over from his version of Servius. The clause, like *haec quae dixi* (256.9) and *sicut . . . diximus* (275.6), is only one more example of a habit first discerned in Pompeius long ago. The most notorious instance is found where Pompeius says, *sed diximus in illa priore parte artis, id est in superioribus* (208.11f.), a reference to a comment on the *Ars minor* that of course does not occur earlier in Pompeius's text: Servius had already made the cross-reference (cf. 436.7, *qua ratione fiant, diximus superius*) to a passage in his commentary on the *Ars minor* (cf. 410.32ff.).[19]

---

17. Cf. also Pomp. 243.23, *legimus in principio*, referring to material provided at Pomp. 149.19ff. that remedies an omission for which Donatus is criticized (Pompeius cannot therefore refer to what was read in Donatus); Pomp. 274.4f., *nam legimus praepositionem adverbio non iungi*, referring to the lesson presented at Pomp. 255.6ff.

18. Cf. Serv. 443.9f.: *"in" autem et "sub" qua ratione servantur, in superiore arte tractatum est.*

19. See Keil, *GL* 5.90; Jeep, *Zur Geschichte der Lehre* 44; Schindel, *Figurenlehren* 21; Holtz, *Donat* 237 n. 45. For such confusions, see also Pomp. 135.36, *et iam saepius hoc tractavimus*, with Serv. 416.19ff.; Pomp. 227.4, *diximus etiam in principio*, with Serv. 413.35–38. A similar borrowing may explain the inconsequence of Pomp. 199.10f., *dixi hoc saepius: multi dicunt, utrum "lac" dicamus an "lact"* (contrast Pomp. 165.15); cf. also the appendix to Part II no. 125.

At times, then, Pompeius seems to remember that he is drawing on the commentary open before him, referring to its doctrine impersonally (*traditum est*) or to its author in the third person singular (*dixit, habet*). At other times, perhaps more frequently, that awareness seems completely submerged—he simply borrows his source's references, apt or not. The vagueness makes itself felt in another, more unsettling form: Pompeius's inconsistent discrimination between Donatus and Servius, the text on which he is supposed to be commenting and the commentary he is using as his source. In this respect, his use of *dixit* and *habet* is a disturbing sign. Although one might naturally expect that the subject of those verbs is Donatus, whose text he is ostensibly reviewing, sometimes such statements can only refer to Servius, and much more often the subject remains ambiguous.[20]

Pompeius is capable of drawing the distinction. When he says, for example, *Donatus ait, "quinque sunt adverbia, quae non debemus iungere nisi positivo tantum, 'tam' 'magis' 'maxime' 'minus' et 'minime.'"* . . . *et reddita est ratio non a Donato, sed ab aliis, quare non iunguntur ista adverbia comparativo et superlativo, sed tantum positivo* (156.1–8), the former reference must look back to the text of Donatus,[21] and the latter statement—despite the generalizing *ab aliis*—is clearly Pompeius's way of referring to Servius.[22] But Pompeius attaches little significance to the distinction, or at least he is concerned to maintain it only flickeringly. At one point Pompeius assures his reader, *hoc quod dicit tenendum nobis fideliter: omnis pars orationis, cum desierit esse quod est, adverbium est* (250.36f.). Although it becomes plain farther on in the paragraph that Pompeius is in general dealing with a Donatan doctrine (cf. 643.4–8H.), the specific lesson introduced by *hoc quod dicit* corresponds to nothing in Donatus; it is the formulation of Servius.[23] Yet at the end of the same paragraph Pompeius reports, *"sed plane," ait, "in his rebus aliqua discernimus accentu, sensu aliqua"* (251.33–34), referring to Donatus's *horum quaedam accentu discernimus, quaedam sensu* (643.7–8H.). In this instance we can follow the shift that occurs in the space of less than a page from *dicit* to *ait*, from Servius to Donatus.

Whether Pompeius himself was aware of the shift is much more difficult to determine; the distinction is effaced often enough to indicate he was not. For example, when introducing his discussion of adverbs ending in -*ē* and -*ĕ*, Pompeius remarks, *tractat de duabus regulis optime* . . .

20. Cf. Keil, *GL* 5.91f.

21. Don. 618.14–15H., of which Pompeius's text is an accurate paraphrase; see below at n. 26.

22. So Serv. 431.15ff., giving the explanation reproduced by Pompeius, beginning *ea scilicet ratione, quoniam.* . . .

23. Cf. Serv. 439.22f., and above at n. 16.

et ait sic, "omnia adverbia 'e' terminata producuntur, omnia penitus . . . exceptis tribus regulis" (244.21–26). The statement after *ait sic* corresponds in substance to Donatus: *adverbia quae in "e" exeunt produci debent praeter illa quae aut . . . aut . . . aut . . .* (640.12–14H.). But in form it much more closely resembles—and must surely refer directly to—the formulation in Servius, *omnia adverbia "e" terminata in positivo semper producuntur . . . exceptis tribus regulis eorum adverbiorum quae aut . . . vel . . . vel . . .* (438.22ff.). This example in effect shows Pompeius commenting on the commentary, and the examples could easily be multiplied.[24]

Such confusions may tell us something not only about Pompeius's work habits but about his resources as well. Even the most careless of men would not blend *Ars* and source commentary so frequently if he were constantly reminded of the distinction as he turned from the text of Donatus spread open before him to his copy of Servius. But the confusion would be readily explained if Pompeius did not have separate copies of the two works. One is tempted to suggest, therefore, that Pompeius was not reading Donatus independently but was working directly from a version of Servius that like Cledonius's commentary had lemmata from Donatus's text.

The instances where Pompeius's text coincides with Donatus against Servius seem to guarantee that he had at least lemmata before him.[25] But there is much evidence that Pompeius was not following Donatus line by line, hanging on every word. He can, for example, be hair-raisingly inexact, even when he clearly has Donatus in mind, especially in his tendency to paraphrase instead of quoting.[26] This habit is harmless when the paraphrase is tolerably accurate. Less innocuous, however, and

24. For clear instances of this sort of confusion, see Pomp. 103.22–24, with Serv. 421.26–28 vs. Don. 604.1–2H.; Pomp. 135.8ff., with Serv. 436.25f. vs. Don. 631.12–632.1H.; Pomp. 219.10f., with Serv. 412.29ff. and *Explan.* 505.15ff. vs. Don. 633.6–7H.; Pomp. 232.16–17, with Serv. 437.23f. vs. Don. 636.8–9H. (remarked by Holtz, *Donat* 237 n. 43); Pomp. 241.11–12, with Serv. 415.7–8 and 438.7 vs. Don. 640.2–3H.; Pomp. 274.17–19, with Serv. 442.23–25. Probable or possible instances also occur at Pomp. 98.21, with *Explan.* 519.11f. vs. Don. 605.5–6H.; Pomp. 189.35–37 (contrast Don. 626.19–627.6H.); Pomp. 225.16f., *dicit*, correcting Donatus; Pomp. 278.24ff. (contrast Don. 651.9–10H.); Pomp. 298.10f. (see Schindel, *Figurenlehren* 25 n. 42).

25. E.g., Pomp. 281.9f., on the definition of the interjection, with Don. 602.2H. and 652.5–6H. vs. Serv. 420.19f. and 443.19f.; Pomp. 269.22ff., on the irregular use of conjunctions, with Don. 648.1–2H. vs. Serv. 441.30.

26. Cf. above at n. 21; and for this feature of Pompeius's text in general, see Keil, *GL* 5.91 and, e.g., Pomp. 164.13ff. vs. Don. 621.7–9H.; Pomp. 170.2ff. vs. Don. 624.5 and 10–11H.; Pomp. 188.28ff. vs. Don. 626.5–7H.; Pomp. 177.20f. vs. Don. 623.6H.; Pomp. 186.34ff. vs. Don. 625.10H.; Pomp. 240.3–5 vs. Don. 639.8–10H.; Pomp. 279.14ff. vs. Don. 651.11–12H.; Pomp. 288.6–8 vs.

perhaps more revealing, are the places where Pompeius offers an inaccurate, interpretive version of Donatus's words and then criticizes Donatus on the basis of the inaccurate interpretation. Thus in his chapter on the pronoun Donatus observed, *sunt alia demonstrativa, quae rem praesentem notant, ut "hic" "haec" "hoc"* (629.12–13H.), and went on to add, *sunt alia magis demonstrativa, ut "eccum" "ellum" "ellam"* (630.1–2H.). The corresponding passage in Pompeius reads, *sunt aliqua pronomina quae rem praesentem significant, ut diximus* [= 203.10ff.], *"hic" "haec" "hoc." sunt aliqua quae magis significant* (205.25–26). Pompeius then continues, *hoc quid sit nescio. omnis res aut praesens est aut non est praesens: "magis praesens" quid sit nescio* (205.26–28). The absurdity of *magis praesens* that troubled Pompeius does not of course appear in Donatus's text; it is a careless combination— based, moreover, not on Donatus's *ipsissima verba* but on the version of Donatus that Pompeius transmits: *rem praesentem significant* blended with *magis significant*, so that the latter is taken to mean *rem magis praesentem significant*.[27]

Whether Pompeius would have stumbled here if he had been reading the text of Donatus is difficult to say. But the error is indistinguishable from the confusions and imprecisions in other passages where Pompeius was obviously commenting on Donatus only through Servius. For example, *semper Donatus "clam" conputat inter ablativas praepositiones: et in alia parte artis* [= Ars min. 601.1, 3H.] *hoc fecit, et hic* [= Ars mai. 649.17, 19H.] *fecit hoc. . . . falsum est, sed est utriusque casus* (274.33ff.). The criticism has been taken over directly from Servius (cf. 419.25–27), as has a cross-reference farther on in the discussion that cannot be Pompeius's.[28] Pompeius has not noticed that Servius missed a statement by Donatus, *"clam" praepositio casibus servit ambobus* (650.2–3H.), which undercuts the criticism (contrast Pompeius's *semper Donatus*, evidently a case of second-hand confidence). Or, *omne verbum aut agere aliquid aut pati significat* (213.21). The statement corresponds to the second half of Donatus's definition of the verb, *aut agere aliquid aut pati aut neutrum significans* (632.5–6H.), except that it omits *aut neutrum*—no doubt because Servius had already rejected that part of Donatus's definition.[29] But Pompeius betrays no knowledge that he is departing from Donatus and commenting on an improved version. In such places (and again the examples could be multiplied) it is

Don. 655.1–2H.; Pomp. 292.8–11 vs. Don. 658.1–2H.; Pomp. 302.3–4 vs. Don. 664.9–10H. (but cf. also Schindel, *Figurenlehren* 32 n. 75).

27. For another criticism based on an inaccurate paraphrase, see Pomp. 117.29–118.28, with reference to Don. 606.11–12H., and cf. Serv. 424.21–28.

28. Pomp. 275.6f.: *sicut in illis diximus.* See p. 144 above.

29. Cf. *Explan.* 503.6ff., with Serv. 413.35ff., *Explan.* 507.3ff., Pomp. 227.3ff.

difficult to believe Pompeius was consulting the full text of Donatus directly, independent of his source.[30]

There is little question, then, that Pompeius was hugely indebted to Servius for much of the substance of his commentary; and the preceding paragraphs argue that Pompeius more than occasionally misunderstood or poorly presented or ill digested that substance.[31] It would be a mistake, however, to conclude that Pompeius was merely reproducing Servius, that he did not use other sources, or that he brought nothing of his own to the work. Eclecticism is characteristic of the late-antique grammarians: heirs to a long tradition, they could draw on large resources, adapting to their own purposes the variations they found in one branch of the tradition or another. For the individual grammarian, the question was not whether he would help himself to this varied heritage, but how much, and how; depending largely on circumstances and inclinations, the answer could differ considerably from one man to the next.

For example, we have noted that Donatus drew on a fairly small number of sources for his *Ars* and attempted to weave them seamlessly together. Diomedes, in contrast, had very different intentions and methods: expansive where Donatus is terse, Diomedes wished to produce a wide-ranging collection of excerpts from earlier works in order to display to its best advantage the tradition that (he said) "the brilliance of human talent has brought to a state of high polish" (*GL* 1.299.3). Where Donatus had tried to achieve a tight weave, Diomedes created from his excerpts a mosaic, in which the junctures between the individual pieces remain visible while the pieces combine to form a coherent pattern. He plainly exerted himself in hunting out the byways of the tradition, so that, for example, his long treatment of verbal *coniugatio* (1.346.30–388.9) can be seen to derive from at least five different major sources and an indeterminate number of lesser works. Whether because of his own inertia or (at least equally possible) because of limited resources,

30. Compare esp. Pomp. 217.28–219.4, a vindication of the *gerundi modus,* after Servius (cf. Serv. 412.18–26 and *Explan.* 504.30–505.2; Donatus ignored this *modus*); Pomp. 293.14ff., on three kinds of *cacenphata* (cf. Serv. 447.16f.; Donatus had recognized only two, 658.11–12H.); Pomp. 298.32ff., a double departure from Donatus's comments on *antithesis* (663.1H.; Pompeius gives no hint that he is aware of any such departure). See also Pomp. 100.5f., with *Explan.* 519.29f.; Pomp. 200.5–7, with Keil, *GL* 5.91 and his *app. crit.* on p. 200; Pomp. 164.28–165.18, where Pompeius cannot be following the order or substance of Donatus's text.

31. Note that Pompeius sometimes ignores in his own usage the *regulae* he transmits: e.g., contrast 157.20ff., Pompeius's strictures on the proper use of cases with the comparative degree (after Servius: cf. Serv. 407.28f.; *Explan.* 492.11ff.), with his phrasing at 110.18 [*regula*] *melior ab antiqua* (similarly Pomp. 127.6, 10; 148.2, 5; 151.28; 155.5f.; 280.15f.).

Pompeius does not show anything like the eclecticism of a Diomedes.[32] But that characteristic is nonetheless discernible in his work.

So, for example, Ulrich Schindel has demonstrated that Pompeius exploited Donatus's commentaries on Vergil and Terence in order to supplement the literary examples with which he corroborated various lessons.[33] He used still other sources to expand or refine the lessons, most obviously in the case of Astyagius.[34] Pompeius cites this otherwise unknown authority twice. On the first occasion, he provides an expanded argument to demonstrate that the first-person-singular pronoun does not possess a vocative.[35] The second citation shows that Astyagius like Pompeius must have been active after Servius and must have been influenced by him.[36]

More tentatively, we can point to a deficiency of Servius that Pompeius criticized and remedied in a matter of prosody: *et nusquam voluerunt hoc dicere isti qui instituerunt artem, quare quattuor breves pro duabus longis ponantur. legimus tamen in antiquis, quae sit ratio* (119.32ff.). Pompeius does not make plain just what distinction he has in mind in the antithesis *isti qui instituerunt artem* versus *in antiquis*.[37] But with the former phrase, "those who have drawn up the *ars*," he appears to be referring to his source commentary: for when he goes on to unveil the *ratio* he has found, Pompeius applies that explanation to the same examples (except one) that had already been noted, without explanation, by Servius (425.17–19). A similar supplement seems to occur, with less fanfare, at 197.24ff.: here Pompeius announces eight *modi* of analogy and proceeds to review them as they occur in Servius (cf. 435.16ff.); but Pompeius ultimately includes a ninth *modus* (cf. 197.28–29, 198.14–15), not found in Servius and presumably imported from another source.[38]

---

32. For Pompeius's dependence on Servius for his knowledge of much of the pre-Donatan scholarship, see above at n. 9. For Diomedes, see Part II no. 47. For brief accounts of his method, see Jeep, *Zur Geschichte der Lehre* 59f., and "Jetzige Gestalt" 408f.; Barwick, *Remmius* 11f.

33. Schindel, *Figurenlehren* 29ff., 101ff., esp. 113f.

34. See Part II no. 189.

35. Pomp. 209.3ff. The vocative was already denied to *ego* by Servius (cf. 436.7), whom Astyagius here supplements.

36. Pomp. 211.5ff. Pompeius quotes Astyagius's definition of the pronoun—precisely the same definition, illustrated by the same example, that Pompeius himself elsewhere reproduces from Servius: cf. Pomp. 96.32f. and 199.26, with Serv. 409.35f., *Explan.* 488.18f. and 499.12.

37. With the latter phrase, cf. Pomp. 141.12, *habes in antiquis artibus*; Pomp. 150.34, *ita definierunt antiqui*; Pomp. 151.14, *habes hoc in antiquo tractatu*.

38. Note also Pomp. 284.30–285.9, Pompeius's comments on the form of barbarism that occurs *pronuntiatu*, which differ both from the meaning of Don. 653.5–7H. and from the doctrine of Serv. 444.13–14.

At other times Pompeius seems to furnish differences in judgment or extensions of a lesson that may be all his own. Some of these are little more than departures in minor details.[39] In other places, however, more substantive issues are involved. At 214.33ff. Pompeius comes to accept the *promissivus modus* as an authentic part of the verbal system, although Donatus had rejected it out of hand (632.10H.) and Servius had apparently left the question open, merely noting the arguments on both sides.[40] Pompeius similarly stakes out a position independent of Servius at 273.25ff., when he confronts the problem of *usque* in the Vergilian phrase *ad usque columnas* (*Aen.* 11.262). Pompeius first applies the rule (273.25) that a preposition cannot be joined with a preposition, in order to show that *usque* here cannot be a preposition. Then, recalling the principle that if any part of speech "ceases to be what it is," it becomes an adverb,[41] he shows that this in turn is in conflict with the rule (274.4–5; cf. 255.6ff.) that a preposition (here, *ad*) cannot be joined with an adverb. He therefore concludes that since the rules are in conflict, *usque* can be regarded as either an adverb or a preposition:

> ob hanc causam, quoniam nec illud nec illud verum est, utrumque accipitur. habemus enim hoc in iure: in plerisque regulis, ubi neque illa firmissima est neque illa firmissima est, utrique consentimus. quoniam nec illud firmissimum est nec illud firmissimum est, ita fit ut defendatur utraque pars. (274.9–14)

Although Pompeius knew Servius's discussion of this problem,[42] the last rule of thumb has no counterpart here or elsewhere in Servius, who takes a different position on the matter.[43] Moreover, Pompeius applies that same rule of thumb at one other point in the commentary, where again he appears to be independent of Servius.[44]

39. E.g., Pomp. 288.28–35 vs. Serv. 445.36–446.2 (with Schindel, *Figurenlehren* 22), on the origins of the term *soloecismus*; Pomp. 269.22ff. vs. Serv. 441.30f., a license granted by Servius but emphatically denied by Pompeius.

40. Cf. Serv. 412.6–12; *Explan.* 503.30–504.3. Note that one of Pompeius's arguments (215.10–17) shows no trace in the surviving versions of Servius's commentary and may be Pompeius's invention.

41. Pomp. 273.34f., *legimus enim talem regulam*, referring to Pomp. 250.36ff. Cf. pp. 143ff. above.

42. Cf. Pomp. 274.17–19, with Serv. 442.23–25.

43. See Serv. 419.16–21 and 442.15–25, denying that *usque* can be an adverb and identifying it as a *praepositio novo modo sibi aliam [coniungens] praepositionem*.

44. See Pomp. 166.6ff., on the accusative forms *duo/duos, ambo/ambos*. Neither the extant version of Servius nor *Explan.* contributes anything on this point, and Servius is silent on the morphology of *duo(s)* and *ambo(s)* in his commentary on Vergil; contrast DServ. at *Ecl.* 5.68 and 6.18, and at *Aen.* 12.342 (on this form of

Pompeius's independent forays are not all equally successful. When discussing how the doubling of medial consonantal -i- can lengthen the preceding syllable in a word such as *Troi(i)a*,[45] Pompeius cites *arma virum tabulasque et Troia gaza per undas* (*Aen.* 1.119). He appears to have chosen the example himself; he also appears to be unaware that *Troia* in that verse cannot possibly be scanned to support his point.[46] Pompeius stumbles similarly elsewhere.[47] And in at least one place, we can watch as Pompeius's self-sufficiency rebounds to leave him noticeably discomfited.

When taking up the topic of barbarism (283.37ff.), Pompeius draws a traditional distinction, noting that what would be a barbarism in prose is regarded as a metaplasm in poetry.[48] But Pompeius goes on to add, *sed plerumque contingit ut etiam in versibus deprehendamus barbarismos* (283.37f.), explaining that if a barbarism in verse is not justified by the demands of meter, it is a barbarism no less than in prose and cannot be passed off as a metaplasm (284.3ff.).[49] Pompeius here is extending the doctrine of barbarism in the direction of greater strictness; he goes on to make the analogous claim when he comes to the section on solecism (289.2-6), insisting that a solecism remains such in verse and cannot be excused as a *figura* if it is not justified *metri necessitate*. The unusual stringency of Pompeius's teaching in both places is owed to no one else—certainly not to Servius[50]—and it causes Pompeius difficulty when he encounters the different doctrine of solecism that Servius transmitted from the elder Pliny:

Plinius sic dicit, "quando sit soloecismus, quando sit schema [= *figura*, "figure"], sola intellegentia discernit." noli te referre ad illud, quod

---

the Servian commentary, see Chap. 5, n. 2). Cf. also below at n. 66: Pomp. 136.18ff. vs. Serv. 428.26-31.

45. Pomp. 105.37-106.3. Pompeius, like Servius (cf. 422.6, 423.28ff.), believed that the -o- was short by nature.

46. The example does not occur in the corresponding passages of Servius and *Explan.*; Servius gives a different, if equally false, explanation of the scansion of *Aen.* 1.119 in his commentary *ad loc.*

47. E.g., Pomp. 158.16, an inept and apparently independent citation of *Aen.* 1.343: cf. Serv. 407.32, 431.25; *Explan.* 492.2f. Or Pomp. 210.16ff., where Pompeius adduces *Ecl.* 3.1, *dic mihi, Damoeta, cuium pecus*, to illustrate the supposed genitive forms *cuia* and *cuium*; the example does not appear in Serv. or *Explan.*, and Servius's Vergilian commentary *ad loc.* gives the correct explanation.

48. Cf. Don. 653.2-3H., Serv. 444.8-11.

49. Cf. Pomp. 284.13ff., the examples *Catilinna* vs. *Catilina*.

50. The statement concerning barbarism might be thought a case of Pompeius's making explicit what was implied by Servius; see Serv. 444.8-11, with 447.22f. = Pomp. 296.4f. But the extension to solecism, which corresponds to nothing in Servius and is inconsistent with, e.g., Serv. 447.22f., is certainly Pompeius's.

diximus de metaplasmis. nam [et]⁵¹ in soloecismo hoc quaeritur, utrum sciens hoc fecerit an nesciens: si sciens fecerit, erit schema; si nesciens fecerit, erit soloecismus. (292.13–17 = Serv. 447.5–10 = Plin. frg. 125 della Casa)

Confronted with Pliny's claim, Pompeius begins to thrash about, adverting to his doctrine *de metaplasmis* but insisting it does not apply *in soloecismo*—seeming to ignore the fact that he had himself extended the same doctrine to solecisms a few pages earlier. The reason for Pompeius's uneasiness is clear. In order to extend that doctrine to solecism, Pompeius now realizes, he must be prepared—as he is not—explicitly to convict Vergil of solecism:

in hoc loco quid dicimus? "pars in frusta secant"⁵² et "pars in frusta secat": et ita et ita stat versus, unde apparet quoniam adfectavit novitatem.⁵³ nefas est autem de isto tanto viro credere per inperitiam hoc fecisse, non per scientiam adfectasse novitatem. (292.20–23)

According to Pompeius's earlier lesson, Vergil's coupling of a singular subject with a plural verb should be judged a solecism in this line, since it plainly cannot be justified *metri necessitate*: *et ita et ita stat versus*. But Pompeius recoils—*nefas est*—and in excusing Vergil must swallow his own inconsistency. The disgruntled note on which he ends the discussion shows that he is conscious of doing so, and not entirely pleased:

hoc [= the restatement of Pliny's formulation, 292.23–27] quidem dixit [sc. Plinius]. tamen quivis potest facere soloecismum et dicere "figuram feci," si noluerit rationem reddere. nihil est hoc, licentia est prava. (292.27–29)

Pompeius's piety before Vergil may overcome the logic of his rule, but he is not willing to let go of the rule gracefully.

These displays of independence, if they do not uniformly increase our regard for Pompeius as a scholar, should nonetheless soften the impression that he was a simple plagiarist. They scarcely touch at all, however, on what is distinctly Pompeius, the tone and style of the text. More than any other Latin grammatical work, the commentary allows us to hear a

---

51. Although printed by Keil, *et* here cannot be correct.
52. *Aen.* 1.212, from Servius; cf. Serv. 447.11, with 446.37f. = Pomp. 291.20; and Serv. 448.2f. On this stock example, see also Chap. 5 n. 77.
53. Cf. Serv. 447.8: *novitatis cupidi.*

living, idiosyncratic voice.[54] To that voice and its nuances we can now turn our attention.

The most conspicuous characteristic, perhaps already revealed in some of the excerpts above, is Pompeius's prolixity. Pompeius evidently believed that he had not made his point unless he had made it at least twice. He repeats himself launching a piece of instruction; he repeats himself referring to scholars; he repeats himself registering approval. So in his pleasure that the pronoun stands second in the order of the parts of speech—*et hoc bene secundum est. bene secunda est ista particula* (97.3–4)—he sounds uncannily like a distant ancestor of Polonius: "That's good. 'Mobbled queen' is good."[55] Above all, he repeats himself to make certain the abstract principle he is stating does not merely receive the necessary stress but is given specific application through an example: a typical passage will find him first stating the rule twice, once with direct reference to his audience and himself (*tu hoc scire debes; conputamus*) and again with reference to the world at large (*quisquis vult*), then repeating the rule twice more with a specific example, as he responds to an imagined request from his audience (*quando dicis mihi . . .*).[56]

Often the examples are vivid and seem to bubble up spontaneously, to reveal now a taste for the amenities (*bene olebant in hospitio meo rosae*),[57] now a touch of the macabre: when he wants to clarify the meaning of *totus*, he says, "What's this that I've said? Pay attention. Take, for example, 'The whole man was eaten up by a bear': look now, what does it mean? The whole man all at once, so that nothing was left. 'The whole man was eaten up,' that is, his hands, feet, back, everything" (204.11–14). In like fashion Pompeius tosses off allusions to simple features of contemporary life as he flows along. He expects his audience to regard "Gaudentius" as a typical slave name or to recognize that *birrus* was a corrupt noun in the *communis sermo*.[58] When he comes to the treatment of proper names in the *Ars*, he passes along the traditional distinction between *nomen* and *cognomen*—then in the same breath acknowledges

54. Cf. Holtz, "Tradition" 50, *Donat* 236f.

55. Cf., e.g., Pomp. 182.30–32, 184.12–15, 227.23–25, 249.13–19; examples could be gathered from any page.

56. See, e.g., Pomp. 112.6–15, his instructions for distinguishing the length of syllables; and contrast the parallel passage at Serv. 423.14–15.

57. Pomp. 102.8, prompted by the single word *rosa*, which appears to have stood as the example in Servius: cf. Serv. 428.18f.; *Explan.* 520.30f.

58. Slave name: Pomp. 141.13f., 142.16; cf. the remarks of Schindel, *Figuren-lehren* 29f., on the distinctively African names "Aventius" and "Amantius" used in an example at Pomp. 286.7–9. *Nomen corruptum*: Pomp. 178.30–33, referring to *birrus* as a corruption of *burrus*, πυρρός; cf. Pompeius's use of the word as a proper name at 210.11, *Birrus* (= *Burrus*, Πυρρός; cf. *TLL* 2.2252.31ff.).

that the old system of nomenclature has passed out of use: "We can't nowadays say, 'What is your cognomen?' We'd get laughed at if we did" (140.35–141.3). Similarly, he breaks off a discussion of nouns that occur only in the plural to pursue a tangent—a *quaestio* concerning the morphology of *Pascha*—in a way that suggests the matter was of some personal interest:

> idcirco etiam debemus hoc animadvertere, quod aliquis obiecit. quaerebatur "Pascha" cuius est numeri. dies festus est: omnia nomina dierum festorum numeri sunt tantum pluralis, "Vulcanalia," "Compitalia." dicebat ille qui obiciebat etiam hoc numeri esse tantum pluralis. sed sunt causae quae repugnant: primo, quod. . . . deinde. . . . unde constat non esse numeri pluralis. (177.3ff.)

This is the only indication in the work that Pompeius was a Christian (as we should anyway expect), and it is probably fair to infer that he himself had been nettled by *ille qui obiciebat*. The passage suggests a vignette from the life of Pompeius's African town, a group of local learned men in conversation, perhaps, falling into debate over a matter of grammatical detail: *quaerebatur* . . . A reminder of the time that Gellius and his mentors spent pondering the sense of *nani* in the vestibule of the imperial palace or that Libanius and his friend Eudaemon of Pelusium spent discussing the vocative of "Heracles" while awaiting the arrival of the governor at Antioch, the passage is also a token of the continuity that can be traced through changes of place and time.[59]

To match emphatic repetitions and vivid examples, there are turns of phrase to rivet his audience. Most common is Pompeius's beloved *ecce*, his constant gesture of satisfaction, whether in producing an illustration, launching into an explanation he likes, or rounding off a lesson.[60] Only slightly less constant, and equally flexible, is Pompeius's *vide*, now warning, now peremptory, now patently excited.[61] He conveys a similar excitement in the clipped *quare . . . ? quare? quoniam . . . ,*[62] or in the questions (or statements, or commands) cast in the form *numquid* [or *non*, or *ne*] . . . ? *non. sed* [or *nam*, or *autem*] . . . —a question, when Pompeius is

---

59. Gell. *NA* 19.13; Lib. *Ep.* 255.6–7, with Part II no. 55. Cf. also the disagreement between Aetius and his γραμματικός at Anazarbus, "Prologue" p. 6 above; and the scene imagined by Macrobius, *Sat.* 1.4–5, with Chap. 5 p. 171.

60. E.g., Pomp. 103.14, 123.20f., 128.37, 129.12f., 134.23f., 194.36f., and *passim*.

61. E.g., Pomp. 104.16f.: *quando "u" nihil est? tunc "u" nihil est—vide qua subtilitate nihil est!—si dicas "quoniam."* Cf. Pomp. 127.25ff., 139.26f., 144.16f., 163.7, 184.17, 224.36, 227.23, and *passim*.

62. E.g., Pomp. 116.33f.; cf. Pomp. 149.37ff.

trying to make plain the sound of vocalic *u*;[63] a flat statement, when he is
treating the quality of the letter *a*;[64] or an abrupt command, when he is
discussing the prosody of *cano* in the first line of the *Aeneid*.[65] These and
other features of Pompeius's language can best be savored in a characteristic passage such as the following, in which Pompeius discusses the
questions that arise when a *nomen* (i.e., an adjective) is used as an adverb,
or an adverb is used as a *nomen* (i.e., a noun):[66]

> Don't let anyone tell you, "If we sometimes use an adverb as a noun,
> we are also obliged to decline the adverb itself." Impossible. For when
> a *nomen* is put in place of an adverb, it maintains its cases; but when an
> adverb passes into the place of a *nomen*, there's no way it can take on a
> case. Don't say to me, "*hoc mane*:[67] now, if *hoc mane* is a noun, you
> ought to decline *huius manis, huic mani*." We don't find that sort of
> explanation [*ratio ista*]; it can't follow that it's declined. "Nonetheless,
> we read that very declension, *a primo mani*, in Plautus.[68] Where did *a
> mani* come from, if there isn't the declension *mane, manis, mani*?" *mane*,
> from which *a primo mani* came, produced the declension. But we still
> shouldn't decline it. Why? You want to know why? Because an adverb
> absolutely cannot be declined. . . . When we say *torvum clamat*,[69] *torvum*
> is now an adverb, and *torvum* stands for *torve*. I'm not allowed, am I, to
> say, for example, *torvi clamat, torvo clamat, a torvo clamat*? I'm not, but I
> pick up that one case for the special use [*ad usurpationem*]. If, therefore, I
> pick up that one case when I produce the adverb, and I can't pick up
> the other cases, so too when I use an adverb in place of a noun, I'm
> not allowed to decline it, but have to put the adverb itself in place of
> the noun. (136.18–35)

Logic is not the argument's strong point: "But we still shouldn't decline
it. Why? You want to know why? Because an adverb absolutely cannot
be declined." The passage does have a brute movement about it, though,

63. E.g., Pomp. 103.34ff.; cf. Pomp. 143.22f., 230.1–3.
64. E.g., Pomp. 106.16f.; cf. Pomp. 138.36ff., 139.16f.
65. E.g., Pomp. 118.7f.; cf. Pomp. 138.2f., 191.31ff., 240.10ff., 252.30f.
66. The discussion is directed implicitly against Servius's position; cf. Serv.
428.26–31. Pompeius probably has Servius in mind when he begins, *nequi tibi
dicat, "si aliquotiens fungimur adverbio pro nomine, debemus etiam declinare hoc ipsum
adverbium"* (Pomp. 136.18–20): cf. Serv. 428.26f., *item adverbium si transeat in sig-
nificationem nominis, non nunquam declinatur*; and cf. n. 68 below.
67. Alluding to *Georg.* 3.325, *dum mane novum*, cited earlier at Pomp. 136.3f.
68. *Most.* 767, *usque a mani ad vesperum*, the example on which Servius based
his case; see Serv. 428.28–30.
69. *Aen.* 7.399, cited earlier at Pomp. 135.38.

as the repetitions, warnings, and emphatic questions hammer the point home.

In this passage, as in any number of others, it is also notable that Pompeius speaks as though to one other person, the second person singular, *tu*.[70] Here he imagines the reader offering an objection or counter-example—*ne dicas mihi, "hoc mane"*—or exposed to some third-party influence: *nequi tibi dicat, "si aliquotiens. . . ."* Similar turns of thought appear frequently in the small dialogues with which Pompeius spices the commentary. Compare, for instance, Pompeius's ruminations on the letter *u*,

> puta si dicas mihi, "'unus,' 'u' qualis est?" dico tibi, "nescio utrum brevis sit an producta, nisi . . ." (106.31ff.),

or on barbarisms,

> et dico tibi, "in versu barbarismus est." tu dicis mihi, "quo modo mihi dixisti . . . ? quo modo?" (284.38ff.).

Such dialogues, to which we shall return below, reinforce the impression Pompeius's discourse creates with its freely flowing repetitions, its spontaneous tangents, or its abrupt questions and commands. Pompeius is a man talking, not writing, and talking with his audience either face-to-face or vividly fixed in his imagination. The impression has been noted before,[71] although doubtless these features of Pompeius's style could equally occur in a work composed at the writing desk. It is, however, possible to go beyond the mere impression that Pompeius was speaking, with his words taken down by a notary; for Pompeius has left unequivocal indications that that is just what he was doing.

The best evidence occurs where Pompeius takes up the notion of *vox* and the distinction between *vox articulata* and *vox confusa*:

> vox dicitur quicquid sonuerit, sive strepitus sit ruinae sive fluvii currentis, sive vox nostra, sive mugitus boum: omnis sonus vox dicitur.

70. Against the several hundred times that the second person singular occurs, the second person plural is found in just over two dozen places, mostly in references either to *auctores* (e.g., Pomp. 167.10, *legite in Petronio et invenietis*, a citation certainly taken over from Servius [cf. Serv. 432.24f.]; Pomp. 186.2, *habetis in ipso Cicerone*; sim. Pomp. 153.12, 242.5, 293.27f., 305.7f., 306.17ff.) or to the technical literature (e.g., Pomp. 114.1, *habetis hanc rationem in Iuba*; Pomp. 138.20, *legite artem Probi et invenietis*; sim. Pomp. 109.34, 137.33, 139.34f., 246.34f., 269.10, 280.12f., 295.34ff., 297.34f.), only once in one of Pompeius's warnings to the reader (253.23f.), never in one of the characteristic dialogues.

71. Cf. Holtz, "Tradition" 50, *Donat* 236f.

verum hae duae sunt partes, articulata et confusa. articulata est vox
quae potest scribi: ut ecce hoc ipsum quod dixi potest scribi. (99.9–12)

As the characteristically extended list of examples shows, Pompeius is
thinking of *vox* as real sound, the physical phenomenon; and when he
exemplifies *vox articulata* by saying, *ut ecce hoc ipsum quod dixi*, he must be
referring self-consciously to his own speech, the *sonus* he is making—
which, as he is also aware, is being written down as he speaks: *potest
scribi.*[72] The statement scarcely makes sense otherwise, and some other
passages are most naturally interpreted in the same way.

Listen, for example, to the following, where Pompeius expands on
Donatus's mention (612.7–8H.) of the *periodos*:

et non dixit quem ad modum fiant, aut quare quaerantur periodi, aut
qui sint periodi—vel quae periodi (nam feminino genere dicimus hoc
nomen). (281.22–24)

Here Pompeius realizes he has made a slip in the gender of *periodos*, and
we can suppose it was more likely a *lapsus linguae* than a *lapsus stili*:
although the error obviously occurred to him immediately, he did not
simply remove it with a stroke, but flowed right along, adding the correct
phrase in midstream.[73] Another, perhaps still better sign of oral composition comes in Pompeius's treatment of iotacism:[74]

iotacismi sunt qui fiunt per "i" litteram, siqui ita dicat "Titius" pro
eo quod est "Titius" [i.e., "Titsius"], "Aventius" pro eo quod est "Aventius" [i.e., "Aventsius"], "Amantius" pro eo quod est "Amantius" [i.e.,
"Amantsius"]. . . . non debemus dicere ita, quem ad modum scribitur
"Titius," sed "Titius" [i.e., "Titsius"]: media illa syllaba mutatur in
sibilum. ergo si volueris dicere "ti" vel "di," noli, quem ad modum
scribitur, sic proferre, sed sibilo profer. (286.7–9, 14–16)[75]

72. With *ut ecce hoc ipsum quod dixi potest scribi* contrast the parallel passage at
Explan. 519.15–18: *articulata est quae scribi potest, quae subest articulis* [= Pomp.
99.12ff.], *id est digitis, qui scribunt, vel quod artem habeat aut exprimat. . . . ergo si dicas
"orator," articulata vox est.*

73. Compare Pomp. 252.14–18, 297.19–27: in both places Pompeius begins
to illustrate a lesson with an example, then realizes that the example was not
well chosen and abruptly shifts to another, leaving the inept example in his
wake. Cf. also the shift from *quo vadis?* to *quo festinas?* in the example used at
Pomp. 235.16ff., quoted at p. 158 below.

74. Pompeius here reverses the correct doctrine concerning iotacism (contrast
Serv. 445.8–10), but the confusion does not affect the point under discussion.

75. See also Pomp. 286.20–24, on *dies* vs. *meridies*; Pomp. 286.24–28, on *castius*.
For *Titius*, see also Pomp. 104.6f.

The passage makes sense only if Pompeius distinguished the forms as he spoke: evidently Pompeius did say "Titsius," but his amanuensis simply rendered the word in its usual written form, *quem ad modum scribitur.*[76] It is appropriate, therefore, to note that elsewhere one of Pompeius's illustrations for the *nomen proprium* presumes he would as a matter of course have had a notary.[77]

We can pause here to piece together the picture of Pompeius that has emerged so far. We should first of all imagine Pompeius sitting with his version of Servius open before him, a version probably supplied with lemmata from Donatus's text. He sometimes reads directly from his Servius, but more commonly he paraphrases or elaborates upon it; at times he ignores the distinction between what his source has said and what he is saying himself, and at times he confuses Donatus with Servius. As he goes along, he might supplement or alter the commentary in front of him, relying on a few written sources at hand, or on his memory, or on his own mother wit, striking out on tangents or repeating and emphasizing his point *ad libitum* in his own distinctive voice, while his notary takes it all down. The picture is consistent and almost complete: one question remains, concerning his audience. Who, after all, are "you"?

We can begin to sketch an answer by recalling Louis Holtz's sympathetic observation that more than any other Latin grammatical work, Pompeius brings us directly into the grammarian's classroom.[78] The remark is just, in the sense that we hear in Pompeius's text a teacher's voice, speaking with some immediacy. But I would like to suggest that the text does not bring us directly into the classroom—the second person singular by itself tells against this—and to refine Holtz's observation by drawing attention to a set of passages in which Pompeius reveals the audience he has in mind.

Consider, for example, the implications of the following vignettes Pompeius uses to illustrate the proper application of the future tense:

> festinanter vadis nescio quo per plateam, occurrit tibi amicus et dicit tibi, "quo vadis?"—ut advertas, quam gravia sic fiunt vitia—dicit tibi, "quo festinas?," dicis, "ad auditorium festino." "quare?" melius, si

---

76. Keil resisted the urge to print *Titsius*, etc. (see his *app. crit.*, *ad loc.*), against Lindemann and against Wilmanns, "Katalog" 402.

77. Pomp. 141.28f.: *puta notarium meum volo vocare "Africanum."*

78. Holtz, "Tradition" 50, "ce text n'a pas son équivalent pour nous faire réellement pénétrer dans l'école du *grammaticus*"; and more specifically *Donat* 236, "le seul texte de l'Antiquité romaine qui nous faire entendre les paroles mêmes du maître en présence de ses élèves"; with n. 37, suggesting "un cours publié d'après les notes sténographiques." Cf. also Keil, *GL* 5.89, 90; Helm, *RE* 21.2313.31ff. We should not, however, forget the fragment of the *Ars grammatica accepta ex auditorio Donatiani* (*GL* 6.275.11, with Part II no. 51); and cf. Chap. 5, on Servius.

participialiter utaris et dicas, "quoniam dicturus sum." ecce per participium sane locutus es: dixisti enim te necdum fecisse, sed facturum esse. si autem sic dicas—"quo festinas?" "ad auditorium." "quare?" "hodie dico."—soloecismum fecisti. "dico" enim non est nisi eius qui agit, qui iam facit hoc ipsum. ergo siqui dicit, "hodie dico," qui adhuc vadit ad dicendum, iam videtur soloecismum facere. (235.16–24)

ergo siquis tibi hoc iterum dicat, "exponis mihi hodie lectionem?," si dicam, "expono," soloecismus est. non enim exponis, non adhuc facis, sed facturus es. (236.19–21)

In the first passage the reader is imagined to be hurrying across the town square on his way to speak in the schoolroom (*auditorium*). In the second, related passage, he is asked if he plans to lecture on a text (*exponere lectionem*).[79] In other words, the reader seems to be thought of as a teacher, setting out on his day, fielding questions from fellow townsmen interested in his plans. The scene might remind one of the grammarian in Juvenal, stopped on his way to the baths to answer less innocuous questions (7.232ff.), and such scenes were doubtless a part of Pompeius's own experience.

That the *tu* of the commentary is thought of as a teacher much like Pompeius himself is confirmed in other passages. After setting out the rules of antepenultimate accent, Pompeius advises the reader not to concern himself with unnecessary details when he is discussing the matter: *ergo noli te in diversas ambages mittere, sed tracta quando debeat accentum habere* (129.32f.). The significant word is the verb *tracta*, virtually a technical term of the grammarian's professional activity, applied by Pompeius throughout the work both to himself (e.g., *tractaturus sum*, 98.25) and to Donatus (e.g., *tractaturus est*, 98.21–22).[80]

When explaining how poor punctuation can undermine the rules of accentuation, Pompeius warns the reader of the risk of misleading a student through his own error: *si male distinguas, potest errare puer* (130.31ff.). The reference to the student (*puer*) in the third person shows that the text does not derive from Pompeius's schoolroom; rather, the reader himself appears to be thought of as a teacher, who must guard against setting a bad example for the student.[81] A passage on punctuation

79. On Pomp. 236.20, *dicam*, see below at n. 84. For *lectio* meaning "text" in a similar context, see Pomp. 141.34ff.; and cf. n. 82 below.

80. With reference to Pompeius, see also Pomp. 128.16f., 132.5f., 135.36, 256.18, 289.14; with reference to Donatus, Pomp. 96.10ff., 133.4, 155.1, 156.11, 159.23, 162.3, 164.28, 165.15f., 231.32, 238.38, 244.21, 281.27 (*bis*), 289.15, 292.30f. (*bis*), 305.2, 305.34; similarly Pomp. 180.31, of Probus.

81. For *pueri*, beyond the passages quoted below, see also Pomp. 293.19f.; and cf. the version of the preface published by Holtz, "Tradition" 59f.

proper that follows shortly—*quod si vis codicem distinguere, ita distingue* (132.1)—makes my point plainer still. Once more the reader is warned against leading the student into error: *ne erret puer et male pronuntiet. . . . ne erret puer et dicat . . .* (132.7ff.). And from the context it is clear Pompeius is thinking of the grammarian's task of *praelectio* and of the punctuation of his codex for that purpose.[82]

In discussing the correct definition of the noun, Pompeius stresses the importance of making the definition clear to the student: *ut possit puer intellegere* (137.18). Here again Pompeius is thinking of the reader as a teacher, and note that he immediately thinks of Donatus in the same terms: *idcirco laborat* [sc. *Donatus*] *ut definitionem nominis propriam reddat* (137.20). A few pages farther on, Pompeius offers another bit of coaching, this time in the classroom practice of question and answer (142.35–143.8). Pompeius provides two examples of how a teacher ought to handle the questions put to and by a student. In the first example (142.36ff.) Pompeius plays the teacher as *interrogator*, and the *puer* replies—the format, to take only the most obvious example, of Donatus's *Ars minor*. In the second example, *ceterum, si te interroget* [sc. *puer*] (143.4f.), the reader takes Pompeius's place and responds to the student's question—ineptly, as it happens, so that Pompeius can reinforce his advice by pointing out the correct procedure.[83]

There are other, comparable passages, to which we will come shortly; but these examples should suffice to show how Pompeius thinks of his audience. Pompeius is talking to another *grammaticus*—or, more strictly, he is talking to an imagined audience presumed to share the point of view and concerns of Pompeius himself as *grammaticus*.[84] Notionally, then,

---

82. On punctuation for reading by the grammarian, see Bonner, *Education* 220–22, esp. 221, citing Pomp. 133.4ff. Bonner assumes, no doubt rightly for most circumstances, that only the teacher would have a text: in the *Hermeneumata Pseudodositheana, colloquia Monacensia* (CGL 3.122.26–29 = 3.646), *clamatus ad lectionem audio expositiones, sensus, personas* seems to imply that the student listened while the teacher lectured from his own text; the version of the *Hermeneumata* published by Dionisotti, "From Ausonius' Schooldays?" 100 (line 37, *eunt priores ad magistrum, legunt lectionem de Iliade, aliam de Odysseia*; and cf. line 39, *tunc revertitur quisque, in suo loco consident. quisque legit lectionem sibi subtraditam*), seems to show students reading from a text prepared by the teacher. Cf. also Lib. *Or.* 1.9: Libanius stands by his teacher's chair while reading *Acharnians*.

83. For questions put to teachers by their students, see the general comment of Eutyches, *GL* 5.447.1ff. (quoted at Part II no. 57); and the questions put by Filocalus and Rusticus at *Explan.* 498.23ff., with Part II no. 217.

84. *Tu* does not denote a specific listener but is used in the generalizing sense of "one," "someone in our position": note esp. the shift from second to first person and back again in Pomp. 236.19–21 at p. 159 above (*siquis tibi . . . dicat,* "*exponis mihi hodie lectionem?*," *si dicam,* "*expono*," *soloecismus est. non enim exponis*) and the interchangeability of *probas* and *probamus* in the formulas *unde hoc probas?*

the commentary is a manual for colleagues. In this respect Pompeius's work is comparable to Donatus's variorum commentary on Vergil, expressly composed as an aid "for the *grammaticus* still wet behind the ears."[85] Pompeius no doubt assumed his audience would use his commentary as he used Servius's, as part of the inherited *Gemeingut* of the profession, taking it over as his own. At the same time, and because it is intended as a manual for colleagues, the commentary offers the closest approximation that we have to a grammarian's extended musings on his profession—often oblique, offhand, and rambling, to be sure, but for that reason more unself-conscious, more revealing, than the poise of formal reflection. Whatever its other shortcomings, Pompeius's text is exceptionally vivid evidence for the grammarian's mind-set.

To appreciate this cast of mind we might look first at a passage similar to those just noted. While reviewing the category of nouns defective in two or more cases, Pompeius says, *vide autem, quid dicit ipse Donatus: ait 'sed haec, quae dico deficere, secundum usum dico, ceterum scio me legisse haec ipsa quae deficiunt"* (186.34ff.). The statement attributed to Donatus is in fact an extended paraphrase of *sunt nomina quorum nominativus in usu non est* (625.10H.). Leaving aside the question how far Pompeius has stretched Donatus's intended meaning here, we can identify the motive behind the paraphrase easily enough. For Pompeius soon points out that the nominative forms of certain words (*later, Iovis*), although not in common use, can indeed be found in literary texts (*in auctoritate*); and he concludes, *ideo dixi, ne putes istum* [viz., Donatum] *inperitum esse aut te omnia debere dicere. ita enim locutus est, "sunt aliqua quorum nominativus in usu non est"* [i.e., 625.10H.; see above]; *non dixit "quorum nominativus non est quidem," sed "in usu non est." ergo vides quia docuit lecta esse, sed non debere poni* (187.13–16). Thus the passage has two purposes beyond the stringent lesson of the last sentence, which Pompeius has inferred from or imposed on Donatus's text. First, Pompeius is intent on defending Donatus—*ne putes istum inperitum esse*—by claiming that Donatus of course knew the rare forms and signaled his knowledge in the phrase *in usu non est*. Second, Pompeius takes the opportunity to offer an object lesson to his reader, evidently imagined as a teacher in the same position and subject to the same criticisms as Donatus, by assuring the reader that he is not obliged to tell everything he knows: *ne putes . . . te omnia debere dicere*. A well-chosen formula—like Donatus's *in usu non est*—can make a point clearly, economically, and blamelessly, without a parade of learning that might in the end obscure the teaching.

(Pomp. 114.13, 151.37f., 200.20, 225.23) and *unde hoc probamus?* (Pomp. 159.5, 180.12ff., 185.31f., 196.13); cf. Pomp. 191.38, *unde hoc probem?*

85. Don. *Epist. praef.* 17 Hardie: *grammatico . . . rudi ac nuper exorto.*

The passage is reminiscent of Pompeius's comments, remarked above, on the proper definition of the noun; there his injunction to the reader is linked with praise for Donatus's effort:

> quid si ita definias nomen, ut possit puer intellegere quid sit nomen, ut dicas, "nomen est pars orationis cum casu"? idcirco laborat [sc. Donatus] ut definitionem nominis propriam reddat. (137.18–20)

The two passages are symptomatic of the work's sustained demand for clarity, precision, and logic. (Here, as elsewhere, the disparity between Pompeius's values and his own achievement is not without poignancy.) So, when Donatus is praised, typically the economy and exactness of his organization or his definitions are singled out: in presenting the accidents of the verb, *Donatus tenuit conpendium optimum* (240.3f.); when touching on the period—which strictly "pertains to rhetoricians, not to grammarians"— Donatus *noluit dilatare, ut doceret aperte* (281.27f.); Donatus's definition of the pronoun's *qualitas* is preferred to competing views as *vera . . . et brevis et utilis*, earning Donatus a "well done."[86] Pompeius dispenses similar praise when he thinks he has spotted similar virtues in the doctrine he has inherited from other grammarians, who made their points "carefully" or "plainly" or "vigorously."[87]

Conversely, when Donatus is criticized, the fault is usually superfluity or confusion in presentation, or imprecision in a definition, or the failure to teach *aperte*.[88] Pompeius occasionally softens such criticisms by magisterially assuring the reader that Donatus really did know what he was talking about, even if he expressed himself badly.[89] But he is unforgiving when he finds faults of logic, in explanations or positions that lay themselves open to a *reductio ad absurdum* or are internally inconsistent. His distaste is apparent when he rejects as stupid the belief of many that *de intus venio* is a proper expression and observes that for consistency

86. Pomp. 200.31: *bene hoc fecit Donatus.* See also Pomp. 96.15–17 (with Pomp. 98.6f. and the version of Pompeius's preface published by Holtz, "Tradition" 59f.), 281.9, 289.29, 292.9–11, 307.28f.

87. Pomp. 111.13 and 118.15f. (Terentianus), 139.34 (Apollonius), 154.13f. (Caper), 227.23f. and 283.13f. (Pliny).

88. Superfluity or confusion: Pomp. 140.20, with Don. 614.8–9H. (contrast Pomp. 237.10f., with Don. 638.5–8H.); Pomp. 231.15f., on Don. 636.6–7H. Imprecision: Pomp. 138.12ff., concerning Probus as well. Failure to teach fully and plainly: Pomp. 305.33f., introducing a supplement to Don. 668.7H.; cf. also the omissions criticized at Pomp. 105.19ff., 149.24ff., 151.5ff., 192.12ff., 302.2ff. (with Schindel, *Figurenlehren* 35, 101–2).

89. See Pomp. 279.14ff., a correction already made—but tacitly, it appears, and without the attempted extenuation—in Servius (cf. Serv. 420.8–9, 443.4–5); Pomp. 220.13ff. (a similar correction: cf. Serv. 413.10–13, *Explan.* 506.14–18).

such people would have to embrace the equally awful *ad intro*.[90] So too, it was "extremely stupid" of Probus to include accent among the accidents of the noun, for he might as well have gone on to include letter and syllable and all the other attributes the noun shares with the remaining parts of speech.[91]

A demand for *ratio*—both "reason" and the "clear and systematic account" it provides—pervades the commentary. What does not "make sense" (*habet rationem*) is simply *stultum* and is easily dismissed.[92] But what reason demands is codified in the *ars* and its *regulae*, to produce the *rigor artis* and the *rigor regularum*.[93] It is consistent with this rigor that when faced with the two traditional etymologies of *ars*, from the Greek ἀρετή and from the Latin *artus*, Pompeius should prefer the latter, because of the power of the *ars* to embrace the language with its "tight" or "firm" precepts" (*artis praeceptis*).[94] Surrounded by these, Pompeius is conscious of the special sphere of expertise the *ars* defines for him and other *grammatici*, centering above all on the *partes orationis*, which distinguish the grammarian's territory alike from that of the teacher of letters and from that of the rhetorician.[95] The *ars* fortifies Pompeius and fills him with exuberant confidence: so, for example, he can differentiate between the definitions of the noun according to the *grammatici* and according to the *philosophi*, dismissing the latter as *ridiculum*.[96]

That verdict is characteristic of Pompeius's magisterial tone, as he complacently delights in the support his profession's traditional doctrine lends and in the certain belief that he can separate the precious metal in

90. Pomp. 248.16ff., with 248.38ff.

91. Pomp. 138.22ff., with reference to Prob. *GL* 4.51.22, 74.32ff. (But from Pomp. 139.16ff., *Probus . . . dixit "nomini accidunt qualitas, genus, numerus, figura, casus,"* *et non dat conparationem nomini*, it is clear that Pompeius never set eyes on Probus's text and is probably basing his comments on the report that he found in the full commentary of Servius; this seems preferable to the suggestion of Jeep, *Zur Geschichte der Lehre* 51, that *Probus* in the last sentence is a corruption.) For similar criticisms, see Pomp. 169.19ff. (cf. *Explan.* 495.11, with Jeep, pp. 48f.), 173.26ff. (cf. Jeep, p. 47), 240.34ff. For seeming inconsistencies in Donatus explained away, see Pomp. 170.2ff., 217.10ff.; and cf. below, pp. 164f., on Pomp. 230.19ff.

92. *Stultum est* vs. *habet rationem*, in the vice of *perissologia*, Pomp. 294.11ff.; for the virtue of *rationabiliter dicere* (= *regulariter dicere*, to speak according to the rules laid down by *ratio*), see Pomp. 276.16, 290.31, 310.21f.

93. *Ratio exigit*: Pomp. 185.23, 195.14. *Rigor artis* (vs. *auctores confuderunt*): Pomp. 268.8. *Rigor regularum*: Pomp. 196.9.

94. Pomp. 95.5–96.2, agreeing with the preference of Serv. 405.2.

95. Pomp. 96.2–18. For the sphere of the grammarian distinguished from that of the rhetorician, see also Pomp. 281.25f., 282.34f., 299.20ff. = 300.1ff.

96. Pomp. 137.26f., with 137.36. To judge from *Explan.* 489.22ff., the distinction was already included in Servius's commentary, without the ridicule.

one vein of the tradition from the fool's gold in another. Criticism he
metes out with a curt *stultum* or, if the victim is lucky, a simple *falsum*,
and he adjudicates firmly and surely between competing views.[97] When
the received doctrine works, his pleasure is audible: *vide quam bonam
brevitatem invenerunt Latini*, he exclaims three times in reviewing word
accent (127.25, 128.1, 128.6), and then concludes, *vides quanta brevitate
utantur Latini. Graeci vero chaos fecerunt, totum confuderunt, ut quamvis mille
legas tractatus non te convenias* (130.1f.). And he is plainly satisfied when the
maiores—the ancients, the classical authors—can be thought to have
followed *ratio*.[98] He is satisfied, that is, when the *maiores* seem to behave
as he and his colleagues behave. But when their *auctoritas* goes against
the *regulae firmissimae* he has inherited, his satisfaction gives way to a
strong warning against literary blandishments.[99] The shift is only to be
expected, since the past practitioners who built up the tradition of firm
rules piece by piece have an *auctoritas* of their own,[100] a match for the
auctoritas of antiquity. In the coordination of verbal person and nominal
case, Donatus laid down the law and resolved the *confusiones antiquitatis*:[101]
just so, Pompeius later with a flourish produces a *regula* to resolve a
"great difficulty."[102]

Here as elsewhere we see Pompeius taking his place in the authoritative
tradition and identifying with it. He is ready, not surprisingly, to make
its strengths his own: when he declares, "I have three rules" to deal
with the genitive plural of the third declension, he seems oblivious of
the fact that the rules are not his, but Donatus's.[103] Yet before we
conclude that he is simply pilfering from Donatus, we should remember
that he identifies as readily with the vulnerability of the inherited doctrine
as with its strength. When he touches on the verbs *pudet* and *taedet*
(230.19ff.), he notes an apparent contradiction with what he has said

97. *Stultum*: Pomp. 108.19 (Varro), 110.12 (Iuba), 125.9ff. (*non nulli metrici*),
138.32 and 178.15ff. (Probus), 186.12ff. and 248.17ff. (*multi*), 180.32ff. (Donatus;
subsequently mitigated). *Falsum*: Pomp. 174.21ff. and 222.30ff. (*non nulli*), 193.31ff.
(the elder Pliny), 228.18ff. (*in artibus istis vulgaribus*). Adjudication: e.g., Pomp.
108.29ff. (*multi* and *levis ratio* vs. *multi* and *valentissima* [*ratio*]), 144.14ff. (Caesar vs.
the elder Pliny), 151.18ff. (*multi* vs. *multi*), 164.33ff. (Probus vs. *alii* and *auctoritas*),
209.2ff. (*plerique* vs. Astyagius).
98. Pomp. 193.10ff.; cf. Pomp. 197.4ff., 199.21ff.
99. Pomp. 253.23ff.; cf. Pomp. 232.2–8 and 12–14, 255.31ff., 263.11ff.,
269.22ff.
100. See Pomp. 156.32, *secundum auctoritatem Donati*; Pomp. 159.24, *auctoritatem
ipsius* [viz., *Varronis*]; Pomp. 169.19, *eius* [viz., *Probi*] *auctoritatem*; cf. Pomp. 144.31,
melius est ut sequaris praeceptum tanti viri, Plinii Secundi.
101. Pomp. 237.11–22; cf. Pomp. 110.18.
102. Pomp. 242.15ff., on the derivation of adverbs from proper nouns. On
regulae, auctoritas, maiores, and their interrelation, see Chap. 5 pp. 182ff.
103. Pomp. 191.16ff. = Don. 626.19–627.4H.

previously, then affirms he has not made an error after all: *et illo loco bene . . . dixi et hoc loco bene . . . dixi.* The noteworthy point is that the inconsistency is in fact due to Donatus; but instead of attributing the contradiction to Donatus and treating it in those terms,[104] Pompeius regards the lapse as his own and defends himself.

Pompeius's need for self-defense is virtually a reflex, inseparable from his magisterial tone. His confidence in passing the verdict *stultum* is constantly shadowed by his anxiety in contemplating an attack on his own expertise; his avoidance of *calumnia* and his search for *excusationes*, to show he is not guilty of *inperitia*, are leitmotifs of the commentary.[105] So, for example, in the dialogues with the reader there recur anticipated objections or the dreaded counterexamples that can upset one's *ratio*:[106]

scire debes. . . . ne dicas mihi, "sed. . . . " (138.1f.)

non potest inveniri. . . . ne dicas mihi. . . . (240.10f.)

sed tamen illud meminisse debes. . . . ne dicas mihi ergo, "quoniam. . . . " (269.22ff.)

Above all, Pompeius is intent on preparing the reader, the alter ego of his *tu*, for situations in which he can expect to be put on his mettle. "If anyone asks you" is a constant refrain,[107] together with the negative counterpart, "Take care lest anyone put a question to you in this matter."[108] You must anticipate the question, How do you prove this?[109] and can expect to be challenged especially on doubtful or ambiguous points.[110] As a result, you must also be on guard against being deceived, sometimes by the language itself,[111] but also by the tricks and cross-grained ingenuity of your fellow men:

104. As at Pomp. 217.10ff. (referring to Don. 633.2–4H., 639.10–12H.; cf. Serv. 437.8–10), explaining that the contradiction was only superficial; cf. n. 91 above.

105. *Calumnia*: Pomp. 153.25ff., 158.34ff., 205.7ff., 283.1ff. *Excusatio*: Pomp. 155.1ff., 159.27ff., 229.4f.

106. E.g., Pomp. 138.28., 177.31f., 180.13ff., 191.31ff., 202.1ff., 260.25ff., 263.11ff., 284.38ff., with Pomp. 136.18–35, translated at p. 155 above. For Pompeius's use of counterexamples, see, e.g., 115.15–21, 164.33ff.

107. E.g., Pomp. 160.19ff., 166.6–7, 175.22ff., 230.11ff., 262.40f.

108. E.g., Pomp. 138.15f., 227.36f.; cf. Pomp. 142.23ff., 228.36ff.

109. *Unde hoc probas*: see n. 84.

110. Pomp. 256.20ff.: *plerumque proponitur nobis et dicitur, " 'amans' quae pars est orationis?," et videmus quod et nomen est et participium. videamus ergo discretionem ipsam.*

111. See Pomp. 141.25, *sed non te decipiat ista res nec fallat*, with, e.g., Pomp. 153.15f., 163.7, 175.11, 179.15f., 270.15f. For Donatus so deceived, see Pomp. 243.19ff., 270.27ff.

quare hoc dico? solent aliqui homines plerumque esse callidi, et inter-
rogat te aliquis et dicit tibi, " 'Lucius' quale nomen est?" "proprium."
"quae pars est proprii nominis?" dicis illi, "praenomen." dicit tibi,
"falsum est: nam ecce servus meus ita appellatur et non habet praenomen."[112] (142.8–12)

This anxious hedging against a world of continuous challenges produces an interesting symptom in Pompeius's comments, a tendency
toward plainly subjective interpretations through which he projects his
own concerns and defenses onto Donatus. When, for example, Donatus
takes up the subject of nouns that waver between the feminine and
neuter genders—*sunt incerti generis inter femininum et neutrum, ut "buxus,"*
"pirus," "prunus," "malus," sed neutro fructum, feminino ipsas arbores saepe
dicimus (621.1–2H.)—Pompeius's comment focuses on the phrase *saepe*
dicimus, which Donatus used to qualify his distinction between the neuter
(the fruit) and the feminine (the trees): *et interposuit "saepe dicimus." scit*
enim esse arborem et masculini generis quae sit et neutri, ut "siler" neutri est,
"oleaster" masculini est (163.31–33). In other words, Pompeius takes *saepe*
to be Donatus's means of protecting himself against counterexamples,
which Donatus is also presumed to know: *scit enim*. There is, of course,
no explicit sign of this in Donatus's text.[113]

The concern with counterexamples here is Pompeius's own, imposed
on Donatus's words. Although it is surely possible that Donatus had
some such point in mind in this case, the chance is slim he did in every
other. Reviewing the use of the various cases with various verbs, Donatus
says, *alia* [sc. *verba*] *accusativi* [sc. *casus formulam servant*], *ut "accuso,"*
"invoco" (638.14H.). Pompeius comments:

"accuso" accusativum regit tantum modo, "accuso illum": non possumus dicere "accuso illius." hoc satis latinum est; nemo potest dicere
"accuso illius." quis hoc nesciat? sed timuit vim Graecam. Graeci
enim "accuso illius" dicunt, κατηγορῶ ἐκείνου. ergo ut faceret differentiam propter Graecam elocutionem, ideo huius rei reddit rationem.
ubi enim dubitatum est, utrum hoc sic possit dici? semper "accuso
illum" dicimus. sed propter expressionem verbi Graeci ideo hoc fecit.
(238.19–26)

112. For the principle, viz., that a slave does not possess a *praenomen*, see
Pomp. 141.24ff. For trick questions, see also the exchange just preceding, Pomp.
141.34ff., and, e.g., Pomp. 231.34f.
113. Compare Pomp. 186.34ff., the interpretation of *in usu non est* (Don.
625.10H.), discussed on p. 161 above. With *scit enim*, cf. Pomp. 162.2ff., *sciens . . .*
tractat in the interpretation of Don. 620.1–5H.

Pompeius is evidently surprised that Donatus has bothered to say what every schoolboy knows, and he hits upon an explanation: *sed timuit vim Graecam. . . . ut faceret differentiam propter Graecam elocutionem.* Once again, Donatus's text gives no hint he was motivated as Pompeius suggests; and in this case there is no probability at all that he had the Greek usage in mind, much less that he feared it. In his survey Donatus naturally chose *accuso* as an example of a verb taking the accusative case; the accusative derived its name from it.[114] Pompeius has simply (if unconsciously) used Donatus's text as a peg to hang his lesson on, concerning a topic—the possibly misleading example of Greek usage—that obviously worried him elsewhere.[115]

In this instance Pompeius projected his concerns onto Donatus where a specific point of doctrine was involved; but we can find him behaving much the same way in a passage that reveals the grammarian's anxious turn of mind more generally. When Donatus comes to the category of nouns occurring in the singular or plural only, he follows his usual practice of noting the various subcategories and offering a few examples for each: *sunt semper singularia generis masculini, ut "pulvis," "sanguis," semper pluralia, ut "Manes," "Quirites," "cancelli," semper singularia generis feminini, ut "pax," "lux,"* and so on (623.1–9H.). At this point Pompeius tells his reader, *vide quia, quodcumque tibi dat exemplum, dat secundum artem, ne recurras ad auctoritatem et rumpas hoc ipsum quod proponit. multa enim contraria sunt* (176.6–8). Pompeius is not accusing Donatus of chicanery, as the statement might at first sight suggest, of suppressing information in the interest of preserving an invalid lesson.[116] Rather, Pompeius is again using Donatus as a model of effective teaching, to underscore the principle that one does not need to say everything:[117] Donatus presents his examples *secundum artem,* according to the handbook—that is, as straightforward rules, according to what one is supposed to say. He does not clutter his lesson with the exceptions in the literary texts (*auctoritates*), so that one will not be tempted to point to those exceptions and fractiously challenge the generally valid rule by saying, *ecce . . .*

But as so often, the specter of counterexample preys on Pompeius's mind, and he soon returns to the matter as it concerns Donatus: *ait sic*

114. As Pompeius himself later notes at 171.10f.: *accusativus, quod per ipsum accusemus, "accuso illum."*

115. Cf. Pomp. 259.23f., *Graeci habent* [sc. *praesens participium in passivo et praeteritum in activo*] *et idcirco praemonui, ne quasi trahant te elocutiones Graecae et velis aliter ponere,* and Pomp. 260.31ff., *ne dicas ergo, "licet mihi."* Pompeius shows a similar concern at 232.16–17.

116. As the larger context shows (e.g., Pomp. 176.11ff.), Pompeius approves of Donatus's lesson.

117. See Pomp. 186.34ff., with p. 161 above.

etiam ipse timens (quoniam scit lecta esse multa contra regulas suas), "*sed scire debes multa per usurpationem esse conexa.*" *nam ecce "pulvis" dicimus secundum artem, et tamen invenimus "pulveres," "bigae" debemus dicere, invenimus "biga"* (177.21–24). As in the passage above, what Donatus is alleged to know, and especially what he says fearfully, owe far more to Pompeius's concerns than to his own text. Indeed, Pompeius's subjectivity is particularly evident here, since it has led him to tear from its context the qualification he attributes to Donatus in the paraphrase *sed scire debes* . . . and apply it misleadingly to the whole category of nouns under discussion.[118] Safeguarding one's rules and expertise exacts a price, as Pompeius's agitation eloquently testifies: *ait . . . timens.* With so many worries crowding about, it was not altogether easy being a grammarian.

If Pompeius's free-flowing talk tells us anything, it tells us of values and aspirations, and their cost: the importance placed on the rational mastery of language that is condensed in the grammatical tradition, the desire to set one's own stamp on the tradition even as one merges with it, and the edgy self-concern that those values and desires evoke. It would be possible to elaborate the portrait of Pompeius and trace the qualities we have already seen, as he treats the topic at the heart of the grammarian's authority, the definition of linguistic correctness. There is, however, another text that can teach us more about the criteria of correctness and their dynamics. We will turn, then, to Servius and his commentary on Vergil.

118. Donatus's qualification concerns only *singularia generis neutri*; cf. Don. 623.4–6H.

CHAPTER 5

Servius

We have already encountered Servius as the author of the commentary on Donatus's *Ars* that was Pompeius's main source. That is not, however, the work for which he is best known today. Born probably in the late 360s or early 370s, Servius was a teacher at Rome by the 390s. His only writing datable with any security—a brief treatise *De centum metris*—was probably composed between 400 and 410; its dedication to a *clarissimus Albinus* (a pupil at the time, as the context shows; probably Caecina Decius Aginatius Albinus, *PVR* 414) reveals that Servius had by then become connected with one of the most distinguished families of the old capital. His other surviving works include two other concise pamphlets (*De finalibus, De metris Horatii*) and the abbreviated version of his commentary on Donatus. The great work that has come down to us is the commentary on Vergil.[1]

Here too Servius was following in the tracks of Donatus, using his variorum commentary as a major source. Beyond the dedicatory epistle, a *vita* of Vergil, and the introduction to the *Bucolics*, Donatus's commentary has not survived. We do, however, have significant extracts thanks to a reader of Vergil—perhaps of the seventh century, perhaps Irish—who incorporated other material into his copy of Servius, including notes from Donatus's commentary.[2] In the dedication of his work Donatus had said that his compilation was meant to serve as a resource for

1. See Part II no. 136; for possible evidence of the relative chronology of the commentaries on Vergil and Donatus, see the appendix to Part II no. 125.

2. The product of the compiler is conventionally termed Servius Auctus or Servius Danielis (after its discoverer, P. Daniel), to be distinguished from the vulgate commentary, which is here taken to be Servius's own. On the relations between the expanded commentary (cited here as DServ.) and the vulgate, see Thilo in Thilo and Hagen, eds., 1, v–lxix; and most recently Goold, "Servius"

other *grammatici*,[3] and Servius clearly used the work much as Donatus had intended; the learning his predecessor had gathered is excerpted, simplified, and criticized—Servius tends to mention Donatus only to convict him of error—now suppressed, now supplemented.[4]

It is also clear that Servius's commentary, although a less personal document than the work of Pompeius, is nonetheless the instrument of a teacher.[5] The commentary remains at the level suitable for *pueri* as Servius makes his way word by word and line by line through the text, remarking on punctuation, meter, uncertain readings, myth or other *Realien*, and especially on the language. The last category, in fact, dwarfs all the others, occasioning two notes out of every three. Only one note in seven, by contrast, is concerned with the broader mythical, historical, and literary background of the poetry, and of this small minority only another small proportion amounts to more than perfunctory references or glosses.[6] The disproportion is a sign of the emphasis that the late-antique *grammatici* placed on linguistic instruction, which continued well beyond the study of the *ars*. It reminds us of the distance that separates a modern commentary, given over to exegesis, from its ancient counterpart, in which exegesis coexists—often uncomfortably, as we shall see—with instruction in a living language.

In the central portion of this chapter, then, we shall try to listen to Servius as his students would have heard him, in order to define the impression of Servius's teaching and of Servius himself that would have been fixed in minds more prepared than the modern to appreciate the nuances of his comments and accept them as fresh. Above all, by placing ourselves in the pupils' position we should be able to experience directly one important element of Servius's personality: the grammarian's sense of his own authority. Servius's conceptions of his task and of his status as a cultural figure remain largely unexpressed. Yet in his commentary

---

esp. 102–22; Murgia, *Prolegomena* 3–6; and Marshall, "Servius." A promising method for reclaiming more of Donatus's commentary has lately been elaborated by Schindel, *Figurenlehren*. All references to the commentary below are to the vulgate Servius and the *Aeneid* unless otherwise noted. As in Chap. 4, the extant version of Servius's commentary on Donatus's *Ars* is cited by page and line of Keil, *GL* 4.

3. See Chap. 4 n. 85.

4. Note esp. the suppression of many of the references to republican authors that Donatus had included and the inclusion of citations from the newly fashionable Silver Latin poets. See Lloyd, "Republican Authors," with Kaster, "Macrobius" 257.

5. See Thomas, *Essai* 182; Lloyd, "Republican Authors" 326; Levy, *"To hexês"*; Goold, "Servius" 135.

6. See Kaster, "Macrobius" 256 n. 109.

an individual and often decidedly quirky turn of mind is demonstrably at work, and Servius's implicit self-image at times so influences his comments that they cannot be understood unless it be taken into account.

To begin, however, we will turn briefly away from the commentary to establish a point of comparison with the voice we will later hear and to open a way into Servius's text. It happens that alone of the *grammatici* in the period Servius speaks both in his own works and as a character in imaginative literature, in the *Saturnalia*, Macrobius's recreation of the Roman aristocracy's intellectual life in the *saeculum Praetextati*. Composed just over a generation after the age it celebrates, the *Saturnalia* offers an idealized Servius standing head and shoulders above the *plebeia grammaticorum cohors* (*Sat.* 1.24.8), the good grammarian demonstrating the moral and intellectual qualities desirable in a man of his profession, a teacher "at once admirable in his learning and attractive in his modesty" (*Sat.* 1.2.15).[7] As such, Servius is called upon early in the first book (*Sat.* 1.4) to deal with the *adulescens* Avienus, who at this point in the dialogue wears the character of a young man essentially sound, if somewhat obstreperous and unformed.

On listening to a discourse by one of the aristocratic participants, Caecina Albinus, Avienus has been struck by the untoward quality (*novitas*) of certain turns of phrase the older and more learned man uses. He is moved to question their legitimacy; in effect, he asks why Caecina has committed two solecisms and a barbarism (respectively, *noctu futura* for *nocte futura*, *diecrastini* for *die crastino*, and *Saturnaliorum* for *Saturnalium*). The defense of Caecina is entrusted to the professional, Servius, who explains each of the usages in turn and shows that what Avienus in his ignorance took for *novitas* was in fact *antiquitas*, the usage of the ancients. The appeal to antiquity fails to impress the *adulescens*: Avienus savages the grammarian for using his professional status to encourage a way of speaking that time has rubbed out and cashiered. Avienus calls for current language, *praesentia verba*, until he is brought to heel by the grave rebuke of the group's most distinguished member, Praetextatus himself (*Sat.* 1.5).

In the conflict that arises from Servius's correction of Avienus, two details are especially important. One is general, Avienus's insistence upon *praesentia verba*, which is supposedly antithetical to the grammarian's defense of antiquity: in fact, as we will see shortly, Avienus's demand is rather what one might expect from a pupil of the real Servius. The other detail is specific, the method Servius uses to justify *diecrastini* (*Sat.*

7. For general discussion of Servius's role in the *Saturnalia* and of the context of the incident described below, see Kaster, "Macrobius" 224ff., esp. 243ff.

1.4.20–27), the last of the controversial expressions treated before Avienus's outburst. As commonly elsewhere in the *Saturnalia*, the words of the speaker—here, Servius—are drawn from a chapter of Aulus Gellius (10.24); and, as is his practice, Macrobius substantially rearranges and modifies the chapter to suit his purpose. Servius's defense proceeds from the assertion that the *doctissimus vir* Caecina did not use the expression *sine veterum auctoritate*. The method of the defense, and so the use of *auctoritas* as a criterion of correctness, is essentially analogical; that is, Servius adduces no attested use of *diecrastini* to provide an authoritative precedent, nor does he even claim (as did Gellius) that the form was ever used by the ancients.[8] Rather, the expression is justified solely and explicitly by analogy with such attested archaic forms as *diequinti* and *dienoni*.[9] The fictional Servius's defense of analogical archaism and the respect for the *veterum auctoritas* that it implies conform thoroughly to Macrobius's idealized vision of the literary culture: they are in accord both with Servius's role as the good grammarian, the man who guarantees the continuity of the language, and with the more general notion that stamps each page of the dialogue, the belief that the cultural tradition continues as a living presence, influencing and validating every aspect of a mature and learned man's life. At the same time, the defense of antiquity that Macrobius's Servius offers and the regard for *auctoritas* that analogical archaism implies are directly opposed to the doctrines of the Servius we find in the commentary.

The real Servius's view can be seen in several notes on the *Aeneid*. Characteristically, the instruction appears early in the first book, so that the student may carry the lesson with him as he proceeds:

1.4 MEMOREM IVNONIS OB IRAM constat multa in auctoribus inveniri per contrarium significantia: pro activis passiva, ut [11.660] "pictis bellantur Amazones armis," pro passivis activa, ut [*Georg.* 1.185] "populatque ingentem farris acervum," et haec varietas vel potius contrarietas invenitur etiam in aliis partibus orationis . . . et in nomine, ut "memorem Iunonis ob iram"—non "quae meminerat" sed "quae in memoria erat." de his autem haec tantum quae lecta sunt ponimus nec ad eorum exemplum alia formamus.

---

8. In a sentence omitted by Macrobius, Gellius does offer the assurance that *item simili figura "diecrastini" dicebatur, id erat "crastino die"* (*NA* 10.24.8); the only attested use of *diecrastini* before Gell. *NA* 2.29.7 is Plaut. *Most.* 881, a fact of which Macrobius would almost certainly have been unaware.
9. *Sat.* 1.4.20, with 1.4.25–27. The analogical defense is found clearly at *Sat.* 1.4.25, *verum ne de "diecrastini" nihil retulisse videamur, suppetit Caelianum illud ex libro Historiarum secundo*, citing a passage that contains *diequinti*. Symmachus and Praetextatus then follow with quotations offering *diequinti* and *dienoni*.

The final sentence warns against imitative extension of the peculiar usages found in the text and conveys the main point of the note.[10] The principle found there can be compared with the burden of another note, which occurs not long after:

1.26 ALTA MENTE REPOSTVM. . . . "repostum" autem syncope est: unam enim de medio syllabam tulit. sed cum omnes sermones aut integri sint aut pathos habeant, hi qui pathos habent ita ut lecti sunt debent poni, quod etiam Maro fecit: namque et [6.655] "repostos" et [8.274] "porgite" de Ennio transtulit. integris autem et ipsis utimur et eorum exemplo aliis.

The main thrust of the note (hi . . . poni and integris . . . aliis) moves in the same direction as the comment on Aeneid 1.4. Both notes concern the use and abuse of analogy and the proper relation between analogical formation and auctoritas:[11] the combined lesson is plainly opposed to the validation Servius gives diecrastini in the Saturnalia, where the one odd expression is justified merely by analogy with similar odd expressions in the texts of literary auctores. Such notes represent specific and limiting applications of the general statement concerning figurative usage found later in the commentary:

5.120 PVBES INPELLVNT figura est, ut [1.212] "pars in frusta se-cant." et sciendum inter barbarismum et lexin, hoc est, Latinam et perfectam elocutionem, metaplasmum esse, qui in uno sermone fit ratione vitiosus, item inter soloecismum et schema, id est, perfectam sermonum conexionem, figura est, quae fit contextu sermonum ratione vitiosa. ergo metaplasmus et figura media sunt, et discernuntur [sc. from barbarism and solecism, respectively] peritia et imperitia. fiunt autem ad ornatum.

Compared with the definitions found in the grammatical tradition, Servius's note here is distinctive in several details[12] and can be contrasted

10. In the final sentence I have read ponimus and formamus with Thilo and the manuscripts of Servius, against posita sunt and formata, the readings of codex C of DServ., printed by the Harvard editors: for the reason, see p. 181 and n. 34.

11. For a similar formulation, cf. Servius's comment at 1.587. See also Serv. 441.13–15, with Pomp. 263.11–28 (cf. Pomp. 232.2–8 and 12–14, and the still more stringent formulation at 187.15f.); and the elder Pliny ap. Charis. 151.18–25 Barwick, warning against the analogical extension of archaic nominal forms in -es (i.e., *copies, on the model of amicities) and opposing the rationis via to the veterum licentia.

12. Esp. in its precise tripartite schematization (lexis, metaplasmus, barbarismus, and schema, figura, soloecismus) and in the formal categories of lexis and schema.

with the less precisely worded doctrine in the extant version of his commentary on Donatus's *Ars*:

> quidquid scientes facimus novitatis cupidi, quod tamen idoneorum auctorum firmatur exemplis, figura dicitur. quidquid autem ignorantes ponimus, vitium putatur. (447.8–10)

This last, broad formulation, with its emphasis on novelty—*novitas*, toned down to the less daring *ornatus* in the Vergilian commentary, where little good is said about *novitas*—and with its vague proviso concerning *auctoritas* (*idoneorum auctorum firmatur exemplis*), could perhaps be taken to countenance the kind of analogical argument offered in Macrobius. The comment on Donatus provides a general, liberal alternative to the specific and confining statements found, for example, in the notes on *Aeneid* 1.4 and 1.26. In the latter places, it seems, we hear the authentic and assertive voice of Servius the teacher,[13] a voice distinct from that of the good grammarian of the *Saturnalia*.

There is more at stake here than just another variation in detail between the creation of Macrobius and the author of the commentary.[14] The two figures understand and value in fundamentally different ways the processes of the language, the authority of the culture that stands behind it, and the status of the grammarian himself. The practice of analogy in the *Saturnalia* clearly accords with the ideal of cultural continuity developed in the dialogue. In using that approach, one assumes that the forms guaranteed by *auctoritas* are—to adapt the term Servius used in the note on *Aeneid* 1.26—as "sound" (*integra*) as the forms used in regular speech and thus are as suited to the operations of analogy; through that linguistic exercise one achieves a more intimate and vivid participation with the ancients.

Precisely the opposite is true of the teaching of Servius, for whom *auctoritas* holds no such guarantees: *figurae* (or metaplasms, which operate under the same terms) are a large but finite and isolated repository of ancient expressions.[15] The repository is, above all, controllable; it is not

---

Schema itself is commonly used interchangeably with *figura* to denote what in ordinary discourse would be considered a solecism: e.g., Don. 658.3H.; Serv. 448.1–7; Pomp. 292.13ff. = Plin. frg. 125 della Casa (above, p. 151f.); cf. also Quintil. *Inst.* 9.3.2, with Don. 663.5–6H.

13. On Servius's tendency to vary his teaching in the commentary on Vergil, "where he was not as bound to the [grammatical] tradition" as in his observations on Donatus, see the remarks of Wessner, "Lucan" 329.

14. For such differences in general, see Kaster, "Macrobius" 255ff.

15. Just how finite and isolated can be gauged from such collections as the *Exempla elocutionum* of the rhetorician Arusianus Messius (edited most recently by

to be extended. *Figurae* may be used under certain conditions virtually as literary allusions, but at the same time they exemplify what should be avoided as vicious in general practice. In Macrobius, *figurae* represent a free channel of communication between past and present that the grammarian has modestly and reverently opened; in Servius's commentary, *figurae* represent a nearly closed door over which he stands guard. The ends of immediacy and participation that the grammarian of the *Saturnalia* serves in instructing young Avienus are countered in Servius's own teaching by the preservation of distance and control.

The goals of distance and control are themselves partially the result of an institutional quirk of Roman education. *Figurae* occupied a no-man's-land between the schools of the *grammaticus* and of the *rhetor*, falling a bit short of the latter's main interest but a bit beyond the former's central concern, the correct understanding of the parts of speech and their attributes.[16] This institutional no-man's-land coincided with a no-man's-land of language and method. The ambiguous place of *figurae* in the structure of formal education conditions the ambiguous function of *figurae* in the commentary, where they commonly mark the boundary between two opposing ideas (e.g., exegesis vs. prescription, the ancients vs. "us," the language of Vergil vs. correct language) but at the same time leave it porous or vague. So, for example, in the economy of Servius's commentary, *figurae* mediate between the two main purposes, exegesis and prescription: *figurae* make intelligible what the author is saying (and often defend his way of saying it) while segregating the author's usage from the grammarian's central lesson of correct speech.[17] In any given note, one purpose may predominate, but the boundary between the two is never neat; one should perhaps speak not so much of boundaries as of buffer zones. The institutional niche of *figurae* corresponds to their use as a buffer (compare Servius on *Aeneid* 5.120, quoted above, where such usages are termed *media*): the category *figura* protects

---

A. della Casa [Milan, 1977]), based on Terence, Vergil, Sallust, and Cicero. Cf. the *singularia* gleaned from the works of Cato and Cicero in the second century by Statilius Maximus, discussed by Zetzel, "Statilius."

16. See the remarks of Schindel, *Figurenlehren* 12ff. Servius most often uses *figura* in the sense of the *schema grammaticum*, a deviation from the *loquendi ratio*, as defined by Quintil. *Inst.* 9.3.2; cf. Serv. 448.1–7, opposing the *schema in sermone factum* (= the *figura grammaticalis*) to the *schema in sensu factum* (= figure of thought, the sphere of the *rhetor*). On the place of the parts of speech at the heart of the grammarian's expertise, cf. Chap. 4 pp. 140, 163.

17. This is grammar's *quod licet Iovi, non licet bovi*; cf. Aug. *C. Faust.* 22.25 (*PL* 42.417): *puer in barbarismo reprehensus, si de Vergilii metaplasmo se vellet defendere, ferulis caederetur.* The dispensation is usually but not always extended to Vergil: see Servius at, e.g., 4.355, 8.260, 10.572.

the regular operations of the language against the authority of the text just as it protects the text against the charge of solecism.[18]

As the goals of protection, distance, and control suggest, the commentary is often a scene of conflict, between the ancients and "ourselves," between different forms and sources of authority, between the deference owed to the author's prestige and the grammarian's domination of the text. Understanding the commentary means in large part understanding how the grammarian controls such conflicts, and understanding that control requires us to appreciate the sense of authority that the grammarian derives from his own institutional niche. As is often pointed out, Servius's approach to the text is one of regulations and categories; and this quasi-bureaucratic treatment of Vergil has done little to endear Servius to modern tastes. But bear in mind that controlling regulations and categories carries a power with it. Servius understands whatever comes before his eyes through the rules his institution provides, and he owes whatever authority he possesses to his command of those rules and to his status in that institution. As we shall see, Servius has so thoroughly internalized those rules and the authority of his position that they are at times combined and expressed unconsciously, in ways that offer unexpected glimpses of Servius's personality and self-image.

Before considering his self-image, however, we must try to understand the basis of Servius's rules and authority and how they are deployed in the commentary. Servius's status as a grammarian, his place in the specialized institution of his profession, involves a specific knowledge, *recte loquendi scientia*, which is presumed to rest on the *natura* of the language. *Recte loqui* means *naturaliter loqui*: strictly correct usage is natural usage.[19] *Natura* provides the raw material of the language, from, say, the quantity of the root vowel of *unus* or the correct spelling of *scribo* to the various functions and forms of the parts of speech.[20] This raw

18. See n. 17; compare Servius at, e.g., 1.120, on the construction of *Ilionei*.

19. Compare the phrase *sermo natura . . . integer* (implicitly the claim of the grammarians) in the polemics of Arnob. *Adv. nat.* 1.59: above Chap. 2 p. 85. On the grammarian's presumption of a natural order in language, see most recently Blank, *Ancient Philosophy* esp. 13, 51 n. 1.

20. The most venerable text on this subject is preserved by Diom. 439.16–22 = Varro frg. 115 Goetz-Schoell: *[Latinitas] constat . . . , ut adserit Varro, his quattuor, natura analogia consuetudine auctoritate. natura verborum nominumque inmutabilis <est> nec quicquam aut minus aut plus tradidit nobis quam quod accepit. nam si quis dicat "scrimbo" <pro eo> quod est "scribo," non analogiae virtute sed naturae ipsius constitutione convincitur. analogia sermonis a natura prodit ordinatio est secundum technicos;* Charis. 62.14–63.9B. offers a parallel version. *Ratio* and *analogia* are used interchangeably in the passage; see esp. Diom. 439.16f., with 439.27f. On *auctoritas* and *consuetudo* (= *usus*), see below. The relation between *natura* and *ratio* or *analogia* here was

material is subject for the most part to *ratio* (or *analogia*), which systematically orders the data of nature to provide the *regulae* set down in the *ars*; the *ars* in its turn is the product and property of the grammarian. The nature of the language is thus incorporated in the institution and identified with the grammarian's expertise. The linguistic forces that lie beyond his institutional niche and contradict his expertise are against nature.

Consider, for example, the comments on figurative usage noted above. By definition a deviation from correct usage, *figurae* are also necessarily a deviation from natural usage, the *sermo naturalis*.[21] Inevitably, therefore, the grammarian is as opposed to analogically extending figurative usage as he is to extending any other usage against nature: with Servius's note on *Aeneid* 1.4, we can compare the following, which warns against backformation from a form whose *natura* has been corrupted:

> 2.195 PERIVRI in verbo "r" non habet; nam "peiuro" dicimus corrupta natura praepositionis. quae res facit errorem, ut aliqui male dicant "peiurus."[22]

Here, as in the case of *figurae*, an accommodation must be reached with the corruption already accomplished: Servius is saying, in effect, "This far, but no farther."

Hedged around by the wall of *natura*, Servius deals from a clearly defined position of strength with the other, unruly forces—*auctoritas* (literary authority) and *usus* or *consuetudo* (ordinary, current usage)—that have an impact on the language. These forces are variously treated in the commentary. For example, *auctoritas* serves largely as a court of last resort, defining the periphery of permissible usage rather than the core of what is correct;[23] but *auctoritas* can also appear, now and then, to govern the language when that serves the grammarian's didactic

---

correctly seen by Barwick, *Remmius* 183f.: "*analogia* . . . ist die der *natura* gegebenen Sprache abgewonnene Gesetzmässigkeit. Daher sind *natura* und *analogia* bis zu einem gewissen Grade zwei verschiedene Seiten ein und derselben Sache."

21. So 2.132, *figura* vs. *sermo naturalis*. See also 1.5, expanded at 5.467: usage adopted *causa metri* vs. what one does *naturaliter*; 2.60, *usurpatum* vs. *naturale* (on this comment see below, p. 182); 7.161, *secundum naturam* vs. *figuratum*.

22. See also the comments at 4.427, against the 1st sing. perf. indic. *revulsi* as derived from the "unnatural" form (*re*)*vulsus*; and cf. 2.39 (sim. 1.149), on the declension of *vulgus*.

23. See above, on 1.4 and 1.26; similarly Pomp. 232.2–8 (with Serv. 437.20–23), 237.35ff., 263.11–28 (with Serv. 441.13–15), 273.3ff.; cf. also Diom. 370.19–23 for reliance on *auctores* in a case where *non est inventa ratio*.

purpose.²⁴ Much the same is true of *usus*: what usage has maintained can be a determining factor,²⁵ and can even be credited with altering the nature of the language.²⁶ But throughout, the grammarian, with his understanding—or rather, definitive control—of *natura*, stands watch over *auctoritas* and *usus*, guarding against the perceived abuse, confusion, and corruption that both produce.²⁷

This intricate and often arbitrary interweaving of *natura*, *usus*, and *auctoritas* is tolerably familiar;²⁸ only two tendencies need emphasis here. First, one can reasonably suggest that the authority of the grammarian's own pronouncements would be perceived by his students and by the grammarian himself as dominant and decisive: the grammarian establishes the distinction between "what we read" and "what we say," grants his permission according to his notion of "what we are able to say," determines the propriety of particular usages, and above all issues warnings.²⁹ Second, when that authority is blended with the prescriptive

24. See, e.g., 8.409, 12.587; cf. Servius's comment on *Georg.* 3.124, and, on Servius's often arbitrary invocation of *idonei auctores*, see Kaster, "Servius." For *auctores* or *veteres* used to confirm a rule reached by way of analogy, cf. Diom. 368.3–11, 375.16–25.

25. Cf. 2.268, where Servius notes the divisions of night and day according to Varro and concludes, *de crepusculo vero, quod est dubia lux, . . . quaeritur, et licet utrique tempori* [i.e., twilight or daybreak] *possit iungi, usus tamen ut matutino iungamus obtinuit.* The meaning "daybreak" authorized by *usus* according to Servius in fact first appears outside Servius in Latin of the fourth and fifth centuries; see *TLL* s.v. *crepusculum* 1175.39ff.

26. Cf. 5.603, *HAC CELEBRATA TENVS tmesis est, "hactenus." et hic sermo, quantum ad artem* [i.e., *naturam*] *spectat, duas continet partes orationis, ut "hac" pronomen sit, "tenus" praepositio. . . . sed iam usus obtinuit ut pro una parte habeatur. ergo adverbium est: omnis enim pars orationis, cum desierit esse quod est, in adverbium migrat;* for the principle, see above at Chap. 4 n. 16. Here again the connection between the *ars* and the essence of the language, *quod est*, is plain.

27. To select from only the first book a few examples in which *auctoritas* and *usus* are found *abuti* or *confundere* or *corrumpere*. For *auctoritas*, see 1.118, 185 (on the distinction between *totus* and *omnis*, never very firm, and weakened further in the common speech of late antiquity [see Löfstedt, *Late Latin* 22]: Servius here urges against the improper usage of the text as a way of undermining a bad habit of common speech; cf. pp. 187–89 below), 334, 590. For *usus*, see 1.319, 410, 480, 697 (*sane sciendum malo errore "cum" et "dum" a Romanis esse confusa*—again touching upon an authentic feature of late Latin; see Adams, *Text* 77). For *regula* or *ratio* corrupted by *consuetudo* or contradicted by the license of the *veteres* or of current usage, cf. Diom. 348.24f. (cf. 349.6f., 15f.), 365.25f., 398.9, 400.3, 406.11–12.

28. On how the scholars of the first century B.C. and first century A.D. balanced the components of the language, the general discussion of Barwick, *Remmius* 203–15, remains fundamental; also valuable, esp. for the Greek background, is Siebenborn, *Sprachrichtigkeit* esp. 108–15 and, a bit less satisfactory, 151–54, on *natura*. For an accessible and useful introduction, see Bonner, *Education* 204–8.

29. "What we read" vs. "what we say": e.g., 2.487, 3.278, 7.605. *Possumus uti* or *licenter utimur* or *pro nostro arbitrio utimur*: e.g., 1.47, 96, 159, 177, 194, 343, 430,

purposes of the commentary, Servius's manufacture of the language for his students' benefit can produce observations on Vergil's language that sound absurd to the modern ear, attuned as it is solely to the commentary's exegetic purpose. Neither tendency can be separated from the other, but the effects of the second are more easily seen in individual notes. We can therefore examine this second tendency and identify a few of the strategies Servius used in his instruction, before returning to consider the implications of the first.

We must accustom ourselves to hearing Servius with a student's ear when he says, for example:

10.526 PENITVS DEFOSSA TALENTA. . . . sane melius [i.e., rectius] "infossa" diceret quam "defossa," ad quod est metri necessitate conpulsus.

Or:

11.468 ILICET "confestim," "ilico": quod ne diceret, metri necessitas fecit. nam "ilico" dicimus.

These and other notes invoking the necessity or compulsion of meter (and anyone familiar with the commentary knows how common they are) were not intended, and would not have been understood, as purely or even primarily exegetic. They are not earnest but superficial attempts to judge or explain Vergil's own choices and technique; rather, the force of these observations is directed largely at the student, telling him what he should or should not do. That the words are Vergil's is virtually incidental. Freely paraphrased, these lessons would be understood to mean something like, "Don't get it into your head that you should do what Vergil has done here; your usage should be such only when all other options have been closed."[30] The text serves as an instrument; the author, as dummy. Both are exploited to meet Servius's purpose.

451, 484; 2.610. Sphere of usage: cf. 1.251, 2.18, 6.79, 10.481. Warnings: cf. 2.513, *VETERRIMA usurpatum est. ergo, ut supra diximus, hoc tantum uti si necesse sit licet*, with 1.253, *HONOS cum secundum artem* [i.e., *naturam*] *dicamus "honor," "arbor," "lepor," plerumque poetae "r" in "s" mutant causa metri. . . . hoc quidem habet ratio: sed ecce in hoc loco etiam sine metri necessitate "honos" dixit. item Sallustius paene ubique "labos" posuit, quem nulla necessitas coegit. melius tamen est servire regulae* [i.e., *naturae*]. Compare the still stricter position of Pomp. 283.37ff.

30. Cf. 2.513 and 1.253, cited in the preceding note; and esp. 1.3, p. 187 below. With the paraphrase offered in the text, compare what Pompeius says at, e.g., 269.22ff., *ne dicas mihi ergo, "quoniam usus est Vergilius . . . , debeo et ego ita facere." nequaquam licet.* Cf. n. 17 above.

The exploitation recurs over a wide range of Servian rhetorical ploys. A similar and, again, essentially negative tactic involves the use of the phrase *debuit dicere*. For example:

> 1.16 HIC ILLIVS ARMA figura creberrima adverbium pro adverbio posuit, praesentis loci pro absentis: debuit enim dicere "illic."

Or:

> 9.467 CINGITVR AMNI "amne" debuit dicere: numquam enim bene [i.e., recte] in "i" exeunt nisi quae communis sunt generis, ut "docilis," "agilis." sed ideo ausus est ita ponere ablativum, quia, ut supra diximus [9.122], apud maiores "hic" et "haec amnis" dicebatur.

Again, *debuit dicere* is directed more at the student than at the text. Servius is not literally contending at *Aeneid* 1.16 that Vergil should have said *illic*; he is making plain to the students what they should use. At stake is not so much a fault worthy of criticism or demanding correction in Vergil—*figura* provides the necessary protection against that—but a deviant usage the student should avoid.[31] Similarly, *ausus est* in the note on *Aeneid* 9.467 is not meant to describe Vergil's behavior, for his daring is immediately denied by the explanation that his words simply reflect the usage current *apud maiores*, of whom he is one. Rather, *ausus est* is directed at the student, to impress upon him what should be avoided as bold.[32] *Debuit dicere* urges against the bad example of the text and has the effective meaning in the commentary of *debemus dicere*.[33] Such notes drive

31. But clearly *debuit dicere* could be construed as an adverse criticism of the author; cf. especially Aug. *C. Faust.* 22.25, quoted below, n. 77, and note Servius and DServ. at 1.273: where Servius offers GENTE SVB HECTOREA *id est* "Troiana." *sed debuit dicere* "Aeneia." *diximus superius* [1.235] *nomina poetas ex vicino usurpare*, explaining and defending as a poetic usage the deviation from what should have been said, the same idea appears in DServ. as GENTE SVB HECTOREA *id est* "Troiana." *sed quidam reprehendunt quod* "Hectorea" *et non* "Aeneia." *mos est poetis nomina ex vicinis usurpare*; here *quidam reprehendunt* is probably a generalizing inference drawn from Servius's *debuit dicere* by the compiler of DServ. (the last clause is certainly no more than a finicky rewriting of Servius typical of the compiler). *Debuit dicere* seems to be located, like *figura*, in a gray area: although the practical or monitory purpose of the phrase dominates in its many appearances in the commentary, it would be wrong to deny out of hand that *debuit dicere* could connote some criticism of Vergil.

32. Cf. 2.610 (concerning a point of usage similar to that in 9.467), where each of the three parts of Servius's statement, *"tridente" debuit dicere; sed novitatem adfectavit, nulla cogente necessitate*, is intended more as a warning for his pupils than as an objective interpretation or evaluation of the verse.

33. Cf. 1.319, *facere non debemus*, referring to a *Graeca figura*.

home their lessons through the use of the third person singular, segregating the author's usage from the Latin that Servius wants to teach.

In these examples, prescription proceeds obliquely, yet nonetheless clearly, as Servius plays his own views off against the text. But prescription is at work in another element of Servius's style, one that is not at all apparent on the surface of his language but is wholly implied in his role. It is a nuance that again requires us to hear Servius with the ear of his pupils and that, not incidentally, adds to the difficulty of teasing apart the strands of *natura, usus,* and *auctoritas* in Servius's weave.

We might look again at the notes on *Aeneid* 1.4 (for its last sentence) and 1.26:

de his autem haec tantum quae lecta sunt ponimus nec ad eorum exemplum alia formamus.

sermones . . . qui pathos habent ita ut lecti sunt debent poni. . . . integris autem et ipsis utimur et eorum exemplo aliis.

As noted earlier, we should accept the readings of Servius's manuscripts at 1.4, *ponimus* and *formamus,* against *posita sunt* and *formata,* the readings of Servius Danielis, which some editors have imposed on Servius.[34] The reason for following the manuscripts of Servius is simple. They bear witness to a constant feature of Servius's language, the use of the first-person-plural indicative in a prescriptive sense.[35] That is, *ponimus,* unless otherwise qualified, would tend to mean *ponere debemus,* or *formamus* to mean *formare debemus,* or *utimur* to mean *uti debemus*—compare the parallel uses of the verbs at 1.4 and 1.26, *ponimus . . . formamus* and *debent poni . . . utimur.* This thoroughly natural overtone is unmistakable as soon as one listens to Servius as a teacher of his native language and not simply as a descriptive, objective commentator in the modern vein. The nuance occurs throughout the commentary, as in some of the notes already cited.[36] It is found most easily, perhaps, in one of Servius's more striking

34. See above at n. 10. The alteration of Servius's active forms to the passives in DServ. is comparable to the systematic alteration of Servius's formula of cross-reference, *ut supra diximus,* to the impersonal *ut supra dictum est* in DServ., revealing the hand of the compiler. Cf. Goold, "Servius" 107–8; Murgia, *Prolegomena* 100–101.

35. This nuance was clearly understood by Thilo: see his remarks in Thilo and Hagen, eds., 1, lxxii.

36. E.g., 11.468, nam *"ilico"* dicimus, where *dicimus* plainly serves the purpose for which *debuit dicere* is used elsewhere. The nuance is of course not peculiar to Servius. A striking example occurs at Pomp. 238.17–19, *est verbum quod regit dativum, "maledico tibi." et hoc in usu pessime habemus: nemo dicit "maledixit me ille," sed dicimus "maledixit mihi" tantum modo.* The sense of *hoc in usu pessime habemus* here

pieces of instruction, where he urges the obsolete pronominal form *ipsus* against the common but irregular *ipse*:

> 2.60 HOC IPSVM "ipsum" autem per "m," quia usurpatum est "ipse," et est naturale "ipsus," ut [Ter. *Andr.* 576] "ipsus mihi Davus." dicimus ergo "ipsus, ipsa, ipsum," ut "doctus, docta, doctum."

Here, as Servius stresses what is regular and natural, the meaning of *dicimus* slides entirely into the realm of what should be, leaving simple description behind.[37]

Beyond demonstrating how readily description is subordinated to prescription, this last example deserves attention for a related feature, the nonchalance with which Servius identifies a palpable archaism (*ipsus*) with what "we [ought to] say." Or perhaps it is more accurate to say that *ipsus* would seem to us moderns a palpable archaism; for in Servius's language, both *dicimus* and *naturale* effectively deny that *ipsus* is an archaism at all. Rhetorically, as a means of confirming the lesson, *naturale* plays the more important role: by associating *ipsus* with nature, the epithet distinguishes the form from ambivalent usages like *figurae* and guarantees its simple, regular validity. There is, plainly, a fair amount of room for eccentric judgment in such matters as this, in part because the concept of *natura* is itself a bit vague about the edges and has its own eccentricities.

So much becomes apparent as soon as one tries to pin the concept down. The *natura* of the language cannot be defined historically in any straightforward way, as something that once came into being with specific characteristics, some of which have endured through the passage of time while others have become obscured or distorted. As we shall see just below, Servius does not believe that the farther back in time one probes the closer one comes to *natura*, or that the usage of the ancient authors, the *maiores*, reveals the language in a pure or more natural state. Yet the *natura* of the language is not timeless, an abstraction somehow outside history, for it can be affected in and over time: not only can *natura* be corrupted, and not only can *usus* change the nature of parts of speech,

---

becomes clear only once one realizes that Pompeius is saying, with notable compression, *et hoc in usu pessime habemus: [multi enim "maledixit me ille" dicunt, sed vitiose. nam] nemo dicit [= debet dicere] "maledixit me ille," sed dicimus [= debemus dicere] "maledixit mihi."* The usage with the accusative does appear to have been vulgar; see *TLL* 8.164.13ff., and cf. *CGL* 3.112.19, 49.

37. An obvious variant of the prescriptive indicative—what might be called the permissive indicative—is found in notes where such phrases as *dicimus et . . . (et)* and *utrumque dicimus* in effect mean *licet* or *possumus dicere et . . . (et)*, and *licet* or *possumus utrumque dicere*: e.g., 1.484; cf. Serv. 418.33f. and 442.1f., with Pomp. 269.32–34.

but Servius's treatment of archaism even implies at times that in its nature the ancients' language overlaps only partially with his own.[38] When the shift is imagined as having occurred, or whether it has ceased to occur, is not made clear, although, as we shall see, a primary agent of the change would appear to be the grammarian himself. At this moment, however, the points to be emphasized are these: to the extent that *natura* inheres in the grammarian's institution, in the form of rules (*regulae*, the guarantee of what is *rectum*), it provides the grammarian with a stable place to stand; and like *figurae*, archaisms, where they are noted, implicitly involve usages that not only contradict the lesson Servius wishes to teach but also run against nature. In our attempt to gauge Servius's sense of his control of the language, therefore, it is important to understand what he has in mind when he deals with archaism in the opposition between *antiqui* and *nos*.

It is evident that when Servius identifies one of Vergil's usages as *antiquum*, an archaism, he does not mean that it was an archaism in Vergil's time (although it might have been that as well) but that he judges it to be obsolete when tested against his own complex sense of acceptable current usage. Vergil was himself one of the *antiqui* (*maiores*, *veteres*) and was grouped as such, in a broad stroke characteristic of ancient scholarship, with the classical and preclassical authors; although Servius was generally aware of the chronological relationships among the various literary figures, the distinction drawn today between archaic and classical usage was not functional in his work.[39] Further, a necessary corollary derives from this repeated testing of Vergil's language for the obsolete: as in the identification of *figurae*, the identification of *antique dicta* has a prescriptive purpose. The basic relationship between the function of *figurae* and the function of archaism in the commentary can be stated fairly simply: as the demarcation of *figurae* is an attempt to deal with deviant usage synchronically, by applying the standards of correct usage to the author as though he were a contemporary, so the identification of archaism is an attempt to isolate such deviations diachronically, by constructing a temporal barrier between the author and the student.

Since the two approaches have such similar goals, we should expect them to be expressed in similar language. In fact, the associations that

38. Corruption of *natura*: see the note at 2.195, p. 177. Change of the nature of parts of speech: cf. the comment at 5.603, n. 26 above. On the mutability of nature, see Barwick, *Remmius* 184 n. 1; Siebenborn, *Sprachrichtigkeit* 108–9; Blank, *Ancient Philosophy* 41ff.; and contrast Varro *ap.* Diom. 439.17f., above, n. 20.

39. Lebek, *Verba* 18 n. 22, has well remarked the importance of understanding that "archaic" in a grammarian's comment means archaic relative to his own time and perception, and likewise the imprudence of accepting such distinctions at face value.

form in Servius's mind as the two approaches melt one into the other can be seen in the trend of his own rhetoric of instruction. In the examples listed below, we can watch Servius's thought pass from the synchronic to the diachronic, with an intermediary blending of the two, from figurative use versus what "he should have said," through figurative use versus what "we now [ought to] say," to archaism versus what "we now [ought to] say." The examples also further illustrate the inter-changeability of *debuit dicere* and the prescriptive indicative *dicimus*:

figura. . . . nam debuit dicere. . . . (1.16)

figurate dixit. . . . nam dicimus. . . . (6.435)

figura. . . . nam modo dicimus. . . . [40] (11.73)

antique dictum. . . . nam nunc dicimus, nec iungimus. . . . (6.544)

debuit dicere. . . . ideo ausus est . . . quia . . . apud maiores . . . dicebatur. (9.467)

archaismos. . . . debuit enim dicere. . . . (10.807)

The instability of the distinction is demonstrated by the progression of the notes and is especially evident in the last two. On *Aeneid* 9.467, as we saw above, *debuit dicere* and *ausus est* look to the present and are intended to have their impact on the student; but the explanation, *quia . . . dicebatur*, looks to the past: it effectively isolates Vergil's usage and at the same time negates any suggestion that he was in reality bold; his usage, a function of his being one of the *maiores*, appears bold only when measured against the current state of the language. In the comment on *Aeneid* 10.807, *dum pluit in terris, ut possint sole reducto / exercere diem*, the operation is even more striking:

DVM PLVIT hic distinguendum: nam si iunxeris "dum pluit in terris," erit archaismos: debuit enim dicere "in terras." tamen sciendum est hemistichum hoc Lucretii [6.630] esse, quod ita ut invenit Vergilius transtulit.

Here the text is in effect moved into the present and punctuated as though it were a contemporary work in order to arrive at what should have been said and avoid an archaism.[41] The blending of the two ap-

---

40. Cf. 1.75, *notanda . . . figura: frequenter enim hac utitur. nam quod nos . . . dicimus, antiqui dicebant . . .* , concerning the use of the ablative for the genitive; see further p. 186.

41. On the series of notes to which 10.807 belongs and with which it must be read to be understood, see further pp. 188f. and n. 55.

proaches is inevitable and derives from the system Servius inherited, in which the categories of *auctores* (associated with figurative usage) and *antiqui* (the sources of archaic usage) had long since fallen together: *auctoritas* and *vetustas* are for Servius essentially one and the same[42] and are equally under constraint.

Like the subordination of description to prescription, this fusion of *auctoritas* and *antiquitas*, of figures and archaism, necessarily diminishes the precision of Servius's statements and the subtlety or consistency of his response to the text.[43] The fusion should not, however, obscure Servius's real sense that the *antiqui* used a language alien, in some fundamental ways, from his own. More than three centuries earlier, Quintilian had observed, "If we compare the language of the ancients with our own, almost everything we say nowadays is a *figura*" (*Inst.* 9.3.1). Servius would have agreed, although he would have altered *quidquid loquimur* to *quidquid loquebantur* in the second half of the statement.

The strain that shifts in usage produced is perhaps most evident when Servius is faced with a corruption in the received text. In such places we can see him struggling mightily but in vain to heave a line across the abyss: thus, commenting on *Aeneid* 9.486–87, *nec te tua funere mater / produxi* (as printed by Mynors, with Bembo's emendation), he attempts the following:

NEC TVA FVNERA MATER id est "funerea": nam apud maiores "funeras" dicebant eas ad quas funus pertinet, ut sororem, matrem. nam praeficae, ut et supra [6.216] diximus, sunt planctus principes, non doloris. "funeras" autem dicebant quasi "funereas," ad quas pertinet funus.

The first sentence here offers a wholly fictive explanation according to what "the ancients used to say"; the second introduces an irrelevancy recalled from an earlier comment; and the third simply restates the first by way of conclusion.

Most often, however, Servius's command of *natura* and his awareness of its changes provide a more useful (if still shaky) bridge. Consider, for example, his note on the difficult bit of phrasing at *Aeneid* 11.149–50, *feretro Pallante reposto / procubuit super*:

42. The only important exceptions to this statement are the so-called *neoterici*, i.e., the post-Vergilian poets, especially Lucan, Juvenal, and Statius, who were *auctores* without being *veteres*. As exceptions, they caused Servius some difficulty; see Kaster, "Servius." The early collapse of *auctoritas* and *vetustas* into a single category was well noted by Barwick, *Remmius* 215.

43. For treatment of the same usage now synchronically, now diachronically, compare Servius's remarks at 3.359 with those at 12.519; similarly 8.168 (on the use of *bina*) in conjunction with the notes at 1.93 and 313.

FERETRO PALLANTE REPOSTO posito Pallantis feretro: nam antiptosis est.

Servius explains the phrase by invoking antiptosis, the use of one case in
place of another (here, ablative for genitive). The explanation is evidently
wide of the mark, but the reason for Servius's error is sometimes
misunderstood. Perhaps naturally, the modern reader assumes that the
technical term is used "as a joker card" to avoid the problem, and that
"the ablative for Servius has the meaning of the possessive genitive."[44]
Servius's own thoughts, however, move in precisely the opposite direction: Servius is certain of the nature and function of the ablative and
genitive in his own language, and is also certain that in the language of
Vergil and the *antiqui* these amounted to something very different. It is
Vergil for whom the ablative had the meaning of the genitive, as Servius
had occasion to remark early on:

1.75 PVLCHRA PROLE. . . . notanda tamen figura: frequenter enim
hac utitur. nam quod nos per genitivum singularem dicimus, antiqui
per septimum dicebant, ut hoc loco "parentem pulchra prole," id est,
"pulchrae prolis."

The belief is hardly unique to Servius and could only be reinforced by
Vergil's repeated practice.[45]
That the manipulations of Vergil could appear more odd at a distance
of four hundred years than they do at a distance of two thousand—quite
as odd as the archaic usage (in our sense) of Ennius—is a quirk of
language and history not always fully appreciated. Thus Richard Bentley,
observing Servius's note on *Aeneid* 10.710, PASTVS pro *"pastum." nam
supra ait "quem": ergo antiptosis est,* reacted with characteristic vigor to
what he took to be a grammarian's sleight of hand: "What the hell is
that antiptosis?"[46] Both Servius and Bentley were attempting to treat a
passage where, again, the received text was corrupt:

44. Williams, "Servius" 52.
45. With Servius's interpretation of 11.149, cf. the alternative explanation of
2.554–55, *hic exitus illum / sorte tulit*, noted by DServ., *quidam "exitus sorte" pro
"sortis" tradunt, ablativum pro genetivo.* Such interpretations were no doubt encouraged by the grammarians' belief that the Romans invented the ablative so
that it could share the burden of the original, i.e., Greek, genitive; cf. Pomp.
171.18–20. For the recognition of archaism implied in claims of antiptosis, see
especially Nonius Marcellus, Book 9, "De numeris et casibus," which is wholly
concerned with instances of antiptosis and presents vividly the distance between
the language of the *antiqui* and the perceptions of late antiquity.
46. *Quae malum illa antiptosis!* in his comment at Hor. *Epod.* 5.28.

> aper, multos Vesulus quem pinifer annos
> defendit multosque palus Laurentia silva
> pastus harundinea.   (*Aen.* 10.708–10)

True to himself and to his sense of independence and authority, Bentley emended *pastus* to *pascit* or *pavit* (the former is printed by Mynors). Servius, also true to himself, interpreted the passage according to his own sense of the language and its changes, relying on an inference drawn from passages where Vergil does use the nominative in place of the accusative.[47] Bentley here was right, Servius wrong.[48] But we should understand that in such cases Servius is using the technical terms not to conceal his difficulties but to acknowledge the discontinuity between the Latin of the *antiqui* and his own. The technical term is simply an economical device provided the grammarian by his profession. Its meaning is condensed, its function in the commentary both expressive and effective: it simultaneously reveals to and impresses upon the student the distance that separates him from Vergil. Offering a guarantee that carries the weight of Servius's institutional authority, the technical term both conveys and enforces the lesson to be learned.

The examples in the last three paragraphs are extreme cases, finding Servius at or near the point of helplessness, and show his method at its worst, measured against modern expectations. But the extreme cases only highlight the normal practice. Servius's narrow historical perspective and his largely prescriptive concerns anchor him in the present moment, the *nunc*, of his teaching. His purpose is to anchor the student in the same rather strange slice of time. So one finds early in the commentary the following note, of a very common type transparent in its intentions:

> 1.3 MVLTVM ILLE. . . . "ille" hoc loco abundat. est enim interposita particula propter metri necessitatem, ut stet versus: nam si detrahas "ille," stat sensus. . . . est autem archaismos.

This comment, with, for example, that on *Aeneid* 5.540, *PRIMVM ANTE OMNES unum vacat*, or on 5.833, *PRINCEPS ANTE OMNES unum vacat*,

---

47. See DServ. on 2.377, *delapsus*; cf. also the *Grammatica Vergiliana* attributed to Asper (Thilo and Hagen, eds., *Servii . . . Commentarii* 3.534) on 1.314, *obvia*. Cf. also Servius at 11.775, *cassida*, for the accusative used in place of the nominative; morphologically his description of Vergil's neologism is not far off.

48. Note, however, that Servius was only more obviously wrong than the large majority of modern editors, who solve the problem by punctuating after *Laurentia*, thus producing for *pastus* a variety of colon whose disposition in the hexameter is thoroughly at odds with Vergil's practice, as Bentley himself was later to show in his comment on Lucan 1.231; see also Townend's valuable paper "Some Problems" esp. 339–43 for Vergil.

should be understood as aimed at the tendency of the common language to add unnecessary words or to use synonymous pairs for intensification.[49] The note, with its concluding sentence, is meant to suggest, "This sort of excess baggage [abundat] is obsolete: that is not the way we [ought to] speak or write nowadays." And it is with the message of this note in mind that one must read, as Servius's students would have heard, the long series of notes of the abundat or vacat type that follows.[50]

The purpose and net effect of such notes is to place the unwanted usage of the auctores firmly in the past:

> 1.176 RAPVITQVE IN FOMITE FLAMMAM paene soloecophanes est. nam cum mutationem verbum significat, ablativo usus est. sed hoc solvit aut antiqua circa communes praepositiones licentia, ut est [Georg. 1.442] "conditus in nubem," contra [Aen. 2.401] "et nota conduntur in alvo" . . . ; aut "rapuit" "raptim fecit" flammam in fomite, id est, celeriter.

The note regards the coordination of prepositions with the case system and is cast in effect in the form of a quaestio—Why is this not a solecism?—to which two solutions are offered. The second is specific, explaining that the ablative is correct by current standards because no change of place occurs.[51] The first is general and more interesting, the invocation of the antiqua licentia: the standard that today would mark the usage as a solecism does not apply to the antiqui, whose language did not draw the same distinctions Servius's does in the use of communes praepositiones.[52] The note, which has as a variant the type found on Aeneid 9.467,[53] is meant to fix the distinction in the minds of Servius's students even as it exempts the antiqui by drawing a line between the past and the present.

49. For the text used to exemplify and so to undermine bad habits of common speech, see n. 27 and below, p. 189. On pleonastic intensification, see Löfstedt, Late Latin 21–24.

50. Compare 1.12, TYRII TENVERE COLONI deest "quam," with the generalization concerning what amant antiqui dicere vs. nos exprimimus: the generalization is clearly meant to enforce the proper use of the relative pronoun; cf. the large number of other notes of the deest type, the complement of the vacat type.

51. Cf. Servius at 2.401 (cited in his comment), and at 5.332, 6.51, or 10.305.

52. The lesson is expanded at 1.295 to include the assertion that the natura of certain communes praepositiones has changed over time. For the antiqua licentia, see also 1.253, on the phrase in sceptra reponis, 6.203, on super arbore; and Serv. 419.27–36, 443.7–10, Pomp. 275.19ff., 276.28ff. Cf. Chap. 4 at n. 101, on Pomp. 237.10–22, contrasting the confusiones antiquitatis (the product of a time when adhuc indefinita erat ista ratio) with the regula of Donatus.

53. Debuit dicere. . . . ideo ausus est . . . quia . . . apud maiores . . . dicebatur; see pp. 180, 184 above.

Yet the blurring of distinctions in this matter—and above all the haphazard use of *in* with the ablative and accusative—was much more characteristic of late Latin than of the ancients.[54] Once more the undesirable practice of common speech is put off on the *antiqui*. And to provide reinforcement, a series of scholia proceeds from this note, reminding the student that the lack of proper distinction belongs to the past, is obsolete, *archaismos*.[55] We have come a long way since then, the grammarian says: the movement of the language under the grammarian's guiding hand, toward greater refinement and regularity and away from ancient confusion or licence or harshness, is not doubted, and is a source of no little satisfaction.[56]

Servius's insistent and complacent didacticism makes his observations unreliable and sometimes bizarre, but not disingenuous. The distinction needs to be emphasized not only for a fair reading of Servius but, more important, for the reasons underlying it. When a usage is explained as arising *metri necessitate*, when Servius suggests what Vergil *debuit dicere*, when he comments on what "we say," when he distinguishes "what we say now" from archaism, the text of Vergil and the general state of the language are subordinated to Servius's sense of his own function and authority. Instead of being real objects that one tries to explain or describe historically, text and language become ciphers, assigned whatever validity or significance Servius chooses. The choice is complex and subjective, but it is not a matter of raw and conscious manipulation: it is expressed impersonally, through appeals to *natura* and the use of technical terms, the guarantees provided by his institutional niche; but Servius not only accepts those guarantees, and the authority they provide, as useful tools, he absorbs them into his personality. Servius believes what he says—about Vergil, the *antiqui*, the language, and *nos*—because he simply cannot believe otherwise. He has been fused with the institution he represents.

That the impersonal guarantees, rules, and authority have all been internalized is evident when we find the workings of Servius's mind displayed unself-consciously in that habit of projection we have already seen at work in Pompeius.[57] Like Pompeius, Servius most reveals himself when he explains someone else's actions and motives. To bring the

54. Cf. Adams, *Text* 54–55.

55. See 2.541, *aut archaismos aut* . . . , the general and specific, similar to 1.176; 6.639, *archaismos*, contradicting Donatus; 9.442, with additional reference to 9.347; 10.387; 10.838; and 10.807 (*archaismos* vs. *debuit dicere*), the matter of punctuation discussed above, p. 184.

56. Beyond the references in nn. 50–53 and 55, see, e.g., Diom. GL 1.374.5ff., 400.1ff., 427.15, 435.22ff. (and cf. 371.16ff., 381.12ff.); Mar. Vict. *Ars* 4.84 Mariotti (p. 85).

57. See Chap. 4 pp. 166ff.

chapter to a close, we can examine three passages that both betray this habit of mind and draw together several of the points remarked above—the use of the text as dummy, the nuance of the prescriptive indicative, and Servius's conception of his own status.

The first example is straightforward:

> 8.435 TVRBATAE pro "turbantis": nam timuit homoeoteleuton et fecit supinam significationem.

The note combines exegesis (it explains and justifies Vergil's use of the wrong participle) with prescription, and is thus a variation on the *metri causa* or *debuit dicere* type; whereas the latter sort is essentially negative, obliquely warning the student against a given usage, the comment on *Aeneid* 8.435 is largely positive. Servius projects his own values and concerns onto Vergil in order to inculcate the lesson in his students: as Servius is and as he would have his students be, so Vergil "was afraid of homoeoteleuton" (the collocation *turbant̲i̲s̲ Pallad̲i̲s̲*), because homoeoteleuton represents a *vitiosa elocutio*, a flawed form of expression, to be avoided in polished speech or writing.[58]

This instance of projection does not require much comment, but it should be compared with our second example, where the same tendency is present in a more interesting if less obvious form. The scholium involves the normative force of *dicimus*. The person who serves this time as the medium of Servius's message is Valerius Probus:

> 10.444 AEQVORE IVSSO pro "ipsi iussi." et est usurpatum partici-pium: nam "iubeor" non dicimus unde potest venire "iussus." sic ergo hic participium usurpavit, ut Horatius verbum, dicens [*Epist.* 1.5.21] "haec ego procurare et idoneus imperor et non invitus." ergo satis licenter dictum est, adeo ut huic loco Probus [hic corruptum] alogum adposuerit.[59]

---

58. For criticism of homoeoteleuton as a *vitiosa elocutio*, see the notes at 4.504, 9.49 and 606; cf. Pomp. 304.10, *antiquum est hoc totum, hodie nemo facit. siqui fecerit, ridetur.* With the function of the phrase *timuit homoeoteleuton* at 8.435, cf. 3.663, 10.571, 11.464, 12.5 and 781, and Schindel, *Figurenlehren* 27. With *timuit,* cf. also Serv. 409.17f.; and Pompeius on the fear of Donatus, Chap. 4 pp. 167f.

59. The text given is that of Thilo, who seems to have made the best of the general corruption in his manuscripts by treating the phrase *hic corruptum* (appear-ing only in M of the manuscripts he used) as an interpolated note originally intended to describe the state of Servius's text itself, where the nonsensical reading *.a. longam* in M (*a longam* or *ad longam* in the other manuscripts) occurs instead of *alogum,* an emendation of Burmann. Alternatively, *hic corruptum* could have found its way into the text at an earlier stage as a gloss on an original reading *alogum.*

The didactic intent of the note concerns the form *iubeor* and could be paraphrased, "We do not [ought not] use the passive *iubeor* or forms derived from it. Look: Vergil did, and his use is so odd that Probus even marked the passage as flawed."[60] But Probus likely did nothing of the sort. This is not to say that Servius invented Probus's annotation, but that the concerns of the two men were probably not so congruent as Servius in the urgency of making his point came to suggest. Where Servius reacts to the question of morphology, Probus was probably reacting to the sense, the figure of thought—the epithet transferred in using *aequore iusso* in place of *socii . . . iussi*.[61]

Several considerations suggest that Servius has gone astray in referring to Probus. First, the thought rather than the verbal form seems to have attracted earlier comment. That is the concern of the (no doubt traditional) gloss that begins Servius's own note; moreover, this particular figure of thought seems to have stood prominently in collections of such passages: when Macrobius's Servius enthusiastically recites expressions allegedly coined by Vergil, it occurs near the head of the list (*Sat.* 6.6.3), where again it is the transfer of the epithet that is noted. Second, in contrast to the foregoing, there is the singularity of Servius's own teaching. His condemnation of *iubeor* (and so *iussus*) is unique among the grammarians, but his citation of Horace's *imperor* suggests his train of thought clearly enough.[62] *Iubeor* is proscribed according to the principle that a verb governing the dative in the active voice (e.g., *impero tibi, invideo tibi, obicio tibi*; cf. Diom. *GL* 1.399.13–32 for a full account)

---

60. For the *alogus*, see Isid. *Orig.* 1.20.17: *alogus nota quae ad mendas adhibetur*; the *alogus* is listed among the critical signs, but is not glossed, in the *Anecdoton Parisinum* (*GL* 7.533–36). On this and the other *notae* said to have been used by Probus, see now Jocelyn, "Annotations" (I–III). My thanks to Prof. Jocelyn for showing me the proofs of "Annotations III," with his discussion of *Aen.* 10.444 (p. 472), in advance of publication: though he doubts (*per litt.*) that we can establish anything at all about Probus's reasoning here, there is no great difference between us in the interpretation of Servius's remarks.

61. So already Ribbeck, *Prolegomena* 151; but his prior assumptions regarding Servius's learning, derived from the portrait in Macrobius, made him unwilling to believe that Servius himself could have been concerned with the mere grammatical point. He therefore regarded the note as an interpolation; a similar conclusion was reached, for slightly different reasons, by Georgii, *Antike Äneiskritik* 454–55. Cf. also Scivoletto, "Filologia" 117.

62. With Servius on *iubeor*, cf. ps.-Acro at Hor. *Epist.* 1.5.21 (cited by Servius), "*imperor*" *finxit ex Graeco* κελεύομαι, *ut in arte poetica* "*invideor*" <φ>θονοῦμαι; and at *AP* 56, *mire dum de fingendis verbis loquitur, secundum Graecos ipse finxit* "*invideor.*" "*invideor,*" *id est,* "*invidiam patior*": *nam* "*invideor*" *negatur posse dici.* The verbs *invideo* and *impero*—and, according to Servius, *iubeo*—can be united in only one respect: their construction with the dative in the active voice and their consequent lack of a personal passive.

should be construed impersonally in the passive: *imperatur mihi,* not *imperor.* Since *iubeo* came to be used with the dative under the influence of *impero,* it should be governed, Servius reasons, by the same rule: *iubetur mihi,* not *iubeor*—a bit strict, but certainly unexceptionable Latin. Servius's prohibition of the passive participle *iussus* is a further, less-than-thoughtful regularization.

But that leads to the final consideration. The attempt at regularity that inspired Servius's remarks on *Aeneid* 10.444 is unlikely to have appealed to Probus.[63] In line with his taste for older authors unfashionable in his day, Probus's views ran in the direction of anomaly. His opinion concerning "those rotten rules and cesspools of grammar" is on record and accords with Suetonius's portrait of the man as something of an anomaly in the world of the *grammatici,* with interests and practices that deviated from the norm.[64] It would seem certain that the licence that disturbed Probus concerned the idea, the nonsensical (ἄλογον) collocation of *aequor* and *iussum* (the bidden plain).[65] But Servius seized upon the grammatical form; finding in one of his sources a reference (probably vague) to Probus's annotation, he instinctively assumed their concerns were identical and saw support for his own eccentric position on the question of what "we say." Servius's treatment of his scholarly predecessor is precisely the same as his treatment of Vergil.

Servius's capacity for misunderstanding or misrepresenting his sources has been remarked before,[66] although not for the reason involved here. The note on *Aeneid* 10.444 takes us beyond casual manifestations of carelessness or animus to a distortion that, like the nuance of *dicimus,* is built-in and automatic. Conditioned by Servius's devotion to his professional role, the distortion is virtually a reflex, and as such brings us close to the center of Servius's identity.

63. Although Aistermann, *De M. Valerio* 11, connected the scholium at 10.444 (= frg. 36 = frg. 98) with the view attributed to a Probus in cod. Paris. lat. 7491 fol. 92 (= GL 4, xxiii–xxiv = frg. 97), the latter probably does not go back to Valerius Probus but represents an inference drawn from Probus *Inst. art.,* GL 4.156.33–157.3, on *verba neutralia.*

64. See Chap. 2 at nn. 84, 85.

65. The Homeric scholia (where to my knowledge ἄλογος is never used for purely morphological matters) are helpful here: with the question of *iusso* vs. *iussi* at 10.444, compare esp. schol. A at *Il.* 18.198, on αὕτως vs. αὐτός and the criterion of οὐκ ἄλογος: the scholium reads, αὕτως· παρὰ Ζηνοδότῳ καὶ Ἀριστοφάνει διὰ τοῦ "ο," "αὐτός," ἵν᾽ ᾖ αὐτὸς χωρὶς ὅπλων. καὶ λόγον ἔχει χαρίεντα, καὶ οὐκ ἄλογός ἐστιν ἡ γραφή. See also schol. bT at *Il.* 21.86, on the readings ἀνάσσει and ἄνασσε; schol. A at *Il.* 8.73–74 and 186–88; schol. bT at *Il.* 24.23.

66. See Goold, "Servius" 134–40, concerned mostly with pure blunders; and cf. Zetzel, *Latin Textual Criticism* 105f., suggesting that Servius's notes at 3.535 and 636 are a malicious distortion of Donatus.

We can perhaps take the last step by looking at our third example, another instance of projection, which seems to define Servius's view of his own status:

4.9 INSOMNIA TERRENT et "terret" et "terrent" legitur. sed si "terret" legerimus, "insomnia" erit vigilia: hoc enim maiores inter vigilias et ea quae videmus in somnis interesse voluerunt, ut "insomnia" generis feminini numeri singularis vigiliam significaret, "insomnia" vero generis neutri numeri pluralis ea quae per somnum videmus. . . . sciendum igitur quia, si "terret" dixerimus, antiqua erit elocutio: "insomnia" enim, licet et Pacuvius et Ennius frequenter dixerit, Plinius tamen exclusit et de usu removit.

Servius's note on the variant readings is set squarely amid a minor bog of Latin lexicography, the distinction between the feminine singular *insomnia*, "sleeplessness," and the neuter plural *insomnia*, "(disturbing) dreams."[67] The lexical point, however, is not the central problem here, but the final clauses of Servius's note, *sciendum . . . removit*. These must ultimately derive from the elder Pliny's *Dubii sermonis libri VIII* and are included by Servius to inform his students that the feminine singular *insomnia* would involve an archaic form of expression.[68] The precise moment when the usage became obsolete is pinpointed, in Servius's understanding, by the magisterial act of Pliny—*exclusit et de usu removit*.

The statement and the idea behind it are intriguing: why—and more to the point, how—did Pliny treat the word so that it was excluded and removed from use? How did he express himself? We cannot know for certain, and there is room for various conjectures concerning the distinction Pliny made.[69] It does seem most likely, however, that Pliny's differentiation of the two ambiguous forms, one feminine singular only, the other neuter plural only, was intended primarily to emphasize the

67. See Getty, "Insomnia" (similarly DeRuyt, "Note"); and the lengthy rejoinder in Ussani, *Insomnia* esp. 77–113. The disposition in *TLL* s.vv. *insomnia* (*-ae*, 1935.75–1936.61) and *insomnium* (*-i*, 1937.70–1938.76) is the most sensible both in classifying the forms and in noting uncertainties.

68. Della Casa printed *insomniam*, the reading of cod. F. of DServ., in her edition of the *Dub. serm.* (frg. 15, *"insomniam" enim . . . removit*) and may have been correct: Servius normally accommodates the case of the word he quotes to the syntax of his sentence. Regardless of whether one reads *insomnia* or *insomniam* in Servius, however, the context makes it plain that he means the feminine singular.

69. For example, Barwick, *Remmius* 206, suggested that the statement represented a preference for *ratio*, analogy, over *vetustas*. Yet the principle of analogy scarcely seems relevant to this problem: more significant are the examples Barwick adduced (p. 207) to show Pliny's special interest in *consuetudo*.

distinction in meaning, which is the center of attention in Servius and other grammarians as well. In that case, the distinction was probably grounded in Pliny's sense of *consuetudo*—the usage current in his own day—set against *vetustas*.

Pliny, in other words, was probably attempting to do no more than clarify an existing situation. In the literary language, the feminine singular was an archaism well before Pliny's day; it is attested only in the older republican poets, of the second and early first century B.C., and thereafter in the archaizing authors of the second century A.D.[70] The neuter plural, though, appears to have been used regularly in the literary language of the first century A.D., including that of Pliny himself, and to have enjoyed even greater currency in ordinary speech.[71] If it is reasonable, then, to believe that Pliny's remarks simply recognized and defined the *status quo*, we might even suggest how Servius found those remarks transmitted in one of his sources—probably something along the lines of the following: *Plinius* [or *sic Plinius* or *Plinius ait*]:[72] *"insomnia," licet et Pacuvius et Ennius dixerit, penitus tamen de usu recessit* [or *exclusa est* or *remota est*].[73]

The precise form of the notice is not crucial; in distinguishing the usage of the *antiqui*, Pliny no doubt used some such phrase as *hodie non utimur* or *abolevit* or *in usu non est*, the kind of phrase that abounds in Servius. The point is this: the magisterial act—*exclusit et de usu removit*— was probably not Pliny's at all, but the product of Servius's interpretation, the act of a Pliny created by Servius in his own image, with his own prescriptive use of such phrases as *hodie non utimur* in mind. The chain of events suggested above, it is fair to say, accurately reflects both Servius's method and his self-image. There is no question who, in Servius's mind, has the final say in the life of the language: the simple observation of another man concerned with the language is translated by Servius, removed in time and imbued with the sense of his own authority, into an act of verbal extinction. *Ipse dixit.*

The grammarian's control of the language was something very personal. He was, to be sure, following a professional tradition of long standing when he offered his students a version of "Received Standard

70. For *insomnia* (*-ae*), see TLL 1935.75–1936.61.

71. See Getty, "Insomnia" 21–22; TLL s.v. *insomnium*, 1939.9–10.

72. The formula *"Plinius: . . ."* is of the kind commonly used to introduce the views of an individual in, e.g., the *Scholia Veronensia.*

73. Cf. Servius at, e.g., 7.626; 9.4; or 12.298, *TORREM erit nominativus "hic torris," et ita nunc dicimus: nam illud Ennii et Pacuvii penitus de usu recessit*; and Pomp. 187.10–12, *legimus in Capro. . . . etiam Naevius, Attius, Pacuvius, omnes isti utuntur hoc exemplo. tamen ista de usu remota sunt.* The citation of Caper is particularly suggestive, since Caper in his turn used Pliny as a major source.

Imperial" Latin,[74] expressed in the impersonal terms of his craft—*natura,
regula,* and the like. But as he filtered that version through his own
idiosyncratic preferences, choices, and distinctions, the grammarian presented and thought of himself as the maker of the *lingua aetatis suae,*
superior to the claims of *auctoritas* or *antiquitas.* Those dissatisfied with
the grammarian's personal control could circumvent it only by insisting
upon a higher authority: that of God, for example,[75] or the more diffuse
authority of the *maiores.* Macrobius's Servius took the latter course in
the incident from the *Saturnalia* with which we began this chapter; and
for his efforts, the grammarian there was roundly abused by the youth
Avienus for purveying the obsolete.

I have already emphasized the radical difference in this regard between
the figure Macrobius created and the man who speaks in the commentary.
It remains to underline one additional point. When Avienus demands
that the participants in the symposium use *praesentia verba,* the *aetatis suae
verba* (*Sat.* 1.5.1–2), he is demanding in effect that they speak natural,
regular Latin, the Latin covered by the *nunc dicimus* of the commentary.[76]
In other words, despite the conflict between youth and teacher that
Macrobius imagined, Avienus speaks much more in the manner we
should expect of a student of the real Servius than of an opponent; were
Avienus not meant to prove himself a basically decent sort, it would be
easy to imagine him behaving like grammarians' pupils who delight in
pointing out what Vergil *debuit dicere.*[77] Avienus's rudeness in his clash
with Servius is part of his characterization, a prelude to the broader
education he receives in the symposium.[78] But that Avienus should speak
as he does at the outset is appropriate in another respect: his initial

74. The phrase is Löfstedt's, *Late Latin* 48.

75. See Gregory the Great's challenge in *Ep.* 5.53a: *situs motusque et prae-
positionum casus servare contemno, quia indignum vehementer existimo, ut verba caelestis
oraculi restringam sub regulis Donati.* Cf. Smaragdus of St. Michel (s.IX): "I disagree
with Donatus, because I hold the authority of Scripture to be greater," cited by
Robins, *Ancient and Medieval Grammatical Theory* 71 (his translation).

76. In addition to the remarks above, see Pomp. 186.34–187.16 for *usus*
falling together with *ars;* cf. the revealing comment of Porphyrio on Hor. *AP*
70–71: "*cadentque / quae nunc sunt in honore vocabula, si volet usus*": *hoc est, ratio
loquendi.* [*usus*] *nihil enim aliud est quam regula sermonis Latini.* Petschenig correctly
secluded *usus* in the note; the whole scholium is clearly a comment on *usus* in
Horace's verse. See also ps.-Acro *ad loc.,* and Brink's valuable note, *Horace*
2.158–59.

77. Thus the *pueri* scorned by St. Augustine, *C. Faust.* 22.25 (*PL* 42.417), in
a comparison with those who find fault with the prophets: *similes sunt, qui in
magnis ista reprehendunt, pueris inperitis in schola, qui cum pro magno didicerint nomini
numeri singularis verbum numeri singularis esse reddendum, reprehendunt Latinae linguae
doctissimum auctorem, quia dixit* [1.212] "*pars in frusta secant.*" *debuit enim, inquiunt,
dicere "secat."* On *debuit dicere* as a criticism, see n. 31.

78. See Kaster, "Macrobius" 242ff.

deficiencies are precisely comparable to those of the *plebeia grammaticorum cohors*, whose inadequate knowledge and narrowly defined expertise Macrobius repeatedly criticized. In the *Saturnalia*, the members of that *cohors* are despised for shutting themselves off, as though in a box sealed by their ignorance of the culture's roots, whereas the idealized grammarian uses the language to bring past and present together. But the Servius of the commentary limits the language's scope and personally guards all approaches to it. He is in fact just another member of the troop, using the box—his institutional niche—as his position of strength.

*   *   *

In these last two chapters we have reviewed some of the elements that contributed to this position of strength: the accumulation of learning preserved in the tradition on which the grammarian could rely; the confidence in the rational ordering of the language's nature and in the greater sophistication, relative to the ancients, that it brought; the ability to apply one's own learning and *ratio* to decide between competing views, or even to add a new or more solid piece to the great edifice here or there; and the anxious need to protect the nature of the language—and, closely linked to it, one's own expertise—from assault. There was in all this a nice cooperation between the grammarian and his tradition. The tradition fortified the grammarian in the authority and security of his niche; the grammarian preserved the tradition and paid it the compliment of his improvements.

Such cooperation made for an enduring equilibrium. The grammarian was not about to criticize the tradition in any basic and general way or to be encouraged by his fellows to do so. The obvious urge to be right was independent of any drive to say what was both true and fundamentally new in the conception of the language or in the methods of discussing it. In its broad outlines and in much of its detail, the truth had already been found, in Diomedes' phrase, through "the brilliance of human talent" (*GL* 1.299.3). Such confidence perhaps led to what modern scholars often see as stagnation and a failure to evolve. But in the eyes of the grammarian, that stagnation was nothing other than the stability of lasting achievement; the failure to evolve, a satisfaction with what was already effective. It is worth remembering that even the most significant innovation in the late-antique *ars*—Priscian's treatment of syntax—is self-consciously presented as an infusion of earlier learning from a branch of the tradition that his Latin colleagues had previously neglected:[79] what had worked before would continue to work, but would work even better for the adjustment.

79. Prisc. *GL* 2.2.2ff., on the incorporation of the work done by Apollonius Dyscolus and Herodian.

From this point of view, grammar's failure to evolve is not attributable to some failure of nerve or intelligence but is a measure of its success. It remained as it was not because it was exhausted but because it worked so well and so smoothly. Perhaps the grammarians' satisfaction with the forms of analysis and the conceptual categories they had inherited over the centuries, and likewise their confidence in the familiar ordering of the language's nature, would have been shaken if they had had to confront more unruly data, derived, say, from the vulgar language of the market or of the suburban countryside. At very least, their thinking might have been modified and might have been forced to move in new directions. But of course those strata of the language not only received no sustained and systematic attention; they were effectively beneath interest. Indeed, they were not just beneath interest; they were what the inherited forms of analysis and conceptual categories, with their heavily normative emphasis, were meant to rise above. And that normative emphasis derived in turn from the embedding of the grammarians' position of strength in a larger structure of status and honor. So, after examining the grammarians' understanding of their skill and of their authority within the confines of their niche, we are reminded that this niche did not exist in a vacuum. In the next chapter we will ask how the grammarians' authority served them when they moved beyond the classroom to make their way in the world at large.

Gentlemen and Scholars

CHAPTER 6

The Social Relations of the Grammarians

*cum . . . Servius a Symmacho rogatus esset quidnam de his existimaret:
"licet," inquit, "in hoc coetu non minus doctrina quam nobilitate
reverendo magis mihi discendum sit quam docendum, famulabor tamen
arbitrio iubentis, et insinuabo."*

When Symmachus requested his judgment on these matters,
Servius said, "Although it is more fitting for me to learn than
to teach in this gathering, to which reverence is due no less for
its learning than for its nobility, I shall nonetheless obey the
will and bidding of Symmachus, and speak."

—*Macrobius*, Saturnalia 1.4.4

Within his classroom, the grammarian was the master of his craft, a
commanding figure, raised up by his texts, his tradition, and reason, just
as he was exalted by the *cathedra* on which he sat. Still, he could enjoy
this mastery for only a fraction of his waking hours, and each day he
had to descend from his throne and lift the curtains at the school's
threshold.[1] What happened when he stepped outside?

There was, to begin with, a significant carry-over of honor from the
classroom. To be called *magister* was a mark of respect, a reminder that
one was engaged in a *splendida ars* and was one of the better sort of
person (οἱ σεμνότεροι).[2] The grammarian, set apart from the mob by his
expertise, belonged to the *Kulturwelt* and shared its pride.[3] As we saw in
Chapter 2, that distinction was a target for some Christian writers in

1. *Grammaticarum scholarum liminibus appensa vela*: Aug. *Conf.* 1.13.22; cf. *De util. ieiun.* 9, *Serm.* 178.8.
2. For *magister* and *splendida ars*, see Don. *Comm. Ter.* at *Ad.* 288 (4 Wessner), with *Ad.* 210 (3 W.). For οἱ σεμνότεροι, see Chap. 3 n. 127.
3. οἱ πολλοί vs. οἱ γραμματικοί: Olympiod. *Comm. Alcib.* 1 95.17ff. Westerink.

their polemics against the traditional culture. The problem, to all appearances, did not much faze the grammarian, conscious of his prestige and unwilling to swallow embarrassment, whatever his religious affiliations.[4] Reputation, after all, was a commodity not to be trifled with: it provided the great name that would be boasted on one's epitaph; it was something on which one's native town could preen itself, whether one taught at home or abroad; it might even catch the ear of the emperor.[5]

Not surprisingly, therefore, grammarians could occasionally serve, like other men of standing, as public spokesmen or conduits of patronage. Early in the reign of Anastasius, probably in 491 or 495, Timotheus of Gaza directed to the emperor a composition concerned with the horrors of the *collatio lustralis*, an especially hated tax that bore most heavily upon merchants and small tradesmen. (Timotheus's action can be called disinterested, since teachers were not subject to the levy.) We might doubt Cedrenus's bald claim that Anastasius abolished the tax because of Timotheus's composition; other considerations aside, the chronology of his account is obviously confused. But it does appear that the tax was abolished not very long after Timotheus's plea.[6]

If Timotheus's intercession must remain a bit obscure, a more detailed case study is available from the fourth century in the person of Nicocles.[7] Having his origins in Sparta, Nicocles chose Constantinople as the place to make his career, and apparently he chose well. By 340 he was successful enough to promise to supply Libanius with forty students, when Libanius was only a budding private teacher of rhetoric in the new capital.[8] The offer highlights two elements in the relations between men at different levels of the teaching profession: not only the cooperative channeling of students from grammarian to rhetorician,[9] but also the use of such favors as a club—for Nicocles hoped simultaneously to oblige Libanius and, by establishing Libanius as a rival, to spite a sophist who

4. Cf. "Prologue" p. 6, on Aetius's teacher at Anazarbus.

5. Epitaph: see from the earlier empire Kaibel 534 = *GVI* 1479; *GVI* 1182 = *IKyzik.* 515 (Miletoupolis / M. Kemalpaşa, s.II); and cf. Heberdey and Kalinka, *Bericht* no. 65, a posthumous decree for Aelius Lucius Pilius Evarestus of Oenoanda, a document concerned as much with his benefactions as with his profession. Glory brought to home town: Lib. *Ep.* 969.4, 337.1; cf. *FD* 3:1.206, with "Prologue" pp. 4f., on Naevianus of Anazarbus. κλέος and the emperor: Agath. *Hist.* 5.6.5f. Keydell, with Part II no. 101.

6. See Cedren. 1.627.7–10 Bekker, where Anastasius is also said to have been swayed by a delegation of monks from Jerusalem; *Suda* T.621; and Part II no. 156.

7. See, in addition to nn. 8–17 following, the full analysis of the sources in Part II no. 106.

8. Lib. *Or.* 1.31.

9. Cf. also Lib. *Ep.* 832, to Nicocles, *Ep.* 398.2, to Acacius (see Part II no. 1).

had wronged him.[10] But Nicocles' moment as a man of consequence only came two decades later, during the reign of Julian. The stage had been set in late 347 or early 348, when the prince, released from his exile at Macellum, had been allowed by his uncle Constantius to continue his education in relative freedom at Constantinople. There he was taught by Nicocles and the sophist Hecebolius; and when Julian reached the throne thirteen years later and came east, Nicocles was not slow to exploit the friendship he could claim with the emperor for his tuition.[11] Doubtless because of Nicocles' favor, his brother Sozomenus appears as governor of Lycia early in 363.[12]

Others, too, were quick to see the potential in the situation. So Libanius evidently managed to forget an old grudge and make friendly overtures to Nicocles, who finds a place in Libanius's correspondence—and so in his network of useful connections—for the first time in 363. Nicocles is thanked for his efforts in spreading Libanius's fame, and Libanius promises to return the favor.[13] Letters of recommendation make their way from Antioch to Constantinople in behalf of a wandering poet or of men hoping to make a public career.[14] And perhaps most significant, Libanius attempts to enlist Nicocles' help in dissuading Julian from moving his court to Tarsus from Antioch.[15] As a known friend of the emperor, however, Nicocles was clearly not confined to serving Libanius's interests: when rioting at Constantinople had set the city prefect and the population against each other, Nicocles helped bring about a reconciliation; and he expected to represent the city in an embassy to Julian at Antioch concerning the same matter.[16]

But Julian went to Persia and died before the embassy occurred, and Nicocles' influence died with him.[17] Based on the loyalty of his extraordinary pupil, Nicocles' prominence was as unexpected as Julian's reign,

10. Lib. *Or.* 1.31; cf. *Ep.* 557.1–2, regarding Nicocles' apparent participation in the conspiracy of sophists and grammarians to drive Libanius from Constantinople ca. 343 (*Or.* 1.44).

11. Lib. *Ep.* 1368.4, the φιλία between Julian and Nicocles, sprung from Julian's admiration (θαῦμα) for Nicocles' teaching.

12. Lib. *Ep.* 1383, with *Bull. ép.* 1979, 509 no. 4.

13. Lib. *Ep.* 810.1–3.

14. Poet: Lib. *Ep.* 816, including the none-too-subtle hint that Nicocles should pay him well; for the type, cf. Lib. *Ep.* 969, in behalf of Diphilus, 632, in behalf of Eudaemon of Pelusium; Aen. Gaz. *Ep.* 9, 10. Hopes for a career: see esp. Lib. *Ep.* 832, in behalf of Theodorus, a former pupil of both Nicocles and Libanius; 810, in behalf of Hyparchius (= *PLRE* I s.v., p. 449); with 1119.1–2, in behalf of Hercul(i)anus (= *PLRE* I s.v. Herculanus 1, p. 420).

15. Lib. *Ep.* 1368.3.

16. Lib. *Ep.* 1368.1.

17. See esp. Lib. *Ep.* 1265, 1266, 1492, with pp. 214f. below.

and as evanescent. Nor are there other examples to set beside it.[18] The case of Nicocles is perhaps finally the exception that proves the rule: like the story of the grammarians' origins and social status in Chapter 3, the story of their social relations and of the prestige and influence that they enjoyed in consequence of their profession is largely set within narrow horizons.

The varieties and causes of these restrictions are not far to seek. First and foremost, the grammarian's place on the threshold of liberal disciplines[19] matched his liminal position of social mediocrity, the modest good standing beyond which the status and application of his expertise was not by itself sufficient to raise him. As we have already noted and as we shall see further, neither his origins nor his skills were commonly suited to set him squarely before the public eye. The grammarian Philtatius of Athens (if he was in fact a grammarian) might receive a statue as the city's thanks for putting his skills to public use by reestablishing the colometry of texts in one of the city's libraries; but that honor grew out of uncommon circumstances, reconstruction in the wake of barbarian devastation. It is unparalleled.[20] In more ordinary conditions, the grammarian might claim a moment as a quasi-public figure by stepping out of his professional role to become an encomiast.[21] But when the city needed the combination of standing and eloquence that made for an effective spokesman or ambassador, the choice fell naturally on the rhetorician.[22]

Moreover, the grammarian's place on the threshold of liberal culture made it difficult for him to develop a cluster of former students who had gone on to become influential men. The grammarian's role was propaedeutic: his students were *parvuli*; the rhetorician's were *perfecti*.[23] In practical terms this meant that, though some of the grammarian's stu-

---

18. Cf. Chap. 3 p. 130, on the status and rewards of imperial tutors in more ordinary circumstances, and p. 132, on Simplicius and Pamprepius and their careers as ex-grammarians dependent on a single powerful patron.

19. Ennod. *Dict.* 10.4: *liberalium disciplinarum limen.* Cf. id. *Opusc.* 6.11.

20. Olympiod. frg. 32. For the historical setting, see Thompson, "Athenian Twilight"; Frantz, "Honors." On Philtatius's service and the question of his profession, see Part II no. 119.

21. See Chap. 3 pp. 123f., with nn. 131, 132.

22. See esp. Lib. *Or.* 19–23, on the Riot of the Statues (cf. *Or.* 1.252–54); and, e.g., *PLRE* I s.vv. Eusebius 24 (p. 305, with pp. 219–20 below), Firminus 3 (p. 339; on his career, see also Basil *Ep.* 116, 117, and Kopaček, "Curial Displacements" 327ff.). For the sophist's intercession with the praetorian prefect, cf. Lib. *Or.* 1.109, *Ep.* 833.1–2; Theodoret. *Ep.* LII, to Isocasius.

23. Pelag. *Expos. in Rom.* 6.14 (p. 52.1ff. Souter). In the analogy around which the passage is built, the Christians stand in the same relation to the Jews as the rhetorician's students do to the grammarian's.

dents might begin careers with no further training,[24] most went on to the rhetorician's school. When they subsequently set about their life's business, their loyalty to their more recent teacher would account for a large part of the influence a rhetorician could claim, as Libanius's network of former students shows.[25] One can surmise that their loyalty to the grammarian, a more distant figure from their earlier years, was more attenuated and remote, less easily mobilized.[26]

Overshadowed by the rhetorician's inevitably greater visibility and prestige, the grammarian's institutional niche gave him his position of strength but also set his limitations. His expertise was esoteric enough to set him apart from the great majority of the population, but within the charmed world of the *litterati* it involved no extraordinary distinction, and little mystery. It was obviously not esoteric at all in the way of modern professions, encapsulated and set off by specialized training as they typically are from even the educated lay public. It was instead eminently accessible to all the educated. The grammarian did not, after all, claim to be a charismatic teacher (as the Christian bishop did) and was not by definition a literary artist as well as a teacher (as the rhetorician was), but was fundamentally and simply a man of *ratio* and *memoria*. The qualities and attainments that gave the grammarian his authority in the classroom, even if not directly transmissible, were nurtured in his pupils by his teaching and, if he taught successfully, ceased to be distinctive to him. Since the grammarian and the educated layman occupied largely common ground, the grammarian's knowledge was not different in kind—or even necessarily in quantity—from that of any well-bred *litteratus*. The talented amateur could stand forth as a questioner and critic (ζητητικός τε καὶ κριτικός) of the professionals on their own ground.[27] Nongrammarians could produce learned works rooted in γραμματική, whether tricked out in literary elegance like the great works of Macrobius and Martianus Capella or straightforward manuals much like the grammarians' own.[28]

24. Cf. Chap. 1 at n. 62.
25. See Petit, *Étudiants* esp. 154ff.
26. Note that Julian was already nearly an adult, with much of his education behind him, when he formed his connection with Nicocles; see the appendix to Part II no. 106. The connection was as extraordinary in this regard as it was in others.
27. Damasc. *V. Isid.* frg. 331 Zintzen = epit. Phot. 298, of Agapius.
28. So the *De metris* of Fl. Mallius Theodorus, the *De differentiis societatibusque Graeci Latinique verbi* of Macrobius, or the handbooks of Charisius (cf. Part II no. 200) and Consentius (cf. Part II no. 203). Note, conversely, the works of general learning produced by grammarians on topics ranging from zoology and medicinal herbs (Part II nos. 61, 156) through a survey of the provinces and cities of the eastern empire (Part II no. 76) to humor (Part II no. 117). Cf. also

It is useful to imagine some of the consequences that might follow from this embedding of the grammarian's profession in the shared life of the elite. To begin with, since the grammarian's knowledge was as fundamental to the distinctive literacy and the prestige of the nonprofessional elite as to his own, the conservatism of his doctrine would be reinforced. The common ground would exercise a strong gravitational pull: the profession would be less free than its modern counterpart to follow its own lead (for better or worse, toward new understanding or the merely faddish), to spin off in the direction of esoteric concerns, or to become fragmented (in the manner of many modern professions) in proliferating subspecialties and techniques. Or to put it another way, two kinds of self-interest would converge to stabilize doctrine: if the grammarian within his institutional niche was not about to challenge or renovate radically the tradition that fortified him, as was suggested at the end of the last chapter, neither would he be expected or encouraged to do so by the *litterati* outside that niche, whose own interests were scarcely less involved. The grammarian's audience did not usually speak the command, Astonish me!

The *litterati* would instead look for qualities other than searching criticism and innovation. When Augustine wants to illustrate the principle that the Word must be loved before it can be understood, he turns naturally to the example of the grammarian's audience, who expect the grammarian to confirm the greatness of the texts on which he comments and so to confirm the assumptions that they bring to the texts even before they have read them.[29] When the grammarians are criticized by the learned elite, as they are, for example, by Tiberius Claudius Donatus and by Macrobius, it is not for offering *crambe repetita*, nor conversely for extending their investigations to a level of expertise beyond the reach of educated laymen, but for superficiality, for falling short of the standards that the educated set.[30] It is not a conceptually fresh and independent approach that is desired, but more of the same; not brilliance, but application, industry, and affirmation. The expectations thus press perceptibly away from the exercise of purely intellectual gifts, and toward intellectual habits that express ethical qualities—qualities that inform a man's behavior overall, that reveal themselves in his personal relations no less

---

the philosophical or theological writings of grammarians and ex-grammarians: Part II nos. 38, 81, 82, 118, 124, 135.

29. Aug. *De util. cred.* 6.13, with which compare Servius's comment at, e.g., *Aen.* 7.647; and cf. Chap. 5 on the function, in part exculpatory, of *figura, antiquitas,* and the like.

30. Ti. Claudius Donatus *Interp. Vergil.* 1.1.5ff. Georgii; Macrob. *Sat.* esp. 1.24.12–13, 5.18–22, with Kaster, "Macrobius" 235f., 252ff.

than in his professional activities, and that lend themselves to personal judgments.

We have already seen an example of how such qualities were viewed by the learned elite, in the *Saturnalia* of Macrobius, where the traits desirable in a grammarian are displayed in a setting of generalized, shared expertise.[31] There the virtues of modesty (*verecundia*) and diligence (*diligentia*) are emphasized above all: they are displayed not only by the good grammarian, represented by Servius, but by all the invited participants; they are assumed to have been the controlling virtues of Vergil, as well, whose text is at the center of the discussion. The virtues in fact hold the world of the dialogue together, since they impel men to maintain their contacts with their culture's past at the same time that they allow harmonious and fruitful conversation to proceed. Each member has a special contribution to make out of his own learning; and the dignity of each man's learning corresponds to his place in a hierarchy of birth and age, from the linguistic expertise of the grammarian, the humblest of the group, through the religious knowledge of the great figure, Praetextatus. But at the same time individual knowledge is not stressed, and the express belief is that learning is distributed broadly throughout the gathering, so that one man is prepared to refine or to add to another's contribution without rancor or self-aggrandizement. It is thoroughly appropriate that when analogy is used, one of the conceptual foundations of the grammarian's skill, other members of the group in addition to the grammarian apply it and simultaneously extend it to ratify usages that the grammarian in his own work would not embrace; the sources of linguistic authority are broadened, just as authority in the dialogue as a whole is diffused throughout the group, not focused in one man.

The display of virtues and the diffusion of expertise and authority are part of Macrobius's ideal in his admiring portrait of the aristocracy of birth and letters at Rome. As we shall see, however, the ideal makes contact with facts of life that would affect the professional teacher wherever he taught. Not least important of these was the judgment of professional competence, which rested fundamentally with laymen. A *professio* at base was no more than a public statement made by men offering "their services . . . at their own discretion."[32] In a world without specialized training and certification, without formal and rationalized means of establishing standards within the profession comparable to the institutions that serve those purposes today (graduate or professional schools, learned associations and journals, for example), no mechanisms

31. See Chap. 2 pp. 60–62; Chap. 5 pp. 171f., 195.
32. Lewis, *Atti* 516.

were commonly available for reaching impersonal judgments, or judgments that at least aimed at being objective in principle. Inevitably—and
in the circumstances, not unreasonably—one could claim to be competent
because the community at large believed one was competent, and especially because respected and prominent members of the community said
so. For private teachers, what mattered was the word of mouth passed
by fathers willing to send their sons to one's school or by patrons
suggesting they should. For teachers aiming at a publicly supported post,
what mattered was the approval (*probatio*, δοκιμασία) of the town council
or, correspondingly, of the senate at Rome or Constantinople.[33]

Even for the formal *probatio*, the teacher necessarily depended on the
good opinion of others outside the profession: in the absence of a formal
test, general reputation and the recommendation of well-placed supporters were paramount.[34] A rhetorician would make his name in part
by displaying his literary talents in public contests: such opportunities
for star turns and for building an independent reputation were part of
the rhetorician's greater visibility;[35] in this respect as in others, the
grammarian's trajectory was lower. His expertise did not lend itself to
public displays from which stellar reputations could be won, and in fact

33. Jones, *LRE* 707–8, 998–99; Lewis, *Atti* 515ff.; Nutton, "Two Notes."
Appointment by town council: *CJ* 10.53.2 (Gordian), with *Dig.* 27.1.6 (Mod.), 4,
and 50.9.1 (ps.-Ulp.); *PCollYoutie* 2.66 = *POxy.* 47.3366, B28f.; Aug. *Conf.* 5.13.23
(Milan); Lib. *Or.* 1.48 (Nicaea and Nicomedia), *Or.* 31.21, *Ep.* 209 (a teacher of
law), 539, 907.3 (Antioch), *Or.* 2.14 (καλούμενος ὑπὸ τῆς βουλῆς at Athens, with
Or. 62.61 and Norman, *Autobiography* at *Or.* 1.82 [p. 170]; cf. also Eunap. *V. phil.*
10.3.8–9), *Ep.* 1366.1 (Apamea; cf. 1391.2), *Or.* 31.42 (Caesarea); and generalized
in Lib. *Or.* 55.36, ψηφίσματι καὶ γνώμῃ κοινῇ πρὸς θρόνον ἀγόμενος. Appointment
by senate: Cassiod. *Var.* 9.21.5ff. (cf. Symm. *Ep.* 1.79 [Rome]); *CTh* 6.21.1 (an.
425; cf. Lib. *Or.* 1.35 [Constantinople]).

34. Well observed by Nutton, "Two Notes" 54f. Lewis, *Atti* 515ff., correctly
stresses that *probatio* or δοκιμασία was normally an administrative process admit-
ting the privileged to immunity—a vote of confirmation for someone already
practicing his profession—not a test of competence conducted by the council
(against Zalateo, "Nuovo significato"; similarly, e.g., Marrou, *Histoire*[6] 440, and
Langhammer, *Stellung* 69, the latter mistakenly defining *probatio* as "eine Art
Probevorlesung" presented by the teacher to the council). Of course we need
not deny that the question of competence, however defined (see below), would
arise at the time of the *probatio*; but we should not think that the question would
typically be answered by the close examination of skills associated with professional certification today. Explicit provision for *reprobatio*, the reconsideration
of teachers' appointments *si non se utiles studentibus praebeant* (*CJ* 10.53.2 [Gordian]),
would seem to acknowledge that the initial *probatio* could be rather loosely
grounded.

35. E.g., Lib. *Or.* 1.35, 37; Aug. *Conf.* 4.1.1, 4.3.5. See also Walden, *Universities*
218ff.; Petit, *Étudiants* 96ff.; and in general on ἀκροάσεις *Bull. ép.* 1958, 347
(p. 281).

the evidence for such displays of the skills and knowledge specific to his profession is virtually nonexistent.[36] Instead, his expertise lent itself to displays in private settings and accumulated its reputation less dramatically through contacts made face to face.

As a result, we commonly see the grammarians playing the part of private consultants, a role comparable to that at the beginning of their history, when they were typically attached as slaves or freedmen to the great houses of late-republican Rome. That the role remains, despite the general rise in the grammarians' social status, can be attributed to the nature of their expertise. The idealized picture of Macrobius's Servius, making his modest contribution to the discussion of the learned *nobiles* in the intimacy of the salon, where his *mores* are as much on display as his learning, is not far removed from the scenes glimpsed in life. Faustus in Africa receives the *liber epigrammaton* of Luxurius for vetting. Sidonius Apollinaris in Gaul relies on Domitius for a similar service and invites him to share the *contubernium* of his estate. In Syria, Libanius recalls the advice he received in conversations with Eudaemon. Diomedes dedicates his compilation to Athanasius, a work written in lieu of conversation (which he also promises when they are together again) and in answer to Athanasius's interest.[37] So, more generally, there is the typical claim that a work was undertaken at the suggestion or request of the dedicatee.[38] The stimulus professedly comes primarily from the outside rather than from the writer's desire or duty to make a professional

36. Only Gell. *NA* 16.6.1–12 might be so interpreted, concerning *quispiam linguae Latinae litterator* [= *grammaticus*; see ibid. 11], *Roma a Brundisinis accersitus*, who made himself available for public tests of his expertise (*experiundum sese vulgo dabat*). The passage shows, however, that these occasions were later than and independent of his summons to the town. Contrast Pamprepius, given a post at Constantinople after reciting either a poem or a discourse on the soul (Malch. frg. 20 and Damasc. *V. Isid.* frg. 178 Zintzen, with Part II no. 114); or Ioannes Lydus, given a chair of Latin at Constantinople by Justinian after delivering an encomium of the emperor (*De mag.* 3.28, with Part II no. 92); or Phoebicius of Bordeaux, gaining his chair through the patronage of a son (Auson. *Prof.* 10.29–30), probably the rhetorician Attius Patera; and see further below.

37. Faustus (Part II no. 58): Luxurius *Anth. Lat.* 1:1.287. Domitius (Part II no. 50): Sidon. Apoll. *Carm.* 24.10ff., *Ep.* 2.2. Eudaemon (Part II no. 55): Lib. *Ep.* 255. Diomedes (Part II no. 47): *GL* 1.299.2–10, 391.16–17. Cf. also Chap. 4 for the vignettes of consultation and questioning Pompeius inserted in his work, probably as a reflection of his own experiences.

38. Besides Diomedes, see Don. *Epist. praef.* 15f. Hardie; Serv. *De fin.*, *GL* 4.449.3, Cledon. *Ars*, *GL* 5.92.2ff.; Prisc. *Inst.*, *GL* 2.2.24ff. and 194.2ff., *De fig. num.*, *De met. Terent.*, *praeex.*, *GL* 3.405.8ff.; Eutych. *Ars de verb.*, *GL* 5.447.8ff. This ancient convention was of course firmly rooted in *belles lettres*: see the examples collected by Gudeman, *Tac. Dial.*[2] 41 n. 1; Janson, *Prose Prefaces* (esp. 116ff. for late-antique texts); Murgia, "Date" 124f.

contribution to his field:[39] the work itself forms part of the grammarian's social relations, as a token or gift that tightens the bonds between the dedicator and the recipient.[40]

Several strands in these relations are brought together in the brief story that the grammarian Sacerdos sketches at the beginning of Book 3 of his *Artes grammaticae*.[41] Sacerdos dedicated his first book to the *vir clarissimus* Gaianus, a companion of long standing (*contubernalis*), his contemporary and onetime fellow student. Gaianus's father, Uranius, learned of the book and was pleased by it—either, as Sacerdos charmingly remarks, because it was "not put together ineptly" or because it was dedicated to his son—and compelled Sacerdos to undertake a second book. Sacerdos gladly obeyed Uranius's commands and was subsequently commended by him to two other gentlemen of senatorial rank, whose commands Sacerdos then satisfied in his third book. What began as a perhaps well-calculated act of friendship, growing out of the intimacy of *contubernium*, thus developed into a series of relations that allowed the grammarian to increase the number of his patrons.

For Sacerdos, his long-standing comradeship (*contubernium*) with Gaianus was evidently the key: it provided the initial opportunity to display his skills; and it acted as an implicit guarantee, a social code that could assure Gaianus's father and friends that Sacerdos—although certainly not a *vir clarissimus* himself—was still in some sense a gentleman, one of them, a decent and respectable sort to whom they could deign to give their attention.[42] It served the purpose, in other words, that is served in different circumstances by stressing *mores*. Recent research on patronage and public careers under the empire has properly emphasized the importance attached to personal qualities in, say, letters of recommendation, and has noted the weight given good character in appointments and promotions—a weight apparently at least equivalent to specialized competence and merit, as those qualities might be judged in technical or impersonal terms.[43] In connection with teachers and others in the liberal professions, we have already had occasion to remark the

39. The only significant exception—and that only partial—is provided by Prisc. *Inst.*: besides noting the urgings and commands of Iulianus (see n. 38), Priscian speaks of the undertaking (*GL* 2.2.2f.) as a *rem . . . officio professionis non indebitam*. For still a different note—the grammarian's work presented as the fruit of gentlemanly leisure—see Serv. *De met. Hor.*, *GL* 4.468.6, with Chap. 2 p. 66.

40. Cf. also Chap. 2 p. 68 for comments on teachers' dedications to their pupils.

41. *GL* 6.496.5ff. The significance of the passage, and especially the importance of *contubernium*, are well brought out by Champlin, *Fronto* 45.

42. Cf. *GL* 6.497.1: *quoniam iubere dignati estis.*

43. See Pedersen, *Public Professionalism* 30f.; and esp. Saller, *Personal Patronage* 95ff.; note also the implications of Campbell, "Who Were the 'Viri Militares'?,"

importance of such personal criteria: the infrequency with which professional skills are singled out as the sole or primary grounds of commendation, and the regularity with which *mores* receive equal or greater
emphasis, so that the distinction between technical attainments and
personal qualities is blurred and the notion of competence embraces
both.[44] This union of ethos and expertise derived from the learned elite's
traditional and comforting assumption that not only were the good to be
identified with the learned, but true learning must proceed from good
character. Gellius's famous definition of *humanitas*, equating it with
learning and education (*eruditio institutioque*) on the one hand and with
such ethical qualities as devotion and discipline (*cura et disciplina*) on the
other, generalizes what Ausonius surely had in mind when he described
one grammarian of *implacidi mores* as also (and inevitably) *doctrina exiguus*.[45]

In everyday usage, the stress on good *mores* offered the assurance that
the man so described would fit in and not disrupt the stately world of
learned gentlemen. Here again the literary description of the good grammarian Servius, "at once admirable in his learning and attractive in his
modesty" (*Sat.* 1.2.15) as he takes his place inconspicuously in the placid
microcosm of the symposium, makes contact with the real world of
social relations, since that description conforms to the terms used in
letters of commendation.[46] Meeting the need to establish that their
subjects are the right sort, such letters run heavily to the praise of
personal attributes. Writing in behalf of Eudaemon of Pelusium, Libanius
emphasizes his family's respectable standing (εὐγένεια) and virtuous
restraint (ἐπιείκεια).[47] On another occasion, Libanius refers again to
the same characteristics, using them to bracket the observation that
Eudaemon is "one of the eloquent," and goes on to add that Eudaemon
"is fairer in my eyes than a brother."[48] In a letter that can stand as a

---

and of Brunt, "Administration." Personal or ethical criteria, though almost
inevitably subjective in their application, were not therefore arbitrary in themselves; for they made sense (even if it was not our kind of sense) in their social
setting, and a coherent account of them can be given. It seems necessary to
stress this point, in view of a tendency simply to link or identify the subjective
and the arbitrary—so, e.g., Frei-Stolba, reviewing Saller in *Gnomon* 55 (1983)
142, speaks of "durchaus subjektiven und willkürlichen Kriterien."

44. Chap. 2 pp. 65f., with nn. 137, 138, 140.

45. Gell. *NA* 13.17, Auson. *Prof.* 10.37–41. For the union of culture and
virtue, see also the honorific inscriptions cited at Chap. 1 nn. 65, 76; and cf. the
inscription commemorating Evarestus of Oenoanda (n. 5 above): γραμματικὸς
ἀλειτούργητος, ἐπὶ ἤθει . . . ἐπαινετός.

46. See Chap. 2 n. 137.

47. Lib. *Ep.* 108.2.

48. Lib. *Ep.* 164.1, 2. Cf. the letter of commendation to the grammarian
Nicocles, in which Libanius says that he regards the subject as "no different
from a son": αἴτιον δὲ ⟨ἡ⟩ ἐπιείκεια καὶ τὸ αἰδεῖσθαί τε καὶ δόξης ἐπιθυμεῖν καὶ

concise example of the genre, written to Alexander of Heliopolis in behalf of an homonymous teacher, Libanius says, "As for the grammarian who shares your name, consider him a good man and one very well versed in literature, and enroll him among those who know how to be a friend."[49]

When Libanius promises this magnate of Heliopolis that the grammarian Alexander knows how to be a friend, he is promising in effect that Alexander will fit snugly into the man's network of connections and dependents: as a worthy recipient of his favor and protection, one prepared to make what return he could. Alexander was moving from Antioch to Heliopolis, and Libanius here is smoothing the way, enlisting a powerful patron for Alexander, passing him along in much the same way that Gaianus's father passed Sacerdos along to his friends, and probably in much the same terms. The patron could presumably be relied on, for example, to spread the word among his connections in order to guarantee Alexander a healthy number of students in his new position; in return, Alexander could be relied on, if needed, to put his knowledge at the patron's disposal, and in general to play the part of a friend by spreading the word of his patron's loyalty and influence.[50] The letter would thus ease Alexander into a position of genteel dependence as the lesser member of a patronage relationship—what has recently and well been described as the continuing, reciprocal, but asymmetrical exchange relationship between men of unequal social status.[51]

The importance of the relationship can be inferred in the case of Sacerdos. It is glimpsed directly in the case of Alexander or of Iulianus Pomerius, who enjoyed the protection of the *potens* Firminus at Arles late in the fifth century.[52] It is perhaps attested most warmly by Augustine, when he recalls the patronage of Romanianus at the early stages of his career. A dominant figure of Thagaste, Romanianus gave Augustine his protection and intimacy when Augustine returned home to teach: he entrusted Augustine with the education of his son, and he even helped

---

λαβεῖν ἐπαινέτας τοὺς γέροντας, ὧν καὶ πρῶτον καὶ μάλιστα τὸν θεῖον τὸν ἐμόν, ὃν εἰδὼς εἰδείης ἂν καὶ τοῦτον. οὐ γὰρ ἂν ἐκεῖνος τὸ οὐκ ἀγαθὸν ἐθαύμασε (*Ep.* 810.6).

49. Lib. *Ep.* 1256.3.

50. Cf. Lib. *Ep.* 467, thanking a patron for his help at court and promising to make a return through his attentions to the man's son, his pupil; similarly *Ep.* 491.3.

51. See Saller, *Personal Patronage* 1ff., after J. Boissevain. The lesser member of the pair could make his exchange concretely, e.g., by presenting a composition to his patron; or, something intangible but perhaps even more important, by publicizing the greater man's excellence whenever the opportunity arose. For a blending of both types of return, see Lib. *Or.* 1.111, a panegyric of the PPO Strategius Musonianus explicitly undertaken to repay an earlier favor.

52. *V. Caes.* 1.8f., with Part II no. 124.

Augustine in his ambition to seek a more prestigious position at Carthage, although Romanianus would have preferred him to remain in his *patria*.[53]

Such relations (and we shall examine other cases below) were crucial to the teacher's professional life—but not only to his professional life, a point that should be emphasized immediately. Just as the line between professional and personal qualities is blurred in the language of approbation and commendation, so the exercise of patronage ignores any distinction between the professional and the personal spheres of the teacher's life: it embraces both and confounds them. In 361 the grammarian Calliopius and his father were teaching Libanius's son at Antioch; Libanius wrote to Iulianus, the *praeses Euphratensis*, asking him to show favor to Calliopius's brother-in-law, for by doing so, Libanius said, Iulianus would dispose the teachers more favorably toward the son.[54] In 358, the grammarian Tiberinus, a native of Arabia teaching at Antioch, turned to Libanius when his son was the object of a lawsuit in his native province: Libanius wrote to the governor Maximus, told him that Tiberinus was "a good man and a teacher of the poets," and tried to engage his good will for Tiberinus's son, basing his appeal on Maximus's respect for culture, his respect for Tiberinus's native and adopted cities, and his respect for Libanius himself.[55]

The same years find Libanius exerting himself in behalf of the grammarian Cleobulus, who had been Libanius's teacher and whom Libanius therefore looked on "as a child does his father."[56] The extent of Libanius's efforts suggests that this was more than just a form of words. On two occasions we can see Libanius mediating between one or another of Cleobulus's relatives and a pair of imperial officials, seeking a staff position in one case and special favor in the other.[57] Particularly revealing is a group of eight letters that show the persistence of a good patron at work.[58] In 359 Cleobulus was being hounded with a suit that threatened a fine he could not afford if it went against him. He turned to a man he regarded as a friend (φίλος) and protector (φύλαξ), Themistius, who at the time was proconsul of Constantinople, but Themistius was unresponsive.[59] Libanius then entered the affair, sending a series of letters in the course of the year to Themistius, to Clearchus, who held an official

53. Aug. *C. Acad.* 2.2.3.
54. Lib. *Ep.* 678; cf. Chap. 2 p. 69; and cf. n. 50 above.
55. Lib. *Ep.* 337. Cf. *Ep.* 431, promising the intervention of Libanius and others in a suit lodged against the grammarian Acacius, who had in the past sent some of his students on to Libanius: *Ep.* 398.
56. Lib. *Ep.* 361.2; cf. *Ep.* 231.1. The documentation for what follows is discussed fully at Part II no. 32.
57. Lib. *Ep.* 361, 82.
58. Lib. *Ep.* 52, 67–69, 90, 91, 155, 231.
59. See esp. Lib. *Ep.* 67.

position of some sort, and to the physician Hygi(ei)nus, a friend of
Themistius. Libanius's repeated petitions had no effect beyond causing
his irritation to mount, and the suit finally went against Cleobulus.
Changing his strategy to meet Cleobulus's need, Libanius appealed to
his own relative Bassianus, who was also a former pupil of Cleobulus.
Reminding Bassianus of "the labors of the good Cleobulus" in his behalf,
Libanius called on him to reciprocate.[60] The appeal worked, and Bassianus
gave Cleobulus the money to pay his fine, saving him from ruin.

These examples suggest the range of needs served by the teacher's
patronal connections; and the case of Cleobulus perhaps best shows the
real strength of the conventional pieties through which such connections
were expressed: the stress on personal relationship, the pressure toward
reciprocity and loyalty, the desire to show oneself a good man by helping,
on a variety of fronts, the good man under one's protection. But the
case of Cleobulus also clearly suggests the limits of the conventions:
although Cleobulus thought he could call on Themistius as friend and
protector, Themistius felt free to turn a deaf ear; and Libanius's influence
was plainly too weak to move the greater man.

A similar lesson is still more vividly drawn in the case of Nicocles. We
have already remarked what prominence Nicocles enjoyed during Julian's
reign on the strength of his connection with his former pupil. But the
death of his great protector exposed Nicocles to men ready to cut him
down to size, or who at least were no longer inclined to pay him respect.
Nicocles' isolation is seen in his relations with his former pupil Clearchus,
who as *vicarius Asiae* turned on his old teacher after Julian's death to get
his own back for some wrong he believed Nicocles had dealt him in the
past.[61] The precise form of Clearchus's harassment is not clear, but it
was sufficiently serious that Nicocles called on Libanius to mediate.
Libanius first wrote a letter of rebuke to Clearchus, by turns warning
him that Fortune is fickle—"The goddess delights both in raising up the
fallen and in bringing down the proud"—and reminding him that he had
once been Nicocles' "child" (παῖς), that Clearchus's father had entrusted
him, as Clearchus had entrusted his brother, to Nicocles.[62] The latter
appeal, of the sort that had worked with Bassianus, had no effect.
Although Clearchus's reply is not preserved, one can guess that it put
Nicocles and Libanius alike in their places; for the tone of Libanius's
second letter is dramatically different, fawning where he had earlier

60. Note esp. Lib. *Ep.* 155.2, μὴ τῶν τοῦ καλοῦ Κλεοβούλου περὶ σὲ πόνων
ἀμνημόνει; with ibid. 3, ὃν [viz., Κλεόβουλον] . . . ἀντευποίει.

61. Lib. *Ep.* 1265, 1266, 1492. For vague reference to Clearchus's motives,
see *Ep.* 1266.3; and cf. n. 64 below.

62. Lib. *Ep.* 1266.5, 7, the ἐπιστολὴ μεμφομένη promised in *Ep.* 1265.3.

been reproachful, and with a sneer for Nicocles: "Granted that Nicocles is otherwise worthless [φαῦλος], he at least deserves respect [τίμιος] because he 'made you such as you are, godlike Achilles.'"[63] On the most charitable interpretation, the letter shows Libanius trying to salvage a bad situation by taking the tack least likely to offend Clearchus.[64]

Nicocles' vulnerability after Julian's death reminds us again of the perils of dependence on a single patron.[65] It was a lesson Pamprepius had a chance to learn early on, when he fell afoul of the magnate Theagenes at Athens and was forced to quit the city.[66] It was a lesson, too, that must gradually have impressed itself on Lollianus of Oxyrhynchus when in making his petition to the emperors he pinned his hopes on the only man of consequence he knew, the courtier he calls "Brother": the surviving draft of Lollianus's letter represents his third attempt to enlist "Brother's" help, and the presumption is strong that the man had simply ignored the first two, as Themistius ignored Cleobulus's appeal.[67]

But even a more differentiated network of relations did not guarantee success or peace of mind; most notably, one risked being squeezed between feuding patrons. So, for example, Diphilus had the misfortune to be the protégé of Libanius when the latter was on wretched terms with another of Diphilus's patrons, Eustathius, governor of Syria. Eustathius promised a favor to Diphilus, who was uncertain whether or not he should accept. (It was less than he had hoped for, and he was a bit put out as a result.) Diphilus turned for advice to Libanius, who persuaded him to take what had been offered. Eustathius thereupon reneged, in order, so Libanius says, to make fools of both of them: "For he thought it would be a terrible thing if Diphilus could spread the word to Palestine [the province where Diphilus taught] that I have enough power to benefit a friend."[68] Clearly, genteel dependence in any form was not without its drawbacks.

63. Lib. *Ep.* 1492.2, quoting *Il.* 9.485. With εἰ καὶ τἆλλα φαῦλος, Libanius may repeat an epithet Clearchus had used in his reply; in any case, it should give a hint of the tone that Clearchus had used.

64. Note that Clearchus, like Nicocles and Libanius, was a pagan; his persecution of Nicocles therefore cannot be ascribed to an antipagan reaction after Julian's death. For Nicocles' paganism and Libanius's allusions to a backlash, see Part II no. 106; for Clearchus, see von Haehling, *Religionszugehörigkeit* 118f.

65. Cf. Chap. 2 p. 132, on Simplicius and Pamprepius.

66. Malch. frg. 20, with Part II no. 114. To judge from his subsequent career (see n. 65), he did not take the lesson to heart.

67. PCollYoutie 2.66 = POxy. 47.3366, B23. For the level of Lollianus's other connections, see Chap. 3 n. 138.

68. Lib. *Or.* 54.56–57, with Part II no. 49. The incident concerns Diphilus *qua* poet, but that should not alter the general point made here.

In the discussion so far we have been concerned almost exclusively with private patronage and mediation. But the presence of the governor Eustathius in the incident just noted and the desirability of an extended network of patrons raise another issue: the place of official patronage and state intervention in the lives of our grammarians. It is time, then, to shift our attention from private to ostensibly public connections: in the rest of the chapter we shall consider the involvement of imperial officials in the schools of the provinces, the apparent blurring of the distinction between municipal and imperial authority in scholastic matters, and the implications for the kinds of relationship we have examined in the pages above.[69]

Evidence for such involvement is not lacking; we should note first, however, that the most notorious piece of evidence is in fact of little consequence. I refer, of course, to Julian's law of 17 June 362, which was intended, as he subsequently made clear, to drive Christian teachers from the schools.[70] By this law, Julian commanded that all teachers be approved first by a decree of the town council, with the agreement of the best men of the town, and that the decree then be sent for his own review and judgment. The demand was unprecedented in two regards. First, it asserted explicitly that in the matter of education the local council merely acted as the emperor's proxy.[71] Second, and perhaps more striking, it extended the scope of the council's *probatio* to include not only teachers seeking municipally funded positions and immunities[72] but all teachers, public and private.[73] This amounted to a clear restriction of what had hitherto been a free *professio*.

But neither this broad limitation nor the principle of imperial review of local *probationes* (in any application of the term) appears to have outlived Julian's equally unprecedented sectarian purposes. The law, it is true, was incorporated in the Code; but in 438 it could only have been a dead letter, with little more meaning for the conduct of affairs than the old command of Constantine (*CTh* 16.10.1) that if the palace or any other public building were struck by lightning the *haruspices* should be consulted *retento more veteris observantiae*. In fact, we do not know of a single case before or after Julian's reign in which the normal *probatio* of a provincial

---

69. The role of the state in late-antique education has often been discussed. In the notes below I have limited my citations to the most recent or most important secondary works. See also the survey in Walden, *Universities* 130ff.

70. *CTh* 13.3.5, with Julian. *Ep.* 61c Bidez.

71. Thus the initial *decretum curialium* and subsequent dispatch to the emperor is justified *quia singulis civitatibus adesse ipse non possum*.

72. As was already customary; see above, n. 33.

73. Plainly implied by the generalized command *iubeo, quisquis docere vult, non repente nec temere prosiliat ad hoc munus, sed iudicio ordinis probatus decretum curialium mereatur optimorum conspirante consensu*.

curia was reviewed by the emperor or in which a private teacher needed to undergo such *probatio*.[74] And for private teachers we have a text more eloquent than this silence. In 425 private teachers in Constantinople were prohibited from using the *auditoria* reserved for those the city senate appointed as public teachers and were compelled to do all their teaching in private houses.[75] Intended to limit the competition that publicly appointed teachers faced, the law is the most explicit attempt (beyond Julian's) to regulate private teachers;[76] but it shows no interest whatever in determining who might teach, merely where. If even so stringent a measure at the heart of the empire did not impose greater control than this, then we should assume *a fortiori* that there was still less regulation in the provinces. Private teachers, who probably made up the majority of the profession, would thus have stood entirely outside the state's concern.

The case of public teachers in the municipalities is, however, more complex; for although we find no general *iudicium* by the emperor of the sort Julian envisioned, there are a number of specific episodes that reveal the hand of imperial authority. Governors and other officials play important roles in appointments, either making recommendations or approving curial decrees.[77] Teachers at Athens are removed from their chairs by the governor, and others are installed in their places.[78] The emperor himself is called on to approve immunities already decreed to a rhetorician of Antioch by the town council.[79] Salaries, too, show the reach of the central government. Down to the end of the third century salaries drawn from imperial funds are attested only for the chairs of Greek and Latin rhetoric established by Vespasian at Rome and for the chairs of rhetoric and philosophy created at Athens through the benefaction of Marcus

74. Note that the clause concerning imperial review (*hoc enim decretum . . . accedant*) was dropped from the version of the law entered at *CJ* 10.53.7; and with the clause quoted in n. 73, contrast *CTh* 13.3.6 (an. 364), *si qui erudiendis adulescentibus vita pariter et facundia idoneus erit, vel novum instituat auditorium vel repetat intermissum*, intended to cancel the effects of Julian's law.

75. *CTh* 14.9.3.

76. Restraint of competition: so correctly Speck in his review of Lemerle, *BZ* 67 (1974) 386–87, also noting that it is incorrect to speak of a monopoly given to the public teachers (against Lemerle, *Premier humanisme* 364; cf. also Jones, *LRE* 999).

77. Lib. *Or.* 1.48, 82–83, 106 (cf. *Ep.* 1255.2–3); Aug. *Conf.* 5.13.23. These instances, and the others remarked in nn. 78, 79, 81, and 82, will be discussed below.

78. Lib. *Or.* 1.25.

79. Lib. *Ep.* 870.1, 905.2–3, 906.1, 907.3. Cf. Lib. *Or.* 54.48, a special honor voted for the sophist Domninus by the βουλή of Syrian Chalcis, needing the confirmation of the governor Eustathius; the episode is difficult to evaluate, since the τιμή in question is not specified.

Aurelius.[80] Beginning in 299, however, we find more such salaries in the provinces: they are received by Eumenius at Autun, by Eudaemon of Pelusium at Elusa, by Libanius and one of his rivals at Antioch; supplementary payments to teachers at Ancyra are arranged by the governor Maximus; salaries from the fisc are ordained by Gratian for grammarians and rhetoricians at the capital cities of the northern Gallic diocese, as they are a century and a half later by Justinian at Carthage.[81] Finally, state intervention in salaries could take still another form, as we see at Antioch around 360: there the teachers drawing municipal salaries were paid from the city's funds, but the funds were administered by imperial officials.[82]

Such evidence—combined with the continuing, indeed expanded, immunities granted to *professores*—has been taken to demonstrate imperial encroachment on a sphere of activity formerly belonging to the cities, an "étatisation" of education, in fact, that was part of a general characteristic of late antiquity, the increased centralization of power.[83] Now I do not propose here to deny that imperial authority seems to have been more intrusive in our period than previously; it is difficult to believe that it was not, but the range of evidence available from early and late empire alike does not provide the grounds for solid proof. I would, however, like to suggest that it is mistaken to think that any effective "étatisation" occurred, and I would like to show that such notions as encroachment and intrusion must be set in their historical context and must be modified.

80. Suet. *Vesp.* 18, in a general account of Vespasian's benefactions; Dio Cassius 72.31.3, similarly for Marcus; Philost. *V. soph.* 2.2 (p. 566); Lucian *Eun.* 3, 8; with the comments of Parsons, *PCollYoutie* 2, pp. 445f. Note esp. the observation of Parsons that the notices for this earlier period in the *Historia Augusta*, when they are not uselessly vague (*Hadr.* 16.8), are either probably (*Pius* 11.3) or certainly (*Alex. Sev.* 44.4) anachronistic; on the last passage see also Nutton, "Archiatri" 216. Chairs of rhetoric, at least, seem to have been established at Constantinople soon after its founding, with pay from the emperor, presumably on the model of Rome; see Lib. *Or.* 1.35, 37, with Kaster, "Salaries" 39ff.

81. Eumenius: *Pan. Lat.* 5.14.14 Galletier; see Chap. 3 n. 87. Eudaemon: Lib. *Ep.* 132. Libanius: *Ep.* 28, 740, 800. Libanius's rival: *Or.* 1.110. Maximus at Ancyra: Lib. *Ep.* 1230.2. Gratian: *CTh* 13.3.11; see Chap. 3 pp. 116f. Justinian: *CJ* 1.27.1, 42; see Chap. 3 pp. 117f.

82. Lib. *Or.* 31.19; see Liebeschuetz, *Antioch* 152f., though caution is needed concerning some details of his discussion and the scope of his conclusions; Kaster, "Salaries" 57f. Note, however, that there is no evidence that the emperors or their subordinates ever attempted to set the amount that a city could pay its teachers from municipal funds; cf. Kaster, "Reconsideration" 102 n. 9.

83. See esp. Marrou, *Histoire*[6] 434ff., esp. 441f., with, e.g., Wolf, *Schulwesen* 41f., Riché, *Education* 7, Kirsch, "Cura" 284–86.

When we look more closely at our evidence, we see, first, that some distinctions are needed, since not all the evidence points in the same direction. Take, for example, perhaps the most drastic and commonly noted case, Libanius's report (*Or.* 1.25) that in 339 or 340 the provincial governor at Athens simply removed the three sophists who held the public chairs in the city and saw to their replacement by three other professors. This episode plainly has little to do with the control of education as such, but it has a great deal to do with the maintenance of public order, which was a governor's oldest and most critical responsibility: in their self-absorbed rivalries the teachers had allowed their students to run riot, and the governor decided to control the disturbances by removing their most conspicuous cause.[84] Other evidence clearly involves extraordinary circumstances. Thus, it is true that the βουλή of Nicomedia asked the governor of Bithynia to confirm their decree inviting Libanius to assume the town's chair of rhetoric. But it is also true that the governor's authority met a special need at that time; for Libanius was removing himself from Constantinople, where he had been brought under a charge of magic by his rivals, and Limenius, the proconsul of Constantinople, had written to Nicomedia in an attempt to deter the town from making the appointment. The council evidently thought it prudent to meet that attempt by adding the governor's support to their decree; and it is noteworthy that when the town council of Nicaea passed a similar decree for Libanius, at just about the same time and in the same circumstances, it had not bothered to involve the governor.[85]

Similarly, it is true that the immunities voted by the town council for Eusebius, a teacher of rhetoric at Antioch, required the confirmation of the emperor,[86] although the regular approval of immune status had been established as a council's responsibility since the reign of Antoninus Pius, more than two centuries earlier. But again, the case of Eusebius was clearly not at all regular. Eusebius was evidently not a full-fledged sophist of the city, qualified to stand among the statutory number of teachers who might receive immunity; rather, he was merely the assistant of Libanius, who as a sophist of the city of course enjoyed immunities of his own. In other words, Eusebius stood *extra numerum*: in voting him immunities the council had gone beyond its customary powers, and the

84. So similarly Eunap. *V. phil.* 9.2, the actions of the proconsul after fighting between the students of Apsines and Iulianus. Cf. Himer. *Or.* 48.37, on the role of the proconsul Hermogenes in "keeping the students in line," τὰς τῶν νέων εὐθύνειν ἀγέλας; cf. also Lib. *Or.* 1.19.

85. Lib. *Or.* 1.48, with Martin and Petit, *Libanios* 1.218f. *ad loc.*; and cf. Norman, *Autobiography* 161 *ad loc.*

86. See n. 79 above.

grant of extraordinary immunities required imperial confirmation.[87] In fact, the entire episode in which Eusebius was involved under Theodosius recalls nothing so much as the case of the sophist Claudius Rufinus nearly two hundred years earlier, under Septimius Severus and Caracalla. Both teachers—Eusebius certainly, Rufinus probably—received extraordinary grants of immunity to begin with; both voluntarily undertook a single liturgy for their cities (Eusebius an embassy) after they had received their grants; in both cases the towns subsequently attempted to impose further liturgies once a chink in the armor of immunity had been opened; and both men succeeded (Eusebius with Libanius's patronage) in having the immunity reaffirmed by the emperors.[88]

Against these special cases there is much evidence that attests both the cities' ordinary freedom to appoint or depose their public teachers[89] and the laxity of imperial control. A governor might be asked to lend his authority to a council's decree in delicate circumstances, as in the case of Nicomedia's invitation to Libanius; but then again he might not, as in the case of Nicaea. A governor might be called upon to confirm a special honor for a sophist[90] or to intervene so that a dilatory council would pass its decree inviting a sophist to assume a chair.[91] But when a sophist

87. Assistant of Libanius: Lib. *Ep.* 908.3, 909. Note esp. that Libanius gives the game away when, recalling the episode at *Or.* 54.52, he speaks defensively of Eusebius as τὸν σοφιστήν, τὸν οὐχ ἧττον ἄξιον ἢ 'γω καλεῖσθαι σοφιστήν. Although Libanius (whose patronage was no doubt important in securing immunity for Eusebius) holds him out to be a sophist here as elsewhere, others evidently thought that Eusebius was indeed less worthy of being called a sophist; and since Eusebius was only the assistant of Libanius, they would have been correct. The status of Eusebius is well analyzed by Petit, *Étudiants* 91. On the council's responsibility for granting immunity and on the *numerus*, see *Dig.* 27.1.6 (Mod.), 2–4, and p. 226 below.

88. For Rufinus (= *PIR*[2] C.998), see *CIG* 3178 = *IGR* 4.1402 = *Syll.*[3] 876 (Smyrna), with Bowersock, *Greek Sophists* 41, and Nutton, "Two Notes" 54. Eusebius's tale is most easily followed in Lib. *Ep.* 907.3–5. For Libanius's patronage, see *Ep.* 870 and 904–9, enlisting the aid of officials and other influential men at Constantinople; *Ep.* 918–21 and 960, thanking some of the same men, and others, for their help.

89. See the references at n. 33 above.

90. Lib. *Or.* 54.48; cf. n. 79 above.

91. Lib. *Ep.* 1366.1–3: ἐπὶ τὸν αὐτὸν αὖθις ἡμῖν ὁ Γερόντιος κατηνέχθη φόβον καί φησιν ἄκλητος μὲν οὐχ ἥξειν, κλῆσιν δὲ ἡγήσεσθαι μόνην, εἰ ψήφισμα αὐτῷ παρὰ τῆς πόλεως ἔλθοι.... σὺ τοίνυν ... λῦσον τὸν φόβον καὶ τὸ ταχέως προσέστω.... οἶμαι μὲν οὖν σε τῆς αὐτῆς ἡμέρας καὶ δέξεσθαι τὴν ἐπιστολὴν καὶ πέμψειν τὴν καλοῦσαν. *Pace* Wolf, *Schulwesen* 42, the letter does not show "dass ein Wahlakt der städtischen Curie von Provinzstatthalter genehmigt werden muss, um rechtsgültig zu sein"; it seems rather to attest the state's "policy of treating the council as a real and responsible government" (Liebeschuetz, *Antioch* 104), with officials waiting until the council had shown itself inert before taking the initiative. Cf. below at nn. 101, 103.

can reject a praetorian prefect's request that he move from one city to another and can selectively respect letters from the emperor himself according to his own convenience or will, we are clearly not witnessing the iron-fisted exercise of central authority.[92]

This is obviously not to say that the provincial governors and other officials were of no consequence; the instances already noted suggest quite the opposite. But these and other cases available for inspection also suggest the need for a more delicate and differentiated view. First, we might note that what has broadly been regarded as encroachment can often on closer examination be seen to be the result of invitation, a teacher's or a town's willing exploitation (whether benign or malign) of an official's formal authority or informal influence. For instance, a teacher knew that he could appeal to the governor if an action of the council displeased him.[93] He might even petition to bring the emperor's authority directly to bear on the βουλή.[94] In their squabbles with one another, too, the teachers were not slow to make an ally of the local imperial authority. So Eunapius retails at length how the proconsul of Achaea was drawn into the rivalries that centered on Prohaeresius, after the sophist's competitors at Athens had bribed an earlier governor to secure his exile;[95] Prohaeresius's enemies probably arranged his conviction on some trumped-up charge, in much the same way as Libanius's rivals at Constantinople tried to suppress him by bringing a charge of magic with the

---

92. Lib. *Or.* 1.74, Libanius refuses the prefect's invitation to return to Constantinople from Nicomedia but accedes to an invitation from the emperor; *Ep.* 405, 432, 438, 439, Libanius later refuses to heed letters from the emperor demanding his return to Constantinople when he wishes to remain in Antioch; cf. *Or.* 1.100; and see Kaster, "Salaries" 41ff.

93. See the generalization at Lib. *Or.* 25.49, a passage that also plainly stresses the council's freedom in its ordinary dealings with its appointed teachers. Such intervention in council business as Libanius posits here was hardly new; cf. Bowersock, *Greek Sophists* 38; Burton, "Proconsuls" 104f.; and esp. C. P. Jones, *Roman World* 99ff., 111ff., with the references at p. 112, nn. 69, 70.

94. So Lollianus of Oxyrhynchus, *PCollYoutie* 2.66 = *POxy.* 47.3366, with Part II no. 90. As Parsons correctly concluded (*PCollYoutie* 2, pp. 441ff.), there would seem to have been no precise precedent in law or in fact for Lollianus's specific request that the emperors compel the council of Oxyrhynchus to make the arrangements necessary for the payment of his salary. For appeals to the emperor, see also the cases of Eusebius and Claudius Rufinus at n. 88 above.

95. Eunap. *V. phil.* 10.3.8–5.5. Note esp. that Prohaeresius was exiled (10.3.15, τῶν ἄλλων ἁπάντων ἐς τοσόνδε ἴσχυσεν ἡ σύστασις, ὥστε τὸν ἄνδρα ἐξόριστον τῶν Ἀθηνῶν εἰργάσατο δεκάσαντες τὸν ἀνθύπατον; the classicizing Eunapius pointedly uses the proper verb to denote the bribery of a judge, δεκάζειν), which must imply some formal action at law before the proconsul; he was not simply deposed or removed from his chair, as is often said, as though the governor had some direct administrative authority over professorial posts. Cf. at n. 84 above.

aid of the proconsul Limenius.[96] As we have just seen, the latter case caused the town council of Nicomedia to take the unusual step of seeking a governor's approval for their decree of appointment; for a similar initiative by a town council—but undertaken in more placid circumstances and more informally—we can recall an episode in the career of Augustine, the request by the curia of Milan that Symmachus, then prefect of Rome, provide a man to fill their chair of rhetoric.[97]

Little in these dealings is fundamentally new, or peculiar to late antiquity; and this touches on a second point worth emphasizing, the continuity apparent from the early empire to the late. Consider the example just mentioned. It is true that in his official capacity as city prefect Symmachus would have been unusually well informed about the teachers of Rome, in consequence of the law of 370 that made the prefect and the *magister census* responsible for keeping track of all students arriving in the city.[98] But his action apparently had little to do with his official powers, which of course had no connection with Milan; further, it must be remembered that, his official position aside, Symmachus was at the time one of the most prominent orators and men of letters at Rome—just the sort of man whose judgment would be valued in such a matter. This personal standing is surely adequate in itself to explain the request of Milan's council; the episode, in fact, is reminiscent of the request Pliny once made of Tacitus to send a suitable teacher from Rome for the position that Pliny was trying to establish at Comum.[99]

In other cases, of course, the official status of the man making a recommendation was evidently more pertinent to the matter at hand, but here too it is difficult to find a clear break from precedent to set the late-antique experience apart. Libanius, for instance, recalls that the proconsul of Achaea, Strategius Musonianus, was responsible for a decree of the βουλή at Athens inviting Libanius to take up a chair of rhetoric in the city.[100] It is not clear whether Strategius formally introduced the motion for curial action or informally (but no less influentially) recommended Libanius to the council's attention. From what Libanius says,

96. Lib. *Or.* 1.43ff. For the governor's involvement in teachers' quarrels, cf. perhaps also Himer. *Or.* 46.1–2, in a speech "against his enemies and against the proconsul Basilius," produced in the midst of what Himerius calls a war that the entire people is waging against him at Athens.

97. Aug. *Conf.* 5.13.23.

98. *CTh* 14.9.1.

99. Plin. *Ep.* 4.13.10. Note, however, that Pliny, writing as a private person, offers no guarantee that the man Tacitus sends will get the position, but stresses that he is leaving the choice open to the parents.

100. Lib. *Or.* 1.82–83, 106.

the former seems marginally more likely,[101] but the distinction does not much matter for the point being made here; a governor's ability to make formal proposals for curial vote is attested already in the reign of Pius.[102] And with Libanius's anecdote we may compare a letter of Fronto to his son-in-law, Aufidius Victorinus, governor of Germania Superior at the time, in which Fronto asks him to use his influence to secure a public appointment for a rhetorician in one of the cities in his province: although Fronto is careful to note that he has not heard the man speak but is relying on the judgment of others, he says nothing to suggest that the request itself is extraordinary, and he takes it for granted that Victorinus would simply have this sort of favor within his power.[103] In another connection, we have already seen that the emperor might grant extraordinary immunities to a favored teacher; here again, the record extends back to the second century.[104]

Such continuity is of course most apparent in the formal measures that fixed the regular immunities of teachers from the end of the first century onward. These measures, moreover, raise a final point concerning the actions of the state; for where those actions can be seen to take on a broad pattern, as opposed to the particular actions of individual officials, or where they sketch a general tendency that might be termed "policy," their chief characteristics are reticence and a rather spotty internal consistency.

As they are first attested for the principate in Vespasian's grant of A.D. 74, these immunities grant freedom from taxation and from the quartering of soldiers.[105] They were, however, considerably expanded within

101. If εἰσηγούμενος at *Or.* 1.82 *fin.* is meant technically, to denote the introduction of a proposal for curial vote. In any case, the council accepted the admonition (νουθεσία) of Strategius and quickly drafted their ψήφισμα (*Or.* 1.83). Since Libanius elsewhere (*Or.* 62.61) attributes the invitation to the action of his friend and former pupil Celsus, it has been assumed that "Celsus made the unofficial approach, Strategius gave it official confirmation" (so Norman, *Autobiography* 170 *ad loc.*, following Sievers); but I see no grounds for putting the matter in those terms.

102. Implied by *Forsch. Eph.* 2 no. 19 = Abbott and Johnson, *Municipal Administration* no. 98 = *Inschr. Eph.* 1a (*IGSK* 11:1) 21; see Burton, "Proconsuls" 105.

103. Fronto *Ad amic.* 1.7 (p. 169 van den Hout): *velim, domine, ut adiuves eum, quo facilius in civitate aliqua istius provinciae publice instituendis adulescentibus adsciscatur.* Compare Lib. *Ep.* 1366.1–3, quoted at n. 91 above.

104. See above, pp. 219f., on Eusebius of Antioch, with Philost. *V. soph.* 2.10 (p. 589), 2.30 (p. 623) (Marcus Aurelius to the sophist Hadrian; Caracalla to Philostratus of Lemnos).

105. Herzog, "Urkunden" 970f. = McCrum and Woodhead, *Select Documents* no. 458. The ordinance also provided protection against ὑβρίζειν and κατεγγυᾶν; cf. *CTh* 13.3.1. Vespasian intended these to be blanket grants to all liberal

the next two generations, so that by the time Hadrian early in his reign confirmed his predecessors' acts, the list included a wide range of exemptions from potentially time-consuming or expensive offices and *munera*.[106] The grants were continued throughout the third century[107] and confirmed under Constantine, who declared that the favored teachers and their possessions in their cities were exempt from all public service (*omnis functio*) and extended the exemption to their wives and children.[108] They were later reconfirmed under Gratian, Valentinian II, and Theodosius in 382,[109] under Honorius and Theodosius II in 414,[110] and again under Theodosius II and Valentinian III in 427.[111]

Throughout their history these immunities were regarded as the favors (*beneficia*) grateful emperors bestowed as a return for and to facilitate the exercise of the teachers' serviceable skills.[112] As practitioners of *necessariae artes*, the teachers were useful (χρήσιμοι) to the cities in which they worked, like the physicians with whom they are commonly paired in the laws or like the *navicularii* and *negotiatores* who sustained the grain supply

---

teachers and physicians; for their subsequent limitation to a fixed number in each city, see at n. 119 below. For their restriction to teachers of liberal letters, see also *Dig.* 50.4.11 (Caracalla *ap.* Mod.), 4; cf. 50.5.2 (ps.-Ulp.), 8. For a similar grant of immunities to teachers, sophists, and physicians already under the triumvirate of 43 B.C., see the new inscription from Ephesus published by Knibbe, "*Quandocumque.*"

106. *Dig.* 27.1.6 (Mod.), 8, quoting Commodus, who is citing a letter of Pius that refers to Hadrian: ὁμοίως δὲ τούτοις ἅπασιν ὁ θειότατος πατήρ μου παρελθὼν εὐθὺς ἐπὶ τὴν ἀρχὴν διατάγματι τὰς ὑπαρχούσας τιμὰς καὶ ἀτελείας ἐβεβαίωσεν κτλ. On the implications of ἐβεβαίωσεν, "confirmed," see Herzog, "Urkunden" 993f.; Griffin in her review of Bowersock, *JRS* 61 (1971) 279f. See also *Frag. Vat.* 149 Bethmann-Hollweg (Ulp.); *Dig.* 50.4.18 (Arcadius Charisius), 30; 50.5.10 (ps.-Paul.), 2; *Inst. Iust.* 1.25.15.

107. Implied by *CJ* 10.53.2 (Gordian), 10.47.1 (Diocletian and Maximian), beyond the writings of Ulpian and Modestinus.

108. *CTh* 13.3.1 (an. 321/24) + 13.3.3 (an. 333) = *CJ* 10.53.6; cf. *CTh* 13.3.10 (an. 373 [Seeck]) for *medici et magistri urbis Romae* and their wives. Teachers' sons of curial status were declared liable for *curialia munera* in 383; thus *CTh* 12.1.98, *ipsos quin etiam filios magistrorum, qui ex curiali stirpe descendunt, simili modo obnoxios esse decernat* (if *magistri* here = "teachers"); but see also *CTh* 13.3.16 (an. 414) *ad fin.*

109. *CTh* 11.16.15 (on the exemption of certain functionaries and officials from *sordida munera*), which includes the clause *circa ecclesias* [om. *CJ* 10.48.12], *rhetores atque grammaticos eruditionis utriusque vetusto more durante*; cf. *CTh* 11.16.18 (an. 390).

110. *CTh* 13.3.16–17.

111. *CTh* 13.3.18.

112. *Beneficia divorum retro principum*: see *CTh* 13.3.3. The grounding of immunities in the recipients' utility is especially well emphasized by Kuhn, *Städtische und bürgerliche Verfassung* 1.83, the introduction to what is in many ways still the best general survey of the subject; and by Herzog, "Urkunden" 981ff.

of Rome.[113] Indeed, the teachers could speak of their very profession as a λειτουργία or *munus*, and reasonably enough.[114] Immunity from further personal and financial obligations in theory left them free to devote themselves to maintaining the stable, civil life of their cities by producing a class of men *honesti* and *docti*. Secondarily—a point emphasized far more in modern accounts than by the emperors and the jurists—they might contribute to the well-being of the empire as a whole by educating the men who would become worthy members of the bureaucracy.[115]

The granting of these immunities is commonly regarded as the center-piece of the emperors' educational policy—*Hochschulpolitik, politique uni-versitaire*, or the like—and there may in fact be little harm in speaking of "policy" (rather than, say, "the expression of partially articulated atti-tudes and impulses"), as long as we recognize that this policy ran heavily to laissez-faire and involved some noteworthy contradictions. For example, despite the fact that the immunities touched both imperial and municipal burdens,[116] the choice of immune teachers was left to the cities; in this respect, the occasional involvement of provincial governors is perhaps less surprising than the fact that their involvement was not regular and formal. Or again, the exemptions were meant to encourage teachers to devote themselves to their own *civitates*, since their enjoyment of immune status was conditioned on teaching there;[117] but exception was made for those who came to teach at Rome, encouraging the best or

---

113. *Necessariae artes*: see CTh 13.3.18. χρήσιμοι: *Dig.* 27.1.6 (Mod.), 11 *ad fin.* Immunity of *navicularii* and *negotiatores*: see *Dig.* 50.6.6 (Callist.), 3.

114. Note Auson. *Prof.* 20.2, *docendi munus* (cf. *Praef.* 1.24, *municipalem operam*); Lib. *Or.* 31.17, on his assistants, οὓς εἴ τις φαίη λειτουργεῖν, ἴσως οὐκ ἂν ἁμάρτοι; *Or.* 11.9, his advice to the city as the equivalent of a λειτουργία performed with money; *Or.* 2.54, οὐ βουλεύω [= act as a member of the βουλή] μέν, ἀλλ᾽ ἀφεῖμαι ταῖς περὶ τοὺς λόγους φροντίσιν; with Lib. *Ep.* 723, ὁ νόμος τοὺς ἰατροὺς μίαν ἀπαιτεῖ λειτουργίαν τὴν ἀπὸ τῆς τέχνης; and cf. CTh 13.3.3 *ad fin.*: *nec ullo fungi munere, quo facilius . . . instituant.*

115. On the former point, see Chap. 1 above. The latter motive (on which see, e.g., Walden, *Universities* 265ff.; Marrou, *Histoire*[6] 446f.; Nellen, *Viri* 15ff.; Klein, "Kaiser Julians Rhetoren- und Unterrichtsgesetz" 90ff.; Nixon, "Latin Panegyric" 95f.) is mentioned in a measure in support of teachers for the first time in the sixth century, and then concerning only the teachers at Rome (Cassiod. *Var.* 9.21.8). Although the emperors, their ministers, and their pane-gyrists were hardly unaware of the schools' usefulness in this regard (cf. CTh 14.9.1 [an. 370] *ad fin.*, Eumen. *Pan. Lat.* 5.5.3f. Galletier, Anon. *Pan. Lat.* 7.23.2, Prisc. *De laud. Anast.* 248ff.), the modern emphasis seems to confuse results with intentions; it must certainly be wrong to project the intention back, for example, to Vespasian's funding of chairs of rhetoric at Rome (so, e.g., Steinmetz, *Unter-suchungen* 85). The emphasis in the codes and jurists falls on the teachers' services to their own localities, through which they gain the *beneficia* of the emperors.

116. See Neesen, "Entwicklung" 204f.

117. See esp. *Dig.* 27.1.6 (Septimius Severus and Caracalla *ap.* Mod.), 9.

at least the most ambitious teachers to leave their homes for the capital and its greater prestige.[118]

Perhaps most important, the policy might jeopardize the cities it was meant to help, by removing from the list of potential liturgists members of the upper classes whose contributions would matter most for the cities' well-being. As G. W. Bowersock has rightly emphasized, it was for this reason that Pius circumscribed his predecessors' more extravagant gestures by establishing that each city's council could designate only a small number of teachers and physicians to receive immunity.[119] Yet even this impulse toward consistency and restraint is joined by a contradictory measure, for which Pius himself was responsible: those who were exceptionally learned (ἄγαν ἐπιστήμονες) would be entitled to immunity even beyond the number of teachers with ordinary immune status.[120] Since a claim of exceptional learning would be based on the testimony of influential friends,[121] and since those best placed to secure such testimony would be the most prominent and wealthy among the learned, the measure would provide a loophole for the very men whose services would most benefit their cities.[122] It is therefore not surprising to find from the second century onward that cities could be altogether reluctant or inconsistent in recognizing immune status—especially of those *extra numerum*—and that immunity could be revoked and at times might drive a wedge between the teachers and their towns.[123] Nor is it surprising that the provision of immunity needed to be repeated and reconfirmed so often by the emperors.[124]

The immunities, an indirect subvention of teachers by the state, represent something less than a consistent and clearly thought-out policy;

118. So another ruling by Septimius Severus and Caracalla; see *Dig.* 27.1.6 (Mod.), 11, with Nutton, "Two Notes" 61ff.

119. On the *numerus*, set according to the size of the city, see *Dig.* 27.1.6 (Pius *ap.* Mod.), 2; with Modestinus's elaboration, ibid. 3, noting that the number must not be exceeded but could be diminished, ἐπειδήπερ ὑπὲρ τῶν πολιτικῶν λειτουργιῶν τὸ τοιοῦτο γινόμενον; and Bowersock, *Greek Sophists* 31ff., pointing out, *int. al.*, that it would be to the council's advantage to see that the wealthiest teachers did not receive immunity: "As far as we can tell, no important and wealthy rhetor is known ever to have received immunity *as one of the statutorily permitted number* in a city" (p. 42, emphasis mine: see following).

120. *Dig.* 27.1.6 (Mod.), 10.

121. See the case of Aelius Aristides (well analyzed by Bowersock, *Greek Sophists* 36ff.), who rounded up letters from Pius, Marcus Aurelius, and a former prefect of Egypt while making his case before a succession of provincial governors.

122. On this exemption, see esp. Nutton, "Two Notes" 52ff.

123. See Bowersock, *Greek Sophists* 34ff.; the case of Eusebius, pp. 219f. above; and Lib. *Ep.* 293, 723.

124. Remarked by Marrou, *Histoire*⁶ 435.

but the other, direct, state support—salaries granted from the imperial fisc to provincial teachers—was still less coherent. As was noted above, such salaries are more visible in the late empire; but the central government appears at the same time to have been unsystematic in its grants, which at least throughout the fourth century seem to have been treated as an exceptional privilege. This point is perhaps especially to be emphasized in view of a common belief that imperial officials normally had a voice in selecting teachers precisely because they administered a generalized system of state salaries.[125]

If we look at the known cases, we see two circumstances in which imperial funds were applied to provincial teachers. First, there were occasions when emperors wished to support teachers in a specific region: thus, Gratian's measure for the provincial capitals in the northern diocese of Gaul when the imperial court was resident at Trier;[126] or Justinian's for Carthage when teachers were made part of the imperial apparatus after the reconquest.[127] Beyond that, we find what amount to *ad hoc* or *ad hominem* grants. Eumenius at Autun receives a salary from the fisc as a sign of the favor he enjoyed with the imperial masters he had lately served as *magister epistularum* and with the understanding that he was to apply the money to revive the school of Autun as his own benefaction to the city;[128] the salary thus provided a way of rewarding a faithful client—*ut intellegas meritis tuis etiam nostram consuluisse clementiam*— and of channeling imperial funds to the city through a prominent citizen who would gain in prestige thereby. At Ancyra, the governor Maximus provides supplements for the teachers' (presumably local) income; the supplements, it is important to note, are mentioned as extraordinary benefactions deserving special praise, along with the literary contests, prizes, and public works Maximus also provided.[129] Imperial salaries in kind (τροφή, σῖτος, πυρός) were granted to Eudaemon at Elusa and Libanius at Antioch; the latter case, which is the better known, shows clearly that the grant depended on the personal relations between the

125. On this *Mitsprachrecht* see, e.g., Wolf, *Schulwesen* 42; Kirsch, "*Cura*" 284.
126. *CTh* 13.3.11 (an. 376). Even this measure does not seem to suppose that the selection of teachers would be taken out of the cities' hands, and the clause *ut singulis civitatibus . . . nobilium professorum electio celebretur* (see Kaster, "Reconsideration" 107f.) may well suppose the opposite.
127. *CJ* 1.27.1, 42 (an. 534). With these localized measures contrast the generalized grant of imperial *salaria* to churches, confirmed at *CJ* 1.2.12, 2 (an. 451); cf. Theodoret. *HE* 1.11, with Jones, *LRE* 898f.
128. *Pan. Lat.* 5.14.14 and 11. 3 Galletier. There is no suggestion that other cities in the region enjoyed similar benefits.
129. Lib. *Ep.* 1230.2, cataloguing διδασκάλων . . . προσθήκαις with τοῖς τούτων [sc. διδασκάλων] πρὸς ἀλλήλους ἀγῶσι καὶ τῷ τοὺς . . . νικῶντας τιμᾶν and τοῖς οἰκοδομίαις καὶ κρήναις καὶ νύμφαις.

recipient and the official in charge (in this instance, the praetorian prefect) and that the salary could be bestowed, diminished, and restored according to the favor or hostility of the official of the moment.[130]

It is possible, of course, that such subsidies became more widespread over time. Nearly all our precise evidence dates from the fourth century; and if, as has sometimes been argued, the cities exerted ever less control of their revenues and contributed less to the maintenance of their services,[131] the imperial government may have picked up more of the slack. Some indirect evidence points in this direction. Procopius reviles Justinian for abolishing all the imperial salaries for teachers and physicians that his predecessors had established;[132] although this is a patent distortion by a notoriously hostile source, the charge should suggest that a significant number of such salaries did exist.[133] Much the same seems to be implied by a law of 531 that grants a privilege to *memoriales, agentes in rebus*, and all others *qui salaria vel stipendia percipiunt publica*, mentioning teachers of liberal studies in that number.[134] Still, it would certainly be mistaken to suppose that the cities withered, and the state extended its support, uniformly and universally. In this regard, as in virtually all aspects of life in antiquity, the fact of local variation must be kept in mind. We know that even as some cities did decline, others maintained a good measure of independent prosperity in the late fifth century and well into the sixth.[135] Just so, we know that some cities continued to provide their teachers' salaries in the same period.[136]

Much of the aid that the imperial government provided was no doubt well intentioned, and a good bit of it no doubt gave welcome additional

130. Eudaemon: Lib. *Ep.* 132. Libanius: *Ep.* 28, 740, 800, with Kaster, "Salaries" 50ff. (It is clear that this τροφή could not have been tied directly to Libanius's selection as a public teacher, since it postdates that selection by several years; cf. above at n. 125.) Cf. Lib. *Or.* 1.110, where Libanius claims to have used his influence with the praetorian prefect to increase the πυροί received by his rival at Antioch.

131. See Jones, *LRE* 733f.; and esp. Liebeschuetz, *Antioch* 153ff.

132. *Anecd.* 26.5.

133. Procopius's statement plainly contradicts the known directives of Justinian, for teachers at Carthage in 534 (*CJ* 1.27.1, 42) and at Rome in 552 (*Nov.* "App." 7.22; the conflict with the latter was already noted by Nutton, *"Archiatri"* 211 n. 144). If it has any basis in fact, the charge probably grows out of some attempt to limit such salaries for economy's sake.

134. *CJ* 3.28.37, 1e–f.

135. See Roueché, "New Inscription" esp. 183ff.

136. Implied by Choric. *Or. fun. Procop.* 12 (p. 113.21f. Foerster-Richtsteig), referring to the attempt by Caesarea to snatch Procopius away from Gaza: τὰ δὲ πειρωμένη χρυσίῳ πολλῷ δελεάζειν. For an earlier example of a city using the promise of a higher munipical salary to lure a teacher from a rival town, see Lib. *Or.* 31.42.

support to local institutions: so, for example, A. H. M. Jones may well have been correct to suggest that Gratian's measure of 376 enabled some towns of northern Gaul to boast endowed chairs where they had had none before.[137] But imperial intervention cannot have resulted in imperial control in any substantive sense. There was certainly no control of curriculum; nor did the state attempt to make the professions of grammar and rhetoric hereditary, as it did for so many occupations and statuses. And whatever form the imperial presence took—making itself felt, say, by subsidizing teachers or in a governor's influence—and whether that presence was invited or provoked, novel or traceable through long-standing precedent, it was typically no more than sporadic or indecisive or formless.[138] It is difficult to discover in the evidence examined above an *étatisation* of education newly developed in late antiquity, and it is still more difficult to think that such *étatisation* could have come about in the absence of a bureaucratic structure—a specialized, formalized, rationalized mechanism of the central administration—through which the state could effectively assume responsibility for organized education. No such structure existed at any time in antiquity. In late antiquity, when a governor spent vast amounts of his time hearing cases and overseeing tax collection, and when a governor typically held office for no more than a year, he could scarcely have spared much time to supervise education, and any supervision that a given governor might have cared to exercise could have had little long-term impact. The question whether imperial officials became more intrusive is therefore finally secondary.

It is secondary because in the circumstances such involvement could not help but be—as to all appearances it was—haphazard and particular, circumscribed by the same kinds of personal connections as those discussed earlier in this chapter. Whether one was dealing with local or imperial authorities, with a *principalis* in the town council or with the aloof and powerful governor, those dealings would not go far unless one were well supplied with patrons. Our analysis of the state's role thus brings us back full circle. One can surely speak of a mingling of authority, municipal and imperial, formal and informal. But as virtually all the evidence surveyed in the preceding pages shows or implies, it was an authority exercised unpredictably or *ad hoc*, harnessed or combatted by mobilizing personal relations.

137. See Jones, *LRE* 998, with Kaster, "Reconsideration" 108f.
138. Cf. the remark of Speck in his review of Lemerle, *BZ* 67 (1974) 392, concluding his discussion of the so-called university of Constantinople: "Staatlich institutionalisierte und geförderte Bildung aber blieb in der Spätantike ein Versuch, der sich nur partiell und vorübergehend durchsetzen konnte."

A teacher receiving an imperial salary in kind at Elusa desires the
privilege of commuting the salary to cash: we find his case being put
by his friend Libanius, who approaches an influential private citizen of
the town and asks him to do what he can to secure the favor.[139] A
teacher about to move from Antioch to Heliopolis has the way prepared,
again by Libanius: letters solicit the favor of Domninus, the governor of
Phoenice, and the local *potens* Alexander, himself a former governor of
Syria now living in retirement in his home town.[140] The differences in
the formal status of one's supporters are finally less significant than
the general and enduring patterns of patronage and personal connections, which remain the same regardless of the circumstances in which
they are found. In the fourth century, Augustine begins his career at
Thagaste, and then moves on to Carthage, with the help of his local
supporter, Romanianus, as he later makes his way from Rome to Milan
with the support of the city prefect Symmachus.[141] In the fifth century,
Pamprepius's lot at Athens is linked to his relations with the magnate
Theagenes; when he is driven from Athens to Constantinople after
falling out with Theagenes, he gains a public salary as a grammarian at
the capital through the patronage of Illus, whose official career thereafter largely determines the course of Pamprepius's fortunes.[142] In the
sixth century, Ioannes Lydus begins his career by being drawn into the
imperial service by a cousin and by a home-town acquaintance who
is praetorian prefect at the time; when he later grows dissatisfied with
the service, he is appointed to a chair of Latin grammar by Justinian
himself—a connection perhaps mediated by another patron, Gabriel, to
whom Lydus presently dedicates his first works when Gabriel is the
city prefect.[143] This last detail is worth savoring. It calls to mind another
small piece of information that we owe to Lydus: the notice that
Suetonius dedicated his *Caesares* to his patron Septicius Clarus when the
latter was prefect of the praetorian guard.[144] These two dedications to
patrons by sometime imperial servants and antiquarians bridge more
than four hundred years in the life of the empire, reminding us how
much that life remained cast in the same mold.

139. Lib. *Ep.* 132, to Eutocius of Elusa, in behalf of Eudaemon of Pelusium.
140. Lib. *Ep.* 1255, to Domninus; 1256, to Alexander. On the latter, see also
above at n. 49; and for Alexander's governorship, see *PLRE* I s.v. Alexander 5,
pp. 40f.
141. See nn. 53 and 97 above. Note esp. the role of Augustine's Manichaean
friends in arranging a display before Symmachus, *Conf.* 5.13.23: *ego ipse ambivi per
eos ipsos manichaeis vanitatibus ebrios . . . ut dictione proposita me probatum . . . Symmachus
mitteret.*
142. See Part II no. 114.
143. See Part II no. 92.
144. Ioan. Lyd. *De mag.* 2.6. On Suetonius and Septicius, see Syme, *Tacitus*
501, 778f.; Wallace-Hadrill, *Suetonius* 6; and more guardedly Baldwin, *Suetonius*
36ff.

PART II
Prosopography

This prosopography primarily surveys the grammarians known between A.D. 250 and A.D. 565, and is the product of a fresh review and analysis of the sources for the period. To control my findings in Part I, I have here set the chronological limits a generation or two on either side of the period with which the body of the book is concerned. Thus the grammarians of the fourth and fifth centuries hold center stage in Part I, but the earliest figure in the prosopography is Lollianus *signo* Homoeus (no. 90), who taught as municipal grammarian of Oxyrhynchus in the reign of Valerian and Gallienus (253–60), and the latest is Flavius Cresconius Corippus (no. 37), still active, although apparently not as a grammarian, early in the reign of Justin II (ca. 566). Consequently, the prosopography also straddles the lower and upper limits of *PLRE* I and II, which cover the period A.D. 260–527.

Although the grammarians are the focus of this compilation, it seemed prudent to include other teachers of letters below the level of rhetorician (i.e., those commonly called "primary" teachers: γραμματοδιδάσκαλοι, γραμματισταί, *magistri ludi*, etc.), both because the grammarians would not be uniformly distinct from the latter group either pedagogically (see esp. Kaster, "Notes") or socially, and because information on the second group is collected nowhere else. I have also included a number of persons called simply διδάσκαλοι; since from the contexts in which they are found it seems possible that they were secular teachers of letters (not, e.g., Christian teachers or rabbis, nor craftsmen in γραφαὶ διδασκαλικαί), they too appear to merit inclusion. But because the title is so vague and could well be applied to anyone from a teacher of elementary letters to a philosopher or physician, I have placed them in the second section of the register.

The prosopography is in two sections. The first contains the men known or likely to have been teaching as grammarians in the period, as well as the so-called primary teachers; the second section, "*Dubii, Falsi, Varii*," contains those whose chronology, profession, or (in a few cases) existence is less certain, or those who have incorrectly been treated as grammarians by one or another standard reference work, or those who are termed simply διδάσκαλοι. Cross-references to the persons entered in the second section are given in the first, which accordingly also serves as an index to the whole collection.

It has not always been possible to decide neatly to which section an individual belongs, or whether he should be included at all, and in more than one case there is room for disagreement. But a line must be drawn somewhere, and a number of names that might have found their way into the second section have been omitted, either because there is no good evidence that they taught as grammarians,[1] or because they cannot be shown to belong to our period,[2] or for both reasons.[3] I have made an exception for Georgius Choeroboscus (no. 201), the important grammarian who is assigned to the sixth century in some standard reference books but who can now be dated securely to the first half of the ninth century.[4]

1. For example, Lactantius Placidus, the commentator on Statius; Eugraphius, author of a rhetorical commentary on Terence; or, in Greek: Demo, the allegorical commentator on Homer; Eucleides; and Eulogius Scholasticus.

2. For example, the scholiasts to Dionysius Thrax: Diomedes, Gregorius, Heliodorus, Melampus, Porphyrius, and Stephanus.

3. For example, the lexicographer Methodius, of uncertain profession, dating to some time after s.V 2/2 and before s.IX 1/2.

4. Note also the following papyri and inscriptions concerning teachers not included in the present register, although they may belong to our period: *PGrenf.* 1.67 = *Stud. Pal.* 3 (= *PKlForm.* 1) 317, s.VI / s.VII; *PStrass.* 484, διδασκαλ.[...] in a document of 6 June 548 (date: Sijpesteijn and Worp, "Chronological Notes" 275); *CIL* 6.10008 = *ILCV* 721, perhaps not before s.IV 2/4, to judge from the names, Fl. Sabinianus and Aur. Gerontius; *CIG* 4278e = *IGR* 3.632 = *TAM* 2:1.315, Aur. Prytanicus, probably not before 212; *TAM* 3:1.439, Aur. Hermadion, of similar date; *RICM* 231, Aur. Cyriacus, of similar date (probably a Christian); see also *RICM* 123, the epitaph (s.IV?) of Eutychius, a "newly baptized Christian teacher" (διδασκάλου χρηστιανοῦ . . . νεοφωτείστου).

I have not included in "*Dubii, Falsi, Varii*" two alleged teachers noted by Baldwin, "Some *addenda*" (1982): no. 43 Gelasius (p. 106) and no. 92 Sophronius (p. 110). The first, the otherwise unknown recipient of Sidon. Apoll. *Ep.* 9.15, mentioned also at 9.16.3, is said to be "possibly a *grammaticus*," although Sidonius's letters give no solid reason to think so. Of the second, Baldwin writes: "A complainant against bishop Dioscorus [of Alexandria] at the Council of Chalcedon; *ACO* 2, 2, 2 [rather: 2, 1, 2] pp. 23–24. Apparently a layman, Sophronius was deprived of all his property and forced to become a teacher; cf. Gregory, *Vox Populi*, 177." The last part of the statement, however, is an error, reproducing a slip Gregory made: the verb διδάσκειν does occur in Sophronius's *libellus*—see *ACO* 2:1.2, p. 23.13, 15, 19; p. 24.24; so (*e*)*docere* in the Latin translation, 2:3.2,

An asterisk (*) appears in the margin before 51 entries, signifying that the person is not found in *PLRE* I or II although he certainly or probably falls within the period A.D. 260–527; in another 34 cases, a plus sign (+) denotes an individual who certainly or probably falls outside the chronological limits or otherwise fails to satisfy the criteria of *PLRE* I or II. Some in this latter group will presumably appear in *PLRE* III.

The prosopography has a threefold purpose: to simplify the main exposition; to avoid unnecessary duplicate references elsewhere in the book; and to serve as a useful repertory for other students of late-antique education. I have therefore presented and discussed the primary sources as extensively as seemed necessary in each case. For the same reasons, I have attempted to offer a guide to the most recent or most important secondary literature. References to the latter are found at the top or in the body of each entry; though not intended to be exhaustive, they should reliably mark the trail for readers interested in compiling a complete bibliography.

The headline for each entry regularly notes the person's profession and other indications of status, the place of his activity, and his date; omission of any of these items implies that the information is not available. Most abbreviations for imperial office or rank (*PVR, PPO, v.c.,* etc.) appear as in *PLRE*; and as in *PLRE*, names are alphabetized on the Latin principle, so that "IOANNES," for example, precedes "ISOCASIUS" and "URBANUS" follows "VICTOR." Other abbreviations used are either conventional or, it is hoped, self-evident. Note that the shortened form "gramm." most frequently means "grammarian" or "grammarians"; less usually, "grammatical." An arrow (→) between professions, ranks, or place names indicates sequence in a career; a virgule (/) similarly placed indicates different stages in a career for which a precise sequence cannot be determined. An en dash (–) placed between two dates signifies inclusiveness; a virgule (/) similarly placed signifies indeterminacy: 336–61 means "from 336 through 361"; 336/61 means "sometime between 336 and 361."

Readers who wish to study the teachers in specific areas of the empire will want to consult the geographical-chronological lists in Appendix 5.

---

p. 38.21, 23, 27; p. 40.12—but it merely refers to the information that Sophronius lays in his complaint; it has nothing to do with his profession. Nor is there any other indication in the document that he became a teacher.

Grammatici, Γραμματοδιδάσκαλοι, *Magistri Ludi*, and the Like

1. ACACIUS.   Gramm.   Constantinople?   s.IV med.
Seeck, *Briefe* 46f.; *PLRE* I s.v. 5, p. 6.

Recipient of Lib. *Ep.* 398 and perhaps of *Ep.* 431 (both an. 355). That A. was a teacher is evident from *Ep.* 398.2: δείκνυται δὲ καὶ ἐν ταῖς τῶν νέων ψυχαῖς ἡ τέχνη. That he was a gramm. is likely since some of his pupils went on to study with Libanius; cf. ibid., continuing from the sentence above: ὡς οὐ πολλοὶ παρ᾽ ἡμᾶς ὧδε ἔχοντες τάξεως ἦλθον (cf. Seeck, *Briefe* 47).

Seeck, *Briefe* 47 and 320 (followed by Festugière, *Antioche* 105 n. 7), locates A. in Constantinople, because *Ep.* 398 stands just before a series of letters addressed to correspondents in Constantinople and its environs (*Ep.* 399–402, 404) and because Libanius had recently been teaching in Constantinople, until 354. But *Ep.* 398 stands just after an equally long series of letters addressed to correspondents in Bithynia, *Ep.* 394–97. (*PLRE* I is wrong to state that the letter "falls within" a group of letters addressed to Constantinople.) A. could therefore have been active in Nicomedia, where Libanius had also taught successfully for a number of years. The matter seems incapable of resolution: note that five of Libanius's students are known to have come from Bithynia, ten from Constantinople; cf. Petit, *Étudiants* 114. Libanius's more recent tenure in the capital might, however, tip the balance in favor of Constantinople. See also below.

Seeck, *Briefe* 47, identifies A. with the Acacius of *Ep.* 431, whom one Daphnus subjected to trial before the *PPO* Strategius Musonianus at Antioch in the autumn of 355. The nature of the case is obscure: Libanius says only that Daphnus had posted a surety in the case despite Musonianus's attempt to discourage him and was awaiting Acacius's arrival, and that Acacius was being aided by the intervention of Clematius, Apodemius, and Libanius himself. Clematius is evidently Clematius 2 (*PLRE* I p. 213), an *agens in rebus*(?) at the time, who returned to Constantinople shortly thereafter; Seeck (*RE* 1.2819.21ff.; cf. *PLRE* I s.v. 1, p. 82) identified Apodemius with the *agens in rebus* instrumental in the death of Gallus and active in Gaul earlier in 355. Apodemius may therefore have traveled to Antioch with Clematius, who had come from Italy by way of Constantinople. If so, and if the gramm. A. (above) was the recipient of *Ep.* 431, the route of Clematius and Apodemius would favor locating the gramm. in Constantinople.

2. ADAMANTIUS.   Lat. gramm.   Sardis?   Before 580; s.V ex. / s.VI init.?
   RE 1.343–44 (Goetz); *PLRE* II s.v. 3, p. 7; cf. Sch.-Hos. 4:2.220.

A *doctor . . . elocutionis Latinae* (*GL* 7.165.14f.); father of Martyrius (q.v., no. 95). The latter is called *Sardianus* in the subscr. to one ms of his work and might be dated to s.VI 1/2 – med. If the epithet is accurate, A. was possibly of Sardis also; if the dating of Martyrius is correct, then A. should be dated to s.V ex. / s.VI init.

   A. provided the inspiration for his son's treatise on *b* and *v*: *GL* 7.165.13f., *hoc commentario nostro acceptis seminibus ab Adamantio meo patre*. He was confused with his son by Cassiodorus, whose use of Martyrius's treatise provides a *term. a. q.* for the pair.

   See further s.v. Martyrius, no. 95.

AEGIALEUS: see no. 179.

+   AETHERIUS: see no. 180.

3. AGATHODAEMON.   Gramm.   Egypt?   s.IV ex. / s.V 1/3.
   PLRE II s.v., p. 33.

A γραμματικός: inscr. Isid. Pel. *Ep.* 3.303; 5.55, 334, 439, 454; cf. also a reference to his students in *Ep.* 5.55 and Isidore's reflections on the effectiveness of his παίδευσις in *Ep.* 5.334. Recipient of several letters from Isidore of Pelusium involving moral exhortation (*Ep.* 3.303; 5.55, 454) and discussion of style (*Ep.* 5.439). *Ep.* 5.444, a protreptic letter with a literary conceit, may be to the same man: it is addressed simply Ἀγαθοδαίμονι, without the title γραμματικῷ; cf. also *Ep.* 1.270, 435, similarly inscribed. The recipient of the latter two epistles was a Christian (1.270, ἡ ἡμετέρα θρησκεία vs. ὁ Ἑλληνισμός) critical of the ascetic life (1.435).

   His school's location cannot be determined. It was evidently in the same place as that of Ophelius (q.v., no. 109), with whom A. received *Ep.* 5.439; it therefore presumably was in a good-sized town, since a small town would not likely have two γραμματικοί. His name suggests Egyptian origin; cf. Ganschinietz, *RE* Suppl. 3.58.33ff.

AGROECIUS: see no. 181.

ALBINUS: see no. 182.

ALETHIUS: see no. 183.

4. ALEXANDER. Gramm. Heliopolis → Antioch → Heliopolis. s.IV 2/3.
Seeck, *Briefe* 56; *PLRE* I s.v. 7, p. 41.

The subject of Lib. *Ep.* 1255, 1256 (both an. 364); called γραμματιστής in
Ep. 1256.3. As is clear from *Ep.* 1255.1, ἐν Ὀδυσσείᾳ ζῶν καὶ σὺν τοῖς
παισὶν ᾄδων καθ' ἡμέραν τὸ ἔπος, this is Libanius's normal use of γραμματιστής to mean γραμματικός (see Appendix 2). A. had already taught
for a long time in Antioch (*Ep.* 1255.1, πολὺν ἤδη χρόνον) and was
returning in 364 to his πατρίς (*Ep.* 1255.2), which must have been Heliopolis in Phoenice; cf. *Ep.* 1256, to Alexander of Heliopolis (= Alexander
5 *PLRE* I, p. 40). He appears to have received an official appointment as
teacher in Heliopolis: *Ep.* 1255.3, to Domninus, *cons. Phoenices*, οὗτος μὲν
οὖν σοῦ τε ἕξεται καὶ τῆς αὐτοῦ πόλεως, σὺ δὲ αὐτὸν κινεῖν καὶ ἀναγκάζειν
καὶ πέμπειν ἐπὶ τοὺς νέους. A. is also commended to Alexander (see
above; *Ep.* 1256.3), a local power at Heliopolis who had shown himself
well disposed toward the literary culture and its teachers during his
governorship of Syria in 363: cf. Lib. *Ep.* 838, 1361, 1366, 1390, and esp.
1370, on Gerontius's appointment to the chair of rhetoric at Apamea.

5. ALEXANDER. Gramm. → monk. s.V 1/3.
PLRE II s.v. 7, p. 56.

Addressee of Nil. Ancyr. *Ep.* 2.49, Ἀλεξάνδρῳ μοναχῷ ἀπὸ γραμματικῶν,
on the theme "the wisdom of the world is folly in the eyes of God." The
letter is among those whose inscr. may have been derived entirely or in
part from their contents: cf. Alan Cameron, "Authenticity" 185f.; and
s.v. Asclepius, no. 18. For other letters addressed Ἀλεξάνδρῳ μοναχῷ,
see *Ep.* 1.129, 2.120–23, all possibly to A.; compare esp. the themes of
Ep. 2.49 and 2.120.

6. ALYPIUS. Gramm. Seleucia (Isauria). s.V med.
PLRE II s.v. 3, p. 62.

Gramm. (γραμματιστής; cf. Appendix 2) teaching at Isaurian Seleucia.
When near death he was cured after incubation in the shrine of St.
Thecla, with whom he communicated by quoting a verse of Homer, *Il.*
1.365: [Basil. Sel.] *Vie et miracles de Sainte Thècle* 2.38 Dagron. On the source
(contemporary with Basil, but not by him), cf. Dagron, "Auteur."
    A.'s son, Olympius (q.v., no. 108), was also a gramm.; see also s.v.
Solymius, no. 259.

7. ALYPIUS.   Gramm.   Gaza → Antioch.   s.V 4/4 / s.VI 1/4.
   PLRE II s.v. 6, p. 62.

Α γραμματικός; recipient of Procop. Gaz. *Ep.* 13 with Stephanus and
Hierius (qq.v., nos. 141, 75): *Ep.* 13 tit. With the other two men A. had
gone from Gaza to Antioch (Daphne): *Ep.* 13.1ff.; cf. s.vv. Hierius,
Stephanus. Procopius's phrasing suggests that the two Greek gramm.
(A. and Stephanus) and the one Latin gramm. (Hierius) constituted the
entire corps of gramm. at Gaza; cf. esp. *Ep.* 13.11ff.: εἰ ἑνὸς ἀνδρὸς [viz.,
Solon] ἀπόντος ἐδάκρυσαν Ἀθηναῖοι, καίτοι σοφοὺς ὡς εἰκὸς εὐτυχοῦντες
ἑτέρους, τίνες ἂν γενοίμεθα τὸ κεφάλαιον ὅλον ἀφαιρούμενοι;

8. AMMONIANUS.   Gramm.   Egypt; probably Alexandria.   s.V med.
   RE 1.1861 (Cohn); *PLRE* II s.v., p. 70.

Gramm.: *Suda* A.1639, Ἀμμωνιανός, γραμματικός; O.391, Ἀμμωνιανῷ τῷ
γραμματικῷ; cf. Damasc. *V. Isid.* epit. Phot. 60 = frg. 111 Zintzen = *Suda*
A.1639, quoted at Appendix 1.3e. Relative of the philosopher Syrianus
(and so of Aedesia, wife of Hermias and mother of Ammonius and Heliodorus; cf. Damasc. *V. Isid.* frg. 124), whom he resembled spiritually and
physically: Damasc. *V. Isid.* frg. 111. His name and relation to Syrianus
make it clear that he was Egyptian, presumably of Alexandria. If Asmus
was correct in making him the teacher of Isidore ("Rekonstruktion"
454f.; *Leben* 37f.), he will have been active (again, presumably at Alexandria) ca. s.V med.
   He is said to have owned an ass that was mad for poetry: Damasc. *V.
Isid.* epit. Phot. 60 = frg. 111; cf. *Suda* O.391.

9. AMMONIUS.   Gramm.   Bordeaux.   s.IV 1/3.
   PLRE I s.v. 1, p. 54.

The name "Ammonius" appears in the tit. of Auson. *Prof.* 10: *Grammaticis
Latinis Burdigalensibus* [cf. *Prof.* 8] *Philologis / Ammonio Anastasio / Grammatico
Pictaviorum.* It is supplied thence by all editors at v. 35, where some name
is plainly missing, to designate the teacher who precedes Anastasius
(vv. 42ff.) in the catalogue. It has been suggested (Booth, "Notes" 243)
that *Ammonio Anastasio* in the tit. is the name of one man, viz., Anastasius
(q.v., no. 11), in which case the name of the teacher commemorated in
vv. 32ff. would be lost beyond retrieval. Note, however, that Ammonius
Anastasius would itself be an unusual name and that the only *grammatici*
Ausonius commemorated who have two or more names—Pomponius
Maximus Herculanus and Acilius Glabrio, the former a *curialis*, the latter
possessing claims to nobility (see s.vv., nos. 70, 64; the second name of
Leontius [q.v., no. 89] Lascivus was a playful *supernomen* and so is irrele-
vant here)—were both probably of higher status than the teacher of

vv. 32–41: see below. It is probably best to retain the traditional solution noted above; for a survey of other solutions to the problems the tit. of *Prof.* 10 presents, see Booth, "Notes" 243.

A. was a *grammaticus* (v. 31) *Latinus* (tit.) who taught *rudibus pueris / prima elementa* (vv. 36–37); cf. s.v. Crispus (no. 40) and Appendix 4. He had *famam tenuem* because he was *doctrina exiguus* (see preceding) and because he had *mores implacidi* (vv. 38–41). He was active probably very early in s.IV and in any event before the time of Ausonius's own tenure at Bordeaux, which began ca. 336/37; see further s.v. Concordius, no. 35. His name points to a non-Gallic—specifically, Egyptian—background.

10. AMMONIUS. Gramm. Alexandria → Constantinople. s.IV ex.
RE 1.1866.8ff. (Cohn); Chr.-Sch.-St. 2:2.1080; PLRE I s.v. 3, p. 55.

A γραμματικός: Soc. HE 5.16.10, 15. Active at Alexandria, whence he fled with the gramm. Helladius (q.v., no. 67) to Constantinople after the desecration of the Serapeum at Alexandria in 391: Soc. ibid. = Phot. Bibl. cod. 28 (1.16 Henry) = Nic. Call. HE 12.25.

A. was a pagan and a priest of the ape: Soc. HE 5.16.11, πίθηκος (for which cf. John Chrysost. Ad pop. Ant. hom. 10.3, In Gen. serm. 1.2; Zach. Schol. Vie de Sévère p. 35.4). The ape meant is probably the πίθηκος κυνοκέφαλος, sacred to Hermes-Thot as god of the moon and, esp. appropriate here, of πάντα γράμματα; cf. Horapollon Hieroglyph. 1.14 Hopfner (Fontes historiae religionis Aegyptiacae 4.582.8f.), with Hopfner, Tierkult 26ff. The historian Socrates, who was a pupil of both Ammonius and Helladius at Constantinople, heard A. indignantly recount the events of 391: HE 5.16.15.

A. is probably not the author of an epic poem on Arcadius's victory over Gainas in 400 (cf. Soc. HE 6.6.37, with Alan Cameron, "Wandering Poets" 480 n. 63, 483 n. 81): "Ammonius" is among the commonest of names; and Socrates dates the poem to 438, rather late for A., who can hardly have been born much later than ca. 370. He is certainly not the author of the lexicon De adfinium vocabulorum differentia surviving under the names of Ammonius and of several others (cf. most recently Nickau, ed., Ammonius lxvi–lxvii); and he is probably not the reviser, who quotes Luke 7.3.

11. ANASTASIUS. Gramm. Bordeaux → Poitiers. s.IV 1/3.
PLRE I s.v. 1, p. 59.

Anastasius: Auson. Prof. 10.42; on the names Ammonio Anastasio in the corrupt tit. of Prof. 10, see s.v. Ammonius, no. 9. Grammaticus (ibid. tit., v. 45) Latinus (ibid. tit.). A native of Bordeaux (v. 46; cf. 51–53), where he apparently taught for some time (v. 53: it was only in senio, when he moved to Poitiers, that he suffered his reverses). He moved to Poitiers out of *ambitio*: vv. 47–48; cf. tit., *Anastasio grammatico Pictaviorum*. His ambition must have been frustrated, since Ausonius says that he lived *ibi et tenuem / victum habitumque colens* having lost the *gloriolam exilem / et patriae et cathedrae*, vv. 49–53.

He was active at Bordeaux probably very early in s.IV and in any event not later than s.IV 1/3; see s.v. Concordius, no. 35. His name suggests that he was a Christian or at least born of Christian parents.

+ 12. ANATOLIUS.   Gramm.   Alexandria.   s.VI med.
RE 1.2073 (Cohn).

Gramm. who enhanced his reputation (ηὐδοκίμησεν) at Alexandria by applying a line of Homer, *Il.* 18.392, to Hephaestus, *praefectus Augustal.* 546–51: Olympiodorus *Comm. in Alc.* 1 2.80ff. Westerink; for the date of Hephaestus's prefecture, see Stein, *Histoire* 2.754 n. 1; for a comparably literary play on the name of the same Hephaestus, see Ioannes Lydus (q.v., no. 92) *De mag.* 3.30. A. is very likely the gramm. Anatolius at whose request Cosmas Indicopleustes composed the seventh book of the *Christ. topogr.* not long after 547: 7.97.12f., Χριστιανοῦ πρὸς Ἀναστάσιον περὶ οὐρανοῦ, τοῦ γραμματικοῦ αἰτησαμένου Ἀνατολίου; cf. Westerink, *Anonymous Prolegomena* xiv; Alan Cameron, "Last Days" 11f.; Wolska, ed., *Christ. topogr.* vol. 3 p. 167 n. 2; for the date, cf. Wolska, ed., *Christ. topogr.* vol. 1 p. 16. In view of the subscription and of the highly polemical character of *Christ. topogr.* 7, A. must have been a Christian.

13. ANAXAGORAS.   Gramm.   s.V 1/3.
PLRE II s.v., p. 86.

Addressee of Nil. Ancyr. *Ep.* 1.195 (Ἀναξαγόρᾳ γραμματικῷ), 196. The second letter purports to answer a question concerning the interpretation of Proverbs 1.9, which is quoted in the first letter.

ANTIOCHUS: see no. 184.

* 14. APOLLINARIUS.   Gramm. and presbyter.   Alexandria → Berytus → Laodicea.   Born not after 290, probably before; dead probably before 362.
RE 1.2842 (Jülicher); Leitzmann, *Apollinaris* 1ff., 43ff.; cf. Barnes, "More Missing Names" 140.

Father of Apollinarius the heresiarch: born in Alexandria (Soc. *HE* 2.46) probably ca. 280, certainly no later than 290. The birth of the son, who died 383/92, is to be dated ca. 310; cf. below.

A gramm.: Soc. ibid., Ἑλληνικῶν λόγων διδάσκαλος ... γραμματικῶν, and 3.16; Soz. *HE* 6.25.9 (cf. Jer. *De vir. ill.* 104, on the younger A., *magis grammaticis in adulescentia operam dedit*, perhaps confusing him with his father). He taught at Berytus and then at Laodicea: Soc. *HE* 2.46. At Laodicea he married, had a son (Soc. ibid.), and served as presbyter in the church (Jer. ibid.; Soc. ibid.; Soz. *HE* 6.25.11). His son taught rhetoric (Soc. ibid. and 3.16) and was early on reader (Soc. *HE* 2.46; Soz. ibid.) and later bishop of the church at Laodicea.

Under the bishop Theodotus, the two Apollinarii associated with the pagan sophist Epiphanius (= *PLRE* I s.v. no. 1, pp. 280f.), teacher of the younger A. at the time: ἔτι γὰρ νέος ἦν, Soz. *HE* 6.25.9; Sozomen's chronology is consistent with a date of birth for the younger A. of ca. 310, since Theodotus is known to have been bishop at least 325–30. The association led to their temporary excommunication: so Soz. *HE* 6.25.12; according to Soc. *HE* 2.46, the break did not come until later (see below). But their association continued under the bishop George, who may have excommunicated them a second time—that is, Soc. and Soz. differ: according to Soz., there were two excommunications, under Theodotus (ended by the repentance of father and son), and under George (for which only the younger A. is mentioned); according to Soc., the warnings of Theodotus were ignored, and the excommunication did not occur until the time of George, when both Apollinarii were affected.

According to Soc. (*HE* 3.16) both Apollinarii turned to the task of adapting Scripture to use in the schools after Julian's school law of 362; according to Soz. (*HE* 5.18), only the younger A. was involved in this venture. Sozomen is probably correct; the elder A. would have been near eighty at the time, if indeed he was still alive. Neither A. had anything to do with the hexameter paraphrase of the Psalter that survives under the name of Apollinarius; cf. Golega, *Homerische Psalter* 5ff.

15. APOLLONIUS. Gramm. Athens. 260/68.

PLRE I s.v. 1, p. 85.

Participant in a memorial celebration of Plato hosted by Longinus and attended by, *int. al.*, Porphyrius, Nicagoras the sophist (omitted from *PLRE* I; but cf. s.v. Nicagoras 1, p. 627), Demetrius the γεωμέτρης (= *PLRE* I s.v. 1, p. 247), Prosenes the Peripatetic (= *PLRE* I s.v., p. 751), and Callietes the Stoic (= *PLRE* I s.v., p. 173): Euseb. *Praep. ev.* 10.3, from Porphyr. Φιλολογ. ἀκρόασ. 1. He is represented as speaking at length on the subject of plagiarism in various authors—Ephorus, Theopompus, Menander, et al.

ELIUS APRILICUS: see no. 185.

AQUILA: see no. 186.

16. ARCADIUS.   Gramm.   Antioch.   *Aet. incert.*: s.II ex. / s.VI 1/2.
    RE 2.1153–56 (Cohn); Chr.-Sch.-St. 2:2.1077f.; Hunger 2.13, 15, 19;
    PLRE II s.v. 3, p. 130.

Called γραμματικός, Ἀντιοχεύς in the *Suda*, A.3948; included in the catalogue of gramm. in Kröhnert, *Canones* 7, under the heading ὅσοι γραμματικοί. The notice in the *Suda* attributes to him the following works: Περὶ
ὀρθογραφίας, Περὶ συντάξεως τῶν τοῦ λόγου μερῶν, Ὀνοματικὸν θαυμά-
σιον. The Ὀρθογραφία is cited in the epitome of Steph. Byz. Ἐθνικά s.v.
Ἄκτιον; the other citations of A. in the Ἐθνικά probably derive from the
same source (see below). The citations of A. in Choerobosc. *Schol. in
Theodos.* (*GG* 4:1.196.33, 205.28f.) derive from the Ὀνοματικόν, if one can
judge from their content and from the section of the scholia in which
the citations occur. A. is not the author of the epitome of Herodian's
Καθ. προσ. (ed. M. Schmidt [Jena, 1860]) attributed to him in two late
Paris mss; cf. Lentz, *GG* 3:1, cxxx–cxxxv; Egenolff, *Orthoepischen Stücke* 5f.;
Galland, *De Arcadii qui fertur libro* 12ff.; Cohn, *RE* 2.1154.4ff.; see also s.vv.
Aristodemus, Theodosius, nos. 188, 152.

    Evidence for precise dating is absent, but a date sometime in the
period s.II ex./s.VI 1/2 seems secure. Although A. is not the author of
the epitome of Herodian, the titles of the works attributed to him suggest that he was an epigonus of Herodian and of Herodian's father,
Apollonius Dyscolus. (Kröhnert, *Canones* 46, placed A. before Herodian;
for what reasons it is not clear.) A. is cited several times in the epitome
of Steph. Byz.: in addition to the citation s.v. Ἄκτιον, see also s.vv.
Αἰγόσθενα, Δασκύλιον, Ζεφύριον, Λυρνατία, Μολυκρία, Νιφάτης, Χαιρώνεια. If these are not interpolations—and it seems unlikely that they all
are: see esp. s.vv. Νιφάτης, Χαιρώνεια—they would provide a likely *term.
a. q.* of s.V ex./s.VI 1/2; for the date, see s.v. Stephanus, no. 144. I
suspect but cannot prove that A. lived closer to the end than to the
beginning of the period defined by those *termini*: he is cited in the company of Orus (q.v., no. 111) at both places in Choeroboscus, and with
Eudaemon (presumably of Pelusium, q.v., no. 55) in the second; he is
cited again with Eudaemon at Steph. Byz. s.v. Δασκύλιον.

*   ARETHUSIUS: see no. 187.

*   ARISTODEMUS: see no. 188.

17. ASCLEPIADES.   Gramm. or philosopher, or both.   Alexandria.   s.V
    2/3–3/4.
    Cf. *RE* 2.1631 no. 35 (Freudenthal); *PLRE* II s.v. 2, pp. 158f.

Son of the gramm. Horapollon, father of the gramm. and philosopher Fl. Horapollon (qq.v., nos. 77, 78), he is said by the latter to have taught all his life at Alexandria (*PCairMasp.* 3.67295.i.15) and to have been linked with his brother by the "Muse of philosophy" (ibid. i.18f.). As son and father of these two Horapollones, he should have his *floruit* placed ca. s.V 2/3–3/4; he was dead at least by the time (early in the reign of Anastasius) that the document represented by *PCairMasp.* 3.67295 was drafted; cf. i.15. On the suggestion that he was dead by 485, see below.

His brother was perhaps the philosopher Heraiscus; see further s.v. Fl. Horapollon. A. himself is perhaps to be identified with the Asclepiades referred to by Damascius as a philosopher and as the author of several works on the pharaonic religion and on Egyptian history; cf. *V. Isid.* epit. Phot. 93–94, frgs. 161, 164, 165, 174 Zintzen; *Dub. et solut.* 125 *quater*, 1.324.2ff. Ruelle. But note, in addition to the remarks s.v. Fl. Horapollon, that Maspéro ("Horapollon" 180) concluded that A. must have been dead by 485/87 since he is not found among the philosophers at Alexandria named in the account of Zach. Schol. *Vie de Sévère* pp. 14ff., though Heraiscus and Fl. Horapollon are mentioned there. If Maspéro is correct, A. cannot be the egyptianizing philosopher Asclepiades, who is known to have survived Heraiscus (Damasc. *V. Isid.* frg. 174).

18. ASCLEPIUS. Gramm. s.V 1/3.
PLRE II s.v. 3, p. 163.

Addressee of Nil. Ancyr. *Ep.* 3.24, Ἀσκληπίῳ γραμματικῷ, on the folly of ζητήματα ἀνωφελῆ. The letter presents as its central questions ποῦ εἰσιν οἱ γραμματικοί; ποῦ εἰσιν οἱ πάνσοφοι σύμβουλοι καὶ διδάσκαλοι;—cf. Isaiah 33.18, ποῦ εἰσιν οἱ γραμματικοί; ποῦ εἰσιν οἱ συμβουλεύοντες; (and cf. Isaiah 19.11f.). It is among those letters of Nilus whose inscr. may have been derived from their contents; on this problem, cf. Alan Cameron, "Authenticity" 185f.; cf. also s.v. Alexander, no. 5. Of course, Nilus's variation on Isaiah may have been motivated by A.'s profession.

19. ASMONIUS. Gramm.? s.IV 2/4–2/3.
RE 2.1702f. (Goetz); Sch.-Hos. 4:1.142; *PLRE* I s.v., p. 117.

Author of an *ars* dedicated to Constantius: Prisc. *GL* 2.516.6, *Asmonius in arte, quam ad Constantium imperatorem scribit.* The quotation concerns a question of verbal morphology; thus, the work was either a general *ars grammatica* or an *ars de verbo.* He also wrote on meter (Prisc. *De metr. Terent., GL* 3.420.1), drawing on Iuba; cf. Goetz, *RE* 2.1702f. Although Prisc. does not call A. *grammaticus* (*vel sim.*), the composition of an *ars,* esp. one dedicated to a person outside his own family (contrast s.v. Fl.

Sosipater Charisius, no. 200), makes it likely that A. was a gramm. by profession.

ASTYAGIUS: see no. 189.

AUDAX: see no. 190.

20. AUR. AUGUSTINUS. Gramm. → rhetorician → presbyter → bishop of Hippo.   Thagaste → Carthage → Rome → Milan (until 387) → Thagaste → Hippo.   13 Nov. 354 – 28 Aug. 430.

RE 2.2363–67 (Jülicher); Sch.-Hos. 4:2.398–470; *PLRE* II s.v. 2, pp. 186ff.

Born 13 November 354: *Beat. vit.* 1.6, with Possid. *V. Aug.* 31; Prosper *Chron.* 1304, *Chron. min.* 1.473. Son of Monica and Patricius, a *curialis* of Thagaste (Numidia) of modest means: *Conf.* 2.3.5; Possid. *V. Aug.* 1. In his education and early secular career he enjoyed the patronage of Romanianus of Thagaste; cf. esp. *C. Acad.* 2.2.3; and, most recently, Gabillon, "Romanianus." Educated by his "first teacher" at Thagaste (*Conf.* 1.9.14ff.) and then at Madaurus (*Conf.* 2.3.5) in grammar and rhetoric; his teacher of grammar was perhaps Maximus (q.v., no. 96). After his studies had been interrupted for lack of funds in his sixteenth year (*Conf.* ibid.), his rhetorical training was continued at Carthage (*Conf.* 3.1.1ff.).

A. dates his activity as teacher and Manichee from his nineteenth year (= 372/73; *Conf.* 4.1.1). He taught first at Thagaste (*Conf.* 4.4.7); his general statement at *Conf.* 4.2.2, *docebam in illis annis artem rhetoricam*, could suggest that he taught rhetoric at Thagaste; but Possidius says grammar: *V. Aug.* 1, *nam et grammaticam prius in sua civitate et rhetoricam in Africae capite Carthagine postea docuit.* Possidius's assertion is confirmed by Paulin. Nol. *Ep.* 7.3 and 8.1, to Romanianus and Licentius, respectively. A. was the first teacher of Licentius; see Kaster, "Notes" 333.

Soon after beginning his career at Thagaste, A. went to Carthage, where he taught rhetoric: *Conf.* 4.7.12ff.; cf. *Conf.* 5.7.13; *C. Acad.* 2.2.3. He apparently had a municipal appointment there: *Conf.* 6.7.11, *publica schola uterer.* In 383 he went to teach in Rome (*Conf.* 5.8.14, 5.12.22), and in 384 Symmachus recommended him for the post of public rhetorician in Milan: *Conf.* 5.13.23; cf. below. He was converted to Christianity in August of 386 and resigned his teaching post in the autumn of the same year; he was baptized on Easter 387: *Conf.* 8.6.13ff.; cf. also s.vv. Nebridius (no. 104); Verecundus (no. 159); Anonymus 5 (no. 171), 6 (no. 172).

Early in his teaching career he formed a liaison with a concubine who bore him a son, Adeodatus (*Conf.* 4.2.2, 9.6.14); Adeodatus was with A. in Milan (*Beat. vit.* 1.6) and was baptized with him (*Conf.* 9.6.14ff.). While

A. was at Milan, he was joined by his mother (*Conf.* 6.1.1), at whose urging he contracted an honorable marriage (*Conf.* 6.13.23). He sent away his concubine, the mother of Adeodatus, because she was regarded as an *impedimentum* to his marriage (*Conf.* 6.15.25); but since the girl to whom he was betrothed was still two years under marriageable age (*Conf.* 6.13.23), A. took another concubine for the interim (*Conf.* 6.15.25). The marriage was never realized.

Besides Licentius, his pupils included Alypius (at both Thagaste and Carthage: *Conf.* 6.7.11) and his fellow *civis* Trygetius (*Beat. vit.* 1.6). To the period before his conversion belongs the lost *De pulchro et apto*, written during his tenure at Carthage and dedicated to Hierius, *Romanae urbis orator* (*Conf.* 4.14.20f.; cf. *PLRE* I s.v. Hierius 5, p. 431); while at Carthage he also won a literary contest (*Conf.* 4.3.5; cf. 4.1.1). During his tenure at Milan he delivered panegyrics of Valentinian II (*Conf.* 6.6.9) and the consul Bauto (1 Jan. 385; *C. litt. Petil.* 3.25.30) and entertained hopes of a provincial governorship (*Conf.* 6.11.19). Among the works written at Milan while A. was awaiting baptism (cf. *Retract.* 1.1–6) was a treatise on grammar, which A. later lost (ibid. 1.6). The gramm. treatises now extant under his name (*GL* 5.494ff.) are supposititious.

He became presbyter of Hippo in 391 and bishop in 395; he died 28 August 430 (Possid. *V. Aug.* 31; Prosper *Chron.* 1304, *Chron. min.* 1.473). For further details, see esp. H.-I. Marrou, *Saint Augustin*; Brown, *Augustine*.

21. DECIMUS MAGNUS AUSONIUS. Gramm. → rhetorician → imperial tutor → QSP → PPO Gall. Ital. Afr. → consul. Bordeaux → Trier. Ca. 310 – ca. 394; dead not before 393.

RE 2.2562–80 (Marx); Sch.-Hos. 4:1.21–43; Jouai, *Magistraat*; Stroheker, *Senatorische Adel* 150ff. no. 51; Hopkins, "Social Mobility"; Étienne, *Bordeaux* 335ff.; Booth, "Academic Career"; *PLRE* I s.v. Ausonius 7, pp. 140f.

Decimus Magnus Ausonius: *Decimi Magni Ausonii*, inscr. of *Mosella* and some mss of the *Caesares*; cf. *Decii Magni Ausonii*, inscr. of the *Ordo urb. nob.* The only evidence for "Decimius" is his son's name, Decimius Hilarianus Hesperius: cf. Green, "Prosopographical Notes" 26 n. 32.

Born at Bordeaux (*Praef.* 1.7 *et saep.*) ca. 310 (hardly before); son of the physician Iulius Ausonius and Aemilia Aeonia: cf. esp. *Par.* 1, 2; *Epiced. in patrem.* A. was educated first at Bordeaux (*Prof.* 10.11ff., 8.9–12, 3.1f.), then at Toulouse in the school of his uncle (and soon imperial tutor) Aemilius Magnus Arborius: cf. esp. *Prof.* 16 and *Par.* 3.7–14. He is sometimes thought to have been taught at Bordeaux by Ti. Victor Minervius (cf. *Prof.* 1.9–11, 25f.), but Minervius was perhaps rather a patron than a

teacher; cf. Booth, "Notes" 247 n. 37. After completing his education he
perhaps tried, but failed, to gain the chair of rhetoric vacated by his
uncle at Toulouse ca. 330(?: see Booth, "Academic Career" 330ff.).

When A. began to teach as gramm. at Bordeaux, he managed also, if
less earnestly, to appear as an advocate in the courts; cf. *Praef.* 1.17–18,
nec fora non celebrata mihi sed cura docendi / cultior. Despite *PLRE* I, p. 140, it
is not certain that he practiced at the bar before turning to teaching;
nec . . . non celebrata . . . sed . . . cultior suggests two concurrent activities,
with the second more zealously pursued (*cultior*). This would probably
have been ca. 336/37; see below concerning his tuition of Gratian. His
marriage, to Attusia Lucana Sabina of Bordeaux (*Par.* 8.1; *Par.* 9), probably belongs to this same period.

As gramm. he first taught the elements to the youngest pupils but
soon advanced to the upper level of grammatical instruction: *Epist.*
22.67–72 (on the distinction, see Appendix 4; for a different reconstruction of this stage of A.'s career at Bordeaux, see Booth, "Academic
Career" 332ff.). After some time, A. advanced to the teaching of rhetoric
(*Epist.* 22.73–76; *Prof.* 24.5–6); he was succeeded as *grammaticus* by Acilius
Glabrio (q.v., no. 64).

His tenure at Bordeaux lasted thirty years (*Praef.* 1.23–24), during
which his pupils included his nephew Herculanus (also a gramm.; cf. s.v.,
no. 70), the teacher Tetradius (q.v., no. 263), and Paulinus of Nola
(Paulin. Nol. *Carm.* 10.93ff.).

He was then summoned to the imperial court to be Gratian's tutor,
first in grammar, then in rhetoric (*Praef.* 1.24–27). The summons is often
dated ca. 365 (summary: Jouai, *Magistraat* 47 and n. 4), when Gratian
(b. 18 April 359) would have been six. A more likely date is 366, when
Gratian was seven (see Booth, "Academic Career" 332 n. 12), or 367,
when Valentinian's court was installed at Trier (see Étienne, *Bordeaux*
342f.; Matthews, *Aristocracies* 51).

Subsequently he was made *comes* and *QSP*, 375–76: *comes et quaestor,*
Praef. 1.35. That he became *quaestor* while Valentinian was still alive, therefore before 17 November 375, is stated in *Grat. act.* 2.11 and *Epist.* 22.90;
that he was still *quaestor* in 376 is shown by Symm. *Ep.* 1.13 (cf. also *Epist.*
13 tit., and see s.v. Harmonius, no. 65). In 377–79 he was *PPO Galliarum*
and *PPO Galliarum, Italiae et Africae*; the latter post he held jointly with
his son Hesperius: cf. *Epist.* 22.91, *praefectura duplex*; see also *Grat. act.*
2.11, *cum teneamus duo.* He was *consul prior* in 379: *prior, Praef.* 1.27–28; cf.
Epist. 22.93. For details, see Jouai, *Magistraat* 146ff.; *PLRE* I s.vv. Iulius
Ausonius 5, Decimius Magnus Ausonius 7, Decimius Hilarianus Hesperius
2 (with Green, "Prosopographical Notes" 24); Matthews, *Aristocracies*
51ff., 69ff.

It is unclear whether he was involved in the education of Valentinian II (b. 371), as is sometimes assumed: A. himself is silent; and it is perhaps the natural inference from *Dom.* 1 praef., *de palatio post multos annos honoratissimus, quippe iam consul,* that soon after his consulship he returned to the *villula* inherited from his father near Bordeaux. He was again at Trier under Maximus in 383: *Epist.* 20 tit. Of his correspondence with Symmachus, no piece can be dated later than the consulship. His correspondence with Paulinus, *Epist.* 23–31, shows him alive in 393.

For a stemma of the family, see Jouai, *Magistraat* at end; Étienne, *Bordeaux* 365; *PLRE* I stemma 8, pp. 1134–35 (with Étienne, "Démographie"; cf. *Bordeaux* 362ff.). On the property of Ausonius and his family, see Hopkins, "Social Mobility" 240ff.; Étienne, *Bordeaux* 362ff.; with Chap. 3 pp. 102–3.

AUXILIUS: see no. 191.

* BABYLAS: see no. 192.

*22. BONIFATIUS. Gramm. Rome. s.IV ex. / s.V init.

Bonifatius *sc*[*holasticus?*] *grammaticus: CIL* 6.9446 = 33808 = *ILCV* 726 = *ICVR,* n.s., 1.1549. With the restoration suggested by Henzen at lines 1f., BONIFATIO SC[HOLASTICO] GRAMMATICO, compare the styles σχολαστικὸς χαμαιδιδάσκαλος and σχολαστικὸς σοφιστής cited s.v. Philagrius, no. 117. B. taught at the *forum Traiani* at Rome in the late fourth or early fifth century: lines 6–7, *Traiani qu<a>eren<t> atria m*[--- / *tota Roma flebit et ipse* [--- (cf. Marrou, "Vie intellectuelle" 97ff., revised and reprinted in *Patristique* 70ff.). The epitaph was set up by B.'s wife, Aeliana. B. was a Christian.

* CABRIAS: see no. 193.

23. CALBULUS. Gramm. Africa? s.V ex. / s.VI init.?

Sch.-Hos. 4:2.72f.; Szövérffy, *Weltliche Dichtungen* 1.178, 187; *PLRE* II s.v., p. 250; *Prosop. chrét.* I s.v., p. 182.

Calbulus *grammaticus* (*Anth. Lat.* 1:1.378 inscr.), author of two poems in the codex Salmasianus, one (no. 379) on the Holy Cross, the other (no. 378) on the sacrament of baptism (vv. 1–10) and the baptistery itself, which C. had evidently donated: vv. 11–13, *marmoris oblati speciem, nova munera, supplex / Calbulus exhibuit. fontis memor, unde renatus, / per formam cervi gremium perduxit aquarum.* For comparable donations, cf. s.vv. Clamosus, nos. 29, 30.

The headings that set off the verses of *Anth. Lat.* 1:1.378 suggest that the lines were originally found on the four sides and the circumference of the baptistery, which was evidently designed for immersion baptism and so must have been a considerable structure: *a parte episcopi*, vv. 1–4; *descensio fontis*, 5–6; *ascensio fontis*, 7–8; *econtra episcopum*, 9–10; *et in circuitu fontis*, 11–13. C. was therefore a Christian, presumably active at an episcopal see. The inclusion of the verses in the cod. Salmas. suggests that he lived in Africa not later than s.VI init.; but see the caution of Clover, "Carthage" 20f., and see Averil Cameron, "Byzantine Africa" 43 n. 132; C. is firmly dated to the reign of Hilderic (523–30), as a contemporary of Luxurius, by Szövérffy, *Weltliche Dichtungen* 178 and 187, though for what reason is not clear.

For C.'s provenance, cf. the name "Cambulus" in a Christian inscr. from Carthage(?), *CIL* 8.1167; this perhaps derives from "Calbulus," being an example of regressive dissimilation of the type $l + l \rightarrow n + l$ (see Schopf, *Konsonantischen Fernwirkungen* 96) and the assimilation $nb \rightarrow mb$.

24. CALCIDIUS.   Gramm.   Africa.   s.V 2/2 / s.VI.

Sch.-Hos. 4:2.199, 202; *PLRE* II s.v. Chalcidius, pp. 282f.

Calcidius *grammaticus*, dedicatee of the *Expositio sermonum antiquorum* of Fulgentius the mythographer (i.e., Fabius Planciades Fulgentius or Fabius Claudius Gordianus Fulgentius) according to the inscr. in the majority of the mss: see esp. Wessner, ed., "Fabii Planciadis Fulgentii expositio" 130ff.; Pizzani, ed., *Fabio* 18ff. C. is also found incorrectly in the inscr. of one ms of Fulgentius's *Expositio Vergilianae continentiae*. (According to Pennisi, *Poeti* 287–90, C. is a phantom generated by the corruption of *Catus presbyter* to *Calcidius grammaticus*.) He is addressed as *domine* in the prefatory epistle to the *Exp. serm. antiq.* (p. 111.1 Helm).

He should presumably be placed with Fulgentius in Africa (cf. Fulg. *De aet. mund. et hom.* 131.5ff. Helm), not before s.V 2/2 (cf. the citation of Martianus Capella in *Exp. serm. ant.* 45, p. 123.4ff. Helm), regardless of the question concerning the identity of the two Fulgentii, the mythographer and the bishop of Ruspe (467–532). C. did not know Greek, unless a convention of the genre motivates the scruple of *Exp. serm. ant.* 16 (p. 116.14ff. Helm), *unde et Demostenes pro Philippo ait—sed ne quid te Graecum turbet exemplum, ego pro hoc tibi Latinum feram—ait enim . . .* ; cf. Terent. Maur. *GL* 6.389, vv. 2127f., *plurimus hoc pollet Siculae telluris alumnus: / ne Graecum immittam versum, mutabo Latinum.*

25. CALLIOPIUS.   Gramm. → advocate → *mag. epist.*   Antioch → Constantinople.   Born not later than ca. 340; still alive in 390.

Seeck, *Briefe* 102; Bouchery, *Themistius* 272ff.; Wolf, *Schulwesen* 34, 69–70; Petit, *Étudiants* 85–86; *PLRE* I s.v. 3, p. 175.

Recipient of Lib. *Ep.* 18 (an. 388); subject of *Ep.* 625, 678 (both an. 361), 951 (an. 390).

An Antiochene of distinguished, presumably curial, family: *Ep.* 18.2, πολίτης τ᾽ ἐμὸς καὶ τῆς πόλεως τὰ πρῶτα. His father was a teacher; see below and s.v. Anonymus 3, no. 169. C. was a brother-in-law of Seleucus (cf. s.v., no. 253) and so brother of Alexandra: *Ep.* 625.4, 678.2. If Seleucus has been correctly identified, C. will have been the uncle of John Chrysostom's protégée Olympias; see *PLRE* I stemma 6, p. 1132, and s.vv. Olympias 2, Alexandra, Seleucus 1.

At one time a student of the sophist Zenobius; cf. *Ep.* 625.4, Καλλιοπίου τοῦ τραφέντος ἐν τοῖς Ζηνοβίου λόγοις; with *Ep.* 18.2, ἐκ ταὐτοῦ μοι κρατῆρος ἐν Μουσῶν κήποις πιών. The latter does not mean that he was a fellow pupil of Libanius (C. was probably younger), only that C., like Libanius, was a student of Zenobius. He is therefore unlikely to have been born later than ca. 340, since Zenobius died in 355; cf. below.

He served as a teacher in Libanius's school (*Ep.* 625.4, κουφίζοντος δὲ ἐμοὶ τὸ περὶ τοὺς νέους ἄχθος) and with his father taught Libanius's son, Cimon (Arabius): *Ep.* 625.6, 678.2. Since Cimon is unlikely to have been more than seven years old in 361, Calliopius and his father must have been lower teachers in Libanius's school, of the type Libanius elsewhere calls γραμματιστής (= γραμματικός; cf. Appendix 2, and note the reading Καλλιοπείου τοῦ γραμματικοῦ, probably a scribal inference from the context, found in one of the mss at *Ep.* 625.4; cf. also Wolf, *Schulwesen* 34).

C. subsequently, *ut vid.*, practiced as an advocate; cf. *Ep.* 18.2, πρῶτον μὲν δίκας λέγων. N.B. πρῶτον: looking back from the year 388—and from the eminence of C.'s position in the bureaucracy—Libanius passes over C.'s more humble teaching thirty years earlier and chooses the semipublic activity of the advocate to mark the start of his career (cf. below). Compare the references to C.'s oratorical ability, ῥητορείαν, at the end of *Ep.* 18.

C. was *mag. epist.* in 388: *Ep.* 18.2, νῦν δ᾽ ἐπιστολὰς γράφων ἄμφω παρὰ βασιλεῦσιν, τῷ μὲν πατρί, τῷ δὲ υἱεῖ. C. is represented as being responsible for mediating between Libanius and Tatianus (*PPO Or.*, an. 388), possibly with the help of Themistius, in 388: see *Ep.* 18, though the text is not clear; cf. Bouchery, *Themistius* 272ff. He was in Constantinople in 390; cf. *Ep.* 951.

C. was one of the Eastern opponents of Latinity and esp. of the attraction of Eastern students to Rome: *Ep.* 951.1. The opening conceit of *Ep.* 18, τίς θεῶν ἢ δαιμόνων κτλ, suggests that C. was a pagan, as was his brother-in-law, Seleucus.

Note that the reconstruction above depends upon Seeck's identification of the Calliopius of *Ep.* 625 and 678 with the Calliopius of *Ep.* 18 and 951 (*Briefe* 102). But the appearance of the lowly διδάσκαλος of 361 as the man of affairs and *mag. epist.* of 388 has not unreasonably caused the identification to be questioned; cf. Wolf, *Schulwesen* 70. Three points are worth making.

First, if the Calliopius of *Ep.* 18 and 951 is to be found among the other Calliopii of Libanius's correspondence, the teacher of *Ep.* 625 and 678 is the most likely candidate. Seeck's Calliopius III is absolutely ruled out; Calliopius IV, virtually so. Calliopius I and II (= *PLRE* I s.v., nos. 1, 2) are possible but unlikely; their careers were already in full bloom in the late 350s and early 360s, and the men were probably too old, if not dead, by 388. C., however, need not have been more than twenty-one in 361, and would have been in his prime in the 380s; cf. above.

Second, the references to the school of Zenobius in the letters from both periods provide a direct link; and the earlier letters' mention of the marriage connection with Seleucus, a man of substance and standing, indirectly confirms the praise of the social standing of C.'s family found in the later *Ep.* 18, τῆς πόλεως τὰ πρῶτα.

Third, the fact that Libanius emphasizes C.'s advocacy as the beginning of his career (see above) might well mean that C. did not teach long: unlike Ausonius, who preferred the classroom to the bar (see s.v., no. 21), C. may have taught only until the opportunity arose to turn his rhetorical education to forensic use. Ausonius's career also provides another comparison: one would not have predicted the *QSP* of the mid-370s from the *grammaticus* of the late 330s.

CALLIOPIUS: see no. 194.

+   CARMINIUS: see no. 195.

*26.   CASSIANUS.   Schoolmaster and martyr.   Forum Cornelii.   s.IV init.

Cassianus: Prudent. *Perist.* 9 tit., vv. 6, 94, 106. Schoolmaster: cf. *Perist.* 9.21–24, *praefuerat studiis puerilibus et grege multo / saeptus magister litterarum sederat, / verba notis brevibus conprendere cuncta peritus / raptimque punctis dicta praepetibus sequi;* 35–36, *agmen tenerum ac puerile gubernat / fictis notare verba signis inbuens.* Since vv. 23–24 and 35–36 clearly refer to shorthand, and since *magister litterarum* by itself never means "teacher of shorthand," we should probably conclude that C. taught both regular letters and shorthand in his school. Compare the Christian Protogenes, who opened a school at Antinoopolis in which he taught both shorthand and τὰ θεῖα λόγια: Theodoret. *HE* 4.18.

C. was martyred at Forum Cornelii (mod. Imola), evidently during the Great Persecution; cf. vv. 29–30, *ecce fidem quatiens tempestas saeva premebat / plebem dicatam Christianae gloriae.* After refusing to sacrifice (v. 32), C. was handed over to his students, who stabbed him to death with their *stili:*

vv. 13ff., 37ff. For the instrument, cf. Evag. *HE* 3.10 (*PG* 86:2.2613f.), Theoph. *Chron.* p. 128.17ff. de Boor, on the death of Stephanus of Antioch; Greg. Naz. *C. Iulian.* 4.89, on the death of Marcus Arethusius; and see s.v. Felix, no. 216.

The *passio* first appears in Prudentius (*Perist.* 9), who visited C.'s martyrium (vv. 5ff.); a *passio* based on *Perist.* 9 and composed before Bede's time is found at Mombritius, *Sanctuarium*² 1.280. There was a *basilica Cassiani* at Imola by s.V med. according to Agnellus, *Lib. pontif. eccl. Ravennae* 52 (*MGH* SS. rer. langob., p. 314).

On the medieval tradition concerning C., cf. *LThK* 3.969 (Sparber); *Bibliotheca Sanctorum* 3.911 (Gordini); Delehaye, *Passions*² 288ff.

CATO: see no. 196.

ARRUNTIUS CELSUS: see no. 197.

*   CHABRIAS: see no. 198.

CHALCIDIUS: see no. 24.

+   IOANNES CHARAX: see no. 199.

FL. SOSIPATER CHARISIUS: see no. 200.

+   GEORGIUS CHOEROBOSCUS: see no. 201.

27. CHRESTUS.   Gramm.   Africa → Constantinople.   358.

RE 3.2449 (Seeck); *PLRE* I s.v., p. 202.

Latin gramm. brought from Africa to Constantinople to fill the place of Evanthius (q.v., no. 54) on the latter's death: Jer. *Chron.* s.a. 358. Otherwise unknown.

With three exceptions, all the mss of Jer. *ad loc.*, including the codex Bodleianus (s.V.), give the man's name as *C(h)restus* (*Chretus* L); of the exceptions, two omit the name entirely, one (B, written sometime between 627 and 699) reads *Charistus*. On the basis of the last, Usener emended the name to "Charisius" (see s.v., no. 200). This conjecture is not impossible, given what little we know of Charisius's life; but *uter in alterum abiturus erat*? "Charistus" looks very much like the idiosyncratic result of a scribal error or a botched interlinear correction, with the name "Charisius" failing in the attempt to drive out the unknown "Chrestus"; the reverse corruption is more difficult to imagine. Usener's conjecture should be rejected.

28. CITARIUS.   Gr. gramm. and poet.   Sicily (Syracuse?) → Bordeaux. s.IV 2/3.

PLRE I s.v., p. 205.

Citarius: Auson. *Prof.* 13 tit., v. 1. A Greek gramm.: *Prof.* 13 tit., *Grammatico Burdigalensi Graeco*; cf. vv. 1f., *dignus / grammaticos inter qui celebrere bonos*, a comparison with Aristarchus and Zenodotus; cf. also s.v. Harmonius, no. 65. From Sicily: v. 7, *urbe satus Sicula*; the tit. specifies *Syracusano*. He came to Bordeaux a *peregrinus*.

As an *amicus* of Ausonius (v. 12; cf. v. 1), C. must have been active at Bordeaux during Ausonius's own tenure, ca. 336–67. He was also a poet; Ausonius compares his *carmina* favorably with the poetry of Simonides (vv. 5–6).

C. married well soon after his arrival in Bordeaux: v. 9, *coniugium nanctus cito nobilis et locupletis*. He died before becoming a father (v. 10).

On the grounds of C.'s poetic talents, *PLRE* I suggested identification with the *Citherius rhetor* who composed an epitaph preserved in *Anth. Lat.* 1:2² 484b. But, apart from the fact that the name and titulatur are against the identification, one would expect a poet compared with Simonides to have written in Greek; note above that he is compared *qua* Greek gramm. with Aristarchus and Zenodotus.

*29. CLAMOSUS.   Schoolmaster.   Parentium (Histria).   s.IV 3/4 / s.V init.

Clamosus, *magister puerorum*, commemorated with his wife, Successa, in a mosaic of the *basilica primitiva* at Parentium, in Histria, for donating 100 feet of pavement: *ILCV* 719 = *Inscr. Ital.* 10:2.58, [*Lu*]*picinus et Pascasia p(edes) CCCC f(ecerunt). Clamosus mag(ister) puer(orum) et Successa p(edes) C. Felicissimus cum suis p(edes) C*; photograph in *Inscr. Ital.* 10:2, p. 27; Molajoli, *Basilica*² 16, fig. 9.

That C. was a schoolmaster is shown by the analogous style of Philumenus (q.v., no. 120), viz., παιδοδιδάσκαλος; likewise by Martial 5.84.1f., *puer . . . clamoso revocatur a magistro*. From the latter, Diehl (at *ILCV* 719) concluded that "Clamosus" was not C.'s "*verum et proprium nomen*" but a *supernomen*, or name assumed from his profession; cf. *SEG* 13.472 (s.II, Ostia), the epitaph of the sophist P. Aelius Samius Isocrates, with the comments of J. and L. Robert, *Bull. ép.* 1949, 233; cf. also *Bull. ép.* 1970, 422 no. 63, a sophist Menecrates ὁ καλήμενος Ποσειδώνιος; and cf. s.v. Arethusius, no. 187. The name indicates that C., and so presumably his instruction, had some contact with the classical tradition.

A *term. p. q.* is provided by a coin of Valens found under the mosaic; a *term. a. q.* is provided by another mosaic, *Inscr. Ital.* 10:2.62, bearing the names of Lupicinus and Pascasia (cf. above) found in the annex added to the *basilica primitiva* probably in s.V init.; cf. Degrassi, *Inscr. Ital.* 10:2, p. 26; Molajoli, *Basilica*² 11ff. If the mosaic is to be dated to s.IV 3/4 / s.V init., then C. must be the father of, not identical with, the Clamosus (q.v., no. 30) commemorated in a similar mosaic of the *basilica praeeuphrasiana* (s.V med.).

For the donation, cf. s.v. Calbulus, no. 23.

*30. CLAMOSUS. Schoolmaster. Parentium (Histria). s.V med.

Clamosus, *magister puerorum*, commemorated with his wife, Victorina, in a mosaic of the *basilica praeeuphrasiana* at Parentium, in Histria, for donating 111 feet of pavement: *Inscr. Ital.* 10:2.74, [C]*lamosus magister puerorum et Victorina f(ecerunt) p(edes) CXI*; photograph in *Inscr. Ital.* 10:2, p. 35; Molajoli, *Basilica*² 22, fig. 24. The construction of the basilica should be dated to s.V med. or not long after; cf. Degrassi, *Inscr. Ital.* 10:2, p. 31; Molajoli, *Basilica*² 17ff. The name of C.'s wife, Victorina, and the date suggest that C. is the son of, not identical with, the Clamosus (q.v., no. 29), husband of Successa, commemorated in a similar mosaic of the *basilica primitiva* (s.IV 3/4 / s.V init.). On C.'s name and the style *magister puerorum*, cf. s.v. Clamosus; cf. also Appendix 1.1c.

ARRUNTIUS CLAUDIUS: see no. 202.

31. CLEDONIUS (ROMANUS ?). Gramm. and senator. Constantinople. s.V med. – 2/2?

RE 4.10 (Goetz); Sch.-Hos. 4:2.207–8; *PLRE* II s.v. 2, p. 302.

Cledonius, styled *Romanus senator, Constantinopolitanus grammaticus*, inscr. cod. Bern. 380. It is possible, however, that the inscr. should be punctuated *Cledonius Romanus, senator Constantinopolitanus, grammaticus*; cf. *CIL* 9.1654 = *ILS* 6497: *M. Rutilius Aelianus, decurio Beneventanus, grammaticus*. That C. taught is suggested by a lesson his *Ars* introduces with an anecdote from the classroom: *GL* 5.14.3ff., *et quia praetermittendum mihi non visum est quod eventus admonuit, quodam tempore, dum ars in Capitolio die competenti tractaretur, unus e florentibus discipulis Iohannes a grammatico venia postulata intendens in alterum sciscitatus est, qua differentia dici debeat.* . . . But given the state of the text (see below), the episode may be an interpolation; note esp. the shift from first person, *mihi*, to third person, *a grammatico venia postulata*. His location can be deduced from his style, *Constantinopolitanus*. If the anecdote cited above is genuine, the *Capitolium* referred to will be that of Constantinople; cf. *CTh* 14.9.3 (an. 425); Ioann. Lyd. *De mag.* 3.29.

    C. must be dated after s.IV med., since he comments on Donatus (q.v., no. 52), and in fact after s.V 1/4, since he appears to have used the commentary of Servius (q.v., no. 136) on Donatus: cf. Holtz, "À l'école de Donat" 526; a date after 425 is also consistent with the reference to the *Capitolium* as the site of instruction (see above, with *CTh* 14.9.3). Since C. styles himself *senator*, and since the title *senator* had come to be reserved for *illustres* by 530 at the very latest, and possibly as early as the reign of Zeno or even of Leo (Jones, *LRE* 529), we should conclude either that C. was an *illustris* or—far more likely—that he cannot be dated later than s.V 2/2. In any case, he must be dated earlier than cod.

Bern. 380 (s.VI – s.VII, *CLA* 7.864); the state of the text therein (see below) suggests that C. composed the work considerably before this copy was made.

C. composed a commentary on the two *artes* of Donatus (*GL* 5.9–79; also ed. H. Bertsch, "Cledonii ars grammatica," diss. Heidelberg, 1884). The work as now preserved is defective at beginning and end, with lacunae throughout; the relation between the lemmata of Donatus and the text of C. is often confused, and there are obvious interpolations. The work was written at the prompting of, and was dedicated to, a certain man of learning whose name is lost with the beginning of the preface, *GL* 5.9; a later hand added the phrase *ad Fidum* to the inscr. in cod. Bern. 380, a guess based on the phrase *o fide omnibus et in omnibus fide* in the preface, *GL* 5.9.6.

32. CLEOBULUS. Gramm. Egypt → Antioch. Born not after 300; dead not before 360.

RE 11.672 (Seeck); Bouchery, *Themistius* 128ff., 135, 154ff.; Wolf, *Schulwesen* 34f., 71–73; Petit, *Étudiants* 85, 86; *PLRE* I s.v. 1, pp. 215f.

Mentioned in or subject of Lib. *Ep.* 361 (an. 358), 52, 67–69, 82, 90, 91 (all an. 359), 155 (an. 359/60?), 231 (an. 360).

C. had come from Egypt to Antioch: *Ep.* 361.2; cf. 361.4, his sister's son in Egypt seeking a position on the staff of the *praef. Aegypt.* Parnasius. He was a poet (*Ep.* 361.2, ποιητής τε ἀγαθός) and teacher (διδάσκαλος, *Ep.* 361.2, 52.3, 91.1, 231.1; cf. 82.2, ὁ παιδευτής). As a teacher, C. took on few pupils because of his physical frailty (*Ep.* 361.2), but had had Libanius as a student (*Ep.* 68.1; cf. *Ep.* 361.2, and esp. the conceit that opens *Ep.* 82.1–2, to Libanius's former pupil Ambrosius: teachers are pleased to ask former pupils for favors, and pupils are glad to help; Cleobulus asks me for help; I ask you), as a result of which Libanius regarded him as a child does his father (*Ep.* 361.2; cf. 231.1, the same feeling imputed to Bassianus). C. had also been the teacher of Bassianus (Phoenix to the latter's Achilles, *Ep.* 155.2; cf. 231.1) before Bassianus studied rhetoric with Libanius, and Bassianus owed his very knowledge of τὰ τοῦ Φοίνικος to C. (*Ep.* 155.3)—i.e., C. had taught Bassianus Homer. C. therefore was a gramm. (see also s.vv. Didymus and Anonymus 2, nos. 46, 168; for the analogy with Phoenix, cf. s.v. Nicocles, no. 106). By the late 350s C. was perhaps one of the gramm. teaching in Libanius's school; cf. *Ep.* 69.2 ἑταῖρον; *Ep.* 155.2; Petit, *Étudiants* 84. The evidence, however, is not decisive.

As Libanius's teacher, C. must have been active at Antioch in the early to mid-320s and so is unlikely to have been born much later than 300; a slightly later date would be possible, however, if C. is identical with Anonymus 2: his instruction of Libanius would then date to the early 330s. He was still active in the period 358–60 and was by then old enough to have a nephew seeking a position on the staff of the *praef. Aegypt.* (see above); note, however, that Libanius does not mention extreme old age as an added cause of sympathy when requesting assistance for C. in his lawsuit (see below). He is therefore perhaps unlikely to have been born much before 300.

C. is said to have had means sufficient to avoid base (ἀγεννές) employment but insufficient "to bear unjust penalties": *Ep.* 52.3; on the latter part of this statement, see below. He is also said to have had enough influence to protect his rights: *Ep.* 52.4, ῥώμη . . . ἀρκοῦσα τὰ δίκαια βεβαιοῦν. He was a φίλος of Themistius: *Ep.* 68.1, 91.4; cf. 68.3, τοσοῦτόν σοι χρόνον συγγεγενώς; for Themistius as his φύλαξ, see 68.5. He was also known to Aristophanes (*Ep.* 361.3; on the latter's career in this period, see *PLRE* I s.v., pp. 106f.) and was patronized by Libanius.

All ten letters involving C. find Libanius interceding with one person or another in C.'s interest or his family's. Two letters concern his kin: *Ep.* 361 intercedes with Parnasius, *praef. Aegypt.*, in behalf of C.'s nephew, who was seeking a post on Parnasius's staff; *Ep.* 82 seeks favor with Libanius's former pupil Ambrosius (holding an ἀρχή of uncertain description) for C.'s relative (συγγενής) Antiphilus, who is described as ἐν πρώτοις . . . τῶν σοι διακονούντων, i.e., already a member of the *officium* of Ambrosius. It is not known whether the nephew of *Ep.* 361 is the Antiphilus of *Ep.* 82. The remaining letters concern C. himself and should be treated together: thus Bouchery, *Themistius* 156.

One group (*Ep.* 52, 67–69, 90, 91), all of 359 and all, *ut vid.*, addressed to Constantinople, concern a suit being brought against C. by one Severus, who is described in *Ep.* 52.1 as long a thorn in Libanius's side; he cannot easily be identified with any other Severus in the correspondence. In *Ep.* 52.2 and 91.2 Severus is said to be acting in collusion with Alexander (= Alexander 9 *PLRE* I, p. 41); an otherwise unknown pair, Antipater and Parmenio, are said in *Ep.* 52.3 to promise trouble in the future. Against Severus, Libanius attempts to enlist the aid of Clearchus (*Ep.* 52, 67, 90), evidently an official—his exact post is unknown, but it was such that Libanius could ask him to threaten Severus with prison in *Ep.* 52.2—and of Themistius, then *procos. Const.* (*Ep.* 67, 91; in *Ep.* 69 the physician Hygi(ei)nus is asked to use his influence with Themistius), to save C. from having to pay insupportable fines (*Ep.* 52.3, and above).

The nature of the suit is unknown, but it may have involved an inheritance; cf. the reference to κληρόνομοι in *Ep.* 52.2. Libanius says that the matter had had a promising beginning from C.'s point of view but had deteriorated (*Ep.* 67.3). As the correspondence drags on through 359 Clearchus and Themistius are evidently unresponsive, and Libanius becomes increasingly impatient in his pleas; see esp. the letters to Clearchus. Although the disposition of the suit is not stated, the course of the correspondence and the absence of any concluding letters to Clearchus and Themistius thanking them for assistance (contrast the case of Bassianus, below) suggest that the suit went against C.

Further, Libanius writes not long thereafter to his relative and fellow Antiochene Bassianus, asking him to help his former teacher C.: *Ep.* 155, late 359 or early 360; the last letters to Clearchus and Themistius belong to autumn 359. The nature of the favor sought is not stated, but from the letter thanking Bassianus for his aid (*Ep.* 231, early autumn 360), it appears to have been a subvention of money: *Ep.* 231.1, ἃ περὶ τοῦ θαυμαστοῦ Κλεοβούλου πρὸς τὴν τήθην [= Bassiana] ἐπιστέλλεις δεόμενος αὐτῷ τὴν σὴν οὐσίαν ἀνεῷχθαι; cf. at ibid. 3 a reference to οὐδὲ ... φαύλους παρὰ τῶν Μουσῶν τοὺς μισθούς. Bassianus thus saved C. from ruin: *Ep.* 231.2, ἔχομεν ... τὸν Κλεόβουλον πάντως ἂν ἀποπτάμενον, εἰ μὴ τοιοῦτος ἦσθα. We can surmise that C. needed the money to pay the fines Libanius had feared.

+ 33. COLUTHUS.   Gramm.   Egypt?   s.VI init.?

RE 1.1177f., s.v. Akoluthos (Crusius).

Recipient of a poem in cod. Barb. 310 (*olim* 246), *PLG*⁴ 3.362ff., where the inscr. runs εἰς τὰ βρουμάλια ἀκολούθου τοῦ γραμματικοῦ. Weil, "Vers," realized that the gramm. (cf. v. 13, σοφέ, γραμμάτων ἀνάσσεις) in whose honor this poem was composed (cf. vv. 41f., ὅτε σὸν πάρεστιν ἦμαρ, / λογικαὶ πάρεισι Μοῦσαι, and *passim*) must be named Κόλουθος: cf. esp. vv. 15–16, μετὰ γὰρ σὸν οὖν τὸ κάππα / τότε τῶν λόγων τὸ γράμμα; v. 71, Kypris called ὁμογράμματος. The poem was thus written for 3 December, the tenth day of the festival of the Brumalia.

Bergk incorrectly printed the poem as an adespoton in *PLG*⁴; it follows without break or distinction the other anacreontic pieces of Georgius the gramm. (q.v., no. 63) in cod. Barb. (cf. Matranga, "Praefatio" xxxiii–xxxiv) and should be attributed to that author; cf. Nissen, *Byzantinische Anakreonten* 13, 16; Anastasi, "Giorgio" 211f. The authorship provides a probable date of s.VI init. (see s.v. Georgius), and C.'s name points to Egypt. From the latter fact flowed Weil's suggestion ("Vers") that C. is the epic poet Col(l)uthus of Lycopolis; but given that no name is more common in Egypt (cf. Crum, "Colluthus") and that the poet is nowhere called γραμματικός, the identification must remain uncertain. At vv. 27–30 C. is called the pride or honor (ἄνθος) of Homer, a compliment that would be as suitable for a γραμματικός, i.e., a learned (v. 29, σοφίης ἄνακτα) expositor of Homer, as for an epic poet. The identification has been accepted most recently by Anastasi, "Giorgio" 214f.

*34. COMINIANUS. Gramm. s.IV init.

RE 4.606 (Goetz); Sch.-Hos. 4:1.141–42, with an important misprint corrected at p. 177 n. 5.

C. is known by name only from Charisius (q.v., no. 200), who cites him nine times (see below); in the Middle Ages Charisius himself is frequently cited under the name of Cominianus; cf. s.v. Iulius Romanus, no. 249, and see Hagen, *Anecd. Helv.* = *GL* 8, clv–clvi. In his first four citations Charisius calls him *Cominianus grammaticus* or *Cominianus disertissimus grammaticus* (*GL* 1.147.18 = 187.8 Barwick, 175.29–30 = 225.23B., 180.11 = 232.9B., 181.15 = 233.24–25B.), which might suggest that *grammaticus* was part of the titulatur of his work; contrast the case of Iulius Romanus, of whom Charisius uses only the vague title *disertissimus artis scriptor* at *GL* 1.232.7 (= 301.17B.), and that only once. His work, a brief and spare treatment of the basics (see below), was probably meant for the schools; cf. the judgments of Keil, *GL* 1, xlviii; Tolkiehn, *Cominianus* 169f.; Barwick, *Remmius* 16. Tolkiehn, *Cominianus* 2 and n. 3, suggested that Charisius refers to C. as *magister noster* at *GL* 1.189.9–10 (= 245.8–9B.), but the conjecture has little to recommend it.

A *term. a. q.* is provided by Charisius (s.IV med.); C. perhaps knew the work of Sacerdos (q.v., no. 132; on Dosith. *GL* 7.393.12 = *Exc. Bob.*, *GL* 1.534.34 = Diom. *GL* 1.318.7, and likewise on Dosith. *GL* 7.407.18 with Charis. *GL* 1.253.26 = 332.8–9B. = Diom. *GL* 1.399.12, see Tolkiehn, *Cominianus* 107f., 157). He should probably be placed toward the beginning of s.IV.

From the excerpts of Charisius it is evident that C.'s work was a basic handbook, treating the parts of speech (*GL* 1.147.18ff. = 187.8–188.10B., on the ablative, i.e., the noun; 175.29ff. = 225.23–226.7B., on the conjugations, i.e., the verb; 180.11ff. = 232.9–30B., on the participle; 180.27ff. = 233.2–25B., on the adverb; 224.24ff. = 289.19–290.11B., on the conjunction; 230.4ff. = 298.2–299.13B., on the preposition; 238.19ff. = 311.4–9B., on the interjection) and the *vitia orationis* (*GL* 1.265.2ff. = 349.18–350.23B. "De barbarismo"; 266.15ff. = 351.13–352.31B. "De soloecismo").

35. CONCORDIUS. Gramm. Bordeaux → *urbs alia*. s.IV 1/3.

PLRE I s.v. 1, p. 219.

Concordius (Auson. *Prof.* 10.18), a *grammaticus Latinus* (ibid. tit.) *qui profugus patria / mutasti sterilem / urbe alia cathedram* (ibid. 19–21). Despite the reserve of *PLRE*—"whether from or to Bordeaux is not clear"; cf. also Étienne, *Bordeaux* 252—this almost certainly means that Concordius left his unprofitable chair at Bordeaux. If instead C. came to Bordeaux, it would be strange for this to be signaled by so offhand a reference as the perfunctory *urbe alia*—at very least, *nostra*, or some metrically compatible equivalent, would seem to be called for; cf. *Prof.* 13.7, of Citarius (q.v., no. 28). Further, at *Prof.* 20.1–2, Ausonius states that it has been his *lex* thus far (i.e., *Prof.* 1–19) to celebrate only *cives*, whether they taught at home or abroad; here *cives* means those who have a *communis patria* with Ausonius: so *Prof.* 19.3, addressing the rhetorician Sedatus, a native of Bordeaux who went to teach at Toulouse. One may point to Citarius (above), Patera, and his father, Phoebicius (*Prof.* 4 and 10.22ff.), who shared that *patria*, and were *cives*, by virtue of their move to Bordeaux (note that the number of such transplants is strikingly small; the number of natives who appear from the *Prof.* to have gone away to teach is twice as large, even if C. is not counted); nonetheless, in the fifteen other places in the *Prof.* where *patria* is used, including twice more in *Prof.* 10, the word, with or without a modifier, can only refer to Bordeaux: cf. praef. 2; 1.4, 6; 6.4, 22; 10.34, 52; 16.4, 17; 17.16; 18.4; 19.3, 8; 25.2; and esp. 23.6–10, where *profugus* and *patria* are also used in close proximity, of a teacher who went from Bordeaux to Spain. There must, then, be a strong presumption that *patria* at 10.19 also refers to Bordeaux. C. therefore was probably a native of Bordeaux who went elsewhere to teach; accordingly, he is possibly identical with the L. Terentius Iulianus *signo* Concordius, a *v.p.*, *magister studiorum*, *grammaticus Latinus* who died at Trier (see s.v., no. 87).

All the gramm. of *Prof.* 10 likely belong to a period well before Ausonius's tenure at Bordeaux, i.e., before ca. 336/37. Macrinus and Phoebicius, the only two of the six who can be dated, certainly belong to that period. (The former was Ausonius's first teacher; the latter was Attius Patera's father; see s.vv., nos. 93, 122.) Further, none of the six is spoken of as an *amicus*—in contrast, e.g., with the *grammaticus Graecus* Citarius (q.v., no. 28), who appears to have been Ausonius's contemporary at Bordeaux; cf. also Iucundus in *Prof.* 9 and s.v., no. 86—and the tone of the poem as a whole is impersonal: Ausonius emphasizes his *officium* in recalling these teachers out of loyalty to Bordeaux; cf. vv. 1–10, 32–34. One senses that Ausonius is using *Prof.* 10 to dispose of a group of teachers from before his time, whom he did not know well, if at all. It may be significant that there is not even the qualifying phrase *nostro . . . in aevo*, which is found in poems about teachers who belonged to the Bordeaux of Ausonius's earliest years; cf. *Prof.* 8.7, 12.7.

CONSENTIUS: see no. 203.

36. CORINTHUS.   Gr. gramm.   Bordeaux.   s.IV 1/4.
PLRE I s.v., p. 229.

Corinthus (Auson. *Prof.* 8.1), *grammaticus Graecus* at Bordeaux (ibid. tit.); cf. vv. 1–4, *Corinthi / . . . / Atticas musas . . . / grammatic[i]*. With Spercheus (q.v., no. 139), C. was one of Ausonius's teachers *primis . . . in annis*; cf. vv. 1–4 with 9–10, and see s.v. Romulus, no. 250. Therefore he was active at least in the second decade of s.IV.

With Spercheus (q.v.) and Menestheus (q.v., no. 99), the other two Greek gramm. celebrated in this poem, C. is said to have possessed *sedulum . . . studium docendi, / fructus exilis tenuisque sermo* (vv. 5–6). Ausonius's *tardior sensus* and *puerilis aevi / noxius error* (vv. 13–16) prevented him from fully appreciating and profiting from their efforts.

See further s.v. Romulus.

37. FL. CRESCONIUS CORIPPUS. Gramm. and poet → *palatinus.* Carthage → Constantinople. s.VI init. – 3/4; dead not before 566/67.

RE 4.1236–46 (Skutsch); Sch.-Hos. 4:2.78ff.; Averil Cameron, "Byzantine Africa" 36ff.

Fl. Cresconius Corippus: the first two names are known only from the lost codex Budensis, reported by J. Cuspinianus; cf. Partsch, ed., *MGH AA* 3:2, xlvii n. 2. Poet and gramm. from Africa: cod. Matrit. Caion. 14 Num. 22, *incipit liber primus Corippi Africani grammatici*; cf. *Laud. Anast.* 36ff. and the typically African name "Cresconius." C. claimed to have his origins in the back country: *Iohan.* praef. 25f., *quid <quod ego> ignarus, quondam per rura locutus, / urbis per populos carmina mitto palam?* (cf. vv. 28, 37). He presented the first book (praef. 39) of his poem on the victories of the *mag. mil.* Ioannes Troglita, *Iohannidos seu de bellis Libycis libri VIII* (ed. Diggle and Goodyear [Cambridge, 1970]), at Carthage (praef. 35) not long after 548. He migrated sometime later to Constantinople, where in 566/67 he composed the panegyric of Justin II, *In laudem Iustini Augusti minoris* (ed. Averil Cameron; also ed. Stache). Perhaps shortly before, in 565/66, he wrote a brief panegyric (now standing as part of the introduction of the *Laud. Iust.*) on Anastasius, QSP (*Laud. Anast.* 17, 31, 41) and *magister* (sc. *officiorum*, ibid. 26, 44; cf. 31f.).

On the date: Anastasius's tenure as *mag. off.* must be dated to 565/66; cf. Averil Cameron, ed., *Laud. Iust.* p. 123. Consequently, if the *Laud. Anast.* is to be regarded as contemporary with the *Laud. Iust.* (as usually), we must assume that the references to Anastasius as *magister* are retrospective, since Theodorus was already *mag. off.* on the occasion of the poem on Justin (see below). Alternatively, since C. stresses Anastasius's tenure of a double office (v. 32, *gemino . . . honore*) and addresses him indifferently as both *quaestor* and *magister* (see *Laud. Anast.* 17, 31, 41; 26, 44), we may conclude that Anastasius was holding both offices at the time of the poem and that the panegyric of Anastasius was originally

composed slightly earlier than the *Laud. Iust.*; cf. Averil Cameron, ed.,
Laud. Iust. p. 123. The second alternative seems more likely; see further
below.

C. appears to have been commended to Anastasius by an imperial
letter (*sacri apices*) during a time of personal difficulty and to have held a
palatine office under him; cf. *Laud. Anast.* 36–48:

generaliter orbi

> quam providens, miseri specialiter Afri
> in te oculos atque ora ferunt: agit Africa grates
> et vestram iam sentit opem, gaudetque quod ampla
> 40 semper Anastasii referunt solacia cives:
> me quoque gaudentem, quaestorum maxime, redde.
> quod labor indulsit, quod fessis provida Musis
> alma per insomnes meruit vigilantia noctes,
> hi sacri monstrant apices. lege, summe magister,
> 45 et causam defende meam. tibi sanctio vestrum
> commendat famulum. vestro de fonte creatur
> rivulus iste meus, sub cuius nomine gesto
> principis officium.

On vv. 42–48, an awkward and obscure passage on any reading, I align
myself with the interpretation presented by Averil Cameron, ed., *Laud.
Iust.* pp. 125f. (and, in part, by Stache, ed., *Laud. Iust.* pp. 2f., on v. 48,
principis officium), although I believe that *sacri apices* (v. 44) must refer to a
letter of Justin, not of Justinian (see now Averil Cameron, "Career"
536ff.). An alternative interpretation, which would equate both *sacri apices*
and *principis officium* with the panegyric of Justin itself, and which consequently would deny an office to C. (see Baldwin, "Career"; and, on
sacri apices, see Stache, ed., *Laud. Iust.* pp. 61f.), has been refuted by Averil
Cameron, "Career" 536ff. Note also that if the remarks above concerning the date of the *Laud. Anast.* are correct, any argument that *sacri apices*,
etc., refer to the *Laud. Iust.* would be weakened significantly, since the
two poems would not be contemporary. Since C. claimed to be an old
man at the time (*Laud. Iust.* praef. 37; *Laud. Anast.* 48), his birth should be
placed toward the beginning of s.VI.

In addition to Anastasius (*Laud. Iust.* 1.15–17) C. names, as those who
have urged him to compose the panegyric on Justin, Thomas (*PPO Afr.*;
ibid. 18–21), Magnus (*CSL*; ibid. 22–24), Theodorus (*mag. off.*; ibid. 25–
26), and Demetrius (*a secretis?* ibid. 26; cf. Averil Cameron, ed., and
Stache, ed., *ad loc.*). He speaks vaguely of some personal misfortune,
which he begs Justin to relieve at *Laud. Iust.* praef. 41ff.; Stein, *Histoire*
2.693, connected C.'s plea with the woes caused in Africa by the revolt

of the sons of Coutsina in 563. The panegyric of Anastasius includes a plea for patronage at vv. 36ff.; see above.

C. was a Christian; cf. *RLAC* 3.428 (Krestan).

CORONATUS: see no. 204.

38. CRESCONIUS. Gramm. and Donatist. Africa. s.V init.

PLRE II s.v. 1, p. 329; *Prosop. chrét.* I s.v. 4, pp. 230ff.; cf. Weissengruber, "Augustins Wertung."

Cresconius, a *grammaticus*, the object of Augustine's tract *Contra Cresconium grammaticum et Donatistam*; for the name and style, cf. also *Retract.* 2.52.1. C. *Cresc.* is probably to be dated ca. 405/7, and in any case not before 405; cf. *Retract.* ibid., *hos autem quattuor libros quando scripsi, iam contra Donatistas dederat leges Honorius imperator.* At C. *Cresc.* 3.47.51 the laws are called *recentissimae*; at C. *Cresc.* 1.1 Augustine says that C.'s rebuttal of the C. *litt. Petil.* (see below) had taken some time to reach him.

A layman, C. had responded to Augustine's attack on Petilianus, the Donatist bishop of Cirta. Some of his arguments, to the extent that they can be reconstructed from the C. *Cresc.*, bore the stamp of his profession; cf. Weissengruber, "Augustins Wertung" esp. 104ff.

The Cresconius mentioned in a catalogue from the library of Lorsch as the author of several poems of Christian content—*In Evangel., De diis gentium, De principio mundi vel de die iudicii et resurrectione carnis*—was identified with C. by Manitius, *Geschichte der christlich-lateinischen Poesie* 314; but the Christian Cresconii of North Africa in this period are legion.

39. CRISPINIANUS. Gramm. Rome. Born not after ca. 336; dead not before 372.

AE 1969-70, 71 (p. 22) = Ferrua, "Nuove iscrizioni" 187 no. 4 = Inscr.; Martindale, "Prosopography" 247.

Crispinianus (Inscr. 3), a *grammaticus* (Inscr. 4), according to the funerary inscription of his daughter, Crispina. The inscription is dated 372 (Inscr. 5, *Modesto et Harintheo coss.*), when the girl was nearly sixteen: Inscr. 2-3, *quae vixit annos XV menses VIII dies XII.* C. cannot therefore have been born much later than ca. 336. He was a Christian: the inscription was found in the catacombs of St. Felicitas and has a Christian monogram and *chrismon.* He was probably a widower: the mother of Crispina is not mentioned, and Inscr. 4 shows *pater . . . curavit,* not, e.g., *parentes curaverunt.*

40. CRISPUS. Gramm. Bordeaux. s.IV med.

PLRE I s.v. 3, p. 232.

Crispus: Auson. *Prof.* 21 tit. and vv. 1, 13. A gramm. who taught both Greek and Latin: ibid. tit., *Crispus et Urbicus grammatici Latini et Graeci.*

Evidently he taught at Bordeaux: the locality is not stated; but since Staphylius is noted as the single exception to Ausonius's *lex commemorandi* in the *Prof.* (cf. *Prof.* 20.1-4 and s.vv. Concordius, Staphylius, nos. 35, 140), and since C. and Urbicus are not specifically said to have been *Burdigalenses* teaching elsewhere, they must be understood to have taught at Bordeaux.

No clear indication of C.'s date is given. Since Ausonius is very well informed about C. (contrast s.v. Thalassus, no. 148) but gives no sign that C. was of the generation of his own teachers (cf. s.vv. Corinthus, Macrinus, Spercheus, nos. 36, 93, 139), he was presumably active after Ausonius's school days and contemporary with Ausonius's tenure at Bordeaux, ca. 336-67.

C. taught *primaevos fandique rudes* the *elementorum prima . . . signa novorum* (vv. 4-6), presumably in both languages. He was therefore a gramm. who gave the youngest students their elementary lessons in letters; cf. Appendix 4 and s.vv. Ammonius, Ausonius, nos. 9, 21. He was also a poet, thought to fortify himself with wine to produce passages rivaling Vergil and Horace: vv. 7-9 (reading *locis* in v. 8 with V and Evelyn-White, against *iocis*, Heinsius's conjecture printed by Schenkl and Peiper).

With his colleague Urbicus (q.v., no. 165; cf. vv. 25, 27, *ambo*, and see below), C. is credited with fluency in speech (*loqui faciles*) and learning in *omnia carmina* and in *mython plasmata et historiam* (vv. 25-26)—i.e., all the appurtenances of the grammarian's craft—and is said to have been of libertine birth (v. 27, *liberti ambo genus*). It is, however, almost certainly incorrect to say with *PLRE* I that C. "declaimed in prose and verse." The statement is evidently based on vv. 13-15, concerning Urbicus: *nam tu Crispo coniuncte tuo / prosa solebas et versa loqui / impete eodem.* (On the exercise involved, see s.v. Urbicus.) But *Crispo coniuncte tuo* probably means no more than "when you were the colleague of your friend Crispus"; and making C. a partner in these performances destroys the clearly articulated structure of the poem, whereby the individual qualities of each man are first celebrated separately—vv. 1-9 for Crispus, including his tipsy excellence as a Latin poet; vv. 10-24 for Urbicus, including his inferiority in Latin and his special excellence in Greek—before the two are finally brought together, with a change of meter and the emphatic triple *ambo*, for the enumeration of their shared qualities in vv. 25-28. Thus vv. 10-12, *et tibi . . . carmen sic* ἐλελείσω, clearly mark the part of the poem set aside for Urbicus—in fact, his part is called a *carmen* in itself—and the statement that Urbicus was *Grais celebris* (v. 11) is continued and expanded by *nam* (v. 13), which introduces the lines that explain Urbicus's special glory. C. should not be allowed to steal his thunder.

‑ 41. AUR.? CYRUS. Gramm. (and poet?); decurion? Antaeopolis? s.VI
1/2; probably dead by 539?

PCairMasp. 2.67134 (= Pap. 1), 2.67135 (= Pap. 2), 2.67139 (= Pap. 3),
3.67326 (= Pap. 4), 3.67327 (= Pap. 5).

Aur. Cyrus: Pap. 2.1; elsewhere Cyrus; on the identification on which
the authenticity of the name "Aurelius" depends, see below. Mentioned
as γραμματικός "of blessed memory" in a receipt his heirs issued to
Apollos of Aphrodito (Antaeopolite nome), father of the poet Dioscorus
of Aphrodito, for rent on land at Piase in the territory of the village
Phthla (Pap. 4). He is likely to be identical with Aur. Cyrus, decurion
(πολιτευόμενος, πολιτευσάμενος) of Antaeopolis, known from similar
receipts he or his heirs issued to the same Apollos or to his heirs for rent
on land in the same place (Pap. 1, 2, 5; cf. also Pap. 3, vi^{v}4, another
receipt); but apart from the difference in style, γραμματικός vs. πολιτευόμενος, note that a Christodorus acts as agent in Pap. 4, whereas the
comparable party in Pap. 1, 2, and 5 is a different man, the προνοητής
Victor.

C. is perhaps the poet Cyrus of Antaeopolis, whose works—an iambic
encomium of the *dux* Mauricius (for the type, cf. Heitsch, *Griechische
Dichterfragmente* XLII.9 [Dioscorus]), other ἐγκωμιαστικοὶ λόγοι, and
letters—were known to Photius, *Bibl.* cod. 279 (8.188 Henry). The identification would, however, be ruled out if the *dux* Mauricius turned out
to be Fl. Mauricius, *v.c., comes et dux* in the Thebaid in 367/75 (= *PLRE* I
s.v. 2, p. 570), as suggested by Baldwin, "Some *Addenda*" (1982) 104f.

C. was dead before 547: in Pap. 4, C. is already dead, and Apollos is
still alive; but Apollos was dead in 547 (Bell, "Egyptian Village" 26). C.
was dead by 539, the probable date of Pap. 5, if he is identical with
Cyrus the decurion. If Maspéro's restoration of the name "Flavius" for
Apollos at Pap. 2.2 is correct, Cyrus the decurion would still have been
alive after 536: Apollos still bore the name "Aurelius" in 536 (*PFlor.*
3.283.4), and the name "Flavius" is otherwise attested for him only in
541 (*PCairMasp.* 3.67126.3); on the change, cf. Bell, "Egyptian Village"
26; Keenan, "Names" (1974) 298f. But Maspéro's restoration is very
doubtful.

42. DAMOCHARIS. Gramm. and poet; *procos. Asiae*? (very unlikely). Cos
→ (?) Constantinople. s.VI 2/3.

RE 4.2067 (Reitzenstein); Chr.-Sch.-St. 2:2.980; cf. *RE* Suppl. 14.110
(Eck).

The author of several epigrams (*Anth. Gr.* 6.63, 7.206, 9.633, 16.310)
from the Cycle of Agathias; he was a contemporary of the latter and of

Paul the Silentiary, who composed an epigram on his death (7.588). He was dead, therefore, before ca. 568: for the date, see Cameron and Cameron, "Cycle"; differently Baldwin, "Four Problems" 298ff., "Date" 334ff.

A γραμματικός of or from Cos: thus the lemma of 7.588, εἰς Δαμόχαριν τὸν γραμματικὸν, τὸν Κῷον, τὸν φίλον καὶ μαθητὴν Ἀγαθίου; the corrector of the codex Palatinus added καὶ μαθητοῦ αὐτοῦ (viz., Ἀγαθίου) to the lemma Δαμοχάριδος γραμματικοῦ of 7.206 (the addition was omitted by Planudes). But note that since Agathias is not otherwise known to have taught, it is not evident in what respect D. would have been his pupil; all other details in the lemma of 7.588 are derived from the poem itself. (On such descriptions of teacher-pupil connections, see also s.vv. Romanus, Timotheus, nos. 129, 156.) Δαμοχάριδος γραμματικοῦ appears in the lemmata of 7.206 and 9.633; the name only is found at 6.63 and 16.310. D.'s acquaintance with Agathias and Paul is probably evidence of a move from Cos to Constantinople.

D. is almost certainly not to be identified with the homonymous proconsul of Asia known from an inscription on a reused base from Ephesus (τὸν σοφίῃ κρατέοντα καὶ εὐνομίῃ καὶ ἀοιδῇ / ἐξ ἀγαθῶν πατέρων ἀνθύπατον πρύτανιν / Δαμόχαριν: see Miltner, "Bericht" 84ff. = id., "Vorläufiger Bericht" 347 = Inschr. Eph. 4 [IGSK 14] 1302, with the remarks of J. and L. Robert, Bull. ép. 1959, 382, and 1960, 347; since the base was originally set up for the proconsul of Asia L. Artorius Pius Maximus [= PIR² A.1187; PLRE I s.v. Maximus 43, p. 589], it can hardly have been reused before s.IV 2/2) or with the benefactor of Smyrna known from Anth. Gr. 16.43, Δαμόχαρι κλυτόμητι, δικάσπολε (the second epithet suggests that he too was a governor; cf. Robert, Hellenica 4.62f.), who was honored for his efforts in rebuilding Smyrna after an earthquake. Damocharis the proconsul and Damocharis the benefactor were considered identical by Malcus, "Proconsuln" 132f., and more tentatively by Eck, RE Suppl. 14.110 (cf. also Bull. ép. 1959, 382); they were identified with D. by Cameron and Cameron, "Cycle" 11, and by Merkelbach, "Ephesische Parerga," who adduces Inschr. Eph. 4.1303, ἀγαθῇ τύχῃ / [Δ]αμόχαρις με [---, as the beginning of a fourth epigram concerning D. Note, however, that it is at least slightly curious that Paul should make no mention of this distinction of his friend in Anth. Gr. 7.588. Further, pace Cameron and Cameron—"There would be nothing at all strange in a poet and grammarian serving as a provincial governor" ("Cycle" 11, citing Alan Cameron, "Wandering Poets" 497f.)—the examples of gramm. flourishing in the imperial service are not plentiful: there is only one example of a gramm. tout court serving as a provincial governor during the period covered by this prosopography; cf. s.v. Fl. Simplicius, no. 137, and Chap. 3 p. 131. Last, the style of the draping of the pallium on the statue of the proconsul Damocharis that surmounts the inscription at Ephesus suggests a date not later than s.V; see McCail, *"Cycle"* 89. A date for the proconsul "bis spätestens um 400" was suggested by Malcus, "Proconsuln" 133.

43. **DANAUS.** Gramm. Oriens (probably: province uncertain; see below and s.v. Diphilus, no. 49). Born not after ca. 348; dead not before 390. *PLRE* I s.v., p. 242.

Father of the gramm. Diphilus (q.v.); mentioned in Lib. *Or.* 54.55 (an. 389), *Ep.* 969 (an. 390). Danaus: *Or.* 54.55; *Ep.* 969.1, 4. A gramm.: *Or.* 54.55, Δαναοῦ τοῦ γραμματιστοῦ νέους πολλοὺς πεπαιδευκότος. Since his son is said to be πράττων . . . ταὐτὸ τὸ πατρί (*Or.* 54.55; cf. *Ep.* 969.1), with the further specification τοὺς παλαιοὺς . . . ποιητὰς εἰς τὰς τῶν νέων ψυχὰς εἰσάγων (*Ep.* 969.1), both father and son must have been gramm.; and γραμματιστής in *Or.* 54.55 must mean γραμματικός, as it usually does in Libanius; cf. Appendix 2. Since his son was professionally active at least by 388, and almost certainly earlier, D. cannot have been born much later than ca. 348; he was still alive, and apparently was still active, in 390 (*Ep.* 969; see further s.v. Diphilus).

His son was a native of the province governed by Heraclianus in 390 (*Ep.* 969.4), probably in Oriens; on the difficulty of identifying the province, see s.v. Diphilus. D. would therefore have been active in that province at the time of his son's birth. There is no evidence that he moved; the statement in *PLRE* I that D. was teaching in Palestine is an error. Rather, his son is said to be teaching in Palestine (*Ep.* 969.4, *Or.* 54.55; cf. ibid. 57); but that was not the province of his birth, and there is no indication that the father followed the son, who was obviously very mobile (see s.v.). The evidence associates D. only with the province of his son's origin.

D. had taught many pupils (*Or.* 54.55) and evidently was of some renown: the opening sentence of *Ep.* 969 suggests that Heraclianus was expected to know of D. and his teaching; and see ibid. 4. He is perhaps identical with Danaus the dedicatee of an epitome of Herodian's Καθολικὴ προσῳδία made by Aristodemus (q.v., no. 188): *Suda* A.3915, ἔγραψε πρὸς Δαναόν.

FABIUS? DEMETRIUS: see no. 205.

44. **DEUTERIUS.** Gramm., rhetorician, poet, *vir spectabilis.* Milan. 503–6(–12?).

RE Suppl. 3.334 (Kroll); Sch.-Hos. 4:2.142f., 145; Sundwall, *Abhandlungen* 72ff. (for the dates of the documents noted below), 113; *PLRE* II s.v. 3, pp. 356f.

Gramm. (Ennod. *Carm.* 1.2 tit., *MGH* AA 7.170; and see below) and poet
(Ennod. *Epist.* 1.19.3, p. 26) who also taught rhetoric (see below). Styled
vir spectabilis: Ennod. *Carm.* 1.2 tit., p. 170, *Deuterio v.s. grammatico*; cf. *Dict.*
8 tit., p. 78, *Deuterio v.s.* (I. Sirmond: *Deutericium* cod. Bruxell., om. cett.).
He taught at Milan when Ennodius was deacon there, ca. 496–513. The
compositions that certainly or probably refer to him or that he received
all date from spring 503 through the middle of 506; *Dict.* 13, which may
also allude to him (see below), dates from early 512. Besides being mentioned in connection with the education of various wards of Ennodius
(see below and Riché, *Education* 25), he received *Epist.* 1.19 (p. 26; spring
503) from Ennodius and suggested that the latter compose a declamation
on the cuckolded Diomedes: *Dict.* 24, pp. 167f., *Dictio ex tempore quam ipse
Deuterius iniunxit*; cf. *Carm.* 2.90.7–8, p. 168, *exactam . . . vocem, / extortis . . .
dictis* (both spring 506). He is also mentioned in connection with *Carm.*
1.2, an encomium of and appeal to Eugenes (or Eugenetes), *QSP* (p. 170;
spring 506), *Dictio data Deuterio v.s. grammatico nomine ipsius Eugeneti v.i.
mittenda*, and he is the subject of *Carm.* 2.104 (pp. 182f.; mid-506).

D. appears as the teacher in Ennodius's declamation *Dict.* 9 (pp. 112ff.),
Praefatio quando Arator auditorium ingressus est, composed when Arator,
ward of Ennodius, began his rhetorical studies. D. is named at 9.11, and
so he must be the *venerabilis magister* addressed at 9.5; on the nature of
the studies, see below. D. is also named as the teacher in the tit. of *Dict.*
8, composed for Ennodius's nephew Lupicinus on a similar occasion,
Praefatio dicta Lupicino quando in auditorio traditus est Deuterio v.s.; the *quando*
clause is found only in the oldest ms, cod. Bruxell. (s.IX), where D.'s
name and style appear as *Deutericium* (see above). D. is addressed or
referred to as *doctissime hominum* (8.5), *doctor optimus* (8.12), *venerabilis
magister* (8.13); cf. *doctor optime* in *Epist.* 1.19.2 (p. 26), to D. He is therefore
probably the *doctorum optime, optime magister*, and sim. addressed in the
following contemporary declamations of Ennodius on similar themes:
Dict. 7 (pp. 6ff.), *Dictio . . . in dedicatione auditorii quando ad forum translatio
facta est*; *Dict.* 10 (pp. 118ff.), on Ennodius's nephew Parthenius, *Gratiarum
actio grammatico quando Partenius bene recitavit* (cf. 10.4, a reference to
another declamation, not preserved, on Parthenius's entry into school);
Dict. 11 (pp. 132f.), on Ennodius's ward the son of Eusebius, *Dictio quae
dicta est quando Eusebii filius traditus est ad studia*; and perhaps also the later
Dict. 13 (pp. 309f.; early 512), on Paterius and Severus.

It would appear from these declamations that D. taught both gramm.
and rhetoric. The latter is clearly involved in *Dict.* 7–9; cf. *Dict.* 7.8,
where D. is *praevius eloquentiae morumque doctor*, and 7.4, on the student
who one day *citaturus reum causidicus inter atria iam probata dictionem metuen-
dus incipiet*. In *Dict.* 8 and 9, Lupicinus and Arator are no longer *pueri* but
adulescentes (cf. 8.4, 10, 12; 9.9, 10, 20), i.e., of an age for the school of

rhetoric; and *Dict.* 9.6 refers to D.'s school as a *palestra*, a metaphor
usually associated with oratory (but cf. Sidon. Apoll. *Carm.* 23.212). But
a stage of education earlier than rhetoric—viz., grammar—must be supposed in *Dict.* 10, 11, and 13: note *Dict.* 10 tit., *Gratiarum actio grammatico;*
and cf. 10.4, where Parthenius is said to have only recently crossed the
liberalium disciplinarum limen. Similarly, in *Dict.* 11 and 13 the students are
in the very early stages of their liberal education: cf. *Dict.* 11.6, [*Eusebii
filius*] *cui saporem vitae labris primoribus contingenti gustum deprecor libertatis
infundi;* 11.7, [*idem*] *cuius prosapiem splendidam tempus postulat scientiae te radiis
adornare;* 13.4, *Paterius et Severus . . . eruditionem originariam in ipsis vitae prae-
stulantur exordiis.*

It also appears that D. taught both subjects concurrently: the works
that allude to rhetorical instruction, *Dict.* 7–9 (spring 503, early 504, and
after Easter 504, respectively; D. is named in *Dict.* 8 and 9), belong to
much the same period as two of the works that allude to grammatical
instruction, namely, *Dict.* 10 (after Easter 504; later than *Dict.* 9, but not
much, since Parthenius is said in 10.4 to have begun his studies only
recently—i.e., probably in autumn 503) and *Dict.* 11 (505); *Carm.* 1.2 tit.,
in which D. is styled *grammaticus,* belongs to spring 506. It does not seem
likely that D. would have descended from a chair of rhetoric to a chair of
grammar. The combination is also suggested by *Carm.* 2.104 (pp. 182f.),
a satirical poem of mid-506 that backhandedly attests D.'s involvement
with both grammar and rhetoric (vv. 5–10). Cf. also s.vv. Iulianus
Pomerius, Staphylius, nos. 124, 140.

Since D. was already of an age to be bald (*Carm.* 2.104.10) and plagued
with bad eyesight (*Epist.* 1.19.2ff.) in the first years of s.VI, he probably is
not the Deuterius *scholasticus* mentioned as a *discipulus* of the Roman
rhetorician Securus Melior Felix in the subscription to Martianus Capella,
whether that subscr. is dated to 534 (cf. Jahn, "Subscriptionen" 352–54)
or to 498, as is more likely correct (see Alan Cameron, "Martianus").

45. DEUTERIUS. Gramm. Rome. s.IV 2/2 / s.VI.
PLRE II s.v. 5, p. 357.

Teacher of poetry and so presumably a gramm.: *ILCV* 729 = *Anth. Lat.*
2:3.1964.1, *priscorum interpres vatum doctorq*[*ue* ˘ - x]. A Christian (ibid.).
Not identical with Deuterius (q.v., no. 44) the gramm. and friend of Ennodius, D. is conceivably the Deuterius *scholasticus* mentioned as a *discipulus*
of the Roman rhetorician Securus Melior Felix in the subscription to
Martianus Capella (an. 498); see the preceding entry *ad fin.*

46. DIDYMUS. Gramm. Egypt → Antioch → Constantinople. Born not
later than ca. 300; dead by 357.

Seeck, *Briefe* 251; Wolf, *Schulwesen* 32; *PLRE* I s.v. 1, p. 252.

The father of Libanius's pupil Rhetorius: *Ep.* 317, 318 (an. 357); cf. *Ep.* 404 (an. 355).

Didymus (*Ep.* 318.2), a teacher (*Ep.* 318.2, διδάσκαλος). At *Ep.* 317.1 Libanius says that D. had taught him τοὺς ποιητάς, as Libanius had taught Rhetorius τοὺς ῥήτορας; D. was therefore a grammarian. Cf. Wolf, *Schulwesen* 32; and s.vv. Cleobulus, Anonymus 2, nos. 32, 168.

As Libanius's teacher, D. must have been active by the early to mid-320s and so is unlikely to have been born much later than ca. 300; a slightly later date is possible, however, if D. is identical with Anonymus 2: his instruction of Libanius would then date to the early 330s. His son, a student of Libanius at Nicomedia (*Ep.* 317.1), i.e., in 343/48, was probably born ca. 328/33. D. was dead, evidently recently, in 357 (*Ep.* 317, 318; see below) but not, apparently, before spring 355 (cf. *Ep.* 404).

A native of Egypt, where he had retained a small parcel of land (*Ep.* 317.2, 318.3, and below), D. was teaching at Antioch probably by the 320s (see above) but subsequently taught at Constantinople; cf. *Ep.* 318.2, πάντως δὲ τὸν Δίδυμον οὐκ ἀγνοεῖς, εἰ μὴ καὶ τὴν μεγάλην ἀγνοεῖς πόλιν, ἐν ᾗ τῆς αὐτοῦ παιδείας ἐκεῖνος μετεδίδου. In context "the great city" is presumably Constantinople (cf., e.g., *Ep.* 454); it is certainly neither Antioch nor Alexandria. There is no firm evidence for when the move to Constantinople took place; if D. is Anonymus 2 (q.v.), then not before 334. The move may have occurred even later in his career: at *Ep.* 404.2, Libanius says that Rhetorius, who was at the time probably in Constantinople, used to make frequent trips to Antioch when Libanius himself was not there; this refers presumably to the period after Rhetorius's schooldays and before Libanius's return to Antioch, i.e., to any time between the mid- to late 340s and 354. The trips were perhaps visits to his father.

Two letters, *Ep.* 317, to Clematius governor of Palestine, and 318, to Sebastianus *dux Aegypti*, were given to Rhetorius when he was traveling to Egypt to claim his patrimony; they were intended, respectively, to ease his journey and to facilitate his mission. It should be noted that although the estate is said to be small (*Ep.* 317.2, 318.3), a mere "solace for a poor man" (*Ep.* 318.3; cf. ibid., Rhetorius one of τῶν οὐκ εὐπόρων), Rhetorius had been able to receive a full literary education; cf. esp. *Ep.* 318.2.

* DIOCLES: see no. 206.

DIOGENES: see no. 207.

47. DIOMEDES. Gramm. s.IV 2/2 / s.V.

RE 5.827–29 (Goetz); Sch.-Hos. 4:1.169–72; *PLRE* I s.v., p. 257.

Diomedes: *GL* 1.299.1, *Diomedes Athanasio salutem dicit*; "Diomedes" in Rufinus, Priscian, Cassiodorus (see below). Not called a gramm., but his activity as a teacher is suggested by the arrangement of the material in his *Ars* (see below).

The dating of D. depends on one's view of his sources. The direct use of Charisius and Donatus (qq.v., nos. 200, 52) that has been detected would produce a *term. p. q.* of s.IV med.; cf. Sch.-Hos. 4:1.169–72; Goetz, *RE* 5.827–29. But D. appears to have used Donatus's main source, not Donatus himself (see esp. Barwick, *Remmius* 10f.); and though Barwick's arguments that D. drew directly on Charisius, not on the main source of the "Charisius-group," have had considerable influence (see Barwick, *Remmius* 8f.; id., "Zur Geschichte" 335f.; and cf. Holtz, *Donat* 81, 85; De Nonno, *Grammatica* xvii), the matter should be regarded as still *sub iudice* (see esp. I. Mariotti, ed., Mar. Vict. pp. 60f.; Ballaira, "Sulla trattazione" 183ff.).

D. certainly wrote before s.V med. or s.VI, when he is cited by Rufinus (q.v., no. 130), *GL* 6.555.5–10 = 1.515.3–8, 6.568.12–18 = 1.469.3–8; cf. 6.565.4, 573.26. (He is also cited five times by Priscian—*GL* 2.470.13, 485.20, 499.19, 515.16, 535.12—each time in company with Charisius, and once by Cassiodorus, *Inst.* 1.30.2.) Note also the abstract form of address or "Ehrenprädikat," *excellens facundia tua*, that occurs in the preface to his work: *GL* 1.299.4, *hanc* [sc. *artem*] *cum cognovissem excellentem facundiam tuam plurimi facere*; cf. Symm. *Ep.* 1.79, *eruditio tua*, addressing Ausonius's son Hesperius; Aug. *Ep.* 187.3, 229.2, *eruditio tua*, addressing in the latter the *vir inlustris* Darius (an. 429/30); Prisc. *GL* 3.405.14f., *sapiens eloquentia vestra*, addressing his dedicatee, Symmachus. Such phrasing points to a date in the second half of s.IV rather than in the first half (if not in s.V): see also the datable examples of the Greek counterparts, e.g., λογιότης, παίδευσις, below; and cf. O'Brien, *Titles* 44, 162, on *eruditio*; Zilliacus, *Untersuchungen* 46, 51ff.; id., "Anredeformen" 167ff.

Author of an *ars grammatica* in three books, D. describes his efforts as a matter of arranging and setting out what *humanae sollertiae claritas expolivit*, *GL* 1.299.2ff. (cf. Charisius *GL* 1.1.4f., *artem . . . sollertia doctissimorum virorum politam et a me digestam*; D.'s method of compilation is, however, much less straightforward than Charisius's). The work is divided into three books according to the age of the audience: *GL* 1.299.10, *secundum trina aetatis gradatim legentium spatia*. Therefore it was composed with an eye to the schools. The material of Book 1, described (*GL* 1.420.2f.) as *sermonis universi membra, quae prima legentibus artis grammaticae studia praecipua esse videbantur*, includes the parts of speech, the case system with exercises, and the verbal system; Book 2 presents basic definitions *de voce*, etc., which are thus placed out of the order normal in such *artes*, and the *vitia et virtutes orationis*; Book 3 considers meter.

The *Ars* is dedicated to one Athanasius; the abstract form of address, *excellens facundia tua*, may indicate that he was a member of a learned profession—esp. a rhetorician or advocate—or belonged to a branch of the imperial service that recruited heavily from the learned professions, e.g., assessors to provincial governors: cf. ἡ λογιότης σου or ἡ σὴ λογιότης in Greg. Naz. *Ep.* 148 and Basil *Ep.* 77, letters to the assessors Asterius and Helpidius; Isid. Pel. *Ep.* 5.125 and Nil. Ancyr. *Ep.* 3.153, letters to σχολαστικοί; *SB* 12.11084 (s.V 2/2), a letter sent by one advocate or rhetorician to another, with Maehler, "Menander" 306. Compare also the use of παίδευσις applied especially to advocates in the papyri, e.g., "your brotherly brilliant learnedness," *POxy.* 8.1165.2, τὴν ὑμετέραν ἀδελφικὴν λαμπρὰν παίδευσιν; see Preisigke, *WB* Abschn. 9, p. 198 s.v.; and add *POxy.* 16.1883.7, a σχολαστικός and ἔκδικος; 1884.10, 14, an ἔκδικος; 1886.12, the same; *PSI* 8.872.3, the same; *Fest. Berl. ägypt. Mus.* 459, a σχολαστικός: none of these documents is earlier than s.V. The locutions need not be tied to a specific profession, however: cf. for λογιότης Basil *Ep.* 1 and 7, the philosopher Eustathius and Gregory Nazianzen; for παίδευσις, *PSI* 4.297.1, a physician.

48. DIOSCORIUS.   Gramm. → *PVC*(?), *PPO*(?)(*Or. ?*), *cons.*(?), *patricius*(?) Myra (Lycia) → Constantinople.   s.V 2/4–2/2.

PLRE II s.v. Dioscorus 5, pp. 367f.

Dioscorius: *Suda* Δ.1208 (cf. 2.732.25f. Adler); Const. Porph. *De cer.* 1.87, below. Also Dioscorides (in the genitive, Διοσκορίδου, presumably an error for Διοσκορίου): *Suda* Ν.395. Α γραμματικός from Myra in Lycia (*Suda* Δ.1208, Ν.395), said to have been the brother of the rhetorician Nicolaus of Myra (Ν.395) and to have taught the daughters of Leo I (Ariadne and Leontia) in Constantinople (Δ.1208).

According to the *Suda*, he was *PVC* and *PPO* (Δ.1208, ὕπαρχος πόλεως καὶ πραιτωρίων) or "prefect, consul, and patricius" (Ν.395, καὶ ὕπαρχος καὶ ὕπατος καὶ πατρίκιος). It is uncertain which of these titles is authentic.

D. is probably the Διοσκόριος, ἀπὸ ἐπάρχων πόλεως, who delivered an encomium of Leo and Anthemius at Constantinople on the occasion of the latter's accession in 467 (Const. Porph. *De cer.* 1.87, p. 395.15f. Reiske). The style, "ex-prefect of the city," allows for the possibility that the prefecture was honorary. In fact, it may have been not only honorary but a reward precisely for his tuition of Leo's daughters, which must have occupied D. in the years just preceding 467; D. probably would not have become tutor of Ariadne and Leontia before the early or mid-460s, since Leontia was not born until after Leo's accession in 457: Ariadne married in 466/67; Leontia, for the first time, in 470/71. For another ex-teacher at Leo's court in this same period, see s.v. Isocasius, no. 85.

If D. received the consulship, it must have been honorary, since no Dioscorius is known to the consular *fasti*. D. cannot be Fl. Dioscorus, *cons. ord.* (West) in 442 (= *PLRE* II s.v. 6, p. 368), although he may have been confused with him; cf. below. If honorary, the consulship could not have been received before the reign of Zeno and would possibly have been purchased; cf. Jones, *LRE* 533.

If the name "Dioscorius" is correct, D. presumably cannot be the bearer (or bearers) of the name "Dioscorus" who was (or were) *PPO Or.* under Leo and Zeno; cf. Seeck, *Regesten* 418–19; *RE* 5.1086.36ff. Attribution of the praetorian prefecture to D. in the *Suda* may be the result of a confusion with Dioscorus; for the error compare Chr.-Sch.-St. 2:2.1075 n. 3, where D. is called "Dioskoros" and is said to have been a poet, evidently out of confusion with the poet Dioscorus of Aphrodito (s. VI 2/3–3/4; there is no evidence D. was a poet). *PLRE* II s.v. Dioscorus 5, pp. 367f., assumes that the correct form of D.'s name was "Dioscorus" and identifies him with the *PPO* Dioscorus.

49. DIPHILUS. Gramm. and poet. *Prov. incert.* → Palestine; also Cilicia and Antioch (origin uncertain and movements varied; see below). Born not after ca. 368; dead not before 390.

PLRE I s.v., p. 261.

Diphilus, son of the gramm. Danaus (q.v., no. 43): Lib. *Or.* 54.55, *Ep.* 969.1, Δίφιλον τὸν Δαναοῦ. Gramm.: see the texts quoted s.v. Danaus. Poet: *Or.* 54.55–57, *Ep.* 969.1, 3.

D. was a native of the province governed by Heraclianus in 390; see s.v. Danaus and below. Since D. was professionally active by 388 at the latest (see below), he cannot have been born later than ca. 368.

Our glimpses of D.'s career are limited to 388 and the summer of 390, and are provided by Lib. *Or.* 54.55–57, composed not long after March or April 389, and *Ep.* 969, respectively. The reconstruction below differs from Seeck, *Briefe* 171, which was followed by Festugière, *Antioche* 105 n. 7, and by *PLRE* I s.vv. Danaus, Diphilus, Heraclianus 3. For full discussion, see Kaster, "'Wandering Poet.'"

Already established as a gramm. in one of the provinces of Palestine, D. embarked on a tour of the cities of Cilicia, where Eustathius, *cons. Syriae*, had promised to arrange "audiences and the income from them" for D.'s poetry; but Eustathius did not keep his promise. The tour was a failure, and D. returned from Cilicia in despair (*Or.* 54.55).

Shortly before the Olympic Games, in July or August of 388, D. was in Antioch or its environs. Eustathius again promised to help D. by making a place for him as a poet in the games and again broke his promise (*Or.* 54.56–57).

In the summer of 390, D. was still teaching in Palestine and was still trying to promote his career as a poet. Libanius commended him as an encomiast to one Heraclianus, the governor of D.'s native province (*Ep.* 969); we do not know that D. was now successful. The province governed by Heraclianus in 390 is also unknown; it was certainly not one of the Palestines, nor was it Syria or Phoenice. If it was in Oriens, as seems most likely, then it was perhaps Arabia or Cilicia; but the question must remain open. See Kaster, " 'Wandering Poet' " 156f.

50. DOMITIUS.   Gramm.   Clermont-Ferrand.   s.V 3/4.

Sch.-Hos. 4:2.268; *PLRE* II s.v. 2, p. 371.

Friend of Sidonius Apollinaris: cf. *sodalis* and *amici* in *Carm.* 24.3, 9. Taught in Clermont-Ferrand (see below) in the 460s: *Ep.* 2.2 belongs to the period of Sidonius's retirement, 461–67 (ca. 465, according to Loyen, ed., *Sidoine* vol. 2 p. 246); *Carm.* 24, to 469 (cf. Loyen, ed., *Sidoine* vol. 1 p. xxx). D. taught Terence (*Ep.* 2.2.2) and therefore was presumably a gramm.

The place of his instruction is not specified but is almost certainly Clermont. Sidonius, writing from his estate, Avitacum, in the Auvergne, refers to D.'s discomfort in the *anhelantes angustiae civitatis*, which in context should refer to the *civitas Arvernorum*, i.e., Clermont; cf. Fournier, "Noms" 553ff. This is all the more likely if Avitacum is Aydat, some 19 km SW of the city; cf. Stevens, *Sidonius* 185ff. Further, Sidonius's *Carmina* make their first stop at D.'s home (*Carm.* 24.10f.), after which they are imagined as following a southerly route from Brionde (*Carm.* 24.16), ca. 58 km SSE of Clermont, to Narbo (*Carm.* 24.90ff.); cf. Loyen, *Sidoine . . . et l'esprit* 64 n. 2.

D. was invited by Sidonius to escape the heat of late spring in the city where he was teaching (*Ep.* 2.2.1) and join him at Avitacum: ibid. 3, *contubernio nostro aventer insertus.* He received the collected poems of Sidonius (*Carm.* 24.10ff.); he is described as a demanding critic (vv. 12–15). Possibly he had been the teacher of Sidonius's brother-in-law Ecdicius; cf. Loyen, *Sidoine . . . et l'esprit* 65. It is not clear whether he was a public or private teacher; for argument that D. had a municipally funded chair, see Riché, "Survivance" 421ff.

51. DONATIANUS.   Gramm.   *Aet. incert.*; perhaps not before s.IV 2/2.

Cf. *RE* 5.1532 (Goetz); Sch.-Hos. 4:1.169; *PLRE* I s.v. Donatianus 6, p. 268.

Scholar to whom the *Donatiani fragmentum* is attributed (*GL* 6.275.10–277.15); according to the fragment, he was a teacher: *GL* 6.275.11, *ars grammatica accepta ex auditorio Donatiani.* The heading also suggests that the fragment is from an ἀπὸ φωνῆς treatise; as such, it is the only identifiable representative of the type in Latin (for the type in Greek, cf. s.vv. Ioannes Charax, Georgius Choeroboscus, nos. 199, 201). The fragment bears a marked resemblance to sections of Charisius: cf. *GL* 6.275.16–276.8 with 1.116.30–117.5 (= Iulius Romanus); *GL* 6.276.10–277.9 with 1.52.6–53.6; *GL* 6.277.9–15 with 1.53.30–54.5. If it depends on Charisius (q.v., no. 200) and not on Charisius's sources, then it must not be dated before s.IV 2/2.

D. is perhaps, though not very probably, Ti. Claudius Maximus Donatianus (q.v., no. 208).

TI. CLAUDIUS MAXIMUS DONATIANUS: see no. 208.

52. AELIUS DONATUS.   Gramm. → (?) *v.c., orator* (unlikely).   Africa? → Rome.   s.IV med.

RE 5.1545–47 (Wessner); Sch.-Hos. 4:1.161–65; *PLRE* I s.v. 3, p. 268; Holtz, *Donat* 15ff.

Aelius Donatus: *Comm. Terent.* cod. Dresden. Reg. Dc132 fol. 1ʳ, 4ʳ; likewise in the subscr. to the commentary on *Phorm.* in cod. Cors. 43 E 28 fol. 294ʳ (cf. Warren, "On Five New Manuscripts" 32) and in the codex Cuiacianus reported by J. Gronovius, on which see now Reeve, "Textual Tradition" 324ff.; cf. also *APLI* [< *AELI*?] *DONATI* in the subscr. to the commentary on *And.*, cod. Paris. lat. 7920 fol. 51ʳ, and *AFRI DONATI* in the subscr. *ad loc.* found in cod. Vat. lat. 2905 fol. 76ᵛ; *FL.* [<? *EL.* = *AEL.*] *DONATVS* in the salutation of the prefatory epistle to the Vergilian commentary. Claudius Donatus (in confusion with Ti. Claudius Donatus): tit. in cod. Oxon. Lincoln. 45. Elsewhere simply Donatus. Note that the name "Aelius" is thus not unequivocally attested before s.XV, though it probably lurks beneath the form *APLI DONATI* found in cod. Paris. lat. 7920, of s.XI; and apart from the form *FL.*, which has been assumed to be a corruption of *AEL(IVS)*, in the *Comm. Verg.* epist. praef. (above), the only evidence for "Aelius" is found in the same mss of the *Comm. Terent.* that carry the very suspect style *v.c., orator*, on which see below.

Styled *grammaticus urbis Romae* in numerous codd. of the *Ars* (see Holtz, *Donat* 354ff.); *grammaticus* at Jer. *Chron.* s.a. 354, *Victorinus rhetor et Donatus grammaticus, praeceptor meus, Romae insignes habentur,* and *praeceptor meus* also at Jer. *C. Rufin.* 1.16, *Comm. Eccles.* 1; *grammaticus excellentissimus* or *clarissimus grammaticus* or *honoratissimus grammaticus* or *grammaticus* in some codd. of the *Comm. Terent.* (see Wessner, ed., 1, x–xxiv). Also styled *v.c., orator urbis Romae* in cod. Paris. lat. 7920 fol. 51ʳ (subscr. to the commentary on *And.*), cod. Cors. 43 E 28 fol. 294ʳ, and cod. Cuiacian. according to Gronovius (the latter two in subscr. to the commentary on *Phorm.*); *orator Urbis* in cod. Vat. lat. 2905 fol. 76ᵛ (subscr. to the commentary on

And.). Also *Donatus V.C.D.* at "Sergius" *Explan.*, *GL* 4.486.8; the meaning is obscure (see below).

Active at Rome at least in the mid- to late 350s and doubtless in the early 360s: see Jer. *Chron.* s.a. 354, *C. Rufin.* 1.16, *Comm. Eccles.* 1; cf. Booth, "Date." The name "Donatus" suggests that D. may have been of African origin; see Syme, "'Donatus'" 589ff. = *Roman Papers* 3.1106ff.; cf. Holtz, *Donat* 19f. If he did pursue a career as a rhetorician, which is unlikely despite the titulatur (see below), he did not do so before 366, when Jerome's schooldays at Rome ended. Jerome clearly knew D. only as a grammarian.

Author of an *ars grammatica*, in the form of an *Ars minor* on the parts of speech, in one book *per interrogationem et responsionem*, and an *Ars maior*, in three books: *GL* 4.355–402; Holtz, *Donat* 585–674. The work was the subject of numerous commentaries, including those by Servius, *GL* 4.405–48 (with "Sergius" *GL* 4.486–562); by Cledonius, *GL* 5.9–79; and by Pompeius, *GL* 5.95–312 (qq.v., nos. 136, 255, 31, 125). Cf. also Schindel, *Figurenlehren*; with Holtz, "À l'école de Donat."

D. also compiled a variorum commentary on the works of Vergil, from which only the prefatory epistle dedicating the work to a certain L. Munatius, the *V. Verg.*, and the preface to the *Buc.* survive independently; the commentary was an important source for Servius, Macrobius, and others. It is now generally agreed that considerable fragments of the commentary are embedded in the interpolated version of Servius discovered by P. Daniel; see s.v. Servius and Chap. 5 n. 2. D. also wrote a commentary on Terence; cf. Priscian *GL* 3.281.14f., 320.13. For the commentaries on Terence and Vergil, see Jer. *C. Rufin.* 1.16; "Sergius" *GL* 4.486.8f. The Terentian commentary that now passes under Donatus's name issues from a later process of abridgement and reconstitution; cf. Sabbadini, "Commento" 4ff.; Wessner, ed., 1, xliv–xlvii. On the transmission of the *Comm. Terent.*, see now Reeve and Rouse, "New Light"; Reeve, "Aelius." For the suggestion that Donatus wrote works on rhetoric now lost, see Sabbadini, "Scolii" 339f.; *contra*, Keil *GL* 4, xxxvi–xxxvii; Holtz, *Donat* 251 n. 34, correctly.

The different styles in D.'s titulatur should properly denote two different periods of his teaching career: as a gramm. (*grammaticus urbis Romae*); and, presumably later, as a rhetorician, when he would also apparently have been honored with the clarissimate (*v.c.*, *orator urbis Romae*). For *orator* or *rhetor urbis Romae*, cf. *PLRE* I s.vv. Hierius 5 (p. 431), Magnus 10 (p. 535); Marius Victorinus, *Expos. in Rhet. Cic.* tit.; the *rhetor* Felix in the subscriptions to Martianus Capella and Horace edited by Jahn, "Subscriptionen" 351ff. (Note that the heading *v.c.*, *grammaticus* in *PLRE* I is misleading, since the evidence for D.'s possession of the clarissimate is—except for the puzzle in "Sergius"—connected only with his supposed status as *orator*.) Since the style *grammaticus urbis Romae* is associated with the mss of the *Ars*, whereas *v.c., orator urbis Romae* appears only in certain mss of the Terentian commentary—including the oldest, cod. Paris. lat. 7920, of s.XI—the natural inference was drawn by Sabbadini, "Scolii" 337ff., who dated the *Ars* to the time of Donatus's activity as a gramm., and the Terentian commentary to a subsequent period, when D. would have been *v.c., orator urbis Romae.*

The evidence of Jerome, however, tells decisively against that inference. First, Jerome preserves a comment D. made while teaching Terence in the classroom as a gramm.: *Comm. Eccl.* 1, on *Eun.* prol. 41, *nihil est dictum, quod non sit dictum prius: unde praeceptor meus Donatus, cum istum versiculum exponeret, "pereant" inquit "qui ante nos nostra dixerunt."* Given the fortunes of the commentary, the absence of the witticism from the surviving text does not prove that Jerome is reporting a *viva voce* remark, but Jerome's tenses and the nature of the remark—more risqué and personal than the ordinary fare of a commentary—make it likely that Jerome is recalling a piece of oral instruction that had stuck in his mind. Moreover, Jerome also makes it plain that the commentaries on Vergil and Terence were both already in circulation when he was a *puer*; cf. *C. Rufin.* 1.16, *puto quod puer legeris Aspri in Vergilium et Sallustium commentarios, Volcatii in orationes Ciceronis, Victorini in dialogos eius, et in Terentii comoedias praeceptoris mei Donati, aeque in Vergilium, et aliorum in alios.* The *puer* here of course is Rufinus, but since he and Jerome were nearly exact contemporaries, the remark will apply to Jerome's own *pueritia* as well—that is, to the very time when, as *puer*, Jerome was a student of D. the *grammaticus*; cf. *Chron.* s.a. 354, and, for Jerome's use of *puer* to denote the time of his own grammatical studies at Rome, *In Abacuc.* 2.3.14 and *Comm. Galat.* prol. Plainly, then, D. both lectured on Terence and published his commentary when still a gramm., not as a rhetorician; and this is only what we should expect, since Terence was traditionally associated with the grammarian's school, not the rhetorician's.

Consequently, either the style *v.c., orator urbis Romae* is genuine and was somehow preserved apart from the original *Comm. Terent.*, which it could not have adorned, ultimately to find its way anachronistically into one branch of the commentary's tradition; or else the title represents a later misunderstanding or invention. No mechanism for the first alternative immediately suggests itself, but later fictions concerning D.'s life are not unknown; cf. the *V. Donati* edited by Hagen, *Anecd. Helv.* = *GL* 8, cclx–cclxi. The mysterious *V.C.D.* in "Sergius" *GL* 4.486.8f., *hic enim Donatus V.C.D. Vergilianum carmen vel [et Ribbeck] Terenti comoedias mirifice commentavit*, may be part of this same problem if *V.C.D.* has its origin in *v.c.o.* or *v.c. or.*, i.e., *v(ir) c(larissimus) o(rator)*; cf. the style in the tit. of the *Exempla elocutionu..* of Arusianus Messius, *v(iri) c(larissimi) or(atoris)*. But

V.C.D. may be a fusion or confusion of *v*(*ir*) *c*(*larissimus*) and *v*(*ir*) *d*(*isertis-simus*); cf. s.v. Rufinus, no. 130. Note also the reference of "Sergius" to D.'s commentary on *Vergilianum carmen*, not *carmina*, implying that D. commented on only one of Vergil's compositions; the reference might further suggest that "Sergius" is not a well-informed witness for D.'s life and work. The question of D.'s correct *titulatur* does not permit an unequivocal solution; that D. became an *orator* and gained the clarissimate must, however, be regarded as at best unlikely.

TI. CLAUDIUS DONATUS: see no. 209.

53. DOSITHEUS.   Gramm. (*magister*).   s.IV, perhaps 2/2.

RE 5.1606-7 (Goetz); Sch.-Hos. 4:1.177-79; *PLRE* I s.v., p. 271.

Dositheus *magister* (*Ars* tit., *GL* 7.376.2), usually taken to be the man responsible for both the composition of the Latin *Ars* and its translation into Greek. The dependence of the *Ars* on the common source of the "Charisius-group" (cf. Barwick, *Remmius* 4ff.) suggests that it was not composed much before s.IV med. It is possible but less likely that D. also drew directly on Cominianus (q.v., no. 34); cf. Tolkiehn, *Cominianus* 79ff. The name "Sacerdos" (q.v., no. 132) is used in examples in a way that might refer to a contemporary; cf. esp. *GL* 7.407.18f., *bene apud Sacerdotem studetur*. But these examples were probably already found in D.'s source; note *GL* 7.393.12f. = *Exc. Bob.*, *GL* 1.534.34 = Diom. *GL* 1.318.7. If the citation of Donatus's *Ars* at *GL* 7.424.9ff. (= 4.391.27ff. = 652.6–13H.) belongs to the treatise as originally written, then a *term. p. q.* of s.IV med. would be established (cf. Tolkiehn, "Apex"); but the citation could be a later addition. A sure *term. a. q.* is lacking. D.'s origin and place of activity are unknown; there is some slight reason to think that he was a Greek-speaker from Asia Minor; cf. Tolkiehn, ed., *Dosithei ars* xii.

D. composed an *Ars grammatica* in Latin, originally with word-for-word (interlinear?) translation in Greek. The work was presumably intended for speakers of Greek who were learning Latin.

He was possibly a Christian; cf. Tolkiehn, *Cominianus* 96. The suggestion of Baldwin, "Some *addenda*" (1976) 119, that D. was an acquaintance of the emperor Julian and was the recipient of Iul. *Ep.* 68 Wright (= 200 Bidez) would have little to recommend it even if the letter were not of doubtful authenticity. The suggestion of Tolkiehn, ed., *Dosithei ars* xii, that D. is to be identified with the homonymous ecclesiastical writer of Cilicia does not have much more chance of being correct.

54. EVANTHIUS.   Lat. gramm.   Constantinople.   s.IV 1/2; died 358.

RE 6.847 (Wessner); Sch.-Hos. 4:1.179-80; *PLRE* I s.v. 2, p. 287; cf. Cupaiuolo, "Antiche edizioni" 42f.

Evanthius, *eruditissimus grammaticorum*: Jer. *Chron.* s.a. 358; cf. Rufin. *GL* 6.554.4, 565.5. Died at Constantinople in 358 (Jer. ibid.); succeeded by Chrestus (q.v., no. 27).

Rufinus, *GL* 6.554.4ff., cites *Evanthius in commentario Terentii de fabula*, quoting two brief passages that now stand in the introduction to the Terentian commentary that has come down under the name of Donatus: *GL* 6.554.5–6 = *Comm. Terent.* ed. Wessner 1.17.16–18; 6.554.6–9 = 19.6–9. It is clear, then, that Evanthius wrote a commentary on Terence that included or was introduced by a general discussion of the genre, but it is uncertain how Evanthius's work is related to the original commentary of Donatus (q.v., no. 52) or to the abridged and reconstituted version that survives.

55. EUDAEMON.   Gramm. (or sophist?); poet; advocate.   Egypt (Pelusium) → Elusa → Egypt → Antioch → Constantinople → Egypt.   Born not after ca. 337, probably well before; dead not before 392.

RE 6.885 (Cohn); Chr.-Sch.-St. 2:2.1075 n. 3, 1077, 1081 n. 3; Seeck, *Briefe* 131; Wolf, *Schulwesen* 37, 39; Hunger 2.13, 18; *PLRE* I s.v. 3, pp. 289f.

The recipient or subject of Lib. *Ep.* 315 (an. 357 not later than summer), 108 (an. 359/60), 132 (an. 360 init.), 164, 167 (both an. 360 spring), 255 (an. 360/61), 632, 633 (both an. 361 summer), 826 (an. 363), 1057 (an. 392); cf. *Suda* E.3407.

From Egypt (*Ep.* 132.1, 255.3), specifically, from Pelusium (*Ep.* 108.2; *Suda* E.3407); of good birth but modest estate (*Ep.* 108.2; sim. 164.1). Since he was an advocate by 357 (see below), he will not have been born much after 337. In fact, he was probably not too far from Libanius's age, since the latter speaks of him as "better than a brother in his behavior toward me" (*Ep.* 164.2); were E. much younger, we would expect Libanius to have chosen "son" as the appropriate image of familial piety: cf. *Ep.* 1428.2 and s.v. Eudaemon (no. 210) *ad fin.* If so, he was perhaps born ca. 314/24; this rough date would be consistent with his father's old age in 359/60 (*Ep.* 108.2). E. cannot have been much older than Libanius (314–93), since he was alive in 392 (*Ep.* 1057). He was active as a poet before he arrived at Elusa (*Ep.* 132.1–2, quoted below) and still at the time of our latest notice of him: *Ep.* 1057; cf. also *Ep.* 108.4, Μουσῶν ἑταῖρος; 255.9ff. (an obscure passage); 632.4; 633; 826.4; *Suda* E.3407, οὗτος ἔγραψε ποιήματα διάφορα.

His teaching career and movements are problematic; as attested by Libanius, they can be presented tentatively in the following stages.

E. received his education in poetry, i.e., his grammatical education, in Egypt but did not receive his rhetorical education until he went to Elusa:

Ep. 132.1–2, τὸ μὲν γὰρ τὰ τῶν ποιητῶν ἐπίστασθαι καὶ γενέσθαι ποιητὴν ἐκεῖθεν [i.e., in Egypt] αὐτῷ, τὸ δὲ τὰ τῶν ῥητόρων εἰδέναι καὶ γενέσθαι ῥήτορα παρ᾽ ὑμῶν αὐτῷ. τοῦτόν τε οὖν ἀνάγκη τὴν παιδεύουσαν φιλεῖν ὑμᾶς τε εἰκὸς ᾧ δεδώκατε τοὺς λόγους καὶ τὰ ἄλλα συμπονεῖν. The letter is addressed to Eutocius, a *principalis* of a city that is not named, doubtless Elusa; cf. Seeck, *Briefe* 151; and below.

By 357 he was active with his cousin Eunomus as an advocate (ῥήτωρ) in Elusa; cf. *Ep.* 315.5, commending to the governor Clematius τοὺς ἑταίρους μοι καὶ φιλτάτους, Εὔνομόν τε καὶ Εὐδαίμονα, τοὺς ἐξ Ἐλούσης. . . . ῥήτορες δὲ ἄμφω καὶ ποιοῦνται τὸν βίον ἀπὸ τοῦ συναγορεῖν. Cf. ῥήτωρ also at *Ep.* 132.1, 164.2, the latter again involving Eunomus. Note that if the suggestions above concerning E.'s chronology are valid, we must assume either that he had first come to Elusa sometime before 357, or that a fair amount of time had intervened between his grammatical studies in Egypt and his rhetorical education in Palestine, or some combination of the two; for he would have been of quite mature age by 357.

His activity as advocate at Elusa can be traced through the spring of 360; cf. *Ep.* 164.2, commending him to Cyrillus the governor of Palaestina Salutaris. *Ep.* 167, addressed to E., presumably at Elusa, on a private matter unrelated to his profession, belongs to the same period. By that time he had also gained a teaching position there; cf. *Ep.* 108.1 (late 359 or early 360), Ἑλλήνων παισὶν ἄξιος. (Since E. was still in Elusa in spring 360, Seeck, *Briefe* 214 and 362, must be wrong in saying that this letter, which introduces E. to the *comes Or.* Modestus and requests his favor for E.'s family, was received by Modestus at Pelusium. The letter, like *Ep.* 100, 101 and 105, was probably sent to Modestus when the latter was still in Palestine; it anticipates his trip to Egypt.) E.'s post at Elusa carried an imperial salary: in *Ep.* 132.3 (an. 360 init.) he is a παιδευτής, and Libanius enlists the aid of Eutocius in winning E. the privilege of converting his salary in kind (τροφή) to cash.

E. cannot have stayed at Elusa much beyond spring 360, for by the time we next hear of him (*Ep.* 255; late 360 or early 361) he has had time to go to Egypt, return to Antioch to respond to a suit, become an intimate of Libanius, advising him on numerous questions, do some teaching at Antioch, and leave again, probably for Constantinople. For the summons from Egypt and the suit, see *Ep.* 255.3; for his friendship with Libanius and his advice, ibid. *passim*. For his teaching at Antioch, see ibid. 4, ἐπὶ συνουσίᾳ σοὶ τῶν νέων καθημένῳ; and cf. ibid. 6, ταὐτὰ δέ, ταὐτὰ ἡμῖν καὶ τὰ προάστεια σύνοιδεν, ἐφ᾽ ὧν καθήμενοι τοὺς ἄρχοντας ἀναμένοντες ἐξ ἀποδημίας ἰόντας εἴχομεν ὅ τι ἐργασόμεθα, referring to the participation of the teachers of Antioch in the ceremonial *adventus* of the governors; cf. Liebeschuetz, *Antioch* 208f. Regarding his departure from Antioch, Seeck, *Briefe* 375, assumed that E. received *Ep.* 255 at

Elusa; but since we know that E. soon visited Constantinople, and since *Ep.* 251–53 are also addressed to recipients there, to assume that E. went to the capital directly from Antioch and there received *Ep.* 255 seems better than to add one more trip—in the opposite direction—to an already crowded itinerary; see immediately below.

Sometime toward the end of 360 or the beginning of 361 E. traveled to Constantinople, only to return to Egypt by the summer of 361; cf. *Ep.* 632, 633, Libanius commending E.'s poetic talents to the *praef. Aegypt.* Gerontius and urging E. to exploit the connection. For the sojourn at Constantinople, see *Ep.* 633.2.

His whereabouts and activity thereafter cannot be traced, although he is referred to again, as poet only, in 363 (*Ep.* 826) and 392 (*Ep.* 1057).

Here is clearly a cluster of difficult questions, an answer to any one of which different from that proposed above would materially alter the reconstruction. Most noteworthy is the flurry of activity that took E. within a year from Elusa to Egypt to Antioch to Constantinople and back to Egypt, a sequence especially disconcerting since it means that E. could only have taught in Antioch for a few months; this is the necessary conclusion from *Ep.* 255. It should be remembered, however, that Libanius had a similarly brief tenure at Nicaea (implied by Lib. *Or.* 1.46–48). The alternative date for *Ep.* 255, an. 357/58 (Foerster), might avoid some of the difficulty but in fact raises more problems than it solves. The most difficult question, however, derives from data that are indisputable. E. certainly taught at Elusa and Antioch; cf. the texts cited above. But was he a gramm., or a teacher of rhetoric?

Libanius offers no sure indication, but his emphasis on E.'s activity as a ῥήτωρ (meaning "advocate" everywhere in these letters) might suggest that he taught rhetoric. The *Suda*, however, terms E. a γραμματικός— though this description is by no means decisive, given the source. More compellingly, the *Suda* states that he wrote a Τέχνη γραμματική and an Ὀναμαστικὴ ὀρθογραφία. Note that these works, esp. the latter, concern the very topics on which Libanius consulted E. while the two were together in Antioch: *Ep.* 255.6–7; see esp. ibid. 7, where Libanius praises at some length E.'s judgment concerning the proper vocative forms of Ἡρακλῆς.

Answers to the question of E.'s metier accordingly differ depending on whether one prefers to draw one's conclusions from Libanius—so, apparently, *PLRE* I, which states that he was a sophist at Elusa; similarly, e.g., Liebeschuetz, *Antioch* 155 n. 6—or from the *Suda*: thus Cohn, *RE* 6.885; Chr.-Sch.-St., 2:2.1075 n. 3, 1077; Wolf, *Schulwesen* 37, 39. Seeck, *Briefe* 131, calls him a gramm., referring to the *Suda* and to *Ep.* 132, 255, 1057, although *Ep.* 132 and 1057 offer nothing useful, and *Ep.* 255 is inconclusive. I am inclined to think that E. taught gramm. at Elusa and Antioch, although I would not be surprised to learn that he taught rhetoric. One should also bear in mind that our detailed evidence, such as it is, for E.'s activity covers only four years, 357–61, in the middle of what would seem to have been a long and busy life, during which E. could have appeared in a number of different professional guises.

The Ὀρθογραφία significantly influenced later gramm.; for details, see RE 6.885. E. is probably the Eudaemon included in the catalogue of gramm. in Kröhnert, Canones 7; cf. ibid. 38ff. That he composed a completely unattested work Περὶ διαλέκτων is a modern conjecture.

EUDAEMON: see no. 210.

56. EUGENIUS. Gramm. and poet. Augustopolis (Phrygia Salutaris) → Constantinople. s.V 2/2 / s.VI init.

RE 6.987–88 (Cohn); Chr.-Sch.-St. 2:2.1075f.; PLRE II s.v. 2, p. 416.

Eugenius son of Trophimus: Suda E.3394. From Augustopolis in Phrygia (Salutaris): Suda ibid. and praef. Taught as a gramm. in Constantinople in the reign of Anastasius when already elderly: Suda E.3394; cf. Stephanus (q.v., no. 144) of Byzantium s.v. Ἀνακτόριον: Εὐγένιος . . . ὁ πρὸ ἡμῶν τὰς ἐν τῇ βασιλίδι σχολὰς διακοσμήσας. He is credited in the Suda (E.3394) with works metrical, ἔγραψε Κωλομετρίαν τῶν μελικῶν Αἰσχυλοῦ, Σοφοκλέους, Εὐριπίδου, ἀπὸ δραμάτων ιε′, Περὶ τοῦ τί τὸ παιωνικὸν παλιμβάκχειον; orthographical, Περὶ τῶν τεμενικῶν, ὅπως προφέρεται [cf. s.v. Horapollon, no. 77], Περὶ τῶν εἰς ια ληγόντων ὀνομάτων; lexicographical, Παμμιγῆ λέξιν κατὰ στοιχεῖον (cf. Suda praef.; this is probably the Συλλογὴ λέξεων cited by Stephanus s.v. Ἀνακτόριον); and poetical, καὶ ἄλλα τινὰ τρίμετρα ἰαμβικά. Named as a source in the preface to the Suda, but the authenticity of the preface is doubtful; see Adler RE, 2. Reihe, 4.681.7ff.

FL. EUGENIUS: see no. 211.

EUSEBIUS: see no. 212.

* EUTROPIUS: see no. 213.

* EUTYCHES: see no. 214.

57. EUTYCHES. Lat. gramm. Constantinople(?). s.VI 1/2.

RE 6.1529 (Goetz); Sch.-Hos. 4:2.238–40; PLRE II s.v. 2, pp. 445f.

Eutyches: in genitive, Eutychis, Euticis, or sim. in some early mss of the Ars and in mss of Cassiodorus De orth. at GL 7.147.12, 199.4 (the form Euticis is presumably the starting point for the nominative Eutex in the commentary of Sedulius, Anecd. Helv. = GL 8.2.1ff.); Euticii in most early mss of the *Ars* (see Jeudy, "Manuscrits"), hence *Eutitii duo* (sc. *libri*) in the catalogue of gramm. in cod. Bern. 243, *Anecd. Helv.* = *GL* 8, cxlix; cf. also *GL* 8.1.13ff.

Called *grammaticus* in some mss of the *Ars*. More reliable evidence of the profession is E.'s dedication of the *Ars* to a pupil, Craterus: *GL* 5.447.9, *meorum dilectissime discipulorum Cratere*; cf. also ibid. 1ff., *cum semper novas quaestiones doctoribus auditorum acutiora commovere solent ingenia . . . , inexcusabilis quodam modo respondendi necessitas praeceptoribus iure videtur inponi.* It is tempting, incidentally, to see in E.'s dedicatee a member of the family of Craterus (= *PLRE* II s.v., p. 328) and his son Phocas (*PPO Or.* 532, = Phocas 5 *PLRE* II, pp. 881–82), the former possibly the rhetorician and advocate who is the subject of *Anth. Gr.* 7.561–62, 9.661 (cf. McCail, "Cycle" 88), the latter known as a patron of Latin studies (cf. s.v. Speciosus, no. 138). E.'s pupil could not, however, have been Phocas's father, whose schooldays must on any reckoning have fallen before E.'s time. Perhaps he was a son of Phocas?

E. was a pupil of Priscian, presumably at Constantinople: *GL* 5.456.29ff., *Romanae lumen facundiae, meus, immo communis omnium hominum praeceptor . . . grammaticus Priscianus.* It is likely that E. taught there as well. As a pupil of Priscian, E. should be dated to s.VI 1/2 – med. Cassiodorus is clearly mistaken in placing him among the *orthographi antiqui* he names at *Inst.* 1.30.2; cf. Cassiod. *De orth.* praef., *GL* 7.147.12, where E. is implicitly distinguished from Priscian, the *modernus auctor*.

Author of an *Ars de verbo* or *de discernendis coniugationibus* in two books (*GL* 5.447–88). Book 1 is entitled "De coniugationibus verborum"; Book 2, "De finalitatibus." There is an extant commentary by Remigius of Auxerre; and one by Sedulius Scottus, *Anecd. Helv.* = *GL* 8.1–38 (cf. ibid. lxxiii–lxxix), with a new edition by B. Löfstedt, *CC CM* 40C, pars 3.2 (Turnhout, 1977). A lost work *De aspiratione* was excerpted by Cassiodorus, *De orth.*, *GL* 7.199–202.

Cf. also s.v. Ter(r)entius, no. 262.

EUTYCHIANUS: see no. 215.

FABIUS: see s.v. Flavius, no. 61.

58. FAUSTUS. Gramm. (and poet?). Africa, perhaps Carthage. s.VI init. – 1/2.

PLRE II s.v. 3, p. 451.

Friend of the poet Luxurius (q.v., no. 235) and a gramm.: *Anth. Lat.* 1:1.287 (= 1 Rosenblum), 4, *tantus grammaticae magister artis*. At F.'s urging Luxurius undertook the publication of his *liber epigrammaton* (ibid. 1ff., 19f.), and Luxurius sent him the poems to review and approve before

their wider circulation (ibid. 10ff.; and see s.v. Luxurius). Connection
with Luxurius (cf. s.v.) suggests F.'s place and date, but note that although Luxurius was probably a man of Carthage, it need not follow
that F. should be placed there as well. It is conceivable that he was the
teacher of Luxurius, but, *pace* Riché (*Education* 38), *Anth. Lat.* 1:1.287.5,
[*versus*] *quos olim puer in foro paravi*, does not have that meaning; and
Luxurius seems to address F. rather as a friend and peer than as an older
man and onetime teacher: cf. ibid. 1, *amice*; 3, *nostro Fauste animo probate
conpar.*

F. is possibly the Faustus whose poetry is quoted in a glossary of s.XII
(cf. Rosenblum, *Luxorius* 44 n. 44; Happ, "Zur Lisorius-Frage" 200),
although he is by no means the only possible candidate from this period;
cf. Ennod. *Carm.* 2.3 (*MGH* AA 7.80).

59. FELICIANUS.   Gramm.   Carthage.   s.V 2/2.

Sch.-Hos. 4:2.58f., 66; Szövérffy, *Weltliche Dichtungen* 1.178f.; *PLRE* II s.v.,
p. 458.

Teacher of the poet Dracontius, who praises F., no doubt with a touch
of encomiastic exaggeration, as the man responsible for recalling Latin
letters from their exile under the Vandals: *Rom.* 1.13f., *qui fugatas
Africanae reddis urbi litteras, / barbaris qui Romulidas iungis auditorio.* When
still his pupil, *ut vid.*, Dracontius addresses him in *Rom.* 1 (tit., *Praefatio
Dracontii discipuli ad grammaticum Felicianum*) and *Rom.* 3 (tit., *incipit praefatio
ad Felicianum grammaticum, cuius supra in auditorio*; cf. ibid. 14–20). These
are the covering or dedicatory pieces for *Rom.* 2, *Fabula Hylae*, and 4,
Verba Herculis. (For classroom compositions of the sort implied by the tit.
of *Rom.* 1 and 3, where note esp. *Dracontii discipuli* and *in auditorio*, see s.v.
Ioannes of Gaza, no. 83.) As products of the time when Dracontius was
still a schoolboy, *Rom.* 1–4 must antedate by some years *Rom.* 7, written
by Dracontius in prison ca. 490, when he was already of a mature age.

Cf. Kuijper, "Varia" 7ff.; Díaz de Bustamente, *Draconcio* 37ff.

+   FELIX: see no. 216.

60. IUNIUS FILARGIRIUS.   Gramm.   Milan.   Not active before s.V 1/4?

RE 10.1077–79 (Tolkiehn); Sch.-Hos. 2.108f.; *PLRE* II s.v. Iunius Philargyrius, p. 874.

Iunius Filargirius: I. Filargirius, subscr. *Explan. 1 in Buc.* codd. NP, subscr.
Explan. 2 in Buc. cod. P; I. Filagirius, subscr. *Explan. 2* codd. P²NL;
I. Filargius in Manitius, *Handschriften* 267; Iunilius or Iunilius Flagrius,
Scholia Bernensia; cited as "Iunilius" in a commentary on Orosius: cf.
Lehmann, "Reste" 200. For the name "Philargyr(i)us," cf. Thilo, "Bei-

träge" 135; Ferrua, "Nuova regione" 178; and Pape and Benseler, *Wörter-buch*; Preisigke, *Namenbuch*; Foraboschi, *Onomasticon* s.v. The form "Filag-rius" was urged by Heraeus, "Drei Fragmente" 391 n. 1.

A gramm. (*grammaticus*, subscr. *Explan. 1* and *2*) at Milan: *Iunilii Flagrii Mediolanenses* [sic], subscr. to *Buc.* in *Schol. Bern.* (printed as inscr. to *Georg.* by Hagen; see below); cf. *Iunilius Flagrius Valentiano Mediolani*, inscr. of *Georg.* in *Schol. Bern.* Author of a commentary on the *Bucolica* and *Georgica* of Vergil, dedicated to a certain Valentinianus: so subscr. to the *Buc.* in *Explan. 2*; *Valentiano*, inscr. of *Georg.* in *Schol. Bern.*, above. Note that even if the form "Valentinianus" is correct, the absence of appropriate orna-ment in the dedication makes it unlikely that one of the three emperors of that name is meant, as has sometimes been supposed. The commen-tary is preserved in two different recensions: recension a, ed. H. Hagen, in Thilo and Hagen, eds., *Servii . . . commentarii* 3:2, contains *Explan. 1* and *2* on the *Buc.*, and the *Brevis expositio* (transmitted without attribution) on the *Georg.*; recension b is the *Scholia Bernensia ad Vergili Bucolica atque Georgica*, ed. H. Hagen, *Jahrbuch für classischen Philologie* Suppl. 4.5 (Leipzig, 1867); cf. Barwick, "De Iunio"; Funaioli, *Esegesi*.

F.'s use of the variorum commentary of Donatus (cf. Funaioli, *Esegesi* 233ff.) provides a *term. p. q.* of s.IV med.; his apparent use of Servius, a *term. p. q.* of s.V 1/4. Funaioli believed F. to be ignorant of Servius; but as C. E. Murgia has emphasized to me, Funaioli's treatment of the evidence was often arbitrary: note esp. that Servius's introduction to the *Georg.* (ed. Thilo and Hagen, *Servii . . . commentarii* 3.128–29.16) is repeated al-most verbatim in both recensions and is attributed to "Iunilius" in re-cension b; so *Schol. Bern.* p. 841.3, *hucusque Iunilius*. For an attempt at more exact dating, see Funaioli, *Esegesi* 399f. A reliable *term. a. q.* is lack-ing; on the identification of the Adamnanus mentioned in *Explan. 1* (*Ecl.* 3.90) with the homonymous abbot of Iona (679–704), cf. Lehmann, "Reste" 197f., and Wessner's review of Funaioli, *PhW* 51 (1931), 209.

Cf. also s.vv. Titus Gallus, Gaudentius, nos. 222, 223.

FILOCALUS: see no. 217.

FIRMIANUS: see no. 218.

FLAVIANUS: see no. 219.

61. FLAVIUS? (FABIUS?). Lat. gramm. Africa → Nicomedia. s.III ex. / s.IV init.

PLRE I s.v. 1, p. 349.

Flavius: "Flavius" and "Fabius" appear in the mss of Jer. *De vir. ill.*, as does "Flavus"; cf. "Flavum" in the mss of Jer. *C. Iovin.*; and Barnes,

"More Missing Names" 144. Latin gramm. invited by Diocletian to teach at Nicomedia: Jer. *De vir. ill.* 80. Since he is said to have been summoned with Lactantius, he was presumably from Africa.

F. wrote a treatise *De medicinalibus* in hexameter verse: Jer. *De vir. ill.* 80; *C. Iovin.* 2.6.

Perhaps a Christian; cf. Jer. *C. Iovin.* 2.6, *noster.* But since F. here is named fourth in a list that begins with three Greeks—Aristotle, Theophrastus, Marcellus of Side—*noster* may instead mark him as a Latin writer.

*   FLAVIUS: see no. 220.

ATILIUS FORTUNATIANUS: see no. 221.

* 62. FL. FORTUNATUS.   Schoolmaster.   Aquileia.   s.IV 2/2 / s.VI.

Fl. Fortun[atus], called [magiste]r litterar[um] on a Christian epitaph from Aquileia; see Brusin, "Nuove epigrafi" 40f. = *AE* 1968, 191–98 n. (p. 72). His religion and the name "Flavius" suggest a date not before s.IV 2/2. His use of the Flaviate is noteworthy as evidence of incomplete social differentiation between *magistri litterarum* and *grammatici*, and might suggest a date of s.V or VI; cf. Chap. 3 pp. 109–11.

TITUS GALLUS: see no. 222.

GAUDENTIUS: see no. 223.

\+ 63. GEORGIUS.   Gramm.   Egypt? Palestine (Gaza)? (very uncertain).   s.VI 1/2?

Nissen, *Byzantinische Anakreonten* 13ff.; Anastasi, "Giorgio" 209ff.; Hunger 2.93f.

A γραμματικός, author of nine surviving anacreontic poems, *PLG*⁴ 3.363ff.: 1–6, exercises in ethopoeia on the theme of the rose, for the Rosalia; 7–8, epithalamia; plus the poem in honor of the Brumalia of the gramm. Coluthus, on the attribution of which cf. s.v. Coluthus, no. 33. Two other poems listed in the index of cod. Barb. 310 (*olim* 246) have not survived; cf. Nissen, *Byzantinische Anakreonten* 13; Anastasi, "Giorgio" 207ff. An Italian translation of the poems, with brief, largely textual notes, is given by Anastasi, "Giorgio" 234ff.

G. appears to have been at one time a pupil of the gramm. Coluthus (q.v.); cf. *PLG*⁴ 3.364, vv. 65–68. The place of G.'s activity cannot be identified with certainty; for some evidence that he might be claimed by Egypt or Gaza, see Nissen, *Byzantinische Anakreonten* 19; Anastasi, "Giorgio" 215ff., and cf. ibid. p. 227, where G. has become a representative of the "Egyptian School." He is probably to be dated roughly contemporary with Ioannes (q.v., no. 83) of Gaza, with whom he shares in the anacreontic pieces certain features distinct from the earlier technique of Gregory Nazianzen and Synesius; cf. Nissen, *Byzantinische Anakreonten* 19ff.; Anastasi, "Giorgio" 217ff. That dating would be established more firmly if the gramm. Coluthus were certainly the poet of Lycopolis; on the identification, see s.v.

It does not seem possible to determine whether G. is the same man as Georgius γραμματικός, author of two unpublished encomia of St. Barbara (*BHG* 218a–b). G. cannot be Georgius Choeroboscus (q.v., no. 201); cf. Chr.-Sch.-St. 2:2.1079 n. 10.

GEORGIUS CHOEROBOSCUS: see s.v. CHOEROBOSCUS, no. 201.

64. ACILIUS GLABRIO.   Gramm. and advocate.   Bordeaux.   s.IV 1/2.

RE 7.1372 (Seeck); *PLRE* I s.v. 2, p. 397.

Acilius Glabrio: Auson. *Prof.* 24 tit.; *Glabrio †Aquilini*, ibid. 4 Schenkl (*Aquilini* V: *Acilini* Heinsius, *Advers.* lib. 4, cap. 5, p. 601, followed by most edd.). The quantity of the second syllable of *Aquilini* is incorrect; *Acilini* as the genitive of his father's name ("Glabrio, son of Acilinus," Evelyn-White in his Loeb translation) is difficult, since if the *iun*(*iori*) of the tit. is correct, G. was possibly the son of an homonymous father, and the name *Acilin*(*i*)*us* does not in any event seem to be otherwise attested. Pastorino (*Opere* 196) conjectured that an imagined Trojan ancestor of the family, Acilinus, was meant; but the family traced its origin back to Anchises and Aphrodite, i.e., through Aeneas (see below).

A *grammaticus* (ibid. tit., v. 6) and advocate (ibid. 7, *inque foro tutela reis*) at Bordeaux (ibid. tit.); coeval with and a fellow student of Ausonius, therefore born ca. 310: ibid. 5, *tu quondam puero conpar mihi, discipulo mox* (*discipulo* Scaliger: *discipulos* V: *discipulus* Corpet, edd.). The reading adopted by modern editors, *discipulus*, would on its most natural and usual interpretation make G. a pupil of Ausonius—although that would have G. still or again studying grammar well into his twenties, the earliest time at which he could have had Ausonius as his teacher, since Ausonius began teaching ca. 336/37. This is not impossible—cf. Libanius aged twenty reading Aristophanes with a gramm., *Or.* 1.9—but it would certainly have been unusual. Scaliger's *discipulo* is much to be preferred: note that the line is articulated naturally by the caesura and diaeresis around *conpar mihi*, which should thus be construed in common with both the preceding and the following phrase. Pastorino seems to have recognized the chronological problem but solved it by reading *discipulus* and punctuating *tu quondam puero conpar mihi discipulus; mox / meque dehinc facto rhetore grammaticus*, where the strong punctuation after *discipulus* and before *mox / meque dehinc* is plainly intolerable; he also ignores his own text when he calls G. "one of [Ausonius's] own first pupils," *Opere* 19.

G. became *grammaticus* when Ausonius was made *rhetor* (ibid. 6), i.e., sometime after ca. 336 and before ca. 367; see following. He died when both his parents were still living (ibid. 13). It is not likely that both parents would still have been alive later than ca. 360 if G. was born ca. 310; and G. almost certainly died well before 360, not long after becoming a gramm., since his premature death receives special emphasis: ibid. 11f., *mox dolor . . . / . . . funere praereptus*; cf. v. 1, *doctrinae vitaeque pari brevitate caducum.*

He claimed descent from the Acilii Glabriones: ibid. 3–4, *stemmate nobilium deductum nomen avorum / . . . Dardana progenies.* For the alleged Trojan origin of the family from Anchises and Aphrodite, cf. Herodian 2.3.4, with *PIR*[2] A.69, *PLRE* I s.v. Glabrio 1, p. 396. He was a landowner: ibid. 7, *cultor in agris.* Ausonius praises him for his character, good counsel, and discretion (ibid. 9–10). He left a wife and children (ibid. 13).

* GORGON(I)US: see no. 224.

GRILLIUS: see no. 225.

65. HARMONIUS.   Gr. and Lat. gramm.   Trier.   376.
RE 7.2389 (Seeck); *PLRE* I s.v. 2, p. 408.

Harmonius (Auson. *Epist.* 13.26, 27), colleague (ibid. 26) of the gramm. Ursulus (ibid. tit.; cf. s.v. Ursulus, no. 166), said to rival the great gramm. of Rome (Claranus, Scaurus, Asper, Varro: ibid. 27–28; cf. s.v. Nepotianus, no. 105) and of Greece (Crates, Zenodotus, Aristarchus: ibid. 28–30). He taught both Greek and Latin poetry: ibid. 30–31, *Cecropiae commune decus Latiaeque camenae, / solus qui Chium miscet et Ammineum.* The reference to Chian wine, like the comparison with Zenodotus and Aristarchus, presumably means that he taught Homer; if *Ammineum* involves a specific reference, presumably Vergil is meant: see *Georg.* 2.97–98, where the wine of Chios (*rex ipse Phanaeus*) is said to rise in deference to the *Aminneae vites.*

H. was at Trier (Auson. *Epist.* 13 tit.) when Ausonius was *QSP* (ibid. tit., with v. 3), probably not long after 1 January 376: Ausonius was certainly *quaestor* in January 376; and since *Epist.* 13 seems to allude to only one Augustus (cf. ibid. tit., with v. 2), Valentinian (d. 17 Nov. 375) was probably already dead at the time it was written.

66. HARPOCRAS.   Gramm.   Egypt, probably Alexandria.   s.V 3/3.
PLRE II s.v. 3, p. 528.

Egyptian gramm. in the reign of Zeno: *Suda* A.4010 = Damasc. *V. Isid.* frg. 313 Zintzen. Since he was an intimate of Ammonius Hermiou (ibid.), and since he associated with Isidore, Heraiscus, and Fl. Horapollon (q.v., no. 78; see below), he was presumably active at Alexandria.

He escaped arrest during the persecution of the philosophers under Zeno; Heraiscus and Horapollon were tortured in an attempt to make them disclose the whereabouts of H. and Isidore: Damasc. *V. Isid.* frg. 313, 314 Zintzen.

HARPOCRATION: see no. 226.

HELLADIUS: see no. 227.

67. HELLADIUS. Gramm. → *com. ord. pr.* Alexandria → Constantinople. s.IV 3/4 – s.V 1/4.

RE 8.102–3 no. 3 (Gudeman), 103–4 no. 8 (Seeck; cf. *Briefe* 167); Chr.-Sch.-St. 2:2.1075, 1080; *PLRE* I s.v. 4, p. 412; cf. ibid. II s.v. 2, p. 534.

A gramm. in Alexandria at the time the pagan temples were desecrated, in 391, when he killed nine men with his own hands: Soc. *HE* 5.16 = Nic. Call. *HE* 12.25; *Suda* E.732 (Ἀλεξανδρεύς). He fled with Ammonius (q.v., no. 10) from Alexandria to Constantinople, where the two later had the historian Socrates among their pupils: Soc. ibid. = Phot. *Bibl.* cod. 28 (1.16 Henry). He is usually identified with the Greek gramm. Helladius who taught in Constantinople and received the *comitiva ordinis primi* and the rank of ex-vicar on 15 March 425; cf. *CTh* 6.21.1. The law (*ad fin.* = *CJ* 12.15.1) establishes that the same honors are to be given thereafter to other teachers who will have satisfied certain conditions, including twenty years' tenure. It is not evident, however, that the last condition is applicable to, and therefore useful in dating the service of, the teachers honored in 6.21.1; cf. s.vv. Syrianus, Theofilus, nos. 147, 154.

H. was active in Alexandria by 391, when he was still young and sturdy enough to work the mayhem noted above; he was possibly of an age to retire by 425. The *Suda*, E.732 and praef., dates him to the reign of Theodosius II, referring to the latter part of his career.

Author of an alphabetical lexicon known to Photius in seven volumes, concerned mostly with the diction of prose: Phot. *Bibl.* cod. 145 (2.110 Henry); cf. *Suda* praef., E.732. The preface to the *Suda* names him as a source, but the authenticity of the notice is doubtful; see s.v. Eugenius, no. 56. H. also produced an Ἔκφρασις φιλοτιμίας, a Διόνυσος ἢ Μοῦσα, an Ἔκφρασις τοῦ λουτροῦ Κωνσταντινιανῶν, and an encomium of Theodosius (presumably Theodosius II).

H. was a pagan, priest of Zeus-Ammon at Alexandria: Soc. *HE* 5.16; cf. s.v. Ammonius, no. 10.

68. FL. HER... Gramm.(?) Hermopolis. s.V 2/2.

Fl. Her..., son of ...philos, gramm.(?), the first of three witnesses to a lease at Hermopolis dated 452, 467, 482, or 497; see *BGU* 12.2152 with p. 36 n. 1 for the date. At line 17, Φλ(άυιος) Ἐρ[– – –]φίλου γρα[.. μ]αρτυρῶ κτλ, the editor suggests the restoration γρα[μμ(ατικός), "wie in Z. 19," i.e., as the papyrus shows for Fl. Pythiodorus (q.v., no. 128), another witness to the lease. If the restoration is correct in line 17, this is the only documented case of more than one gramm. at the same time in the same place in Egypt outside Alexandria. The signature of the third witness, a presbyter, is preceded by a Christian monogram; the signatures of the two gramm. are not.

H. is conceivably the Hermias of Hermopolis who wrote πάτριά τε τῆς Ἑρμουπόλεως καὶ ἕτερά τινα in iambics, Phot. Bibl. cod. 279 (8.187 Henry); but note also that the gramm. Heraclammon (q.v., no. 69) is also a candidate, since he seems to have been at Hermopolis at some indefinite time after 391; and cf. s.vv. Hermias, Anonymus 7, nos. 71, 173.

* 69. HERACLAMMON.   Gramm.   Hermopolis.   s.IV ex. / s.V; after 391.

Heraclammon γραμματικ(ός), registered as the recipient of 20 artabae of wheat (σῖτος) in an account of six months' payments in kind, λόγου ὀψωνίου σμίνου (i.e., ἑξαμήνου), made to various persons, mostly tradesmen: PRossGeorg. 5.60. The term. p. q. and probable place are indicated by the recto of the papyrus, which contains fragmentary records of the exactor of the Hermopolite nome, the first of them carrying the date 391. The payment is among the largest recorded in the account—e.g., five times larger than the payment to the veterinarian Isidorus, line 4; twice as large as the payment to the physician Heraclammon, line 3—and is exceeded only by a payment of 22 artabae to an ὀνηλάτης. The account does not specify the services for which the payments are made, nor is it clear whether the payments come from a private or from a public source. For payments in kind made to teachers from public resources, see s.v. Lollianus, no. 90; for such payments by private individuals, see PGiss. 80 (s.II; Hermopolite nome?), POsl. 3.156 (s.II; the Fayûm), and perhaps POxy. 24.2421 (payment to the γραμματοδιδάσκαλος Sarapion, on which see s.v., no. 133). For payments to teachers in six-month installments, cf. Cassiod. Var. 9.21.6.

He is conceivably the gramm.(?) Fl. Her… (q.v., no. 68) at Hermopolis, s.V 2/2.

70. POMPONIUS MAXIMUS HERCULANUS.   Gramm.   Bordeaux.   s.IV 2/4.

RE 8.549 (Seeck); PLRE I s.v. Herculanus 3, p. 420.

Pomponius Maximus Herculanus: Auson. Par. 17 tit.; Maximus, Par. 17.11; Herculanus, Prof. 11 tit., v. 1. Son of Pomponius Maximus, an important curialis of Bordeaux (Par. 15), and his wife, a sister of Ausonius who must be Iulia Dryadia (Par. 12). He was first a pupil of Ausonius (Prof. 11.1), in whose school he later taught as a gramm. (Prof. 11.3, *particeps scholae*; tit., *grammaticus*). Had he lived long enough, H. would have succeeded to Ausonius's chair of grammar (*Prof.* 11.3; on the implications see Appendix 4); but because of H.'s early death the chair instead went to Acilius Glabrio (q.v., no. 64).

He died very young, *in tempore puberis aevi* (*Par.* 17.9), evidently as the result of a youthful indiscretion: *Prof.* 11.4–5, *lubricae nisi te iuventae praecipitem flexus daret / Pythagorei non tenentem tramitis rectam viam.* Whatever this was, it apparently involved some disgrace: *Par.* 17.6–7, *verum memorare magis quam / functum laudare decebit*; cf. s.v. Marcellus, no. 94. His birth, education, brief career, and death are all probably to be assigned to the second quarter of s.IV.

71. HERMIAS.   Gramm.   s.IV ex. / s.V 1/3.

PLRE II s.v. Hermeias 2, p. 547.

Hermias γραμματικός, recipient of Isid. Pel. *Ep.* 3.350 ('Ερμείᾳ γραμματικῷ), on the deceit of poets. H. is possibly Hermias of Hermopolis, whose πάτρια of Hermopolis and other poems in iambics were known to Photius in a volume containing the works of several poets of s.IV / s.VI, *Bibl.* cod. 279 (8.187 Henry). Note, however, that Photius does not style this poet γραμματικός as he does Serenus and Horapollon (qq.v., nos. 134, 77). Cf. also s.v. Fl. Her..., no. 68.

72. HERMOLAUS.   Gramm.   Constantinople.   s.VI 2/3?

RE 8.891 (Gudeman); cf. *RE*, 2. Reihe, 3.2374.59ff. (Honigmann); Chr.-Sch.-St. 2:2.1084; Hunger 2.37.

According to the *Suda*, E.3048, a gramm. of Constantinople who produced an epitome—not certainly the extant epitome—of the Έθνικά of Stephanus (q.v., no. 144) of Byzantium and dedicated it to the emperor Justinian. The last piece of information has often been doubted on the grounds that it would be strange for an epitome to be produced so soon after the original work. But if the epitome is placed *ex hypothesi* toward the end of Justinian's reign, it could be separated by one generation or more from the work of Stephanus, which is itself difficult to date; cf. s.v.

The dedication has also been doubted because it would be strange for a gramm. to dedicate to the emperor an epitome of another man's work. But if one could dedicate an anthology to an empress (cf. s.v. Orion, no. 110), one could presumably dedicate an epitome to an emperor; for the dedication of epitomes or extracts of grammatical works, cf. s.vv. Aristodemus, Ioannes Charax, Theodoretus, nos. 188, 199, 265. It has also been suggested that the reference to Justinian is an error for Justin or should be understood to mean Justinian II (both notions refuted by Müller, "Zu Stephanos" 347f.), or that the dedication to Justinian was Stephanus's own, mindlessly copied by H. into his epitome and then falsely attributed to H. himself; cf. Honigmann, *RE*, 2. Reihe, 3.2375.10ff. But even if the latter, unlikely, series of events took place, we still have a probable date for H.'s epitome no later than the reign of Justinian, since the notice in the *Suda* is likely to have been drawn from the Ὀνοματο-λόγος of Hesychius Illustrius, who was active under Justinian and was possibly H.'s contemporary. It is best to accept the notice as it stands.

* AUR. HERODES: see no. 228.

HESPERIUS: see no. 229.

73. HESYCHIUS. Gramm. Alexandria. s.V / s.VI.

RE 8.1317–22 (Schultz); Chr.-Sch.-St. 2:2.1083; Latte, ed., 1, vii–li; Hunger 2.35f.; *PLRE* II s.v. 15, p. 555.

Compiler of the lexicon Συναγωγὴ πασῶν λέξεων κατὰ στοιχεῖον surviving in abridged and interpolated form in cod. Marc. gr. 622 (s.XV). H. styles himself γραμματικὸς Ἀλεξανδρεύς in the salutation of the prefatory epistle, addressed to one Eulogius. H. is probably to be dated to the fifth or sixth century: cf. Latte, ed., 1, vii–viii, expressing a slight preference for the former date and rejecting identification of the dedicatee with Eulogius Scholasticus, whose date (s.V 2/2 at the earliest) can in any event only be determined very approximately; cf. Reitzenstein, *Geschichte* 358. Both H.'s religion (see following) and, e.g., the abstract form of address in the epistle, ἀπέστειλα πρὸς τὴν σὴν ἀναμίλλητον φιλίαν (1.2.46f. Latte), urge against a significantly earlier date.

Although the biblical glosses found in the lexicon are interpolated, H. was certainly a Christian; cf. his name and the closing formula of the epistle, εὔχομαι δὲ τῷ θεῷ σωζόμενόν σε καὶ ὑγιαίνοντα χρήσασθαι τοῖς βιβλίοις (1.2.48f.).

74. HIERAX. Schoolmaster. Alexandria. s.V init.

PLRE II s.v. 2, p. 556.

According to Soc. *HE* 7.13.7ff., a schoolmaster: γραμμάτων . . . τῶν πεζῶν διδάσκαλος, "teacher of common [or: "vulgar"] letters." The phrase γράμματα πεζά means γράμματα κοινά, i.e., *litterae communes* or *viles*, as opposed to liberal studies, for which see Socrates' usual phrasing, Ἑλ-ληνικοὶ or Ῥωμαϊκοὶ λόγοι, at, e.g., 2.46, 5.25.1, 7.17.2; cf. *LSJ* s.v. πεζός II.3 and Kaster, "Notes" 326 n. 9. The phrase does not mean "teacher of prose," as if γράμματα πεζά meant λόγοι πεζοί, i.e., *sermo pedestris*: since the teacher of poetry was the gramm., we would expect the teacher of prose—according to the traditional distinction of skills—to be the rhetorician. But from Socrates it is clear that H. was not anything so grand as a teacher of rhetoric, and the phrase is in any case not so used elsewhere.

The leader of a claque for Cyril, bishop of Alexandria, H. was set upon by Jews in the theater and tortured there by the *praef. Aug.* Orestes not long after Cyril became bishop (an. 412).

75. HIERIUS. Lat. gramm. Gaza → Antioch. s.V 4/4 / s.VI 1/4.
PLRE II s.v. 8, p. 559.

The recipient of Procop. Gaz. *Ep.* 13 jointly with Alypius and Stephanus (qq.v., nos. 7, 141): Ἀλυπίῳ καὶ Στεφάνῳ γραμματικοῖς καὶ Ἱερίῳ Ῥωμαϊκῷ (sc. γραμματικῷ). H. taught Latin at Gaza: *Ep.* 145.1, τὸν λογιώτατον Ἱέριον τὸν τῆς Ἰταλῶν παρ' ἡμῖν προβεβλημένον φωνῆς. Later, apparently, he taught at Antioch (Daphne), where he had gone with the Greek gramm. Stephanus and Alypius: *Ep.* 13; cf. s.vv. Alypius and esp. Stephanus.

He was commended in *Ep.* 145 by Procopius to Eudaemon, a provincial governor (so *PLRE* II s.v. 5, p. 407, correctly). Eudaemon has otherwise been identified as a teacher of law (Garzya and Loenertz, eds., *Procopii . . . epistolae* 104) or an advocate (Seitz, "Schule" 15). But the description of Eudaemon as one who administers justice for a fortunate people (εὐδαίμονες ὄντως οἷς διέπεις τὰ δίκαια) and ensures the rejuvenation of a formerly withered Δίκη rather conforms to the conventional praise of a governor; cf. *Ep.* 145.5ff., with Robert, *Hellenica* 4.62ff., 99ff.; and esp. Ševčenko, "Late Antique Epigram" 30f. The commendation to Eudaemon might indicate that H. combined legal or forensic expertise with his knowledge of Latin.

HIEROCLES: see no. 230.

76. HIEROCLES. Gramm.(?) s.VI 1/3(?); possibly s.V med.
RE 8.1487–89 (Kiessling); Hunger 1.531, 2.399.

Hierocles, compiler of the Συνέκδημος, a list of provinces and cities of the eastern empire perhaps drawn up early in the reign of Justinian, ca. 527/28; cf. Honigmann, ed., 1f.: only one of Justinian's foundations is recorded, and his reorganization of the provinces is ignored. Note, however, that the list in its present form is dependent on a register drawn up in the reign of Theodosius II. Accordingly, it is possible that H. himself composed the latter register, to which additions were made unsystematically by a later hand; see Jones, *CERP*[2] 514ff.

H. is styled ὁ γραμματικός by Constantine Porphyrogenitus (*De them.* 1, p. 85.36; 4, p. 89.6f. Pertusi), who can be shown to have known a different (longer) version of H.'s work than is now preserved; see Jones, *CERP*[2] 514; cf. Kiessling, *RE* 8.1488.39ff. The style is not otherwise attested.

HIERONYMUS: see no. 231.

* HIERONYMUS: see no. 232.

HOËN(I)US: see no. 233.

77. HORAPOLLON. Gramm. Phenebythis (Panopolite nome) → Alexandria → Constantinople. s.IV ex. / s.V 1/3.

Maspéro, "Horapollon" (fundamental); PLRE I s.v., p. 442; ibid. II s.v. 1, p. 569; cf. RE 8.2313–14 (Roeder).

From Phenebythis, a village of the Panopolite nome: Suda Ω.159; cf. s.v. Fl. Horapollon, no. 78. He taught as a gramm. in Alexandria—"in Alexandria and in Egypt," Suda ibid.—and then in Constantinople under Theodosius (Suda ibid.: this was probably Theodosius II; see below). Credited by the Suda with a Τεμενικά, of uncertain character but probably on the morphology of temple names: cf. Suda E.3394 = Eugenius (q.v., no. 56), with Reitzenstein, Geschichte 313 n. 1. The Suda also mentions H.'s commentaries on Sophocles, Alcaeus, and Homer; if he is the Horapollon γραμματικός mentioned by Photius at Bibl. cod. 279 (8.187 Henry), he wrote δράματα and a πάτρια of Alexandria in verse. The latter genre points to a date early in the Byzantine era; this may, however, be the work of Fl. Horapollon or of a third man of the same name.

H. is probably not Horapollon Neiloios, author of the Hieroglyphica. It has been suggested that H. was the Egyptian νεανίσκος known for his poetic talents at Constantinople in 377 (Them. Or. 29.347A; cf. PLRE I s.vv. Horapollon, Andronicus 5; and Alan Cameron, "Wandering Poets" 487f.); but if H. was the grandfather of Fl. Horapollon (see below and s.v.), that date is almost certainly too early for him to have been active at Constantinople even as a νεανίσκος. The identification is questioned in PLRE II s.v.

Said to have been λαμπρὸς ἐπὶ τῇ τέχνῃ and comparable to the most brilliant gramm. of old (Suda Ω.159), H. is probably the Horapollon of the catalogue of gramm. in Kröhnert, Canones 7. His Τεμενικά, even if concerned only with morphology, and his probable family relations suggest that he was a pagan.

In all likelihood the father of Asclepiades (q.v., no. 17) and another son (Heraiscus?), and the grandfather of the gramm. and philosopher Fl. Horapollon active under Zeno and Anastasius (see following and s.v. Fl. Horapollon). His floruit therefore should probably be placed in s.V 1/3. Accordingly, he will have taught at Constantinople under Theodosius II (see above). Note esp. that, in the legal petition he drafted in the reign of Anastasius, Fl. Horapollon says he has spent his career in Alexandria (see s.v.); he therefore cannot be identified with H., who taught in Alexandria and then under Theodosius in Constantinople.

Confusion of the two Horapollones goes back at least as far as the *Suda*, Ω.159, where excerpts from Damasc. *V. Isid.* concerning Fl. Hora-pollon (3.615.6–18 Adler) are appended to the notice of H. drawn from the Ὀνοματολόγος of Hesychius Illustrius (3.615.1–6 Adler). The two Horapollones are treated as one man by Chr.-Sch.-St. 2:2.1076f., follow-ing Reitzenstein, *Geschichte* 312; similarly *FGrH* IIIc 630; Alpers, *Attizist-ische Lexikon* 93 n. 41, 96 n. 52; and, *ut vid.*, Hunger 2.18.

78. FL. HORAPOLLON.   Gramm. and philosopher; *v.c.*   Phenebythis and Alexandria.   s.V 3/3.

PLRE II s.v. 2, pp. 569f.

Fl. Horapollon: *PCairMasp.* 3.67295 (= Pap.) ii.24; elsewhere Horapollon. Son of Asclepiades (q.v., no. 17): Pap. i.1, 15, 26; and see below. He styles himself *v.c.*: Pap. i.1, [το]ῦ λαμπροτάτου. It is not clear how H. would have gained the rank, but the context in which it appears, a legal petition, shows that it must be intended as a formal designation of his status. He taught as a distinguished gramm. at Alexandria: Zach. Schol. *Vie de Sévère* pp. 14.2, 15.4–10. He associated there with a number of Neoplatonist scholars: ibid. pp. 15.10ff., 16.10–12, 22.14f., 23.6f.; Damasc. *V. Isid.* frg. 314, 317 Zintzen (see further below). His pupils perhaps included Timotheus (q.v., no. 156) of Gaza; for the evidence, see s.v. Timotheus. He calls himself [ἐλλογ]ιμώτατος φιλόσο[φος], Pap. i.1 (cf. ibid. ii.24), and says [ἄγω]ν σχολὴν περὶ τὰς ἐκε[ῖσε] [i.e., Alexandria] ἀκαδημ[ί]ας . . . τὴν φιλόσοφον ἐπε[ύθυ]νον [*l.* ἐπηύθυνον] τοῖς βουλομέ-νοις πα[ιδ]είαν, Pap. i.13–14; cf. Ὡραπόλλων ὁ φιλόσοφος, Steph. Byz. s.v. Φενέβηθις. The evidence is not contradictory, *pace* Maspéro, "Hora-pollon" 178 n. 1. We may conclude that "philosopher" and "philosophi-cal" are used in a broad, nontechnical sense not uncommon in the period (cf., e.g., Ioannes Lydus's characterization of his cousin, the *exceptor* Ammianus, as φιλομαθής τε καὶ φιλόσοφος τὸν βίον at *De mag.* 3.28; cf. also s.vv. Isocasius, Nicocles, Manippus, nos. 85, 106, 236), so that H. would be a gramm. as a matter of profession, but a philosopher—i.e., a lover of wisdom and learning—in his general interests and personal associations; cf. esp. Zach. Schol. and Damasc. as cited above (and see below). For such associations, see s.v. Asclepiades, no. 17; and for a gramm.-philosopher(?), cf. s.v. Ioannes Philoponus, no. 118. Or else we may conclude that H. taught gramm. in the 480s but later came to teach philosophy. For the dates, see below.

An Egyptian (*Suda* Ω.159, 3.615.6 Adler); he owned inherited property in Phenebythis in the Panopolite nome (Pap. i.1 and *passim*) and taught at Alexandria (Zach. Schol.; Pap. i.13, 16, 29). He was teaching by ca. 485; Zach. Schol. *Vie de Sévère* pp. 14–39 sets the struggle for the soul of H.'s pupil Paralius of Aphrodisias during the episcopacy of Peter Mongus

(482-90) and shortly after the arrival of Zach. and Severus in Alexandria (ibid. p. 14.1), therefore in 485/86; cf. *Suda* Ω.159, ἐπὶ Ζήνωνος βασιλέως. H. was still active under Anastasius; cf. Pap. ii.17, with i.29. Maspéro was probably correct in suggesting that the original document was composed closer to the beginning than to the end of Anastasius's reign, but his attempt at more precise dating (491/93: "Horapollon" 190) is not compelling.

Suspected of trafficking with demons and magic (Zach. Schol. *Vie de Sévère* p. 15.10f.), H., along with the Neoplatonist philosophers Asclepiodotus, Heraiscus, Ammonius Hermiou, and Isidore, was mocked by his pupil Paralius, who was then beaten by H.'s other students. The affair came before the prefect, a crypto-pagan, through whose collusion H. and the others escaped (ibid. pp. 22-27). At Easter 486(?) the Christian population of Alexandria cursed H., calling him "Soul Destroyer," Ψυχαπόλλων, and rioted (ibid. p. 37). For the date of the episode, cf. above.

H. is said to have been tortured during the persecution of the pagans under Zeno: Damasc. *V. Isid.* frg. 314 Zintzen, in connection with Heraiscus, Isidore, and Harpocras (q.v., no. 66). Nonetheless, he was not thought to be a true philosoper. Heraiscus (his uncle and father-in-law? see below) foretold that H. would "desert to the others and abandon the ancestral ways"—i.e., he would become a Christian—and this proved correct (ibid. frg. 317). The prophecy, if of the type found, e.g., at Eunap. *V. phil.* 6.9.17, may have been confirmed after Heraiscus's death; H.'s conversion could then be dated after 487/91 and sometime before 526. Regarding the lower limit, 487/91, note that Heraiscus was still alive when Zach. and Severus were in Alexandria (485-87) but died while Zeno was still emperor; cf. Damasc. *V. Isid.* frg. 334 Zintzen. For the upper limit, note that Damascius can have written the *V. Isid.* no later than, and perhaps well before, 526; *V. Isid.* epit. Phot. 64 refers to Theoderic, ὃς νῦν τὸ μέγιστον ἔχει κράτος Ἰταλίας ἁπάσης.

H. was very possibly a Christian by the time he drafted the document represented by Pap.: cf. the Christian formula in i.15, [τῷ ἐν] ἁγίοις μακαριωτάτῳ μου πατρί, though ἁγίοις is obviously uncertain; cf. also the monogrammatic cross at the end of i.30, though since the document as preserved is a later copy the monogram may not be original; and cf. an oath κατὰ τοῦ παντοκράτορος Θεοῦ in ii.15f. (not decisive). If he was Christian, we have in Pap. an example of the flexible, subjective use of the term φιλόσοφος noted above; for after conversion H. would have ceased to be a philosopher in the sense recognized by, e.g., Damascius.

H.'s chronology, his ancestral property in Phenebythis, his claim in Pap. i.14f. that his vocation to teach was received ἐκ πατέρων καὶ προγόνων, and the name "Horapollon" itself make it virtually certain that H.

was a descendant of the gramm. Horapollon (q.v., no. 77), probably his grandson; see Maspéro, "Horapollon" 176ff. His father, Asclepiades (q.v., no. 17), had been a teacher all his life (Pap. i.15, when he is already dead), linked with his brother (H.'s uncle and father-in-law) by the "Muse of philosophy." The brother was perhaps Heraiscus; cf. Maspéro, "Horapollon" 179ff. The identification of Heraiscus is not certain: for Asclepiades and Heraiscus, cf. Damasc. *V. Isid.* frg. 160–65, 174 Zintzen, with Asmus, *Leben* 60.10ff., and Zintzen, ed., *Damascii . . . reliquiae* p. 135. But frg. 160, the crucial link, might refer instead to Ammonius and Heliodorus, the sons of Hermias; cf. Tannery, *Mémoires* 1.114ff.; Prächter, *RE* 8.422.36ff.; and s.v. Asclepiades. For a stemma, see *PCairMasp.* 3, p. 48 = *PLRE* II, p. 1326, where a change should be made to indicate the possibility that Asclepiades and his brother were born of the same father but different mothers; cf. Pap. i.18.

H. married his cousin (Pap. i.18), who abandoned him and attempted at law and through other means to acquire some of his property (Pap. i.20ff.).

H. is not certainly known to have left any writings. He is perhaps the Horapollon γραμματικός of Phot. *Bibl.* cod. 279 (8.187 Henry), author of δράματα and a πάτρια of Alexandria in verse; or he may be Horapollon Neiloios, author of the *Hieroglyphica.* Both identifications are uncertain. For an attempt to identify both of the latter with H. and to place the works in the egyptianizing milieu of s.V, see esp. Maspéro, "Horapollon" 181ff., whose assertions and argument are to be treated with some caution; sim. Rémondon, "Égypte" 63ff.

See also s.v. Horapollon.

79. HYPERECHIUS.   Gramm.   Alexandria? → Constantinople?   s.V 3/4.
RE 9.281 (Funaioli); Chr.-Sch.-St. 2:2.1073; *PLRE* II s.v., p. 581.

Gramm. of or from Alexandria in the reign of Marcian according to *Suda* Y.273; he was still active in the reign of Leo, by whom he was banished: *Suda* Λ.267, 3.248.27f. Adler = ?Malch. frg. 2a, *FHG* 4.114. His banishment by Leo may mean that he was active at Constantinople, in which case Ἀλεξανδρεύς in *Suda* Y.273 will indicate his origin and possibly the site of his earlier activity. The statement of Ioannes Tzetzes, *Chil.* 10.48ff. (pp. 388f. Leone), that H. was the teacher of "Eudocia, daughter of the great Leo," is likely a garbled invention; see s.v. Orion, no. 110.

Grammatical work of several kinds is attributed to him in the *Suda* (Y.273): ἔγραψε τέχνην γραμματικήν, περὶ ὀνομάτων, περὶ ῥήματος καὶ ὀρθογραφίας. A trace of his doctrine περὶ ὀνομάτων may be preserved in Choerobosc. *Schol. in Theodos.*, *GG* 4:1.292.6ff.: καὶ λέγει ὁ Ἡρωδιανός, ὅτι (NC) vs. καὶ λέγουσιν ὅ τε Ὑπερέχιος καὶ Ἡρωδιανός, ὅτι (V).

80. IOANNES.   Gramm. (or rhetorician?).   The Auvergne?   Ca. 476/80.
RE 9.1747 (Seeck); Sch.-Hos. 4:2.269; *PLRE* II s.v. 30, p. 601.

A teacher, recipient of Sidon. Apoll. *Ep.* 8.2, ca. 476/80, in which he is
praised (8.2.1) as the [*litterarum*] *quodammodo iam sepultarum suscitator, fautor,
assertor*, who has postponed the obliteration of the literary culture under
the barbarians; for the date, see Loyen, ed., *Sidoine* vol. 3 p. 216. Sidonius's
assertion that I. should be honored as "a second Demosthenes, a second
Cicero" may mean that he was a rhetorician. The comparison may,
however, be inspired primarily by I.'s status as a figure of resistance
rather than by his specific metier; and Sidonius's reference to a *competens
lectorum turba* issuing from his school (8.2.3) may suggest that the aims of
his instruction were modest. It is also possible in this period that I.
taught both gramm. and rhetoric (cf. s.v. Deuterius, no. 44) or that, in
the reduced circumstances Sidonius sketches, the traditional distinction
between the stages of gramm. and rhetoric was somewhat effaced.

With the praise of I., compare Dracontius's praise of the gramm.
Felicianus (q.v., no. 59).

81. IOANNES.   Gramm. → presbyter.   *Antiochenae parochiae.*   s.V 4/4.
RE 9.1806 (Jülicher); *PLRE* II s.v. 36, p. 603.

Ioannes: Gennad. *De vir. ill.* 94 = Marcellin. *Chron.* s.a. 486, *Chron. min.*
2.93.14–16 (the first sentence of Gennadius, through *confitentes naturas*).
Presbyter and former gramm. (*ex grammatico presbyter*) in the district under
the ecclesiastical jurisdiction of Antioch (*Antiochenae parochiae*): Gennad.
ibid. He wrote against Monophysitism and against certain anti-Nestorian
pronouncements of Cyril of Alexandria that were providing aid and
comfort to the Theodosiani.

Placed by Marcellinus s.a. 486; according to Gennadius, he was still
alive at the time of the composition of the *De vir. ill.*—i.e., before ca.
480?

Not to be confused with the Neo-Chalcedonian Ioannes (q.v., no. 82),
the gramm. of Caesarea.

82. IOANNES.   Gramm. and (or →) presbyter.   Caesarea (Palestine?).
s.VI 1/4.
PLRE II s.v. 74, pp. 611f.

Ἰωάννης (ὁ) γραμματικός: Ephraem. Ant. *PG* 86:2.2109B = Ioan. Damasc.
Parall. Rupef., *PG* 96.481C; Eustath. mon. *Epist. de duabus naturis*, *PG*
86:1.912A, 913B, 933A; also in two excerpts in the *Catena* on the Gospel
of John (see below). Also ὁ γραμματικός: Severus of Antioch *passim* in the
C. impium grammaticum (cf. Leont. Byz. *C. monophys.*, *PG* 86:2.1841B–
1845D, 1848A); John of Beith-Aphthonia, *Vie de Sévère*, *PO* 2.248ff.;

Ephraem. Ant. in *Conc. Constant. III, Actio* X, Mansi 11.436A (for the same work of Ephraem, see above; ὁ γραμματικός is here incorrectly identified with Ioannes Philoponus [q.v., no. 118] in Mansi; cf. Helmer, *Neuchalkedonismus* 162 n. 334); Eustath. mon. *Epist. de duabus naturis, PG* 86:1.908A, 912D. Also Ἰωάννης πρεσβύτερος ἀπὸ γραμματικῶν in the Πρὸς ἀφθαρτοδοκήτας, tit.; Ἰωάννης γραμματικὸς καὶ πρεσβύτερος in the Πρὸς τοὺς ἀκεφάλους, tit.; Ἰωάννης ἀπὸ γραμματικῶν and ὁ αὐτὸς Ἰωάννης πρεσβύτερος, titt. of the two homilies against the Manichaeans.

From Caesarea: Ἰωάννης ὁ Καισαρεὺς ὁ γραμματικός, Anast. Sinait. *Viae dux* 6, *PG* 89.101D; cf. 104A, 105D; cf. also Leont. Byz. *C. monophys., PG* 86:2.1845C. Also ὁ ἐπίσκοπος Καισαρείας, *vel sim.*, an apparent confusion with Ioannes Khozibites, in Leont. Byz. *C. monophys., PG* 86:2.1848D; cf. *Conc. Lateran., Secretarius V*, Mansi 10.1116D. It is not known which Caesarea is meant; cf. Moeller, "Représentant" 103 n. 1, suggesting Caesarea of Cappadocia; Helmer, *Neuchalkedonismus* 160, Caesarea of Palestine. The latter is more likely.

Not long before 518, I. wrote a defense of the Council of Chalcedon, for which Severus, Monophysite bishop of Antioch, made him the object of the *C. impium grammatium* ca. 520. On the date of the apologia, cf. Lebon, *Monophysisme* 137ff. On the circumstances of its composition, see Richard, ed., pp. vi–xii; *contra*, Halleux, "Synode." The Syriac version of Severus's polemic is published with Latin translation by Lebon, *CSCO* Scr. Syr., 4th ser., vols. 4–6. Lebon's Latin translations of extracts from I.'s apologia as quoted by Severus and some fragments preserved in Greek are published by Richard, ed., 6ff., along with the following works attributable to I. with varying degrees of certainty: two Christological tracts, Πρὸς τοὺς ἀκεφάλους (cf. Helmer, *Neuchalkedonismus* 172ff., 255f.) and Πρὸς ἀφθαρτοδοκήτας (cf. above); two comments on the Gospel of John from a *Catena* in cod. Valicallan. E 40; and four works of anti-Manichaean polemic, viz., two homilies attributed to I. by Richard, ed., p. xli, on the basis of the titt. (cf. above), a Διάλεξις Ἰωάννου Ὀρθοδόξου πρὸς Μανιχαῖον (on the attribution, compare Richard, ed., pp. xlv–liv, with Aubineau *ap.* Richard, ed., pp. 112ff.), and Συλλογισμοὶ ἁγίων πατέρων.

Not to be confused with the anti-Monophysite writer Ioannes *ex grammatico presbyter* of the *Antiochena parochia* or with Ioannes Philoponus (qq.v, nos. 87, 118).

83. IOANNES. Gramm. and poet. Gaza. s.VI 1/2?

RE 9.1747–48 (Thiele); Chr.-Sch.-St. 2:2.977; Downey, "John of Gaza"; Hunger 2.93f., 110.

Gramm. of Gaza: γραμματικὸς Γάζης, inscr. and subscr. of the Ἔκφρασις and inscr. of the anacreontic pieces; γραμματικός, lemma of *Anth. Gr.*

15.1. Poet: six brief poems in anacreontic meter are extant, PLG⁴ 3.342ff. (a seventh, listed in the index of cod. Barb. 310, *olim* 246, is lost), as well as the Ἔκφρασις τοῦ κοσμικοῦ πίνακος, a verse description in two books of a painting of the cosmos in the Winter Baths of Gaza; the Ἔκφρασις is preserved only in the codex Palatinus between Books 14 and 15 of the *Anthology* (cf. *Anth. Gr.* 15.1), ed. P. Friedländer, *Johannes* 135ff. The baths and painting in question were located in Gaza, according to the inscr. and subscr. of the Ἔκφρασις and a marginal note at the beginning of the poem; a note added to the subscr. says ἢ ἐν Ἀντιοχείᾳ, apparently referring to the representation of the cosmos that has been discovered at Antioch, on which see Downey, "John of Gaza" 205ff. Since the work at Antioch is a mosaic (s.IV 1/2, on archaeological grounds), whereas I. appears to have described a painting (cf. P. Friedländer, *Johannes* 220ff.), and since I.'s description differs in several respects from the Antiochene piece, the two must have been different works; the mosaic at Antioch was perhaps the model for the painting at Gaza.

Beyond the title γραμματικός, the lemmata of two of the anacreontic pieces show that I. was a teacher; see Nissen, *Byzantinische Anakreonten* 13ff. These ascribe the poems to the spring festival Rosalia—ἐν τῇ ἡμέρᾳ τῶν ῥόδων—and place the poems in the context of I.'s school: no. 5, ἐν τῇ ἑαυτοῦ διατριβῇ (cf. the address to the παῖδες, vv. 37ff.); no. 4, μετὰ τὸ εἰπεῖν τοὺς φοιτητάς, apparently referring to the students' recitation of display pieces of the type (also in anacreontics) found in Pack² 1945 = PLaur. 2.49 Hermopolis (s.V). For students' compositions, cf. the titt. of Dracont. *Rom.* 1, 3; and cf. s.v. Felicianus, no. 59. For school festivals or holidays at Gaza, cf. Choric. *Apol. mim.* 104 (p. 368.8ff. Foerster-Richtsteig).

The evidence does not allow us to date I. precisely. A *term. p. q.* of 526/36 for the Ἔκφρασις has been deduced from certain passages in Choricius; cf. Seitz, "Schule" 33f.; P. Friedländer, *Johannes* 111. But this is by no means certain: the baths, with the paintings, may well have been older, and it is not necessary to tie I.'s poem to their construction or dedication; cf. Downey, "John of Gaza" 211 n. 25. The influence of Nonnus found in the Ἔκφρασις, however (cf. P. Friedländer, *Johannes* 112ff.; Wifstrand, *Von Kallimachos zu Nonnos* 19, 24, 62, 73), suggests a date ca. s.V ex. / s.VI 1/2, and the metrical technique of the anacreontic pieces may point in the same direction; see Nissen, *Byzantinische Anakreonten* 19ff.; and cf. s.v. Georgius, no. 63.

If the latter dating is correct, I. would have been a contemporary of Choricius (cf. above) and could be the unnamed encomiastic poet referred to at Choric. *Laud. Summ.* 2 (p. 70.6ff.); cf. ibid. 21 (p. 75.14f.). Two of the anacreontic pieces apparently derive from comparable occasions, when I. produced poems for prominent men: cf. the lemma of no. 2, λόγος εἰς τὸν ὑπερφυέστατον Ζαχαρίαν τὸν Δοῦκα τὸν Ἀσκαλωνίτην. ἔχει δέ τινα καὶ εἰς τὸν μεγαλοπρεπέστατον Ζαχαρίαν τὸν Γαζαῖον παρόντα τῇ ἀκροάσει; and the lemma of no. 3, ἐπιθαλάμιος σχεδιασθεὶς εἰς τὸν θαυμασιώτατον Ἀνατόλιον Φαύστου τὰ πρῶτα φέροντα Γάζης. Identification with the gramm. Ioannes, author of *Anth. Gr.* 9.628 and possibly 629, from the Cycle of Agathias, has also been suggested; cf. Cameron and Cameron, "Further Thoughts"; and cf. s.v. Ioannes, no. 84.

+ 84. IOANNES. Gramm. Alexandria(?) Before ca. 568.

Ioannes γραμματικός: according to the lemmata, author of *Anth. Gr.* 9.628 (on the Horse Baths at Alexandria, if the lemma can be trusted) and 629, both from the Cycle of Agathias, thus earlier than ca. 568; for the date, see Cameron and Cameron, "Cycle" 6ff.; differently Baldwin, "Four Problems" 298ff., and "Date." *Anth. Gr.* 9.629 recurs in the codex Palatinus after 9.680, where it is attributed to John Barbucallus, i.e., John the Poet. If that is an error, and if the two Johns are distinct (cf. Cameron and Cameron, "Cycle" 12), I. may be the poet and gramm. Ioannes (q.v., no. 83) of Gaza, as suggested by Cameron and Cameron, "Further Thoughts." But the difficulty involved in establishing the latter's date (cf. s.v.) and the number of gramm. with this most common of names make the identification necessarily uncertain.

IOANNES CHARAX: see s.v. CHARAX, no. 199.

IOANNES LYDUS: see s.v. LYDUS, no. 92.

IOANNES PHILOPONUS: see s.v. PHILOPONUS, no. 118.

85. ISOCASIUS. Gramm. → sophist → *QSP*. Aegeae (Cilicia) → Antioch → Constantinople. s.V 2/4–3/4.

RE 9.2146 (Seeck); *PLRE* II s.v., pp. 633f.

Originally from Aegeae in Cilicia: John Malalas 369.18f. Dindorf; *Chron. Pasch.* 1.595.7f. Dindorf; and cf. below. He later was a citizen of Antioch: Malal. 369.19; *Chron. Pasch.* 1.595.8f.; cf. Theoph. *Chron.* p. 115.9ff. de Boor; Cedrenus 1.612.21 Bekker. According to the *acta* of the synod of Ephesus of 449 (ed. J. Flemming, *Abhandlungen der Königlichen Gesellschaft der Wissenschaften zu Göttingen, Philologisch-historische Klasse*, n.s., 15.1 [1917] 127.14ff.), he was at Antioch by 441/42, when, although still a pagan, he allegedly helped contrive the ordination of the bishop Domnus (441/42–449).

According to the author of the *Vie et miracles de Sainte Thècle*, he was a gramm. before becoming a sophist: [Basil. Sel.] *Vie et miracles* 2.39 Dagron, ἀπὸ γραμματιστοῦ [on the term here, see Appendix 2.2a–b] σοφιστὴς γεγονώς. A nonbeliever, he fell ill at Aegeae, where a cure was revealed to him by incubation at the shrine of St. Thecla. He persisted in his ἀπιστία nonetheless; cf. above and below. The author of the *Vie et miracles* alleges a certain Eudocius of Tarsus, a man ἀληθείας μηδὲν μᾶλλον πρεσβεύων, as his source.

As a σοφιστής, presumably at Antioch, I. received five letters from Theodoret of Cyrrhus: *Ep.* XXVII, XXVIII, XXXVIII, XLIV, LII ed. Azéma, vol. 1; for the date of *Ep.* XLIV, perhaps before 446, cf. Azéma, ed., p. 108 n. 1. Theodoret sent him pupils (*Ep.* XXVII, XXVIII; cf. XLIV), and a woodcarver to decorate his home (*Ep.* XXXVIII), and requested that he intercede with the court of the praetorian prefect in behalf of a young heir burdened by taxes (*Ep.* LII). I. is also called ὁ φιλόσοφος at Malal. 369.18, *Chron. Pasch.* 595.6, Theoph. *Chron.* p. 115.9ff. de Boor, and Cedrenus 1.612.21f.; he is called σφόδρα λογικός at Malal. 370.1f. and *Chron. Pasch.* 595.9f.

Said to have held many offices with honor (Malal. 370.1; *Chron. Pasch.* 595.9), I. was *QSP* under Leo (Malal. 369.17f.). While *quaestor* he was denounced as a pagan: Malal. 369.17ff.; placed s.a. 467 in *Chron. Pasch.* 595.6ff.; in the eleventh year of Leo, 467/68, by Theophanes, *Chron.* p. 115.9f. de Boor; in the tenth year, 466/67, by Cedrenus, 1.612.21. Arrested at Constantinople and stripped of his office, he was sent for interrogation to Theophilus, governor of Bithynia, at Chalcedon: Malal. 370.2ff.; *Chron. Pasch.* 595.11ff. Through the intervention of Iacobus, *comes* and *archiatros* (= Iacobus 3 *PLRE* II, pp. 582f.), his case was returned for hearing at Constantinople before the senate and *PPO*: Malal. 370.5ff.; *Chron. Pasch.* 595.14ff.; cf. Theoph. *Chron.* p. 115.10ff. de Boor; Cedrenus 1.613.1 says παρὰ τῷ ἐπάρχῳ Κωνσταντινουπόλεως, incorrectly. When I. was questioned by the prefect Pusaeus (= *PLRE* II s.v., p. 930), his humility and candor won him the favor of the multitude and his freedom: Malal. 370.16ff.; *Chron. Pasch.* 596.3ff. After being forcibly baptized (Malal. 371.2ff.; cf. *Chron. Pasch.* 596.12), he was sent back "to his own country," presumably to Antioch: Malal. 371.4; *Chron. Pasch.* 596.12; Theoph. *Chron.* p. 115.17f. de Boor; Cedrenus 1.613.7.

86. IUCUNDUS. Gramm. Bordeaux. s.IV 1/2 or 2/3.

PLRE I s.v., p. 467.

Iucundus (Auson. *Prof.* 9 tit., v. 4), *grammaticus* (ibid. tit., v. 2) at Bordeaux (tit.). He was the brother of another gramm. of Bordeaux, Leontius (q.v., no. 89) Lascivus: *Prof.* 9 tit. I. probably taught as a contemporary of Ausonius, who calls him *amicus* and *sodalis* (cf. s.v. Citarius, no. 28), therefore between ca. 336 and ca. 367. His brother was older than Ausonius and was perhaps dead by 355/60; cf. s.v. Leontius.

I. was thought unqualified for the chair he occupied (vv. 1-2), an opinion with which Ausonius evidently agreed: vv. 5-6, *quamvis impar* vs.

meritos . . . viros; compare the language used to describe I.'s brother's attainments in *Prof.* 7.9–19 (below, s.v. Leontius).

* 87. L. TERENTIUS IULIANUS *signo* CONCOR[DIUS]. Gramm.; *v.p.*
Trier. s.III / s.IV.

L̞. Terentius Iulianus *qui et* Concor[dius], commemorated on an epitaph at Trier; cf. Cüppers and Binsfeld, "Zweiseitig beschriftete Grabplatte"; Schillinger-Häfele, "Vierter Nachtrag" 453. Styled *v(ir) p(erfectissimus)*, *magister s[t]udiorum, grammaticus Latinus* (lines 7–8); the end of his *signum* and his rank, *v.p.*, restored by Schillinger-Häfele, in tacit correction of Cüppers and Binsfeld, "Zweiseitig beschriftete Grabplatte" 136 n. 5. For his status as teacher, cf. lines 4–5 in the text of Schillinger-Häfele, *doctor Rom[ani n]ob[ilis] eloqu[i]i*. I. is dated to s.III by Cüppers and Binsfeld, "Zweiseitig beschriftete Grabplatte" 138; the stone is dated to s. IV by Schillinger-Häfele.

Despite the fact that I. seems to have possessed the perfectissimate, the style *magister studiorum, grammaticus Latinus* is probably a designation of his *condicio* (for *condicio*, cf. *Gesta apud Zenophilum, CSEL* 26.185.9f., and below s.v. Victor, no. 161, *professor . . . Romanarum litterarum, grammaticus Latinus*; for *magister studiorum*, cf. s.v. Annius Namptoius, no. 103) rather than a reference to the equestrian secretariat *a studiis* or *magister a studiis* or *magister studiorum*. Cf. Schillinger-Häfele, "Vierter Nachtrag" 453; the form of the title *magister studiorum* is securely attested only for the last man known to have held the secretariat, C. Caelius Saturninus (under Constantius I?); cf. *PLRE* I s.v. Saturninus 9, p. 806.

I. was presumably not a Christian; cf. *D(is) M(anibus)* in line 1 and the absence of Christian formulas throughout. If I. was active at the beginning of s.IV, and if the restoration of his *signum* is correct, he is possibly the Concordius (q.v., no. 35) who Ausonius says left Bordeaux to teach elsewhere.

88. IULIUS. Gramm. Antioch. Died 355/56.

RE 10.107 (Seeck); Chr.-Sch.-St. 2:2.1075 n. 4; Seeck, *Briefe* 193; Petit, *Étudiants* 86; *PLRE* I s.v. 1, p. 481.

Iulius, a gramm. whose death is mentioned in Lib. *Ep.* 454.4 (an. 355/56), Ἰούλιος δὲ ὁ γραμματιστὴς ὑπὸ λύπης οἴχεται; Libanius normally uses γραμματιστής in the sense of γραμματικός (cf. Appendix 2). Since Libanius seems to be informing his uncle Phasganius of matters affecting his own school—ibid., τὰ δὲ περὶ τοὺς νέους τὰ μὲν ἄλλα ᾗ πρὸ τοῦ, Ἰούλιος δὲ κτλ—I. probably taught in that establishment; cf. s.vv. Calliopius, Cleobulus, nos. 25, 32; for gramm. having a place in Libanius's school, see Petit, *Étudiants* 85ff.

*   LEONTIUS: see no. 234.

89. LEONTIUS *signo* LASCIVUS.   Gramm.   Bordeaux.   Born before 310;
    dead probably by 355/60.

    RE 12.2052 (Tolkiehn); *PLRE* I s.v. Leontius 17, p. 502.

    Leontius . . . cognomento Lascivus, Auson. *Prof.* 7 tit.; Leontius, ibid. vv. 3, 16;
    Lascivus, vv. 5–8, an incongruous nickname that tickled his friends'
    fancy. Brother of Iucundus (q.v., no. 86): *Prof.* 9 tit. A gramm. (*Prof.* 7
    tit.) whose achievements in letters (ibid. vv. 9–12) were sufficient for a
    "meager chair," *posset insertus numero ut videri / grammaticorum.* The phras-
    ing seems to suggest that he was something of a marginal figure; cf. the
    case of his brother Iucundus, s.v. Since he was the brother of Iucundus
    (*Prof.* 9 tit., *Burdigalensis*) and a companion of Ausonius's *iuventa* (see
    below), and since he is not said to have taught elsewhere, he must in
    accordance with *Prof.* 20.1–2 have taught at Bordeaux.

    L. was older than Ausonius (*Prof.* 7.14), who calls him *meae semper socius
    iuventae.* If this is limiting—i.e., *socius* when Ausonius was a *iuvenis,* but
    not later—the *term. a. q.* of his death would be ca. 355/60, when Ausonius
    was forty-five or fifty years old, the lower and upper limits, respectively,
    in the traditional reckoning of when one ceased to be a *iuvenis*; cf. Cens.
    Die nat. 14.2; Isidore of Seville *Etym.* 11.2.1–8. He probably did not begin
    to teach at Bordeaux much before ca. 325; Ausonius does not suggest
    that the association extended back to his *pueritia* or that L. had been his
    teacher. His teaching career would therefore have fallen mainly in s.IV
    2/4, and he would have been Ausonius's companion during the first two-
    thirds (ca. 336/37–ca. 355) of the latter's tenure at Bordeaux.

    Identification of L. with the Leontius whose name can be made out in
    a fragmentary verse inscription (epitaph?) found in the vicinity of
    Bordeaux, *CIL* 13.911 (Loupiac), is very uncertain.

+ 90. LOLLIANUS *signo* HOMOEUS.   Gramm.   Oxyrhynchus.   253/60.

    PCollYoutie 66, ed. Parsons (page numbers below refer to the discussion
    of Parsons there) = *POxy.* 47.3366 = Pap.

    Lollianus ὁ καὶ Ὅμοιος: Pap. A5, B35, C44. Son of Apolloni...: Pap. B35.
    Municipal gramm. (δημόσιος γραμματικός, Pap. A5–6, B29; cf. A12, C53)
    of Oxyrhynchus, with an appointment from the βουλή: Pap. B28–29.
    The documents that concern him date from the reign of Valerian and
    Gallienus (Pap. A2–3, C41–42), perhaps 258 or 259; cf. Parsons, p. 419.

    L. drew a municipal salary (σύνταξις), which was set in cash but paid
    spottily in kind (Pap. B29–30). Because of the irregular payments, L.
    requested the use of public lands (an orchard), the rents on which would
    serve as his salary (Pap. B31–34, C61–68); Parsons, pp. 413f., compares

the similar arrangement proposed at Antioch by Libanius in behalf of his assistants (*Or.* 31). L.'s salary was 2,000 *dr.* (per annum?), whereas the orchard was expected to bring in 2,400 *dr.*; cf. Pap. B34, C65. L. addressed his appeal not to the βουλή but directly to the emperors—Pap. A and C are drafts of his petition—with vague reference to the precedent for imperial intervention allegedly established by earlier emperors in such circumstances; cf. Pap. A12–16, C50–56(?). On the procedure L. followed and the doubtful strength of his argument from precedent, cf. Parsons, pp. 416f., 441ff. At the same time, L. wrote a letter (= Pap. B) to an unnamed friend at court whom he calls "brother" (Pap. B23), asking him to use his influence to secure a favorable decision and an unambiguous response; cf. Pap. B36–37. Note that this was the third letter L. had written to the "brother" on this matter; cf. Pap. B23. The would-be patron had perhaps ignored the two prior requests.

L. was married, with children (Pap. B22–23, 28). He calls himself σχολαστικός: Pap. B36, ὑπὲρ σχολαστικοῦ καὶ φίλου. The term is evidently still used at this date in the general sense, "educated man," "scholar"; for similar usage in a comparable context, see *PSI* 13.1337.23, with Claus, "ΣΧΟΛΑΣΤΙΚΟΣ" 43f. The draft of the letter to his patron (Pap. B) may be in L.'s own hand.

91. LUPERCUS. Gramm. Berytus. Born or *floruit* shortly before 268/70. *RE* 13.1839–41 (Gudeman); Chr.-Sch.-St. 2:2.889; *PLRE* I s.v. 1, p. 519.

Lupercus, gramm. of Berytus, whose birth or *floruit* (γεγονώς) is placed shortly before the reign of Claudius ὁ δεύτερος (i.e., Claudius Gothicus) by the *Suda*, Λ.691. His works, listed in the *Suda* (ibid.), include a Κτίσις τοῦ ἐν Αἰγύπτῳ Ἀρσινοήτου, a work on a standing literary puzzle Περὶ τοῦ παρὰ Πλάτωνι ἀλεκτρυόνος, presumably on *Phd.* 118a, and a number of technical works of philology: three books on ἄν, one on ταώς, a Περὶ τῆς καρίδος (on the quantity of the iota?), Ἀττικαὶ λέξεις (noted as a source in the preface to the *Suda*, though the authenticity of the notice is doubtful; see s.v. Eugenius, no. 56), a Τέχνη γραμματική, and thirteen books on the three genders, "in which [ἐν οἷς; the antecedent is controversial] he surpasses the renown of Herodian" (*Suda* Λ.691 *ad fin.*). For a critical review of the catalogue, see Gudeman, *RE* 13.1840.5ff.

Despite those words of praise, his influence on later gramm. appears to have been minimal; for later references to him, see Gudeman, *RE* 13.1840.54ff. and 1841.29ff. His works may, however, have been extant as late as s.XIII ex., when "the sixth of the books of Lupercus" was cited by Planudes (if it is his hand) in a scholium on Plutarch; cf. Paton, "Simonides."

LUXORIUS: see s.v. LUXURIUS, no. 235.

LUXURIUS: see no. 235.

92. IOANNES LYDUS. *Praefectianus, palatinus,* and Lat. gramm. → *com. ord. pr.* Philadelphia (Lydia) → Constantinople. Born 490/91; died 557/61.

RE 13.2210–17 (Klotz); *RE* Suppl. 12.521–23 (Carney); Chr.-Sch.-St. 2:2.1041–44; Stein, *Histoire* 2.729ff., 838ff.; Carney, *Bureaucracy* 2.3ff.; Bandy, *Ioannes* ix–xxxviii; Hunger 1.250f., 2.427f.; *PLRE* II s.v. Ioannes 75, pp. 612ff. (The accounts of Klotz and Chr.-Sch.-St. are worthless for L.'s career; some of their errors are repeated in the more recent study of Tsirpanlis, "John Lydos." The best brief account remains that of Stein.)

Ἰωάννης (ὁ) Λυδός: *Suda* I.465; Leo *Tactic. epilog.* 67, *PG* 107.1092B; Const. Porph. *De them.* I, p. 63.78 Pertusi; anon. *ap.* Cramer *Anecd. Oxon.* 3.187.4ff.; cod. Vat. 1202 chartac. (excerpt of *De ostent.*). Also ὁ Λυδός, Theophylact. Simocatt. *Hist.* 7.16, p. 186.21 Bekker. Also Ἰωάννης: Justinian *ap.* Ioan. Lyd. *De mag.* 3.29; Hephaestus ibid. 3.30. The inscr. Ἰωάννου Λαυρεντίου (τοῦ) Λυδοῦ appears in some mss (cf. *De ostent.* ed. Wachsmuth, p. xiv; *De mens.* ed. Wünsch, pp. xvi–xvii) and in Phot. *Bibl.* cod. 180 (2.187 Henry). The second name is probably that of I.'s father, i.e., Ἰωάννης Λαυρεντίου (ὁ) Λυδός; cf. Chr.-Sch.-St. 2:2.1041.

Bureaucrat, antiquarian, and poet. Born 490/91 (see below) in Lydian Philadelphia: *De mag.* 3.26, ἐκ τῆς ἐνεγκούσης με Φιλαδελφείας τῆς ὑπὸ Τμώλῳ ἐν Λυδίᾳ κειμένης; cf. ibid. 3.58, 59; *De ostent.* 53; *De mens.* 4.2. Cf. Φιλαδελφεύς: *Suda* I.465; Phot. *Bibl.* cod. 180 (2.187 Henry); some mss of L.'s works (see the edd.); Const. Porph. *De them.* I, p. 63.78 Pertusi.

L. left his birthplace in 511, when he was in his twenty-first year: *De mag.* 3.26, ἕνα καὶ εἰκοστὸν τῆς ἡλικίας ἄγων ἐνιαυτὸν ἐπὶ τῆς Σεκουνδιανοῦ ὑπατείας. He intended to obtain a place as *memorialis* in the palatine service at Constantinople: ibid., παρῆλθον εἰς ταύτην ⟨τὴν⟩ εὐδαίμονα πόλιν· καὶ . . . ἐπὶ τοὺς μεμοριαλίους τῆς αὐλῆς συνεῖδον ἐλθεῖν. While awaiting an appointment, he read Aristotle and Plato with Agapius, a pupil of Proclus (ibid.). He soon received a position, though not the one he had expected. Under the influence of his patron and fellow Philadelphian the *PPO* Zoticus, L. was "forced" probably late in 511 or very early in 512 to become an *exceptor,* a shorthand clerk, in the praetorian *officium* (ibid.); his cousin Ammianus was already enrolled among the *exceptores.* This shift from his initial ambition was not of great consequence for the early part of his career, in which L. can be seen now to have combined and now to have chosen between posts in the central (palatine) administration and in the *officium* of the praetorian prefect, i.e., in the αὐλή and in the στρατεία. Within a year, still during Zoticus's prefecture, L. made a brilliant start in the civil division of the judicial branch in the praetorian *officium* (ibid. 3.27), being chosen by the assistants of the *ab actis* to become one of the three πρῶτοι χαρτυλάριοι. (On the gradations within the *officium*, see Jones, *LRE* 587ff.; Morosi, *"Officium"* 103ff.) At the same time he drafted *suggestiones* to the senate and served as an *exceptor* in the sacred consistory, where he was soon being groomed for the palatine secretariat *a secretis*: *De mag.* 3.27, ἐπεσηκρήτευον παρὰ τοῖς ταχυγράφοις, ἔτι καὶ βοηθῶν ἑτέροις ἐν τῷ τεμένει τῆς δίκης ταχυγραφοῦσιν, ὃ καλεῖται σήκρητον, . . . ἔνθεν ὥσπερ ἀναπτερωθεὶς ἐπὶ τοὺς λεγομένους ἃ σηκρήτις τῆς αὐλῆς ἐπειγόμην.

L. decided, however, to withdraw from the αὐλή and to concentrate all his energies in his service as *praefectianus* (ibid. 3.28). His progress there can be traced through his service as *chartularius* to the *commentariensis*; cf. ibid. 3.17, where the text must be corrupt: although as *chartularius* to the *commentariensis* L. would have had a higher rank than in his initial post with the *ab actis*, the passage as it stands appears to date this service to a time when L. could have been only about fifteen years old; cf. Stein, *Histoire* 2.838 n. 4. L. also describes his dealings with the prefect Phocas (an. 532), although it cannot be said in what capacity: *De mag.* 3.73; cf. s.v. Speciosus, no. 138. But L. came to hate the στρατεία and resolved to devote himself entirely to his books (ibid. 3.28). This decision was probably made sometime during the second prefecture of John the Cappadocian (532–41), who is the object of much abuse on L.'s part. The passage in which L. states his reasons is obscure: τῶν οὖν κοινῶν τοιούτων ἀποτελεσθέντων ἐπὶ πᾶσιν, ὁποίων ὁ λόγος ἐμνημόνευσε, καὶ τὸ λοιπὸν τοῖς λογικοῖς, <οὐχ> ὡς τὸ πρίν, τῆς τύχης ἀπαρεσκομένης, ἐμίσησα τὴν στρατείαν. A comma should be placed before (so now the text of Bandy) rather than after the <οὐχ>, and the passage should be understood as follows: "When in all respects public affairs [τὰ κοινά] had been brought to such a state as this account has recorded, and when in addition fortune was showing disfavor to men of literary attainments—something that had not happened before—I came to hate the service." The passage would thus be in line with L.'s other complaints about the state of the service under John, particularly the loss of prestige suffered by men with literary training; cf. esp. *De mag.* 2.17, 21; 3.65–66, 68.

Nonetheless, L. gained or retained the favor of Justinian, who allowed L. to deliver an encomium of him (ibid. 3.28), presumably in verse: cf. Justinian's praise of L.'s ἐν ποιητικοῖς χάριν, ibid. 3.29. Further, Justinian invited L. to compose a history of his campaign at Daras (ibid. 3.28) and appointed L. to a post as a Latin gramm. in the Capitoline school. On the appointment and status, see ibid. 3.29, Justinian's directive to the praetorian prefect: Ἰωάννῃ τῷ λογιωτάτῳ πολλὴν μὲν σύνισμεν τὴν ἐν λόγοις παιδείαν τήν τε ἐν γραμματικοῖς ἀκρίβειαν τήν τε ἐν ποιητικοῖς χάριν καὶ τὴν ἄλλην αὐτοῦ πολυμάθειαν. . . . ἴστω δὲ ὁ εἰρημένος σοφώτατος ἀνήρ, ὡς . . . ἀξιώμασι καὶ ἱεραῖς μείζοσι φιλοτιμίαις τιμήσομεν αὐτόν, . . . ἐπαίνοντες αὐτόν, εἰ καὶ πολλοῖς ἑτέροις τῆς οὔσης αὐτῷ μεταδοίη παρασκεύης (see further below). For Latin as the language of his instruction, cf. Justinian's reference to L.'s labors with ἡ ῾Ρωμαίων φωνή (ibid.).

Justinian's actions cannot be dated with great precision—after 532, or after 540 (cf. Carney, *Bureaucracy* 2.10 n. 13), depending on which campaign at Daras is meant; probably before 543: see below on the dedication to Gabriel the city prefect. But L. gives the impression that they came in quick succession. The last guaranteed that L. could devote himself to his books while remaining nominally enrolled in the στρατεία, retaining his seniority and claims to promotion; cf. again Justinian's statement at *De mag.* 3.29, Ἰωάννῃ . . . σύνισμεν . . . , καίτοι τῆς στρατείας αὐτῷ τῆς ἐν τοῖς δικαστηρίοις τῆς σῆς ὑπεροχῆς [= the *PPO*] ὀρθῶς φερομένης, ἑλέσθαι μετ' αὐτῆς καὶ τὸν ἐν βιβλίοις ἀσκῆσαι βίον καὶ ὅλον ἑαυτὸν ἀναθεῖναι τοῖς λόγοις; see also L.'s own remarks ibid. *ad fin.*, καὶ [sc. Ἰουστινιανοῦ] τόπον διδασκάλοις ἀπονενεμημένον ἀφορίσαντός μοι ἐπὶ τῆς Καπιτωλίδος [cf. s.v. Cledonius, no. 31] αὐλῆς, ἐχόμενος τῆς στρατείας ἐπαίδευον. The post as gramm. was evidently no mere sinecure; cf. L.'s own statement, ibid. 3.29, ἐπαίδευον; see also the reference to his pupils made by the prefect Hephaestus when L. retired from the στρατεία, ibid. 3.30, πολλοὺς ἑτέρους, οἳ δὴ τῆς αὐτοῦ διδασκαλίας ἔργον γεγόνασι. It is therefore likely that he was in effect an absentee *praefectianus* for all or part of the latter years of his career, a suggestion borne out by L.'s statement (ibid. 3.30 init.) that toward the end of his service he received the salary but not the fees associated with the στρατεία. Such payment was the regular lot of the absentee; cf. Jones, *LRE* 605.

It seems clear in any case that L. was eventually promoted through all the grades of the *officium*; cf. L.'s references to his reaching retirement, *De mag.* 3.30, παρὰ μέντοι τῆς στρατείας βαθμῶν τε καὶ πόρων ἄνευ τινὸς ἐλαττώσεως . . . ἐπὶ τὸ πέρας τῆς στρατείας ἀνῆλθον and τυχὼν τοῦ εἰωθότος παρὰ τῆς βασιλείας ἀξιώματος τοῖς πληροῦσιν ἐπιδίδοσθαι; with Hephaestus's reference to his service, ibid., τοὺς ἐν τοῖς ἡμετέροις δικαστηρίοις βαθμούς τε καὶ πόνους διανύσας. L. finally retired from the στρατεία after forty years and four months (ibid. 3.30 *ad fin.*; cf. also 3.67)—i.e., probably ca. April 552—as *cornicularius*, with the ranks of *tribunus et notarius (vacans)* and *comes ordinis primi*; cf. esp. ibid. 3.4, 24–25; and Stein, *Histoire* 2.731. The latest references in the *De mag.* suggest that he died sometime between 557 and 561; cf. Stein, *Histoire* 2.839f.

Probably beginning before his retirement (see above and following), L. composed the *De mensibus* and the *De ostentis*, and, after his retirement, the *De magistratibus*. The three were read and excerpted by Photius, *Bibl.* cod. 180 (2.187ff. Henry); the first two are listed in the *Suda*, I.465, which refers to ἄλλων τινῶν ὑποθέσεων μαθηματικῶν but not specifically to the *De mag.* The *Suda*, ibid., says that L. dedicated these (ταῦτα) to

Γαβριηλίῳ τινὶ ὑπάρχῳ, presumably the city prefect Gabriel (cf. *De mag.* 3.38), himself a poet (cf. *Anth. Gr.* 16.208), whose prefecture of 543 (Stein, *Histoire* 2.441 n. 4) was celebrated by Leontius Scholasticus in *Anth. Gr.* 16.32. Gabriel's prefecture thus provides a *term. a. q.* for when L. came to hate the στρατεία and devoted himself to his books. In addition to the encomium of Justinian (see above), L. wrote a brief encomium of his early patron, Zoticus, for which he was rewarded at the rate of one *solidus* per line (*De mag.* 3.27).

L. remarks (ibid.) that during the brief prefecture of Zoticus, while still an *exceptor*, he was able to make no less than 1,000 *solidi*. As *chartularius* in the *scrinium* of the *ab actis*, L. received a salary of 24 *solidi* per year. The opportunity for extraordinary income was considerable; cf. his use of the euphemism παραμυθία, ibid., and his remarks ibid. 3.24–25. At the prompting of L.'s cousin Ammianus, Zoticus had provided L. with a wife, who in turn provided a dowry of 100 lb. of gold (*De mag.* 3.28, ἑκατὸν . . . χρυσίου λιτρῶν φερνήν). If it could be inferred from *De mag.* 3.26 that all L.'s prior education had taken place in Philadelphia, then that city could be added to the list of places in the East where instruction in Latin was available.

From L.'s works Photius, *Bibl.* cod. 180 (2.181 Henry), concluded that he was a pagan, probably incorrectly; cf. esp. *De mag.* 3.73 *fin.* and 3.74, L.'s concern to demonstrate the εὐσέβεια of Phocas; and cf. the judgment of Carney, *RE* Suppl. 12.523.5ff., with *Bureaucracy* 2.49f. n. 11. Bandy, *Ioannes* xvi, claims that L.'s "appointment to the university required a religion test"; but it is not clear what that statement means or on what evidence it is based.

93. MACRINUS. Gramm. Bordeaux. s.IV 1/4.
PLRE I s.v. 1, p. 529.

Macrinus (Auson. *Prof.* 10.11), Latin gramm. (ibid. tit.; cf. vv. 5–10) at Bordeaux (ibid. tit.), the first teacher of Ausonius (ibid. 12–13); since Ausonius was born ca. 310, M. was active in s.IV 1/4.

MANIPPUS or MARSIPUS: see s.v. MANIPPUS, no. 236.

94. MARCELLUS. Gramm. Bordeaux → Narbo. s.IV med.?
RE 14.1492 (Ensslin); *PLRE* I s.v. 4, p. 551.

Marcellus (*Prof.* 18 tit., v. 1), son of Marcellus (ibid.); a gramm. (ibid. tit., vv. 7–8, 13–14) who taught at Narbo (ibid. 4–8) after leaving his *patria*, i.e., Bordeaux (cf. *Prof.* 20.1–2; and cf. s.v. Concordius, no. 35). There is no indication of his date, though like all the other subjects of the *Prof.* he was dead by the time the poems were composed. If Ausonius speaks of the scandal (see below) from firsthand knowledge, then M. presumably dates to s.IV med.; but that is not certain.

Driven from Bordeaux by his mother, M. was received at Narbo, where he married the daughter of the *nobilis* Clarentius, who is said to have been impressed by M.'s *indoles egregia* (ibid. 5–6). He acquired *grammatici nomen divitiasque* (ibid. 7–8); but because of his *pravum ingenium* he was ruined in a scandal, which Ausonius forbears to retail (ibid. 9–12; cf. s.v. Herculanus, no. 70). Ausonius places him *inter grammaticos praetenuis meriti* (ibid. 14).

NONIUS MARCELLUS: see no. 237.

MARCIANUS: see no. 238.

95. MARTYRIUS.   Lat. gramm.   Sardis?   Before 580; s.VI 1/2 – med.?

RE 14.2041–43 (Wessner); Sch.-Hos. 4:2.219; *PLRE* II s.v. 6, p. 732.

M.'s treatise on *b* and *v* bears the attribution *Adamantii sive Martyrii* in the mss used by Keil; Cassiodorus calls him both "Adamantius Martyrius" (*De orth.*, *GL* 7.147.8, 167.1, 178.10, 193.8; *Inst.* 1.30.2; cf. also Manitius, *Handschriften* 267) and "Martyrius" (*De orth.*, *GL* 7.143.9ff., 185.9). From the preface to the treatise, *GL* 7.165.13f., *hoc commentario nostro acceptis seminibus ab Adamantio meo patre*, it is clear that the author was Martyrius, son of Adamantius (q.v., no. 2).

He is styled *grammaticus* in an *explicit* (*GL* 7.178.14) in cod. Monac. 766, the copy of an *antiquissimus codex* made by Politian in 1491; cf. Keil, *GL* 7.136. This is not solid evidence in itself, but note that his father was a *doctor . . . elocutionis Latinae*: *GL* 7.165.14f. He is called *Sardianus* in the same *explicit* (see also below); he clearly knew Greek.

M. is to be dated certainly after Herodian, to whom he refers at *GL* 7.166.13f. His use of the name "Valentinianus" in an example at *GL* 7.173.1 (bracketed by Keil), like his own name, suggests a date not earlier than s.IV / s.V. At *GL* 7.175.9ff. he refers to the opinion of a certain Memnonius on the correct spelling of *berna* (vs. *verna*): *illustris memoriae audivi Memnonium, omnis hominem facundiae iudicem, se dicentem de hoc reprehensum a Romano quodam disertissimo*. Bücheler, "Coniectanea" 330f., identified this Memnonius *facundiae iudex* with the father of Agathias, Memnonius ῥήτωρ ἐξ Ἀσίης—specifically, Myrina: *Anth. Gr.* 7.552, with Agathias, *Hist.* praef. 14, p. 6.10 Keydell; cf. also Michael the Grammarian, *Anth. Gr.* 16.316. The identification is attractive, esp. if M.'s designation as *Sardianus* is correct. The treatise could then be dated sometime after 534/35: Agathias was born ca. 531/32 (for the date, see McCail, "Earthquake" 241ff.; Averil Cameron, *Agathias* 1f., with 138f.); Memnonius survived his wife, who died when Agathias was three years old (*Anth. Gr.* 7.552.3–8), i.e., 534/35; but the Memnonius known to M., *illustris memoriae . . . Memnonius*, was dead by the time M. wrote. Against the identification one can adduce the evident belief of Cassiodorus that "Adamantius Martyrius" was one of the *orthographi antiqui*: so *Inst.* 1.30.2; cf. *De orth.* praef., *GL* 7.147.8ff., where M., along with the other men listed there, is implicitly distinguished from Priscian, the *modernus auctor*. But Cassiodorus may be no more reliable concerning M.'s date than he is concerning his name; cf. esp. s.v. Eutyches, no. 57, for Cassiodorus's error concerning the date of Priscian's pupil; and cf. s.v. Phocas, no. 121. M. can at any rate be dated before ca. 580, the date of the *De orth.* and of the revision of the *Inst.*

M.'s treatise on *b* and *v* was excerpted by Cassiodorus (*GL* 7.167–99) and has been transmitted independently (*GL* 7.165–99).

96. MAXIMUS.   Gramm.   Madaurus.   s.IV 2/2-ex.

RE 14.2571 (Wendel); *PLRE* I s.v. 28, p. 585; *Prosop. chrét.* I s.v. 3, pp. 733f.

Maximus, gramm. of Madaurus who corresponded with Augustine: inscr. and subscr. of Aug. *Ep.* 16, 17. The letters are to be dated ca. 390, by which time M. was a *senex*: *Ep.* 16.4; cf. ibid. 1, *seniles artus*. The beginning of their correspondence precedes the extant letters; cf. *Ep.* 16.1. It has sometimes been suggested that M. had been Augustine's gramm. at Madaurus in the late 360s; cf. *Conf.* 2.3.5. The suggestion is plausible, although obviously not capable of proof.

After expressing allegiance to a civic-spirited paganism and a belief in a number of *numina* worshiped as the *membra* of a single, highest god (*Ep.* 16.1; cf. 17.1), M. goes on to condemn the cult of martyrs (*Ep.* 16.2; cf. 17.2) and the exclusivity and secrecy of Christian worship, which he compares unfavorably with the public cult of pagans (*Ep.* 16.3; cf. 17.4). The charges are commonplace in the polemics of this and earlier periods, as are the rebuttals Augustine presents point by point in his heavily sarcastic reply, *Ep.* 17. The correspondents do show some individuality, however, in their concern with and view of local African martyrs (Miggines, Sanames, Namphamon, Lucitas). For a full study of these letters, with text and translation, see now Mastandrea, *Massimo*.

97. MELLEUS.   Schoolmaster.   Centum Cellae.   s.IV 2/2 / s.VI.

Melleus, a *magister ludi*, Christian, dead aged 30: *CIL* 11.3568 = *ILCV* 718 (Centum Cellae).

98. MEMNON.   Teacher of letters.   s.V 1/3.

PLRE II s.v., p. 753.

A γραμματοδιδάσκαλος, addressee of Nil. Ancyr. *Ep.* 2.326, on repentance. The first and last sentences correspond in reverse order to the first two sentences of John Chrysost. *Hom. in seraphim* 6.4, *PG* 56.140; cf. Heussi, *Untersuchungen* 54ff.

99. MENESTHEUS.   Gr. gramm.   Bordeaux.   s.IV 2/4.

RE 15.852 (Ensslin); Martindale, "Prosopography" 249; cf. *PLRE* I s.v. Spercheus, p. 851.

Menestheus (Auson. *Prof.* 8.3), Greek gramm. (ibid. tit., vv. 1–8) at Bordeaux (ibid. tit.). Third in the list of Greek gramm., he did not teach Ausonius (ibid. 1–3, with v. 9); Spercheus (q.v., no. 139), M.'s father (ibid. 2–3), did. M. therefore was probably not yet active in the second decade of s.IV but belonged to the next generation of teachers; cf. ibid. 7, *nostro . . . in aevo.* His career accordingly should be placed ca. s.IV 2/4. Like all the other subjects of the *Prof.,* M. was dead by the time the poems were composed.

With the two other Greek gramm. celebrated in this poem, M. is said to have possessed *sedulum . . . studium docendi, / fructus exilis tenuisque sermo* (ibid. 5–6).

On the teachers of *Prof.* 8, cf. also s.v. Romulus, no. 250.

100. METRODORUS.   Gramm.   Constantinople.   s.V / s.VI?

PLRE II s.v., p. 762.

Metrodorus γραμματικός, author of *Anth. Gr.* 9.712, on a lawyer Ioannes; according to the poem's lemma, Ioannes was ἐν Βυζαντίῳ. Ioannes' name, his profession, and the place combine to suggest a date of s.V / s.VI.

M. may be the gramm. Metrodorus (q.v., no. 101) of Tralles and Constantinople (s.VI 1/3–1/2); he is probably not to be identified either with Metrodorus the author or collector of *Anth. Gr.* 14.116–46 or with Metrodorus the author of *Anth. Gr.* 9.360. The latter was imitated in *Epigr. Bob.* 26 and therefore must be dated before ca. 400; cf. Weinreich's review of Munari, *Gnomon* 31 (1959), 245f.

+ 101. METRODORUS.   Gramm.   Tralles → Constantinople.   s.VI 1/3–1/2.

Gramm.: Agath. *Hist.* 5.6.4 Keydell, ἐν τοῖς καλουμένοις γραμματικοῖς; cf. Appendix 2 *ad fin.* on the phrasing. From a talented family of Tralles— M.'s father, Stephanus, was a physician there (Alexand. Trall. Book 4, Περὶ συνάγχης, vol. 2 p. 139 Puschmann); M.'s brothers were the lawyer and advocate Olympius, the physicians Dioscorus and Alexander, and the architect Anthemius: Agath. *Hist.* 5.6.3ff. According to Agathias, he was a gramm. of some renown and with Anthemius was summoned by the emperor to Constantinople, where they remained the rest of their lives: *Hist.* 5.6.5f., τὸ κλέος ἁπανταχοῦ περιαγόμενον καὶ ἐς αὐτὸν ἀφῖκται τὸν βασιλέα. τοιγάρτοι μετάπεμπτοι ἐν Βυζαντίῳ παραγενόμενοι καὶ αὐτοῦ τὸν λειπόμενον διανύσαντες βίον . . . ὁ μὲν [= M.] νέους πολλοὺς τῶν εὐπατριδῶν ἐκπαιδεύσας καὶ τῆς παγκάλης ἐκείνης μεταδοὺς διδασκαλίας, ὡς καὶ πόθον ἅπασι τὸ μέρος ἐμβαλεῖν τῆς ἀμφὶ τοὺς λόγους ἐπιμελείας. Although it is not clear which emperor is meant, M.'s *floruit* should probably be placed in the first third or first half of s.VI since Anthemius was apparently already at Constantinople when Justinian commissioned him to rebuild St. Sophia in the wake of the Nika Revolt of 532 (cf. Agath. *Hist.* 5.9.2; Procop. *De aed.* 1.1.20ff.) and was long dead when an earthquake damaged St. Sophia in 557: Agath. *Hist.* 5.9.4, ἐκ πλείστου ἐτεθνήκει. On the latter date, see Averil Cameron, *Agathias* 142.

M. is perhaps the otherwise unknown gramm. Metrodorus listed in the catalogue of gramm. in Kröhnert, *Canones* 7, under the heading ὅσοι <περὶ> ἐθνικῶν, or he may be Metrodorus γραμματικός the author of *Anth. Gr.* 9.712 (see s.v., no. 100); he may even be both. He cannot be identified confidently with Metrodorus the author or compiler of *Anth. Gr.* 14.116–46; he is certainly distinct from Metrodorus the author of *Anth. Gr.* 9.360, who is datable before ca. 400: see s.v. Metrodorus, no. 100, *ad fin.*

+   "METRORIUS": see no. 239.

102. MUSAEUS.   Gramm. and poet.   s.V 2/2–3/3.

RE 16.767–69 (Keydell); Chr.-Sch.-St. 2:2.972; Hunger 2.109; PLRE II s.v., p. 768.

Author of Τὰ καθ᾽ Ἡρὼ καὶ Λέανδρον, in hexameters; styled γραμματικός in three mss of s.XIV, but not in the oldest, cod. Barocc. 50, of s.X / s.XI init.; cf. Kost, ed., p. 16.

Later than Nonnus, by whose poetry he was influenced; before the epic poet Col(l)uthus, who probably used him; therefore to be dated s.V 2/2–3/3: cf. Keydell, *RE* 16.767.34ff.; Gelzer, "Bemerkungen" (1967) 133ff., (1968) 11ff.; Kost, ed., pp. 15f., who dates him to 470/510.

Presumably a Christian, since he appears to have known Nonnus's paraphrase of the Gospel of John (cf. Kost, ed., at vv. 19, 42, 138–39, 233, 242, 255, 293, 295), the ps.-Apollinarian Psalter (cf. Golega, *Homerische Psalter* 104), and the poetry of Gregory Nazianzen (cf. Kost, ed., at vv. 17 [p. 159], 173, 274).

He is perhaps the Musaeus who received Procop. Gaz. *Ep.* 147, 165; the identification is proposed most forcefully by Gelzer, "Bemerkungen" (1967) 137ff.; cf. also Minitti Colonna, "De Musaeo" 65ff. It remains no more than plausible.

103. ANNIUS NAMPTOIUS. *Magister studiorum*, jurisconsult, *flamen perpetuus, curator rei publicae.* Thuburbo Maius (Africa Proconsularis). 361.

PLRE I s.v., p. 615; Bassignano, *Flaminato* 169, 170, 172f.; *AE* 1916, 87, 88 (= 20 *bis*) = *ILAfr.* 273a, b = Inscr. a, b.

Annius Namptoius: Inscr. a; Annius Namptoivius, Inscr. b. Styled *fl(a)-m(en) p(er)p(etuus), iurisconsultus, magister studiorum, cur(ator) rei p(ublicae).* Mention of the proconsulship of Clodius Hermogenianus Olybrius (= *PLRE* I s.v. 3, p. 640) dates Inscr. b. to 361; mention of Constantius as emperor dates the inscr. to sometime before November of that year (Constantius died 3 Nov. 361).

The date makes it impossible for *magister studiorum* to refer to the imperial secretariat *a studiis*. N. presumably was a local teacher of liberal studies, with some legal expertise as well (cf. *iurisconsultus;* Lepelley, *Cités de l'Afrique* 2.200 n. 11, has suggested that N. was a professor of law at Carthage). The style *magister studiorum* is not common, but it is found in the nearly contemporary law of Julian on the schools: *CTh* 13.3.5 (an. 362), *magistros studiorum doctoresque excellere oportet moribus primum, deinde facundia;* cf. *CJ* 3.28.37, 1e (an. 531), *magistri studiorum liberalium.* See also esp. s.v. L. Terentius Iulianus, no. 87: *magister studiorum, grammaticus Latinus.*

Since the positions of *flamen perpetuus* and *curator r.p.* are otherwise unexampled in this period for a man of N.'s profession, his holding them is especially noteworthy. On the former title, cf. Bassignano, *Flaminato* 10ff., 371ff.; on the latter, see Lucas, "Notes"; Jones, *LRE* 726ff.; Burton, "Curator." The two titles together imply that N. was a *curialis.*

Similarly unusual is the scale of the undertaking (reconstruction of baths) recorded in Inscr. a and b. Note also that, if N. was a teacher, he appears either not to have received or else to have declined immunity. For the relationship in this period among the *cura civitatum*, curial status, and the *munera*, see *CTh* 12.1.20 (an. 331), with Lucas, "Notes" 62ff.

104. NEBRIDIUS. Assistant gramm. Carthage (environs) → Milan → Carthage. s.IV 2/2; dead by 390?

RE Suppl. 7.550f. (Ensslin); *PLRE* I s.v. 4, p. 620; *Prosop. chrét.* I s.v., pp. 774ff.

Friend and correspondent of Augustine: *Conf.* 4.3.6; 6.10.17, 16.26; 7.2.3, 6.8; 8.6.13; 9.3.6; *Ep.* 3–14 (author of *Ep.* 5, 6, 8; recipient of the rest). He taught as assistant (*Conf.* 8.6.13, *subdoceret*) to the gramm. Verecundus (q.v., no. 159) at Milan; he could have held a better position but did not have the ambition (ibid.). He is almost certainly not the *proscholus grammatici* Augustine refers to at *Serm.* 178.7.8 (see below).

A near contemporary of Augustine, N. followed him to Milan ca. 385: *Conf.* 6.10.17, 8.6.13. He died not long after Augustine's baptism in 387; at the time of his death, probably no later than 390, he was back in Africa: *Conf.* 9.3.6; cf. *Ep.* 5, 10.1.

His family possessed a substantial estate in the vicinity of Carthage: *Conf.* 6.10.17, *rus optimum*.

An intimate of Augustine at the time of the latter's spiritual odyssey, N. had no patience for astrology or Manichaeism: *Conf.* 4.3.6, 6.16.26, 7.2.3, 6.8; cf. *Ep.* 3, and *Ep.* 4–14 *passim*. Not yet a Christian at the time of Augustine's baptism, he had become one, and had converted his entire family in Africa, by the time of his death: *Conf.* 9.3.6.

The *PLRE* regards as probable the identification of N. with a pagan gramm.'s anonymous assistant (*proscholus*) at Milan (= Anonymus 5, no. 171), the hero of an edifying tale Augustine sets during his tenure there: *Serm.* 178.7.8 (*PL* 38.964), *nobis apud Mediolanum constitutis*. This is very likely incorrect. The *proscholus* is described as *plane Christianus*, but N. was not yet a Christian during Augustine's time in Milan (see above); Augustine resigned his chair of rhetoric in autumn 386, was baptized at Easter 387, and left Milan soon after (see s.v., no. 20). Further, the *proscholus* is described as a *pauperrimus homo* who had taken his position out of desperation—*tam pauper ut proscholus esset grammatici*—but this is quite at odds with what we know of N.'s circumstances, esp. his family's *rus optimum* near Carthage (see above); note that at *Conf.* 8.6.13 Augustine says N. did not take his position out of *cupiditas commodorum*. Unless Augustine is embellishing his story, then, N. was not the *proscholus* involved. The identification could be ruled out at once if Clarke, *Higher Education* 27 n. 105, were correct in drawing a sharp distinction between the positions of *subdoctor* and *proscholus*; but the distinction was not everywhere so clear. Cf. also Heraeus, *Kleine Schriften* 93f.

See further s.vv. Verecundus, Anonymus 5, 6, nos. 159, 171, 172.

NEPOS: see no. 240.

105. NEPOTIANUS. Gramm. → rhetorician and provincial governor. Bordeaux. s.III ex.–s.IV 2/2.

RE 16.2513 (Ensslin); Green, "Prosopographical Notes" 23; *PLRE* I s.v. 1, p. 624.

Nepotianus: Auson. *Prof.* 15 tit., v. 4. A gramm. and rhetorician: ibid. tit., *grammatico eidem rhetori*. The phrase should mean "gramm. and also [i.e., subsequently] rhetorician," not "gramm. and at the same time rhetorician," as in, e.g., Marrou, *Histoire*[6] 597 n.1; such simultaneous tenure of teaching positions is unparalleled in the period for Bordeaux. For the same use of *idem*, applied by Ausonius to himself to indicate serial—not concurrent—tenure of teaching positions, see *Epist.* 22. 73. N.'s teaching career was therefore probably comparable to Ausonius's. Cf. *Prof.* 15.10 and 12, where N. is said to have had a rhetorical style second to none and to have rivaled the gramm. Scaurus and Probus; for the latter compliment, cf. s.vv. Harmonius, Staphylius, nos. 65, 140. He is also said to have been a master of logic: ibid. v. 11, *disputator ad Cleanthen Stoicum.*

N. became a provincial governor: ibid. v. 18, *honore gesti praesidiatus inclitus*; the province is not specified. The governorship probably capped his teaching career, as commonly in such cases; since N. was a native of Gaul, his province was more likely in the West than in the East. He is perhaps Nepotianus the *praeses* of Tripolitania known from *AE* 1952, 173 (Lepcis Magna; = Caputo, "Flavius" 234ff.); cf. Guey, "Note"; *PLRE* I s.v. Nepotianus 4, p. 624. If so, his official style thereafter would have been *Fl. Nepotianus, v.p., ex comitibus et praesidibus*, the Flaviate presumably being acquired simultaneously with the governorship; cf. Keenan, "Names" (1973).

An intimate and adviser of Ausonius, who speaks more warmly of N. than of any other gramm. (cf. esp. *Prof.* 15.1–8, 14–17), N. was evidently a friend of Ausonius's mature years; he would therefore probably have been a colleague in his teaching at Bordeaux. Ausonius's use of *sodalis* points in the same direction; cf. s.vv. Citarius, Iucundus, nos. 28, 86. Consequently, his governorship, on the assumption that it followed his teaching, has a likely *term. p. q.* of ca. 336/37, when Ausonius's tenure began at Bordeaux. By that time N. was probably not younger than forty: since he had died, aged ninety (ibid. v. 19), by the time Ausonius wrote the *Prof.*—which was probably completed not very long after 385/86 (the execution of Euchrotia is referred to at *Prof.* 5.35ff.)—N. was born probably not much later than ca. 295. If, however, both his death and the *Prof.* are put as late as possible, his birth could be pushed to ca. 304; but even then, *pace* Caputo, "Flavius" 240f., a date for his governorship later than the death of Valentinian (Nov. 375) is scarcely conceivable; cf. also Appendix 4.

If N. was born ca. 295, he was about fifteen years older than Ausonius. He was probably not a full generation older: Ausonius speaks of him as an older friend or alter ego and does not use metaphors appropriate to a father figure; cf. s.v. Staphylius, no. 140, *ad fin.* He was not, as is sometimes claimed, one of Ausonius's teachers during his schooldays at Bordeaux, from ca. 317 through the mid-320s.

N. was survived by two sons (*Prof.* 15.20), one of whom was perhaps the homonymous bishop of the Arverni in this period; cf. Greg. Tur. *Hist. Franc.* 1.46, with Green, "Prosopographical Notes" 23.

106. NICOCLES. Gramm. Sparta → Constantinople. s.IV 2/3–3/3.
RE 17.352–56 no. 9 (Laquerer), no. 10 (Stegemann); Seeck, *Briefe* 221f.;
Wolf, *Schulwesen* 37ff.; *PLRE* I s.v., p. 630; Bradford, *Prosopography* s.v. 11,
p. 306.

Mentioned in Lib. *Or.* 1.31, 15.27, *Ep.* 557 (the last an. 357); subject or
recipient of *Ep.* 810, 816, 832, 1368, 1383, 1411, 1119 (all an. 363), 1196,
1211, 1265, 1266 (all an. 364), 1487, 1492, 1533 (all an. 365); cf. Soc. *HE*
3.1.10.

Confusion about N.'s profession has been the rule for at least a century:
e.g., rhetorician in Sievers, *Leben* 50; sophist and philosopher in *PLRE* I
s.v.; rhetorician in Bowersock, *Julian* 27; philosopher, rhetorician, and
grammarian in Bradford, *Prosopography* 306. Yet despite his wide interests
(see below), and despite the fact that Libanius—our only firsthand source;
see below—nowhere calls N. a gramm., that is doubtless what he was.
The following are the most revealing passages, which deserve to be
presented in some detail.

Or. 1.31: Libanius had dealings with N., one of the teachers (τῶν τις
διδασκάλων) at Constantinople, ca. 340. At that time N. promised to
supply Libanius with forty pupils on the spot and presented the arrangement as a matter of mutual advantage: μήτε σαυτὸν μήτε ἡμᾶς ἀδίκει—
"Don't put a spoke in your wheels or mine," in Norman's translation.
N.'s design in this was to foil a sophist who had betrayed him. By
channeling the students to Libanius, N. would hurt his enemy both
directly—since he would have fewer pupils—and indirectly, by giving
him a rival in Libanius. The promise itself, the arrangement it sketches,
and its darker motive make sense only if N. was a gramm., not another
sophist; cf. Norman, *Autobiography* 156 *ad loc.*

Or. 15.27: when speaking of N.'s stint as Julian's teacher, Libanius
specially mentions his expertise in Homer. This again suggests that N.
was a gramm.; thus the inference of Soc. *HE* 3.1.10, τῶν μὲν οὖν γραμματικῶν λόγων Νικοκλῆς ὁ Λάκων ἦν αὐτῷ παιδευτής, ῥητορικὴν δὲ παρὰ
Ἐκηβολίῳ κατώρθου. Just as Socrates certainly depends on Lib. *Or.*
18.11ff. for knowledge of Hecebolius's position and the general shape of
Julian's education (cf. Baynes, "Early Life"), so he must depend on *Or.*
15.27 for knowledge of N.'s position and his Spartan origin. For allusion
to N. as teacher of Homer with Julian, see also *Ep.* 1368.4: Ἰουλιανῷ δὲ
τῷ καλῷ πάλαι μὲν ἦσθα φίλος . . . καὶ ἔτι γε πρότερον ἀπὸ τοῦ θαύματος
ἐν ᾧ σε κατέστησεν ἡνίκα ἦρχε Φρυγῶν.

Ep. 832: Libanius commends to N. a certain Theodorus, who had been
one of Libanius's first pupils at Antioch (cf. *Ep.* 831.1)—although, as
Libanius says, there is no need to introduce them, because N. had

previously taught Theodorus: ὃν αὐτὸς ἐξέθρεψας, with the common metaphor of teacher as (foster) father; for another instance of the metaphor involving N., cf. *Ep.* 1266.5; and in general see Petit, *Étudiants* 31ff. Since Theodorus was evidently N.'s pupil before going to Libanius's school at Antioch, the natural inference is that he learned gramm. with N. and subsequently learned rhetoric with Libanius.

Ep. 1492.2: in a letter to Clearchus, another of N.'s former pupils (cf. *Ep.* 1266.5), Libanius, quoting *Il.* 9.485, says that N. had been Phoenix to Clearchus's Achilles—a metaphor that Libanius uses once elsewhere, to describe the relationship of the gramm. Cleobulus with his student Bassianus; cf. *Ep.* 155 and s.v. Cleobulus, no. 32, with Kaster, "Notes" 332, 333 n. 40.

By way of negative demonstration, *Ep.* 810.2 may be added. Libanius says that N.'s high opinion of his oratory could not be flattery, for N. would not grovel before "a king's lot, much less a sophist": ὃς γὰρ οὔτ' ἂν κολακεύσαις—οὐδὲ γὰρ βασιλέως σύ γε τύχην, μὴ ὅτι γε σοφιστήν— οὔτε ἂν ἀγνοήσαις λόγου κάλλος ἢ αἶσχος. The passage should imply that N. was no more a sophist than he was a king.

As a "friend of the Muses" (*Ep.* 816.1), N. could claim attainments that certainly extended beyond grammar. In rhetoric, he was a connoisseur of Libanius's speeches (*Ep.* 810.2, just quoted) and was capable of serving on an embassy to the emperor (*Ep.* 1368.1). He also prided himself on his reputation for philosophy; cf. esp. *Ep.* 1119.2, with *Ep.* 1383.5, Νικοκλέα τὸν σοφώτατον. Though this interest in philosophy may have influenced his teaching of Homer (see the appendix at the end of this entry), Libanius says N.'s love of σοφία was manifest in a nontechnical or nonprofessional way—N. was wise like Socrates, in his conversation and his way of life: *Ep.* 1487.1–2, κέρδος οὐ μικρὸν . . . τὸ σέ τε ἰδεῖν καὶ τῶν σῶν ἀκοῦσαι λόγων, οὓς οὐκ ἀπὸ βιβλίου δεικνύεις τοῖς ἀνθρώποις, ἀλλὰ τὸν Σωκράτους τρόπον. ἔδειξας δὲ τὴν σαυτοῦ φιλοσοφίαν εὖ τε φερόμενος καὶ μεταπεσόντος τοῦ πνεύματος οὔτε τότε ὁρμήσας ἐπὶ πλοῦτον οὐ καλὸν τὸν χειμῶνά τε ἐνεγκὼν ἀνδρείως. (Cf. the description of Libanius attributed to Julian at *Or.* 1.131.) Neither rhetoric nor philosophy was central to his professional life as it can be more narrowly defined; he was certainly a gramm. His career can be sketched as follows.

A native of Sparta—cf. *Or.* 1.31, 15.27 (the source of Soc. *HE* 3.1.10); *Ep.* 810.2 and 4, 1368.2, 1383.4, 1119.4—N. was well enough established as a gramm. in Constantinople by 340 to have acted as patron for one sophist, to offer to provide pupils to another, and thus to play a part in the professional rivalries of the city (*Or.* 1.31; cf. above). Libanius's behavior toward N. on that occasion was less than candid; cf. *Or.* 1.32ff., a case of *qui s'excuse, s'accuse* (see Norman, *Autobiography* 156 *ad loc.*).

N. perhaps resented this; for at the time of Libanius's troubles in Constantinople (ca. 343), N. was among his enemies (*Ep.* 557.1–2), presumably as one of the gramm. who joined the conspiracy of Bemarchius to drive Libanius from the city. For the involvement of the gramm., τοὺς ἀμφὶ τοὺς ποιητάς, see *Or.* 1.44.

N. remained at Constantinople, where ca. 348 he had the prince Julian as a pupil: *Or.* 15.27; *Ep.* 1368.4; for the date, see the appendix below. Another of his pupils, Theodorus, probably was with him in the early 350s; cf. *Ep.* 832, and see above.

By early 363, when we can start to follow his correspondence with N., Libanius had evidently resolved his differences with the gramm., and (or because) N. was now a person of some influence with his former pupil the emperor Julian. The familiar moves of friendship and patronage are then played out, and N.'s prestige makes itself felt in other ways as well: N. acts as publicist for Libanius, and Libanius returns the favor (*Ep.* 810.1–3); N. is in Antioch early in 363 on the occasion of Libanius's speech (*Or.* 12) in honor of Julian's consulship, reconciles the population of Constantinople and the city prefect in the wake of rioting, and anticipates going on an embassy to Julian at Antioch on the same matter (*Ep.* 1368.1); Libanius hopes that N. will join those trying to dissuade Julian from moving his court from Antioch to Tarsus (*Ep.* 1368.3); N.'s influence is made evident in the letters of recommendation he receives (*Ep.* 810, 816, 832, 1119) and in a recommendation made in his name to his brother, Fl. Sozomenus, *v.c.*, governor of Lycia in 363 (*Ep.* 1383; for the name and rank, see *Bull. ép.* 1979, 509 no. 4).

All that ended with Julian's death. For a time in 364 N. gave up teaching, forced out by an antipagan reaction, Libanius seems to imply, or by a general evaporation of patronage, or by both these causes; he resumed teaching by early 365. For the resumption, see *Ep.* 1487; for N.'s paganism, *Ep.* 810.7, 1411.3, with which compare Libanius's veiled but increasingly obvious references to a backlash, *Ep.* 1196, 1211, 1265; and cf. *Ep.* 1533.1–2. How wanting for patronage N. was during 364 and into 365 can perhaps be gauged from his harassment at just this time by a former pupil, Clearchus, then *vicarius Asiae*; cf. *Ep.* 1265, 1266, 1492, with Chap. 6 pp. 214–15.

N. was probably still alive in 388, since he is probably the dedicatee of Lib. *Or.* 32. Since N. was well established at Constantinople by 340, he cannot have been born much later than ca. 315. He was probably, therefore, a close contemporary of Libanius.

N. is possibly the Nicocles found in the catalogue of gramm. in Kröhnert, *Canones* 7.

Appendix: Nicocles and the Early Chronology of Julian

The analysis of N.'s career is necessarily involved with the chronology of his best-known pupil. There are two competing views of the latter problem, that of Seeck, *Untergang* 4.205ff., and that of Baynes, "Early

Life." To follow Seeck, one must place Julian's exile to Macellum in the years 345–51, assigning his education under N. and Hecebolius at Constantinople and his first acquaintance with Libanius's work at Nicomedia to the four years preceding, 341–44. To follow Baynes, one must place the latter events after the exile, in the years 347/48–349. Seeck's chronology has been followed most recently by *PLRE* I; by Browning, *Emperor* 34ff. (intermittently and with some confusion); by Bradford, *Prosopography* 306 (*ut vid.*); and by Braun, *Empereur* 10. The most recent adherents of Baynes's view include Norman, *Libanius* (Loeb) vol. 1 p. ix; Head, *Emperor* 20ff.; Bowersock, *Julian* 22ff.; Athanassiadi-Fowden, *Julian* 27.

Baynes's position is certainly correct. At *Or.* 18.13, Libanius says that Julian ἤδη . . . πρόσηβος ἦν, "was already near manhood," when Constantius decided that he was a threat and sent him from Constantinople to Nicomedia, where he first came to know of Libanius; cf. esp. Norman, *Libanius* vol. 1 p. ix. Since Seeck had to place that event ca. 344, he also had to assume, *int. al.*, that πρόσηβος could be used here of Julian when he was thirteen or fourteen years old—an evident difficulty. One who is πρόσηβος should be closer to eighteen than to fourteen; cf. a passage in Libanius's epigonus Choricius, *Tyrannic.* 37 (294.13ff. Foerster-Richtsteig), where ἔφηβος and πρόσηβος are used interchangeably. Hence anyone πρόσηβος would be of an age to be leaving the schools, not entering them; cf. esp. Lucian *Somn.* 1, ἄρτι μὲν ἐπεπαύμην εἰς τὰ διδασκαλεῖα φοιτῶν ἤδη τὴν ἡλικίαν πρόσηβος ὤν. Nonetheless one might circumvent the difficulty by pointing to the flexibility of ancient terms for age groups and of ancient educational practices. But *Or.* 15.27, a passage often overlooked in the controversy, shows that Julian was also πρόσηβος when N. took him on as a student—i.e., when, according to Seeck, Julian was ten or eleven; and that is simply impossible.

The impossibility can only be surmounted by the bald assumption that Libanius was exaggerating when he described Julian as πρόσηβος in *Or.* 15.27 and 18.13. This was the contention of, e.g., Richtsteig, "Einige Daten" 429, 430. But such an assumption is methodologically weak; and in any case its implications make little sense. In the gross outlines of his account of Julian's life (*Or.* 18.11ff.), Libanius is concerned to suppress the disgrace of his exile to Macellum and the dislocation it produced from the normal course of his life. The last thing we should expect, then, is that Libanius would intentionally exaggerate that dislocation by making Julian older than the normal age when he encountered N., Hecebolius, and Libanius himself. The occurrence of πρόσηβος should instead be regarded as a small element of truth that Libanius unwittingly let slip amid the larger distortion he was working. The difficulties of course disappear when the evidence of *Or.* 15.27 and 18.13 is applied to Baynes's scheme: Julian was about seventeen when he came to N. and

Hecebolius at Constantinople in late 347 or early 348, and about eighteen when he went from Constantinople to Nicomedia in late 348 or early 349.

One last point, lest it be thought odd that Julian read Homer—usually the first text read in school—and other poets with N. when he was about seventeen. It should be noted that Libanius (*Or.* 15.27) particularly emphasizes N.'s knowledge of the ἀπόρρητα of Homer and other poets— the "mysteries," the deeper, hidden meanings accessible only to the initiated; and Julian, who had long since been introduced to Homer by Mardonius (*Misopog.* 351A–354B), was certainly an initiate. Indeed, given the references to N.'s φιλοσοφία (see above), it is conceivable that Lib. *Or.* 15.27 alludes to allegorical interpretation such as Porphyry had practiced two or three generations earlier. (For contemporary reference to the ἀπόρρητα in poets' works, see Eunap. *V. phil.* 4.1.9; on the need for allegorical interpretation, see Julian himself, *Or.* 5.170A–C, 7.216B– 222D; cf. Greg. Naz. *Or.* 4, *C. Iulian.* 1.118.) But however that might be, we can be sure that N. did not give his extraordinary pupil an everyday schoolboy's first lessons in Homer.

107. NILUS.   Gramm.   s.IV ex. / s.V 1/3.

RE Suppl. 7.561 (Ensslin); *PLRE* II s.v. 1, p. 784.

The recipient of a letter of moral exhortation from Isidore of Pelusium, *Ep.* 3.205, Νείλῳ γραμματικῷ.

108. OLYMPIUS.   Gramm.   Seleucia (Isauria).   s.V med.

PLRE II s.v. 10, p. 803.

Son of Alypius (q.v., no. 6), the gramm. of Isaurian Seleucia, O. was himself a gramm. of some reputation: Ὀλύμπιος . . . ὁ γραμματιστὴς ὁ πάνυ, [Basil. Sel.] *Vie et miracles de Sainte Thècle* 2.38 Dagron; cf. Appendix 2.2a. See also s.v. Solymius, no. 259—the brother of O., according to the received text, but probably O. himself.

109. OPHELIUS.   Gramm. and poet.   Egypt?   s.IV ex. / s.V 1/3.

RE 18.632 (Ensslin); *PLRE* II s.v. 1, p. 806.

A γραμματικός: inscr. of Isid. Pel. *Epp.* (below); cf. also *Ep.* 3.92, παρὰ μὲν ὑμῖν τοῖς γραμματικοῖς [vs. παρὰ τοῖς φιλοσόφοις] τὸ ὁμώνυμον ταὐτόν ἐστι τῷ συνωνύμῳ; 5.245, Isidore's response to O.'s criticism of the use of the superlative degree with reference to fewer than three subjects; 5.317, Isidore's advice συνεχῶς, ὦ ἐλλογιμώτατε, τοῖς φοιτῶσι παισὶ τὰ περὶ ἀρετῆς καὶ σωφροσύνης παραίνει. Also a poet: *Ep.* 1.86, ὦ ἄριστε ποιητῶν (incorrectly punctuated in Migne); cf. 3.31, ὑμεῖς οἱ ὁμηρίζοντες; 3.70, ὡς Ὅμηρος μὲν ἔφη, σὺ δὲ γέγραφας.

Recipient of twenty-odd letters from Isidore of Pelusium involving moral exhortation (1.11, 86; 2.55, 255, 273; 5.66, 317, 517), interpretations of philosophical and scriptural matters (2.119; 3.31, 92–94; 4.105, 162, 200; 5.430, 558), discussions of literary usage and style (2.42, on the style of John Chrysostom, quoting [Lib.] *Ep.* 1553; with 5.121, 133, 245, 439, 544), and a matter of topical concern (3.70). See also 2.154 and 201 and 5.200, addressed Ὀφελίῳ σχολαστικῷ, possibly to O.

O. was a connoisseur of rhetorical texts; cf. *Ep.* 4.162, on O.'s admiration for Isocrates; cf. also the letters on style, above. But he was ignorant of philosophy: *Ep.* 3.92, ἄμοιρος τῶν τοιούτων μαθημάτων.

He was a Christian and on one occasion had debated theology with a Jew: *Ep.* 3.94.

The place of his school cannot be determined; it was evidently in the same place as that of Agathodaemon (q.v., no. 3), with whom O. received *Ep.* 5.439. Presumably it was in a center of some size, perhaps in Egypt; see s.v. Agathodaemon.

FL. OPTATUS: see no. 241.

110. ORION.   Gramm.   Thebes (Egypt) → Alexandria / Constantinople? (very doubtful) / Caesarea?   s.V 1/4–1/2.

RE 18.1083–87 (Wendel); Chr.-Sch.-St. 2:2.1081, 1087; Hunger 2.45; PLRE II s.v. 1, p. 812.

Orion: Marinus *V. Procli* 8; *Suda* Ω.188 (cf. Ω.189 and below); Ioan. Tzetzes *Chil.* 10.52, p. 389 Leone; mss of the *Etym.* and *Anth.* (see below); Ἐπιμερισμοί, Cramer, *Anecd. Paris.* 3.322.11; Kröhnert, *Canones* 7. Called γραμματικός, as teacher of Proclus, by Marinus *V. Procli* 8, and in cod. Vindob. philol. gr. 321 of the *Anth.*, cod. Paris. gr. 2653 of the *Etym.*; on Ioan. Tzetzes *Chil.* 10.52, see below. He is included in the catalogue of gramm. in Kröhnert, *Canones* 7.

A native of Egyptian Thebes: *Suda* Ω.188, Θηβαῖος τῆς Αἰγύπτου; called Θηβαῖος in the catalogue of gramm. in Kröhnert, *Canones* 7, and in the following mss of the *Etym.*—Paris. gr. 2653 (ed. Sturz, pp. 1–2); Darmst. 2773 (cf. Garzya, "Per la tradizione" 216; *Etym. Gud.* ed. Sturz, pp. 611–12); Vat. gr. 1456; Bodl. Misc. 211 = Auct. T II.11; Paris. gr. 464, 2610 (cf. Micciarelli Collesi, "Nuovi 'excerpta'" 521 and "Per la tradizione"). Cf. Marinus *V. Procli* 8, ἣν ἐκ τοῦ παρ' Αἰγυπτίοις ἱερατικοῦ γένους καταγόμενος.

He taught Proclus at Alexandria: Marinus *V. Procli* 8; cf. also on *Suda* Ω.189, below. The evidence for O.'s activity at Constantinople and Caesarea is, respectively, very probably worthless, and slight.

O. has commonly been placed at Constantinople as the teacher of Athenais / Eudocia on the basis of Ioan. Tzetzes *Chil.* 10.48–53, pp. 388f. Leone:

ἐκ τοῦ προφήτου δε αὐτὸς ἐχρήσατο τῷ λόγῳ
ὥς που καὶ ἡ βασίλισσα ἐκείνη Εὐδοκία,
ἡ τοῦ μεγάλου Λέοντος ἡ πάνσοφος θυγάτηρ,
γραμματικοῖς μαθήτρια οὖσα Ὑπερεχίου,
ποτὲ καὶ τοῦ Ὠρίωνος μικρὸν ἀκροωμένη,
ῥητορικοῖς ἑτέρων δε καὶ φιλοσόφοις ἄλλων. . . .

The passage, however, is riddled with confusion. Although, as the rest of the passage goes on to show, Tzetzes clearly has in mind Eudocia, daughter of the sophist Leontius, the wife of Theodosius II and author of the Homer centos, he calls her the daughter of "the great Leo," presumably thinking of the emperor Leo I (457–74) and deriving the name either from an error in his source (Λέοντος for Λεοντίου) or from his own misunderstanding. Further, it would have been very difficult, if not impossible, for Eudocia to have been a pupil both of O., who was established at Alexandria by the mid-420s (see below), and of Hyperechius, who belongs to the third quarter of s.V under Marcian and Leo (see s.v. Hyperechius, no. 79)—especially since Eudocia left Constantinople for Jerusalem in the early 440s, never to return. (The date of her departure is still controversial; see most recently Alan Cameron, "Empress" 259ff., an. 440/41; Hunt, *Holy Land Pilgrimages* 235f., an. 441/42; Holum, *Theodosian Empresses* 193f., an. 443.) Tzetzes' confusion in this passage is still worse at vv. 51–52, where he presents Hyperechius as Eudocia's main teacher and gives a minor role (μικρὸν ἀκροωμένη) to O., her real contemporary. But it is obvious what has happened. Starting with the two pieces of information at his disposal—viz., that Eudocia was a lady of literary attainments and the daughter of "the great Leo"— Tzetzes set out to sketch a proper literary education for her. Although he could provide no details for her training in rhetoric and philosophy— hence the vague statements in v. 53—he could easily learn that one gramm., Hyperechius, had been active under her "father," Leo (*Suda* Λ.267 = ?Malch. frg. 2a, *FHG* 4.114), and that another gramm., O., had dedicated his *Anth.* to her (*Suda* Ω.188 = Hesych. Illust.). Thus Eudocia became a pupil of both. There is, then, no credible evidence that would place O. at Constantinople; he may well have dedicated the *Anth.* to Eudocia, but he did not need to be her teacher or to be teaching in the capital to do so (see below).

The extract of the *Anth.* in Vindob. philol. gr. 321 (s.XIV) carries the tit. Ὠρίωνος γραμματικοῦ Καισαρείας. That last piece of information reappears in the sixteenth century in the tit. of the longest version of the *Etym.*, in Paris. gr. 2653: Ὠρίωνος Θηβαίου γραμματικοῦ Καισαρείας. The other mss that carry extracts of the *Etym.*, which date from s.X (Vat. gr. 1456) to s.XVI (Paris. gr. 464, 2610), have only Ὠρίων (ὁ) Θηβαῖος in their tit. (see above); the version of the *Etym.* in Vindob.

theol. gr. 203 (s.XIV; cf. Cohn, "Nicetae . . . Rhythmi" 661) is without attribution. If that evidence can place O. in Caesarea—the one in Palestine would be a more likely destination than the one in Cappadocia for a native of Egypt teaching in Alexandria—it cannot certainly be determined when in his career O. would have taught there (see below).

O. was already established at Alexandria when Proclus went there to study, sometime in the mid-420s. Proclus had already been taught by a gramm. in Lycia and was ready for rhetorical instruction as well—i.e., he was no more than fifteen, possibly a bit younger—cf. Marinus *V. Procli* 8. This will have been no later than 425 or 427, depending on whether Proclus's birth is put in 409/10 or 412; on the latter dates, cf. Évrard, "Date." If a personal connection with Eudocia is to be inferred from the dedication of the *Anth.*, that connection can most plausibly be dated to the time after Eudocia's withdrawal to Jerusalem (440/43; see above), by which time, it must be supposed, O. will have moved to Caesarea in Palestine nearby: so Alan Cameron, "Empress" 280f.; Holum, *Theodosian Empresses* 220. This reconstruction must be based only on the dedication of the *Anth.* and on the inscr. of Vindob. philol. gr. 321; no support can be sought from the passage in Tzetzes (see above).

Marinus, *V. Procli* 8, speaks of O.'s scholarly activity and legacy: καὶ συγγραμμάτια ἑαυτοῦ ἴδια ἐκπονῆσαι καὶ τοῖς μεθ᾽ ἑαυτὸν χρήσιμα καταλιπεῖν. Identification of O.'s works depends upon the view taken of the information found in the *Suda*, which offers two entries s.v. The first, Ω.188, identifies O. of Egyptian Thebes as the author of an anthology, Συναγωγὴ γνωμῶν ἤγουν Ἀνθολόγιον, dedicated to the empress Eudocia, wife of Theodosius II; but note that Vindob. philol. gr. 321, the ms containing the extract of the *Anth.* (see above), does not attribute the work to an O. of Thebes. The second notice in the *Suda*, Ω.189, concerns an O. Ἀλεξανδρεύς, γραμματικός, author of an Ἀνθολόγιον, an Ἀττικῶν λέξεων συναγωγή, a Περὶ ἐτυμολογίας, and an ἐγκώμιον Ἀδριανοῦ τοῦ Καίσαρος. Because an *Anth.* is found in both notices, and because the *Etym.* is attributed to O. of Thebes in the mss (see above), it has often and probably correctly been concluded that there is a confusion in the *Suda*; the confusion is denied by, e.g., Chr.-Sch.-St. (cf. 2:2.873, 1081, where the two are treated as distinct). The difficulty lies in determining whether the *Suda*'s compilers have made two men out of one (cf. s.v. Triphiodorus, no. 157) or have partially confused two different men (cf. s.vv. Horapollon, Diogenes, nos. 77, 207). According to the first view, O. of Thebes would be the author of all works listed in both entries—so, e.g., Wendel, *RE* 18.1083ff.—and the encomium of Hadrian would be explained as a classroom exercise *vel sim.* According to the second view, O. would have been the author of the *Anth.* and the *Etym.* (and possibly the Ἀττικῶν λέξεων συναγωγή), to be distinguished from an earlier figure of the same name, a contemporary of Hadrian who composed an encomium in his honor (and possibly the Ἀττικῶν λέξεων συναγωγή). Although the problem does not admit of a certain solution, the second view seems more likely. It is also possible that the Ἀττικῶν λέξεων συναγωγή was a work of Orus, which is here incorrectly attributed to O.; see most recently Alpers, *Attizistische Lexikon* 97f. For the confusion of the two men, see s.v. Orus, no. 111.

The *Anth.* survives independently only in an abridged form; it was also used by Stobaeus. There are several more or less extensive versions of the *Etym.* in the mss (see above); the work was also drawn upon by the compilers of the *Etym. Genuin.* and the *Etym. Gud.* O. is included among ὅσοι <περὶ> ἐθνικῶν (sc. ἔγραψαν) in the catalogue of gramm. in Kröhnert, *Canones* 7, but the arrangement of the catalogue there is disturbed; see s.v. Orus *ad fin.*

According to Marinus, *V. Procli* 8, O. was of a priestly family of Egypt.

111. ORUS. Gramm. Alexandria → Constantinople. s.V 1/2–2/3.

RE 18.1177–83 (Wendel); Chr.-Sch.-St. 2:2.1077, 1081f., 1087; Hunger 2.13, 18, 45, 49, 50; *PLRE* II s.v., p. 814; Alpers, *Attizistische Lexikon* 3ff., 87ff.

Orus: *Suda* Ω.201; the various etymological collections that cite him, where he is often confused with Orion (q.v., no. 110; see Reitzenstein, *Geschichte* 9f., on the sign used to designate both gramm. in the *Etym. Genuin.*; cf. Livadaras, "Συμβολή" 182ff., esp. 189ff.); Choerobosc. *Schol. in Theodos.* (*GG* 4:1.138.38, 196.33, 205.28, 360.8; 4:2.73.4, 14), *Schol. in Hephaest.* 185.4ff., 212.25, 248.19ff. Consbruch; Kröhnert, *Canones* 7 (see below). "Aros" in the catalogue of gramm. in Rabe, "Listen" 340.

A grammarian from Alexandria who taught in Constantinople according to the *Suda*, Ω.201. The location is sometimes thought to be the result of a confusion with Orion; but on the supposed activity of Orion in Constantinople, see s.v. Called ὁ γραμματικός at Choerobosc. *Schol. in Theodos.*, *GG* 4:1.138.38, 360.8; Cramer, *Anecd. Paris.* 3.378.16. The designation ὁ Μιλήσιος that appears in *Etym. Genuin.* and other works dependent on it was shown by Reitzenstein, *Geschichte* 10, to be a mistaken expansion of the abbreviation ὁ μελ or ὁ μλ, which appears in the earliest mss of *Etym. Genuin.* Wendel, "Späne II" 351, has suggested that the proper expansion was ὁ μέλας, an epithet referring to his complexion and so to his national origin; Wendel compares Hdt. 2.104.2, μελάγχροες, of the Egyptians; cf. also the description of another Egyptian gramm., Pamprepius (q.v., no. 114), in Damasc. *V. Isid.* frg. 178 Zintzen, μέλας τὴν χροιάν.

O. is certainly to be dated after Phrynichus and Herodian (s.II ex.; see below) and before Timotheus of Gaza (q.v., no. 156; s.V ex. / s.VI init.), probably s.V 1/2-2/3: O.'s work on ethnics can be dated after 438; see Reitzenstein, *Geschichte* 287ff.; cf. Alpers, *Attizistische Lexikon* 89ff. Despite Chr.-Sch.-St. 2:2.1081 n. 3, no chronological conclusions can be drawn from the order in which O. appears in the catalogues of gramm. in Kröhnert, *Canones* 7, and in Rabe, "Listen" 340.

The *Suda*, Ω.201, attributes to O. a work on vowels of ambiguous quantity, Περὶ διχρόνων, also listed in Kröhnert, *Canones* 7 (see below); a work on ethnics, Ὅπως τὰ ἐθνικὰ λεκτέον (cf. Reitzenstein, *Geschichte* 316ff., and below on Kröhnert, *Canones* 7); works against Phrynichus and concerning Herodian, Κατὰ Φρυνίχου κατὰ στοιχεῖον and Λύσεις προτάσεων τῶν Ἡρωδιανοῦ; on enclitics, Περὶ ἐγκλιτικῶν; on orthography, Ὀρθογραφία κατὰ στοιχεῖον and Περὶ τῆς ει διφθόγγου and Ὀρθογραφία περὶ τῆς αι διφθόγγου, the latter two probably part of the first (cf. the ὑπόμνημα τῆς ὀρθογραφίας τοῦ ἡρώων [*l.* Ἡρωδιανοῦ] attributed to O. in the *Etym. Gud.* s.v. ξίρις, p. 415 Sturz; for extracts of O.'s orthographical work, see Rabe, "Lexicon" and "Nachtrag"); and a catalogue of his own works, Πίναξ τῶν ἑαυτοῦ. Extensive fragments of O.'s work Κατὰ Φρυνίχου κατὰ στοιχεῖον, preserved in the Atticist lexicon of "Zonaras," have been identified and published by Alpers, *Attizistische Lexikon*. Other fragments of his work, probably from the Περὶ διχρόνων, are preserved in a compilation inscribed ἀρχὴ τῶν τονιζομένων λέξεων παρεξελεχθέντων τούτων ἐκ τῶν Ὥρου, Χοιροβοσκοῦ, Αἰθερίου γραμματικοῦ, Φιλοπόνου καὶ ἑτέρων (unpublished; see s.v. Aetherius, no. 180); extracts from another work, Περὶ πολυσημάντων λέξεων, are preserved in codd. Paris. gr. 2720 (= Cramer, *Anecd. Paris.* 4.262.4ff.), 2558, and 2830; cf. Reitzenstein, *Geschichte* 335ff. A commentary on Hephaestion seems to be implied by the citations of O. in Choerobosc. *Schol. in Hephaest.* (see above); remnants of it are probably preserved in *Scholia A* to Hephaestion: see Consbruch, ed., *Hephaestionis Enchiridion* pp. xiv, 91ff. The work listed last in the *Suda*, Ω.201, Ἀνθολόγιον περὶ γνωμῶν—incorrectly printed as two titles, Ἀνθολόγιον and Περὶ γνωμῶν, in Adler's ed.—is probably an intrusion, the result of confusion with Orion; cf. *Suda* Ω.188, Συναγωγὴν γνωμῶν ἤγουν Ἀνθολόγιον. Also dubiously ascribed to O. are an Ἰλιακὴ προσῳδία and a Περὶ παθῶν, both perhaps referable ultimately to Herodian; cf. Wendel, *RE* 18.1182.47ff.

In addition to being listed in the catalogue of gramm. referred to above (Rabe, "Listen" 340), O. appears four times in the comparable catalogue in Kröhnert, *Canones* 7, once under the general heading ὅσοι γραμματικοί, once under the rubric ὅσοι περὶ ὀρθογραφίας, and twice more toward the end of the list: ὅσοι περὶ διχρόνων. Ὧρος, Παμπρέπιος, Αἰθέριος Ἀπαμεύς, Ὧρος, Στέφανος ὁ Κωνσταντίνου πόλεως. ὅσοι <περὶ> ἐθνικῶν. Ὠρίων Θηβαῖος, Μητρόδωρος, Φιλόξενος, Λογγῖνος. The repetition of O.'s name under the heading ὅσοι περὶ διχρόνων is obviously intolerable, and attempts at correction were made by Ritschl, who altered the second Ὧρος to Ἡρωδιανός (*Opuscula* 1.623), and by Kröhnert, who changed the same name to Ὠρίων (*Canones* 7; cf. 50). It is very likely, however, that the corruption goes beyond a single name. Specifically, the final heading, on ἐθνικά, has evidently been displaced: not only would one expect Stephanus (q.v., no. 144) of Byzantium to be listed among the authorities on ἐθνικά, but O. himself also composed a work, Ὅπως τὰ ἐθνικὰ λεκτέον, that would fit under this heading. O.'s name should be retained in both its appearances, and the list should be emended as follows: ὅσοι περὶ διχρόνων. Ὧρος, Παμπρέπιος [not otherwise known to have composed a technical treatise on this subject], Αἰθέριος Ἀπαμεύς [cf. s.v., no. 180]. ὅσοι <περὶ> ἐθνικῶν. Ὧρος, Στέφανος ὁ Κωνσταντίνου πόλεως κτλ. If the heading on ἐθνικά has in fact been displaced, the position it now holds, before the last four names in the list, was perhaps originally filled by a different heading entirely, e.g., ὅσοι περὶ ἐτυμολογίας, an important category now missing from the catalogue.

112. AUR. OURSENOUPHIUS. Teacher of letters. Heracleopolite nome. 411.

A γραμματοδιδάσκαλος who wrote a subscription in behalf of Aur. Anoutis, an illiterate party to a sale: *Stud. Pal.* 20.117.18, Αὐρήλιος Οὐρσενούφιος γραμματοδιδάσκαλ(ος) [ἔγραψα ὑπὲρ αὐτοῦ γράμμ]ατα μ[ὴ εἰδ]ότος.

113. PALLADAS. Gramm. Alexandria. Ca. 320?–s.IV ex.
RE 18:2(2).158–68 (Peek); Chr.-Sch.-St. 2:2.979; Irmscher, "Palladas"; Hunger 2.166; *PLRE* I s.v., pp. 657f.

Palladas (lemmata in *Anth. Gr.*), a gramm.; cf. *Anth. Gr.* 9.168, 169, 171, 173–75; 10.97; 11.378; *Epigr. Anth. Pal.* 3.145, p. 314 Cougny.
He despised his profession, calling it a burden of μῆνις οὐλομένη; cf. 9.168, 169, 173, 174. He complained of poverty and of being cheated of his fees (μισθοί) by his students, whom he charged 1 *solidus* a year: 9.174, with Alan Cameron, "Roman School Fees" 257; for payment in monthly installments, see *Anth. Gr.* 9.174.3–8. He also received a salary from public funds, σύνταξις, of which he was deprived (9.175; cf. 9.171) late in life (10.97; see further below). He presents himself variously as distraught (9.175, heavily sarcastic) or relieved (9.171, 11.378) at leaving his post.
He taught in Alexandria: Ἀλεξανδρεύς, lemmata in *Anth. Gr.* A number of his poems refer to the religious upheavals there in the early 390s (see below). There is no good evidence that would place him in Constantinople: on 9.528, cf. Bowra, "Palladas and the Converted Olympians,"

and Alan Cameron, "Notes" 219ff. (differently Irmscher, "Palladas-
Probleme" and "Haus"); on 16.282 and 11.386, see Alan Cameron,
"Palladas and the Nikai" 54ff., 58f.

   Anth. Gr. 11.292 probably lampoons Themistius as PVC in 384; cf.
Alan Cameron, "Notes" 220ff.; this identification was made already in
[Elias] *Lectures on Porphyry's Isagoge* 22.22ff. Westerink (s.VI ex. / s.VIII init.).
A number of poems must allude to the antipagan riots inspired by the
bishop Theophilus in 391 and the changes in the religious climate of
Alexandria in the years immediately following: cf. 9.501 and 10.82, 89–
91 (with Keydell, "Palladas"; Bowra, "Palladas and Christianity"; Alan
Cameron, "Palladas and Christian Polemic" 21ff.); 9.180–83 (with Bowra,
"Palladas on Tyche" 120ff.); 9.528 (with Bowra, "Palladas and the Con-
verted Olympians"); 7.684–85 (with Alan Cameron, "Palladas and the
Fate"); 16.282 (with Alan Cameron, "Palladas and the Nikai" 54ff.;
Irmscher, "Alexandria").

   P. chose to connect his departure from his teaching position with
those changes: cf. 9.175, with Bowra, "Palladas and Christianity" 257,
263ff.; Alan Cameron, "Palladas and Christian Polemic" 26ff.; and Kaster,
"Grammarian," for a survey of P.'s poems from this period. *Anth. Gr.*
10.97, in which P. says that he has lived "a pound of years [= 72] with
grammar," can plausibly be dated to this period; cf. Bowra, "Palladas and
Christianity" 267; Alan Cameron, "Palladas and Christian Polemic" 27f.
His birth could then be placed in 319 or the early 320s.

   There is no good evidence that P. lived into the fifth century. *Anth.
Gr.* 9.400, once thought to be evidence of P.'s friendship with the philosopher Hypatia, has been shown to have no connection with either of
them; cf. Luck, "Palladas" 462ff.; *contra,* Irmscher, "Palladas und Hypatia."
On 9.528, see above.

   Although P. identifies himself with the "Hellenes" (i.e., pagans) of
Alexandria, against the Christians (see poems noted above), that identification is notably attenuated and ambivalent; cf. esp. Luck, "Palladas";
Kaster, "Grammarian." He expresses regard for none of the old gods,
with the possible exception of Serapis (cf. 9.378); his contempt for
Platonism is explicit (cf. 10.45, with 10.75, 84, 85, and 11.349), and he
aligns himself with no school of philosophy. Attempts to find evidence of
a conversion on P.'s part have not been successful; cf. Lacombrade,
"Palladas"; Bowra, "Palladas and Christianity" 261ff.

   P. claims to have been married (cf. 9.168; 11.378; *Epigr. Anth. Pal.*
3.145, p. 314 Cougny), to have had children (10.86), and to have owned
a slave, chickens, and a dog (10.86), and a κέλλιον that he rented out
(11.351).

   His epigrams, of which over a hundred appear in the *Anth. Gr.,* enjoyed some currency in the West at the end of s.IV—imitations can be

found in the epigrams of Ausonius and the *Epigrammata Bobiensia*; cf. Weinreich's review of Munari, *Gnomon* 31 (1959), 241ff.—and were known to Claudian, if P. is the *iratus grammaticus* of *Carm. min.* 24; cf. Alan Cameron, "Notes" 223, 225f., and *Claudian* 308f. One of his epigrams, 10.58, has been found on a Christian epitaph (*RIGCAM* 296 Megiste [Lycia]); perhaps another, 10.87, in modified form, in a toilet at Ephesus; cf. Weisshäupl, "Ephesische Latrinen-Inschriften"; Kalinka, "Palladas-Epigramm"; Bowra, "Palladas on Tyche" 120; but cf. Alan Cameron, "Notes" 226ff.

PALLADIUS: see no. 242.

114. PAMPREPIUS. Gramm. and poet → *QSP, cons., patricius, mag. off.* Panopolis → Athens → Constantinople. 29 Sept. 440–Nov. 484.

RE 18:2(2).409–15 (Keydell); Chr.-Sch.-St. 2:2.961, 1039, 1077; Alan Cameron, "Wandering Poets" esp. 486, 499f.; Livrea, "Pamprepio"; Hunger 2.13, 110, 112; *PLRE* II s.v., pp. 825ff.

An Egyptian: Damasc. *V. Isid.* epit. Phot. 168 = frg. 290 Zintzen; Rhetorius *Catal. cod. astrol. Graec.* 8:4.221.2; Malch. frg. 20 (*FHG* 4.131f. = *Suda* Π.137, 4.13.28–14.33 Adler). From Panopolis: Damasc. *V. Isid.* epit. Phot. 110 = frg. 178; Ioan. Ant. frg. 211.2 (*FHG* 4.619); *Suda* Π.136. A poet (Damasc. *V. Isid.* epit. Phot. 168 = frg. 290; *Suda* ibid.; see further below) and a pagan, believed at various points in his career to dabble in magic and prophecy: Damasc. *V. Isid.* epit. Phot. 109 (cf. 110, 171); Rhetorius *Catal. cod. astrol. Graec.* 221.5; Zach. Schol. *Vie de Sévère* p. 40.3ff., *V. Isaiae* p.7.17f. (*CSCO* Scr. Syr., ser. 3, vol. 25); Josh. Styl. 15, p. 10 Wright; Malch. frg. 20; Candidus *FHG* 4.137 = Phot. *Bibl.* cod. 79 (1.165 Henry); Theoph. *Chron.* pp. 128.10, 130.7 de Boor.

Born 29 September 440; cf. the horoscope of Rhetorius, *Catal. cod. astrol. Graec.* 221.8ff., with Delatte and Stroobant, "Horoscope" 62ff.; abbreviated translation, with comment, also in Neugebauer and van Hoesen, eds., *Greek Horoscopes* 140f. He lived the hard life of a wanderer for his first twenty-five or thirty years; cf. Rhetorius *Catal. cod. astrol. Graec.* 222.8ff.: τὴν πρώτην ἡλικίαν χαλεπὴν ἐκτήσατο, ἀλλὰ δὴ καὶ φυγὰς ἐν πολλοῖς τόποις ἐγένετο. . . . καὶ ταῦτα μὲν περὶ τῆς πρώτης ἡλικίας μέχρι ἐτῶν κε΄ ἢ λ΄. He then went to Athens as a professional poet (Damasc. *V. Isid.* epit. Phot. 168 = frg. 290; cf. Malch. frg. 20), probably ca. 465/70, to judge from Rhetorius (see preceding quotation), and in any case sometime before late 472 (see below).

There he was made a γραμματικός by the city: Damasc. ibid.; Malch. ibid.; cf. Rhetorius *Catal. cod. astrol. Graec.* 221.2, 223.3ff.; Damasc. *V. Isid.* epit. Phot. 110 = frg. 178 (on Damascius's use of γραμματιστής here, see Appendix 2.2e); Ioan. Ant. frg. 211.2. He married (Ioan. Ant. ibid.;

Damasc. V. Isid. frg. 178), and he taught for a number of years (πολὺν χρόνον, Damasc. ibid., Ioan. Ant. ibid.; συχνὰ ἔτη, Malch. frg. 20), apparently enjoying the patronage of the Christian magnate Theagenes. For Theagenes' religion, see Damasc. V. Isid. frg. 258, quoted below ad fin.; for his patronage of teachers, see Damasc. V. Isid. frg. 264, and below.

Since Damasc. and Malch. say that P. taught for a considerable period in Athens before he went to Constantinople (in May 476; see below), he must already have been teaching in Athens before late 472, the end of his thirty-second year; after that, according to Rhetorius, his fortunes changed for the better: Catal. cod. astrol. Graec. 221.2, πένης ὡς ἐτῶν λβ'; cf. 222.8ff. The change in his fortunes should thus be placed during his time in Athens—not at his arrival, as commonly—and is to be associated with his marriage, in his thirty-third year: Rhetorius Catal. cod. astrol. Graec. 221.3, ἀπὸ δὲ ἐτῶν λγ' γήμας ἤρξατο ἀνασφάλλειν ἐν Ἀθήναις. By then he was presumably already established in the city; on his arrival, cf. above. He is also said to have studied with Proclus while at Athens: Malch. frg. 20; cf. Damasc. V. Isid. frg. 289.

Having fallen afoul of Theagenes (Malch. frg. 20, διαβολῆς δὲ αὐτῷ πρὸς Θεαγένην τινὰ . . . συστάσης), he moved to Constantinople in May 476, according to Rhetorius: Catal. cod. astrol. Graec. 224.4-7, with Cumont, app. crit. to line 7. There Marsus introduced him to the Isaurian Illus: Damasc. V. Isid. frg. 178; Candidus FHG 4.137 = Phot. Bibl. cod. 79. He impressed Illus with the public recitation of a poem (Malch. frg. 20) or of a discourse on the soul (Damasc. V. Isid. frg. 178), or perhaps both; he was appointed as a teacher with a public salary (Malch. ibid.; Damasc. ibid.), probably in 477, when Illus was mag. off. Deprived of the protection of Illus when the latter returned to Isauria in 478, P. was accused of magic and treason by "the envious," οἱ βασκαίνοντες (Malch. frg. 20), either his own rivals or Illus's enemies, and he was exiled. He went first to Pergamum and then, on the invitation of Illus, to Isauria; there he was Illus's confidant and agent (Malch. frg. 20).

His fortune and movements thereafter are intimately connected with Illus's. Most important, Illus made him quaestor in early 479 and sometime later(?) consul and patricius. The quaestorship is mentioned by Ioan. Ant. frg. 211.3, where it appears to be placed toward the end of 478 or beginning of 479; it is mentioned with the consulship (presumably honorary; cf. s.v. Dioscorius, no. 48) and patriciate by Rhetorius Catal. cod. astrol. Graec. 221.5f.; cf. 223.9, 224.9-13. P. is called πατρίκιος in Malal. Exc. hist. 3.165.16 de Boor, συγκλητικός in Theoph. Chron. p. 128.10 de Boor, probably after Malal. ibid. 14f. Rhetorius Catal. cod. astrol. Graec. 224.9-13 dates an improvement in P.'s fortunes to January 479—probably the quaestorship, although Rhetorius groups the three honors together. For P. as μέγιστον ἤδη δυνάμενος on his arrival in Alexandria, see Damasc. *V. Isid.* frg. 288.

He was sent to Alexandria: Rhetorius *Catal. cod. astrol. Graec.* 224.13ff.; cf. Damasc. *V. Isid.* epit. Phot. 172, frg. 287; for the date, after September 483 (against Rhetorius), see Keydell, *RE* 18:2(2).412.34ff. Apparently he was to canvass pagan support for the rebellion of Illus and Leontius, in which he had become involved: Zach. Schol. *Vie de Sévère* p. 40.3ff., *HE* pp. 71.17ff., 80.14ff., 98.7f. Ahrens-Krüger, *V. Isaiae* p. 7.15ff. (*CSCO* Scr. Syr., ser. 3, vol. 25); Josh. Styl. 15, p. 10 Wright; Eustathius frg. 4, *FHG* 4.140.

He was made *mag. off.* of Leontius: Malal. *Exc. hist.* 3.166.10f. de Boor; cf. Theoph. *Chron.* p. 130.7 de Boor. This must have been after July 484; cf. Bury, *LRE* 1.397 n. 4. But he proved treacherous: Rhetorius *Catal. cod. astrol. Graec.* 221.6f.; Damasc. *V. Isid.* epit. Phot. 172, 173 (cf. epit. Phot. 110 and frg. 295, 299, 300); Josh. Styl. 15, p. 10 Wright; Malal. *Exc. hist.* 3.166.19f. de Boor. He was executed by Illus in late November 484 at the Isaurian fortress Papyrion, in which Illus and Leontius had taken refuge: Malal. ibid.; cf.(?) Damasc. *V. Isid.* epit. Phot. 110, 174, 291 (= frg. 306). For the date, see Rhetorius *Catal. cod. astrol. Graec.* 221.7, 224.19f.; differently Theoph. *Chron.* p. 130.7 de Boor.

P. is described by Rhetorius (*Catal. cod. astrol. Graec.* 221.5, 7; 223.10ff.) as hypocritical, treacherous, and licentious. His portrait is also harshly drawn by Damascius, largely because of P.'s ambition and his seeming betrayal of the pagans; cf. *V. Isid.* frg. 287 (with 178), 288, 289, possibly frg. 179; cf. Asmus, "Pamprepios" 344ff. But Damascius nonetheless describes him as λογιώτατος and πολυμαθέστατος, skilled beyond all others in ἡ ἄλλη προπαιδεία, i.e., all areas of the literary culture short of philosophy: Damasc. *V. Isid.* frg. 289 = epit. Phot. 168. He is included in the catalogue of gramm. in Kröhnert, *Canones* 7, under the rubric ὅσοι περὶ διχρόνων, i.e., writers on vowels of ambivalent quantity.

The *Suda*, Π.136, besides describing P. as ἐπῶν ποιητής, attributes to him a work on etymology and an Ἰσαυρικά in prose: ἔγραψεν Ἐτυμολογιῶν ἀπόδοσιν, Ἰσαυρικὰ καταλογάδην. In his edition of the *Suda* Bernhardy argued that the last word should be transposed to follow ἀπόδοσιν and suggested that the Ἰσαυρικά was one of P.'s poems; but Bernhardy's premise—that the entry as transmitted necessarily implies that the work on etymology was in verse—is incorrect, and his transposition is accordingly uncertain. Gerstinger, *Pamprepios* 22ff., suggested that remnants of P.'s poetry—an idyll describing a day in spring (so Griffiths, "Alcman's *Partheneion*" 17 n. 29) or late autumn (so most recently Livrea, "Pamprepio" 124f.), an encomium of a πατρίκιος Theagenes, and scraps of the alleged poem Ἰσαυρικά—are preserved in pap. gr. Vindob. 29788A– C (ed. Gerstinger, *Pamprepios*; cf. Page, *Select Papyri* 3 no. 140; Heitsch,

Griechische Dichterfragmente XXXV). P.'s authorship of these poems has most recently been defended by Livrea, "Pamprepio"; doubts were already expressed by Graindor, "Pamprépios (?)."

Attribution of the poems to P. is very uncertain at best. The author is not named, nor is it clear that all the verses are by the same man; Gerstinger made the identification primarily because the poet of the idyll was evidently an Egyptian writing in Athens and on the assumption that the Theagenes of the encomium, also evidently an Athenian, could be identified with the Theagenes involved in P.'s career. The former consideration cannot carry much weight, since there were any number of Egyptian poets prowling the Greek East from the late fourth century onward; cf. esp. Alan Cameron, "Wandering Poets." Theagenes could well have patronized more than one of them; cf. Maas's review of Gerstinger, *Gnomon* 5 (1929), 251; Page, *Select Papyri* 3 p. 565. Note esp. that the poet of the idyll presents himself as about to leave Athens for Cyrene (Gerstinger C.1.193ff. = Page no. 140 a.151ff. = Heitsch XXXV, 3.193ff.); but no such move can reasonably be connected with anything known of P.'s career after his arrival in Athens. Further, there is good reason to doubt the identification of the Theagenes addressed in the encomium. A verse in the introduction of the encomium states that "Helicon, growing old because of outrage," has stored away all its Muses in Theagenes' keeping: Gerstinger C.2.4f. = Page no. 140 b.3f. = Heitsch XXXV, 4.3f., ᾧ [ἔν]ι πάσας / ὕβρει γηράσκων Ἑλικὼν ἀνεθήκατο Μούσας. This phrase has reasonably been read as the complaint of a paganism put on the defensive by the outrage of Christian hostility toward the traditional culture; cf., e.g., Gerstinger, *Pamprepios* 17. If that is correct—and for a distinctly non-Christian note cf. Gerstinger C.2.8ff. = Page no. 140 b.7ff. = Heitsch XXXV, 4.7ff.—it would be strange to find such an attitude if the recipient of the poem was P.'s patron, since that Theagenes was certainly no enemy of the Christians and was himself probably a Christian, not a pagan, *pace* Gerstinger, *Pamprepios* 21f., and, most recently, Livrea, "Pamprepio" 121; see Damasc. *V. Isid.* frg. 258, on Theagenes: καὶ τὰ νέα ἀξιώματα προτιμῶν τῶν ἀρχαίων ἠθῶν τῆς εὐσεβείας, ἔλαθεν ἑαυτὸν ἐμπεσὼν εἰς τὸν τῶν πολλῶν βίον ἀποσπασθεὶς τῶν Ἑλλήνων καὶ τῶν ἔτι ἄνω προγόνων. This should mean that Theagenes accepted Christianity and deserted "Hellenism"; for the phrasing, esp. ἀποσπασθεὶς τῶν Ἑλλήνων καὶ τῶν ἔτι ἄνω προγόνων, cf. Damasc. *V. Isid.* frg. 317, Heraiscus's prophecy concerning the conversion of Fl. Horapollon (q.v., no. 78). Finally, the fragments of the alleged Ἰσαυρικά of P. (Gerstinger frg. 1–3 = Heitsch XXXV, 2 and 1) appear to belong to a poem composed in 489/90, after Zeno had put down the revolt of Illus and Leontius, and thus after P.'s death; see McCail, "P. Gr. Vindob. 29788C."

115. PAMPUS(?). Gramm. s.V ex. / s.VI init.

RE 18:2(2).409 (Ensslin); Chr.-Sch.-St. 2:2.1075 n. 5; *PLRE* II s.v., p. 828.

Pampus γραμματικός, recipient of a letter of consolation (P. had been robbed) from Aeneas of Gaza: *Ep.* 6 tit. For doubts concerning the name, perhaps a corruption of Λάμπος or Πάππος, see Massa Positano, ed., *Enea*² p. 82.

PANISCUS: see no. 243.

PAPIRIANUS: see no. 244.

116. PAULUS. Lat. gramm.(?) → Novatian bishop. Constantinople. s.V 1/2; died 438.

PLRE II s.v. 8, p. 850.

At one time probably a Latin gramm.: Soc. *HE* 7.17.2, ὃς πρότερον μὲν λόγων 'Ρωμαϊκῶν διδάσκαλος ἦν. μετὰ δὲ ταῦτα πολλὰ χαίρειν τῇ 'Ρωμαϊκῇ φράσας φωνῇ. . . . With the phrasing of the relative clause, compare Socrates' description of Fl. Eugenius, whom he believed to be a gramm.: *HE* 5.25.1, 'Ρωμαϊκοὺς παιδεύων λόγους (see further s.v., no. 211); with the participial phrase thereafter, compare the version in the *Suda*, Π.814: τὸν δὲ γραμματικὸν πόνον καταλιπών. It is conceivable, however, that P.'s metier had been rhetoric; cf. Soc. *HE* 5.14.5, concerning Symmachus: ἐθαυμάζετο δὲ ἐπὶ παιδεύσει λόγων.

In 419, P. became Novatian bishop in Constantinople after Chrysanthus, son of Marcianus (q.v., no. 238; Soc. *HE* 7.17.1); just before his death, around 21 July 438, he chose as his successor one Marcianus (Soc. *HE* 7.46.4ff.), perhaps his predecessor's son.

P. organized a monastic community of the eremitic type and devoted himself to good works (Soc. *HE* 7.12.2ff. = *Suda* Π.814). In 428, the bishop Nestorius, intent on rooting out heretics and irked by the high regard in which P. was held, planned an attack on him but was checked by the authorities (οἱ κρατοῦντες, Soc. *HE* 7.29.10). P.'s death was mourned by all sects at Constantinople (Soc. *HE* 7.46.2–3).

PHALERIUS: see no. 245.

117. PHILAGRIUS. Gramm. s.III 2/2 / s.IV?

RE Suppl. 11.1061 (Thierfelder); cf. ibid. 1062–68 (id.); Chr.-Sch.-St. 2:2.1049f.

Compiler of jokes; a gramm., according to the inscr. of the longer version of the Φιλόγελως, cod. Paris. suppl. gr. 690, Φιλόγελως ἐκ τῶν Ἱεροκλέους καὶ Φιλαγρίου γραμματικῶν (or γραμματικοῦ, as reported in the most recent edition, by A. Thierfelder [1968]); cf. cod. Monac. gr. 551, Φιλόγελως ἐκ τῶν Ἱεροκλέους καὶ Φιλαγρίου γραμματικοῦ. A firm *term. p. q.* of 248 is established for the collection by the reference in no. 62 to the millenial anniversary of the founding of Rome. Although the nature of the collection, which evidently brings together material from different periods, makes it difficult to draw further reliable inferences concerning the date, much of the diction, esp. the presence of Latin loan words, and the reckoning of prices in myriads point to a date not before s.IV; cf. Wessely, *Altersindizium* 9ff. But the use of pagan oaths and references to pagan practices and beliefs point to a date not much later than s.IV (cf. Thierfelder, *RE* Suppl. 11.1063.16ff.; idem, ed., 14f.), as does also the frequent use of σχολαστικός as an epithet—i.e., with the undifferentiated sense "student," "learned (man)," "scholar(ly)," as opposed to the quasi-titular sense "lawyer" or "advocate" that becomes normal in Greek by s.V; cf. Claus, "ΣΧΟΛΑΣΤΙΚΟΣ" 64ff. Note esp. no. 54, σχολαστικός meaning "student" and distinct from ῥήτωρ; no. 61, σχολαστικὸς χαμαιδιδάσκαλος; no. 90, σχολαστικὸς σοφιστής; no. 256, σχολαστικὸς παιδοτρίβης; but cf. no. 68, a σχολαστικός and his client, συνηγορούμενος. See further Wessely, *Altersindizium* 4ff.; Thierfelder, ed., 12ff.

IUNIUS PHILARGYRIUS: see s.v. IUNIUS FILARGIRIUS, no. 60.

PHILOCALUS: see s.v. FILOCALUS, no. 216.

PHILOMUSUS: see no. 246.

118. IOANNES PHILOPONUS.   Gramm.(?), philosopher, theologian.   Alexandria.   s.V ex. – s.VI 3/4.

RE 9.1764–93 (Gudeman; defective in many respects), 1793–95 (Kroll); Chr.-Sch.-St. 2:2.1067f.; Boehm, *Johannes Philoponus*; Geerard, *Clavis* 3.366ff.; Hunger 1.25ff. and 520, 2.13, 17, 19, 30f., 221, 228f.; *PLRE* II s.v. Ioannes 76, pp. 615f.

Called Ἰωάννης (ὁ) γραμματικός: Timoth. Constant. *De recept. haeret.* 10, *PG* 86:1.61C; *Documenta ad origines Monophysitarum illustrandas*, *CSCO* Scr. Syr., ser. 2, vol. 37 p. 232; and in the polemics of Alfarabi (cf. the trans. by Mahdi, "Alfarabi" 253ff.); for the mss of P., see below. More frequently Ἰωάννης (ὁ) Φιλόπονος or simply ὁ Φιλόπονος *vel sim.*: Ioannes Charax *GG* 4:2.432.5; Bekker *Anecd.* 3.1150; twenty-seven times in Choerobosc. *Schol. in Theodos.*; Phot. *Bibl.* codd. 21–23, 43, 55, 75, 215, 240; Timoth. Constant. *De recept. haeret.* 10; Leontius *De sect.* act. V, *PG* 86:1.1232D, 1233A–B; Nic. Call. *HE* 18.47–49, *PG* 147.424C–432D; Michael the Syrian *Chron.* 8.13, ed. Chabot, vol. 2 p. 92; the catalogues of gramm. in Kröhnert, *Canones* 7, and Rabe, "Listen" 340 (for the mss of

P., see below). Also Ἰωάννης (ὁ) γραμματικὸς Φιλόπονος *vel sim.*: Timoth. Constant. *De recept. haeret.* 10; Nic. Call. *HE* 18.45 and 49; *Suda* I.464; *Conc. Constant. III, Actio XI* Mansi 11.501A; *Documenta ad origines Monophysitarum illustrandas, CSCO* Scr. Syr., ser. 2, vol. 37 p. 112.

The evidence of the mss is as follows. Among the Ammonian commentaries on Aristotle—*Comm. in Anal. pr., Comm. in Anal. post., Comm. in De an., Comm. in De gen. et corr.* (see below)—only the mss of the first and last regularly include γραμματικός in their inscr.; the mss of the others have only Ἰωάννης or Ἰωάννης ὁ Φιλόπονος. Among the non-Ammonian commentaries—*Comm. in Phys., Comm. in Meteorologic. pr., Comm. in Categ.*—the mss of the first have only Ἰωάννης ὁ Φιλόπονος in their inscr.; the mss of the second have either Ἰωάννης γραμματικός or simply ὁ Φιλόπονος; the mss of the third, either Ἰωάννης ὁ Φιλόπονος or Ἰωάννης γραμματικὸς ὁ Φιλόπονος. Further, γραμματικός appears in cod. Haun. 1965 of the Τονικὰ παραγγέλματα and the mss of the Latin trans. of the *Comm. in De an.* by William of Moerbeke, *CLCAG* 3, ed. Verbeke; the *De opificio mundi*, ed. Corder (an. 1630), has Ἰωάννης ὁ Φιλόπονος, but not cod. Vindob. theol. gr. 29; the *De aeternitate mundi contra Proclum* in cod. Escurial. Σ III 19 (s.XVI) has Ἰωάννης ὁ Φιλόπονος, and the ed. Venet. (an. 1535) has Ἰωάννης γραμματικὸς ὁ Φιλόπονος (on the *De aetern. mundi* see below for the evidence of Simplicius).

The forms with γραμματικός and ὁ Φιλόπονος both occur in the Syriac mss of P.'s Monophysite works (ed. Sanda), in the mss of the grammatical work Περὶ τῶν διαφόρως τονουμένων (cf. Daly, ed., pp. 3, 95, 141, 197 = Recensions A, C, D, E), and in the mss of the commentary on Nicomachus of Gerasa (cf. Hoche, ed., praef., vol. 2 [Leipzig, 1867] p. i; Delatte, *Anecdota* 2.129ff.); in the latter two cases, ὁ Φιλόπονος predominates. Ἰωάννης ὁ σχολαστικός occurs in a number of mss of the *Comm. in Anal. pr.*, the *Comm. in De gen. et corr.*, and cod. Neap. III D7 (incorrectly attributing Simplicius's *Comm. in Phys.* to P.); Ἰωάννης ὁ Τριθεΐστης appears in Ioan. Damasc. *De haeres.* 83, *PG* 94.744A (cf. 744B).

Evidently P. himself adopted the epithet or title γραμματικός, found in the inscr. of at least some of his works already in s.VI: cf. esp. Simplicius *Comm. in De cael.* 1.2 (*CAG* 7.49.10f.), καὶ γραμματικοῦ τὰ συγγράμματα ἐπιγράφων; 1.3 (*CAG* 7.71.8), εἰ καὶ γραμματικός ἐστιν, ὡς ἐπιγράφει; 1.3 (*CAG* 7.119.7), οὗτος ὁ γραμματικὸν ἑαυτὸν ἐπιγράφων. The inscr. was thus found at least in the *De aetern. mundi contra Proclum* (composed in 529; see below) and in the lost *De aetern. mundi contra Aristot.*, the works against which Simplicius was directing his polemic; cf. Wieland, "Ewigkeit." Simplicius elsewhere refers to P. simply as ὁ γραμματικός, e.g., *Comm. in De cael.* 1.2 (*CAG* 7.56.26), 1.3 (*CAG* 7.70.34, 73.10), 1.4 (*CAG* 7.156.26, 162.20f.); *Comm. in Phys.* 8.1 (*CAG* 10.1140.7 and *passim*); see further below.

The name ὁ Φιλόπονος was an honorary surname (ἐπίκλησις): cf. esp. *Suda* I.464; Nic. Call. *HE* 18.45; Timoth. Constant. *De recept. haeret.* 10. It possibly indicates association with the paraclerical group of φιλόπονοι at Alexandria; cf. Saffrey, "Chrétien" 403f. When P.'s works were anathematized, his name was parodied as ματαιοπόνος: cf. *Conc. Constant. III, Actio XI* Mansi 11.501A; *Documenta ad origines Monophysitarum illustrandas, CSCO* Scr. Syr., ser. 2, vol. 37 pp. 135, 212; Phot. *Bibl.* codd. 22, 23, 55.

Christian philosopher and theologian, Monophysite, and ultimately chief representative of the tritheist heresy; for the last, his works were anathematized (cf. above). He is not to be confused with the Neo-Chalcedonian Ioannes (q.v., no. 82) of Caesarea, as he is in, e.g., *Suda* I.464 and in Gudeman, *RE* 9.1764.61ff.

Very little is known of his life. He was born(?) or at any rate was active at Alexandria: cf. mss, *Suda* I.464, Nic. Call. *HE* 18.47, Timoth. Constant. *De recept. haeret.* 10. P. wrote the commentary on Aristotle's *Phys.* in 517 (cf. *Comm. in Phys.* 4.10, *CAG* 17.703.16f. with *app. crit.*) and the *De aeternitate mundi contra Proclum* in 529 (cf. p. 599.14ff. Rabe; for criticism of the common view that the latter work represents the Christianization of the Alexandrian school, cf. Westerink, *Anonymous Prolegomena* xiii). The lost *De aeternitate mundi contra Aristotelem* had already been written by the time of the attack on Proclus; cf. *De aetern.* p. 258.24ff. Rabe. The Τμήματα excerpted by Michael the Syrian (see above) contain references to the second Council of Constantinople (553), which thus provides a *term. p. q.* If, as is likely, the bishop Sergius to whom the *De opificio mundi* is dedicated (p. 2.4ff. Reichardt) is the patriarch of Antioch (557/58–559/60), that work can also be dated with some precision; but cf. *contra* Wolska, *Topographie* 163ff. About 568, P. was engaged in a controversy with Ioannes Scholasticus, patriarch of Constantinople; cf. Phot. *Bibl.* cod. 75 (1.153f. Henry). For further attempts at a chronology of P.'s works, see Évrard, "Convictions"; H. Martin, "Jean Philopon."

The inscr. of four—not, as frequently stated, all—of the commentaries on Aristotle show that they derive from the classroom of P.'s teacher, Ammonius Hermiou. In all but the *Comm. in Anal. pr.*, P.'s contribution is noted as well, e.g., Ἰωάννου Ἀλεξανδρέως εἰς τὴν περὶ ψυχῆς Ἀριστοτέλους σχολικαὶ ἀποσημειώσεις ἐκ τῶν συνουσιῶν Ἀμμωνίου τοῦ Ἑρμείου μετά τινων ἰδίων ἐπιστάσεων, *Comm. in De an.* (*CAG* 15.1); similarly *Comm. in Anal. pr.* (*CAG* 13:2.1), *Comm. in Anal. post.* (*CAG* 13:3.1), *Comm. in De gen. et corr.* (*CAG* 14:2.1, 204). If he was a student of Ammonius in—or rather, before—517, his birth should be placed in the last years of s.V. Saffrey, "Chrétien" 403, dates P.'s birth ca. 490; but Saffrey assumes that P. was still a student of Ammonius in 517, the date of the *Comm. in Phys.* Although the assumption may well be incorrect, since that commentary does not bear the classroom inscription of some of the other commentaries (see above), P.'s birth can hardly be put much before 490, which can be retained as a working date with no difficulty. If P. had been born ca. 490, he could have studied with Ammonius in his early twenties— the common time for such studies—and have put his student days behind him by 517.

There is no evidence that P. was anything but a Christian all his life; cf. Évrard, "Convictions."

We do not know how long P. taught as a gramm.; we cannot even be certain that he did so at all. Gudeman, *RE* 9.1781.11ff., believed that γραμματικός was an epithet (= *litteratus*), not a professional title. The suggestion seems arbitrary, since the only evidence adduced has no probative value, viz., P.'s use of γραμματικός as a simple epithet in an example distinguishing a potential from an actual quality: δυνάμει γραμματικός vs. ἐνεργείᾳ, *De aetern. mundi* 3.2, p. 46.3ff. Rabe. The example is merely conventional, with its origins in Aristotle (cf. *De an.* 417a21ff., *Categ.* 10b26ff.), and can be found in the same or similar application elsewhere in P.—e.g., *Comm. in Phys.* 2.1 (*CAG* 16.209.8f.), 3.3 (*CAG* 16.382.1ff.); *Comm. in De gen. et corr.* 2.7 (*CAG* 14:2.271.19ff.); *Tractat. ad Serg.* 1, p. 127 Sanda—as well as in, e.g., Asclepius *Comm. in Metaphys.* 4.7 and 11 (*CAG* 6:2.317.15f.; 324.36ff.), the anti-Manichaean homily attributed to Ioannes (q.v., no. 82) of Caesarea (*CC SG* 1.86.71ff.), and [Elias] *Lectures on Porphyry's Isagoge* 34.7, 42.34f. Westerink; see further Appendix 3.

Yet there may indeed be some evidence that P. was not a gramm. throughout his life: note the distance implied by *Comm. in Categ.* 1 (*CAG* 13:1.16.8f.), τὴν δὲ αἰτίαν [sc. of the use of singular verbs with neuter plural subjects] γραμματικοὶ λεγόντων. The statement is of the common type that distinguishes the expertise and function of the gramm. from those of the philosopher; cf., e.g., Simplicius's polemic, below. Further, P. seems to be independent of Ammonius here: the statement does not appear in the corresponding passage of Ammonius's commentary on the *Categ.*, *CAG* 4:4.18.7ff.; and the inscr. of P.'s *Comm. in Categ.* does not refer to Ammonius's classroom (see above). In only one ms of the *Comm. in Categ.*, cod. Vat. gr. 246, does γραμματικός appear as part of the inscr.

Simplicius, however, clearly did believe that P. was a professional gramm.; cf. esp. *Comm. in De cael.* 1.2 (*CAG* 7.26.21ff.), οὐ γὰρ ἀπὸ Μενάνδρου καὶ Ἡρωδιανοῦ καὶ τῶν τοιούτων ἦλθεν ἡμῖν ἀκριβέστερον Ἀριστοτέλους τὰ περὶ τῆς φύσεως τῶν ὄντων πεπαιδευμένος; with *Comm. in De cael.* 1.2 (*CAG* 7.49.10f.), καὶ θαυμαστόν, ὅτι καὶ γραμματικοῦ τὰ συγγράμματα ἐπιγράφων οὐδέποτε τοῦ τελείου τὴν ἐτυμολογίαν ἐζήτησε. Cf. also *Comm. in De cael.* 1.3 (*CAG* 7.74.5ff.) and *Comm. in Phys.* 8.10 (*CAG* 10.1326.38ff.), in both of which a distinction is drawn between P. *qua* γραμματικός and ἰδιώται; *Comm. in Phys.* 8.1 (*CAG* 10.1161.32f.), P.

qua γραμματικός distinguished from οἱ φιλόσοφοι; *Comm. in Phys.* 8.1 (*CAG* 10.1168.30ff.), ὡς εἴ γε οὗτος . . . γραμματικευόμενος ἐτεχνολόγει. But Simplicius claims to have had no personal acquaintance with P. (cf. *Comm. in De cael.* 1.2, *CAG* 7.26.19); his highly polemical statements are evidently based on inferences drawn from the inscr. of P.'s works (see above). If P. did choose to style himself γραμματικός in the sense *litteratus,* the inferences would be incorrect.

The evidence does not allow an unequivocal conclusion concerning P.'s metier. All told, however, it seems prudent to regard γραμματικός as P.'s professional title unless weightier evidence to the contrary can be found.

Numerous philosophical and theological works are preserved under P.'s name; for lists, see Gudeman, *RE* 9.1772.42ff.; Hermann, "Johannes Philoponus" 211ff.; and (theological works only) Geerard, *Clavis* 3.366ff. There are also treatises on grammatical subjects ascribed to P.: Τονικὰ παραγγέλματα ἐν ἐπιτομῇ, ed. Dindorf (Leipzig, 1825); Περὶ τῶν διαφόρως τονουμένων καὶ διάφορα σημαινόντων, ed. L. W. Daly, Memoirs of the American Philosophical Society, 151 (Philadelphia, 1983); cf. Περὶ τόνων ἐκ τῶν Χοιροβοσκοῦ, Αἰθερίου, Φιλοπόνου καὶ ἑτέρων, ed. Koster, "De accentibus" 151ff.; with Koster, ibid. 136ff.; Ludwich, *De Ioanne Philopono*; see also s.v. Aetherius, no. 180. A tract on barbarisms and solecisms is attributed to P. in cod. Vindob. phil. gr. 347 (s.XVI); cf. Hunger, *Katalog* 1.440. For extracts from a dialectological work Περὶ Αἰολίδος attributed to a Ἰωάννης γραμματικός (possibly P.), see Hoffmann, *Griechischen Dialekte* 2.204–22. The authenticity of all these tracts has sometimes been doubted, at least in the form transmitted; the treatise Περὶ τῶν διαφόρως τονουμένων is not attributed to P. in the mss of Recension B or in the oldest ms, Bodl. Barocc. 50 (s.X), of Recension A; see Daly, ed., pp. 3, 55.

P. is cited by Ioannes Charax and, more frequently, by Georgius Choeroboscus (qq.v., nos. 199, 201; cf. above). He is listed in the catalogues of gramm. in Kröhnert, *Canones* 7, under the heading ὅσοι περὶ ὀρθογραφίας, and Rabe, "Listen" 340. His teacher was perhaps Romanus (q.v., no. 129).

119. PHILTATIUS. Gramm.(?). Athens. s.V init.

RE 20.203 (Ensslin); *PLRE* II s.v., p. 880.

Friend of Olympiodorus of Thebes; honored ca. 416/17 with a statue at Athens after solving a problem concerning the colometry of texts: Olympiod. frg. 32 = Phot. *Bibl.* cod. 80 (1.179 Henry) = *FHG* 4.64, reading περὶ τῶν κεκωλισμένων βιβλίων . . . τὸ μέτρον τοῦ κώλου with Dindorf, *Hist. Gr. min.* 1.463.9f. and p. lv, after Phot. cod. A; against περὶ τῶν κεκολλημένων βιβλίων . . . τὸ μέτρον τοῦ κόλλου, the reading of Phot. cod. M, adopted by Müller and Henry. For the error, compare κεκόλλισται and κεκόλησται for κεκώλισται in the subscr. to the *Scholia vetera* of Aristoph. *Nub.*, p. 250.2 Koster. It seems unlikely that P.'s skills in γραμματική would have been called into play if the banausic matter of bookbinding were involved (see also below).

The description of P. in Olympiod. frg. 32 as εὐφυῶς περὶ γραμματικῆς ἔχων does not make clear whether he was a professional gramm., or simply a man of literary attainments. If P. was a gramm., the phrase may be a periphrasis chosen for stylistic reasons, to avoid the technical term γραμματικός; cf. Appendix 1.3 and Appendix 2. The mention of γραμματική does, in any case, suggest that the colometry of poetic texts was involved, rather than prose texts written κατὰ κῶλον; cf. *Suda* E.3394, quoted s.v. Eugenius, no. 56; differently Frantz, "Honors," a good treatment of the fragment in its historical context.

120. PHILUMENUS.   Schoolmaster → monk.   Mossyna / Epistraton (Galatia I).   s.VI med. – 2/2.

Schoolmaster (παιδοδιδάσκαλος) at Mossyna / Epistraton, near Syceon in the hinterland of Anastasiopolis. As a young man he became the first disciple of Theodore of Syceon, after the latter had cured P.'s mother: Georg. presb. *Vie de Théodore de Sykéon*, ed. Festugière, Subsidia hagiographica 48, §26.7ff. He came to serve as the scribe of the monastery and instructed the monks, including George, the author of the biography, in letters: ibid. §26.20ff., ἦν ὁ νεανίας καλὸς τῷ εἴδει, πλέον δὲ τοῖς ἤθεσι τῆς γνώμης, πεπειραμένος δὲ κατὰ ἄκρον πάσης τῆς τῶν γραμμάτων σοφίας. ὅστις καὶ τὰς πλείους βίβλους ἰδίᾳ χειρὶ γεγράφηκεν τῆς γενομένης μονῆς, ἐμέ τε τὸν ἀνάξιον καὶ ἄλλους οὐκ ὀλίγους παῖδάς τε καὶ μέσης ἡλικίας τῇ τῶν γραμμάτων παιδεύσας διδασκαλίᾳ. . . .

For his later monastic activities, see ibid. §§30, 41, 54, 70, 130. Cf. also s.v. Anonymus 12, no. 178.

121. PHOCAS.   Gramm.   Rome.   s.IV ex. / s.V.

RE 20.318–22 (Strzelecki); Sch.-Hos. 4:2.215–18; *PLRE* I s.v., p. 699; replaced by *PLRE* II s.v. 3, p. 881.

Phocas, Focas: inscr. *Ars, Vita*; Prisc. *Inst.*, *GL* 2.515.16; Cassiod. *De orth.* praef. (*GL* 7.146.21), *Inst.* 1.30.2. A *grammaticus*: several codd. of the *Ars*; the unique cod. of the *Vita*. That he was a teacher is evident from *Ars de nom. et verbo*, *GL* 5.411.13ff., on *discipuli nostri* and *nostra professio*. The *Ars* was written with a view to the schools (cf. *GL* 5.410.6, 411.2ff., 426.8f.), although a larger audience was anticipated (*GL* 5.410.8–9, 411.8ff.). He seems to have taught in Rome: *grammaticus urbis Romae*, inscr. cod. *Vitae*; cf. Mazzarino, "Appunti" 520 n. 3.

A *term. a. q.* for P. is provided by the citation in Priscian (above), which, incidentally, contradicts P.'s words at *GL* 5.433.24. The *term. p. q.* is controversial. P. has been dated after Donatus, whose *Vita* of Vergil P.

is sometimes thought to have used. The debt is not certain, but the date would be consistent with the fact that traces of Charisius and Diomedes have been detected in the *Ars*; cf. Keil at *GL* 5.407. Note also that Priscian (*GL* 2.515.16) cites P. in the company of Diomedes and Charisius and that P.'s preface at times slightly resembles those of the other two men; cf. *GL* 5.410.4–5, 14–16 with *GL* 1.1.14f., 299.2–7. More cogently, a date after Donatus would consist with P.'s frequent citations of Lucan in the *Ars*: nine times, equaled only by his citations of Vergil; Juvenal is cited three times. For the significance of this frequency, cf. Wessner, "Lucan," with Kaster, "Servius."

Otherwise, P. has been dated before Donatus, perhaps s.III ex. / s.IV init. This dating denies P.'s dependence on Donatus's *Vita* and derives from a notice in Cassiodorus (*GL* 7.214.23ff.) that groups P. with Palaemon, Probus, and Censorinus as an *auctor temporum superiorum*, in contrast to Donatus. Cf. Cassiod. *Inst.* 1.30.2 and the notice in cod. Vat. Regin. 1560, of s.XI (cf. Keil at *GL* 5.407), *Focas iste antiquissimus grammaticus fuit ante Priscianum et Donatum, adeo ut Priscianus multa de eo in libro suo dicat et exempla sumat*; save for the mention of Donatus, a piece of information possibly drawn from Cassiodorus (*GL* 7.214.23ff.), the notice is found in virtually the same form in the commentary on P. by Remigius of Auxerre: cf. Esposito, "Ninth-Century Commentary" 167.

For the former, standard, dating, see Sch.-Hos. 4:2.216; cf. Mazzarino, "Appunti" 526f.; Jeudy, "*Ars*" 61f. For the latter dating, see Strzelecki, *RE* 20.318f.; followed by F. Casaceli, ed. (Naples, 1973); criticized by Mazzarino, "Appunti" 506ff. Cassiodorus is probably mistaken, as he is elsewhere in such matters (cf. s.vv. Eutyches, Martyrius, nos. 57, 95); P. should probably be placed in the late fourth or in the fifth century, primarily because he uses Juvenal and Lucan (cf. above): so, correctly, Jeudy, "*Ars*" 62.

Author of an *Ars de nomine et verbo*, ed. Keil, *GL* 5.410–39, and ed. F. Casaceli (Naples, 1973); for a full account of the medieval reception of the work, see Jeudy, "*Ars*" 62ff. The work is presented as a brief, clear review of the traditional teachings on the subject. Also author of a *Vita Vergilii*, in hexameters, with a prologue in sapphic strophes; the biography derives (through Donatus?) from Suetonius. Two other works, an *Orthographia* and a *De aspiratione*, are wrongly attributed to P. For the former, see Sabbadini, "Ortografia"; for the latter, see *GL* 5.439–41 and, for the mss, Jeudy, "Tradition."

Because P. uses the name *Petrus* in a paradigm (*GL* 5.423.20), Mazzarino suggested that he was a Christian or writing for a largely Christian public ("Appunti" 526f.)—likely enough if P. was active in s.IV ex. or s.V. Note that such religious affiliations would seem not to have prevented P. from referring to the schools of the traditional literary culture as the *gymnasium sapientiae, quo ad beatam vitam semita demonstratur* (cf. *GL* 5.411.2ff.), or to the *Aeneid* as a *carmen sacrum* (*V. Verg.* praef. 24).

122. PHOEBICIUS. Gramm. Bayeux → Bordeaux. s.IV init.

RE 20.322 (Ensslin); *PLRE* I s.v., p. 700.

Phoebicius (Auson. *Prof.* 10.23), a native of Baiocassum (Bayeux), in Armorica (ibid. 28, with *Prof.* 4.7). He taught as a Latin gramm. at Bordeaux (*Prof.* 10 tit., v. 29), where he gained his chair with the help of his son (ibid. 29–30; see below).

P.'s son Attius Patera was a generation older than Ausonius: *Prof.* 4.3–4, *aevo floruisti proximo / iuvenisque te vidi senem.* P.'s grandson, Attius Tiro Delphidius, was Ausonius's contemporary, *floruit* ca. 355 (cf. Jerome *Chron.* s.a.), dead *medio aevi* (*Prof.* 5.36)—which is vague enough—before 381; cf. Booth, "Notes" 239; for the relationships, see below. P. was therefore of the generation of Ausonius's grandfather. Ausonius's notice is very impersonal; we learn nothing about P. from *Prof.* 10 that could not be gathered from the poem on his son Patera, save the exact form of P.'s name and the fact that he gained his post with his son's help. Such distance suggests that Ausonius did not know P. well, if at all; cf. s.v. Concordius, no. 35, on *Prof.* 10 in general. P.'s teaching is to be placed very early in s.IV.

He was the father of Attius Patera and Phoebicius, and was the grandfather of Attius Tiro Delphidius: *Prof.* 4.11–14. It is usually assumed that Patera, the rhetorician, was the son responsible for securing P.'s post at Bordeaux.

He was a priest of Belenus-Apollo at Bayeux (*Prof.* 10.24, with 4.7–9), where his family claimed descent from Druids (*Prof.* 10.27, 4.7), a claim that Ausonius does not present without considerable qualification: *Prof.* 10.26, *ut placitum*; 4.8, *si fama non fallit fidem.*

123. PLACIDUS. Gramm.(?) and glossographer. s.V / s.VI?

RE 20.1937–44 (Dahlmann); Sch.-Hos. 4:2.257–61; Goetz, *CGL* 1.59ff.; Wessner, *CGL* 1.311ff.; Lindsay, *Gloss. Lat.* 4.5ff.; *PLRE* II s.v. 2, p. 890.

Placidus: *libri Romani* = codd. Vat. lat. 1552 (s.XV), 3441 (s.XV), 5216 (s.XVI); on the name "Luctatius Placidus" in the lost cod. Corsianus, see Goetz, *CGL* 1.59. Styled *grammaticus* in the *libri Romani.*

From a note found in a version(?) of the glossary preserved in cod. Paris. lat. n. a. 1298 (= *CGL* 5.147.33), *solaces: quod nos funalia dicimus . . . hos Romani funes et funalia nominabant*, it has been inferred that P. did not write at Rome; but the provenance of the note is uncertain, as are attempts to place P. in Africa, Gaul, or Spain. In the same Paris ms there are three references to Donatus (*CGL* 5.114.4, 123.14, 149.2); in another(?) version, the *Liber glossarum*, there are two allusions to Orosius (*CGL* 5.71.23, cf. *Gloss. Lat.* 4.41 G.1; *CGL* 5.97.23, cf. *Gloss. Lat.* 4.48 S.2). If the references to Donatus are authentic, a *term. p. q.* of s.IV med. is established; if those to Orosius are, s.V init. The influence of some glosses of P.—or ps.-P., according to Lindsay—has been found in the preface of the codex Salmasianus; cf. Goetz, *CGL* 5 pp. vi–vii; Lindsay, *Gloss. Lat.* 4.8f. This would suggest a *term. a. q.* of s.VI. He was in any case a source for Isidore of Seville; cf. Sch.-Hos. 4:2.260; more restrained, Fontaine, *Isidore* 572.

Author of a glossary containing entries of two distinct kinds: brief glosses on archaic words, extant through the letter *P* (treated as ps.-Placidus by Lindsay, *Gloss. Lat.* 4), and more extensive notes of grammatical or antiquarian interest. The glossary is printed as three recensions by Goetz, *CGL* 5: *Placidus librorum Romanorum, Placidus Libri glossarum*, and *Placidus codicis Parisini*. For further details, see Dahlmann, *RE* 20.1938ff.

P. was probably a Christian; cf. references to *pagani* at, e.g., *CGL* 5.4.5 = 49.10 = *Gloss. Lat.* 4.12 A.19; *CGL* 5.19.17 = 63.20 = *Gloss. Lat.* 4.21 E.29; *CGL* 5.25.9 = 74.19 = 109.46 = *Gloss. Lat.* 4.24 H.9; *CGL* 5.27.11 = 90.22 = *Gloss. Lat.* 4.25 I.19.

PLUTARCHUS: see no. 247.

*   AUR. PLUTION: see no. 248.

124. IULIANUS POMERIUS.   Gramm. and rhetorician / presbyter or abbot. Africa → Arles.   s.V ex. / s.VI init.

RE 21.1876 (Ensslin); Sch.-Hos. 4:2.554–56; *PLRE* II s.v., p. 896; cf. Mathisen, "*PLRE*" 382.

Iulianus Pomerius: Isidore of Seville *De vir. ill.* 25.31, *PL* 83.1096A; Pomerius elsewhere. Of African origin ([Gennad.] *De vir. ill.* 99; *V. Caes.* 1.9, 2.299.32 Morin); settled in Arles by ca. 497/98, when he undertook the education of Caesarius of Arles. His migration has been associated in some modern accounts with Vandal persecution of the Catholics. If this is correct, the move should be placed under Huneric (d. 484) or—less likely—very early in the reign of Thrasamund; cf. Victor *Chron.* s.a. 497, 4, *Chron. min.* 2.193.

He appears to have taught both gramm. and rhetoric, although it is not clear whether he taught the two subjects at different points in his career or concurrently: *V. Caes.* 1.9, p. 299.31ff., *Pomerius nomine, scientia rhetor . . . , quem ibi* [= at Arles] *singularem et clarum grammaticae artis doctrina reddebat*. The relative clause makes it clear that P. was teaching grammar at Arles, which would be consistent with the negligible literary attainments attributed to his student Caesarius in the *Vita* up to that point; perhaps P. had taught rhetoric earlier in Africa. While at Arles he was the protégé of the local magnate Firminus and his mother, Gregoria: *V. Caes.* 1.8f., p. 299.23ff. On P.'s achievements in both ecclesiastical and secular studies, *utraque bibliotheca*, cf. Ennod. *Epist.* 2.6.2, 4ff., *MGH* AA 7.38 (mid-503: Sundwall, *Abhandlungen* 73); Ruric. *Ep.* 2.9, *CSEL* 21.385.7ff.

P. is called a presbyter at [Gennad.] *De vir. ill.* 99; Ruricius addresses him as *abbas* in *Ep.* 1.17 (p. 369.13) and 2.10 (p. 385.12). Neither the relationship between the two titles nor the relationship between these titles and P.'s secular career can be determined.

He was invited to Limoges by Ruricius (*Ep.* 2.10, p. 385.13ff.; cf. 2.9, p. 385.2ff.) and to Milan by Ennodius (*Epist.* 2.6.1, pp. 37f.). P.'s acquaintance with Ennodius might have been formed at Arles, the probable place of Ennodius's origin; P.'s patron, Firminus, might in fact be Firminus the learned man and relative of Ennodius known from the latter's correspondence in the first years of s.VI: Ennod. *Epist.* 1.8 (p. 17; early 502, according to Sundwall, *Abhandlungen* 72), 2.8 (pp. 38f.; mid-503, according to Sundwall, *Abhandlungen* 73); cf. *PLRE* II s.v. Firminus 4, p. 471.

In addition to the extant *De vita contemplativa* (*PL* 59.415ff.; Engl. trans. M. J. Suelzer [Westminster, Md., 1947]; cf. Hagendahl, *Latin Fathers* 345f., 372ff.), P. is credited with a dialogue *De natura animae*, in eight books (fragments collected by Solignac, "Fragments"), two *dictata* (*De contemptu mundi, De vitiis et virtutibus*), and a work *De virginibus instituendis*: [Gennad.] *De vir. ill.* 99; Isidore of Seville *De vir. ill.* 25.31–33.

125. POMPEIUS. Gramm. Africa. s.V / s.VI.

RE 21.2313–15 (Helm); Sch.-Hos. 4:2.208–10; Holtz, "Tradition"; Schindel, *Figurenlehren* 19ff.; *PLRE* II s.v. 1, p. 898.

Pompeius: codd.; the catalogues of gramm. in cod. Bonon. 797 (Negri, "De codice" 266) and cod. Bern. 243 (*Anecd. Helv.* = *GL* 8, cxlix). Styled *grammaticus* in the inscr. of several mss; cf. Keil at *GL* 5.83f.; Holtz, "Tradition" 53ff.

Author of a commentary on Donatus's *Ars*, with emphasis on the *Ars maior*; perhaps also of commentaries on Vergil and Terence, but this is extremely uncertain: see the appendix below. That the commentary on Donatus was written with a view to the schools is suggested by the care taken to explain even the most elementary points, by the recurrence of such phrases as *ne puer erret* (e.g., *GL* 5.132.13), and by the fact that the reader, *tu*, to whom P. addresses himself is imagined to be a teacher; see Chap. 4.

P. can be placed in Africa on the basis of *GL* 5.205.4ff., *si interroges verbi causa de Mauro, aut siqui me interroget, "iste homo cuias est?," "nostras est," id est Maurus*; for other, less eloquent evidence, cf. Keil at *GL* 5.93; Sch.-Hos. 4:2.209. He is to be dated after Donatus, on whose *Ars* he commented, and in fact after Servius, whom he does not name but whose unabridged commentary on Donatus he certainly used, very possibly in interpolated form (see Chap. 4 n. 8), and before Isidore of Seville (ca. 560–636), who used him. He is to be placed, therefore, in s.V or early(?) s.VI (s.V 2/2: Schindel, *Figurenlehren* 19ff.; s.V 2/2 or s.VI: Holtz, "À l'école de Donat" 526).

It has been suggested on the basis of *GL* 5.239.16ff., discussing the phrase *Liber pater* and the word *triumphans*, that he was a pagan; but those comments are entirely conventional, and his extended discussion of the word *Pascha*, *GL* 5.177.4ff., shows that he was a Christian.

Appendix: *GL* 5.294.33ff., *quem ad modum diximus in Vergilio*

In his remarks on *tapinosis* in the commentary on Donatus, *GL* 5.294.27ff., P. makes a cross-reference, *quem ad modum diximus in Vergilio* (*GL* 5.294.33f.), apparently drawing attention to statements made in a commentary on Vergil. Since the doctrine and the examples that follow correspond precisely to Servius's commentary on *Aen.* 1.118 and 2.19, and since it is otherwise clear that P.'s massive debt to Servius's *Comm. Don.* extends even to the inept repetition of cross-references found in the latter work (see Chap. 4 pp. 142ff.), Schindel concluded that this cross-reference too was taken directly from Servius (*Figurenlehren* 25f., 132f.; against Fontaine, *Isidore* 135, who posited a commentary on Vergil by P. himself, following "sur les pas de Servius"). If correct, Schindel's conclusion would establish that Servius composed his commentary on Vergil before his commentary on Donatus.

In the absence of other evidence, Schindel's conclusion would appear quite probable. There are, however, two other passages in P. that should be remarked, since they are similar to the cross-reference at *GL* 5.294.33f., and in fact obscure its significance. In the first, after denying (with Servius and Donatus) the existence of a future passive participle in deponent verbs (*GL* 5.228.28ff.), P. attempts to deal with apparent counter-examples of the type *loquendus*; in the course of his comments, he includes the cross-reference (*GL* 5.229.6f.) *habemus usurpandorum participiorum licentiam, ut diximus et in Terentio*. Again, in his comments on verbs that lack one or more moods, P. remarks (*GL* 5.240.18ff.), [*habes verbum defectivum*] *per modos, ut diximus in Terentio, "cedo," non "caedo" ut faciat diphthongon, sed "cedo," id est "dic": hoc enim verbum non habet nisi solum imperativum, "cedo quid attulisti?"* There is no comparable comment on *cedo* in the extant version of Donatus's commentary on Terence.

In both places the reference to what was said *in Terentio* evidently alludes to a commentary on Terence; both references must be compared with the reference *quem ad modum diximus in Vergilio*. Among the conclusions that could be drawn, the following seem most worth noting.

First, despite their formal similarity, the references to a commentary on Terence might have no bearing on the reference to a commentary on Vergil; the latter reference could have been taken over from Servius, as Schindel suggested, and the former passages could refer to a commentary on Terence by P. himself.

Alternatively, the reference to the Vergilian commentary could have been taken over from Servius, and the references to the Terentian commentary could have been taken over from Donatus's commentary on Vergil, to which P. had access. On the latter point, see Schindel, *Figurenlehren* 101ff.; but note the *communis opinio* that Donatus composed his commentary on Terence after his commentary on Vergil—e.g., Wessner, "Bericht" 201f.; Schindel, *Figurenlehren* 11 n. 14.

Or, all three references could have been taken over from Servius; we would then have unique evidence for a Servian commentary on Terence. But, other considerations aside, note that the specific doctrine of *GL* 5.229.6f., concerning the *usurpandorum participiorum licentia*, takes a distinctly un-Servian turn: with the *licentia* claimed there, contrast *GL* 5.263.1ff. with Serv. *GL* 4.441.10–15; cf. Chap. 5 pp. 172ff.

Or again, all three references could have been lifted from the version of Servius's *Comm. Don.* known to P., a version probably already interpolated with extraneous observations and additions by an unknown scholar (see above). None of the passages would then need to refer to works by P.; instead, they could refer to Servius's commentary on Vergil and a commentary on Terence by the unknown intermediary.

Last, all three passages could refer to commentaries by P., whose commentary on Vergil would then have been much indebted to Servius's (or Donatus's).

Of these possibilities, the second and third seem unlikely *prima facie*; our current knowledge does not, I think, allow us to decide confidently among the rest. Concerning the last possibility, however, one can add the following: though Schindel demonstrated that the doctrine introduced by the cross-reference at *GL* 5.294.33f. corresponds to Servius's remarks in his Vergilian commentary, this does not by itself prove that the cross-reference was taken from Servius's *Comm. Don.* or that P. himself did not write a commentary on Vergil. For given P.'s great dependence on a single main source (Serv. *Comm. Don.*) in his commentary on Donatus, we may conjecture that any commentary on Vergil he might have composed would similarly have depended on one main source, whether Servius's Vergilian commentary or Donatus's. The correspondence Schindel noted could therefore be explained if a commentary by P. were based directly on Servius (cf. Fontaine, *Isidore* 135, above) or on Donatus, whose work he knew; in the latter case, the similarity between P. and Servius would be attributable to their dependence on a common source. That a commentary by P. on Vergil or on Terence is otherwise unattested does not count for much, since virtually all our knowledge about P. comes only from his own text. Note too that P. provides evidence for other, post-Servian grammatical work, which is also otherwise unattested; see s.v. Astyagius, no. 189.

126. PRISCIANUS. Lat. gramm. Caesarea (Mauretania Caesariensis?) → Constantinople. s.V ex.–s.VI 1/3.

RE 22.2328–46 (Helm); Sch.-Hos. 4:2.221–38; Glück, *Priscians Partitiones*; Salamon, "Priscianus"; *PLRE* II s.v. 2, p. 905.

Priscianus: codd. of the grammatical works and poems (see *app. crit.* of Keil's ed. in *GL*, and Passalacqua, *Codici*); subscr. of Theodorus to *Inst.* 5, 8, 13, 14 and inscr. and subscr. to *Inst.* 17; Eutyches *GL* 5.456.31 (cf. *Anecd. Helv.* = *GL* 8.1.9f., 2.6f.); Cassiod. *GL* 7.147.15, 207.13, 214.18; "Albinus magister" (= Alcuin) *GL* 7.310.34 and 36, 312.23; Paul. Diac. *De gest. Langob.* 1.25, *MGH* SS. rer. langob. 63. P. also uses his own name in gramm. examples, e.g., *GL* 2.79.9.

Styled *grammaticus*: codd.; subscr. of Theodorus; Eutyches *GL* 5.456.31; Cassiod. *GL* 7.207.13; Paul. Diac. *De gest. Langob.* 1.25. Also called *doctor meus*: subscr. of Theodorus to *Inst.* 8 and 14, and inscr. to *Inst.* 17; cf. *doctor*, Cassiod. *GL* 7.207.14. Or *praeceptor meus*: inscr. of Theodorus to *Inst.* 8; Eutyches *GL* 5.456.29f. Cf. also P.'s reference to his *professio* at *GL* 2.2.3. He is called *sophista* in subscr. to the *Praeex.*

Called *Caesariensis* in the subscr. of Theodorus and in various mss in the inscr. to the prefatory epistle of *Inst.* and in the inscr. or subscr. to *Inst.* 1, 7, 9, 11, 13, 15; at *De figuris* (*ad fin.*); in two mss of the *Periegesis* (see Woestijne, ed., pp. 10ff.); Paul. Diac. *De gest. Langob.* 1.25. Since P. aligns himself with speakers of Latin—*nos* or *nostri* vs. *Graeci*, e.g., *GL* 2.1.12ff., and often—Niebuhr concluded that he must have been a native of Caesarea in Mauretania (*CSHB* 1, xxxiv). The inference was anticipated by the author of the *vita* of P.: *Anecd. Helv.* = *GL* 8, clxviii, lines 6ff.

P. taught at Constantinople: *grammaticus* or *doctor urbis Romae Constantinopolitanae* in the subscr. of Theodorus at *Inst.* 8, 14, 17; cf. also various mss in the inscr. to the prefatory epistle of *Inst.* and in subscr. to *Inst.* 9, 11, 13, 15; Cassiod. *GL* 7.207.13f.; Paul. Diac. *De gest. Langob.* 1.25. For P.'s firsthand knowledge of Constantinople, cf. *GL* 2.17.13f. He was a pupil of Theoctistus (q.v., no. 149), also presumably at Constantinople.

P. was at Constantinople during the reign of Anastasius, for whom he wrote a panegyric, *De laud. Anast.* (cf. esp. vv. 248ff., praise of Anastasius's patronage of learned men), now plausibly dated to 503; cf. Alan Cameron, "Date of Priscian's *De laude*," against the traditional date of 512. A date of 513 has been proposed more recently by Chauvot, "Observations." A *term. a. q.* of 526 is provided for the *Inst.* by the subscr. of Theodorus, which record his progress (*ut vid.*) in copying various parts of the work: the subscr. to *Inst.* 5 is dated to the consulship of Olybrius = 526; the subscr. of *Inst.* 8 is dated 11 January 527; of *Inst.* 13, 5 February 527; the inscr. of *Inst.* 17, 25 February 527; the subscr. of *Inst.* 17, 30 May 527. The dedication of the three minor works (on which see below) to Symmachus, presumably Q. Aurelius Memmius Symmachus, provides a *term. a. q.* of 525 for those pieces. The notice of Cassiodorus is vague: *GL* 7.207.13f., *ex Prisciano grammatico, qui nostro tempore Constantinopoli doctor fuit*; cf. ibid. 147.15, *ex Prisciano moderno auctore.* These remarks are usually taken to refer to the time of Cassiodorus's career at the western court, before 537, rather than to the years he spent at Constantinople, 540–54. P. is dated by Paul. Diac. *De gest. Langob.* 1.25 to the reign of Justinian. If this is correct, the early part of the reign is presumably meant; the dating may, however, be no more than an inference drawn from the subscr. of Theodorus to *Inst.* 17: *scripsi manu mea in urbe Roma Constantinopoli tertio Kal. Iunias Mavortio v.c. consule imperantibus Iustino et Iustiniano PP. Augg.*

P. was the author of the *Institutio grammatica* (= *Inst.*) in eighteen books, in which he intended to apply the teachings of Greek gramm., esp. Herodian and Apollonius Dyscolus, to Latin and to correct the faults of his Latin predecessors; cf. *Inst.* praef. epist., *GL* 2.1.2ff.; for P.'s Greek sources, cf. Luscher, *De Prisciani studiis.* Also author of the *Institutio de nomine, pronomine et verbo*, a compendium drawing upon the preceding work, intended for use in the schools (cf. *GL* 3.449.1); and of the *Partitiones duodecim versuum Aeneidos principalium*, also for the schools. On the background of the exercise *partitio* or ἐπιμερισμός, see Glück, *Priscians Partitiones* 31ff., with Lossau's review of Glück, *Gnomon* 43 (1971), 168f. The relative chronology of the three works can be established, since the *Inst. de nom.* refers eight times to full discussion in the *Inst.*, and the *Partit.* contains references to both of the latter works; cf. Glück, *Priscians Partitiones* 54f., 162ff.

Also author of the *De figuris numerorum*, the *De metris fabularum Terentii*, and the *Praeexercitamina*, all dedicated to Symmachus (for his probable identity see above). The chronological relation of these three to the first three works cannot be established. There are also two poems, viz., the panegyric of Anastasius (see above) and a version of the Περιήγησις of Dionysius. At (*Inst.*) *GL* 3.133.1, P. refers to a *liber . . . de accentibus* that he had written. It is uncertain whether the *De accentibus* now extant under P.'s name (*GL* 3.519–28) is authentic; see most recently Holtz, *Donat* 243. The two poems *De sideribus* and *De ponderibus et mensuris* attributed to P. are not genuine. For the mss of P., see Passalacqua, *Codici.*

Symmachus is the dedicatee of the *De figuris*, the *De metris*, and the *Praeexercitamina*; the dedicatee of the *Inst.* (*GL* 2.2.24ff., with a second dedication at the beginning of *Inst.* 6, *GL* 2.194.2ff.) is *Iulianus consul ac patricius*, not otherwise known. For the suggestion that Iulianus is also addressed in the *Inst. de nom.*, cf. Glück, *Priscians Partitiones* 61. He is perhaps the *Iulianus v.c.* of the subscr. to Stat. *Theb.* 4 found in the cod. Puteanus (Paris. lat. 8051); cf. Vollmer, "Textkritisches zu Statius" 27; Pasquali, *Storia*[2] 175ff. The consulship was presumably honorary, since Iulianus is not known to the *fasti*.

The pupils of P. included the gramm. Eutyches (q.v., no. 57) and the subscriber of the *Inst.*, Fl. Theodorus, who consistently styles himself *v.d. memorialis sacri scrinii epistolarum et adiutor v.m. quaestoris sacri palatii*. The names "Flaccus," "Flavianus," and "Flavius Lucius" that appear in some mss (see Keil's *app. crit.* for the subscr. noted above) are mistaken expansions of "Fl."; he is probably to be identified with the Theodorus *antiquarius qui nunc palatinus est* who appears in the subscr. to Boethius *Hyp. syll.* 3 in Paris. lat. n. a. 1611. For the text of the subscr., see Pagallo, "Per una edizione" 72. Another supposed pupil, Ter(r)entius, is a later invention (see s.v., no. 262).

P. may have had a son who went to Rome; cf. *GL* 2.407.14ff., *ut si, filio meo Romae in praesenti degente, optans dicam.* . . . But the passage could be merely exemplary, i.e., the son or his stay in Rome, or both, might have been invented to illustrate the usage at issue; cf. 3.240.3ff., a similar example with a son now in Athens.

P. was a Christian; cf. *GL* 2.238.5f., *noster praeceptor Theoctistus* . . . *cui quidquid in me sit doctrinae post Deum imputo*; cf. also Christian traits in the *De laud. Anast.*, esp. vv. 211ff.

* 127. PROBUS(?).   Gramm.   Africa? → Rome?   s.IV.

RE 23.59–64 (Helm); Sch.-Hos. 2.738–41; della Casa, "'Grammatica'" 149ff.; Jocelyn, "Annotations III" 468f.

Probus: codd. Paris. lat. 7494 (s.IX), 7519 (s.XV) of the *Inst. art.*; citations of the *Inst. art.* in Servius, Cledonius, Pompeius, Rufinus, Priscian (see further below). *Grammaticus*: inscr. in the Paris mss noted above. The subscr. *Probi grammatici urbis* at the end of the *Catholica* in cod. Neap. lat. 2 (= Vindob. 16; s.V) is probably worthless; in all likelihood the work has been incorrectly attributed to P. and belongs to Sacerdos (see below). The *Inst. art.* gives no clear indication of its author's profession or status and, beyond its fairly elementary exposition, allows no sure conclusions about its intended audience. From the use of the names *Cirta* and *Utica* along with *Roma* in an example (*GL* 4.155.16f.), it has been inferred that the author was a native of Africa; cf. Barwick, "Sogenannte *Appendix*" 422. Reference to the Baths of Diocletian (see below) might suggest residence in the capital.

A *term. p. q.* is established for the *Inst. art.* by the reference (*GL* 4.119.26–27) to the *Diocletianae thermae*, dedicated between 1 May 305 and 24 July 306; cf. Hülsen, *RE* 5.657. *Pace* Barwick, "Sogenannte *Appendix*" 422, the composition of the *Inst. art.* need not be dated precisely to the period of the dedication; but note that the name of Cirta (see above) was changed to Constantina sometime between 310 (cf. Aur. Victor *De Caes.* 41.28) and 320 (cf. the *Gesta apud Zenophilum* of that year, quoted s.v. Victor, no. 161). A firm *term. a. q.* is provided by the citations in Servius (s.IV ex. / s.V init.), who refers to P. by name when citing the work; the probable misattribution of the *Catholica* also presupposes that the *Inst. art.* was circulating under P.'s name by or before Servius's time (see below). Thereafter P. is cited by Cledonius, Pompeius (from Servius), Rufinus, and Priscian; for a list of citations, see Keil, *GL* 4, xvii–xviii; della Casa, "'Grammatica'" 154ff. Cf. also s.vv. Audax, Palladius, nos. 190, 242.

Author of an *Instituta artium* (*GL* 4.47–192), a handbook of the basics that proceeds from definitions *de voce, de arte, de litteris,* and *de syllabis* through the eight parts of speech. The title *Instituta artium* is used by Priscian, *GL* 2.283.7, and indeed was probably known in that form before the end of s.IV; cf. below on the *Catholica.* The work appears without title or attribution in cod. Vat. Urb. lat. 1154 (s.V ex.) and is inscribed simply *Tractatus Probi grammatici* in cod. Paris. lat. 7494; the inscr. *Probi grammatici de octo orationis membris ars minor* occurs in cod. Paris. lat. 7519; part of the *Inst. art.* also appears in fol. 17^r–49^r of cod. Neap. lat. 1 (= Vindob. 17; s.VII / s.VIII), but a quaternion bearing the beginning of the work has been lost, and with it any inscr. that may have appeared.

It has been suggested, most recently by della Casa, "'Grammatica'" 152f. (cf. Jocelyn, "Annotations III" 468f.), that the *Inst. art.* is not the work of a man named Probus but was circulating as an acephalous treatise to which the name of the famous literary man (Valerius) Probus was attached. This is not implausible: cf. esp. s.v. Victorinus, no. 273, and note the lack of attribution in cod. Vat. Urb. lat. 1154, the earliest extant ms. But of that ms, sumptuously produced in uncial script of late s.V (cf. Lowe, *CLA* 1.117), Lindsay, "The Primary MS." 232, remarked: "And yet . . . the scribe has thought more of beauty than of accuracy. He has been guilty of many omissions, some of them very large." The lack of attribution may therefore not count for much, and it is quite possible that the work was written by a gramm. called Probus—a common name in late antiquity—as the citations of Servius, Priscian, and other gramm. (see above) attest; cf. Dionisotti, "Latin Grammar" 206. Whatever the name of the author, the *Inst. art.* is certainly a product of s.IV.

The following works have been associated with P.:

1) The *Catholica* (*GL* 4.3–43), a systematic review of nominal and verbal desinences preserved under the title *De catholicis Probi* in fol.

95^v-111^v of cod. Neap. lat. 2 (= Vindob. 16), is in fact virtually identical to Book 2 of the *Ars* of Sacerdos (q.v., no. 132). It probably came to be attributed to P., as the author of the *Instituta artium*, because of a confusion produced by the closing sentence of Sacerdos's Book 1: *GL* 6.470, *huc usque artium grammaticarum fecimus instituta, de catholicis vero nominum atque verborum latius exponemus*; on the relation between the two texts and the mechanism of the misattribution, see Wessner, *RE*, 2. Reihe, 1.1630.28ff., and Dahlmann, *RE* 21.602.4ff. The *Catholica* was already circulating under P.'s name by the time of Servius; cf. the citation of Probus in his commentary on *Aen.* 2.15 = *Cath., GL* 4.17.1f.

2) The *Appendix Probi* (*GL* 4.193–204) is transmitted without title in fol. 49^r–52^r of cod. Neap. lat. 1 (= Vindob. 17), where it follows the *Inst. art.* It is attributed to Valerius Probus in cod. Montepessulan. 306 (s.IX), fol. 68^r, which contains only the section "De differentiis" (= *GL* 4.199.18–203.34); cf. the notation *secundum Probum* in cod. Paris. lat. 7491, fol. 93^r, at *GL* 4.201.15.

3) The *De nomine excerpta* (*GL* 4.207–16), now reedited by M. Passalacqua (Rome, 1984), is a collection of extracts from various authors, attributed to Valerius Probus in cod. Neap. lat. 1 (= Vindob. 17), fol. 8^r–10^v; for recent argument in favor of attributing the work to P., as a revision of Caper's *De latinitate* (s.II), see Dionisotti, "Latin Grammar" 205f.

4) The *De ultimis syllabis* (*GL* 4.219–64), dedicated to a certain Caelestinus, is transmitted without attribution in cod. Neap. lat. 2 (= Vindob. 16), fol. 76^r–95^v, where it precedes the *Catholica*. It was printed as *Probi grammatici instituta artium ad Caelestinum* by Parrhasius and as *M. Valerii Probi grammatici institutionum liber I* by van Putschen.

For details of nos. 2–4, see Helm, *RE* 23.62f.; della Casa, " 'Grammatica' " 150f.

The identification—revived most recently by Bartalucci, " 'Probus' " 248ff.—of P. with the Probus to whom G. Valla attributed a set of scholia on Juvenal, or with the homonymous correspondent of Lactantius (cf. s.v. Firmianus, no. 218), or with both, has little to recommend it beyond the similarity of the not uncommon name.

* 128. FL. PYTHIODORUS. Gramm. Hermopolis. s.V 2/2.

Fl. Pythiodorus γραμματικός, third and last witness to a lease at Hermopolis dated 452, 467, 482, or 497; see *BGU* 12.2152, with p. 36 n. 1, on the date. See further s.v. Fl. Her..., no. 68; cf. s.v. Anonymus 7, no. 173.

129. ROMANUS. Gramm. Alexandria? s.V ex. / s.VI init.?

Ludwich, *De Ioanne Philopono* 5ff.; *PLRE* II s.v. 6, pp. 947f.

The teacher of Ioannes Philoponus (q.v., no. 118), according to Georgius Choeroboscus: *Schol. in Theodos., GG* 4:1.106.3f., ὁ Φιλόπονος καὶ ὁ Ῥωμανὸς ὁ τούτου διδάσκαλος; ibid. 309.28f., Ῥωμανὸς ὁ τοῦ Φιλοπόνου διδάσκαλος. Cited also by Choeroboscus ibid. 108.13f., οἱ δὲ περὶ Ἀπολλώνιον καὶ Ἡρωδιανὸν καὶ Ῥωμανόν; ibid. 314.34, κατὰ Ῥωμανὸν καὶ τοὺς δοξάζοντας (sc. γραμματικούς); cf. also ibid. 254.7, 311.8; 4:2.189.15, 229.3f. Also cited by Ioannes Charax in the *Sophron. exc. (GG* 4:2.407.16f.) and in the Περὶ ἐγκλινομένων (Bekker, *Anecd.* 3.1150); not mentioned in extant grammatical works attributed to Philoponus. He is included in the catalogue of gramm. in Kröhnert, *Canones* 7, under the heading ὅσοι περὶ ὀρθογραφίας.

If Choeroboscus's statements are to be taken at face value, R. will have taught, most likely at Alexandria, at the end of the fifth and beginning of the sixth century, the probable time of Philoponus's education; cf. s.v. Note, however, that Choeroboscus may have been speaking loosely or may have been drawing an inference from some conventional phrase in Philoponus such as the one Choeroboscus himself uses at *Schol. in Theodos., GG* 4:2.229.3f., ὁ Ῥωμανὸς ἡμᾶς ἐδίδαξεν; compare *GG* 4:1.333.10f., Φιλητᾶς ὁ διδάσκαλος Θεοκρίτου, plainly no more than an inference drawn from Theoc. *Id.* 7.40. On the difficulty of evaluating third-party statements that establish teacher-student relationships in such contexts, see s.vv. Damocharis, Timotheus, nos. 42, 156.

C. IULIUS ROMANUS: see no. 249.

ROMULUS: see no. 250.

130. RUFINUS. Lat. gramm. / *v.c.* Antioch. s.V med. / s.VI init.; after Servius.

RE Suppl. 5.842f. (Wessner); Sch.-Hos. 4:2.213; *PLRE* I s.v. 8, p. 775.

Rufinus, *grammaticus (Comm.* tit., *GL* 6.558.7); he also calls himself *litterator*: *GL* 6.565.9, 566.6. For the use of these two terms interchangeably, cf. Appendix 2.3. For R.'s profession, cf. also the dedication to his pupils that stands between his two works: *GL* 6.565.7f., *haec ego Rufinus collegi mente benigna / discipulisque dedi munera pulchra libens* (printed as the subscr. to the *Comm.* by Keil, it could equally well have been intended as an inscr. of the work on prose rhythm that follows immediately, *GL* 6.565.9ff.).

R. styles himself *v(ir) c(larissimus)* at *GL* 6.565.9, 566.6, and 575.26; cf. also *Rufinus v(ir) d(isertissimus)*, codd. *Comm.* tit., where Keil restores *v.c.*, probably correctly. For another possible confusion of *v.c.* and *v.d.*, see s.v. Aelius Donatus, no. 52, *ad fin.* R. is called *Antiochensis* in the tit. of the *Comm.*

A *term. p. q.* of s.IV ex. / s.V init. is provided by a reference to Servius at *GL* 6.573.26; cf. references also to Evanthius, Charisius, Diomedes, and Donatus (qq.v., nos. 54, 200, 47, 52) *passim* in the two works. A reliable *term. a. q.* is lacking; Keil, *GL* 6.553, thought that R. was a source of Priscian *De metris fab. Terent.*, but cf. Sch.-Hos. 4:2.233. As a Latin gramm. at Antioch, R. is perhaps more likely to belong to the fifth than to a later century, although s.VI is also possible. For Latin gramm. in the East outside Alexandria and Constantinople in s.V / s.VI, see s.vv. Hierius (no. 75: Gaza, Antioch) and Adamantius and Martyrius (nos. 2, 95: perhaps Sardis); cf. also s.v. Ioannes Lydus, no. 92, *ad fin.*, and *PNess.* 3, pp. 11–13.

R. composed a *Commentarium*—rather, a collection of excerpts—*in metra Terentiana* (*GL* 6.554–565.8). Some *versus . . . Rufini de compositione et de metris oratorum* are quoted at the beginning (565.9–567.29) and in the body (575.26–576.7) of a collection of critical comments on prose rhythm drawn largely from Cicero but with references ranging up through Servius (*GL* 6.565.9–578.8 = *Rhet. Lat. min.* 575–84 Halm); the collection is transmitted without break after the dedication noted above, and was evidently R.'s own compilation. Note that R. also quotes his own verse at (*Comm.*) *GL* 6.558.7ff.; he might therefore also be supposed to have written a more extensive work on meter, in verse, which is now lost.

131. DOMITIUS RUFINUS.   Teacher of liberal letters.   Iomnium (Mauretania Caesariensis).   s.IV / s.V?

PLRE I s.v. Rufinus 16, p. 777.

[Christian monogram] *Domitio Rufino, magistro liberalium litterarum, homini bono, v(ixit) a(nnis) LXXV*: *BCTH* 1896, 218 no. 184 = *ILS* 7762 Iomnium (Tigzirt). The date is to be inferred from R.'s religion, indicated at the top of the inscr. For the identification of the site, modern Tigzirt (= ancient Iomnium, not Rusucurru), on the coast of Mauretania Caesariensis roughly midway between Icosium (Algiers) and Saldae (Bejaïa), see P.-A. Février, *PECS* 777 s.v. Rusucurru.

SABINUS: see no. 251.

132. MARIUS PLOTIUS SACERDOS.   Gramm.   Rome.   s.III 2/2?

RE 21.601–8 (Dahlmann), 2. Reihe, 1.1629–31 (Wessner); Sch.-Hos. 3.169–72; De Nonno, "Frammenti"; *PLRE* I s.v. Sacerdos 3, p. 795.

Marius Plotius Sacerdos: inscr. *Ars* 3, *GL* 6.497.4, *Marius Plotius Sacerdos composui Romae docens de metris*; cf. the use of "Marius" in an example at *GL* 6.504.19, *non me Musarum comitem* [*Aen.* 9.775] *Marium non laudo*. The form of the name given in the subscr. to *Ars* 1 and 2, M. [Book 1; M̄., Book 2] *Claudius Sacerdos*, is in all likelihood a corruption. On the possible citation of S. from *Ars* 1 and 2 as "Claudius" in later gramm. treatises, cf. Hagen, *Anecd. Helv.* = *GL* 8, lxxxvi–lxxxvii; Sabbadini, "Spogli" 179f. The form "Cassius Sacerdos" also occurs; cf. Manitius, *Handschriften* 162. He appears as *Marius Plocius pontifex ac sacerdos maximus* in the subscr. to cod. Valentin. N. 5. 1 of *Ars* 3.

No titulatur appears in his mss to indicate his profession; but the inscr. to *Ars* 3 (quoted above), the identity and status of his dedicatees together with the phrasing of his dedication (see below), and the gram- matical example at Dosith. *GL* 7.407.18f., in which his name is used, *bene apud Sacerdotem studetur*, combine to make it clear that he was a professional gramm., at Rome.

A probable *term. a. q.* of s.IV init. is provided by Cominianus, who seems to have known S.'s work (see s.v., no. 34). A probable *term. p. q.* of s.III med. would be established if the Aquila mentioned at S. (= [Probus]) *Cath.*, *GL* 4.19.32, is Aquila Romanus, who is later than Alexander Numenius (s.II med.) and before Iulius Rufinianus (s.III ex. / s.IV init.); but this identification is not certain. The citation of Iuba *metricus* (s.II) at *GL* 6.546.8 provides a definite *term. p. q.* Similarly, S. could be dated around or just before s.III ex. / s.IV init. if his contemporary and dedicatee, Gaianus *v.c.* (see below), were known to be the addressee of several imperial rescripts belonging to that period; cf. *PLRE* I s.v. Gaianus 2, p. 378. But that is also uncertain.

S. was the author of a grammatical treatise in three books, *GL* 6.427– 546. Book 1 treats the parts of speech, *vitia*, and *virtutes*; Book 2, "De catholicis nominum atque verborum," contains a systematic review of desinences and a brief treatment of prose rhythm; Book 3 considers meter. Book 3 is transmitted separately, with the original preface by S.; Books 1 and 2 are transmitted together in fragmentary form in cod. Neap. 2 (= Vindob. 16). There is also a virtually identical version of Book 2 transmitted as the *Catholica* of Probus (q.v., no. 127), *GL* 6.471–95 = 4.6.25–10.20, 25.13–43.10. The version of Book 2 preserved in cod. Neap. 2 has suffered a loss corresponding to the central portion of the *Catholica*, 4.10.21–25.12; *membra disiecta* of this lost section of cod. Neap. 2 have now been recognized in the so-called Turin Fragment formerly assigned to the *Catholica*: see De Nonno, "Frammenti" 393ff.

S. presents himself as having written for or at the request of several men of senatorial rank (6.496.5ff.). Book 1 was dedicated to his *contuber- nalis*, Gaianus, a contemporary and onetime fellow student; Book 2 was written at the "order" of Gaianus's father, Uranius; Book 3 is dedicated to Maximus, *nobilitatis splendore praedito*, and Simplicius, *omni laude praedica- bili*, to both of whom S. was commended by Uranius. All four are called *viri clarissimi* or *amplissimi*.

MARCIUS SALUTARIS: see no. 252.

* 133. SARAPION.   Teacher of letters.   Oxyrhynchus.   s.III ex. / s.IV init.

Registered in an account of payments in kind, *POxy*. 24.2421, as the recipient of ¹/₁₂ *artaba* of wheat (σῖτος) with a cash value of 82 *den*. and 1 *artaba* of barley with a cash value of 655 *den*.: col. ii.48, Σαραπίων γραμματοδιδάσκαλος σ(ί)τ(ου) (ἀρτ.) ι̅β̅ (δην.) πβ κρ(ι)θ(ῆς) (ἀρτ.) α (δην.) τνε. The ratio of values here—wheat @ 984 *den./artaba* : barley @ 655 *den./ artaba* :: 3 : 2—is constant throughout the account.

A *term. p. q.* of 290 is provided for the account by *POxy*. 24.2422 (an account of beef and pork dated to 290), on the verso of which it is written; the account on the verso must date to the very end of s.III or the very beginning of s.IV, i.e., one generation later than *POxy*. 12.1413, 1414, 1496, 1497, all an. 270/80; cf. *POxy*. 24, pp. 185f. This dating is consistent with the cash values noted in the account, which show a marked inflation over grain prices known from the third century (e.g., *POxy*. 14.1733, dated to late s.III by its editor, barley at 40 *den./artaba*; cf. Jones, *LRE* 109 and n. 69) but fall well short of the prices known from the first six decades of s.IV: grain at 2,000–3,000 *den./artaba* in 314, wheat at 37,000 *den./artaba* and barley at 20,000 *den./artaba* in 338 (cf. Bagnall and Sijpesteijn, "Currency" 116–17); wheat at 1,268,966 *den./ artaba* in 357/58 (?: cf. Bagnall and Worp, "Commodity Prices").

Since the account must be nearly contemporary with Diocletian's Edict on Maximum Prices, it is worth noting that the equivalent of 737 *den*. set down to S.'s account would nearly equal the monthly fees payable to a teacher of letters from fifteen students under the schedule prescribed by the edict (7.66). But since neither the purpose of the account nor the period covered by its entries is specified, it is difficult to draw any conclusions concerning the payment made to S. The quantity of grain involved suggests a month's rations: note the dole of 1 *artaba* of σῖτος per month at Oxyrhynchus under Claudian II and Aurelian; cf. *POxy*. 40, p. 6; Hopkins and Carter, "Amount" 195. But contrast the 20 *artabae* of σῖτος received as six months' payment in kind by the gramm. Heraclammon (q.v., no. 69) at Hermopolis, s.IV ex. / s.V. For references to other payments in kind to teachers, see s.v. Heraclammon.

SELEUCUS: see no. 253.

VIBIUS SEQUESTER: see no. 254.

134. SERENUS.   Gramm.   Egypt?   s.IV / s.VI?

Chr.-Sch.-St. 2:2.686; Alan Cameron, "Wandering Poets" 488; *PLRE* I s.v. 2, p. 826.

Serenus, mentioned by Photius as a γραμματικός and author of various δράματα in various meters, *Bibl.* cod. 279 (8.187 Henry). His works were known to Photius in a volume containing the works of four other poets, Hermias of Hermopolis, Andronicus of Hermopolis, Horapollon, and Cyrus of Antaeopolis (cf. s.vv. Aur. Cyrus, Hermias, Horapollon, nos. 41, 71, 77), all Egyptians datable certainly or probably to s.IV / s.VI. S. can therefore probably be assigned to the same general place and time. If so, he cannot be the gramm. Aelius Serenus of Athens; cf. *RE* 1.532. If S. is the Serenus whose Ἀπομνημονεύματα were excerpted by Stobaeus, Photius was unaware of it, since he classes the latter among the philosophers used by Stobaeus: *Bibl.* cod. 167 (2.156 Henry).

"SERGIUS": see no. 255.

135. SERGIUS.　Gramm.　Northern Syria? (Beroea?).　s.VI init.
PLRE II s.v. 9, p. 995.

Eutychianist and γραμματικός who engaged in theological debate with Severus of Antioch ca. 515 and immediately thereafter. The Syriac version of the three letters of S., the replies of Severus, and the *Apologia Sergii ad Severum* are found with Latin translation in the edition of Lebon, *CSCO* Scr. Syr., ser. 4, vol. 7; cf. id., *Monophysisme* app. 2, pp. 538–51; Brock, "Some New Letters" 19ff. For the date, cf. Lebon, *Monophysisme* 163ff.

S. styles himself (in Lebon's translation) *humilis grammaticus*; cf. Σέργιος ὁ γραμματικός, Leont. Byz. *C. Monophys.*, PG 86:2.1848A; *Conc. Lateran.*, *Secretarius V* Mansi 10.1116D; similarly Phot. *Bibl.* cod. 230 (2.56 Henry); cf. also Σέργιος . . . γραμματικὸς Εὐτυχιανιστής, Eustath. mon. *Epist. de duabus naturis*, PG 86:1.909A. He was probably the object of the Christological treatise Πρὸς Σέργιον τὸν γραμματικόν of Anastasius I, orthodox patriarch of Antioch (558–70, 593–99; fragments in PG 89.1285–86). If this is S., and if the attribution to Anastasius is valid, the work must have been composed in Anastasius's youth or, more likely, after S.'s death, as a later response to his correspondence with Severus; cf. Weis, *Studia Anastasia* 1.104.

S. is confused with Ioannes (q.v., no. 82) of Caesarea in [Zach. Rhet.] *PO* 2.271.1ff. (cf. ibid. 321.11ff.), where he is made the object of Severus's *C. impium grammaticum*; for the latter polemic, see s.v. Ioannes, no. 82.

S. has been identified with Sergius (q.v., no. 257) the lector of Emesa in southern Syria and author of an epitome of Herodian. The identification, suggested before the letters of S. were published, is based on the coincidence of the very common name and is probably incorrect. Nowhere does S. or Severus indicate that S. was a member of the clergy; further, S.'s first letter was addressed not to Severus but to Antoninus, bishop of Beroea, which may well indicate that S. was active in northern Syria rather than farther south, perhaps in Beroea or its diocese.

+   SERGIUS: see no. 256.

+   SERGIUS: see no. 257.

        SERVILIO: see no. 258.

136.   SERVIUS.   Gramm.   Rome.   s.IV 3/3 – s.V 1/3.

RE, 2. Reihe, 2.1834–48 (Wessner); Sch.-Hos. 4:1.172–77; Georgii, "Zur Bestimmung der Zeit"; Alan Cameron, "Date and Identity" 29ff.; Goold, "Servius" 102ff.; Marinone, "Per la cronologia"; *PLRE* I s.v., p. 827.

Servius: Macrob. *Sat.* 1.2.15 and *passim*; Rufin. *GL* 6.573.26; Prisc. *GL* 2.8.15, 106.1 (= 242.5), 233.14, 256.14, 259.22, 515.22, 532.22, all but the first clearly referring to the commentary on Vergil (see below); the subscr. to Juvenal in cod. Leid. 82 (s.X), *apud Servium magistrum* (cf. cod. Laurent. 34.42 [s.XI], *apud M. Serbium*); the mss of the commentary on Vergil (cf. Thilo, in Thilo and Hagen, eds., 1, lxxvii–xci; Savage, "Manuscripts"; Murgia, *Prolegomena* 72ff.; on the evidentiary value of the titles in the ms families of the commentary, cf. Murgia, ibid. 117ff.); cod. Paris. lat. 7530 (s.VIII) of the commentary on Donatus and the *De metris Horatii* and several mss of the *De centum metris* (inscr. to the praef. in codd. Darmstadt. 1283 [s.IX / s.X], Berol. Sant. 66.4 [s.VIII], Neap. Borbon. IV. A 8 [s.VIII], Paris. lat. 7530 [s.VIII]; subscr. cod. Leid. 135 [s.X]). "Sergius," an error: *Comm. Don.* tit., cod. Paris. lat. 7530; *Comm. Verg.* tit., codd. Neap. Bibl. Publ. 5 and Bern. 363; also in the *Comm. Bern.* on Lucan 3.402, 7.633. On "Sergius," see below.

        Save for its appearance in the tit. of the folia added in s.XIII to cod. Laurent. Bibl. S. Cruc. XXII.1, a hybrid ms of the *Comm. Verg.*, the form "Servius Honoratus" or "Honoratus" is associated with only three works. First, the tit. of *Comm. Don.* gives the name thus in the early printed editions; the references to "Honoratus" in the catalogues of gramm. in codd. Bonon. 797 (Negri, "De codice" 266) and Bern. 243 (cf. *Anecd. Helv.* = *GL* 8, cxlix) perhaps involve the *Comm. Don.*—alternatively, the *De finalibus*—as do the references to an *Ars Honorati* and a *Commentum Servii Honorati* in two medieval library catalogues (cf. Manitius, *Handschriften* 196f.). Second, the *De finalibus* has "Servius Honoratus" in the tit. of codd. Neap. lat. 2 (= Vindob. 16; s.VII / s.VIII), Monac. 6281 (= Frising. 81; s.X), Leid. Bibl. Publ. 122 (s.X); also "Honoratus grammaticus" in an inscr. in the text (= *GL* 4.449.6) in the first two of these mss and in the subscr. of the last. Third, the *De centum metris* has "Servius Honoratus" in the inscr. to the praef. in cod. Paris. lat. 7730 (s.X).

With two insignificant exceptions—"Marius Servius" in cod. Leid. Bibl. Publ. 5 (s.XII) and "Servius Maurus" added in the hand of Bongars in cod. Bern. 363, both in the tit. of the *Comm. Verg.*—the form of the name with "Maurus" or "Marius" is associated with only two of these works. First, the *De finalibus* has "Servius Maurus Honoratus" in the tit. in cod. Monac. Emmeran. G. 121 (s.X) and in the early printed editions. Second, the *De centum metris* has "Maurus Servius grammaticus" in the tit. in codd. Darmstadt. 1283 and Leid. 135, and in the subscr. in codd. Darmstadt. 1283 and Valentin. N. 5. 1 (s.IX); also "Marius Servius grammaticus," tit. in codd. Valentin. N. 5. 1 and Paris. lat. 7491 (s.X), subscr. in codd. Neap. Borbon. IV. A 8 and Paris. lat. 7491; "Marius Servius Honoratus grammaticus," subscr. in cod. Paris. lat. 7730; "Marius Servius Honoratus grammaticus. . . . Marius Servius grammaticus," tit. and inscr. to the praef. in the early printed editions.

It is very uncertain which (or whether any) of the names "Maurus," "Marius," or "Honoratus" is authentic. "Honoratus" may be an epithet misunderstood as a name; compare *Donati honoratissimi grammatici* in the tit. of Donatus's *Comm. Terent.* in cod. Oxon. Lincoln. 45, with, e.g., "Honoratus grammaticus" or "Marius Servius Honoratus grammaticus" above. "Maurus" may be an attempt to supply an ethnic, with "Marius" a subsequent corruption, or the two may have arisen independently from the sort of confusion found in the subscriptions to Juvenal; there the phrase *apud Servium magistrum* of cod. Leid. 82 reappears as *apud M. Serbium* in the later cod. Laurent. 34.42.

A gramm.: Macrob. *Sat.* 1.2.15, *Servius inter grammaticos doctorem recens professus*; also *grammaticus* or *litterator* or *doctor* at *Sat.* 1.24.8, 1.24.20, 2.2.12, 6.7.2ff.; *grammaticus* in a number of mss of the *Comm. Verg.* and in some mss of the *De finalibus* and *De centum metris*, quoted above; *magister* in the subscr. to Juvenal in cod. Leid. 82 and in the subscr. to the *Comm. Don.* in cod. Paris. lat. 7530; *magister Servius . . . dictavit* in "Sergius" *Explan. in Don.*, GL 4.496.26f. (see below); *Servius magister exposuit* at [Acro] *in Hor. Serm.* 1.9.76 (*magister Urbis* or *magister Romae* in a later recension of the scholia *ad loc.*).

S. taught at Rome: so Macrob. *Sat.* (see the passages cited just above; the dialogue is set in Rome); cf. the dedication of the *De centum metris* below. He was active later than Donatus, on whose *Ars* he commented, whose commentary on Vergil he used, and to whom he refers in one of his minor works: *De fin.*, GL 4.449.6. He antedates Rufinus and Priscian, who cite him.

The only other source of useful information on Servius's date is Macrobius's *Saturnalia*, in which Servius appears as an *adulescens* (7.11.2) recently established in his profession (1.2.15)—i.e., he is probably imagined as being in his early twenties. The dramatic date, 383 or 384, might therefore be thought to establish a *term. a. q.* ca. 364 for his birth; but since Servius's presence in the *Sat.* is an anachronism, defended by Macrobius at 1.1.5, *nec mihi fraudi sit, si uni aut alteri ex his . . . matura aetas posterior saeculo Praetextati fuit* (only Servius and the other *adulescens,* Avienus, can be meant), ca. 364 should rather be a *term. p. q.,* with his birth perhaps falling sometime in the next decade and his teaching not begun until the last decade of s.IV. If, as is likely, the dedicatee of the *De centum metris* (*GL* 4.456.3f.), a *clarissimus Albinus* addressed as *praetextatorum decus* (i.e., a boy of the age of one of S.'s pupils), is Caecina Decius Aginatius Albinus, who was *PVR* as a young man in 414, that work should be dated to the first decade of s.V. Cf. Georgii, "Zur Bestimmung der Zeit"; Alan Cameron, "Date and Identity" 29ff.; Marinone, "Per la cronologia"; Barnes, "Late Roman Prosopography" 264f.

The argument of Alan Cameron, "Date and Identity" 31, that Servius was dead by the time of the composition of the *Sat.* (ca. 430) is plausible but not certain, esp. if the other *adulescens* of the *Sat.,* Avienus, was still alive at that time; cf. Alan Cameron, "Macrobius" 386ff. The fact that Macrobius did not use Servius's commentary on Vergil cannot reliably be taken to date the latter work after 430, *pace* Marinone, "Per la cronologia" 198ff. For possible evidence that the *Comm. Verg.* was written before the *Comm. Don.,* see the appendix s.v. Pompeius, no. 125.

S. was the author of a commentary on the poems of Vergil, extant in a vulgate and in an interpolated form. The latter is the so-called Servius Danielis, not attributed to Servius in the mss; cf. Goold, "Servius" 102ff.; and now briefly Marshall, "Servius," on the transmission of the two forms of the commentary. S. also wrote several brief treatises, *De finalibus, De centum metris, De metris Horatii* (*GL* 4.449–72), and a commentary on the *Ars* of Donatus (*GL* 4.405–48; cited by Priscian, *GL* 2.8.15), now preserved only in an abridgment; see most recently Schindel, *Figurenlehren* 21ff.; Holtz, *Donat* 228f.; and Chap. 4 n. 8. The *Explanationum in Donatum libri II* (*GL* 4.486ff.; cf. *Anecd. Helv.* = *GL* 8.143ff.), which is variously attributed to "Servius," "Sergius," or "Seregius" in the mss, is not by S. but is the work of a later compiler, or more than one, drawing on Donatus and on S.; cf. esp. *GL* 4.496.26f., *haec sunt quae Donatus in prima parte artium tractavit, haec magister Servius extrinsecus dictavit.* On the *Explan.* see further s.v. "Sergius," no. 255.

The name "Servius" or "Sergius" is also attached to several other works that do not belong to S.: a treatise *De litt., de syll.,* etc. (*GL* 4.475ff.); a version of the *De finalibus metrorum* of "Metrorius" (q.v., no. 239) onto which the first two paragraphs of S.'s *De finalibus* have been grafted and to which the heading *ad Basilium, amicum Sergii* has been attached (*GL* 6.240ff.; Basilius is incorrectly identified as the "dedicatee of Servius's *De*

Arte Donati" at *PLRE* I s.v. Basilius 4, p. 149); a work *De idiomatibus casuum et generum* (*GL* 4.566ff.; cf. Keil, *GL* 4, li–lii, lv); and some medieval glosses.

The *De centum metris* is dedicated to the boy Albinus, probably S.'s pupil (see above); the dedicatees of the other brief treatises, Aquilinus (*De finalibus*) and Fortunatianus (*De metris Horatii*), cannot be identified with any certainty. Holtz, *Donat* 227, incorrectly treats (*ut vid.*) the scribal subscr. at cod. Paris. lat. 7530 fol. 46ʳ, *feliciter Iuliano scolastico Sardiano*, as an authorial dedication; for the type, cf. s.v. Calliopius *scholasticus*, no. 194.

S. possessed or had the use of (cf. s.v. Domitius, no. 50) a place of retirement in Campania: *GL* 4.468.6, *Horatium, cum in Campania otiarer, excepi.*

It is doubtful that S. is Servius the addressee of Symm. *Ep.* 8.60.

137. FL. SIMPLICIUS.   Gramm. → assessor → *cons. sexfasc. Numid.* → *vic. urb. Rom.* (the last three positions ca. 364–75).

RE, 2. Reihe, 3.203 (Seeck); *PLRE* I s.v. 7, p. 844.

From Emona; at one time a gramm.; protégé of the Pannonian Maximinus, whom he served as assessor, thereby gaining entry to the imperial service: Amm. Marc. 28.1.45, *Emonensis Simplicius, Maximini consiliarius ex grammatico*; ibid. 52, *pronuntiante Simplicio et consiliario suo et amico*. For S. and Maximinus presented in the darkest colors, cf. also ibid. 46. Since the *consiliarii* of provincial governors were heavily recruited from the ranks of the advocates, S. had perhaps combined advocacy with his teaching: see s.vv. Ausonius, Acilius Glabrio, Aur. Theodorus, nos. 21, 64, 150; cf. s.vv. Calliopius, Eudaemon, nos. 25, 55.

The phrase *Maximini consiliarius ex grammatico*, with specification of former profession, is noteworthy (cf. Amm. Marc. 14.11.30, where Dionysius's fall from tyrant to head of a *ludus litterarius* is presented as one type of extreme change in fortune); in its hostile context the reference to S.'s profession is perhaps intended to reproach and contemn him as a parvenu. The function of the *consiliarius* was largely judicial, and S.'s subsequent exercise of judicial authority, overseeing as vicar the trials for adultery and treason to which his social superiors were subject at Rome, especially aroused Ammianus's anger; cf. 28.1.45–46. Further, Ammianus regarded Maximinus himself as socially unfit for his duties; cf. 28.1.2, *quosdam despicatissimae sortis*, referring to Maximinus and the equally despised Leo. The phrase *Maximini consiliarius ex grammatico* may be meant to suggest that Maximinus and S. were in this respect birds of a feather. It is not known where S. taught as a gramm.

For the Flaviate, see *CIL* 8.8324 = *ILS* 5535, S.'s dedication of a basilica at Cuicul while *consularis sexfascalis* of Numidia. For details of his later career, see *PLRE* I s.v. 7, p. 844; and Seeck, *RE*, 2. Reihe, 3.203.

SOLYMIUS: see no. 259.

*   SOSISTRATUS: see no. 260.

+ 138. SPECIOSUS.   Lat. gramm. or rhetorician.   Africa → Constantinople. s.VI 1/3.

Introduced by Ioannes Lydus (q.v., no. 92) to the praetorian prefect Phocas, therefore sometime between late January and mid-October 532 (for the date of Phocas's prefecture, cf. Stein, *Histoire* 2.784), as a teacher of Latin: *De mag.* 3.73. He was evidently from Africa; Phocas had expressed a preference for a Λίβυν, and S. was immediately suggested. It is not clear whether he was a gramm. or a rhetorician, but it appears that he was a teacher by profession. He received an initial payment of 100 *solidi* from Phocas but was not, *ut vid.*, required to perform any extended services.

139. SPERCHEUS.   Gr. gramm.   Bordeaux.   s.IV 1/4.

PLRE I s.v., p. 851.

Spercheus (Auson. *Prof.* 8.2), a Greek gramm. (ibid. tit.; cf. vv. 2-4, *Sperchei . . . / Atticas Musas . . . / grammatic[i]*) at Bordeaux (ibid. tit.). With Corinthus (q.v., no. 36), S. was one of Ausonius's teachers *primis . . . in annis* (vv. 1-4, with 9-10) and was therefore active at least in the second decade of s.IV. S. was also the father of the Greek gramm. Menestheus (q.v., no. 99; vv. 2-3).

  With the other two Greek gramm. celebrated in *Prof.* 8, S. is said to have possessed *sedulum . . . studium docendi, / fructus exilis tenuisque sermo* (vv. 5-6). Ausonius's *tardior sensus* and *puerilis aevi / noxius error* (vv. 13-16) prevented him from fully appreciating and profiting from their efforts.

  See also s.v. Romulus, no. 250.

140. STAPHYLIUS.   Gramm.(?) and rhetorician.   Auch (Novempopulana) → Bordeaux? (not likely).   s.IV 1/2.

RE, 2. Reihe, 3.2149 s.v. Staphylos no. 4 (Seeck); *PLRE* I s.v., p. 852.

Staphylius (Auson. *Prof.* 20 tit., v. 4), a gramm. (v. 7, *grammatice ad Scaurum atque Probum*; cf. s.vv. Harmonius, Nepotianus, nos. 65, 105) and rhetorician (ibid., *promptissime rhetor*; tit., *rhetor*). Since the tit., which seems to be well informed about S.—it calls him *civis Auscius*, information not derived from the poem itself, unless it was divined from v.4, *genitum stirpe Novem populis*—calls him *rhetor* only, there is reason to doubt that S. taught grammar. His expertise in that field (see above) may be included as a token of his polymathy, not directly connected with his teaching; he is said in the following verses (8-10) to own well-thumbed copies of Livy and Herodotus, whom Ausonius does not mention here as school authors, and to know "all the learning stored away in Varro's innumerable volumes." This doubt may, however, be excessively skeptical; note that the other figures whom Ausonius compares with Probus and Scaurus, *vel sim.*, were certainly gramm. For the combination of the two disciplines, cf. s.v. Deuterius, no. 44.

S. was a *civis Auscius*—i.e., he belonged to the Ausci of Elimberris (modern Auch)—in the province of Novempopulana (ibid. tit., v. 4). In view of vv. 1–4, where Ausonius states that by including S. he is violating his own *lex commemorandi*, S. must not have been a *Burdigalensis* on any reckoning, and the common assumption (in *PLRE* I, p. 852; *RE*, 2. Reihe, 3.2149; and Étienne, *Bordeaux* 252) that he taught at Bordeaux must be mistaken. On the *lex* and S.'s status as an exception see Booth, "Notes" 248f.; cf. s.v. Concordius, no. 35.

S. was older than Ausonius, who says that S. was like a father or uncle to him (vv. 5–6). S. enjoyed a *pulchra senecta* before dying a peaceful death (vv. 13–14).

STEGUS: see no. 261.

241. STEPHANUS. Gramm. Gaza → Antioch. s.V 4/4 / s.VI 1/4.

Garzya and Loenertz, eds., *Procopii . . . epistolae* p. xxvii, s.v. Étienne A; *PLRE* II s.v. 8, p. 1029.

A Greek gramm. at Gaza and later at Antioch, recipient of Procop. Gaz. *Ep.* 13 (jointly with Alypius and Hierius, qq.v., nos. 7, 75), 71, 89, 105.

With Alypius and Hierius, S. went from Gaza to Antioch (Daphne) (*Ep.* 13.1ff., 71.1ff.), where he taught (*Ep.* 89.7ff.) as a γραμματικός: *Ep.* 13 tit.; on the corruption of his name in one group of mss there, cf. s.v. Stegus, no. 261. Procopius perhaps suggests that S. made the move with expectations of greater financial success; cf. the references to πλούτῳ κομᾶν and the Pactolus in *Ep.* 13.4f., 89.9f. He borrowed a book from Procopius and promised to return it within three months, but kept it for three or four years (*Ep.* 71.10ff.; cf. *Ep.* 89.5ff., 105.4ff.); Procopius says that when S. borrowed the book he himself had not yet finished paying for it (*Ep.* 71.14ff.).

S. had a brother: *Ep.* 105.1f.; the context of the notice makes it clear that ἀδελφός is used literally.

242. STEPHANUS. Gramm. Gaza(?) → Alexandria. s.V 4/4 / s.VI 1/4.

Garzya and Loenertz, eds., *Procopii . . . epistolae* p. xxix, s.v. Étienne E ou Jérôme; cf. ibid. pp. xxxi–xxxii.

The recipient of Procop. Gaz. *Ep.* 57 while teaching at Alexandria: *Ep.* 57.1, παρὰ τὸν Νεῖλον οἰκεῖς; 4, τοῦ Μακεδόνος ἡ πόλις. A gramm.: *Ep.* 57.9, ταῦτα τοῖς παισὶ καθηγούμενος, followed by a quotation of

Callimachus—i.e., a teacher of poetry; cf. Appendix 1.3. He had evidently abandoned his wife and child (ibid. 1, 10f.). His origin is not stated, but Procopius's conceit and phrasing imply that S. was from Gaza: Procopius urges S. to imitate Odysseus and reseek his Ithaca, adding καὶ γάρ σε νῦν ἐπιθυμῶν . . . ἰδεῖν κέχηνα τῇ θαλάττῃ καὶ περισκοπῶ τὰς ὁλκάδας, εἴποτε παρόντα θεάσομαι (ibid. 4ff.).

By the conjecture of Garzya and Loenertz, eds., *Procopii . . . epistolae* pp. xxix, xxxi–xxxii, S. is identified with Hieronymus (q.v., no. 231) the recipient of *Ep.* 2, 9, 81, 86 and 124, because both are said to have abandoned their families and to have gone to Egypt to teach: for S., see above; for these and the following details concerning Hieronymus, see s.v. This is almost certainly incorrect, since, in the comparable periods of their careers (i.e., when each already had a family and was away in Egypt), S. was teaching at Alexandria, whereas Hieronymus taught at Hermopolis; and S. was clearly a gramm., whereas Hieronymus was probably a teacher of rhetoric. In addition, Hieronymus was certainly a native of Elusa, but the available evidence suggests that S.'s "Ithaca" was Gaza (see above). The mss unanimously make S. the recipient of *Ep.* 57.

143. STEPHANUS.   Gramm.   Alexandria?   519/38.

PLRE II s.v. 23, p. 1032.

"The learned and believing grammarian Stephen," who brought a letter from "Thecla the Countess" to Severus of Antioch in the period of the latter's banishment (519–38) at Alexandria; cf. *Ep.* 9.3, trans. E. W. Brooks, *The Sixth Book of the Select Letters of Severus Patriarch of Antioch* (London, 1903–4) 2.423f. S. was perhaps therefore active at Alexandria also. The style Severus gives him suggests that S. was a Monophysite Christian.

144. STEPHANUS.   Gramm.   Constantinople.   s.V ex. / s.VI 1/2.

RE, 2. Reihe, 3.2369–99 (Honigmann); Chr.-Sch.-St. 2:2.1084f.; Hunger 1.530f., 2.36f.; *PLRE* II s.v. 24, p. 1032.

A gramm. (*Suda* E.3048: Στέφανος γραμματικός) at Constantinople; see the catalogue of gramm. in Kröhnert, *Canones* 7, quoted s.v. Orus, no. 111, *ad fin.*; cf. also below. Author of the Ἐθνικά (title: cf. Steph. Byz. s.v. Αἰθίοψ; Choerobosc. *Schol. in Theodos.*, GG 4:1.305.4; *Suda* E.3048), a work on toponyms in over fifty books, of predominantly grammatical (etymological, orthographical, morphological) interest, surviving in abridged form.

Information concerning the date and activity of S. must be drawn entirely from references in the Ἐθνικά, a task made difficult by the presence of some certain interpolations; for an example, which cannot be earlier than s.IX 1/2, see s.v. Georgius Choeroboscus, no. 201. If the entry s.v. Ἀνακτόριον is original, S. taught at Constantinople after Eugenius (q.v., no. 56, for the entry), who is otherwise known to have been active, when already elderly, under Anastasius. The Ἐθνικά might then be dated late in Anastasius's reign or to the reign of Justinian. If the latter, then more likely early than late in the reign, since Hermolaus (q.v., no. 72) is said to have dedicated an epitome of the work to Justinian. If Hermolaus in fact did so (on the problem, see s.v.), then he might also have added at least some of the references that cannot antedate the reign of Justinian—e.g., s.v. Θεούπολις, the name given to Antioch after 526; s.v. Ἀκόναι, a notice of Peter the Patrician as a contemporary *mag. off.* and *patricius*, which must have been written sometime during or after the period 539–50: Peter was appointed *mag. off.* in 539 and is first attested as *patricius* in 550 (Procop. Caes. *BG* 4.11.2); the notice was treated as an interpolation by Meineke in his edition of Stephanus (Berlin, 1849) but was defended as authentic by B. A. Müller, "Zu Stephanos" 339ff. Finally, if Hermolaus added such references, then the reference to Eugenius (above) may have been among them. The problem scarcely allows a certain solution: see further B. A. Müller, "Zu Stephanos"; Honigmann, *RE*, 2. Reihe, 3.2369.38ff.; *PLRE* II s.v., noting a *term p. q.* in the citation of the geographer Marcianus (s.V init.); Baldwin, "Some *addenda*" (1982) 101, noting a possible *term. p. q.* in the citation of the historian Priscus (s.V med.).

S. refers s.v. Γότθοι to a discussion ὡς εἴρηταί μοι ἐν τοῖς Βυζαντιακοῖς; it is not clear whether this refers to a longer notice s.v. Βυζάντιον than is now preserved or to an independent work Βυζαντιακά. The Ἐθνικά seems originally to have been provided with a methodological or analytical preface; cf. s.v. Αἰθίοψ: περὶ τοῦ Αἰθιόπισσα πλατύτερον ἐν τοῖς τῶν ἐθνικῶν προτεχνολογήμασιν εἴρηται. It is perhaps to this preface rather than to another grammatical work that the analysis (τεχνολογία) of the name "Thecla" cited by Choeroboscus belonged; cf. *Schol. in Theodos.*, *GG* 4:1.304.26ff.

S. appears to have been a Christian; cf. s.v. Βήθλεμα: ἐν ᾗ γέγονεν ἡ κατὰ σάρκα γέννησις τοῦ θεοῦ καὶ σωτῆρος ἡμῶν (treated as an interpolation by Meineke in his edition). Cf. also the citations of Eusebius and Synesius s.vv. Βίεννος, Εὐκάρπεια, respectively.

It is no doubt mere coincidence that S. concerned himself with a grammatical analysis of the name "Thecla" (see above) and that the gramm. Stephanus (q.v., no. 143) brought a letter from "Thecla the Countess" to Severus of Antioch in perhaps the same period.

45. STEPHANUS. Gramm. s.IV / s.VI?

PLRE II s.v. 17, p. 1031.

Author of *Anth. Gr.* 9.385 (Στεφάνου γραμματικοῦ in the lemma), a summary of the *Iliad* in twenty-four lines. Identification of S. with Stephanus (q.v., no. 144) of Byzantium (e.g., by Beckby, ed.) is arbitrary, though S. may belong to the late Roman or early Byzantine period.

146. SUCURO. Gramm. Bordeaux. s.IV init.

PLRE I s.v., p. 859.

Sucuro (Auson. *Prof.* 10.15), a Latin gramm. of Bordeaux (ibid. tit., vv. 5–10), probably early in s.IV; on the gramm. of *Prof.* 10, cf. s.v. Concordius, no. 35. He was of libertine birth and a sober and effective teacher (vv. 14–17).

147. SYRIANUS. Gramm. → *com. ord. pr.* Constantinople. s.V 1/4.

PLRE II s.v. 2, p. 1050.

A *grammaticus Graecus* awarded the *comitiva ordinis primi* and rank of exvicar, 15 March 425 (*CTh* 6.21.1); honored with the Greek gramm. Helladius and the Latin gramm. Theofilus (qq.v., nos. 67, 154), the sophists Martinus and Maximus, and the *iuris peritus* Leontius.

+   TER(R)ENTIUS: see no. 262.

TETRADIUS: see no. 263.

148. THALASSUS. Gramm. Bordeaux. s.IV init.

PLRE I s.v., p. 889.

Thalassus: Auson. *Prof.* 12 tit., v. 1; cf. Green, "Prosopographical Notes" 23. Latin gramm. (*Prof.* 12 tit.; cf. v. 5) at Bordeaux (ibid. tit.); he was teaching as a *iuvenis* (v. 5; cf. v. 1, *primaeve*) when Ausonius was *parvulus* (v. 2; cf. v.7, *nostro . . . in aevo*). Since Ausonius emphasizes that he has only hearsay knowledge (v. 2, *audivi*, with v. 5, *tantum te fama ferebat*) and virtually no recollection (vv. 2f.) of T., it is no doubt safe to assume that T. was no longer teaching when Ausonius began his education at Bordeaux, in the middle or the latter part of the second decade of s.IV.

T.'s reputation was slight when he was alive (v. 6) and nonexistent by the time Ausonius composed the *Prof.* (vv. 4, 6).

149. THEOCTISTUS. Lat. gramm. Constantinople? s.V 2/2.

RE, 2. Reihe, 5.1704–5 (Wessner); Sch.-Hos. 4:2.221; *PLRE* II s.v. 5, p. 1066.

Theoctistus: Prisc. *Inst.*, *GL* 3.148.2, 231.24; Cassiod. *Inst.* 1.30.2. Also Theotistus: some mss of Prisc. *Inst.*, *GL* 2.238.6, 3.231.24; [Acro] *in* Hor. *Serm.* 1.5.97. Also Theuctistus or Thostistus: some mss of Prisc. *Inst.*, *GL* 2.238.6.

The teacher of Priscian (q.v., no. 126): *Inst., GL* 2.238.5f., *noster praeceptor Theoctistus, omnis eloquentiae decus, cui quidquid in me sit doctrinae post Deum imputo; Inst., GL* 3.231.4, *teste sapientissimo domino et doctore meo Theoctisto;* cf. in an example, *Inst., GL* 3.148.2f., *ut "ego doceo illum" vel "Theoctistus docet Priscianum."* It is usually assumed that T. taught Priscian at Constantinople, not at Caesarea. As the teacher of Priscian, he must be dated to s.V 2/2.

The author of an *Institutio artis grammaticae;* cf. Prisc. *Inst., GL* 3.231.24f., *teste . . . Theoctisto, quod in institutione artis grammaticae docet.* The other reference of Priscian, *Inst., GL* 2.238.5f., *doctissime attendit noster praeceptor Theoctistus,* on the feminine *satura,* is probably attributable to the same source; likewise T.'s remarks on orthography alluded to at Cassiod. *Inst.* 1.30.2. The citation of T. in the scholia of ps.-Acro to Horace, *Serm.* 1.5.97, [*Bari*] *civitas est, quae Atbaris dicitur hodieque, ut dixit grammaticus Theotistus,* has invited broad speculation concerning T.'s involvement in a fifth-century redaction of the scholia; cf. Wessner, *RE,* 2. Reihe, 5.1704.55ff.; more skeptically Noske, *Quaestiones* 271f. But no certain or even very probable conclusions can be drawn, save that the note provides a *term. p. q.* for recension § of the scholia.

His name suggests that T. was a Christian.

THEODORETUS: see no. 264.

THEODORETUS: see no. 265.

150. AUR. THEODORUS.   Gramm. and advocate.   Hermopolis.   398.
    PLRE II s.v. 60, p. 1097.

Aur. Theodorus, son of Periodos: *PLips.* 56 (= Pap.) lines 6, 23. The name "Periodos" is very rare, but a Periodos appears as the father of one Achilleus in the Hermopolite land register of s.IV, *PFlor.* 1.71.108 = *PLandlisten* F.108. T. was a gramm. and advocate (σχολαστικός) at Hermopolis (Pap. 7f.; cf. 24f.); he acted as guarantor for the appearance of his brother, Aur. Taurinus, in an unspecified matter before Aur. Cyrus son of Philammon, decurion (πολιτευόμενος) and νυκτοστράτηγος of Hermopolis (Pap. 13ff.; cf. 24ff.). This is presumably the Aur. Cyrus son of Φ[ιλάμμ]ων who is attested in *PLips.* 39 as νυκτοστράτηγος at Hermopolis in 390.

The document is dated to 398 (Pap. 1–2). This date and the form of T.'s titulatur, σχολαστικὸς καὶ γραμματικός, suggest that σχολαστικός, like γραμματικός, is used here to denote an occupation, meaning "advocate," and not as a general epithet, "learned (man)," "scholar(ly)"; cf. Claus, "ΣΧΟΛΑΣΤΙΚΟΣ" 57f.; for contrasting examples, see s.vv. Bonifatius, Philagrius, nos. 22, 117. T. is therefore the last σχολαστικός known to bear the name "Aurelius" instead of the higher-status name

"Flavius"; cf. Keenan, "Names" (1973) 60. For the combination gramm. and advocate, see s.vv. Ausonius, Acilius Glabrio, nos. 21, 64. No conclusions concerning T.'s religion can be drawn from his oath by the Τύχη of the emperors; cf. *POsl.* 3.113.5ff. and comment ibid. p. 166; cf. also de Kat Eliassen, "Five Papyri" 55f.

+   THEODORUS: see no. 266.

151. THEODOSIUS.   Gramm.   Alexandria.   s.IV ex. / s.V init.
     PLRE II s.v. 3, pp. 1099f.

     Theodosius, ὁ θαυμάσιος γραμματικός, friend of Synesius, mentioned by the latter in a letter to his brother, Euoptius, at Alexandria in 402: *Ep.* 4, p. 645 Hercher. On the date of the letter, cf. Lacombrade, *Synésios* 131ff.
     He is perhaps to be identified with Theodosius (q.v., no. 152) the gramm. of Alexandria and author of the introductory rules (Κανόνες εἰσαγωγικοί) on nominal and verbal flexion.

152. THEODOSIUS.   Gramm.   Alexandria.   s.II ex. / s.V ex.; perhaps s.IV ex. / s.V init.
     RE, 2. Reihe, 5.1935 (Gudeman); Chr.-Sch.-St. 2:2.1078f.; Hunger 2.11ff.; cf. *PLRE* II s.v. 3, p. 1099.

     Theodosius, γραμματικὸς Ἀλεξανδρεύς: inscr. of the Κανόνες. Also ὁ Θεοδόσιος or ὁ τεχνικός frequently in Choerobosc. *Schol. in Theodos.*, *GG* 4:1.103–417, 4:2.1–371; similarly in Sophronius's excerpts from the scholia of Ioannes Charax, *GG* 4:2.375–434. Also Θεοδόσιος (ὁ) γραμματικός: cod. Paris. gr. 2542, fol. 11ʳ, inscr. of a version of the Περὶ προσῳδίας of Choeroboscus (cf. Hilgard, *GG* 4:2, lxx); codd. Matrit. 38, Barocc. 179, Haun. 1965 of the epitome of Herodian (see below). Also Θεοδόσιος ὁ τοῦ * * * : catalogue of gramm. in Kröhnert, *Canones* 7. Some mss of the Κανόνες have Θεόδωρος, a name under which T. is sometimes cited by Urbanus Belluensis; cf. Hilgard, *GG* 4:2, vii–viii.
     T. is later than Herodian, whom he cites (*GG* 4:1.97.1f.) and of whose Καθολικὴ προσῳδία he perhaps made an epitome (see below). T.'s paradigmatic analysis of τύπτω (*GG* 4:1.43–82) had been excerpted and added as a supplement to the Τέχνη of Dionysius Thrax (*GG* 1:1.125ff.) by the end of s.V, when the Armenian version of Dionysius was written; cf. Merx, *GG* 1:1, lxxii–lxxiii. He is perhaps to be identified with ὁ θαυμάσιος γραμματικός Theodosius (q.v., no. 151) mentioned by Synesius in a letter to his brother at Alexandria in 402 (*Ep.* 4, p. 645 Hercher). On the identification, see esp. Oguse, "Papyrus" 85ff.
     Author of Κανόνες εἰσαγωγικοὶ περὶ κλίσεως ὀνομάτων καὶ ῥημάτων, an extension of Dionysius Thrax used as a school text by Ioannes Charax, Georgius Choeroboscus (qq.v., nos. 199, 201), and many later gramm.

(*GG* 4:1.3–99). Also conjecturally the author of the treatise Περὶ προσῳ-διῶν appended as a supplement to the text of Dionysius Thrax: so Laum, *Alexandrinische Akzentuationssystem* 27f. Very doubtfully the author of an epitome of Herodian's Καθολικὴ προσῳδία attributed to T. in three mss (listed above) of s.XV / s.XVI; cf. Cohn, *RE* 2.1154.4ff.; cf. also s.vv. Arcadius, Aristodemus, nos. 16, 188. On the *farrago commentationum gram-maticarum* falsely attributed to T. in codd. Paris. gr. 2553 and 2555, see Uhlig, *GG* 1:1, xxxvi–xxxvii. He is listed under the general heading ὅσοι γραμματικοί in the catalogue of gramm. in Kröhnert, *Canones* 7. On the relationship between the Κανόνες and the grammatical papyri, see Roberts, *PRyl.* 3 p. 170, with the amplifications and corrections in *PHamb.* 2.166 (p. 116 n. 1); Oguse, "Papyrus" 86; P. J. Parsons, "School-Book" 145f. Cf. also Wouters, *Grammatical Papyri.*

153. THEODOSIUS.   Gramm.   Panopolis(?).   Not before s.IV?
PLRE I s.v. 2, p. 902.

Theodosius γραμματικός, on a stele of unknown provenance, *RIGCE* no. 325; cf. Crum, *Coptic Monuments* no. 8361 p. 84. Lefebvre assigned the stele on stylistic grounds to Akhmîm (Panopolis; cf. *RIGCE* p. xxvii).

   The inscr. shows that T. was a Christian; he is therefore probably to be dated to s.IV / s.VI. The second column of the inscr. contains mostly illegible remains of an epitaph in verse. T.'s name and a reference to his σοφί[η] can be distinguished in lines 2 and 5, respectively.

154. THEOFILUS.   Lat. gramm. → *com. ord. pr.*   Constantinople.   s.V 1/4.
PLRE II s.v. Theophilus 4, p. 1109.

Theofilus, [*grammaticus*] *Latinus*, awarded the *comitiva ordinis primi* and the rank of ex-vicar, 15 March 425 (*CTh* 6.21.1); honored with the Greek gramm. Helladius and Syrianus (qq.v., nos. 67, 147), the sophists Mar-tinus and Maximus, and the *iuris peritus* Leontius.

THEON: see no. 267.

THEOPHILUS: see s.v. THEOFILUS, no. 154.

THESPESIUS: see no. 268.

155. TIBERINUS.   Gramm.   Arabia → Antioch.   358.
RE, 2. Reihe, 6.790 (Ensslin); Wolf, *Schulwesen* 32; Petit, *Étudiants* 85; *PLRE* I s.v., p. 913.

The subject of Lib. *Ep.* 337 (an. 358), Tiberinus (*Ep.* 337.1, 2) taught the poets: *Ep.* 337.1, τοὺς ποιητὰς εἰσάγοντος εἰς τὰς τῶν νέων ψυχάς. He was therefore a gramm.

T. was a native of the province governed by Maximus (= Maximus 14, *PLRE* I, p. 582) in 358, viz., Arabia; cf. *Ep.* 337.1, οὐ παρ' ἡμῖν μόνον ἀλλὰ καὶ οἴκοι τιμᾶσθαι; ibid. 2, ταῖς πόλεσι τῇ τε ἡμετέρᾳ καὶ ἐξ ἧς ἐστιν. When Libanius wrote the letter T. was teaching in Antioch: *Ep.* 337.1, παρ' ἡμῖν ἄνθρωπος τὸ αὐτοῦ ποιεῖ.

Since T.'s son, Archelaus, was of an age to be sued or otherwise harassed on his own account in 358 (*Ep.* 337.2), T. was probably at least middle-aged at the time, and so roughly contemporary with Libanius.

T. is said to bring glory to his homeland by his teaching: *Ep.* 337.1, τῇ δόξῃ δὲ κοσμῶν τὴν οἰκείαν. His enemies are said to show no respect for the business of culture or, consequently, for T.: *Ep.* 337.2, οἱ περὶ τὸ χρῆμα τῶν λόγων ἀσεβοῦντες . . . Τιβερῖνον οὐκ αἰσχυνόμενοι.

156. TIMOTHEUS.   Gramm. and poet(?).   Gaza.   s.V ex. / s.VI init.

RE, 2. Reihe, 6.1339–40, concerned almost exclusively with the zoological work (Steier); Chr.-Sch.-St. 2:2.974f., 1077; Hunger 2.13, 18f., 265; *PLRE* II s.v. 3, p. 1121.

Gramm. of Gaza in the reign of Anastasius: *Suda* T.621, Τιμόθεος, Γαζαῖος, γραμματικός, γεγονὼς ἐπὶ Ἀναστασίου βασιλέως; cf. Ioan. Tzetzes *Chil.* 4.171f., p. 132 Leone, Τιμόθεος γραμματικὸς Γαζαῖος / Ἀναστασίῳ βασιλεῖ σύνδρομος ὢν ἐν χρόνοις.

Gaza: scholium to the Ἔκφρασις of Ioannes (q.v., no. 83) of Gaza, p. 135 Friedländer, ἐλλόγιμοι ταύτης τῆς πόλεως Ἰωάννης, Προκόπιος, Τιμόθεος; cod. Coislin. 387 = Cramer, *Anecd. Paris.* 4.239.14, Τιμόθεος Γάζης; cod. Barocc. 50 = Cramer, *Anecd. Oxon.* 4.263.17, Τιμόθεος γραμματικὸς Γάζης; scholia to the glossary falsely attributed to St. Cyril (see below), Τιμόθεος ὁ Γαζεὺς γραμματικός; Cedrenus 1.627.8f. Bekker, Τιμόθεος ὁ Γαζαῖος ἀνὴρ τὰ πάντα σοφός; the catalogue of gramm. in Kröhnert, *Canones* 7, Τιμόθεος ὁ Γαζαῖος; also Τιμόθεος in the extracts of the Περὶ ζῴων in *Suppl. Aristot.* 1:1 and in Graff, "Mittheilung" (see below).

According to the *Suda* and Cedrenus he composed a τραγῳδία addressed to Anastasius on the quinquennial tax in gold (*collatio lustralis*); cf. *Suda* T.621, εἰς ὃν [sc. Ἀναστάσιον] καὶ τραγῳδίαν ἐποίησε περὶ τοῦ δημοσίου καλουμένου χρυσαργύρου; Cedrenus 1.627.8f., Τιμοθέου . . . τραγῳδίαν ποιήσαντος ὑπὲρ τοῦ τοιούτου. This was probably an oration lamenting the horrors of the tax; for this sense of τραγῳδία, cf. Dion. Hal. *De Thuc.* 18 (p. 351.22f. Usener), noted at Chr.-Sch.-St. 2:2.974 n. 9; cf. also *LSJ* s.v. II, 2. Compare Philost. *V. soph.* 2.9 (p. 582), where μονῳδία is used of Ael. Arist. *Or.* 19, Aristides' letter to Marcus concerning aid for earthquake-stricken Smyrna (Philostratus quotes a phrase from *Or.* 19.3); μονῳδία is also given as the title of Ael. Arist. *Or.* 18 (Ἐπὶ Σμύρνῃ μονῳδία) in the paradosis. For recent dissent, see Baldwin, "Some *addenda*" (1982) 101, who would prefer to see in T.'s τραγῳδία "a rare example of dramatic writing in early Byzantium." The question of genre should be able to be resolved, since this is presumably the work noted as partially preserved in a ms "ἐν τῇ λαύρᾳ τοῦ ἁγίου Ἀθανασίου" on Mt. Athos: Sathas, Μεσαιωνικὴ Βιβλιοθήκη 1.271, Τιμοθέου Γραμματικοῦ, πρὸς τὸν αὐτοκράτορα Ἀναστάσιον· ἀτελές. Anastasius abolished the *collatio lustralis* in May 498 (cf. Stein, "Kleine Beiträge" 583; *Histoire* 2.206f.); Cedrenus therefore cannot be correct when he places both the τραγῳδία and the abolition in the first year (*ut vid.*) of Anastasius's reign (491/92), attributing the abolition to the effects of T.'s work. Since the *collatio lustralis* was levied at an emperor's accession and then every four or five years during his reign (cf. Jones, *LRE* 431f., with ibid. 432 n. 52 for evidence of quadrennial levies in s.V), T.'s efforts were probably occasioned by a levy marking Anastasius's accession in 491, or perhaps by a levy ca. 495, which would then have been the last. In either case, Cedrenus has misleadingly associated the abolition with the composition in Anastasius's first year.

T. was also the author of a Περὶ ζῴων in four books, in hexameters according to the *Suda* T.621: ἔγραψε δὲ καὶ ἐπικῶς περὶ ζῴων τετραπόδων θηρίων τῶν παρ' Ἰνδοῖς καὶ Ἄραψι καὶ Αἰγυπτίοις καὶ ὅσα τρέφει Λιβύη καὶ περὶ ὀρνέων ξένων τε καὶ ἀλλοκότων καὶ ὄφεων βιβλία δ'; cf. cod. Barocc. 50 = Cramer, *Anecd. Oxon.* 4.263.17ff., Περὶ ζῴων τετραπόδων καὶ φυσικῶν αὐτῶν ἐνεργειῶν θαυμαζομένων ποιητηκῶς [*sic*] αὐτοῦ καλλιεποῦντος; scholium to Ioan. Gaz. Ἔκφρασις, p. 135 Friedländer, Τιμόθεος ὁ γράψας περὶ ζῴων Ἰνδικῶν; Ioan. Tzetzes *Chil.* 4.169ff., p. 132 Leone. The work survives only in extracts or paraphrases: Lampros, *Suppl. Aristot.* 1:1; Haupt, "Excerpta" 8ff., trans. Bodenheimer and Rabinowitz, *Timotheus*; Graff, "Mittheilung" 23ff., reprinted in Haupt, "Excerpta" 29f.; Cramer, *Anecd. Oxon.* 4.263.17ff. These give no sign that it was originally composed in verse. On the work, cf. Steier, *RE*, 2. Reihe, 6.1340.5ff.; Bodenheimer and Rabinowitz, *Timotheus* 7ff.

T. composed Κανόνες καθολικοὶ περὶ συντάξεως, dependent on Herodian; cf. Cramer, *Anecd. Paris.* 4.239.15ff., with Egenolff, *Orthographischen Stücke* 6ff. Note also the Περὶ ὀρθογραφίας πρὸς Ἀρκεσίλαον cited under T.'s name in the scholia to the so-called Cyril-glossary in codd. Vallicell. E 11, Laurent. LIX 49; cf. Reitzenstein, *Geschichte* 296. A ms inscribed Τιμοθέου Περὶ ὀρθογραφίας is listed in Spyridon of the Laura and S. Eustratiades, *Catalogue* 177 no. 1113, cod. I 29 fol. 52ʳff.

In various scholia to the Cyril-glossary T. is identified as the student of Horapollon, and Horapollon is identified as his teacher; see Reitzenstein, *Geschichte* 296. If this is correct, chronology requires that the younger gramm. of that name be meant; cf. s.v. Fl. Horapollon, no. 78. How much the information can be trusted, however, is unclear. As Reitzenstein pointed out, although the scholiast refers to Diogenianus, Herodian, Aristophanes, and Horapollon as well as to Timotheus, he appears to have had firsthand knowledge only of T.'s work and to owe his references to the others to citations embedded therein. If the younger Horapollon is meant, T. may have referred to him as ὁ ἡμέτερος διδάσ-καλος or the like in the course of transmitting some pieces of *viva voce* instruction, since Fl. Horapollon is not otherwise known to have left any technical writings; cf., e.g., s.v. Aelius Donatus, no. 52, for Jerome's calling Donatus *praeceptor meus* when repeating one of the gramm.'s class-room comments. Alternatively, T. may have referred to one or another of the technical writings of the elder Horapollon, perhaps the Τεμενικά; see s.v., no. 77, and Reitzenstein, *Geschichte* 313–16. The teacher-student relationship, that is, may be merely an inference of the scholiast; cf. the catalogue of gramm. in cod. Bern. 243, *Anecd. Helv.* = *GL* 8, cxlix, where "Honoratus" (= Servius), "Sergius," Maximus (= Maximus[?] Victor-inus), and "Metrorius" (qq.v., nos. 136, 255, 274, 239) are all called the *discipuli* of Donatus. On the difficulty of evaluating third-party allegations of teacher-student relationships, see also s.vv. Damocharis, Romanus, nos. 42, 129.

157. TRIPHIODORUS.   Gramm. and poet.   Panopolis(?).   s.III / s.IV.

RE, 2. Reihe, 7.178–80 (Keydell); Chr.-Sch.-St. 2:2.971; Hunger 2.109; cf. *PLRE* II p. 1126.

Tryphiodorus: mss of the Ἅλωσις Ἰλίου (ed. Gerlaud); *Suda* T.1111. Probably incorrectly for "Triphiodorus," a name derived from the god-dess Triphis, worshipped at Panopolis and its environs; cf. Keydell, *RE*, 2. Reihe, 7.178.28ff. A γραμματικός and epic poet from Egypt: *Suda* T.1111.

T. was formerly dated to s.V 2/2 on the basis of his alleged dependence on Nonnus in the Ἅλωσις Ἰλίου and of his alleged influence on Col-(l)uthus. That opinion must be revised because of the discovery of a papyrus fragment of vv. 391–402 of the Ἅλωσις, *POxy.* 41.2946; cf. the remarks of the editor, J. R. Rea, pp. 9f. The fragment is datable on paleographic grounds to s.III / s.IV. Also important for a revised dating is the conspectus of the relationship between Nonnus and T. presented by Alan Cameron, *Claudian* app. D, 478ff.; cf. also Livrea, "Per una nuova edizione." Nonnus must now be regarded as later than T. The influence of T. on Gregory Nazianzen that has been detected (cf. Gerlaud, ed., *Triphiodore* 55 n. 3) would establish a *term. a. q.* of s.IV med.–2/2. A *term. p. q.* for T. is provided by his familiarity with the work of Quintus of Smyrna, who is to be dated to s.III; cf. Vian, ed., *Quintus* 1, xxi–xxii.

Besides the extant Ἅλωσις Ἰλίου, other works attributed to T. at *Suda* T.1111 are Τὰ κατὰ Ἱπποδάμειαν, a Μαραθωνιακά, and an Ὀδύσσεια λειπογράμματος. For the character of the last, cf. *Suda* N.261. He is probably to be identified with the second Tryphiodorus catalogued in the

Suda, at T.1112, διάφορα ἔγραψε δι' ἐπῶν. παράφρασιν τῶν Ὁμήρου παραβολῶν, καὶ ἄλλα πλεῖστα; cf. Keydell, *RE*, 2. Reihe, 7.181.1–6.

TROILUS: see no. 269.

158. AUR. TROPHIMUS. Teacher. Altıntaş (Kurtköy; Phrygia). s.III 2/2 / s.IV.

Aur. Trophimus son of Eutyches, subject of one of three funeral epigrams inscribed on an altar belonging to a single family at Altıntaş (Kurtköy), in central Phrygia, ca. 35 km SSE of Kütahya (Cotyaeum): Kaibel 372 = *SEG* 6.137. Speaking as the author of his own epitaph and of that of his wife, Aur. Tatia (= *SEG* 6.138), T. describes himself as τὸν σοφίης . . . διδάσκαλον ἔν(v)ομον, *SEG* 6.137.4f.; cf. ibid. 28f., τὸν π[ρὶν] σοφίης ἐμὲ διδάσκαλον, ὅς ποτ' ἐκλήθην. Since T. was apparently not a Christian (cf. ibid. 6ff.), σοφίη should mean secular wisdom, and T. was probably a small-town schoolmaster; cf. Buckler, Calder, and Cox, "Asia Minor" 53ff. This is a common meaning of σοφίη; compare, e.g., s.vv. Coluthus, Theodosius, Timotheus, nos. 33, 153, 156. For the phrase, cf. σοφίης πανάριστε / διδάσκαλε, Dörner, *Bericht* no. 137, 1f. (Bithynion / Claudiopolis).

A *term. p. q.* of s.III med. is provided by the devotion of T.'s granddaughter to the Novatian sect (*SEG* 6.140.32f.). The religious history of T.'s family, which finds T. a pagan and the next two generations openly Christian, might suggest that the group of inscriptions belongs to the end of s.III and the first half of s.IV; cf. Buckler, Calder, and Cox "Asia Minor" 53ff., with discussion and stemma of the family; for other Novatian inscriptions in Phrygia, see Calder, "Epigraphy," in Buckler and Calder, eds., *Anatolian Studies* 74ff.; Haspels, *Highlands* app. 3 no. 50, with p. 207.

T. evidently died at an advanced age; cf. *SEG* 6.138.2ff., his wife dead at age seventy in the same year; with ibid. 137.24–25.

STATIUS TULLIANUS: see no. 270.

CURTIUS VALERIANUS: see no. 271.

159. VERECUNDUS. Gramm. Milan. 384–87.

RE, 2. Reihe, 8.2419 (Ensslin); *PLRE* I s.v., p. 950; cf. Martindale, "Prosopography" 251.

An intimate (*familiarissimus noster*) of Augustine; a *civis* and gramm. of Milan during Augustine's time there. Nebridius (q.v., no. 104) was his assistant teacher; cf. *Conf.* 8.6.13.

V. possessed an estate outside Milan, Cassiciacum, which Augustine used as a place of rest and study in preparation for his baptism; cf. *Conf.*

9.3.5, *De ord.* 1.2.5, *De beat. vit.* 4.31. He is praised for his *benevolentia singularis* at *De ord.* 1.2.5.

V. very much desired to join Augustine in baptism but could not bring himself to abandon his marrige (*Conf.* 9.3.5–6). In 387, when Augustine had left Milan for Ostia, V. fell ill, was baptized, and died: *Conf.* 9.3.5; cf. *Ep.* 7.4, where V. is mentioned as *familiaris quondam noster* in a parallel with *mortuae res.*

V. has been identified with the unnamed *grammaticus* of Milan (= Anonymus 6, no. 172) to whom Augustine refers at *Serm.* 178.7.8 (*PL* 38.964); cf. Courcelle, *Recherches* 84 n. 2. Note, however, that the gramm. of the anecdote is emphatically described as *paganus* and is sharply distinguished from his *proscholus* (assistant), who is a Christian: *sed plane Christianus, quamvis ille esset paganus grammaticus: melior ad velum quam in cathedra.* The description scarcely suits V., who is described at *Conf.* 9.3.5 as *nondum Christianus*, a phrase that in Augustine's usage denotes one who is neither *paganus* nor *plane Christianus* but is decidedly closer to the latter; cf. *nondum Christianus* of Nebridius, *Conf.* 9.3.6. The identification is likely wrong; the identification of the Christian assistant with Nebridius (q.v., no. 104) is certainly wrong. There was presumably more than one gramm. active at Milan in the late 380s.

See further s.v. Nebridius; cf. s.vv. Anonymus 5, 6, nos. 171, 172.

160. VERONICIANUS.   Gramm.   Antioch.   s.VI init.

RE 3.309 (Schmid); *PLRE* II s.v. 3, p. 1157.

A gramm., mentioned in Dionysius of Antioch *Ep.* 3 Hercher; the phrasing suggests that he was at Antioch with Dionysius: ὡς δὲ ἠσθόμην ἀφ᾽ ὧν ὁ γραμματικὸς Βερονικιανός μοι διελέχθη. Schmid, *RE* 3.309, confuses V. with the homonymous successor of the philosopher Chrysanthus mentioned in Eunap. *V. phil.* 24.1–2.

161. VICTOR.   Gramm.   Cirta / Constantina (Numidia).   s.IV 1/4.

RE, 2. Reihe, 8.2058 no. 6 (Ensslin); *PLRE* I s.v. 1, p. 957; *Prosop. chrét.* I s.v. 1, p. 1152.

V.'s interrogation on 13 December 320 by the *consularis Numidiae* Zenophilus is recorded in *Gesta apud Zenophilum*, *CSEL* 26.185ff.; extracts of the *Gesta* are found also in Aug. *C. Cresc.* 3.29.33 = *CSEL* 26.185.4–8, 186.16–187.5, 187.15–21, 188.35–189.8, 192.21–24. The *Gesta* includes quotations from the record of proceedings (*acta*) of 19 May 303 in which V. was also involved; see below.

Questioned about his *condicio* by Zenophilus, V. responded, *professor sum Romanarum litterarum, grammaticus Latinus* (185.9–10); he is called *grammaticus* also at 185.6, 188.15ff., 195.7. Questioned about his *dignitas*, V.

replied (185.10ff.) that his father had been a decurion of Constantina; his grandfather, a soldier in the *comitatus*. His family was of Moorish descent.

V. taught at Cirta (186.20f., the *acta* of 19 May 303) = Constantina (185.11f., the *gesta* of 13 Dec. 320); for the change of the city's name, cf. s.v. Probus(?), no. 127. He was at Carthage for an unknown purpose and length of time in 312; cf. 185.17ff., *cum essem apud Carthaginem, Secundus episcopus cum Carthaginem tandem aliquando venisset, dicuntur invenisse Caecilianum episcopum nescio quibus non recte constitutum, illi contra alium instituerunt*. A gramm. already in 303 (188.15ff., in the *acta* of 303), he was still teaching in 320 (the *gesta* of 320); it is unlikely that he was born much later than ca. 283.

A lector in the church of Cirta at the time of the Great Persecution (186.8–9, 188.29ff.), V. was accused thereafter of being a *traditor* (186.3ff.), i.e., one of those who handed over the Scriptures to the persecutors for destruction. Against the evidence of the *acta*, which implicated him (186.15ff.), V. repeatedly denied the charge, claiming that he had hidden during the persecution and that the sacred codices were removed from his house in his absence (186.4–11, 188.34, 192.21). He did, however, implicate Silvanus (192.21ff.), who had been subdeacon in 303 and was bishop in 320.

Despite his social standing (*honestas*, 185.14), he was threatened with torture by Zenophilus: 186.14–15, *simpliciter confitere, ne strictius interrogeris*.

VICTOR: see no. 272.

VICTORINUS: see no. 273.

MAXIMUS(?) VICTORINUS: see no. 274.

162. VICTORIUS. Assistant teacher. Bordeaux → Sicily → Cumae. s.IV 2/3.

RE, 2. Reihe, 8.2086 (Ensslin); Booth, "Notes" 249; *PLRE* I s.v. 1, p. 965.

Victorius (Auson. *Prof.* 22 tit., v. 1); assistant teacher, *subdoctor sive proscholus* (ibid. tit.), of Ausonius: v. 17, *exili nostrae fucatus honore cathedrae*. On the distinction between *subdoctor* and *proscholus*, cf. s.vv. Nebridius, Anonymus 5, nos. 104, 171. His post gave him a taste of being a gramm.: v. 18, *libato tenuis nomine grammatici*.

I here interpret *nostrae* of v. 17 with Booth, "Notes" 249, as a reference to Ausonius's chair of grammar, not to Bordeaux in general; *contra*, e.g., "in our city," trans. Evelyn-White in the Loeb edition. In either case, V. was certainly teaching in Bordeaux, and the doubts expressed on that point in *PLRE* I s.v. are unfounded. From Bordeaux he went to Sicily and Cumae, where he died (vv. 19–20). It is not clear whether he taught after leaving Bordeaux.

An assistant to Ausonius when the latter was a gramm. (vv. 17–18; cf. above), V. must have taught at Bordeaux between ca. 336/37 and ca. 366/67, presumably—since Ausonius was still a gramm.—nearer the beginning of that period. His death was premature (vv. 15–16).

Ausonius says that V. neglected Cicero (i.e., rhetoric), Vergil (i.e., poetry), and Roman history in favor of his interest in religious antiquities and pontifical law (vv. 3–14). This interest suggests that V. was a pagan.

163. VIRGILIANUS.   Gramm.   Not before s.IV ex. / s.V.

PLRE I s.v., p. 969.

The son of Vibius Sequester (q.v., no. 254), to whom the latter dedicated his glossary *De fluminibus, fontibus, lacubus, nemoribus, paludibus, montibus, gentibus per litteras* (ed. Gelsomino [Leipzig, 1967]). Since the glossary concerns only names that occur in poetry (see s.v. Sequester), and since Sequester promises his son *quo lecto non minimum consequeris notitiae, praesertim cum professioni tuae sit necessarium* (p. 1.13f.), V.'s *professio* would appear to have demanded knowledge of the geographic details contained in poetic texts; i.e., he was probably a gramm. The work is unlikely to have been written before the end of s.IV. On the date, and on the misattribution of V.'s profession in *PLRE* I, see s.v. Sequester.

+   URBANUS: see no. 275.

164. URBANUS.   Lat. gramm.   Alexandria → Constantinople.   s.V 3/3 / s.VI 1/4.

PLRE II s.v. 2, p. 1188.

"L'admirable Urbanus, qui est aujourd'hui, dans cette ville impériale [= Constantinople], professeur de grammaire latine," Zach. Schol. *Vie de Sévère*, p. 37.8f.; cf. Kugener, ibid. n. 4, "mot à mot: 'grammairien (γραμματικός) de la science de la langue des Romains ('Ρωμαῖοι)'"; cf. also p. 15 n. 1.

He was baptized in Alexandria one Easter (Zach. Schol. *Vie de Sévère* p. 37.4ff.) when Zach. and Severus were students there, probably in 486; cf. s.v. Fl. Horapollon, no. 78. If, as is likely, U. also was a student at the time, he was probably born ca. 470. He was a gramm. at Constantinople by the time the biography of Severus was composed, i.e., sometime after 512. He is therefore probably to be identified with Urbanus the gramm. who received a doctrinal letter from Severus in 516/17; an extract preserved in a Syriac version has been published with an English translation as *Ep.* 44 by E. W. Brooks, *PO* 12.310ff. If the identification is correct, U. was a Monophysite Christian; the letter's tone is one of instruction for a coreligionist rather than of polemic against an opponent.

165. URBICUS.   Lat. and Gr. gramm.   Bordeaux.   s.IV med.
PLRE I s.v. 1, p. 984.

Urbicus: Auson. *Prof.* 21 tit., v. 11. A *grammaticus Latinus et Graecus*: ibid.
tit.; cf. below. Where he taught is not stated, but since Staphylius (q.v.,
no. 140) is noted as the single exception to Ausonius's *lex commemorandi*
in the *Prof.* (cf. *Prof.* 20.1–4; cf. also s.v. Concordius [no. 35], s.v. Staphylius), and since U. and his colleague Crispus (q.v., no. 40) are not said
to have taught elsewhere, U. must have taught at Bordeaux; cf. s.v.
Crispus. PLRE I gives Bordeaux as the place where Crispus taught (s.v.,
p. 232) but queries "(?) Bordeaux" s.v. Urbicus, p. 984. U. was probably
active s.IV med.; cf. s.v. Crispus.

On the structure of *Prof.* 21 and the correct attribution of the skills of
U. and Crispus, see s.v. Crispus. Ausonius describes U. in the following
terms. His Greek was superior to his Latin (vv. 10–12). In Greek, he
possessed a skill in prose and verse (v. 14, *prosa . . . et versa loqui*) that was
able to recall the *priscos . . . heroas* of Homer—the brevity of Menelaus,
the volubility of Odysseus, the sweetness of Nestor (vv. 13–24). This is
perhaps a reference to the genre of ethopoeia or to the school exercise of
recasting in prose or in verse select passages from the classical texts; cf.
Aug. *Conf.* 1.17. Together with his colleague Crispus, U. is further
credited (vv. 25–28) with fluency in speech (*loqui faciles*) and with learning
in *omnia carmina*, in the *mython plasmata*, and in *historia*; both men are said
to have been of libertine birth (*liberti ambo genus*).

Perhaps the father of Urbica, a follower of Priscillian stoned to death
at Bordeaux in 385; see Prosper *Chron.* 1187, *Chron. min.* 1.462. Cf.
Prosper ibid. and Auson. *Prof.* 5.35–38, with Booth, "Notes" 238f., for
the involvement in Priscillianism of the wife and daughter of the rhetorician Delphidius of Bordeaux.

166. URSULUS.   Gramm.   Trier.   376.
RE, 2. Reihe, 9.1067–68 (John); PLRE I s.v. 2, p. 988.

Ursulus: Auson. *Epist.* 13 tit., v. 26. A *grammaticus* who taught six hours a
day at Trier: ibid. tit., v. 10. Since his expertise is not specified, he
presumably taught Latin—not Latin and Greek; Ausonius presents that
combination of skills as the special glory of U.'s colleague Harmonius
(q.v., no. 65): vv. 31f., *Cecropiae commune decus Latiaeque camenae, / solus qui
Chium miscet et Ammineum*.

Through the intercession of Ausonius (ibid. tit., vv. 1–4), U. received
the emperor's New Year's gift (*strenae*) in the amount of six *solidi*: v. 5,
regale nomisma, Philippos; cf. Milne, "'Philippus.'" For the amount, cf.
vv. 6–24.

Epist. 13 is probably to be dated not long after 1 January 376, when Ausonius was *QSP*; cf. ibid. tit., with v. 3; see further s.v. Harmonius.

ZOSIMUS: see no. 276.

* 167. ANONYMUS 1. Gramm. Anazarbus (Cilicia). s.IV 1/3.

Gramm. of Anazarbus whose dealings with the Arian Aetius are described in some detail at Philostorg. *HE* 3.15; called σοφιστής in the derivative passage *ap.* Nic. Call. *HE* 9.17 (*PG* 146.289C–D). During Aetius's wanderings, when he was making his living as a goldsmith, the gramm. received him into his house and agreed to teach him his τέχνη in return for Aetius's service as a domestic: εἰσοικισθεὶς ἐθήτευεν, τὰς οἰκετικὰς αὐτῷ τελῶν λειτουργίας. Aetius, however, publicly embarrassed the gramm., who thereupon drove him from his house.

The gramm. was evidently a Christian, perhaps a Homoousianist, since the falling out was occasioned by Aetius's charge that the gramm. misunderstood Scripture: ὅτι μὴ τῶν θείων λογίων ὀρθὴν ἐποιεῖτο τὴν διήγησιν. Aetius was thereupon immediately received by Athanasius the Arian bishop of Anazarbus.

According to the sequence given by Philostorgius, the episode should probably be placed ca. 332. Aetius arrived in Anazarbus soon after being expelled from Antioch by the bishop Eulalius, the short-lived successor of Paulinus of Tyre; Paulinus himself had died only six months after succeeding Eustathius, who had been deposed ca. 330/31: thus Philostorg. *HE* 2.7 and 3.15, with the evidence of Nicetas *Thesaur.* 5.9; see p. 19.23ff. in Philostorgius, *Kirchengeschichte* ed. Bidez and Winkelmann (3d ed., Berlin, 1981). On the date of the deposition of Eustathius, cf. Devreesse, *Patriarcat* 115f.; *LThK* 3.1202 (van Roey). The chronology of the Antiochene see is, however, immensely confused for the periods immediately preceding and following the episcopacy of Eustathius. For different accounts, see Jer. *Chron.* s.a. 328; Soc. *HE* 1.24 and 2.9; Soz. *HE* 2.19; Theodoret. *HE* 1.21; Theoph. *Chron.* p. 29.26 de Boor. On any reckoning, A.'s encounter with Aetius must be dated after the Council of Nicaea (325).

* 168. ANONYMUS 2. Gramm. Antioch. 329–34.

The gramm. (γραμματιστής; for Libanius's usage, see Appendix 2) with whom Libanius read Aristoph. *Acharn.* when he was twenty, i.e., in late 334, by which time he had been studying with the man for five years: *Or.* 1.9. On the chronology, cf. Booth, "À quel âge?" Possibly identical with one or the other of the two gramm. with whom Libanius is otherwise known to have studied, Cleobulus and Didymus (qq.v., nos. 32, 46).

* 169. ANONYMUS 3.   Gramm.   Antioch.   s.IV 1/3 – 2/3.

Father of the gramm. Calliopius (q.v., no. 25) and of Alexandra; teaching with his son at Antioch in 361: Lib. *Ep.* 625, 678. See further s.v. Calliopius, esp. for the family's standing and connections.

* 170. ANONYMUS 4.   Gramm.   Africa → Rome.   s.IV med.

A gramm. from Africa teaching at Rome; described by Jerome, *C. Rufin.* 3.27. He was a *vir eruditissimus*, but his speech was marred by the accents of his native land, *stridor linguae eius et vitia . . . oris*, which one of his students thought it proper to imitate. Perhaps Jerome meant to suggest that the gramm.'s accent showed the influence of Punic; he regularly uses *stridor* or *stridulus* to characterize the sound of Semitic languages, including Punic: see esp. *Ep.* 130.5, *stridor Punicae linguae*, with *Ep.* 125.12, *Comm. Galat.* 3 prol., *V. Hilarion.* 22, *Comm. Is.* 4.11, *Comm. Tit.* 3; cf. also Aug. *De ord.* 2.45.

   The anecdote must date to Jerome's days as a student at Rome, from the mid- or late 350s through the mid-360s; it is conceivable but unlikely that Jerome here refers under the cover of anonymity to his own teacher Aelius Donatus, who was possibly of African origin (see s.v., no. 52).

* 171. ANONYMUS 5.   *Proscholus grammatici*.   Milan.   384/86.

The *proscholus* (attendant or assistant) of a pagan gramm.; hero of an edifying tale told by Augustine, *Serm.* 178.7.8 (PL 38.964), of the time of his tenure at Milan (*nobis apud Mediolanum constitutis*). On the distinction between *subdoctor* and *proscholus*, see Clarke, *Higher Education* 27 n. 105; but cf. also Heraeus, *Kleine Schriften* 93f.

   He was *plane Christianus* and *pauperrimus*. The pagan gramm. was probably not Verecundus; the *proscholus* was almost certainly not Augustine's friend Nebridius; see s.vv. Nebridius, Verecundus, nos. 104, 159; cf. s.v. Anonymus 6, no. 172.

   If *constitutis* in *Serm.* 178.7.8 refers to Augustine's position as an official rhetorician at Milan, the episode can be dated between autumn 384 and autumn 386. If the meaning is less precise, the *term. a. q.* will be mid-387.

172. ANONYMUS 6.   Gramm.   Milan.   384/86.

A gramm. of Milan in a story told by Augustine, *Serm.* 178.7.8 (PL 38.964), of the time of his tenure in that city (*nobis apud Mediolanum constitutis*). A *paganus* himself, he had a Christian assistant (= Anonymus 5, no. 171). It has been suggested that A. is Augustine's friend Verecundus, but that is probably wrong; see s.v. Verecundus, no. 159.

   For the *term. a. q.* of the anecdote, see s.v. Anonymus 5.

* 173. ANONYMUS 7. Gramm. Egypt (Hermopolis?). s.V 2/2.

"The lord grammarian," ὁ κύριος ὁ γραμματικός, mentioned in a letter (*SB* 12.11084 = Maehler, "Menander" 305ff. = Pap.) dated on the basis of the script (Maehler, "Menander" 305) to s.V 2/2 and sent by Victor, apparently an advocate or rhetorician at Hermopolis (cf. Pap. 6–8), to Theognostus, probably of the same profession: cf. Pap. 4, ἡ σὴ λογιότης. Victor reminds Theognostus to return certain rhetorical handbooks that he had borrowed: Pap. 9ff. and verso, with Maehler, "Menander" 308ff. "Elias . . . the slave of the lord grammarian" (Pap. 4ff.) is to act as courier. It is not stated whether Elias has been sent on the errand from Hermopolis or is to come directly from the unnamed place of Theognostus's residence. The former seems more likely, since Victor offers the services of Elias; the opening clause, κατα[ξι]ούτω ἡ σὴ λογιότης διδόναι Ἠλίᾳ . . . τὸ βιβλίον (Pap. 4ff.), might suggest that Elias himself brought the letter to Theognostus. If so, Elias's master is possibly one of the two gramm. attested at Hermopolis in s.V 2/2, Fl. Her. . . and Fl. Pythiodorus (qq.v., nos. 68, 128).

* 174. ANONYMUS (ANONYMI?) 8. Gramm. Egypt. s.V / s.VI.

In an account, *PSI* 8.891.10, γραμματικ^Κ/ ̥̅ α, "one *solidus* to the *grammaticus*"—or *grammatici*? Cf. Vitelli, ed., *ad loc.*, "forse i due κ indicano un plurale (γραμματικοῖς?)." Note, however, that every other payment in the account is to one person, and that no one receives less than one *solidus*. The purpose and the source of the payments are not specified, although the paying agents in the separate parts of the account are named in lines 2, 8, 14, and 17.

* 175. ANONYMUS 9. Gramm. Aphrodito(?). s.VI.

"My master the gramm.," mentioned in a private letter from an unknown writer to an unknown recipient, concerning(?) an accident and injury suffered by another unknown party: *PCairMasp.* 1.67077.13ff., ἐλάλησα δὲ τῷ δ[εσ]πότῃ μου τῷ γραμματικῷ. . . .

* 176. ANONYMUS 10. Schoolmaster. Rome. s.IV 2/2 / s.VI.

A [*ma*]*gister ludi*, Christian: *ICVR* 1.1242 = *CIL* 6.9530 (cf. *ILCV* 718 n.) = *ICVR*, n.s., 2.5129.

* 177. ANONYMUS 11. Schoolmaster. Rome. s.VI init.(?).

A [*m*]*agister ludi litterarii*, Christian, died 516: *ICVR* 1.1167 = *CIL* 6.9529 = *ILCV* 717 = *ICVR*, n.s., 2.5020, line 2, [NO]N̄. FĒB. CŌN. FL. PẸT[RI] = an. 516; so De Rossi *ad loc.* in *ICVR*, against the reading FL. PḤ[ILIPPI] = an. 348 or 408.

- 178. ANONYMUS 12.   Schoolmaster.   Syceon (Galatia I).   s.VI 2/3 – 3/4.

Teacher at Syceon in the hinterland of Anastasiopolis, ca. 19 km from
the city in Galatia I; cf. Georg. presb. *Vie de Théodore de Sykéon*, ed.
Festugière, §5, διδάσκαλος; §7, καθηγητής. He taught Theodore his letters from his eighth until his twelfth year: §5, μαθεῖν γράμματα and ἡ τῶν
γραμμάτων σοφία; §10, μαθὼν δὲ ὁ παῖς τὰ γράμματα πάνυ καλῶς. He was
active, therefore, in s.VI 2/3 – 3/4, since Theodore was born in the reign
of Justinian. He held class in the morning and in the afternoon, with a
break for the midday meal. Theodore's desire to fast and his attempts to
avoid returning home at mealtime brought the teacher into conflict with
Theodore's mother.

Cf. s.v. Philumenus, no. 120.

ANONYMI 13–17: see nos. 277–81.

Dubii, Falsi, Varii

179. AEGIALEUS. Man of liberal education; physician? Carchar (Mesopotamia). 276/82.

PLRE I s.v. Aegialaus, p. 16.

One of four judges in the debate between Mani and the bishop Archelaus (*claruit sub imperatore Probo*, Jer. *De vir. ill.* 72) composed by Hegemonius, which survives in a defective Latin trans., *Acta Archelai* (s.IV 2/2?), and which Epiphan. *Panar. haeres.* 66.10ff. draws upon.

A pagan and *vir primarius* (*Acta Arch.* 12) of Carchar (Κασχάρης, Epiphan. *Panar. haeres.* 66.10.2), A. is described as *archiater nobilissimus et litteris apprime eruditus* in *Acta Arch.* and as φύσει γραμματικόν in Epiphan. The medical expertise attributed to A. in *Acta Arch.* is associated in Epiphan. with a Claudius ἰατροσοφιστής, who in turn appears as a simple *rhetor* in *Acta Arch.*; for the correspondences between the two works, see s.v. Manippus, no. 236. The phrase φύσει γραμματικόν in Epiphan.—"a man of letters by his very nature" or "to the depths of his being," i.e., *litteris apprime eruditus*—probably finds γραμματικός used as a simple epithet, in a nontechnical, nontitular sense; cf. Appendix 3.

The debate is of very doubtful historicity.

+ 180. AETHERIUS. Gramm. (and poet?). Apamea. *Aet. incert.*; probably not before s.V ex. / s.VI init.

RE Suppl. 1.41 (Crusius); Chr.-Sch.-St. 2:2.107–9; Hunger 2.13; Koster, "De accentibus" 133f.

Listed in the catalogue of gramm. in Kröhnert, *Canones* 7, as Αἰθέριος Ἀπαμεύς, under the heading ὅσοι περὶ διχρόνων; cf. ibid. 50ff. Fragments of his work are included in the compilation Περὶ τόνων ἐκ τῶν Χοιροβοσκοῦ, Αἰθερίου, Φιλοπόνου καὶ ἑτέρων published from codd. Urbin. 151

and Laurent. LVII.34 by Koster, "De accentibus." Other fragments are found in a similar compilation inscribed ἀρχὴ τῶν τονιζομένων λέξεων παρεξελεχθέντων τούτων ἐκ τῶν Ὥρου, Χοιροβοσκοῦ, Αἰθερίου γραμματικοῦ, Φιλοπόνου καὶ ἑτέρων *vel sim.* in codd. Paris. suppl. gr. 202 and Laurent. LV.7. The compilation remains unpublished; cf. Cramer, *Anecd. Paris.* 1.397, with Hilgard, *GG* 4:2, xc; Egenolff, *Orthoepischen Stücke* 32; Kröhnert, *Canones* 50.

Evidence for A.'s date is lacking. His presence in the company of Orus, Georgius Choeroboscus, and Ioannes Philoponus (qq.v., nos. 111, 201, 118) may suggest that he should not be set earlier than s.V 2/2 or s.VI init., although like Choeroboscus he could have lived much later. *Pace* Kröhnert, *Canones* 51, no reliable conclusions concerning A.'s date can be drawn from the order of his appearance in the catalogue noted above, esp. since there seems to be a serious corruption in the catalogue's text immediately after A.'s name; see s.v. Orus *ad fin.*

A. is possibly the poet Aetherius mentioned in the *Suda* Αι.116, Αἰθέριος: ἐπῶν ποιητής. ἔγραψε διάφορα, καὶ Ἐπιθαλάμιον δι᾽ ἐπῶν εἰς Σιμπλίκιον τὸν ἴδιον ἀδελφόν. (Cf. *Suda* Π.204 for an Aetherius as dedicatee of a poem by Panolbius [= *PLRE* II s.v., p. 829]; for a discussion placing the poet Aetherius in the context of s.V ex., see Alan Cameron, "Wandering Poets" 505f.). There is no evidence that would allow a certain conclusion. The identification was denied by Kröhnert, *Canones* 52; it was affirmed more or less tentatively by Crusius, *RE* Suppl. 1.41; by Koster, "De accentibus" 133 n. 1; and by Chr.-Sch.-St. 2:2.1079. Note that Crusius and Koster miscontrued the argument of Kröhnert, who proposed that A. was designated γραμματικός in the mss noted above in order to distinguish him from another Aetherius, viz., the poet; Kröhnert did not claim that A. must be distinguished from the poet because he is designated γραμματικός, which would, of course, be absurd. But Kröhnert's argument still falls short of compulsion.

If Simplicius the brother of Aetherius the poet is Simplicius the philosopher, as is often assumed or suggested, the identification of A. with the poet is probably ruled out: A. was an Apamean, whereas Simplicius's brother presumably had the same origin as Simplicius, in Cilicia; cf. Agath. *Hist.* 2.30 Keydell.

181. AGROECIUS. Rhetorician? Bishop of Sens? Gaul. s.V 2/4(–3/4?).

RE 1.902 (Goetz); Sch.-Hos. 4:2.206–7; *PLRE* II s.v. 3, p. 39.

Agroecius: cf. *GL* 7.114.7f., *"Agroecius" cum Latine scribis, per diphthongon scribendum, non, ut quidam putant, per "i," "Agricius,"* perhaps correcting Auson. *Prof.* 15, on Censorius Atticus Agricius; cf. Green, "Prosopographical Notes" 23.

Styled *rhetor* in codd. Bern. 338 and 432. A.'s *Ars* gives no sign of his profession or status beyond the fact that he writes to his dedicatee, the bishop Eucherius of Lyons, as an inferior to a superior; cf. the salutation, *Domino Eucherio episcopo Agroecius*; and cf. esp. *GL* 7.113.1–3, *libellum Capri de orthographia misisti mihi. haec quoque res proposito tuo et moribus tuis congrua est, ut, qui nos in huius vitae actibus corrigere vis, etiam in scribendi studiis emendares*; cf. also the Horatian tag, *decus et praesidium meum*, that closes the prefatory epistle. A. is often identified with Agroecius the bishop of Sens, who received Sidonius Apollinaris *Ep.* 7.5; that Agroecius is probably the learned *metropolitanus* referred to at *Ep.* 7.9.6.

The dedication to Eucherius as bishop dates A.'s *Ars* sometime between 434 and 450; cf. Stroheker, *Senatorische Adel* 168 no. 120. If A. is the recipient of Sidon. Apoll. *Ep.* 7.5, he was still alive ca. 470/71. If the identification of A. with the bishop of Sens is correct, then the early date of the *Ars* relative to Sidonius's letter and the tone of the dedication to Eucherius (see above) suggest that A. composed his work before his elevation to the episcopacy.

Author of an *Ars de orthographia*, or *Orthographia* (the mss have both), presented as a supplement to the work of Flavius Caper, *De orthographia et de proprietate ac differentia sermonum*; cf. *GL* 7.113.8ff. A.'s *Ars* was transmitted with Caper in the mss and is listed with Caper—and with Isidore of Seville, who drew on A.—in the catalogue of gramm. in cod. Bern. 243, *Anecd. Helv.* = *GL* 8, cxlix; the *Ars* is published in *GL* 7.113–25 and was edited most recently by M. Pugliarello (Milan, 1978).

A. was possibly related to other known Gallic Agroecii: the rhetorician of Bordeaux commemorated by Ausonius (see above) and referred to by Sidonius in *Ep.* 5.10.3; or the *primicerius notariorum* of Jovinus noted in Stroheker, *Senatorische Adel* 144 no. 12, and in *PLRE* II s.v. 1, pp. 38f. Cf. also Agroecius the "?wealthy layman" who contributed to the construction of a church at Narbo, noted in *PLRE* II s.v. 2, p. 39.

182. ALBINUS.   *Dign., loc. incert.*   s.IV 1/2 or before?

RE 1.1315.24ff. (Graf); Sch.-Hos. 4:1.142; *PLRE* I s.v. 4, p. 33.

Albinus: Victorinus *De metris et de hexam.*, *GL* 6.211.23f. = Audax *GL* 7.339.1f., *Albinus in libro quem de metris scripsit.* Mentioned in the list of those who *mensuram esse in fabulis . . . Terentii et Plauti et ceterorum comicorum et tragicorum dicunt*, Rufinus *GL* 6.565.4.

The identification of A. with Ceionius Rufius Albinus (= Albinus 15 *PLRE* I, pp. 37f.) has been suggested on the strength of the metrical interests attributed to the latter at Macrob. *Sat.* 1.24.19; cf. *PLRE* I s.v. Albinus 4. Alternatively, identification has been sought with Ceionius

Rufius Albinus, the grandfather(?) of the latter; cf. Graf, *RE* 1.1315; *PLRE* I s.v. Albinus 14 *ad fin.*, p. 37. Evaluation of the probabilities turns on the dating of Victorinus *De metris*, which was almost certainly composed in the first half or not far into the second half of s.IV; see s.v. Victorinus, no. 273. (The identity of the author of the *De metris*—certainly not Marius Victorinus—is irrelevant here.) Further, the fact that a reference to A. is found in the *Excerpta* of Audax (q.v., no. 190), who was not, *ut vid.*, drawing on Victorinus (nor vice versa), suggests that A. was already mentioned in the common source of Victorinus and Audax; and this in turn almost certainly rules out the younger Ceionius Rufius Albinus (= Albinus 15 *PLRE* I).

Identification of A. with Albinus the author of a work on music (= Albinus 5 *PLRE* I, p. 34) has also been suggested in *PLRE* I s.vv. Identification of these two with the elder Ceionius Rufius Albinus (= Albinus 14 *PLRE* I) was proposed by Graf, *RE* 1.1315; Minio-Paluello, "Text" 67 (and others before; cf. Sch-Hos. 4:1.142); differently Pfligersdorffer, "Zur Frage." All these identifications are obviously uncertain.

183. ALETHIUS.   Poet and *quaestor sacri palatii* (*ut vid.*).   s.IV ex. / s.V init.

The subject of Claudian *Carm. min.* 24 = Alethius 1 *PLRE* I, p. 39. A mistaken interpretation of *Carm. min.* 24.6, *irati relegam carmina grammatici*, would make him a gramm.: so most recently Gnilka, "Beobachtungen" 70ff.

184. ANTIOCHUS.   Teacher.   Antioch.   s.IV ex.

Wolf, *Schulwesen* 40; *PLRE* I s.v. 9, p. 72.

The recipient of Libanius's consolation and advice in *Or.* 39. It can be said with certainty only that A. was a teacher (διδάσκαλος), one of whose rivals had been favored with the patronage of the man Libanius calls "Mixidemus": *Or.* 39.2, τῷ δεῖνι μὲν διδασκάλῳ συμμαχεῖν; cf. 39.16, τὰς βλάβας ταύτας δὴ τὰς περὶ τοὺς μαθητάς. There is no decisive evidence A. was a rhetorician, though that is assumed by Foerster, ed., vol. 3 p. 264 (likewise in *PLRE* I s.v.); he may have been a grammarian. Mixidemus's influence in the courts (*Or.* 39.12ff.) might suggest that A. and his rival were concerned with rhetoric; note, however, that in conclusion Libanius advises A. to console himself by writing invective poetry against Mixidemus, καὶ διδάξεις ἐκεῖνον ὅτι ἄρα οἶσθα τὸν Ἀρχίλοχον (*Or.* 39.24). Wolf, *Schulwesen* 40, correctly says that the matter is an open question; Chr.-Sch.-St. 2:2.1075 n. 3 assume that A. was a grammarian.

A. also appears to have been a poet: cf. Lib. *Or.* 39.24, ἔστι δέ σοι δύναμις. ἔστι γὰρ δὴ καὶ γλῶττα καὶ δόσις παρὰ Μουσῶν οἵα ἂν παρὰ

Μουσῶν γένοιτο. But the remark may only be a reference to A.'s general literary attainments, a conceit preparing the way for the specific advice noted above.

A. is probably not to be identified with Antiochus the ῥήτωρ (advocate) of *Or.* 27.10ff., as he is by Foerster and *PLRE* I. The Antiochus of *Or.* 27 was not a teacher; cf. Wolf, *Schulwesen* 40 n. 85.

185. ELIUS APRILICUS.   Scribe.   Rome.   s.III.

PLRE I s.v., p. 86.

Incorrectly identified as a "Jewish *grammaticus*" in *PLRE* I on the basis of *CIL* 6.39085. He was a Jewish scribe, sc. of a synagogue: the inscr. reads γραμματεύς, not γραμματικός; cf. N. Müller, *Jüdische Katakombe* 115f., with Müller and Bees, *Inschriften* 6f.

186. AQUILA.   Gramm.?   Born 335/40?   Still alive in 392.

Seeck, *Briefe* 80; *PLRE* I s.v. 2, p. 90.

Mentioned by Libanius in 355/56; see *Ep.* 469.4, to A.'s father, Gorgonius, assessor to the governor of Armenia, urging him to show favor to the sophist Himerius and thus δίδαξον δὲ τὸν υἱὸν Ἀκύλαν ὡς οὐκ ἄτιμον οἱ λόγοι. This has been interpreted to mean that A. was a student of Libanius at the time; cf. Petit, *Étudiants* 26, 49. If so, he is likely to have been born 335/40.

He reappears some thirty-six years after *Ep.* 469 as the recipient of *Ep.* 1030 (an. 392), in which Libanius praises the long πόνοι—presumably literary labors, the usual sense in Libanius—that A. had conducted as a favor (χαριζόμενος) for Libanius's friend Olympius (= *PLRE* I s.v. 3, pp. 643f.; d. 388/89). The allusive phrasing of the letter suggests that A. was now performing this favor for Libanius—καὶ νῦν περὶ ἡμᾶς εὑρίσκων σε τοιοῦτον καὶ θαυμάζω καὶ χάριν οἶδα—and that the end of the project, whatever it was, was in sight: καὶ βουλοίμην ἂν μὴ καταλῦσαι τὴν προθυμίαν, πρὶν ἂν τέλος ἐπιθῇς τοῖς ἐν χερσὶ τούτοις ἄξιον τοῦ μακροῦ χρόνου. Perhaps with χάριν οἶδα this is a way of saying delicately that Libanius will continue to provide whatever encouragement, material as well as emotional, Olympius provided in the past.

A.'s metier is very uncertain. Seeck, *Briefe* 80, tentatively identified A. with the homonymous φιλόσοφος σχόλια λογικὰ γεγραφὼς περὶ συλλογισμῶν of *Suda* A.1041 or with the γραμματικὸς μουσικός of *Suda* A.1042. The former sounds more like the earlier(?) rhetorician and philosopher repeatedly praised and cited by Syrianus (= *PLRE* I s.v. Aquila 1, p. 90). If the Aquila γραμματικός of *Suda* A.1042 is to be identified with a known Aquila, and if in fact A.1042 refers to an Aquila different from A.1041, then A. is a candidate, nothing more. Even then, there is no guarantee that γραμματικός is being used in a technical or professional sense in the *Suda*; cf. Appendix 3.

187. ARETHUSIUS.   Teacher.   Antinoopolis.   s.IV.

A διδάσκαλος mentioned in the letter of a bridegroom named Papais to his future mother-in-law, Nonna, concerning preparations for the wedding: *PAnt.* 2.93 = Naldini, *Cristianesimo* no. 80. A. had apparently given the gift of a pearl: lines 33ff., δήλωσον εἰ ἐδέξω τὸν δακτύλιον χρυσοῦν παρὰ Δωροθέου βοηθοῦ Ἀνυσίου μετὰ τοῦ πιναρίου Ἀρεθουσίου διδασκάλου [ἵν]α ἀγοράσῃς ἀρώματα. "Arethusius" is not a common name, and, as the editor of *PAnt.* 2.93 (Zilliacus) remarks, it is "an appropriately poetic name for a teacher." Perhaps it is a *surnom de métier*; cf. s.v. Clamosus, no. 29. For other evidence of teachers at Antinoopolis in s.IV, cf. esp. *PAnt.* 3.156: fragments of *Il.* 2, with [---]ῳ διδασκάλῳ on the verso.

188. ARISTODEMUS.   Gramm.?   s.IV 2/2? (probably not before s.IV).

Author of an epitome of the Καθολικὴ προσῳδία of Herodian, dedicated to a certain Danaus: *Suda* A.3915, ἐπιτομὴν τῆς καθόλου Ἡρωδιανοῦ ἔγραψε πρὸς Δαναόν. It has been conjectured that this epitome is the work surviving in some mss of s.XV / s.XVI under the names of Theodosius and Arcadius; cf. Galland, *De Arcadii qui fertur libro* 12ff.; cf. also s.vv. Arcadius, Theodosius, nos. 16, 152. If that Danaus is the gramm. Danaus (q.v., no. 43) known from the correspondence of Libanius—the profession is appropriate, and the name is very rare—then A. could be dated to the second half of s.IV. No epitome of Herodian is known to have been made before s.IV. See further Kaster, "'Wandering Poet'" 157f.

189. ASTYAGIUS.   Gramm.?   s.V?

RE 2.1865 (Goetz); Sch.-Hos. 4:2.210; *PLRE* II s.v., p. 174.

Cited by Pompeius (q.v., no. 125) as an authority on the pronoun; see *GL* 5.209.1–5, 211.8–10. He was therefore possibly a grammarian. The suggestion in Sch.-Hos. 4:2.210 that Pompeius's first citation, *docente Astyagio istam rationem mirifice*, betrays "Gleichzeitigkeit und persönliche Beeinflussung" is conceivably correct in substance; cf. below. But since *docere* or διδάσκειν in such contexts can equally refer to the written works of predecessors with whom one has no personal connection, the phrasing offers no safe grounds for the inference; see esp. s.v. Romanus, no. 129.

A. is probably to be dated in s.V, before Pompeius, who cites him, and after Servius, whose commentary on Donatus he seems to have known.

It is further possible that the interpolated version of Servius's commentary known to Pompeius was A.'s work: see *GL* 5.211.5ff., with Chap. 4 n. 36; cf. Chap. 4 n. 8.

The reference to A. in Mai, *Classicorum auctorum . . . tomus* 5.152 (cod. Neap. Bibl. Reg. IV A 34), is not independent testimony but is derived, like all the other excerpts there, from Pompeius.

190. AUDAX.   *Dign., loc., aet. incert.*: before s.VII; after s.IV 1/2?

RE 2.2278 (Goetz), 14.1845.36ff. (Wessner); Sch.-Hos. 4:2.214–15; *PLRE* II s.v. 2, p. 184.

Author of a work inscribed *De Scauri et Palladii libris excerpta per interrogationem et responsionem* in the mss, published in *GL* 7.320–62. The first sections of the work, *GL* 7.320–48, correspond to the *Ars* of Victorinus; see s.v. Victorinus, no. 273. The nature of the resemblances between the two works, however, rules out the direct dependence of one upon the other, and points to a common source. Later portions of the work, *GL* 7.349–57, show the influence of Probus *Inst. art., GL* 4.143ff. On the sources of the *Excerpta*, see Sch.-Hos. 4:2.214–15; Barwick *Remmius* 77ff. The work is written in question-and-answer form with varying constancy.

A. is to be dated before Julian of Toledo (bp. 680–90), who quotes him in his *Ars* (1.1.8, p. 11.48ff. Maestre-Yenes) and calls him a *grammaticus* (1.1.38, p. 17.193ff.). A *term. p. q.* of s.II would be established if the Scaurus of the title is Terentius Scaurus; Palladius cannot be identified, but cf. s.v., no. 242. If the resemblances of A. and Victorinus are attributable to a common source, it must have existed by the first half or the early second half of s.IV; cf. s.v. Victorinus. If A. relied on Probus's *Inst. art.*, then a *term. p. q.* of s.IV 1/2(?) would be established. If the influence of Diomedes that Keil detected is real (*GL* 7.318f.; cf. Barwick, *Remmius* 77ff.), a still later *term. p. q.* (s.IV 2/2 or s.V) would be provided. And if Hubert, "Isidore" 297ff., is correct, at least a part of the excerpts, the "Recapitulatio de accentibus" (*GL* 7.357.13ff.), depends on Isidore of Seville.

191. AUXILIUS.   Gramm.

PLRE I s.v., p. 142.

Auxilius (Scaliger: *Ausilius* codd.); butt of Auson. *Epigr.* 6. Called *grammaticus* (tit.) and *magister* (vv. 1, 3).

The poem plays on the name "Auxilius" and the noun *auxilium*, branding the gramm. a walking solecism: vv. 3–4, *Auxilium te nempe vocas, inscite magister. / da rectum casum: iam solecismus eris*; in fact, the flaw would strictly be classified as a barbarism, not a solecism—but *barbarismus* is not suited to the meter (*solecismus*, for *soloecismus*, is itself a metaplasm used *metri causa*; cf. Chap. 4 p. 151, Chap. 5, p. 173). As with the other creatures of the epigrams, there is a good chance that Auxilius is a fiction produced for the sake of the conceit; cf. Booth, "Notes" 242 n. 23; cf. also s.v. Philomusus, no. 246.

192. BABYLAS.   Teacher and martyr.   Nicomedia.   304?

A teacher allegedly martyred with eighty-four of his ninety-two pupils at Nicomedia in the Great Persecution: *Inédits byzantins*, ed. Halkin, 330ff., Μαρτύριον τοῦ ἁγίου μάρτυρος Βαβύλα καὶ τῶν σὺν αὐτῷ πδ′ νηπίων.

An old man at the time of his denunciation (§1.19 and *passim*), he is evidently presented as a teacher of letters for very young students; cf. §1.21f., τὴν τῶν γραμμάτων τοῖς παιδίοις ἐν τῇ ἀγορᾷ [cf. §2.7] παραδιδοὺς μάθησιν. Note that out of his class of ninety-two pupils (§4.31ff.) of various ages (§4.9f.) only the ten oldest children are presented before the tribunal "to give answers that seemed to be beyond the reach of the age of the rest" (§5.1ff.), i.e., the others were not yet capable of reasoning; cf. §5.8ff. B. is otherwise called simply ὁ διδάσκαλος: §§1.37; 4.20, 29; 5.40, 46, 48; 7.1f. He was denounced for abusing his profession by teaching the children Christian hymns and the Psalms instead of τὰ Ἑλληνικὰ παιδεύματα: §1.25ff.; cf. §3.23, B.'s crime referred to as τοὺς ἰδιώτας ἐξαπατᾶν; and cf. §2.4ff. Eighty-four of his ninety-two pupils confessed their Christianity (§4.31ff.) and were executed with him (§6.28ff.).

The story in its present form is legendary, and B. himself is probably a doublet of St. Babylas of Antioch; cf. Halkin, ed., *Inédits byzantins* 329f. On the number πδ′ and its connections with the story of St. Babylas, see Delehaye, "Deux Saints." Note, however, that the narrative is not without historical elements, since Priscillianus, the ἡγεμών (i.e., *praeses Bithyniae*) who oversees the executions (§3.38ff., §6), was in fact a persecutor of Christians at Nicomedia in this period: Lact. *De mort. pers.* 16.4; *PLRE* I s.v. Priscillianus, p. 729.

193. CABRIAS.   Teacher.   Panopolis.   Dead by s.IV init.

"The wife of Cabrias the teacher" is registered as the owner of a parcel of land in a list from Panopolis of s.IV init.: *PPanop.* 14.25, γυναικ(ὸς) Καβρία διδασκάλου. For the date and for the reading of C.'s name, see Kaster, "P. Panop." C. is almost certainly the διδάσκαλος Chabrias known from another, contemporary listing of properties in Panopolis, *PBerlBork.* col. 1.18; see Kaster, "P. Panop."; cf. also s.v. Chabrias, no. 198.

The form of the listing suggests that C. was dead at the time of the survey; cf. s.v. Chabrias and s.v. Eutyches, no. 214; cf. also Kaster, "P. Panop." 133 n. 7.

194. CALLIOPIUS. *Scholasticus.* s.V?
RE 3.1361–62 (Wissowa); *PLRE* I s.v. 5, p. 175.

A man of learning (*scholasticus*; see below) attested in the subscriptions in some minuscule mss of Terence that descend from the hyparchetype Σ: *Calliopius recensui* (or *recensuit*) and *feliciter Calliopio bono scholastico*; see Jahn, "Subscriptionen" 362ff.; on the transmission of Terence, see the survey of Reeve, "Terence." The subscriptions and hence their relations to the ms families have never accurately been catalogued; cf. Zetzel, *Latin Textual Criticism* 224. C.'s name has been given to the "Calliopian recension" of the text of Terence.

C.'s responsibility for the text of this so-called recension is controversial. Substantial credit is given to C. by those who believe that the recension was achieved at a single stroke; cf. Wissowa, *RE* 3.1361, following Leo, "Überlieferungsgeschichte"; Wessner's review of Jachmann, *Gnomon* 3 (1927), 343ff.; Lindsay, "Notes" 33ff., with Craig, *Jovialis* 5ff. According to a different, more likely, theory, the recension would be the result of gradual change and accretion, and C.'s importance would be diminished; cf. Pasquali, *Storia*² 361ff. Jachmann, *Geschichte* 120ff., esp. 124ff., also denies C. any substantial role, though he retains the idea of a one-stage recension.

C. is usually dated to the fifth century; attempts at dating again involve assumptions concerning his responsibility for the recension; see esp. Wessner's review of Jachmann, p. 344; Craig, *Jovialis* p. v.

On the strength of the epithet *scholasticus* he has been regarded as a gramm. (so, e.g., Jachmann, Lindsay, Craig, Wessner, Wissowa, above), a "? lawyer or grammaticus" (*PLRE* I s.v.), or a lawyer and gramm. (Seeck, *Briefe* 103). Three points should be noted.

First, *scholasticus* seems to occur here in a scribal subscr., i.e., the epithet is not necessarily C.'s description of himself. The relationship between the two forms of the subscr. is not clear; see Jahn, "Subscriptionen" 362ff.; and cf. above.

Second, although in the East σχολαστικός came to serve predominantly as a professional title equivalent to "advocate" or "lawyer," in the West— where C. is presumably to be located, although not even that is clear— *scholasticus* appears to have stayed in use somewhat longer as a simple epithet, comparable to *doctus* or *litteratus*, with no necessary connotation of a specific profession. So much seems to emerge from the evidence collected by Claus, "ΣΧΟΛΑΣΤΙΚΟΣ" 43ff.; *scholasticus* is, of course, also used as a lawyer's title in the West, esp. in the law codes.

Third, I know of no instance where *scholasticus* by itself clearly serves as a professional title equivalent to *grammaticus*; cf. Lehnert, "Griechisch-römische Rhetorik" 45; Claus, "ΣΧΟΛΑΣΤΙΚΟΣ" 43ff.; cf. also s.vv.

Bonifatius, Coronatus, Lollianus, Philagrius, Aur. Theodorus, nos. 22, 204, 90, 117, 150. It is likely, therefore, that the person who described C. as *bonus scholasticus* meant nothing more specific than "the good man of learning," "good scholar," "good student." For *scholasticus* in subscriptions, cf. esp. the rhetorician Felix's student Deuterius, termed *scholasticus* and *discipulus* in the subscr. to Martianus Capella; see Jahn, "Subscriptionen" 351. For the type of scribal subscr. represented by *feliciter Calliopio bono scholastico*, see s.v. Servius, no. 136, *ad fin*.

195. CARMINIUS. *Dign., loc., aet. incert.*; before s.IV ex. / s.V init.
RE Suppl. 3.235 (Kroll); Sch.-Hos. 4:1.180.

Author of a work *De elocutionibus* cited by Servius at *Aen.* 5.233; also cited by Servius at *Aen.* 6.638, 861; 8.406. The two citations in *Aen.* 6 give no useful indication of their origin; the citation in *Aen.* 8 may come from a commentary: *Probus vero et Carminius propter sensum cacenphaton "infusum" legunt.* All three could, however, be derived from a work *De elocutionibus*.

The mss of Macrob. *Sat.* 5.19.13 present the *Carminii curiosissimi et docti verba* from a work *De Italia* (the phrase *Carminii verba* recurs at the beginning of 5.19.14). Meursius emended *Carminii* at 5.19.13 to *Granii*; Willis emended to *Granii, viri*—probably correctly. That would be the Granius Licinianus or Granius Flaccus cited elsewhere in the *Sat.* (1.16.30, 18.4) on antiquarian matters; cf. *RE* 7.1819ff. nos. 12, 13.

C. must be placed before Servius and probably after Valerius Probus, with whom he is cited by Servius at *Aen.* 8.406. Datable instances of the name "Carminius" cluster in the early empire, and C. is likely to be closer to s.II (so Kroll, *RE* Suppl. 3.235) than to s.IV (as in Sch.-Hos. 4:1.180). His omission from *PLRE* I was probably correct.

196. CATO. Poet. Africa. s.V 4/4.
Sch.-Hos. 4:2.74; Szövérffy, *Weltliche Dichtungen* 1.183; *PLRE* II s.v. 1, p. 272.

Author of a poem on a land-reclamation project of the Vandal king Huneric (477–84), preserved in the codex Salmasianus, *Anth. Lat.* 1:1.387. The allusion to Genesis 1.6 in the poem suggests that he was Christian: vv. 3f., of Huneric, *verbo divisit aquas molemque profundi / discidit iussis.*

C. has been called a gramm. (e.g., Sch.-Hos. 4:2.74; Szövérffy, *Weltliche Dichtungen* 1.183; Riché, *Education* 38) on the basis of an assumed identity with the author of a grammatical *Liber Catonis* from which extracts on adverbs and on *differentiae*—*ad* and *at*, *-ve* and *vae*, etc.—are transmitted in cod. Montepessulan. 306 (s.IX) following extracts from the *Epitomae* of the gramm. Virgilius Maro (s.VII). For the text of the extracts *ex libro Catonis*, see Huemer, "*Epitomae*" 519 n. 1. Nothing further is known of this work. The title *Liber Catonis* might suggest some connection or confusion with the *Dicta Catonis*, which was used as a schoolbook and is often found in the company of grammatical texts; see, e.g., such entries as *Catonis libellus et in eodem ars Phocae* or *Donatus minor et Cato simul* or *primus liber est Donati, in quo continetur liber Catonis, Aviani, atque Prisciani liber minor* in medieval catalogues noted by Quicherat, "Fragments" 125 n. 1, and by Manitius, *Handschriften* 167ff. The *Dicta Catonis* is itself preserved in an earlier portion of cod. Montepessulan. 306, fol. 11^r–13^v. Nothing but the name "Cato" favors the identification with C.

197. ARRUNTIUS CELSUS. Before s.III med.

RE 2.1265 (Goetz); Sch.-Hos. 3.174; *PLRE* I s.v. 6, p. 194.

Arruntius Celsus: Charis. *GL* 1.213.18f. = 276.9–10 Barwick, 222.6f. = 286.13–14B., 222.30 = 287.12B. Celsus: Charis. *GL* 1.200.27f. = 261.1–2B., 207.13f. = 268.19–20B., 212.3f. = 274.18–19B., 214.4f. = 276.24–25B., 214.18 = 277.13B., 223.11f. = 288.1–2B.; Consentius *GL* 5.375.1, 390.6ff.; Priscian *GL* 2.148.16ff. = 215.13 (and four other times). Cited also as Arruntius: Priscian *GL* 2.98.7f., 251.13f.; 3.408.2ff. Cited as Arruntius Claudius (q.v., no. 202) by Diomedes, *GL* 1.321.11f.

A grammatical authority of uncertain date. The citations in Charisius appear only in a section excerpted from Iulius Romanus (q.v., no. 249) on adverbs, *GL* 1.190.8–224.22 = 246.18–289.17B.; they must therefore be assumed to have been present in the work of the latter. Hence C. is probably to be placed in s.III (before s.III med.), or even earlier; see s.v. C. Iulius Romanus; cf. also Sch.-Hos. 3.174, "vor Romanus und wahrscheinlich auch Caper (s.II)"; and cf. Goetz, *RE* 2.1265. C. is dated "? III / IV" in *PLRE* I, although there is virtually no chance of his being as late as s.IV. See also s.v. Arruntius Claudius.

Perhaps to be identified with the Celsus cited in the *Scholia Vaticana* and the scholia of Servius Danielis to *Georg.* 1.277; 2.333, 479; 3.188, 296, 313. In at least some of these citations, however, the person meant may more probably be (A.) Cornelius Celsus, the encyclopedist of early s.I who is cited in *Schol. Vat.* at *Georg.* 4.1; cf. esp. Ribbeck, *Prolegomena* 25f.

* 198. CHABRIAS. Teacher. Panopolis. Dead by s.IV init.

"Another house, belonging to the sons of Chabrias the teacher [διδάσκαλος] and [his] brothers," registered in a topographical listing of properties in Panopolis executed early in s.IV, *PBerlBork.* col. 1.18. For the date, see Youtie, "P. Gen."; Borkowski, *PBerlBork.* p. 13. The listing of the property as the joint possession of C.'s sons and brothers, i.e., of his heirs, shows that C. was dead at the time of the survey; cf. Youtie, "P. Gen." 170; Borkowski, *PBerlBork.* 26ff. For other διδάσκαλοι in this same register, see s.vv. Eutyches, Theon, nos. 214, 267.

C. is almost certainly the διδάσκαλος Cabrias whose wife (i.e., widow) is recorded as the owner of a parcel of land in another, contemporary list from Panopolis, *PPanop.* 14.25; see s.v. Cabrias, no. 193; cf. Kaster, "P. Panop."

199. IOANNES CHARAX. Gramm. s.VI 1/2 / s.IX 1/2.

RE 3.2123-24 (Cohn); Chr.-Sch.-St. 2:2.1077, 1078; Hunger 2.13f., 19.

'Ιωάννης (ὁ) Χάραξ: Choerobosc. *Schol. in Theodos.*, *GG* 4:2.243.8, 245.15 (cf. 297.22); inscr. of the Περὶ ἐγκλινομένων, Bekker, *Anecd.* 3.1149; two mss of the Περὶ ὀρθογραφίας (cf. Egenolff, *Orthographischen Stücke* 4f.); Sophronius in the excerpts of the *Schol. in Theodos.*, *GG* 4:2.375.14, 397.2f.; the catalogue of gramm. in Rabe, "Listen" 340. Also ὁ Χάραξ: Choerobosc. *Schol. in Theodos.*, *GG* 4:2.330.20 = Cramer, *Anecd. Oxon.* 4.210.29 = ibid. 352.4; inscr. of a fragment of the Περὶ ὀρθογραφίας in cod. Taurin. CCLXI C.1.25 fol. 74ʳ; inscr. of the excerpts of the *Schol. in Theodos.*, *GG* 4:2.375.4; Ἐπιμερισμοί, Cramer, *Anecd. Paris.* 3.322.11; the catalogue of gramm. in Kröhnert, *Canones* 7.

Styled γραμματικός: Choerobosc. *Schol. in Theodos.*, *GG* 4:2.243.8, 245.15, 297.22; ms of the Περὶ ἐγκλινομένων (Bekker, *Anecd.* 3.1149) and mss of the Περὶ ὀρθογραφίας (cf. Egenolff, *Orthographischen Stücke* 4f.).

The subject, form, and content of C.'s *Schol. in Theodos.*, excerpted by the patriarch of Alexandria Sophronius (841-60) and dedicated to Ioannes, bishop of Tamiathis, all show that C. was a teacher. The work originated as a series of lectures—not a written treatise—on the basic textbook of Theodosius (q.v., no. 152), and it refers to lectures anticipated or already delivered on other texts or topics in the syllabus: e.g., *GG* 4:2.399.35f., περὶ ὧν σὺν Θεῷ ἐν τῷ μεγάλῳ Ὀνοματικῷ [viz., of Herodian] ἐροῦμεν; 430.6f., ὡς ἐντελέστερον ἐν τῷ ἰδίῳ περὶ αὐτῶν [sc. τῶν ἀπαρεμφάτων] γνωσόμεθα λόγῳ; cf. 375.23f., τὰς δὲ τῆς θέσεως αὐτῶν [sc. τῶν μέρων τοῦ λόγου] αἰτίας ἐν ἄλλοις γνωσόμεθα; 426.15f., ὡς ἐν τοῖς ἄλλοις τεχνικοῖς γράμμασι γιγνόμενοι σὺν Θεῷ μαθησόμεθα; for lectures already delivered, cf. 430.1, ἐδείξαμεν γὰρ ἐν ἄλλοις, on τὰ ἀπαρέμφατα, of which C. also promises a more detailed presentation (cf. 430.6f., quoted above). C.'s *Schol. in Theodos.* thus belongs to the category of ἀπὸ φωνῆς commentaries; the phrasing of 426.15f. shows that the passages cited above refer primarily not to C.'s writings but to the course of his lectures: ἐν τοῖς ἄλλοις τεχνικοῖς γράμμασι γιγνόμενοι, "when we come to the other technical treatises." For other cross-references of this type, and on ἀπὸ φωνῆς commentaries, cf. s.v. Georgius Choeroboscus, no. 201.

In addition to the excerpts from C.'s *Schol. in Theodos.*, Sophronius also preserves a fragment of C.'s Περὶ τῶν εἰς ων (sc. ληγόντων), *GG* 4:2.397.1-398.27, inscribed ἐκ τοῦ μονοβιβλίου τοῦ περὶ αὐτῶν [viz., τῶν εἰς ων] Ἰωάννου Χάρακος and inserted after the scholia on κανών 25 of

Theodosius, on the same subject. Two other works are preserved under his name, Περὶ ἐγκλινομένων (in Bekker, *Anecd.* 3.1149–55) and Περὶ ὀρθογραφίας, both dependent on Herodian; cf. Egenolff, *Orthoepischen Stücke* 36f., *Orthographischen Stücke* 4f., respectively. The Περὶ ὀρθογραφίας is accessible only in the brief excerpt found in Cramer, *Anecd. Oxon.* 4.331f. C. is listed under the heading ὅσοι περὶ ὀρθογραφίας in the catalogue of gramm. in Kröhnert, *Canones* 7.

C. cannot be dated earlier than s.VI 1/2, since he cites Ioannes Philoponus (q.v., no. 118)—twice, as ὁ Φιλόπονος: Bekker, *Anecd.* 3.1150; *GG* 4:2.432.5. He was active before Sophronius (see above) and before Georgius Choeroboscus, who cites C. four times in his own *Schol. in Theodos.* (see above), each time as an approved authority. Choeroboscus must now be dated to s.IX 1/2 (see s.v.). I strongly suspect but cannot prove that C. lived closer to the end than to the beginning of the period defined by those *termini*; note esp. his concern *qua* gramm. with usage in Scripture.

He was a Christian; cf. his opinion on the use of the imperative εἰπόν in Scripture, cited by Choerobosc. *GG* 4:2.245.15f., and his use of the formula σὺν Θεῷ ἐροῦμεν *vel sim.* in the passages cited above.

200. FL. SOSIPATER CHARISIUS.   *v.p., magister.*   s.IV 2/4–2/3?

RE 3.2147–49 (Goetz); Sch.-Hos. 4:1.165–69; *PLRE* I s.v. 3, p. 201.

Fl. Sosipater Charisius: *Ars* tit., *GL* 1.1.1 = 1.1 Barwick; Rufinus *GL* 6.572.18. Also Sosipater Charisius: Rufinus *GL* 6.565.4. Charisius elsewhere in Rufinus and gramm. For citation of C. as "Flavianus," see s.v., no. 219.

Author of an *Ars grammatica* in five books; C. states in the dedication that his labor was largely devoted to compilation and arrangement: cf. *GL* 1.1.4f. = 1.5–6B., *artem grammaticam sollertia doctissimorum virorum politam et a me digestam in quinque libris*; cf. also the phrasing of Diomedes at *GL* 1.299.2–7. That statement is borne out by the contents; see Sch.-Hos. 4:1.168 and esp. Barwick, *Remmius*. On the history of the text, see now briefly Rouse, "Charisius."

C. is styled *v.p., magister* in the tit. of the *Ars*. It is not certain whether *magister* denotes his profession or a palatine office. If the former, perhaps the designation in full would be *magister urbis Romae*, as Keil conjectured: cf. *app. crit.* ed. Keil *ad loc.* (Nellen, *Viri* 99, mistook Keil's conjecture for the transmitted reading). Or the style might denote C.'s profession otherwise, perhaps with the full designation *magister studiorum*: cf. s.vv. L. Terentius Iulianus, Annius Namptoius, nos. 87, 103; cf. also s.vv. Dositheus, Servius, nos. 53, 136. If the style denotes an office, perhaps the office was *magister scrinii*, as suggested in *PLRE* I. The composition of an *ars* might at first sight suggest that C. was a professional gramm.; but cf. s.v. Consentius, no. 203, and note that C. says he compiled his *ars* out of fatherly concern for his son: *GL* 1.1.4–6 = 1.4–7B., *amore Latini sermonis obligare te cupiens, fili karissime, artem grammaticam . . . dono tibi misi.* The dedication of the work to his son appears to place C. in the category of learned amateurs such as, e.g., Aulus Gellius, Ti. Claudius Donatus, and Macrobius; see s.v. Nonius Marcellus, no. 237; cf. Chap. 2 at nn. 142, 152, 153. The use of the name "Flavius" is consistent with tenure of an imperial *dignitas*; cf. Keenan, "Names" (1973) 33ff. The name would place him no earlier than s.IV 2/4, a date likely on other grounds (see below).

C. cites Cominianus (q.v., no. 34) and so is probably later than s.III ex. / s.IV init. His use of *magnus . . . Iulianus . . . Augustus* in a paradigm (*GL* 1.44.28f. = 54.5–6B.) might indicate that he wrote during or not long after the reign of Julian; cf. Tolkiehn, "Lebenszeit" 1055. On the possible significance of the name "Flavius" for dating, see above. His work was perhaps known to Diomedes (q.v., no. 47).

C. may be cited in the scholium of Servius Danielis (not Servius) to *Aen.* 9.329, *"temere" significat et "facile": Plautus* (quoting *Bacch.* 83) = Charis. *GL* 1.221.11ff. = 285.27–29B., *"temere" pro "facile" Plautus in Bacchidibus* (quoting the same verse), in a section from Iulius Romanus. If this were a genuine citation, and if Servius Danielis here represented the commentary of Aelius Donatus, we would be able to locate C. all the more firmly in the middle of s.IV. But the second condition is by no means certainly satisfied; and as for the first, the full forms of the quotations in the two places—Charisius = Plautus + Cato; Servius Danielis = Plautus + Ennius + possibly Cato (see the *app. crit.* in *Servii . . . commentarii* ed. Thilo, *ad loc.*) + Ennius again—make it less probable that Servius Danielis is citing C. If there is any connection at all, the material in the two places probably derives ultimately from a common source that has been more faithfully reproduced in Servius Danielis.

The dedication of the *Ars* shows that C. was not a "Roman of Rome": *GL* 1.1.9ff. = 1.12–15B., *erit iam tuae diligentiae . . . studia mea . . . memoriae tuisque sensibus mandare, ut quod originalis patriae natura denegavit, virtute animi adfectasse videaris*; cf. esp. Macrob. *Sat.* 1 praef. 11. On the conjecture of African origin, see below. The statement *hodieque nostri per Campaniam sic locuntur* (*GL* 1.215.22f. = 279.1–2B.) is not evidence for C.'s *origo*. It may suggest that C. lived in Italy, but it is more likely to have been taken over from his source at this point, Iulius Romanus (q.v., no. 249).

Usener, "Vier lateinische Grammatiker" 492, conjectured that C. is lurking behind the Charistus who appears in one ms of Jer. *Chron.* s.a. 358 as the gramm. who went from Africa to Constantinople to succeed Evanthius (q.v., no. 54). That conjecture is probably correct in the sense that "Charistus" is no doubt a corruption involving C.'s name; but it is also probably wrong, in the sense that the passage in Jerome should not be emended to read "Charisius"; see s.v. Chrestus, no. 27.

+ 201. GEORGIUS CHOEROBOSCUS. Gramm.; "ecumenical teacher"; deacon and ecclesiastical archivist. Constantinople. s.IX 1/2.

RE 3.2363–67 (Cohn); Chr.-Sch.-St. 2:2.1079f.; Hunger 2.11, 13f., 19, 23, 50.

Γεώργιος (ὁ) Χοιροβοσκός: numerous codd. of his works; the catalogue of gramm. in Rabe, "Listen" 340. Also (ὁ) Χοιροβοσκός: some mss of the excerpts of the Περὶ πνευμάτων (cf. Egenolff, *Orthoepischen Stücke* 19f.) and of the Περὶ τόνων (cf. Koster, "De accentibus" 134f., 151); the catalogue of gramm. in Kröhnert, *Canones* 7. Γεώργιος: inscr. in codd. Marc. 489, Paris. gr. 2831 of the *Schol. in Theodos.*; used as an example by C. himself at Ἐπιμερισμοί 35.2 Gaisford.

Styled διάκονος καὶ χαρτοφύλαξ, cod. Marc. 491; διάκονος in four other mss (cf. Hilgard, *GG* 4:2, lxi; the title χαρτοφύλαξ is regarded skeptically by Darrouzès, *Recherches* 22f.); γραμματικὸς καὶ οἰκουμενικὸς διδάσκαλος, codd. Marc. 491, Taurin. 261; Βυζάντιος γραμματικός, codd. Barocc. 50, Paris. gr. 2554; γραμματικὸς ὁ Βυζάντιος τῆς οἰκουμενικῆς διδασκαλίας, cod. Paris. suppl. gr. 1198; γραμματικός, codd. Barocc. 116, Paris. gr. 2758, Vat. gr. 1751, Hamburg. 369; οἰκουμενικὸς διδάσκαλος, cod. Paris. gr. 2008.

From his lectures there survive, in the form of an ἀπὸ φωνῆς commentary, the scholia on the Κανόνες of Theodosius (q.v., no. 152), *GG* 4:1–2, ed. Hilgard; cf. also the excerpts Περὶ τόνων, which derive from the scholia, ed. Koster, "De accentibus" 151ff., with 140ff. Similarly preserved are the scholia on the Ἐγχειρίδιον of Hephaestion (ed. Consbruch, *Hephaestionis Enchiridion* 177ff.), a Περὶ ὀρθογραφίας (an epitome, in Cramer, *Anecd. Oxon.* 2.167ff.; cf. Egenolff, *Orthographischen Stücke* 17ff.; Hilgard, *GG* 4:2, lxxviii–lxxxii), and Ἐπιμερισμοί of the Psalms (Gaisford, *Georgii Choerobosci Dictata* 3.1ff.; for mss of the work found since Gaisford, see Bühler and Theodoridis, "Johannes von Damaskos" 398 n. 7). On ἀπὸ φωνῆς commentaries, see Richard, "ΑΠΟ ΦΩΝΗΣ"; cf. s.v. Ioannes Charax, no. 199. For C.'s in particular, cf. the inscr. ἀπὸ φωνῆς Γεωργίου Χοιροβοσκοῦ *vel sim.* in codd. Neap. Borb. II D.3, Coislin. 176, and Paris. gr. 2831 of the *Schol. in Theodos.*; cod. Paris. suppl. gr. 1198 of the scholia to Hephaestion; cod. Barocc. 50 of the Περὶ ὀρθογραφίας; cod. Paris. gr. 2756 of the Ἐπιμερισμοί.

Also attributed or attributable to C. and transmitted in various states of preservation are scholia to Dionysius Thrax and a commentary, Περὶ προσῳδίας, on the Περὶ προσῳδιῶν appended to the Τέχνη of Dionysius.

The scholia to Dionysius survive only in extracts; see Hilgard, *GG* 1:3, xv–xviii; with Uhlig, *GG* 1:1, xxxiv. For the versions of the Περὶ προσῳδίας see *GG* 1:3.124–28, 128–150; with Uhlig, *GG* 1:1, l–li; Hilgard, *GG* 4:2, lxx–lxxii. A treatise Περὶ πνευμάτων also attributed to C. is accessible as part of a collection of excerpts in Valckenaer, *Ammonius* 188ff.; cf. Egenolff, *Orthoepischen Stücke* 17ff. On the doubtful or pseudepigraphic works Περὶ τρόπων ποιητικῶν (Walz, *Rhet. Gr.* 8.802–20; Spengel, *Rhet. Gr.* 3.244–56), Περὶ τῶν τριῶν σχημάτων τῶν συλλογισμῶν (cod. Brit. Mus. Addit. 5118), and Ἐρωτήματα τῶν προλεγομένων τῶν προσῳδιῶν (cod. Paris. gr. 2090), see Cohn, *RE* 3.2366.67ff.; Hilgard, *GG* 4:2, lxxxviii–lxxxix.

The scholia to Theodosius—and, less frequently, the scholia to Hephaestion and the commentary on the Περὶ προσῳδιῶν—refer to topics or texts either already covered in the syllabus, e.g., *GG* 4:2.192.25, or to be presented in the future, e.g., 4:1.135.5, 200.25ff., 211.37, 286.37f.; 4:2.52.31f., 79.11f., 299.9ff. The references allow us to draw a fairly precise picture of the curriculum C. and his pupils followed; cf. esp. Hilgard, *GG* 4:2, lxviii–lxxxvii.

A *term. p. q.* of s.VI init.–1/2 was long recognized in C.'s citations of Ioannes Philoponus (q.v., no. 118; cf. also s.v. Ioannes Charax, no. 199). C. was dated to s.VI by Cohn, *RE* 3.2363.51f.; the same date was assumed by, e.g., Glück, *Priscians Partitiones* 44ff.; Lemerle, *Premier humanisme* 79. For other estimates of C.'s date, see Wouters, "*P.Ant.*" 603 n. 17; Bühler and Theodoridis, "Johannes von Damaskos" 399 n. 14. B. A. Müller, "Zu Stephanos" 345ff. (accepted by Chr.-Sch.-St. 2:2.1079 n. 4), sought to find a *term a. q.* in the reference to C. in the Ἐθνικά of Stephanus (q.v., no. 144) of Byzantium s.v. Ταμίαθις, arguing against Meineke's seclusion of that reference as an interpolation in his edition of Stephanus (Berlin, 1849). But Müller failed to acknowledge C.'s own citation of Stephanus, *GG* 4:1.305.1ff., a passage that cannot be an interpolation, as Hilgard pointed out; cf. *GG* 4:2, liv. A date for C. in s.IX 1/2 has now been established by Theodoridis, "Hymnograph," who notes C.'s citations of the hymnograph Clemens and of Andreas Peros. Bühler and Theodoridis, "Johannes von Damaskos," already inferred a *term. p. q.* of s.VIII 1/2 from C.'s knowledge of the Κανόνες of John the Damascene; likewise earlier Papadopulos-Kerameus, "Zur Geschichte," noted by Alpers, *Attizistische Lexikon* 91 n. 25. A *term. a. q.* is implied by the citations of the Ἐπιμερισμοί and Περὶ ὀρθογραφίας in *Etym. Gen.* and by the excerpts of the scholia to Theodosius in the Περὶ τόνων published by Koster, "De accentibus," both compiled sometime in s.IX med.–2/2. This date in turn is consistent with the style οἰκουμενικὸς διδάσκαλος; cf. Speck, *Kaiserliche Universität* 74ff. (although Speck places C. in s.VI); Theodoridis, "Hymnograph" 344. A date in s.IX is also consistent with C.'s use of the Psalter

as a grammatical text, which we should hardly expect in the Constantinople of s.VI, and with the form of C.'s name: "Ein Familienname *Choiro-*
ist in den Jahrhunderten 6 und 7 schwer glaublich" (P. Maas, private
communication, quoted by Di Benedetto, "Techne" 797 n. 2).

202. ARRUNTIUS CLAUDIUS.

PLRE I s.v. Claudius 8, p. 208.

Cited by Diomedes, *GL* 1.321.11f., *sicut Arruntius Claudius asserit*, in all
likelihood a mistaken reference to Arruntius Celsus (q.v., no. 197; cf.
Sch.-Hos. 4:1.180). C. was omitted from *RE*, presumably because it was
taken for granted that Diomedes is in error; cf. *RE* 12.1265 (Goetz),
where Diomedes is simply listed among those who cite Celsus. Jeep,
"Priscianus" 7f., suggested that Diomedes misread a reference in his
source in the form *Arruntius teste Claudio* [sc. *Didymo*]; for citation of the
man as Arruntius, see s.v. Arruntius Celsus. If Jeep was correct, then
Celsus could not be dated later than s.I.

203. CONSENTIUS. *v.c.* Narbo? s.V 1/2?

RE 4.911–12 (Goetz); Sch.-Hos. 4:2.210–13; *PLRE* II s.v. 3, p. 310; cf.
Stroheker, *Senatorische Adel* 161f. nos. 95, 96.

Author of a grammatical work parts of which are now preserved as the
De duabus partibus orationis nomine et verbo (*GL* 5.338ff.) and as the *De
barbarismis et metaplasmis* (*GL* 5.386ff.; also edited by M. Niedermann
[Neuchâtel, 1937]). References to preceding and subsequent parts of the
larger work occur in the sections that survive; cf. Keil, *GL* 5.332;
Sch.-Hos. 4:2.211.

Termed *Consentius, v.c.* in codd. Monac. 14666 and Leid. Voss. 37. 8.
The titulatur in cod. Bern. 432, *INCIPIT ARS CONSENTII VIRI CLARI /
U̅C̅ QUINTI CONSULIS [QUINQ CIVITATŪ]*, is gibberish; on its origin
as a scribal *ludus*, cf. Keil, *GL* 5.334. None of the mss calls him *grammaticus*, and there is nothing in the extant work to suggest that he was a
gramm. by profession; rather, his style (cf. Keil, *GL* 5.333), his readiness
to quote from the spoken Latin of his day (e.g., *GL* 5.391.31ff.), and his
independence in organization and judgment (cf. Sch.-Hos. 4:2.211) all
combine to distinguish his work from that of the professional *grammatici*;
cf. also Loyen, *Sidoine* 80; Holtz, *Donat* 83f., 86. On the evidence available,
he should be placed in the class of learned amateurs.

Unequivocal evidence for date and location is lacking; on his possible
sources, see Barwick, *Remmius* 4ff.; Holtz, *Donat* 87ff., the latter esp. on
C.'s use of the main source of Donatus. A *term. p. q.* of s.IV med. is
consistent with his use of Lucan, whom he quotes at least twice: *GL*
5.345.22, 355.17; for use of Lucan as a criterion for dating, cf. s.v.

Phocas, no. 121. An origin in Gaul has been detected in C.'s frequent use of Gallic place names in examples; cf. *GL* 5.346.3ff., 348.35. It has been customary since Lachmann (ed., Terent. Maur. [Berlin, 1836] xiii) to associate C. with the Consentii of Narbo known to Sidonius Apollinaris; cf. *Carm.* 23; *Ep.* 8.4, 9.15.1 v. 22. Attempts at a more precise identification have been made, either with the younger Consentius (= Stroheker, *Senatorische Adel* no. 96 = *PLRE* II s.v. 2, pp. 308f.), poet and influential palatine minister under Valentinian III and Avitus (so Osann, *Beiträge* 2.345ff.); or with the elder Consentius, described as poet, stylist, and polymath by Sidonius Apollinaris, *Carm.* 23.97ff. (= Stroheker, *Senatorische Adel* no. 95 = *PLRE* II s.v. 1, p. 308), father of the younger Consentius and son-in-law of the usurper Iovinus (so Loyen, *Sidoine* 80f.). If either identification is correct, it is probably the latter: C. would then have been dead by 462, the *term. p. q.* of Sidon. *Carm.* 23, and probably would have been born sometime in the last two decades of s.IV—ca. 380, according to Loyen, *Sidoine* 80 n. 144.

204. CORONATUS. *Scholasticus* and poet; *v.c.*   Africa.   s.VI init.

RE 4.1644 (Skutsch); Sch.-Hos. 4:2.74; Szöverffy, *Weltliche Dichtungen* 1.187; *PLRE* I s.v., p. 229, superseded by *PLRE* II s.v., p. 326.

Epigrammatic poet three of whose poems are included in the codex Salmasianus: *Anth. Lat.* 1:1.223 (cf. Cupaiuolo, *"Locus"*), 226, 228. Probably to be identified with Coronatus *scholasticus* the author of a grammatical work on final syllables, dedicated to Luxurius (q.v., no. 235); cf. the dedicatory epistle, with the salutation *Domino eruditissimorum* [cod. Monac. 14252: *domino viro eruditissimo peritissimorum* cod. S. Paul. in vall. Lavant. 24] *atque inlustri fratri Luxorio Coronatus*, published by Keil, *De grammaticis* 4 n. (cf. *GL* 4, 1) = Rosenblum, *Luxorius* 259. His place and date are suggested by his inclusion in the cod. Salmas. and esp. by his probable connection with Luxurius. He is styled *vir clarissimus* in the inscr. of the poems in *Anth. Lat.*

On the strength of the grammatical treatise and the epithet *scholasticus* C. is commonly said to have been a gramm.; cf., e.g., Levy, *RE* 13.2103.23ff., 2104.29ff.; Rosenblum, *Luxorius* 36; Riché, *Education* 38. Skutsch, *RE* 4.1644.15ff., is correctly silent. The designation is far from certain: mere authorship of a grammatical work does not guarantee that the author was a gramm.; nor does C. give any indication in the dedicatory epistle that the work grew out of or was intended for use in the schools. *Scholasticus* is not certainly C.'s self-description but simply occurs in the incipit of cod. S. Paul. in vall. Lavant. 24, fol. 75, *expliciunt finales Sergii, incipiunt Coronati scholastici.* *Scholasticus* here probably means merely "learned man" or "scholar" and is distinct from the professional title *grammaticus*; cf. s.v. Calliopius *scholasticus*, no. 194, *ad fin.* There is no reason to think that C. was anything but a learned amateur, as his friend Luxurius appears to have been (see s.v.).

+ 205. FABIUS(?) DEMETRIUS. Gramm. Tarraco. s.III.

A *magister grammaticus*, on an epitaph found at a level of secondary usage in an early Christian necropolis at Tarraco: *AE* 1928, 200 = *AE* 1938, 17 = *ILER* 5716 = *RIT* 443, D(is) M(anibus) [Fabio? De]metrio [ma]gistro [gramma]tico Q(uintus?) [F]abius [---fra]t(ri?) piiss[imo b]eneme[renti---]. For the style *magister grammaticus*, see Appendix 1.1a. The name "[F]abius" seems uncertain; there is no trace of the -*a*- in the photograph in *RIT*. Alföldy, *RIT* p. 481, dated the inscription to s.III, with a range of s.II ex. / s.IV 1/2.

* 206. DIOCLES. Gramm.? → philosopher? → monk. Arsinoe. Born 347/ 51; dead not before 408/12.

Monk at Arsinoe, formerly a gramm.(?) and philosopher(?): Pallad. *Hist. Laus.* 58, p. 152.5ff. Butler, ἀπὸ γραμματικῆς μὲν ἀχθεὶς τὰ πρῶτα, ἐς ὕστερον δὲ δοὺς ἑαυτὸν εἰς φιλοσοφίαν . . . εἰς εἰκοστὸν ὄγδοον ἔτος ἄγων τὴν ἡλικίαν ἀπετάξατο μὲν τῶν ἐγκυκλίων μαθημάτων, συνετάξατο δὲ τῷ Χριστῷ. It is not clear whether the initial phrases describe the successive professions of D. *qua* gramm. and philosopher or—perhaps more likely— just the course of a liberal education. He made his conversion in his twenty-eighth year (see above) and was spending his thirty-fifth year in the caves when Palladius saw him, 408/12 (p. 152.9–10). His birth can therefore be dated to 347/51; his conversion, to 374/78.

He was chosen by Dorotheus to administer the bulk of a gift of 500 *solidi* sent to Arsinoe by the younger Melania (p. 151.20ff.).

207. DIOGENES. Gramm.? Cyzicus. s.IV / s.VI init.? (before Stephanus of Byzantium).

RE 5.737–38 (Schwartz); Chr.-Sch.-St. 2:2.1077; *PLRE* II s.v. 4, p. 360.

Diogenes: Διογένης, Steph. Byzant. s.vv. Ἀδράστεια, Βέσβικος, Ζέλεια = *FGrH* IIIb, 474F1–3; Διογένης ἢ Διογενειανός, *Suda* Δ.1146, the latter name the result of an evident confusion or partial fusion with Dio-genianus, gramm. of the reign of Hadrian (cf. *Suda* Δ.1139–40, and below). A γραμματικός, *Suda* Δ.1146. Native of Cyzicus: Κυζικηνός, *Suda* ibid.; Steph. Byzant. s.v. Βέσβικος = *FGrH* 474F2.

The citations in the Ἐθνικά of Stephanus (q.v., no. 144) of Byzantium provide a *term. a. q.* of s.VI 1/2 at the latest. If the title Πάτρια Κυζίκου given in the *Suda* (ibid.) is authentic, D. is not likely to have been active before s.IV; cf. Chr.-Sch.-St. 2:2.803 n. 2, 1077 n. 2; Schwartz, *RE* 5.737.63ff. But the authenticity of that title, with πάτρια, is not certain. Note that Stephanus cites the work as ἐν πρώτῃ Κυζίκου s.v. Ἀδράστεια (= FGrH 474F1) and as ἐν γ̄ Κυζίκου s.v. Ζέλεια (= FGrH 474F3); the text of Stephanus s.v. Βέσβικος (= FGrH 474F2) seems to be corrupt, ἐν πρώτῃ †τῶν ἑπτὰ περὶ τῆς πατρίδος νήσων. Compare the case of Theagenes, whose local history of Macedon is cited as Μακεδονικὰ πάτρια by Photius, *Bibl.* cod. 161 (2.127 Henry), but simply as Μακεδονικά by Stephanus (*FGrH* IIIc, 774F2–12, 14, 15). For similar, earlier efforts by a gramm., cf. esp. the case of Ti. Claudius Anteros, gramm. of Mylasa(?), honored ὅτι τὰ τῆς πατρίδος καλὰ εἰς μ[έ]σους τοὺς Ἕλληνα[ς] προήγαγεν διὰ τῶν ἐπιχωρίων ἱστοριῶ[ν] [ἐ]νδοξότερα ε<ἶ>ναι, *Labraunda* 3:2.66.20ff. (s.II; not before 127).

In addition to the work on Cyzicus (in at least three books, in prose, as the citations in Stephanus show), there are three treatises on grammatical subjects attributed to D. in the *Suda* (ibid.): a Περὶ τῶν ἐν τοῖς βιβλίοις σημείων, a Περὶ ποιητικῆς, and a Περὶ στοιχείων. Because the *Suda* appears to confuse D. with the Hadrianic gramm. Diogenianus (see above), Bernhardy conjectured that those works should be attributed to the latter; this was accepted by, e.g., Jacoby, *FGrH* IIIb, 474T1 and commentary. It remains to be pointed out that if in fact the confusion is so severe, there is a very good chance that D. was not a γραμματικός at all.

208. TI. CLAUDIUS MAXIMUS DONATIANUS. Gramm.? *Aet. incert.*; perhaps not before s.IV 2/2.

RE 5.1532 (Goetz); Sch.-Hos. 4:1.169; *PLRE* I s.v. Donatianus 6, p. 268; cf. ibid. s.v. Donatianus 1, p. 267.

Son of Ti. Claudius Donatus (q.v., no. 209), to whom the latter dedicated his *Interpretationes Vergilianae*. Name and filiation: *Interp.* tit., ed. Georgii, 1.1.2f.; cf. postscr. 2.642.5f., *Tiberio Claudio Donatiano filio suo*.

Perhaps D. is the gramm. Donatianus (q.v., no. 51) of the *Donatiani fragmentum*, *GL* 6.275.10ff. On the profession and date of the latter, perhaps not before s.IV 2/2, see s.v. The identification is, however, extremely uncertain: note esp. that if D. was the gramm., he was presumably already active when his father wrote the *Interp.* as a *senex*—in which case his father's very unflattering comments on the *grammatici* and their teaching (see s.v. Ti. Claudius Donatus) would be surprisingly if not impossibly tactless.

Further, if D. is to be dated as late as s.IV 2/2, he is probably not Donatianus the senator cited by Priscian, *GL* 2.225.10, *Donatianus in senatu pro se*. For with the exception of Vegetius, whose work is known to have enjoyed some currency in Constantinople (cf. Jahn, "Subscriptionen" 344f.), Priscian quotes no Latin *auctor*—i.e., no authoritative model other than a technical writer—later than Ulpian.

209. TI. CLAUDIUS DONATUS.   *Aet. incert.*; perhaps s.IV med. – 2/2.

RE 5.1547 (Wessner); Sch.-Hos. 2.105–7; *PLRE* I s.v. Donatus 4, pp. 268f.

Ti. Claudius Donatus, author of the *Interpretationes Vergilianae*: *Interp.* tit., ed. Georgii, 1.1.1; postscr., 2.642.5. The work provides no positive indication of D.'s status; he was almost certainly not a professional gramm., since he explicitly rejects the practices of the schools (proem., 1.1.5ff.) and would even remove Vergil from the sphere of the *grammatici*: 1.4.27f., *intelleges Vergilium non grammaticos sed oratores praecipuos tradere debuisse*. His motives for composing the *Interp.* for his son may be compared in general with those of Macrobius in the *Saturnalia*; cf. Kaster, "Macrobius" 258ff. He was probably, like Macrobius, a learned amateur.

His stated interest in the text is rhetorical; his comment, largely paraphrase. For the suggestion that he had been an advocate, see Georgii, ed., 1, viii–ix.

His promise (2.642.12ff.) to compose a work on the characters and historical details in the *Aeneid* was not to our knowledge fulfilled.

D. composed the *Interp.* as a *senex* (2.642.7f.). He is sometimes dated after Servius (q.v., no. 136) because the *Interp.* allegedly depends on the commentaries of Aelius Donatus and of Servius, and because Servius appears to be ignorant of D. But the dependence is extremely doubtful, a use of common sources at most; see Burckas, "De Tib. Claudii Donati in Aeneida commentario" 10ff.; Hoppe, "De Tib. Claudio Donato" 18ff. Further, since D. self-consciously separated himself from the scholastic tradition (see above), it is not surprising that Servius, writing within that tradition, should not know him. If his son and dedicatee, Ti. Claudius Maximus Donatianus, is the man from whose schoolroom the *Donatiani fragmentum* derives, then D. could possibly be dated to s.IV med. – 2/2. But this too is very uncertain; see s.vv. Donatianus and Ti. Claudius Maximus Donatianus, nos. 51, 208.

210. EUDAEMON.   Gramm. or, more probably, teacher of rhetoric.   Egypt → Antioch →? Tarsus   Born not after ca. 335, and probably not before ca. 324; dead not before 364.

Seeck, *Briefe* 131f.; Petit, *Étudiants* 86; *PLRE* I s.v. 2, p. 289.

Recipient or subject of Lib. *Ep.* 454 (an. 355/56), 364 (an. 358), 66 (an. 359), 1428 (an. 363), 1286, 1300, 1303 (all an. 364); cf. also *Ep.* 368 (an. 358).

E. is firmly identified as a "rhetor" in *PLRE* I, p. 289; cf. Schemmel, "Sophist" 58 (somewhat confused). Petit, *Étudiants* 86, treats him as a gramm. (similarly Norman, *Autobiography* 156); Seeck, *Briefe* 131f., more vaguely speaks of him as a "Lehrer." In fact, explicit and unequivocal indication of E.'s profession is lacking; conclusions must be drawn from the following three passages, which require full presentation.

Ep. 454.4 (an. 355/56), to Phasganius: τὰ δὲ περὶ τοὺς νέους τὰ μὲν ἄλλα ἢ πρὸ τοῦ, Ἰούλιος δὲ ὁ γραμματιστὴς ὑπὸ λύπης οἴχεται, καὶ γνοὺς Εὐδαίμων ὡς οὔπω πάντα αὐτῷ ῥᾴδια, Σεβαστιανὸν πείθει δεηθῆναί μου νεῖμαί τι προνοίας αὐτῷ. Since Libanius appears to be informing his uncle of affairs touching his own school—that is what τὰ δὲ περὶ τοὺς νέους should imply—his remarks might mean that Iulius the γραμματιστὴς (= γραμματικός in Libanius's usage; see Appendix 2) had been a teacher in Libanius's establishment (see further s.v. Iulius, no. 88) and that his passing away had left a gap E. hoped to fill (so Petit, *Étudiants* 86); accordingly E. had called on Sebastianus, who was by this time *dux Aegypti*, to intercede with Libanius and remove an obstacle to his ambition. In that case, E. would also have been a gramm. But Iulius's death and E.'s machinations need not stand in the relation of cause and effect; they could be two different matters concerning Libanius's school. In that case, E. could either already be a member of Libanius's school or be seeking a position in it, and no precise conclusion could be drawn concerning his profession.

Ep. 364.5–6 (an. 358), introducing the poet and teacher Harpocration to Aristaenetus: Ἁρποκρατίων γὰρ οὑτοσὶ καὶ ποιητὴς ἀγαθὸς καὶ παιδευτὴς ἀμείνων, δεινὸς μὲν ἐνθεῖναι τὰ τῶν παλαιῶν νέοις, δεινὸς δὲ ἐκείνοις παρισωθῆναι. . . . οὗτος Εὐδαίμονι κοινωνήσας καὶ τροφῆς καὶ μουσείων πάλαι μὲν ἐν τῷ φοιτᾶν, νῦν δὲ ἐν τῷ παιδεύειν καὶ μικροῦ τῷ φίλῳ συμπεφυκὼς ὑπὸ τῆς ὑμετέρας ἀπερράγη δυναστείας. The passage invites the following conclusions. If Harpocration, "a good poet and a better teacher," was "frightfully clever at instilling in the young the works of the ancients, and clever at equalling the ancients," it is a possible but not necessary inference that the ancients whose works he taught were the same as those he rivaled, viz., the ancient poets: so Petit, *Étudiants* 86; cf. Schemmel, "Sophist" 58. In that case Harpocration would have been a grammarian. Further, since Harpocration was now E.'s fellow teacher, as he had once been his fellow student, E. should also be a gramm.; this conclusion will thus depend on the accuracy of the preceding inference. Note that Εὐδαίμονι κοινωνήσας καὶ τροφῆς καὶ μουσείων πάλαι μὲν ἐν τῷ φοιτᾶν does not mean that Harpocration had been a pupil of E. (*pace* Seeck, *Briefe* 131f., and *PLRE* I s.v. 2, p. 289) or that the two were brothers (*pace* Petit, *Étudiants* 86), but that the two had grown up and gone to school together; i.e., in their schooldays Harpocration had had his upbringing (τροφή) in common with E., as now, in their teaching days, he had a common livelihood (τροφή); cf. τῷ φίλῳ συμπεφυκώς, a phrase that more suitably describes the relations between friends and contemporaries than those between brothers or between pupil and teacher.

Ep. 368.1, 3, to Themistius: τὴν Ἁρποκρατίονος ἡμᾶς ἀφελόμενος γλῶτταν ἔδωκας τοῖς οὐδὲν δεομένοις. . . . εἶτα γνοὺς [sc. Ἁρποκρατίων] ὡς μεταπέμποιο σοφιστάς, "μαθητὰς" ἔφην "ὁ καλὸς ζητεῖ Θεμίστιος." If we take as our premise that μαθητάς is used here figuratively, this should mean that Harpocration went to Constantinople in the person of a sophist. The phrasing of the first clause, esp. ἡμᾶς ἀφελόμενος, might also suggest that Harpocration was teaching in Libanius's school. Since he was teaching with E., then E. would also be a teacher in Libanius's school; cf. *Ep.* 364.7, where Libanius says that he personally will console E. for the loss of his friend Harpocration. In *Ep.* 368.1, however, ἡμᾶς may simply refer to Antioch in general, as opposed to Constantinople.

Clearly, the interpretation of *Ep.* 364.5 is critical. If the inference drawn above is correct, then Harpocration was a gramm. at Antioch but went to Constantinople as a sophist; in that case, E. was a gramm. at Antioch also. If, however, the inference is not correct—if Libanius's words at *Ep.* 364.5 should not be pressed to make τῶν παλαιῶν mean "the ancient poets" exclusively—then there is no evidence that Harpocration was a gramm., and he was probably already a teacher of rhetoric at Antioch; in that case, E. probably taught rhetoric also. Given the risk involved in imposing the required precision on Libanius's words at *Ep.* 364.5—and so the uncertainty of the inference—and given, too, the language of *Ep.* 368, esp. 368.3, γνοὺς ὡς μεταπέμποιο σοφιστάς, I think that the second alternative is on balance marginally more likely to be correct. But I have no great confidence in this conclusion, and I am aware that other alternatives could be squeezed from the data. If, however, it is correct to conclude that Harpocration and E. were teachers of rhetoric, then a further inference follows with regard to the interpretation of *Ep.* 454.4 above: as a teacher of rhetoric, E. would not have been interested in filling the gap left by the gramm. Iulius. In that case, his machinations alluded to in *Ep.* 454 concerned some matter unrelated to Iulius's death, and he might already have been a member of Libanius's school by 355/56, as he perhaps was in 358 (see the discussion of *Ep.* 368.1 and 3 above). This, too, is obviously uncertain. But one further, more firm conclusion can be added: since E. and Harpocration are said to have grown up together (see *Ep.* 364.5–6 above) and since Harpocration was an Egyptian (see s.v., no. 226), E. must also have been an Egyptian. The patronage of Sebastianus, *Ep.* 454.4, might point in the same direction.

Briefly, then, the following seems to have been the course of E.'s career through 358: a teacher of rhetoric and native of Egypt, E. was perhaps in a position by 355/56 to seek or hold a teaching post in Libanius's school at Antioch. He cannot therefore have been born much later than ca. 335; he was not yet married in 355/56 (see below). He remained in Antioch when his long-time friend and fellow teacher Harpocration left for Constantinople in 358.

E. was still in Antioch in 359, enjoying a correspondence with Themistius at Constantinople (*Ep.* 66.5), possibly as a result of the latter's connection with Harpocration; cf. *Ep.* 368 and s.v. Harpocration. Autumn 363 found him away from Antioch but still presumably having that city as his base; in *Ep.* 1428.2 he brings a letter from Libanius to the *PPO Or.* Saturninius Secundus *signo* Salutius, who was making his way with the retinue of Jovian to Antioch. Jovian was somewhere between Edessa and Antioch at the time; cf. Seeck, *Briefe* 412f.

A year later, however, E. was in Cilicia, where he was acting as Libanius's "ambassador" to the god Asclepius at Tarsus—Libanius was suffering from the gout—and looking forward to his own marriage. For Libanius's gout, see *Ep.* 1286.3, 1300, 1303.1; for E. as Libanius's πρεσβευτής, *Ep.* 1300.1; for E.'s marriage, *Ep.* 1300.4, τοῦτο [viz., the cure for the gout] δὲ εἰ γένοιτο, δραμούμεθα παρὰ τὸν φιλόδωρον θεὸν βεβαιωσόμενοί τε τὸ δοθὲν καὶ σοὶ δᾷδα ἄψοντες ἐν τοῖς γάμοις. Libanius evidently expected the marriage to take place in Cilicia. This may mean that E. had left Antioch and had taken up residence in Tarsus. Although that is not a necessary conclusion—πρεσβευτής in *Ep.* 1300.1 might suggest that his return to Antioch was anticipated—it is clear that his stay in Cilicia was long enough for Libanius to correspond with him. (*Ep.* 1300 and 1303 are the only letters addressed to E. in the extant corpus.) E. was closely attached (*Ep.* 1303.2) to Quirinus, a sophist, several times a provincial governor, and a landowner in Cilicia, who evidently died not long before the autumn of 364 (= *PLRE* I s.v., pp. 760f.).

E. was a pagan and dabbled in the interpretation of dreams (*Ep.* 1300.1).

Since he was of an age to teach in 355/56, he is not likely to have been born much later than ca. 335. If *Ep.* 1428.2 can be pressed (Libanius, sending E. to Salutius, uses the simile of fathers who gain vicarious enjoyment by sending their sons to banquets they cannot themselves attend) he is not likely to have been close to Libanius's age, i.e., not likely to have been born before ca. 324.

E. is not to be confused with Eudaemon of Pelusium, who, *int. al.*, was probably older; see s.v., no. 55.

211. FL. EUGENIUS.   Lat. gramm. or rhetorician → *magister* (*scrinii*) → *Augustus* (392–94).
PLRE I s.v. 6, p. 293.

Fl. Eugenius only in two inscr. dated by the consulship (West) of Theodosius and Fl. Eugenius, *ICVR*, n.s., 3.8159, 8430; Eugenius elsewhere.

His chronology is uncertain for the period before his elevation, but he was connected with Ricomer by 385 (see below). His place of teaching is unknown; it was presumably in the West.

Described by Socrates as γραμματικός τις ... Ῥωμαϊκοὺς παιδεύων λόγους, HE 5.25.1; cf. Theoph. Chron. p. 71.2f. de Boor, ἀπὸ τῶν γραμματικῶν. According to Zosimus 4.54, ῥητορικὸν ἐπανελέσθαι βίον καὶ προεστάναι διδασκαλείου, he was a teacher of rhetoric; cf. Ioan. Ant. frg. 187, FHG 4.609, ἐπὶ σοφιστικὸν ἐγκαθήμενον θρόνον. Given the latter evidence, and given the fact that Socrates' expression Ῥωμαϊκοὺς παιδεύων λόγους could refer as well to rhetoric as to grammar (cf. HE 5.14.5; for the expression in Socrates, see s.v. Paulus, no. 116, and Appendix 1.2a), one might think that γραμματικός is used by Socrates here in the nontechnical sense, "man of letters," vir litteratus; cf. Appendix 3. But in fact Socrates otherwise uses the word only in its narrower, titular sense; cf. HE 2.46.3; 3.1.10, 7.18, 16.2–3; 4.9.4, 25.5; 5.16.10, 15. His exact profession therefore seems to be an open question.

Probably before 385 (see below) E. abandoned teaching for the palatine service (Soc. HE 5.25.1), wherein he was respected because of his eloquence and literary attainments: Soc. ibid., διὰ τὸ εἶναι ἐλλόγιμος; Zos. ibid., διὰ παιδείας ὑπερβολήν; Ioan. Ant. ibid., ὑπὸ γλώττης εὐδοκιμοῦντα. He became an ἀντιγραφεύς (Soc. ibid.; cf. Theoph. ibid.), i.e., a magister scrinii (μάγιστρον τὴν ἀξίαν, Philostorg. HE 11.2) overseeing the drafting of ἀντιγραφαί, imperial rescripts. This was probably after 385; in 385 he is referred to as v.c. (Symm. Ep. 3.61), although by that date he would probably have been entitled, if he was a magister scrinii, to the rank of spectabilis; cf. Ensslin, RE, 2. Reihe, 3.156.59ff.

While in the palatine service he became the protégé of Ricomer; cf. Zos. ibid., Ioan. Ant. ibid. This will have been sometime before 385; cf. Symm. Ep. 3.60 (undated) and 61 (an. 385). Both these letters were brought to Ricomer by E., who is referred to in them as dominus et frater meus and v.c., frater meus, respectively. Ricomer introduced him to Arbogast, who intended to use him as a cat's-paw, since he himself could not aspire to the throne because of his barbarian origins (Philostorg. ibid.).

E. was alleged to have been a pagan (Philostorg. ibid.; cf. Soz. HE 7.22.4) or to have served by his usurpation as the rallying point of pagan resistance; see Rufinus HE 2.33; Aug. CD 5.26; Oros. 7.35; cf. also Ambros. Ep. 57.2ff. But the sources may exaggerate the religious motives for the usurpation; cf. Ziegler, Zur religiösen Haltung 85ff.; O'Donnell, "Career" 136ff.; Szidat, "Usurpation."

On E.'s elevation and events through the battle of the Frigidus (5 Sept. 394), see RLAC 6.860–77 (Straub); Matthews, Western Aristocracies 238ff.; RE Suppl. 13.896.64ff. (Lippold); and Ziegler, O'Donnell, and Szidat as cited above.

212. EUSEBIUS.   Rhetorician (probably).   *Aet. incert.*; not later than s.IV / s.V.
RE 6.1445 (Brzoska); Sch.-Hos. 4:1.149; *PLRE* I s.v. 34, p. 307.

A writer on prose rhythm, according to Rufinus, *GL* 6.573.25 = *Rhet. Lat. min.* 581.18; not a "metrical writer," *pace* Sch.-Hos. and *PLRE* I. He appears also to have commented on Cic. *De inv.*; cf. Grillius *Rhet. Lat. min.* 598.20. Both data, esp. the latter, suggest that he was a rhetorician rather than a gramm. Evidence for precise dating is lacking; since he is cited by Rufinus and Grillius (qq.v., nos. 130, 225), he cannot be later than s.IV / s.V.

213. EUTROPIUS.   Gramm.?   *Aet. incert.*; before s.VI init.

Cited by Priscian, *GL* 2.8.19f., on the letter *x*; quoted immediately after Servius.
    The name suggests a late-antique date; identification with any other known literary Eutropii—e.g., the historian, or Fl. Eutropius the subscriber of Vegetius at Constantinople in 450 (cf. Jahn, "Subscriptionen" 344f.)—is not evident.

214. EUTYCHES.   Teacher.   Panopolis.   Dead by s.IV init.

"A house belonging to Casiana, daughter-in-law of Eutyches the teacher [διδάσκαλος]," and "another house belonging to the sons of Eutyches the teacher," registered in a topographical listing of properties in Panopolis executed early in s.IV: *PGen.* inv. 108 = *SB* 8.9902 = V. Martin, "Relevé" 39ff. = *PBerlBork.* A.II.2 and 14. For the date, see references s.v. Chabrias, no. 198. The two houses were evidently located in the same quarter of the town. The manner of the registration shows that E. was no longer alive at the time of the survey; cf. s.v. Chabrias. For other διδάσκαλοι in the same register, see s.v. Chabrias and s.v. Theon, no. 267.

215. EUTYCHIANUS.   Gramm.?   s.IV 1/2–2/3?
PLRE I s.v. 2, p. 319; cf. ibid. s.v. 3.

Called πρωτοασηκρήτης ὁ γραμματικός, *Script. orig. Constantinop.* 2.144.3 Preger; included in a group of authors of autopsy accounts of the dedication of Constantinople and said to have been with Julian in Persia.
    The source is very untrustworthy; note esp. that others included among the supposed eyewitnesses—e.g., Eutropius, Troilus—could not possibly have been present. Its terminology is not likely to be precise; πρωτοασηκρήτης, "first secretary of the sacred consistory," is certainly anachronistic; γραμματικός is perhaps used in a nontechnical sense, "man of letters," as it sometimes is in the *Suda* (cf. Appendix 3). The notice of

E. should therefore be regarded as of very doubtful historicity; there may be a complete or partial confusion with Eutychianus the soldier and historian, who is also said to have accompanied Julian on his Persian campaign; cf. *PLRE* I s.v. 3.

+ 216. FELIX.   Schoolmaster and martyr.

Magister puerorum and martyr; the story of his passion is legendary and a doublet of that of Cassianus (q.v., no. 26) of Imola, possibly borrowed to explain the origin of F.'s name, "St. Felix *in pincis*." See Iacobus de Voragine, *Historia Lombardica seu legenda aurea* (Nuremberg, 1482) fol. 20ᵛ: *Felix pronomine "in pincis" dicitur, vel a loco in quo requiescit, vel a subulis cum quibus passus perhibetur. nam pinca subula dicuntur. aiunt enim quod cum magister puerorum extiterit et eis nimium rigidus fuerit, tentus a paganis, cum Christum libere confiteretur, traditus fuit in manibus puerorum quos ipse docuerat, qui eum cum stilis et subulis occiderunt.*

+ 217. FILOCALUS.

RE 19.2432–33 (Kroll); cf. Barnes, "More Missing Names" 148.

A Filocalus appears three or four times in "Sergius" *Explan. in Don.* in exchanges that take the form *interrogavit Filocalus. . . . respondit* (sc. *Servius*?: see below): *GL* 4.498.23, 501.31, 503.11, 515.30. In the first of these places Keil's text reads *interrogatus Filocalus . . . respondit*; there *interrogatus* should be corrected to *interrogavit* if the name *Filocalus* is to remain. But note that the majority of mss reported by Keil have simply *interrogatus . . . respondit*, perhaps correctly.

Kroll, *RE* 19.2432–33, followed by Barnes, "More Missing Names" 148 (on F.'s omission from *PLRE* I, but the omission is probably correct; see below), assumed that F. was a gramm. and identified him with Furius Dionysius Philocalus, the calligrapher associated with the epigrams of Damasus (cf. Ferrua, *Epigrammata* 21ff.) and with the *Chron. A.D. 354.* This is almost certainly incorrect. It is chronologically difficult to associate a figure active near the middle of s.IV with Servius (on whose involvement here, see following), whose teaching did not begin until the end of the century (see s.v., no. 136). Moreover, Kroll was too hasty in assuming F. was a gramm.; for it seems probable that the subject of *respondit* is supposed to be *Servius magister*; cf. *GL* 4.496.26f., where *magister Servius dictavit* begins the section in which the exchanges appear. It is more likely that F. is here supposed to be a pupil of Servius—in which case the chronological problems would be insurmountable. Finally, we must note that F. is not the only character to appear in these exchanges: one also finds *interrogavit Rusticus* at *GL* 4.499.24. The names "Filocalus" and "Rusticus" thus paired—"Mr. Refined" and "Mr. Uncouth"—should arouse suspicion, and that suspicion should be heightened by the fact that the questions asked by the two correspond to their names. F.'s are fairly involved and show a good grasp of the *ars* and *auctores*; Rusticus's is treated as a bit stupid. It would seem that we are dealing with imagined circumstances here; cf., e.g., Pomp. *GL* 5.142.35ff., with Chap. 4 p. 160; cf. also s.v. Ter(r)entius, no. 262. Both F. and Rusticus should be regarded as fictions, types invented for the sake of the exchanges, which are themselves devised for the sake of illustration. The entire passage, which finds the teacher responding to questions, is comparable to the model exchanges devised *exempli gratia* by Pompeius, cited above. *PLRE* I was correct in omitting F.

218. FIRMIANUS.   Gramm.? Vergilian commentator?   Before s.IV med.?
Cf. *PLRE* I s.v. 1, p. 338.

Author of a commentary(?) on Vergil, responsible for the correct reading of *Aen.* 7.543. The name is preserved *ad loc.* in Servius Danielis (= DServ.): *dicit etiam quidam commentarius—Firmiani* [DServ.]—*"convecta" legendum.* If the name in DServ. is derived from the variorum commentary of Donatus, to which the compiler of DServ. had access, then F. could be placed before s.IV med. On the *commentarius*, see below.

The relation of F. to Firmianus the metrical writer and to the rhetorician and Christian apologist L. Caecilius Firmianus *qui et* Lactantius is uncertain. The former should perhaps be dated before s.IV med., since his remarks to a certain Probus on comic meter not only were excerpted by Rufinus (q.v., no. 130) but also seem to have been drawn on by [Marius Victorinus] = Aelius Festus Aphthonius: *Firmianus ad Probum de metris comoediarum sic dicit.* . . . Rufinus *GL* 6.564.7–20 = [Marius Victorinus] *Ars gramm., GL* 6.78.19–79.1. The excerpts in Rufinus and the text of Aphthonius = [Victorinus] appear to be derived independently from the same source, although this is uncertain, as is the date of Aphthonius.

Firmianus the metrical writer is usually assumed to be identical with Lactantius; cf. s.v. Victorinus, no. 273, for Lactantius quoted on a metrical point. If the two were the same man, then the date of the metrical writer would of course be established independently of the considerations noted above; and the remarks to Probus would probably have been part of Lactantius's correspondence, not a separate metrical treatise; cf. Jer. *De vir. ill.* 80, *ad Probum epistularum libros quattuor*, with *Comm. Galat.* 2 prol., *Lactantii nostri quae in tertio ad Probum volumine de hac gente* (sc. *Gallorum opinatus sit verba*).

If the *commentarius* Servius mentions was in fact a full-scale commentary, its author is likely to have been a Firmianus other than Lactantius. The term *commentarius* may, however, represent nothing more than

Servius's inference; i.e., the reading attributed to F. may have originally stood in a passing observation or quotation—made, say, in a miscellaneous work such as the correspondence noted above—that Servius found in his source (e.g., in the form *Firmianus ait*) and simply assumed was derived from a commentary. (Servius is not completely trustworthy in such matters; cf. Chap. 5 pp. 190ff.) In that case all three Firmiani could be Lactantius.

Other combinations are conceivable: e.g., for the Firmianus on meter identical with the Firmianus on Vergil but not with Lactantius, cf. Ogilvie, *Library* 12f.

219. FLAVIANUS.

Sch.-Hos. 4:1.167; cf. *PLRE* I s.v., p. 349.

Flavianus, listed in the catalogues of gramm. in codd. Bonon. 797 (Negri, "De codice" 266) and Bern. 243 (*Anecd. Helv. = GL* 8, cxlix, *de Italia . . . Flaviani IIII* [sc. *libri*]). Cited by later gramm.; cf. esp. Hagen, *Anecd. Helv. = GL* 8, clxiv–clxvii. The citations appear to be derived from Charisius (q.v., no. 200), and the name "Flavianus" is probably a mistaken interpretation of his nomenclature, "Fl(avius) Sosipater Charisius." Cf. s.v Priscianus, no. 126, for similarly mistaken expansions of "Fl." in the name "Fl. Theodorus."

* 220. FLAVIUS.   Gramm.

A γραμματικός, addressee of a letter on a wooden tablet, *SB* 1.5941 = Maspéro, "Études" 150ff. The letter offers some circumstantial touches: a precise date, 21 September 510 (cf. Sijpesteijn and Worp, "Chronological Notes" 273 n. 21); appropriate honorific titles for the gramm. in lines 1–2 recto, [Φ]λαυίῳ [τῷδε] τῷ εὐλογιωτάτῳ γραμματικῷ [cf. *PMonac.* 14.29f., an. 594] καὶ παιδευτῇ Ἑλληνικῶν λόγων ἐλευθερίων; a specific occupation for the writer in line 3 recto, παρὰ Αὐρηλίου τοῦδε πραγματευτοῦ ὀθονιακοῦ. Nonetheless, the document is revealed to be a practice exercise or formulary by its use of generalized names (Φλαύιος ὅδε, Αὐρήλιος ὅδε), by such expressions as ἐγὼ . . . ὁ δῖνα τοῦδε (lines 2f. verso), and by the verso's disjointed contents. For this kind of practice draft, see *SB* 1.6000 (s.VI), *APF* 1902–3, 183 no. 1 (s.VII); cf. *SB* 4.7433 (s.V med.), 7434 (s.II), 7435 (s.VI). We are therefore not dealing with a real gramm. here. It is worth remarking, however, that this notional gramm. is given the name "Flavius"—and thus a status higher than that of the πραγματευτής, an Aurelius; cf. Chap. 3 pp. 109f.—and that he is presumed to be married and to have some purchasing power; cf. lines 3f. verso, ὑμᾶς τοὺς πριαμένους Φλαύιον τόνδε καὶ τήνδε τὴν γαμετήν σου.

221. **ATILIUS FORTUNATIANUS.** Gramm. *Aet. incert.*; before s.IV?

RE 2.2082–83 (Consbruch); Sch.-Hos. 4:1.148–49; *PLRE* I s.v. 2, p. 369.

Author of an *Ars* on meter, *GL* 6.278–304, dedicated to a member of a senatorial family (6.278.3–5); the exposition emphasizes the *Horatiana metra*. F. was a gramm., the former teacher of the dedicatee; cf. 6.279.3–4, *cum artem grammaticam et intellexeris apud me et memoriae mandaveris diligenter.*

There is no indication of F.'s precise date; Consbruch, *RE* 2.2083, conjectured s.III ex. or s.IV init. But note that F. mentions the praetorship evidently as an important office calling for eloquence and standing high in the traditional senatorial cursus: 6.278.4–6, *ut eloquentia senatoriam cumules dignitatem (quid enim pulchrius disertissimo praetore? aut quid sublimius eloquentissimo consule?).* Such a conception of the praetorship should indicate a date before s.IV, unless the passage is intentionally archaizing. Note also that the only source F. cites by name, Philoxenus (6.302.20), belongs to s.I B.C.; cf. Theodoridis, *Fragmente* 3ff. If these hints suffice to date F. before s.IV, he cannot be the dedicatee of Servius's *De metris Horatii*, named at *GL* 4.468.3, *Servius Fortunatiano D̄N̄*. For a more likely candidate, see *PLRE* I s.v. Fortunatianus 3, p. 369.

222. **T. GALLUS.** Gramm.? Vergilian commentator.   s.V / s.VI?

Sch.-Hos. 2.108f.; *PLRE* II s.v. 2, p. 492.

Titus Gallus: subscr. to the *Buc.* in the *Scholia Bernensia, haec omnia de commentariis Romanorum congregavi, id est Titi Galli et Gaudentii et maxime Iunilii Flagrii Mediolanensis* (-*ses* codd. Bern. BC: -*tium* cod. Voss.); subscr. to *Georg.* 1, †*Titus Gallus de tribus commentariis Gaudentius* [codd. Bern. BC: -*tii* cod. Voss.] *haec fecit.* Elsewhere Gallus.

Commentator on the *Bucolica*(?) and *Georgica*, known only from the *Scholia Bernensia*; cited by name only in the scholia to *Georg.* 1. His contribution to the scholia on the *Buc.* will be established only if the subscr. noted above is in fact that, and not an inscr. to *Georg.* 1; on the problem, cf. Wessner, "Bericht" 208f.

His date can be established only conjecturally and with no great precision—s.V / s.VI? Cf. Funaioli, *Esegesi* 398; cf. also s.vv. Iunius Filargirius, Gaudentius, nos. 60, 223.

223. **GAUDENTIUS.** Gramm.? Vergilian commentator.   s.V / s.VI?

RE 7.857–58 (Funaioli); Sch.-Hos. 2.108f.; *PLRE* II s.v. 10, p. 495.

Commentator on the *Bucolica* and *Georgica*, known by name from the *Scholia Bernensia*: see the subscr. to the *Buc.* and to *Georg.* 1, quoted s.v.

T. Gallus, no. 222; cf. *passim* in the scholia. Also cited by name in a commentary on Orosius, in a note that corresponds to *Schol. Bern.* on *Georg.* 4.387; cf. Lehmann, "Reste" 199.

He can be dated only very tentatively (s.V / s.VI?), on the grounds of his seeming dependence on Servius. Cf. also s.v. Iunius Filargirius, no. 60, and s.v. T. Gallus.

* 224. GORGON(I)US.   Teacher?   Rome.   s.IV / s.VI.

Gorgon(i)us *magister*, a Christian, on an epitaph set up by his wife Ianuar(i)a, *ILCV* 720 (Rome): *Ianuar(i)a co(n)iugi benemerenti Gorgon(i)o magistro primo.* The last word was added by a later hand; between *magistro* and *primo* (i.e., at the end of the original inscr.) and running vertically there is a drawing of what might be a *volumen* or a *capsa*; cf. De Rossi, *Roma* 2, pls. 45–46 no. 43.

225. GRILLIUS.   Rhetorician.   Before Priscian; s.IV / s.V?

RE 7.1876–79 (Münscher); Sch.-Hos. 4:2.263–64; *PLRE* I s.v., p. 404.

Cited by Priscian as *ad Vergilium de accentibus scribens*, *GL* 2.35.24ff. The citation concerns marks of aspiration. Author also of a commentary on Cic. *De inv.*, partially preserved: *Rhet. Lat. min.* 596ff., *Excerpta ex Grilli commento in primum Ciceronis librum de inventione.* The latter evidence esp. suggests that he was a rhetorician rather than a grammarian.

His date is uncertain: before Priscian (q.v., no. 126), who cites him; later than Eusebius (q.v., no. 212), whom he cites. According to the catalogue of Amplonius Ratinck (an. 1412), G. also composed commentaries *super Topicam Marci Tullii Cyceronis* and *super libris 5 Boecii de consolatu philosophico*; cf. Manitius, *Handschriften* 233. (I am indebted to C. E. Murgia and D. R. Shanzer for alerting me to this notice.) The latter, if authentic, could not have been written before s.VI 2/4—a fact difficult to reconcile with Priscian's citation of G., though conceivably consistent with it if G. was Priscian's younger contemporary. The notice, however, is probably worthless. Note that the same source provides other, certainly spurious attributions: a commentary by Fulgentius on the *De nupt. Merc. et Philol.* of "Martialis" and a commentary by Cassiodorus on Boeth. *De consol. phil.*; cf. Manitius, *Handschriften* 302, 320.

226. HARPOCRATION.   Gramm. or, more probably, sophist.   Egypt → Antioch → Constantinople.   Born not after ca. 335, and not before ca. 324; dead not before 363.

RE 7.2410 (Seeck; cf. id., *Briefe* 131, 298); Schemmel, "Sophist" 58; Bouchery, *Themistius* 107ff.; Petit, *Étudiants* 86; *PLRE* I s.v., p. 408.

The subject of Lib. *Ep.* 364, 368 (both an. 358), 818 (an. 363). An Egyptian (*Ep.* 368.2) and a poet (*Ep.* 364.5), H. was an instructor of rhetoric (less likely a gramm.) with his long-time friend and fellow student Eudaemon (q.v., no. 210), at Antioch in 358, perhaps in Libanius's school. In that year Themistius invited him (Libanius says ἐβιάσω, with evident hyperbole) to come to Constantinople as a sophist (*Ep.* 368).

His position at Antioch and his relation to Eudaemon are controversial; for relevant texts and detailed discussion, see s.v. Eudaemon. The reason for Themistius's summons is also a matter of discussion. For the view that H. went to Constantinople to teach, see Seeck, *Briefe* 298; for the view that his summons was part of Themistius's attempt to expand the senate of the new capital, see Bouchery, *Themistius* 107ff.

H. was a friend of both Themistius and Libanius in 363 (*Ep.* 818). Since H. seems to have been a close contemporary of Eudaemon, any conclusions regarding the latter's chronology (see s.v.) should also apply to H.

H. cannot be Aur. Harpocration the panegyrist from Panopolis (s.IV 2/4) mentioned in *PKöln* inv. 4533ᵛ (see Browne, "Panegyrist" and "Harpocration"); the latter was dead before 358. Identification with other literary Harpocrationes is uncertain; cf. *RE* 7.2416f., s.v. nos. 6, 7, 10.

227. HELLADIUS. Gramm.? Antinoopolis. s.IV init.

RE 8.98–102 no. 2 (Gudeman), 8.103 no. 4 (Seeck); Chr.-Sch.-St. 2:2.974; *PLRE* I s.v. 1, p. 412.

Helladius son of Besantinous: Phot. *Bibl.* cod. 279 (8.170 Henry), Ἑλλαδίου Βησαντινόου; Photius mistook Βησαντινόου for a toponym (8.187 Henry), although according to Gudeman, *RE* 8.98.44ff., the error was not new with him.

Author of a Χρηστομάθειαι excerpted by Photius (*Bibl.* cod. 279) and originally written in iambics (8.187 Henry). Photius does not style him γραμματικός, though the excerpts reveal a man with pronounced grammatical interests; this caused Gudeman to imagine that the work was composed for school use (*RE* 8.100.33ff.). Gudeman's comparison with Aulus Gellius (ibid. 28f.) is, however, more apt, and points away from the schoolroom. Note esp. that, like Gellius, H. prefers the usage of the ancients to the rules of the *grammatici*; cf. esp. 8.180 Henry, οἱ Ἀττικοί vs. οἱ γραμματικοὶ τεχνολογοῦντες; 8.181 Henry, Ἀριστοφάνης vs. οἱ γραμματικοί. H.'s views and his manner of expression suggest a distance from the professionals.

A native of Antinoopolis (8.187 Henry; cf. below) "in the time of Licinius and Maximianus": 8.187 Henry, γέγονε δὲ κατὰ τοὺς χρόνους

Λικιννίου καὶ Μαξιμιανοῦ; the verb γέγονε is ambiguous; cf. s.v. Lupercus, no. 91.

In addition to the Χρηστομάθειαι in at least four books (8.170 Henry), H. is credited with eight other poems, also in iambics: 8.187 Henry, Ἀθῆναι, Νεῖλος, Αἰγύπτιος, Προτρεπτικός, ᾽Ρώμη, Φήμη, Νίκη, Πόλις ᾽Αντινόου. Photius inferred that he was a pagan (8.187 Henry). Though Photius's conclusions are not always reliable (cf. s.v. Ioannes Lydus, no. 92), note the passage on the supposed leprosy of Moses (8.170 Henry), which appears to place H. in a long and largely Alexandrian tradition of anti-Jewish exodus stories; cf. Gager, "Moses." The passage in H., with its reference to a Philo, is printed as a fragment of the Περὶ Ἰουδαίων of Philo of Byblos, FGrH IIIc, 790F11; but Gager, "Moses" 248, connected it with Philo Alexand. Mos. 1.79 (4.138.7ff. Cohn), on Exodus 4.6.

* 228. AUR. HERODES.   Teacher.   Karanis.   299.

Signatory of two declarations of land lying in different districts of Karanis, owned by Aur. Isidorus and by Herois, his mother: PCairIsid. 3.41, Αὐρήλιος Ἡρώδης διδάσκαλος· παρ᾽ ἐμοὶ ἐτελέσθη; 4.21 (the same). The declarations were made for the census of 297 and were executed in September 299 for the censitor Iulius Septimius Sabinus (= Sabinus 17 PLRE I, p. 794).

On the διδάσκαλος acting as secretary of the district, cf. PCairIsid. pp. 42f. at line 41; Lallemand, Administration 176; and s.vv. Aur. Plution, Anonymus 14, nos. 248, 278. The διδάσκαλοι in these documents were evidently acting in an unofficial capacity: such declarations are equally valid with or without the signature of the διδάσκαλος; cf. PCairIsid. pp. 42f. Cf. also s.vv. Sosistratus (SB 6.9270), no. 260 = Anonymus 15 (SB 6.9191), no. 279.

229. HESPERIUS.   Gramm.(?) or, more probably, rhetorician.   Clermont-Ferrand.   s.V 2/2.

Sch.-Hos. 4:2.269; PLRE II s.v. 2, p. 552.

Teacher to whom Ruricius of Limoges commended his son: Ep. 1.3, CSEL 21.356.16ff., ita et tenerorum adhuc acies sensuum ignorantiae nubilo quasi crassitate scabrosae rubiginis obsessa, nisi adsidua doctoris lima purgetur, nequit sponte clarescere. It is not clear from the context whether he taught grammar or rhetoric; but since Ruricius's phrasing does not suggest that his son was only beginning his education, and since much is made of H.'s eloquentia in the other two letters he receives from Ruricius (1.4, p. 356.24ff., and 1.5, p. 357.23ff.), he probably taught the latter. H. is styled devinctissimus filius semperque magnificus Hesperius in the salutations.

H. is probably the Hesperius who received Sidon. Apoll. *Ep.* 2.10 (469 or early 470: Loyen, ed., 2.247) and who is mentioned in Sidon. Apoll. *Ep.* 4.22.1 (late 476 or 477: Loyen, ed., 2.254). At the time of *Ep.* 2.10 he was a *iuvenis* (2.10.1) interested in poetry and oratory, apparently still as a student; cf. 2.10.1, *cum videmus in huiusmodi disciplinam iuniorum ingenia succrescere, propter quam nos quoque subduximus ferulae manum.* He was, however, already anticipating marriage: *Ep.* 2.10.5, *propediem coniunx domum feliciter ducenda.* At the time of *Ep.* 4.22 he was evidently settled at Clermont-Ferrand. The letter calls him *vir magnificus* (cf. above) and *gemma amicorum litterarumque.*

230. HIEROCLES.   Gramm.?   s.III 2/2 / s.IV?

RE Suppl. 11.687 (Thierfelder), cf. ibid. 1062–68 (id.); Chr.-Sch.-St. 2:2.1049f.

Compiler of jokes; gramm., according to(?) the inscr. of the longer version of the Φιλόγελως: cod. Paris. suppl. gr. 690, Φιλόγελως ἐκ τῶν Ἱεροκλέους καὶ Φιλαγρίου γραμματικῶν. But γραμματικοῦ is reported for this inscr. in the most recent edition, by A. Thierfelder (1968); cf. cod. Monac. gr. 551, Φιλόγελως ἐκ τῶν Ἱεροκλέους καὶ Φιλαγρίου γραμματικοῦ. The briefer version of the compilation (= recension β) is simply inscribed ἐκ τοῦ Ἱεροκλέους συντάγματα. On the date of the collection, see s.v. Philagrius, no. 117.

231. HIERONYMUS.   Gramm.(?) or, more probably, rhetorician.   Elusa → Egypt → Elusa → Hermopolis.   s.V 4/4 / s.VI 1/4.

RE 8.1565 (Münscher); Chr.-Sch.-St. 2:2.1028; Garzya and Loenertz, eds., *Procopii . . . epistolae* pp. xxxi–xxxii s.v. Jérôme A (cf. also p. xxix); *PLRE* II s.v. 2, pp. 560f.

Recipient of Procop. Gaz. *Ep.* 2, 9, 81, 86, 91, 124. On *Ep.* 57, see below *ad fin.*

From his πατρίς (*Ep.* 2.13f.), Elusa (*Ep.* 9.7, 81.4, 91.21, 124.2), H. went to Egypt, where he taught (*Ep.* 2.2ff.). Procopius suggests that he made the change to improve his prospects (*Ep.* 2.24ff.). He soon returned (*Ep.* 2.1ff., 9.1ff.) and married (*Ep.* 2.28ff., Procopius's congratulations; *Ep.* 9.11f., the anticipation of a child). He returned to Egypt (*Ep.* 81.1ff.; cf. 86.1f.) and taught at a city upriver from Alexandria (*Ep.* 86.3f.), viz., Hermopolis (*Ep.* 124.5). Procopius says that H. had abandoned his wife and child (*Ep.* 91.38f.), although they are with him by the time of *Ep.* 124 (§16).

It is not simply stated whether he taught as a gramm. or as a rhetorician: e.g., he is variously said to be teaching παῖδες (*Ep.* 2.2ff., 91.34ff.), νέοι (*Ep.* 2.6), and μειράκια (*Ep.* 91.14), with no evident distinction. But he was concerned or had occasion in his teaching to use language reminiscent of the sophist Aelius Aristides; cf. *Ep.* 91.14f., τί δῆτα τῶν μειρακίων προκαθεζόμενος οἴει τι μέγα φέρειν Ἀριστείδου . . . , εἰ λέγοις ὡς αὐτός. Further, he could claim a training in rhetoric (*Ep.* 91.27, τὰ Δημοσθένους εἰδέναι ποιουμένου), and he apparently took offense that Procopius addressed him as an inferior (*Ep.* 91.5ff., 24ff.). He is therefore more likely to have been a rhetorician.

H. is not to be identified with Stephanus the recipient of *Ep.* 57, *pace* Garzya and Loenertz, eds., *Procopii . . . epistolae* pp. xxix, xxxi–xxxii; see s.v. Stephanus, no. 142.

+ 232. HIERONYMUS.   Gramm.?   s.IV 2/2 / s.VII 2/2.
Sch.-Hos. 4:1.163.

A grammatical writer, *ut vid.*; cited three times—twice as Hieronimus, once as Hieronymus—in the *Ars Ambrosiana*, an anonymous commentary on Book 2 of the *Ars maior* of Donatus: pp. 22.386, 24.454f., 132.140 ed. B. Löfstedt; cf. Sabbadini, "Spogli" 170; Manitius, *Geschichte der lateinischen Literatur* 1.520f.; Law, *Insular Latin Grammarians* 93–97.

Of uncertain date, probably after Donatus and before the latter part of s.VII, when the commentary seems to have been composed (B. Löfstedt, ed., p. vii). The *term. a. q.* depends on one Old Irish gloss that occurs in the text and is datable to ca. 700. Law, *Insular Latin Grammarians* 94 n. 73, remarks the possibility that the gloss "was present in a source-text and was copied by the author of the *Ars Ambrosiana*. If this is so, the *terminus ante quem* would be set by the date of the manuscript alone" (s.IX / s.X init.).

Cf. s.v. Nepos, no. 240. For suggested identification of H. with St. Jerome, cf. Tolkiehn, "Kirchenvater," with Lammert, "Grammatiker," and Tolkiehn, "Noch einmal."

233. HOËN(I)US.   Gramm.?   Poet.   Gaul.   s.V med.
Sch.-Hos. 4:2.269; *PLRE* II s.v., p. 566.

Gallic poet and apparently a teacher of Sidonius Apollinaris: *Carm.* 9.311ff., *nostrum aut quos retinet solum disertos, / dulcem Anthedion et mihi magistri / Musas sat venerabiles Hoëni.* As teacher of Sidonius he would have been active in the 440s; the connection with poetry might suggest that he was a gramm., but that is not certain. For the suggestion that he taught grammar at Arles, cf. Stevens, *Sidonius* 11.

* 234. LEONTIUS.   Gramm.   Nicomedia.   s.III ex.

Teacher of the saint Eustathius who was martyred with his brothers, Thespesius and Anatolius, in the Great Persecution under Maximian:

Halkin, ed., "Passion" 292 §2, αὐξησάντων δὲ αὐτῶν, δίδωσιν ὁ Φιλόθεος
[sc. ὁ πατὴρ] Εὐστάθιον τὸν υἱὸν αὐτοῦ μαΐστορί τινι γραμματικῷ ὀνόματι
Λεοντίῳ διδάξαι αὐτὸν κατὰ λόγον τὴν γραμματικήν.

The *passio* belongs to the genre of *passions épiques*; cf. Halkin, ed.,
"Passion" 288. Its information is not to be taken at face value; L. may be
a fiction (cf. s.v. Babylas, no. 192). Note, however, that the author probably strives for a degree of verisimilitude in describing the circumstances
of Eustathius's education: the father, a βεστιοπράτης selling his wares in
Nicaea and Nicomedia, gave only Eustathius, his eldest son, a formal
literary education, and that only in grammar; thereafter Eustathius joined
his father and brothers at their trade; cf. the sentence quoted above with
the sentences that follow it, καὶ τοὺς ἄλλους δύο παῖδας [A: παῖδας
ἐκπαιδεύσας P] εἶχεν εἰς τὸ ἐργαστήριον. μαθόντος δὲ Εὐσταθίου, κἀκεῖνον
εἶχεν παρ᾽ ἑαυτῷ.

235. **LUXURIUS.** Gramm.(?: unlikely) and poet; *vir clarissimus et spectabilis.*
Africa, probably Carthage. s.V ex. / s.VI 1/3.

RE 4.2102–9 (Levy); Sch.-Hos. 4:2.73f.; Szövérffy, *Weltliche Dichtungen*
1.178f., 186f.; *PLRE* II s.v. Luxorius, p. 695; *Prosop. chrét.* I s.v. Luxorius,
p. 655.

Luxurius: on the form of the name, against "Luxorius," see Happ,
"Luxurius." Epigrammatic poet (*Anth. Lat.* 1:1.18, 203, 287–375 = 91,
90, 1–89 Rosenblum) and apparently dedicatee of the *Liber de finalibus* of
Coronatus (q.v., no. 204) *scholasticus.*

L. lived in Africa, probably in Carthage; see *Anth. Lat.* 1:1.330.1 = 44.1
R., *Tyriis*; cf. Rosenblum, *Luxorius* 44, who is perhaps too skeptical. He
can be dated to the end of the fifth century and the first third of the
sixth; cf. *Anth. Lat.* 1:1.203 = 90R., written under Hilderic (523–30); cf.
also Rosenblum, *Luxorius* 43.

L. is commonly said to have been a gramm. (see below), but direct
evidence is lacking. He is styled *vir clarissimus et spectabilis* in the inscr. of
Anth. Lat. 1:1.18 = 91R. and of the *liber epigrammaton* = 287–375 = 1–
89R.; contrast the case of Calbulus (q.v., no. 23). The arguments in
favor of the claim that L. was a gramm. fall well short of probability; and
the substance of *Anth. Lat.* 1:1.287 = 1R. shows fairly clearly that L. was
not a gramm.

There are two arguments adduced in favor of L.'s having been a
gramm., for which cf. esp. Schubert, *Quaestionum . . . pars I* 24f., with
Levy, *RE* 13.2104.29ff., and Rosenblum, *Luxorius* 38. The arguments are
as follows.

First, L. is the dedicatee of the grammatical work, *Liber de finalibus*, by
Coronatus *scholasticus*; cf. the dedicatory epistle, with the salutation

Domino eruditissimorum [cod. Monac. 14252: *domino viro eruditissimo peritis-simorum* cod. S. Paul. in vall. Lavant. 24] *atque inlustri fratri Luxorio Corona-tus*, published by Keil, *De grammaticis* 4 n. (cf. *GL* 4, 1) = Rosenblum, *Luxorius* 259. But it is not likely that Coronatus himself was a gramm. (see s.v.), and the references to L.'s learning that occur in the epistle are commonplaces, too vague to have any specific probative value; cf., e.g., *peritiam tuam et ardorem tui excellentiorem ingenii* or *in tuo gremio sofistarum* [N.B.] *novi cuncta versari* or *fallere nequivisset, quod tu proba diligas ac defendas, et quae <in>utilia et inepta cognoscas te saepius damnare cognovi.* Rosenblum's translation of the salutation, *Luxorius* 259, "To Luxorius, most learned teacher," etc., is incorrect.

Second, L.'s status as a gramm. has been inferred from *Anth. Lat.* 1:1.287 = 1R., with L.'s address to the gramm. Faustus (q.v., no. 58) as *nostro . . . animo probate conpar* (v. 3) and his request that Faustus circulate the poems *per nostri similes . . . sodales* (v. 14). But the expressions simply mean that the two were friends, not coprofessionals. Note that the conventional argument, if valid, would necessarily imply that L. had requested his poems be circulated only among his fellow gramm. Note too that on the same argument Sidon. Apoll. *Carm.* 24, with the gramm. Domitius included among the poet's *sodales*, would prove that Sidonius was a gramm. also.

Against these arguments, it is important to notice that L. asks Faustus not simply to circulate the poems but to review and approve them first:

> [versus] transmisi memori tuo probandos
> primum pectore; deinde, si libebit,
> discretos titulis, quibus tenentur,
> per nostri similes dato sodales.
> nam si doctiloquis nimisque magnis
> haec tu credideris viris legenda,
> culpae nos socios notabit index—
> tam te, talia qui bonis recenses,
> quam me, qui tua duriora iussa
> feci nescius, immemor futuri.
>
> (*Anth. Lat.* 1:1.287.11–20)

In other words, L. is emphasizing and relying upon the special compe-tence of Faustus *qua* gramm.—cf. v. 4, *tantus grammaticae magister artis*—to judge the quality of his poetry. The motif is found elsewhere in late-antique Latin poetry; cf. Sidon. Apoll. *Carm.* 24.10ff., where the *libellus* of Sidonius is told to go first to the gramm. Domitius, a stern critic: vv. 14–15, *sed gaudere potes rigore docto: / hic si te probat, omnibus placebis.* The implications are similar: the man who sends the poems (L. or Sidonius) affects to recognize in the gramm. an expertise he himself either does not possess, or possesses in smaller measure. There is a distance established between the sender and the recipient; the poem's implied protocol shows that L. like Sidonius was not a gramm. by profession.

It remains to be pointed out that if L. was not a gramm., one of the main supports vanishes for identifying L. with Lisorius, a poet and writer on orthography of unknown date before s.XI; cf. Happ, "Zur Lisorius-Frage." That identification is unlikely on other grounds; cf. S. Mariotti, "Luxorius."

236. MANIPPUS or MARSIPUS.   Gramm., or rhetorician, or both?   Carchar (Mesopotamia).   276/82.

RE 14.1146 (Dörries); *PLRE* I s.v. Manippus, p. 541.

One of four judges in the debate between Mani and the bishop Archelaus (*claruit sub imperatore Probo*, Jer. *De vir. ill.* 72) composed by Hegemonius, which survives in a defective Latin trans., *Acta Archelai* (s.IV 2/2?), and which Epiphan. *Panar. haeres.* 66.10ff. draws upon.

Manippus: *Acta Arch.* 12. Or Marsipus: Epiphan. *Panar. haeres.* 66.10.2. A pagan and *vir primarius* (*Acta Arch.*) of Carchar (Κασχάρης, Epiphan.). M. is described in the *Acta Arch.* as *grammaticae artis* [*grammaticus* cod. Ambros. O. Sup. 210] *et disciplinae rhetoricae peritissimus*, the phrase corresponding to τὸν . . . τῶν ἐκτὸς λόγων φιλόσοφον in Epiphan.; *peritissimus* corresponds to ὁ φιλόσοφος exactly as *grammatica ars et disciplina rhetorica* does to οἱ ἐκτὸς λόγοι (i.e., ἡ ἔξω παιδεία). M. was therefore either the local teacher of liberal letters or simply a cultured man. The point matters little, however, since the historicity of the debate is very doubtful.

The other judges appear as follows in the two versions: Claudius and Cleobulus, *duo fratres egregii rhetores* vs. τὸν δὲ ἰατροσοφιστήν, . . . καὶ τὸν ἄλλον σοφιστήν; Aegialeus, *archiater nobilissimus et litteris apprime eruditus* vs. τὸν δὲ φύσει γραμματικόν.

Cf. s.v. Aegialeus, no. 179.

237. NONIUS MARCELLUS.   Gramm.? (unlikely.)   Tubursicum Numidarum. s.III init. / s.VI init. (s.IV init.?).

RE 17.882–97 (Strzelecki); Sch.-Hos. 4:1.142; Lindsay, ed., *Nonii . . . libri* pp. xiii–xiv; *PLRE* I s.v. 11, p. 552.

Nonius Marcellus: *De compendiosa doctrina* tit.; Priscian *GL* 2.35.20, 269.20f., 499.20f. Though often assumed to have been a *grammaticus* because of the character of his extant work (see below), he is not likely to have been a professional gramm.; the style *Peripateticus* in *De comp. doctr.* tit., whatever it may have meant to M., suggests that his cultural ambitions lay elsewhere. He is to be associated with the learned amateurs—e.g.,

Aulus Gellius, Ti. Claudius Donatus, Macrobius—who dedicate their works to their sons; cf. *De comp. doctr.* tit., *ad filium*. A professional gramm. dedicates his work to friends, patrons, or pupils; no man known to be a professional gramm. in late antiquity dedicates a work to a son or other family member. Cf. s.v. Fl. Sosipater Charisius, no. 200; Chap. 2 at nn. 142, 152, 153.

Called *Tubursicensis* in *De comp. doctr.* tit., M. is probably identical with or a relative of Nonius Marcellus Herculius of Tubursicum Numidarum, who is honored in *CIL* 8.4878 = *ILS* 2943 = Inscr.

Later than Gellius, whom he does not name but clearly used; likewise later than Septimius Serenus (e.g., 61.26M. = 86L.) and Apuleius (68.21M. = 96L.), whom he cites. Earlier than Priscian, who cites him (see above). Inscr. is probably to be dated to 326/33. Constantine is the sole *Augustus*; Constantine and one of his brothers are *Caesares*: if the brother is Crispus, the date will be between late September and early November 324; or, more likely, if the brother is Constantius, the date will be between 326 and 333. But since M.'s relation to the dedicator is unknown, it is difficult to use Inscr. for dating. On the subscription to Persius, dated to 402 and attached to an abridgment of *De comp. doctr.*, see Clausen, "Sabinus' MS."

Author of the *De compendiosa doctrina* (cited as *de doctorum indagine* by Priscian at *GL* 2.35.20 and 269.20f.), a collection of lexicographical, morphological, and antiquarian lore in twenty books. Also author of *Epistolae a doctrinis de peregrinando*, a lost work of unknown content referred to at *De comp. doctr.* 451.11M. = 723 L.

His family was evidently of some local importance in the early fourth century; Inscr. mentions restorations of a public street and of baths and other buildings by Nonius Marcellus Herculius.

238. MARCIANUS.   Imperial tutor of grammar (ca. 366) and Novatian presbyter → bishop.   Constantinople.   Died 395.
PLRE I s.v. 8, p. 554.

M.'s career is sketched by Socrates *HE* 4.9.4 (= Soz. *HE* 6.9.3; *Suda* M.207), 5.21.1–4 (= Soz. 7.14.2–3), 6.1.9 (= Soz. 8.1.9).

A virtuous and eloquent man: Soc. 4.9.4, εὐλαβὴς ἐν ταὐτῷ καὶ ἐλλόγιμος (in Socrates' usage ἐλλόγιμος regularly means "eloquent" *vel. sim.* rather than "reputable," "well regarded"); cf. the version of Soz. 6.9.3, drawing on Soc., ἐπὶ βίῳ καὶ λόγοις θαυμαζόμενος. M. had been in the palatine service for some time before being chosen to teach γραμματικοὶ λόγοι to Anastasia and Carosa, the daughters of Valens (Soc. ibid.). He was a Novatian presbyter at the time; out of regard for him Valens relaxed his persecutions of the Novatians: Soc. ibid.; cf. 5.21.3. The date will have been ca. 366; cf. Soc. 4.9.7–8.

M. became Novatian bishop of Constantinople in 384 or 385 (Soc. 5.21.1–4); he was succeeded by Sisinnius in November 395 (Soc. 6.1.9), who was in turn succeeded by M.'s son, Chrysanthus, in 407 (Soc. 7.6.10) or 412 (cf. Soc. 7.17.1); the later date is probably correct. For the career of Chrysanthus, cf. Soc. 7.12.1ff., with *PLRE* I s.v., p. 203. In 419 Chrysanthus was succeeded by Paulus (q.v., no. 116; Soc. 7.17.1); Paulus in turn was succeeded in 438 by Marcianus (Soc. 7.46.1), who was perhaps M.'s grandson.

M. is to be treated not as a gramm. but as one of a select group of teachers in the fourth and early fifth centuries, the tutors at the imperial court; none of them came to his position as a gramm. For survey and comment, see Chap. 3 at n. 167; note M.'s prior service as a *palatinus*.

239. "METRORIUS."

A name incorrectly derived from the title of a treatise *De finalibus metrorum*, *GL* 6.229ff., METRORŪ giving rise to METRORII; cf. Wessner, *RE* 14.1847.43ff.; cf. also s.v. "Sergius," no. 255. Apart from the mss that carry the work, the name is also found in the catalogues of gramm. in codd. Bonon. 797 (cf. Negri, "De codice" 266) and Bern. 243 (cf. Hagen, *Anecd. Helv.* = *GL* 8, cxlix–cl) and in a library catalogue of s.IX from Lorsch (Manitius, *Handschriften* 178).

240. NEPOS.　Gramm.?　s.IV 2/2 / s.VII 2/2.

RE 16.2511 (Ensslin); Sch.-Hos. 4:1.163; *PLRE* I s.v., p. 623.

A grammatical writer, *ut vid.*, whose clarifications of Aelius Donatus are twice cited in the *Ars Ambrosiana*, an anonymous commentary on Book 2 of Donatus's *Ars Maior*; cf. pp. 150.226f., 152.266ff. ed. B. Löfstedt. For the date of the commentary, see s.v. Hieronymus, no. 232.

N. is perhaps the Nepos to whom the otherwise unattested neuter form *culmum* is attributed in the *De dub. nom.*: *GL* 5.576.12, *culmum generis neutri, ut Nepos vult*. The work is a compilation concerning nouns of dubious gender, with examples drawn from *auctores* sacred and profane ranging from the Psalms to Isidore of Seville; its date is therefore later than s.VII 1/3. The passage on *culmus*, however, is rather confused—a use of *culmus* in the feminine is mistakenly attributed to Vergil—and the republican author Cornelius Nepos might be meant, since the Nepos who is cited appears in the company of Cicero, Varro, and Vergil; attribution to Cornelius Nepos is assumed by *OLD* s.v. *culmus*.

241. FL. OPTATUS.　Teacher of letters? *Patricius* and *consul*.　Born s.III 3/3; died 337.

RE 18.760–61 (Ensslin); *PLRE* I s.v. 3, p. 650; Booth, "Some Suspect Schoolmasters" 5f.

Uncle of the Optatus who was the target of Lib. *Or*. 42 *Pro Thalassio*; for the relationship, see *Or*. 42.26–27. *Patricius* and *consul prior* of 334; for this part of his career, see Ensslin, *RE* 18.760–61; and *PLRE* I s.v. 3, p. 650.

Libanius says O. began as a γραμμάτων διδάσκαλος, ὃς καὶ Λικιννίῳ τὸν παῖδα ταῦτα ἐδίδασκεν ἀπὸ δυοῖν ἄρτοιν καὶ τῆς ἄλλης τροφῆς ἢ τούτοις συνέζευκται, a "teacher of letters, who taught Licinius's son in return for a couple of wheaten loaves and the other nourishment that goes with them" (*Or*. 42.26). After Licinius fell, in 324, O. allegedly came into prominence thanks to his wife, the daughter of a Paphlagonian innkeeper; she was, Libanius implies, liberal with her favors (*Or*. 42.26).

Since Valerius Licinianus Licinius was born in mid-315, O. would not have had him as a pupil before 321 or 322; he could therefore have been imperial tutor for two or three years before the end of Licinius's reign. Probably born sometime in s.III 3/3, he was executed in 337 (Zos. 2.40.2). But it is difficult to derive other firm conclusions from *Or*. 42.26, for three reasons.

First, some account must be taken of Libanius's exuberant invective, which runs through the speech as a whole; cf. esp. the notorious rogues' gallery of parvenus assembled at *Or*. 42.23–24. The author's animus is manifest in *Or*. 42.26, both in the insultingly low, if not actually servile, wage that Libanius specifies and in his sneers at the origins and behavior of O.'s wife.

Second, the phrase γραμμάτων διδάσκαλος is evidently intended *per se* as a sneer at O.'s origins. The phrase is the peg on which Libanius hangs his elaborate sarcasm at the beginning of *Or*. 42.26, sharply distinguishing his opponent's antecedents from the empire's ruling elite: αὐτὸς τοίνυν οὗτος τίνων ἐστίν; ἆρά γε τῶν ʿΡώμην κτισάντων ἢ τῶν τοὺς νόμους θέντων ἢ τῶν ὑπηκόους κτησαμένων ἢ τῶν τὸ κτηθὲν φυλαξάντων; οὐ μὰ Δία, ἀλλ᾽ ἦν τις ʿΟπτάτος γραμμάτων διδάσκαλος. For the assumption that the offspring of a man who earned his living διδάσκων γράμματα would normally be subject to contempt, see Dio Chrys. *Or*. 7.114; cf. esp. Demosth. *De cor*. 258, Demosthenes' attack on the background of Aeschines, which might have inspired Libanius here. For other evidence of the same social bias, cf. Booth, "Some Suspect Schoolmasters" and "Image" 2. Further, though γραμμάτων διδάσκαλος (= γραμματοδιδάσκαλος) is denotatively equivalent to γραμματιστής, Libanius here notably avoids the latter term, which he regularly uses as an honorable title for teachers of liberal letters, i.e., grammarians; on this see Appendix 2. His use of γραμμάτων διδάσκαλος is probably intended to suggest that O. was nothing more than a lowly teacher of nonliberal letters; see Kaster, "Notes" 340.

But, third, that O.'s estate was so low is difficult to believe. Eunuchs aside, of the seven persons known to have taught the children of reigning emperors throughout the fourth century, not one came to his position as a *grammaticus*, much less as a still humbler "teacher of letters." (For a list, see Chap. 3 n. 167; cf. s.v. Marcianus, no. 238.) Most often, the tutor was a professional rhetorician; in the two decades immediately before and after O.'s tenure, one finds Lactantius, Exsuperius, and Ausonius's uncle Arborius. In view of all the above, then, we should conclude that Libanius is bending the truth: either the claims in the passage are mere fabrications intended to smear Libanius's opponent (so Booth, "Some Suspect Schoolmasters"), or, as seems more likely to me, O. was in fact an imperial tutor and, as such, probably a more prestigious man of letters than Libanius found it useful to admit.

242. PALLADIUS.   *Dign., loc., aet. incert.*; after s.IV 1/2(?); before s.VII ex.
RE 18:2(2).203 (Aly).

Name found in the title of the work of Audax (q.v., no. 190), *De Scauri et Palladii libris excerpta per interrogationem et responsionem*, GL 7.320ff. If P. is to be associated with the latter portion of the work (*GL* 7.349–57; cf. Keil, *GL* 7.318), which resembles sections of Probus *Inst. art.* (cf. *GL* 4.143ff.), then he may be the intermediary through whom the doctrine of the *Inst. art.* was transmitted to Audax. In that case, he could be dated sometime after s.IV 1/2 (?: see s.v. Probus, no. 127) and before s.VII ex., Audax's *term. a. q.* (see s.v.). The name suggests a late-antique date. He is not mentioned elsewhere.

243. PANISCUS.   Teacher.   Egypt (Panopolis?).   s.III med.

Paniscus διδάσκαλος, father of Tamuthes, on a mummy label dated 19 April 256: *Corp. ét.* no. 900, p. 76 = *CRIPEL* 1976–77, no. 563. The theophoric name "Paniscus" is closely associated with Panopolis; cf. V. Martin, "Relevé" 60.

244. PAPIRIANUS.   *Dign., loc., aet. incert.*: before s.VI init.; after s.IV med.?
RE 18:2(2).1001f. (Helm); Sch.-Hos. 4:2.218–19; PLRE I s.v. 2, pp. 666f.

Papirianus: Priscian *GL* 2.27.11, 31.2, 503.16, 593.14; Cassiod. *De orth.*, *GL* 7.158.9, *Inst.* 1.30.2. Also Paperianus: some codd. of Priscian and Cassiod. (see Keil's *app. crit.* at the passages cited just above); on this form of the name, cf. below.
    Author of a treatise *De orthographia*, cited by Priscian—therefore before s.VI init.—and excerpted by Cassiodorus, *GL* 7.158.9–165.6. (For the title, see Prisc. *GL* 2.27.12, 593.15.) An opinion attributed to P.

by Priscian, *GL* 2.503.16f., contradicts the corresponding passage in Cassiodorus's excerpt, *GL* 7.165.6. In the excerpt of Cassiodorus, at *GL* 7.161.14–16, a passage from Book 1 of Donatus's *Ars maior* is paraphrased: *GL* 4.367.12–14 = 604.1–2 Holtz. If the paraphrase stood in P.'s treatise, then he can be dated after s.IV med.; but since the paraphrase is placed at the end of a section to confirm what precedes—*sic et Donatus dicit*—it is equally likely to be Cassiodorus's addition. Cassiodorus felt free to make minor additions to the texts he was excerpting, as, e.g., comparison of the text of Martyrius (q.v., no. 95) with Cassiodorus's excerpts shows.

The other technical writers cited in the excerpt from P. are Velius Longus and Caesellius Vindex—both early s.II—and an unknown Gratus *artigraphus*. In Priscian, P. is cited in the company of Pliny and Probus (*GL* 2.31.2) and of Nisus and Probus (*GL* 2.503.16), all of s.I (if Probus is Valerius Probus). He is listed fourth at Cassiod. *De orth.* praef. (*GL* 7.147.7), after Curtius Valerianus (q.v., no. 271) and before Martyrius. Along with the other men listed there, P. is implicitly distinguished from Priscian, the *modernus auctor*; see also Cassiod. *Inst.* 1.30.2, where again P. stands between Curtius Valerianus and Martyrius and is classed among the *orthographi antiqui*; cf. also s.v. Curtius Valerianus.

P. is probably the Q. Papirius a fragment of whose work *De orthographia* is printed at *GL* 7.216.8–14; cf. *Quinti Papirii orthographia* listed with works of Caesellius Vindex and of Caper in a catalogue from Murbach (Manitius, *Handschriften* 267). The latter Papirius's work *De analogia* is mentioned in a library catalogue of Bobbio (Manitius, ibid.). P. is probably also the Pap(p)erinus—with the form of the name, cf. also "Paperianus" above—to whom an *Analogia* is attributed in the catalogue of gramm. in cod. Bern. 243 (*Anecd. Helv.* = *GL* 8, cxlix) and whose *Artificialia Paperini de analogia* was excerpted by Politian (ed. Pesenti, "Anecdota" 72–85); cf. Tolkiehn, "Grammatiker." Pap(p)erinus is cited in several medieval handbooks in various mss; see Hagen, *Anecd. Helv.* = *GL* 8, cclii–ccliii; Bischoff, "Ergänzungen."

245. PHALERIUS.   Gramm.(?) or, perhaps more likely, rhetorician.   Tavium (Galatia).   393.

RE 6.1971 s.v. Falerius no. 2 (Seeck); ibid. 19.1663 s.v. Phalerios no. 1 (id.); *PLRE* I s.v., p. 692.

Commended by Libanius to the rhetorician Paeonius at Tavium, where P. was intending to teach (*Ep.* 1080). It has been suggested that P. was a gramm.; so Jones, *LRE* 999, presumably in the belief—reasonable enough in itself—that a town the size of Tavium would not have two rhetoricians. But Libanius's words rather suggest that P. was a rhetorician;

note esp. *Ep.* 1080.2, κτήσεται . . . δόξαν ἥν ποιεῖ τὸ λέγειν. Possibly P. was intending to assist rather than to rival Paeonius; Libanius stresses that P. will be the μαθητής of Paeonius (*Ep.* 1080.5–6).

246. PHILOMUSUS.

PLRE I s.v., p. 698.

Auson. *Epigr.* 7:

DE PHILOMVSO GRAMMATICO

Emptis quod libris tibi bibliotheca referta est,
    doctum et grammaticum te, Philomuse, putas?
hoc genere et chordas et plectra et barbita condes:
    omnia mercatus cras citharoedus eris.

Philomusus may be a literary creation, the name invented to suit the conceit; see testimonia in Schenkl, ed., *MGH* AA 5:2.207; cf. Booth, "Notes" 242 n. 22; cf. also s.vv. Auxilius, Filocalus, nos. 191, 217.

Further, despite the lemma *de Philomuso grammatico* (so cod. Voss. 111), P. is presented not as a *grammaticus* but as a man who merely possesses the trappings: thus the lemma in some mss (see *app. crit.* in Schenkl, ed., ibid.), *ad Philomusum qui arbitratur se doctum cum nihil sciret.* The entry in *PLRE* I would more accurately read, "would-be *grammaticus* lampooned by Ausonius."

Finally, *grammaticus* here seems to be used like *doctus* (v. 2), not as a technical term or professional title but as an epithet, "man of letters"—a sense that Greek γραμματικός continued to possess long after the Latin borrowing was largely confined to its technical application. For late-antique examples in Latin and Greek, see Appendix 3. We should probably regard *grammaticus* as a predicate adjective, meant to suggest the Greek equivalent of *doctus*; cf. the Greek terms in the second couplet. The point is that P. fancies himself "learned and *lettré*," in both languages; the books with which he stuffs his library are presumably in Latin and in Greek.

247. PLUTARCHUS.   Gramm.?   Athens.   Before late 472 / May 476.

PLRE II s.v. 4, p. 894.

Plutarchus the son of Hierius: Damasc. *V. Isid.* frg. 289 Zintzen. One of the educated men of Athens, τῶν αὐτόθι παιδείας μετειληχότων, among whom Pamprepius strove to show himself πολυμαθέστατος while a gramm. there. For the date, see s.v. Pamprepius, no. 114.

PLRE is probably right to reject on chronological grounds the emendation of Asmus, according to whom the passage should read "Hierius the son of Plutarchus," so that P. would be identified with the homonymous scholarch. Less likely, however, is *PLRE*'s identification of P. as a gramm. The text of Damasc. *V. Isid.* frg. 289 assigns no specific profession to P.; contrast the case of the other man mentioned there, Hermias (= Hermeias 4 *PLRE* II, p. 548), who is identified as a ῥήτωρ. Moreover, the point of the passage is precisely that Pamprepius, though teaching grammar at the time, was striving to gain a reputation for excellence beyond grammar, in ἡ ἄλλη προπαιδεία, the other branches of liberal learning short of philosophy. The men against whom he is measured here, then, should be men known for the excellence of their general culture—cf. ὧν τὸ κλέος ὑπερβαλεῖν ἐσπουδάκει τῆς πολυμαθίας—not for their skill specifically in grammar.

* 248. AUR. PLUTION.   Teacher.   Philoteris (Arsinoite nome).   300.

Signatory of a declaration of land made by Aur. Kamoutis of Arsinoe for the census of 297, executed sometime between January and August 300 for the *censitor* Iulius Septimius Sabinus (= Sabinus 17 *PLRE* I, p. 794): *PRyl.* 4.656.23 Arsinoite nome, Αὐρ(ήλιος) Πλουτίων διδάσκαλος· παρ᾽ ἐμοὶ ἐτελέσθη. The declaration appears to have been made at Philoteris, west of Theadelphia (cf. line 5, περὶ κώμην Φιλωτέριδα).

For the secretarial function of the διδάσκαλος in this type of document, see esp. s.v. Aur. Herodes, no. 228; cf. s.v. Anonymus 14, no. 278. Cf. also s.vv. Sosistratus (*SB* 6.9270), no. 260 = Anonymus 15 (*SB* 6.9191), no. 279.

249. C. IULIUS ROMANUS.   Gramm.?   Italy?   s.III init. / s.IV med. (s.III 2/3?).

RE 10.788-89 (Tolkiehn); Sch.-Hos. 3.168-69; A. Stein, "Zur Abfassungszeit"; *PIR*² I.520; *PLRE* I s.v. 9, p. 769; della Casa, "Giulio Romano."

C. Iulius Romanus: Charis. *GL* 1.177.6 = 150.3-4 Barwick, 190.8 = 246.18B., 229.3 = 296.14B., 230.1 = 297.26-27B., 236.16 = 307.17B., 239.1 = 311.14B., 254.8 = 332.21B. Iulius Romanus or Romanus elsewhere in Charisius.

Author of a book of Ἀφορμαί, "basics" or "resources," arranged according to topics: cf. *GL* 1.230.1 = 297.26-27B., *libro ἀφορμῶν sub titulo de coniunctione*; 1.238.16 = 311.1B., *libro ἀφορμῶν sub titulo de praepositione*. The words treated under each topic were arranged alphabetically. The work is known only from the extensive excerpts made by Charisius: on the principle of analogy, *GL* 1.116.29ff. = 149.21-187.6B.; on adverbs, 190.8ff. = 246.18-289.17B.; on conjunctions, 229.3ff. = 296.14-297.28B.;

on prepositions, 236.16ff. = 307.17–311.2B.; and on interjections, 239.1ff. = 311.14–315.27B.

His profession and status are not precisely known. Charisius calls him *disertissimus artis scriptor, GL* 1.232.7 = 301.17B.; this probably means that Charisius did not know either. But note that if such expressions as *licet grammatici velint* stood in R.'s work (cf. *GL* 1.129.25–30 = 164.30–165.7B., rejecting the *grammatici* in favor of the elder Pliny), the distance they imply should suggest that he was not a gramm. by profession; cf. s.v. Helladius, no. 227. The statement in Charis. *GL* 1.215.22f. = 279.1–2B., *hodieque nostri per Campaniam sic locuntur*, is probably taken over from R. and may imply that he lived in Italy.

Charisius provides a *term. a. q.* of s.IV med. (see s.v., no. 200). The citations of *auctores* and technical writers of s.II med.–ex. that occur in the excerpts—Fronto (e.g., *GL* 1.197.3f. = 256.8B.), Apuleius (*GL* 1.240.28f. = 314.4–5B.), Fl. Caper (e.g., *GL* 1.145.23 = 184.19B.), Statilius Maximus (e.g., *GL* 1.209.4 = 270.29B.), Helenius Acro (e.g., *GL* 1.210.11 = 272.14B.)—are no doubt attributable to R., and so provide a *term. p. q.* R.'s concern with the forms of the Old Testament names "Adam" and "Abraham" (*GL* 1.118.13f. = 151.15–17B.) would not likely consist with a date earlier than s.III.

Possible grounds for more precise dating are found in two of Charisius's excerpts, where R. cites the opinions of a Marcius Salutaris, *v.p.*: *GL* 1.202.2 = 262.10–11B., 229.19 = 297.8–9B. (where the rank is given). Salutaris is perhaps to be identified with a man of the same name known to have been alive 244/48; see A. Stein, "Zur Abfassungszeit"; cf. s.v. Marcius Salutaris, no. 252. R. may have been a friend and contemporary of Salutaris, who is otherwise unknown to literary history: both the opinions cited concern Vergil and need not reflect anything more than the judgment of a man with the standard literary education. Further, personal connection would account for R.'s accurate knowledge of Salutaris's titulatur: so Stein, "Zur Abfassungszeit"; see s.v. If so, R. could be dated to s.III 2/3. But this is uncertain, and R.'s Marcius Salutaris may have been a descendant or an ancestor of the Salutaris of 244/48.

Further evidence for more precise dating is lacking. The places alleged by Stein, "Zur Abfassungszeit," to show Salutaris's name being used in grammatical examples do not stand up under examination, with the barely possible exception of Charis. *GL* 1.47.9 = 57.28B. = Diom. *GL* 1.307.2 = *Exc. Bob., GL* 1.545.18. Under the name of Cominianus the *Schol. Bern.* to *Ecl.* 3.21 cites the second of the opinions of R.'s Salutaris: though this might seem to provide a *term. a. q.* of s.III ex. / s.IV init. (cf. s.v. Cominianus, no. 34), it is doubtless an instance of Charisius's being cited as Cominianus, a frequent error in medieval sources; cf., e.g., the *Schol. Bern.* at *Georg.* 1.215, 2.84, 3.311.

250. ROMULUS.

PLRE I s.v. 1, p. 771.

Auson. *Prof.* 8, *Grammaticis Graecis Burdigalensibus*, vv. 1–4:

> Romulum post hos prius an [= Hor. *Carm.* 1.12.33] Corinthi
> anne Sperchei pariterque nati
> Atticas Musas memorem Menesthei
>   grammaticorum?

Should I call to mind "first after these Romulus, or" the Attic Muses of Corinthus, or of Spercheus and likewise his son Menestheus, the *grammatici*?

Booth, "Notes" 242f. (following Corpet), and, less decisively, Green, "Prosopographical Notes" 23, are certainly correct in banishing Romulus from the rolls of the Greek gramm. of Bordeaux. The structure and sense of the stanza depend upon the antithesis between the two direct objects, *Romulum* and *Atticas Musas*: as Booth says, Ausonius is "pretending to debate whether to place *Prof.* 10 [on the Latin *grammatici* of Bordeaux] before *Prof.* 8." Accordingly, the only gramm. here are *Corinthi . . . Sperchei . . . Menesthei grammaticorum*. Not incidentally, this relieves Ausonius of an embarrassment of riches, three teachers of Greek *primis . . . in annis* (the necessary count if Romulus were included); vv. 9–10, *tertius horum mihi non magister, / ceteri . . . docuere*, will then mean that Corinthus and Spercheus taught Ausonius, but Spercheus's son, Menestheus, did not, presumably because he was too young. Menestheus will therefore represent the next generation of teachers, after Ausonius's schooldays and before, or partially overlapping with, his own time as teacher. Menestheus will still have been active *nostro . . . in aevo* (v. 7).

Prof. 8 provoked something of a muddle in *PLRE* I. Although Romulus is treated (s.v., p. 771) as real and so, in line with vv. 9–10, as one of Ausonius's teachers, Spercheus "with Corinthus" is also said (s.v., p. 851) to have been one of Ausonius's teachers, which he could not then have been: if Romulus were real, Spercheus would be *tertius*. But *PLRE* I says nothing s.v. Corinthus (p. 229) about his relation to Ausonius; and Menestheus, at first omitted from *PLRE* I, is said in the addenda of Martindale, "Prosopography" 249, to have been one of Ausonius's teachers.

251. SABINUS.   Gramm.?   Before s.V?

RE, 2. Reihe, 1.1599 (Funaioli); *PLRE* I s.v. 2, p. 791.

Known only from a citation in Cledonius (q.v., no. 31; s.V?), *GL* 5.20.19, on the temporal nuance of the Latin optative. Since he is cited with Probus—evidently with a view to Probus *Inst. art.*, *GL* 4.160.28–161.4— and against Donatus, he may belong to early s.IV; cf. s.v. Probus, no. 127. But this is very uncertain.

252. MARCIUS SALUTARIS.   *v.e., procurator* = (?) *v.p.*, gramm.?   s.III med.

RE 14.1590–91 (Stein and Wessner); Sch.-Hos. 3.175, 4:1.167, without the papyri; A. Stein, "Zur Abfassungszeit"; *PLRE* I s.v., p. 800 (cf. Martindale, "Prosopography" 250f.).

Pap.: 1 = *PLond.* 3.1157ᵛ = Wilck. *Chrest.* 375 Hermopolis (an. 246); 2 = *SB* 3.7035 (partial) = *PLeit.* 16 = *PWisc.* 2.86 (an. 244/46); 3 = *POxy.* 17.2123 (an. 247/48); 4 = *POxy.* 33.2664 (ca. an. 247/48); 5 = *POxy.* 1.78 (undated). Inscr. = *Bodl. Gr. Inscr.* 3018, cited at *POxy.* 33 p. 87 nn.1, 2.

S. appears in Pap. 1–4 and Inscr. as an ἐπίτροπος τῶν Σεβαστῶν with the rank of κράτιστος, i.e., *egregius* (Pap. 1–5), together with the *rationalis* Claudius Marcellus (Pap. 1–5, Inscr.; cf. *PIR*² C.923) in the years ca. 244–48.

Identified by A. Stein, "Zur Abfassungszeit" (cf. *RE* 14.1590f.), with Marcius Salutaris the *v.p.* whose opinions on Vergil are twice cited by C. Iulius Romanus (q.v., no. 249) in excerpts in Charisius: *GL* 1.202.2 = 262.10–11 Barwick, 229.19 = 297.8–9B. The rank *vir perfectissimus* appears in the latter place. It has been thought that another source of Charisius alludes to Marcius Salutaris the *v.p.* by using the name "Salutaris" in a grammatical example, Charis. *GL* 1.47.9 = 57.28B. = Diom. *GL* 1.307.2 = *Exc. Bob.*, *GL* 1.545.18. But this conclusion becomes unlikely if the use of the name is viewed in the context of the passage as a whole; cf. *GL* 1.47.3–9 = 57.20–28B., with, e.g., 1.143.5f. = 181.5–6B. If the identification of S. with the Marcius Salutaris known to Romanus is correct, S. must have enjoyed a promotion in rank, from *v.e.* to *v.p.*, after the period documented in Pap. 1–5, and Romanus's references to him will be later than ca. 248; see also s.v. C. Iulius Romanus.

Romanus's references are thought to derive from an *ars* or commentary by S., but this inference is not necessary. Nor is it necessary to think that S. was a professional gramm. (the profession or status of Romanus is similarly uncertain). The two opinions of S. that Romanus cites—on the nuance of *ilicet* at *Aen.* 2.424 and of *an* at *Ecl.* 3.21—concern Vergil, who made up the common ground of all men liberally educated in Latin. They are simply opinions, showing no great learning and, in the second, little sense—although this failure was not peculiar to amateurs. Accordingly, S. may be thought to have written a work after ca. 248, of uncertain description and otherwise unknown, on which his later rank was inscribed; or else he may be thought to have been a contemporary of Romanus, who knew his rank and his opinions through personal connection.

Finally, the identification may be incorrect. In that case the Marcius Salutaris of Romanus could be a son of the procurator; it is less likely that he was S.'s grandson, in view of the constraints imposed by the chronology of Romanus and Charisius. Or he may have been S.'s ancestor, since the rank of *vir perfectissimus* occurs from s.II med. onward.

253. SELEUCUS. Gramm. Emesa. *Aet. incert.*

Seeck, *Briefe* 272f.; *RE*, 2. Reihe, 2.1248f. (id.); *PLRE* I s.v. 3, p. 819.

The *Suda*, Σ.201, gives notice of a Seleucus γραμματικός of Emesa, author of an hexameter (i.e., didactic) poem on fishing, in four books, ἀσπαλιευτικὰ δι᾽ ἐπῶν βιβλία δ'; also of a commentary on the lyric poets, and of a Παρθικά in two books.

He has been identified firmly by Seeck (*Briefe* 272f.; *RE*, 2. Reihe, 2.1248f.) and tentatively in *PLRE* I (s.v. 3) with Seleucus (= *PLRE* I s.v. 1) the brother-in-law of the gramm. Calliopius (q.v., no. 25) of Antioch and correspondent of Libanius, whom Libanius urged in 365 to write a history of Julian's Persian campaign (*Ep.* 1508.6–7). Since Libanius says nothing to suggest that his correspondent was a gramm., there is *prima facie* little reason to identify him with the S. who is styled γραμματικός in the *Suda*. Moreover, even if we ignore the style in the *Suda*, where γραμματικός is sometimes used imprecisely (see Appendix 3), the identification remains unlikely for three reasons.

First, the correspondent of Libanius has no known ties to Emesa, but appears to be most at home in Cilicia; cf. *Ep.* 770, which seems to show Seleucus a provincial high priest, with *Ep.* 771, which mentions his connection with Celsus, governor of Cilicia. At *Briefe* 272f., Seeck dismissed the evidence of the *Suda* and called Seleucus a Cilician, though at *RE*, 2. Reihe, 2.1248 he called Seleucus an Emesene with holdings in Cilicia.

Second, in *Ep.* 1508.6–7, Libanius suggests that Seleucus console himself for his misfortunes in the manner of Thucydides, by writing a history of Julian's Persian campaign—the only possible link with the S. of the *Suda*, author of a Παρθικά. But there is no hint that the suggestion was followed. *PLRE* I twice misstates the contents of *Ep.* 1508: s.v. Seleucus 1, "He undertook the composition of a history of Julian's Persian campaign . . . (nothing more is known of this work)"; and s.v. Seleucus 3, "Possibly to be identified with Seleucus 1, whose history of Julian's Persian campaign is mentioned Lib. *Ep.* 1508."

Third, the S. of the *Suda* was clearly involved with poetry, as author and commentator, and in fact his Παρθικά could well have been a poem. But when Libanius suggests that his friend write a history, he clearly has in mind a work of prose, as the analogy of Thucydides shows; and although Libanius has more than one occasion to refer to Seleucus's literary attainments (*Ep.* 1508.5ff.; cf. *Ep.* 499.3ff.), he mentions no interest in poetry.

254. VIBIUS SEQUESTER.   Not before s.IV ex. / s.V.

RE, 2. Reihe, 8.2457–62 (Strzelecki); Sch.-Hos. 4:2.120–22; *PLRE* I s.v., p. 823.

Author of a glossary of place names found in poetry. Although S. refers to *plerosque poetas* in his preface (p. 1.6f. Gelsomino), he in fact limits himself to Vergil, Lucan, Silius Italicus, and some Ovid (*Met.* 15). He used Lucan extensively, nearly as much as he did Vergil; cf. Pueschel, *De Vibii . . . fontibus* 9ff., 33; Gelsomino, "Studi" (1961, 1962). This use of Lucan suggests that he did not write before interest in that poet revived in the course of s.IV; cf. Wessner, "Lucan"; with Kaster, "Servius."

He is incorrectly presented as "?grammaticus" by *PLRE* I s.v. That title rather belongs to his son and dedicatee, Virgilianus; see s.v., no. 163. The latter is included in *PLRE* I s.v., p. 969, but his profession is not mentioned.

255. "SERGIUS."

Name under which Servius is sometimes cited (see s.v., no. 136) and under which circulate at least four grammatical works not by Servius:

1) *De littera, de syllaba, de pedibus, de accentibus, de distinctione*, GL 4.475–85.

2) *Explanationes in Donatum*, GL 4.486–565, with *Anecd. Helv.* = GL 8.143–58; an edition of the final part of the *Explan.* entitled "De vitiis et virtutibus orationis," published in part by Keil, GL 4.563–64 "De solecismo," is now in Schindel, *Figurenlehren* 258–79. On the compilation and attribution of the *Explan.*, see Schindel, *Figurenlehren* 34ff. To his discussion of the *Entstehungszeit* of the *Explan.* add that a possible *term. a. q.* of s.VI init. is provided by the reference of Coronatus (see below).

3) A work *De grammatica*, GL 7.537.1–539.15; see Finch, "Text."

4) In cod. Vat. Pal. lat. 1753 a version of the *De finalibus metrorum* of "Metrorius" (q.v., no. 239), *GL* 6.240–42, onto which the first two paragraphs of Servius's *De finalibus* have been grafted and the heading *ad Basilium amicum Sergii* has been attached.

The two references to Sergius in cod. Bern. 243, *de Sicilia* [sc. *venerunt ad nos libri*] *IIII discipulorum eius* [viz., *Donati*] *id est Honorati et Sergii et Maximi et Metrorii* and *de Italia . . . Sergii novem de littera et de barbarismo*, cannot be placed with certainty. The former may refer to the version of the *De finalibus* just noted, which is attributed to "Metrorius" in two codd., Neap. lat. 2 (= Vindob. 16) and Monac. 6281 (= Frising. 81), that also transmit the metrical treatise of Maximus Victorinus (q.v., no. 274); the latter may refer to the *De litt., de syll.*, etc., or to the *Explan.* (differently Hagen, *Anecd. Helv.* = *GL* 8, ci). For the catalogue of gramm. in cod. Bonon. 797, see Negri, "De codice" 266. See also the reference to *peritissimus Sergius* by Coronatus (q.v., no. 204) *scholasticus* in the prefatory epistle to his *De finalibus* (Keil, *De grammaticis* 4 n. = Rosenblum, *Luxorius* 259), which is transmitted after the *Explan.* in cod. S. Paul. in vall. Lavant. 24. Cf. also Wessner, *RE*, 2. Reihe, 2.1845.21ff.; Hagen, *Anecd. Helv.* = *GL* 8, lxxxix–xcvi, cxcii–cciii; Holtz, *Donat* 234, 429.

Which (or whether any) of the works noted above was written by a man named Sergius cannot be determined.

+ 256. SERGIUS. Gramm. *Loc., aet. incert.*; before s.IX 1/2.

Cited by Georgius Choeroboscus as ὁ γραμματικὸς Σέργιος, *Schol. in Theodos.*, *GG* 4:2.73.14ff., against Ioannes Philoponus and Orus (qq.v., nos. 118, 111). A *term. a. q.* of s.IX 1/2 is provided by Choeroboscus; cf. s.v., no. 201. He is perhaps to be identified with Sergius (q.v., no. 257) the lector of Emesa and epitomator of Herodian, or with the Σέργιος ὁ νεώτερος mentioned in the catalogues of gramm. in Kröhnert, *Canones* 7, and Rabe, "Listen" 340, or with both.

+ 257. SERGIUS. Lector. Emesa. *Aet. incert.*; perhaps before s.IX 1/2. Chr.-Sch.-St. 2:2.1078.

Lector of Emesa, author of an epitome of Herodian: cod. Vindob. gr. 294, Σεργίου ἀναγνώστου Ἐμισηνοῦ ἐπιτομὴ τῶν ὀνοματικῶν κανόνων Αἰλίου Ἡρωδιανοῦ; a version of the epitome without inscr. is found in cod. Harl. 5656. Cited as Σεργίου ἀναγνώστου Ἐμεσινοῦ εἰς τὰ Αἰλίου Ἡρωδιανοῦ by Pachomius Rhusanus (s.XV–s.XVI); cf. Hilgard, *Excerpta* 3ff. (the text appears ibid. 6–16).

Perhaps to be identified with ὁ γραμματικὸς Σέργιος (q.v., no. 256) cited by Georgius Choeroboscus (q.v., no. 201), *Schol. in Theodos.*, *GG*

4:2.73.14ff., in which case S. would have been active before s.IX 1/2; see s.v. Georgius Choeroboscus. Perhaps also or alternatively identifiable with the Σέργιος ὁ νεώτερος in the catalogues of gramm. in Kröhnert, *Canones* 7, and Rabe, "Listen" 340. He is probably not to be identified with Sergius the Eutychianist, gramm. and correspondent of Severus of Antioch (see s.v. Sergius, no. 135), *pace* Hilgard, *Excerpta* 5; Ludwich, *De Ioanne Philopono* 9f.

258. SERVILIO. Ecclesiastical teacher. s.V ex. / s.VI init.
PLRE II s.v., p. 997.

At one time a teacher of Ennodius; cf. *Epist.* 5.14, *MGH AA* 7.183f. (506; Sundwall, *Abhandlungen* 77). It has been suggested that S. was Ennodius's master in liberal studies; cf. Riché, *Education* 24 n. 44. The text, however, indicates that S. was Ennodius's spiritual or ecclesiastical mentor: *Epist.* 5.14.2, *sic ego sanctitatis tuae adfectione possessus, quamquam me de peritia iactare non audeam, vultum tamen praeceptoris expecto, ne degeneri te credas ecclesiasticum germen filio commisisse, quia quamvis memoria mea ad centenos se non valeat fructus extollere, scit tamen semina multiplicata redhibere cultori.*

259. SOLYMIUS(?). Teacher or student? Seleucia (Isauria). s.V med.
PLRE II s.v., p. 1020.

The son of one gramm., Alypius, and the brother of another, Olympius (qq.v., nos. 6, 108), at Isaurian Seleucia, according to the received text of [Basil. Sel.] *Vie et miracles de Sainte Thècle* 2.38 Dagron. His father fell ill and was cured by Saint Thecla; at the time S. was either a teacher or a student, and devoted half the day to λόγοι, half to tending his father.

Anomalies in the text, however, combine to suggest that some corruption has occurred and that ὁ παῖς ὁ Σολύμιος is a garbling of ὁ παῖς ὁ Ὀλύμπιος: see Kaster, *"Vie."* "Solymius" probably should be regarded as an error for "Olympius."

260. SOSISTRATUS. Teacher. Egypt (Arsinoite nome?). 337.

Teacher who wrote out a loan agreement in 337, probably somewhere in the Arsinoite nome (see Wegener, "Some Oxford Papyri" 209): *PBodl.* inv. e.129 = *SB* 6.9270 = Zilliacus, "Anecdota" 132, lines 22ff., Αὐρήλιος Ἀφροδείσιος Ἀλε[ξάνδρου γραμμα]τεὺς ἔγραψα ὑπὲρ αὐτοῦ [ἀγραμμάτου διὰ Σω]σιστράτου διδασκάλου. On the role of S., Zilliacus remarks, "As for the meaning of the note [διὰ Σω]σιστράτου διδασκάλου I suppose it is equivalent to the usual δι' ἐμοῦ ἐγράφη. . . . Sosistratus presumably works as a private *symbolaiographus*" ("Anecdota" 133 n. 24); cf. *CIL* 10.3969 = *ILS* 7763, with Kinsey, "Poor Schoolmaster?" Cf. also

still earlier *PCairZen.* vol. 3 p. 290 (addendum to *PCairZen.* 2.59257) =
PapLugdBat. 20A.20.9f. (252 B.C.), ἔγραψεν τὸ σύμβολον Ἀρ[......]ης διδάσκαλος Ἀσκληπιάδου συντά[ξαν]τος.

For a different reconstruction of the same passage in *PBodl.* inv. e.129,
see *SB* 6.9191 = Wegener, "Some Oxford Papyri" 209, and s.v. Anonymus 15, no. 279. Though this earlier version was apparently unknown
to Zilliacus, his interpretation of the role of the διδάσκαλος is nonetheless
probably preferable; see s.v. Anonymus 15.

261. STEGUS.

Cf. Chr.-Sch.-St. 2:2.1075 n. 5.

The name appears in one family of mss as a corruption in the tit. of
Procop. Gaz. *Ep.* 13, ἀλύπῳ καὶ στέγῳ γραμματικοῖς; see the *app. crit.* in
the ed. of Garzya and Loenertz *ad loc.* The gramm. in question was
Stephanus (q.v., no. 141), who received *Ep.* 71, 89, and 105 in addition to
Ep. 13. Cf. also s.vv. Alypius, Hierius, nos. 7, 71.

+ 262. TER(R)ENTIUS.

Ter(r)entius *grammaticus*, a pupil of Priscian according to the *Commentum
Sedulii* on Eutyches (q.v., no. 57): *Anecd. Helv.* = *GL* 8.1.11f. = p. 87.15f.
Löfstedt, *Ter(r)entius* [*Terrentius* cod. T: *Terentius* cod. B] *grammaticus "cum
autem" inquit "fuissemus ego et Eutex in schola Prisciani, sic ait nobis. . . ."*

But T. is introduced in the *Commentum Sedulii* only to provide a fanciful
etymology for the equally fanciful name *Eutex*; cf. s.v. Eutyches. For the
etymology, see Keil, *GL* 5.445; Löfstedt, ed., testimonia *ad loc.* T. is in all
likelihood a fiction, to be identified with the gramm. "Terrentius" invented by the gramm. Virgilius Maro (s.VII) along with the fictional
grammarians "Don," brother of Donatus, "Galbungus," et al.; the etymology offered in the *Commentum* may well derive from the same source,
though it is not in the surviving *Epitomae* of Virgilius Maro; cf. Wessner,
RE, 2. Reihe, 5.595; B. Löfstedt, "Miscellanea" 161f. (for other references
to T.), 163.

263. TETRADIUS.   Teacher; perhaps gramm.   Iculisma → Saintes?   s.IV
2/2.

RE, 2. Reihe, 5.1071f. (Ensslin); *PLRE* I s.v., p. 885.

Tetradius: Auson. *Epist.* 11 tit., v. 2. Whether he taught at Iculisma
(Angoulême; vv. 21ff.) as a gramm. or as a rhetorician is not clear; the
fact that T. was a poet (see below) is not much help on the question.
Ausonius's emphasis on Iculisma's obscurity might suggest that it was
not large enough to support a rhetorical school. T. could then have been

a gramm. or a general teacher of liberal letters; cf. s.v. Domitius Rufinus, no. 131; see also Kaster, "Notes" 342ff.

It is also unclear whether T. was still teaching at the time of *Epist.* 11. The sharp antithesis Ausonius draws between his condition at Iculisma and his current state—*docendi munere adstrictum gravi* (v. 21) vs. *floreas* (v. 26)—seems to suggest that he had broken the bonds of the *munus grave* altogether and had gone on to a different, better, fortune rather than that he had simply moved to a more favorable position.

T.'s origins are unknown. He had been a pupil of Ausonius, presumably at Bordeaux (vv. 17–18; the relationship is reversed at *RE*, 2. Reihe, 5.1072.1f.), and had subsequently taught at Iculisma (above). By the time of *Epist.* 11, he had left Iculisma (vv. 19–28). T.'s location is not stated, but Ausonius was writing near Saintes: vv. 11f., *cur me propinquum Santonorum moenibus / declinas . . . ?* Since T. is near Ausonius—vv. 25–26, *nunc frequentes atque claros nec procul / cum floreas inter viros*—it is a reasonable inference that T. was at Saintes; cf. Matthews' review of *PLRE* I, *CR* 24 (1974), 101.

The letter was written in the year of Ausonius's consulship, i.e., 379, or else sometime after: v. 30, *spernis poetam consulem.* If T. was of an age to have been a pupil of Ausonius at Bordeaux sometime in the period 336–67, he cannot have been born before the early 320s or much later than the early 350s—presumably he was born closer to the former *terminus*, since the conceit of the letter, his alleged disdain for Ausonius, would seem more decorously used of someone more nearly Ausonius's contemporary than of someone less than half his age.

T. was a poet (vv. 23–24, 31–32, 37–38); Ausonius specially mentions his skills as a satirist, comparing him to Lucilius (vv. 1–10).

T. is possibly to be identified with Taetradius the *proconsularis vir* who converted to Christianity under the influence of St. Martin at Trier: Sulp. Sev. *V. Martin.* 17; cf. *PLRE* I s.v., p. 873; Green, "Prosopographical Notes" 23.

264. THEODORETUS. Gramm. Asiana? *Aet. incert.*; perhaps before ca. 568.

Θεοδώρητος: *Anth. Gr.* 16.34 tit. (Θεοδωρίτου Planudes). Styled γραμματικός, ibid. Author of an epigram accompanying a statue set up at Smyrna by the city of Philadelphia in honor of the governor Philippus: ibid. lemma, εἰς εἰκόνα ἄρχοντος ἐν Σμύρνῃ.

The epigram may once have been collected in the Cycle of Agathias, which would provide a *term. a. q.* of ca. 568; for the date, cf. Cameron and Cameron, "*Cycle*"; differently Baldwin, "Four Problems" 298ff. and "Date." But the attribution to the Cycle is uncertain; cf. Cameron and

Cameron, "*Cycle*" 20. T. was dated to s.IV / s.V by Beckby, ed., *Anth. Gr.* 4.745; on what grounds is not clear.

Perhaps to be identified with Theodoretus the author of a treatise Περὶ πνευμάτων; cf. s.v., no. 265.

+ 265. THEODORETUS.   Gramm. and poet?   *Aet. incert.*; perhaps before ca. 568.

RE, 2. Reihe, 5.1801–2 (Wendel); Chr.-Sch.-St. 2:2.1080; Hunger 2.12f.

Θεοδώρητος: inscr. cod. Vindob. gr. 240 fol. 47. Θεοδώριτος: most codd. and v. 1 of the dedicatory epigram; cf. Uhlig, "Noch einmal" 791; Egenolff, *Orthoepischen Stücke* 11ff.

Author of a treatise Περὶ πνευμάτων drawn from the twentieth book of the Καθολικὴ προσῳδία of Herodian; cf. Egenolff, *Orthoepischen Stücke* 10ff., *Orthographischen Stücke* 32. As yet unedited, T.'s treatise was used in compiling the *Mischlexicon* ἐκ τῶν περὶ πνευμάτων Τρύφωνος, Χοιροβοσκοῦ, Θεοδωρίτου καὶ ἑτέρων in Valckenaer, *Ammonius*[2] 188ff. It was introduced by a twelve-line epigram dedicating the work to a certain Patricius; for the text of the poem, see Uhlig, "Noch einmal" 791f.; cf. Pachomius Rhusanus (s.XV – s.XVI), in Hilgard, *Excerpta* 5, Θεοδωρήτου περὶ πνευμάτων τῶν ὀκτὼ στοιχείων ἐξ Ἡρωδιανοῦ πρὸς Πατρίκιον.

Because he produced an epitome of Herodian, T. probably cannot be dated before s.IV; cf. s.v. Aristodemus, no. 188. T. may well belong to s.V / s.VI, as the names "Theodoretus" and especially "Patricius" suggest.

Perhaps to be identified with Theodoretus (q.v., no. 264) the gramm. whose epigram on the governor Philippus is preserved as *Anth. Gr.* 16.34. It is probably a coincidence that the *Suda*, Φ.352, records a Φίλιππος, σοφιστής, ὁ γράψας περὶ πνευμάτων, ἐκ τῶν Ἡρωδιανοῦ, κατὰ στοιχεῖον.

+ 266. THEODORUS.   Gramm. or poet, or both.   s.VI 1/2.

Subject of two funerary epigrams by Julian the Egyptian (*Anth. Gr.* 7.594, 595) and possibly of one by Paul the Silentiary (7.606), all from the Cycle of Agathias. His *term. a. q.* is therefore ca. 568; cf. Cameron and Cameron, "*Cycle*"; differently Baldwin, "Four Problems" 298ff. and "Date."

Julian claims that T. "revived" or "rescued from oblivion" the labors of the ancient poets (7.594.3f.) and that the latter are now buried with him (7.595.4.). He was presumably a gramm. or a poet, or both; cf. 7.594.1–4:

μνῆμα σόν, ὦ Θεόδωρε, πανατρεκὲς οὐκ ἐπὶ τύμβῳ,
ἀλλ' ἐνὶ βιβλιακῶν μυριάσιν σελίδων

αἶσιν ἀνεζώγρησας ἀπολλυμένων ἀπὸ λήθης
ἁρπάξας νοερῶν μόχθον ἀοιδοπόλων.

The lines could bear either interpretation. For the phrasing of vv. 1–2, cf. *GVI* 1182 = *IKyzik.* 515.2 (s.II); *SEG* 6.829 = *GVI* 1305.3–4 (s.II 2/2).

Paul's epigram mentions no literary attainments, in notable contrast to the poems of Julian. If T. was nonetheless its subject, he was survived by a son.

267. THEON.   Teacher.   Panopolis.   s.IV init.

Theon διδάσκαλος, registered as the owner of a new house, και(νή) (sc. οἰκία), in Panopolis in a topographical listing of properties executed early in s.IV, *PBerlBork.* col. 12.34. For the date, see references s.v. Chabrias. Note that unlike the other two διδάσκαλοι mentioned in the same register, Chabrias and Eutyches (qq.v., nos. 198, 214), T. appears to have been alive at the time of the survey; cf. Kaster, "P. Panop." 133f.

268. THESPESIUS.   Gramm.(?) or, more probably, rhetorician.   Caesarea (Palaestina).   s.IV 2/3.

RE, 2. Reihe, 6.60 (Stegemann); Hauser-Meury, *Prosopographie* s.v., p. 174; *PLRE* I s.v. 2, p. 910.

Thespesius: Jer. *De vir. ill.* 13; Greg. Naz. *Epitaph.* 4 (*PG* 38.12f.). Called *rhetor* by Jerome; γραμματικός in the lemma of Greg. Naz. *Epitaph.* 4. Gregory's poem praises T. as a glorious example of the σοφίη that was the special pride of Athens: vv. 3–4, ἡ δ' ἐβόησε / Ἀτθίς· τίς ποτ' ἐμῆς δόξαν ἔχει σοφίης. Since this must mean oratory—it can hardly mean grammar—the lemma is probably mistaken. The error was perhaps due to ἐπέεσσι in v. 3, where T.'s skill in improvisation(?) is mentioned: ἀρτιτόκοις ἐπέεσσι τόσος βρύζες. Cf. Hauser-Meury, *Prosopographie* 174.

Active at Caesarea in Palestine: according to Jerome, *De vir. ill.* 13, T. taught Gregory and Euzoius in the city that housed the library of Origen and Pamphilus and that later had Euzoius as its bishop. As teacher of Gregory Nazianzen (born 329) at Caesarea, T. must have been active at least by the mid- or late 340s. The date of his death cannot be fixed; but since the Ἐπιτάφια seem to be arranged chronologically, it can be placed between ca. 357 (*Epitaph.* 1–3) and ca. 367 (*Epitaph.* 5).

269. TROILUS.   Gramm.   *Loc., aet. incert.*

PLRE II s.v. 2, p. 1128.

According to the tit. of *Anth. Gr.* 16.55, a gramm., author of an epigram on the base of a statue raised by a city to the wrestler Lyron. T. is dated by Beckby, ed., to ca. 375; for what reason is not clear. It is possible, however, that he lived in late antiquity.

270. STATIUS TULLIANUS. *Dign., loc., aet. incert.*; before s.IV med.

RE, 2. Reihe, 3.2223-24 (Funaioli); Sch.-Hos. 4:1.180; *PLRE* I s.v., p. 924.

Glossographer or antiquarian; author of a work *De vocabulis rerum* (codd. Macrob.: *deorum* Eyssenhardt). A citation from the first book is found at Macrob. *Sat.* 3.8.6–7 = Servius Danielis *ad Aen.* 11.542. The common source of Macrobius and Servius Danielis here is almost certainly the variorum commentary of Aelius Donatus; cf. Funaioli, *RE*, 2. Reihe, 3.2223–24; Marinone, *Elio Donato* 71, 77; Santoro, *Esegeti* 36ff. T. should therefore be dated before s.IV med. Nothing more is known about him.

271. CURTIUS VALERIANUS. *Dign., loc., aet. incert.*; before ca. 580, and perhaps before s.VI init.

RE 4.1891f. (Wessner); Sch.-Hos. 4:2.218; *PLRE* II s.v. 7, p. 1142.

Writer on orthography excerpted by Cassiodorus, *De orth.*, *GL* 7.155.22ff. Listed third at *De orth.* praef. (*GL* 7.147.6), after Velius Longus and before Papirianus (q.v., no. 244). Along with the other men listed there, V. is implicitly distinguished from Priscian, the *modernus auctor* (cf. *GL* 7.207.3, *nostro tempore*); cf. also *Inst.* 1.30.2, where again V. stands between Velius Longus and Papirianus, and is classed among the *orthographi antiqui*. He may therefore be dated before Priscian; but on Cassiodorus's shortcomings in chronology, see s.vv. Eutyches, Phocas, nos. 57, 121. Though V.'s relation to Papirianus is uncertain, the dependence Keil suggested, *GL* 7.134, seems very doubtful; likewise the date of Papirianus—certainly before Priscian, perhaps after Aelius Donatus; but cf. s.v. Papirianus. V. can at least be dated before ca. 580, the date of Cassiod. *De orth.* and of the revision of Cassiod. *Inst.*.

272. VICTOR. Gramm.? Before s.V med. / s.VI init.

PLRE I s.v. 7, p. 959.

The opinion of a Victor in an *Ars grammatica* is cited by Priscian, *GL* 2.14.13f., under the heading "De syllabis." Rufinus *GL* 6.573.26 lists a Victor as an authority who had written on rhythm, *de numeris* (sc. *oratoriis*), in Latin.

It is not certain that the two are the same man. The second is usually identified with the author of a rhetorical handbook, C. Iulius Victor; cf. Cybulla, *De Rufini . . . commentariis* 39f. The first remains a mystery. If Priscian cites him correctly as the author of an *Ars grammatica*, he probably should not be identified with C. Iulius Victor, Sulpicius Victor, or Claudius Marius Victor. "Victorinus" has been suggested in place of

"Victor"; cf. *GL* 2.14.13f., *app. crit.* But nothing comparable to the opinion Priscian cites can be found either in the extant *Ars* of Marius Victorinus or in the work of Aphthonius that was circulating under Victorinus's name by the middle of s.V.

273. VICTORINUS. Gramm. s.IV 1/2?

Victorinus *grammaticus*, cod. Sangall. 877; Victorinus or Victurinus, codd. Vat. Regin. 1587, Neap. Borbon. IV A 34. Presented as the author of a grammatical *Ars* with metrical appendix, *GL* 6.185–215. The *Ars* is also transmitted without the appendix, and the appendix in turn is found independently; but the common format of the two sections and other features of the paradosis make it certain that the two parts belong to a single whole; for details, see Wessner at *RE* 14.1845.36ff. and in Teuffel 3 §408.4.

Since the work also appears without attribution in cod. Vat. Regin. 251, and since the metrical appendix in cod. Paris. lat. 7559 and the part of the *Ars* preserved in cod. Neap. lat. 2 (= Vindob. 16) are attributed to Palaemon, the whole is possibly an acephalous work ascribed to various well-known authors in the course of transmission. H. van Putschen attached the name "Maximus Victorinus" (q.v., no. 274) to the work in his ed. (Hanoviae, 1605).

The work is written throughout in the question-and-answer format that belongs to the schools; for analysis, see Barwick, *Remmius* 77ff. A reference to Lactantius occurs at *GL* 6.209.11ff.: *nostra quoque memoria Lactantius de metris "pentameter" inquit et "tetrameter."* If the wording, with the phrase *nostra memoria*, indicates that the writer was a contemporary of Lactantius, then the reference should place the genesis of the work in S.IV 1/2. But note also that an allusion to the *Ars* of Aelius Donatus suggests a date after s.IV med.: *GL* 6.200.24f., *de pronomine similiter quoniam Donatus exposuit, ideo praetermisimus.* The latter may, however, be due to revision in the course of transmission; cf. Barwick, *Remmius* 82 n. 1.

Though the *Ars* bears a marked resemblance to the *Excerpta* of Audax (q.v., no. 190), differences between the two suggest reliance on a common source rather than dependence of one on the other.

274. MAXIMUS(?) VICTORINUS.   Gramm. or rhetorician?   *Loc., aet. incert.*; before Bede.

Cf. *RE* 14.1847.27ff. (Wessner); Sch.-Hos. 4:1.154.

Called Maximus or Maximinus or Maximianus Victorinus in the mss (Maximinus Victorinus in the oldest, cod. Neap. lat. 2 [= Vindob. 16, s.VII / s.VIII]): see Keil, *GL* 6, xx–xxi. He is probably the Maximus mentioned in the company of "Honoratus" (= Servius), "Sergius," and

"Metrorius" in the catalogues of gramm. in codd. Bonon. 797 (Negri, "De codice" 266) and Bern. 243 (*Anecd. Helv.* = *GL* 8, cxlix); cf. further s.v. "Sergius," no. 255.

Author of a *Commentum* or *Commentarius de ratione metrorum* (so the mss), *GL* 6.215–28. Of uncertain profession or status, he is styled *Maximianus grammaticus* in the subscr. of cod. Monac. 6281, but he appears to be especially concerned with rhetoric; cf. *GL* 6.227.25–27, *haec prudenti satis sunt, hisque exemplis omnia in promptu habebit. rhetoricam autem eloquentiam, id est veram, nosse non poterit, nisi qui ad eam hoc vestigio venerit.*

His date is likewise beyond determination, save that Bede refers to him (as "Victorinus"), *De orth.*, *GL* 7.248.17ff. = 6.218.16ff.

+ 275. URBANUS.   Gramm.?   Vergilian commentator.   *Loc., aet. incert.*; s.II med. / s.V init.

RE, 2. Reihe, 9.982–86 (Strzelecki); Sch.-Hos. 3.173.

Commentator on Vergil, cited eleven times by Servius. The nature of the citations makes it reasonably clear that U.'s work was a commentary, not some other type of grammatical work. Servius's citations provide a *term. a. q.* of s.IV ex. / s.V init.; though firm evidence for a *term. p. q.* is lacking, there is some reason to suppose U. was later than Velius Longus; cf. Serv. *ad Aen.* 5.517, with *Schol. Veron.* to *Aen.* 5.488; Strzelecki, *RE*, 2. Reihe, 9.983.31ff.

Very little recommends the common suggestion that U. is the M. Damatius Urbanus whose literary attainments are recorded on *CIL* 8.8500 = *ILS* 7761 Sitifis (an. 229): *summarum artium liberalium, litterarum studiis utriusque linguae perfecte eruditus, optima facundia praeditus.* Praise of this type is very common in inscr., and implies no specific accomplishment beyond a liberal education: e.g., for *utraque lingua eruditi* (*vel sim.*) in or from Africa, see the inscr. collected at Champlin, *Fronto* 17 n. 84. Further, the Urbanus of *CIL* 8.8500 died in his twenty-third year.

276. ZOSIMUS.   Sophist.   Ascalon.   s.V ex. / s.VI init.

RE, 2. Reihe, 10.790ff. (Gärtner); *PLRE* II s.v. 4, p. 1206.

A sophist of Ascalon active under Anastasius, according to the *Suda*, Z.169, where he is partially confused, *ut vid.*, with the homonymous and nearly contemporary sophist of Gaza (= Zosimus 2 *PLRE* II, p. 1205). The confusion is inconsequential for our purposes, however; for although Z. is called a gramm. by *PLRE* II—perhaps a slip, after Gärtner, *RE*, 2. Reihe, 10.790ff., where the term seems to be used loosely—no ancient source identifies him as a gramm., and nothing that we know about him or about his homonym suggests that he was one. The work associated with him is wholly concerned with prose, esp. the Attic orators; see Gärtner, *RE*, 2. Reihe, 10.791ff. That by itself indicates he was a sophist.

277. ANONYMUS 13.   Teacher.   Oxyrhynchus.   s.III / s.IV.

In a private account dated by the editor (J. Barns) to s.III / s.IV: *POxy.* 24.2425 col. ii.16, τῷ διδασκάλῳ κβ. The units involved are not specified, but the amounts recorded in the part of the account published are fairly uniform, ranging from 17 to 22.

278. ANONYMUS ("the Elder") 14.   Teacher.   Karanis.   299.

Signatory of a declaration of land owned by Aur. Isidorus, lying in two districts of Karanis: *PCairIsid.* 5.45, [Αὐρ(ήλιος) ± 10] πρεσβύτερος [δι]δάσ-καλος· παρ᾽ ἐμοὶ ἐτελέσθη. The declaration was made for the census of 297 and was executed 11 September 299 for the *censitor* Iulius Septimius Sabinus (= Sabinus 17 *PLRE* I, p. 794). Probably the same man appears as a signatory in a copy of another document of the same type apparently executed at the same time and concerning parcels of land located in the same districts: *PNYU* 1.1.15, [Αὐρ. ± 13 πρεσβύ]τερος διδ[ά]σκαλος· παρ᾽ ἐμοὶ ἐτ[ελ(έσθη)].

Evidently distinct from the διδάσκαλος Aur. Herodes who appears in a similar capacity on two similar documents prepared at the same time in Karanis; see s.v. Aur. Herodes, no. 228. The two men were performing the same job at the same time probably because the parcels of land lay in different parts of Karanis; see *PCairIsid.* p. 48.

On διδάσκαλοι as secretaries, see references s.v. Aur. Herodes, no. 228. Cf. also s.vv. Aur. Plution, no. 248; Sosistratus (*SB* 6.9270), no. 260 = Anonymus 15 (*SB* 6.9191), no. 279.

279. ANONYMUS 15.   Teacher.   Arsinoite nome.   337.

Teacher found performing a notarial function in a loan agreement drafted probably somewhere in the Arsinoite nome in 337: *PBodl.* inv. e.129 = *SB* 6.9191 = Wegener, "Some Oxford Papyri" 209, lines 22ff., Αὐρήλιος Ἀφροδείσιος Ἀμμω[νίου ὑπογραφ]εὺς ἔγραψα ὑπὲρ αὐτοῦ [ἀγραμμάτου ἀξιω]θεὶς ὑπὸ τοῦ διδασκάλου. With the role of the διδάσκαλος here, Wegener compared that of Aur. Herodes (q.v., no. 228) at *SB* 5.7669.41 = *PCairIsid.* 3.41; cf. also *PCairIsid.* 4.21 (s.v. Aur. Herodes); *PRyl.* 4.656 (s.v. Aur. Plution, no. 248); *PCairIsid.* 5.45, *PNYU* 1.1.15 (s.v. Anonymus 14, no. 278). Note, however, that the latter documents belong to a homogeneous set, viz., declarations of land before the *censitor*, distinct from the private agreement found here.

A perhaps preferable reconstruction of this passage would read [διὰ Σω]σιστράτου διδασκάλου for [ἀξιω]θεὶς ὑπὸ τοῦ διδασκάλου; see s.v. Sosistratus, no. 260.

* 280. ANONYMUS 16.   Teacher.   Egypt.   s.IV?

In an account dated to the "fourth (?) century": *OPetr.* 450, τῷ διδασκάλῳ β. The units of payment are not specified, but the same figure is given in the five other entries that are legible.

* 281. ANONYMUS 17.   *Magister (sc. alicuius artis liberalis).*   Rome?   s.V ex. / s.VI init.

Subject of Ennod. *Carm.* 2.96 (*MGH AA* 7.172), with the lemma *de quodam Romano qui magister voluit esse.* The poem's theme is conventional, the ignorant would-be teacher: vv. 2–3, *littera nulla colit brutae commercia linguae. / numquam discipulus, valeas dic unde magister.* Perhaps a literary invention; cf. s.vv. Auxilius, Philomusus, nos. 191, 246.

Appendixes

Titles, Styles, Circumlocutions: A Selection

For literary and institutional reasons, the terms for teachers below the level of rhetorician proliferated in the course of antiquity beyond the simple titles most commonly found, viz., γραμματιστής, γραμματοδιδά-σκαλος, *litterator, magister primus,* or *magister ludi (litterarii)* for the so-called primary teacher;[1] γραμματικός or *grammaticus* for the so-called secondary teacher.[2] The collection below is a sampling of the other titles, styles, and circumlocutions applied to such teachers, especially in sources of the third through sixth centuries. In making my selection I have aimed at variety, not exhaustiveness, and I have attempted to avoid unnecessarily duplicating information already collected elsewhere.[3]

1. Various expansions of *magister*

a. *magister artis grammaticae, magister grammaticus,* etc.: CIL 2.3872 = ILS 7765 = ILER 5715 Saguntum, *magister artis grammaticae* (cf. CIL 3.12702 [with 13822] = ILS 7767 Doclea, *artis grammaticae Graecae peritissimus;* CIL 13.1393 = ILS 7764 Limoges, *artis grammaticae doctor morumq(ue) mag[is]ter; Anth. Lat.* 1:1.287.4, *grammaticae magister artis);* Amm. Marc. 22.10.7, *magistri rhetorici et grammatici* (sim. 25.4.20); cf. AE 1928, 200 = ibid. 1938,

1. Cf. Marrou, *Histoire*[6] 221, 390.
2. On γραμματιστής and *litterator,* see Appendix 2; on the so-called primary and secondary levels, see Kaster, "Notes."
3. In addition to Marrou, *Histoire*[6] 221, 390, see the works cited by Lauffer, *Diokletians Preisedikt* 241, on 7.66, 242, on 7.70; cf. Kuhn, *Städtische und bürgerliche Verfassung* 1.84f., for the usage of the jurists and the Codes. Christes, *Sklaven* 142ff., provides a useful survey of *Berufsbezeichnungen;* for examples of an important style overlooked there, καθηγητής, see Robert, *Collection* 56–57, *Hellenica* 13.53; Robert and Robert, *Carie* 215 no. 6; CIL 6.2210 = ILS 4499 = IGVR 2.707; Mitsos, "Ἐκ τοῦ Ἐπιγραφικοῦ Μουσείου" 79f.; Raubitschek, "Greek Inscriptions" 248f. no. 10; FX 7 no. 64, pp. 157f. (Balland); POxy. 6.930, 18.2190; POsl. 3.156; PGiss. 80.

17 = *ILER* 5716 = *RIT* 443, *magister grammaticus; Anal. Boll.* 93 (1975) 292, μαϊστὼρ γραμματικός; *CIL* 2.2236 = *ILS* 7766 = *ILER* 5717 Corduba, *magister gramm(aticus) Graecus; AE* 1974, 234 Aquinum, *magister Graecus.*

b. *magister liberalium litterarum: BCTH* 1896, 218 no. 184 = *ILS* 7762 Iomnium; cf. Prudent. *Perist.* 9.22, *magister litterarum* (with Part II no. 26); Brusin, "Nuove epigrafi" 40f. = *AE* 1968, 191–98 n. (p. 72) Aquileia, [*magiste*]r *litterar*[*um*] (with Part II no. 62).

c. *magister puerorum: ILCV* 719 = *Inscr. Ital.* 10:2.58 Parentium; *Inscr. Ital.* 10:2.74 Parentium (see Part II nos. 29, 30, with no. 216); cf. διδάσκαλος παιδῶν, *PSI* 3.157; παιδοδιδάσκαλος, Greg. presb. *Vie de Théodore de Sykéon* §26.7ff. Festugière (see Part II no. 120); cf. also [Clement. Rom.] *Testament. D. N. Iesu Christi* 2.2, p. 115 Rahmani = *CSCO* Scr. Syr. 162 p. 49; *CIL* 6.16843 = *IG* 14.1537 = *GVI* 1326 = *IGVR* 3.1189.3–4 (quoted at 3a below); Prudent. *Perist.* 9.21, *praefuerat studiis puerilibus,* of the *magister litterarum* Cassianus.

d. *magister studiorum: TZ* 35 (1972) 136 = *BRGK* 58 (1977) 453 Trier, *magister studiorum, grammaticus Latinus; AE* 1918, 87, 88 (= 20 *bis*) = *ILAfr.* 273a, b Thuburbo Maius, *magister studiorum;* cf. *CTh* 13.3.5 (an. 362), *magistri studiorum doctoresque;* also *CJ* 3.28.37, 1e (an. 531), *magistri studiorum liberalium.*

2. Miscellaneous expressions specifying "teacher" or the like with an objective genitive

a. Ἑλληνικῶν or Ῥωμαϊκῶν λόγων διδάσκαλος γραμματικῶν, etc.: Soc. *HE* 2.46.2, 3.1.10, 4.9.4, 5.25.1; cf. 7.17.2, and Part II no. 116; contrast 7.13.7, γραμμάτων τῶν πεζῶν διδάσκαλος; with Part II no. 74.

b. *doctor eloquii,* etc.: *TZ* 35 (1972) 136 = *BRGK* 58 (1977) 453 Trier, *doctor Rom*[*ani*] . . . *eloqu*[*i*]*i,* of the Latin *grammaticus* L. Terentius Iulianus (cf. 1d above); Martyrius *GL* 7.165.14, *doctor* . . . *elocutionis Latinae,* of Adamantius (see Part II nos. 2, 95); cf. Prisc. *Inst., GL* 2.238.5f., *omnis eloquentiae decus,* of Theoctistus; Eutych. *Ars, GL* 5.456.29f., *Romanae lumen facundiae,* of Priscian. Note also Ennod. *Dict.* 7.8, *praevius eloquentiae morumque doctor,* of Deuterius, who taught both grammar and rhetoric (cf. Part II no. 44); *CIL* 6.9858 = *ILS* 2951, *magister eloquentiae,* of the rhetorician Fl. Magnus (= Magnus 10 *PLRE* I, p. 535).

c. γραμματικῆς ἐπιίστωρ τέχνης: Kaibel 402 = *IGR* 3.118 = *GVI* 1184 Sebastopolis (Cappadocia); cf. Kaibel 848, σοφίης ἐπιίστωρ πάσης; Charneux, "Inscriptions" 616f. = *SEG* 16.261, τὸν πάσης σοφίης ἐπιίστορα, of a governor of s.IV.

d. ὁ εὐλογιώτατος γραμματικὸς καὶ παιδευτὴς Ἑλληνικῶν λόγων ἐλευθερίων: *SB* 1.5941, with Part II no. 220.

e. *professor Romanarum litterarum, grammaticus Latinus: Gesta apud Zenophilum, CSEL* 26.185.9f.; for *professio* or *professor litterarum,* cf. esp. Dahlmann, *Kleine Schriften* 255ff.

f. σοφίης διδάσκαλος: Kaibel 372 = SEG 6.137 Altıntaş (Kurtköy [Phrygia]; see Part II no. 158); Dörner, Bericht 54 no. 13 Bithynion / Claudiopolis; cf. PLG⁴ 3.362ff., v. 29, σοφίης ἄναξ, of the grammarian Coluthus (cf. Part II no. 33).

3. Some circumlocutions

A teacher's activity or status was frequently described allusively or periphrastically, without a precise title. One familiar example involves the teacher's use of the rod; see, e.g., the references Mayor collected in his commentary on Juv. 1.15 (London, 1888). An equally familiar and seemingly antithetical example involves his status as (foster) father; see esp. Petit, Étudiants 31ff., on the use of τρέφειν and θρέμμα in Libanius's letters, with, e.g., Paulin. Nol. Ep. 7.3, 8.1, Dion. Ant. Ep. 24 Hercher, Ennod. Dict. 8.8ff. The most common circumlocutions for "grammarian" involve expertise in poetry.

a. GVI 1182 = IKyzik. 515 Miletoupolis / M. Kemalpaşa (s.II), concerning Magnus: vv. 1–2, τὸν μέγαν ἐν Μούσαισι, τὸν ἐν σοφίη κλυτὸν ἄνδρα, / ἔξοχα Ὁμηρείων ἀψάμενον σελίδων. The inscription concludes, ἀλλά, φίλοι, μνήσασθε καὶ ἐν φθιμέν[οι]σι γεραιοῦ, / πρῶτος ὃς ὑμετέρους υἷας γεῦσε λόγων (vv. 7–8). Magnus gave the sons of Miletoupolis a taste of λόγοι (vv. 7–8), that is, he was their teacher; and he was especially expert in Homer (vv. 1–2), that is, he was a γραμματικός. With vv. 1–2 compare SEG 6.289 = GVI 1305 Kittium (s.II 2/2): vv. 3–4, Κιλικᾶν ἔξοχον ἠϊθέων, ὃς ποθ' Ὁμηρείαισι μετέπρεπον ἐν σελίδεσσιν / δεικνὺς ἡρώων ἠνορέην προτέρων; cf. Part II no. 266, for Anth. Gr. 7.594.1f. With v. 8 compare CIL 6.16843 = IG 14.1537 = GVI 1326 = IGVR 3.1189.3–4: ζωὸς ἐὼν [Μούσαισιν ὁ]μείλεον, ἐν δέ τε παιδῶν / εὐγενέων ἱερῆς ἦρξα διδασκαλίης, of Didius Taxiarches, on whom see most recently Christes, Sklaven 154.

b. Bull. ép. 1939, 447 = Iacopi, Esplorazioni 22 and fig. 88 = GVI 381 (s.II / s.III: Peek), of the teacher Sarapion of Tyana (so the stone in Iacopi's photograph; Σεραπίων in Iacopi, Esplorazioni 22, and in GVI 381): παιδευτῶν ὄχ' ἄριστος . . . παιδεύσας Μούσαις τοὺς Τυανῶν λογίους.

c. Lib. Or. 1.44: οἱ ἀμφὶ τοὺς ποιητάς, of the grammatici of Constantinople.

d. Lib. Ep. 337.1, 969.1: τοὺς (παλαιοὺς) ποιητὰς εἰς τὰς τῶν νέων ψυχὰς εἰσάγων, of the grammatici Tiberinus and Diphilus, respectively; cf. Wolf, Schulwesen 32f. Compare Ep. 398.2: δείκνυται δὲ καὶ ἐν ταῖς τῶν νέων ψυχαῖς ἡ σὴ τέχνη, to the grammarian Acacius. Cf. also Procop. Gaz. Ep. 57.9: ταῦτα τοῖς παισὶ καθηγούμενος, followed by a quotation of Callimachus (see Part II no. 142); Choric. Or. fun. Procop. 5, p. 111.4ff. Foerster-Richtsteig: ἐπὶ θύρας ἥκειν ποιητικάς and τὰ Μουσῶν μανθάνειν, of Procopius's studies at the grammarian's school; similarly Laud. Marc. 2.7, p. 29.20.

e. Damasc. *V. Isid.* epit. Phot. 60 = frg. 111 Zintzen: ἠγάπα τὴν ἐπὶ ποιητῶν ἐξηγήσει καὶ διορθώσει τῆς Ἑλληνικῆς λέξεως καθημένην τέχνην, denoting the profession of the grammarian Ammonianus. Cf. *V. Isid.* frg. 276: ὅσοι ῥητορικῶν προίσταντο διατριβῶν ἢ ποιητικῶν, a circumlocution for ὅσοι ῥήτορες ἢ γραμματικοὶ ἦσαν. On Damascius's periphrastic avoidance of the technical title γραμματικός, see further Appendix 2.2e.

For some other styles, cf. Paul. Silent. *Anth. Gr.* 7.588.3, γραμματικῆς ἱερὴ βάσις, of Damocharis; Olympiod. frg. 32 = Phot. *Bibl.* cod. 80 (1.179 Henry) = *FHG* 4.64, εὐφυῶς περὶ γραμματικὴν ἔχων, of Philtatius (cf. Part II no. 119), perhaps a circumlocution for εὐφυὴς γραμματικός. Compare ἀφυὴς γραμματικός at Hierocles and Philagrius, Φιλόγελως nos. 196, 197.

APPENDIX 2

Γραμματιστής Meaning Γραμματικός

P. Wolf (*Schulwesen* 32ff.) and P. Petit (*Étudiants* 85 n. 194) both independently drew attention to the fact that Libanius avoids the title γραμματικός, preferring various periphrases (cf. Appendix 1.3c, d) or the term γραμματιστής, which elsewhere is commonly applied to the humbler teacher of elementary letters.[1] Among authors earlier than or contemporary with Libanius, Aelius Aristides and Themistius can be shown to have followed a similar practice.[2] This appendix gathers together some of the evidence for the use of γραμματιστής in authors later than Libanius. The first section gives apparent examples of the word in its more common sense; the second, examples of usage similar to Libanius's; a third section briefly describes a similarly flexible usage in Latin.

1. Γραμματιστής meaning "teacher of elementary letters"

a. Isid. Pel. *Ep.* 5.335: γραμματιστής as a teacher of writing.
b. Isid. Pel. *Ep.* 4.134: γραμματιστής opposed to φιλόσοφος in a simile distinguishing προπαιδεύματα from φιλοσοφία. The teacher of elementary letters or writing seems to be meant, associated with τῇ χειρί as opposed to τῇ ψυχῇ.
c. Nil. Ancyr. *Ep.* 2.49: γραμματιστής vs. φιλόσοφος in a context similar to Isid. Pel. *Ep.* 4.134, above.
d. Ioan. Philop. *Comm. in Phys.* 2.8, *CAG* 16.321.1ff., on the proposition οὐδὲ αἱ τέχναι βουλεύονται· ἀλλ' οὐδ' ὁ γραμματιστὴς βουλεύεται πῶς δεῖ τὸ 'α' ἢ τὸ 'β' γράψαι, οὐδ' ὅταν γράφῃ τὸ 'Σωκράτης' ὄνομα βουλεύεται ποῖον δεῖ πρῶτον τῶν στοιχείων γράψαι, ποῖον δὲ δεύτερον καὶ τρίτον. The

---

1. Cf. Lib. *Ep.* 406; Part II nos. 4, 43, 88, 168; with Wolf, *Schulwesen* 32ff. For Libanius's single use of γραμμάτων διδάσκαλος, see Part II no. 241.
2. See Wolf, *Schulwesen* 35 with nn. 62, 63.

first part of the statement demonstrates that "teacher of basic letters" is meant here.[3]

In three further examples, γραμματιστής obviously means "teacher of elementary letters":

    e. Simplic. *Comm. in Categ.* 8, *CAG* 8.230.2ff., on a man who had to repeat his education from the beginning after suffering amnesia: καὶ γὰρ νοσήσαντές τινες ἀπέβαλον τὰς ἐπιστήμας, ὥσπερ ἐφ᾽ ἡμῶν ἐν Παλαιστίνῃ προκεκοφώς τις ἐν λόγοις ἤδη καὶ νοσήσας πάντων ἐπελάθετο, ὡς δεηθῆναι μετὰ τὴν ἀνάληψιν αὖθις εἰς γραμματιστοῦ φοιτῆσαι.

    f. Olympiod. *Comm. Alcib. 1* 2.32f. Westerink, on Plato's education: ἐν ἡλικίᾳ δὲ γενόμενος πρῶτον μὲν ἐφοίτησε Διονυσίῳ τῷ γραμματιστῇ πρὸς μάθησιν κοινῶν γραμμάτων. Compare ibid. 95.17ff., 96.14ff.

    g. Paul. Aeg. 1.14, *CMG* 9:1.13.19ff., prescribing the first two stages of scholastic education: ἀπὸ δὲ τῶν ἓξ καὶ ἑπτὰ ἐτῶν τούς τε παῖδας καὶ τὰς κόρας γραμματισταῖς παραδιδόναι πραέσι καὶ φιλανθρώποις. . . . τοὺς δὲ δυοδεκαετεῖς τῶν παιδῶν πρός τε γραμματικοὺς φοιτᾶν ἤδη καὶ γεωμέτρας καὶ τὸ σῶμα γυμνάζειν. The passage is taken verbatim from Oribasius, *Lib. inc.* 3.9, *CMG* 5:2.2.13f.; cf. *Syn. ad Eustath.* 5.14, *CMG* 6:3.158. Oribasius in turn was drawing on Athenaeus of Attaleia.

2. Γραμματιστής meaning γραμματικός, "teacher of liberal letters" or "teacher of literature"

    a. At [Basil. Sel.] *Vie et miracles de Sainte Thècle* 2.38 Dagron, the father and son, Alypius and Olympius, are each called γραμματιστής; see Part II nos. 7, 108. The expertise of the former—who communicates with St. Thecla by quoting a verse of Homer—and the honorific style of the latter, ὁ γραμματιστὴς ὁ πάνυ, make it clear that γραμματιστής here denotes more than a humble teacher of letters; i.e., it means γραμματικός.

    b. Accordingly, in the following chapter of the *Vie*, on Isocasius, a γραμματιστής turned σοφιστής (*Vie* 2.39; cf. Part II no. 85), the term must have the same meaning. It is worth noting that the author of the *Vie* was a man of some literary pretensions, perhaps a former rhetorician, concerned to present the story of St. Thecla in a polished style.[4]

    c. Zach. Schol. *Disputatio,* PG 85.1061A–1064A: καὶ μοῦ τῆς δεξίας λαβόμενος ἀπάγει παρὰ τὸ τέμενος τῶν Μουσῶν, ἔνθα ποιηταὶ καὶ ῥήτορες

---

    3. Compare Simplic. *Comm. in Phys.* 2.8, on the same proposition, *CAG* 9.385.17ff.: τί γὰρ δεῖται βουλῆς ὁ γραμματικός, ἵνα οὕτως γράψῃ τὸ Δίωνος ὄνομα ὡς γράφει. Both Philoponus and Simplicius clearly have the teacher of beginning letters in mind, as the examples Σωκράτης and Δίων show: for the same names used in this connection, see Headlam, *Herodas* 134. For the grammarian giving elementary instruction, see also Appendix 4; cf. the references at n. 15 below.

    4. Cf. Dagron, ed., *Vie* pp. 17ff.

καὶ τῶν γραμματιστῶν οἱ παῖδες φοιτῶντες ποιοῦνται τὰς ἐπιδείξεις. Here both context and content—the precinct of the Muses; the pupils of γραμματισταί mounting literary displays—strongly suggest that γραμματιστής must mean a teacher of liberal studies, i.e., a γραμματικός. A primary teacher's pupils would have little occasion to present ἐπιδείξεις,[5] but literary exercises and displays by the students in the grammarian's school are well known.[6]

d. Agath. *Hist.* 5.21.3 Keydell, describing the education of Germanus, brought from Bederiana to Constantinople at the end of his eighth year: τοῖς τε . . . τῶν γραμματιστῶν ὡμίλει διδασκαλείοις καὶ πρός γε ἀνὰ τὰ φροντιστήρια φοιτῶν τῆς τῶν Λατίνων μετέσχε παιδείας. Since Germanus was probably unschooled when he arrived in the capital, γραμματισταί could mean "elementary teachers" here. But since only the γραμματισταί and Latin studies are mentioned for an education that apparently spanned about ten years—Germanus was at the end of his eighth year on his arrival; the sentence immediately following the passage above begins ἐπεὶ δὲ ἐς ἥβης μέτρον ἀφίκετο, i.e., around eighteen years of age— γραμματισταί here more likely means both "teachers of elementary letters" and "teachers of literature," in an undifferentiated sense: note the plural. Compare the remarks on Procopius's usage and on the significance of the phrase οἱ καλούμενοι γραμματικοί elsewhere in Agathias, below *ad fin.*

e. Damasc. *V. Isid.* frg. 178 Zintzen describes the grammarian Pamprepius (Part II no. 114) as γραμματιστὴς τὴν τέχνην. Since Damascius is largely a hostile witness for Pamprepius, it has sometimes been thought that he uses γραμματιστής here in the sense "elementary teacher," as a term of invective, with a view to diminishing Pamprepius's stature.[7]

This is probably not correct. Damascius does despise Pamprepius for his ambition and his seeming betrayal of the pagans; cf. *V. Isid.* frg. 287 (with 178), 288, 289, and possibly 179. But he otherwise makes no attempt to conceal or diminish Pamprepius's cultural attainments;[8] it therefore seems unlikely that Damascius would attempt to smear with a phrase a man whose learning he elsewhere establishes at length.

Further, although Damascius does use the word γραμματικά to mean "literary matters" (*V. Isid.* epit. Phot. 298 = frg. 331), the sense that it

5. Cf. Marrou, *Histoire*[6] 240f.
6. For Hellenistic evidence, cf. Marrou, *Histoire*[6] 252; see also, e.g., Part II nos. 59, 83.
7. Cf. Keydell, *RE* 18:2(2).409.64ff.
8. Cf. frg. 289 = epit. Phot. 168: περὶ δ' οὖν τὴν ἄλλην προπαιδείαν [i.e., all literary culture short of philosophy] οὕτω διεπονεῖτο καὶ ἐς τοσοῦτον διεγυμνάζετο ὁ Παμπρέπιος, ὥστε ἐν ὀλίγῳ χρόνῳ λογιώτατος εἶναι ἔδοξε καὶ πολυμαθέστατος τῶν αὐτόθι παιδείας μετειληχότων.

has in classical Greek, he regularly goes out of his way to avoid using the nonclassical technical term γραμματικός to designate the professional grammarian: see esp. the periphrases in *V. Isid.* epit. Phot. 60 (= frg. 111) and frg. 276, both quoted at Appendix 1.3e. In fact, the apparent occurrences of γραμματικός in the remnants of the *V. Isid.* are all the result of additions or rephrasing by Photius or the compilers of the *Suda*. Photius normalizes the phrase γραμματιστὴς τὴν τέχνην at *V. Isid.* frg. 178, replacing it with τέχνην γραμματικός in his epitome (epit. Phot. 110); the remaining appearances of γραμματικός, in *V. Isid.* frg. 111 and frg. 313, referring to Ammonianus and Harpocras, respectively, almost certainly reflect not Damascius's *ipsissima verba* but the *Suda*'s usage: in both cases, γραμματικός occurs as part of an introductory formula of the type regularly found in the *Suda*'s biographical entries.[9]

Damascius avoids yet another technical term in *V. Isid.* frg. 178: note the euphemism παραμυθία in his reference to Pamprepius's public salary at Constantinople; the technical term, σύνταξις, appears in Malch. frg. 20 = *FHG* 4.131f. Probably, then, Damascius uses γραμματιστής in frg. 178 as an alternative for the technical term γραμματικός, like Libanius and the other authors quoted above.

3. Γραμματιστής and *litterator*

With the variable use of γραμματιστής remarked above we should compare the behavior of the corresponding Latin term, *litterator*. In a pair of valuable articles, E. W. Bower and A. D. Booth have drawn attention to how the word is used both to designate the elementary teacher—i.e., *litterator* as one who makes another *litteratus* in the basic sense—and, more commonly, as a synonym for *grammaticus*.[10] Note that an author can use the word unself-consciously in its two different meanings at different points in the same work: thus at *Hist. Aug., M. Ant.* 2.2, the term *litterator* must mean a teacher of *elementa*; but at ibid. *Comm.* 1.6 the term must mean *grammaticus*, since it refers to the stage of education preceding the *orator*.

This same flexibility can be found in the use of γραμματιστής by a Greek author, the historian Procopius. In four of the five places where

9. Frg. 111 = *Suda* A.1639, 1.145.20 Adler, Ἀμμωνιανός, γραμματικός, an inference correctly drawn from the elaborate periphrasis Damascius uses (see Appendix 1.3e); frg. 313 = *Suda* A.4010, 1.366.23f. Adler, Ἁρποκρᾶς: οὗτος συνήθης ἦν Ἀμμωνίῳ, ἀνὴρ Αἰγύπτιος, γραμματικός, ἐπὶ Ζήνωνος τοῦ βασιλέως, where the ethnic and chronological formulas that surround the title clearly reveal the hand of the *Suda*'s compiler.

10. Bower, "Some Technical Terms" 469ff.; Booth, "Litterator"; both discuss passages from the early through the late empire. For *litterator* meaning *grammaticus*, note also Gell. *NA* 16.6.1, 11 and 18.9.2–3.

he uses γραμματιστής, the word is most naturally taken to mean "teacher of basic letters." Thus at *Anecd.* 20.17 Procopius remarks of Iunilius (*QSP* 543), Ἑλληνικῶν μέντοι [sc. γραμμάτων] ἕνεκα οὐδὲ πεφοιτηκότα πρὸς γραμματιστοῦ πώποτε οὐδὲ τὴν γλῶσσαν αὐτὴν ἑλληνίζειν δυνάμενον. Since Iunilius is supposed to be ignorant of Greek, γραμματιστής here should denote the elementary teacher of the language.[11] But at *BG* 1.24.12 Procopius says of John the Cappadocian, λόγων μὲν τῶν ἐλευ-θερίων καὶ παιδείας ἀνήκοος ἦν. οὐ γὰρ ἄλλο οὐδὲν ἐς γραμματιστοῦ φοιτῶν ἔμαθεν ὅτι μὴ γράμματα. Here the logical sequence—note the γάρ—and the substance of the second clause imply that one could learn more than mere elementary letters, that one was in fact expected to become familiar with λόγοι οἱ ἐλευθέριοι καὶ παιδεία under the γραμματιστής. The notion has little to do with the function of the γραμματιστής *qua* elementary teacher, as that is normally conceived, but it makes sense if the meaning of γραμματιστής here approaches γραμματικός. We should conclude, therefore, that Procopius used γραμματιστής as the author of the *Historia Augusta* used *litterator*, to mean "teacher of letters" in a fluid, fairly un-differentiated sense, allowing it to be defined by context and by the kind of letters to which he refers.

The passages surveyed above suggest that Wolf was correct to con-clude that Libanius preferred γραμματιστής to γραμματικός for stylistic reasons; he could thereby avoid a technical term standard only in con-temporary usage and find a substitute sanctioned by classical diction.[12] Similar stylistic considerations probably motivated the post-Libanian examples of γραμματιστής meaning γραμματικός noted in Section 2 above, where all the authors cited aim at literary sophistication.[13] Such concerns perhaps also motivate some of the other peculiarities of style to which I have alluded: for example, frequent periphrasis (see 2e above, on Damascius; cf. Appendix 1.3), or the use of such explanatory or objective—in essence, apologetic—phrases as οἱ καλούμενοι γραμματικοί at Agath. *Hist.* 5.5.4, where the historian tries to forestall any offense at his using the nonclassical technical term.[14] But no such stylistic considerations

11. Compare, e.g., the passage of Simplicius quoted in Section 1e above. For the other, similar uses in Procopius, see *BP* 2.15.7, concerning Peter of Arzanene; *BG* 1.2.6, concerning Athalarich; *BG* 4.19.8, on the Huns' illiteracy.

12. Wolf, *Schulwesen* 35: "Der massgebliche Kreis der klassischen Literatur nur 'Grammatistes' [and not, i.e., γραμματικός] in der Bedeutung Lehrer kennt."

13. Contrast the passages noted in Section 1, which occur either in Christian writings composed by ascetics or in philosophical and medical treatises with no great stylistic ambitions.

14. For the stylistic implications of the phrasing, see Averil Cameron, *Agathias* 75ff., with this example at p. 80; contrast Agathias's use of γραμματιστής, in Section 2d above.

seem to have motivated the variable use of *litterator* noted above; Latin authors have no apparent bias against *grammaticus*. And it must be stressed that to prefer γραμματιστής was probably to modify common usage slightly, not willfully to distort it: γραμματιστής, like *litterator*, could be used so flexibly because the boundary between the activities of the primary and of the secondary teacher, the γραμματιστής and the γραμματικός, was not distinct and absolute.[15]

15. See n. 3 above; with Wolf, *Schulwesen* 34f.; Kaster, "Notes" 325ff.; and Chap. 2 "Some Variable Definitions."

Γραμματικός as Epithet and Personal Name

It is well known that at its first appearance, in Attic Greek of the fourth century B.C., γραμματικός was an epithet with the general sense "literate," "knowing, skilled in, letters or literature," the antonym of ἀγράμματος (in place of *γράμματος), and only later became the title for a professional teacher of language and literature. Latin *grammaticus*, borrowed directly from the Greek of the postclassical period, has the titular force almost exclusively,[1] whereas much of the burden of classical γραμματικός is taken over in Greek by φιλόλογος, which is an epithet or name, never a professional title.[2]

This lexical shift has pleasant consequences for the historian and prosopographer, since γραμματικός and *grammaticus* emerge as perhaps the most differentiated titles in the literary culture of antiquity. Though, for example, *litterator* or γραμματιστής and ῥήτωρ or σοφιστής are all flexible (not to say vague) in their application,[3] one can be nearly certain that from the second century B.C. onward anyone who is called γραμματικός or *grammaticus* is believed to possess a readily definable expertise that he holds in common with anyone else bearing the same title. The differentiation, however, was not complete.[4] Moreover, the original force of γραμματικός, as simple epithet or proper name, persists in Greek and Latin in documents from the fourth through the sixth century and beyond. Some examples follow.

1. With *litteratus* and *litteris eruditus* corresponding to the epithet γραμματικός of classical Greek: cf. below; on *grammaticus* and *litteratus*, see Bower, "Some Technical Terms."

2. Cf. Nuchelmans, *Studien*; Kuch, ΦΙΛΟΛΟΓΟΣ; Robert, *Hellenica* 13.45ff.

3. On γραμματιστής and *litterator*, see Appendix 2. On ῥήτωρ and σοφιστής, see Bowersock, *Greek Sophists* 12ff.; C. P. Jones, "Reliability"; Stanton, "Sophists."

4. For qualification, see the references at Appendix 2 nn. 3, 15.

1. Epithet meaning "literate," "knowing, skilled in, letters or literature"

a. Greek: especially frequent in the late-antique Aristotelian tradition; see Ioan. Philop. *Comm. in Anal. pr.* 1.1 (*CAG* 13:2.21.17f.), 1.15 (ibid. 191.25ff.), 2.6 (*CAG* 13:3.354.1ff.); Simplic. *Comm. in De cael.* 1.2 (*CAG* 7.29.10ff.); cf. also the numerous examples of δυνάμει γραμματικός cited in Part II no. 118. These instances belong to a specialized tradition, conditioned by Aristotle's well-known preference for γραμματικός as an example in his arguments.[5] However, an obvious unspecialized instance can be found at Epiphan. *Panar. haeres.* 66.10ff., where Aegialeus of Kaschares is described as φύσει γραμματικός, corresponding to *litteris apprime eruditus* in the Latin *Acta Archelai*; see Part II nos. 179, 236. Note also the *Suda*'s use of γραμματικός in a loose, nontechnical sense, most clearly perhaps at Γ.450, on Gregory Nazianzen, οὗτος οὐ μόνον γραμματικὸς καὶ τὰ ἐς ποίησιν δέξιος, ἀλλὰ πολλῷ πλεῖον καὶ ἐς φιλοσοφίαν ἐξήσκητο καὶ ῥήτωρ ἦν ἀμφιδέξιος; in the *Suda*, however, it is not always clear whether the word is being used in a nontechnical, nontitular sense, or whether the technical sense is being ineptly applied. From an earlier period, the famous portrait of Hermione with the inscription γραμματική (*SB* 1.5753; photograph in Turner, *Greek Papyri* pl. 3) probably provides another example; likewise perhaps the obscure papyrus published by Coles, "More Papyri" 121f. no. 1 (s.III; Socnopaei Nesus?) = *SB* 10.10569, where γραμματικός means "(speech-?)writer," according to Coles.

b. Latin: Boethius *In Categ.* 3, *PL* 64.257C–D; Mart. Cap. 4.349, p. 113.16ff. Willis; probably Auson. *Epigr.* 7.2 (see Part II no. 246). Note that the Aristotelian tradition is at work in the first two examples— obviously in Boethius, tangentially in Capella—and that the influence of Greek epigram may be suspected in Ausonius.

2. Proper name

Far less common than Φιλόλογος (cf. above, n. 2): Aug. *Ep.* 43 tit., *Grammaticus*, one of Augustine's addressees; *Inschr. Eph.* 6 (*IGSK* 16) 2312, a funeral inscr. to one Tertullianus raised by [Γ]ραμματι[κ]ός; perhaps *CIG* 2169 = Kaibel 828 = *IG* 12:2.129 Mytilene: v. 8, Γραμματικὸς τελέω. Cf. also *CIL* 12.1921 Vienna, the epitaph of one L. Marinus Italicensis *signo* Grammat(i)us; with Kajanto, *Supernomina* 83.

5. For the persistence of the tradition, see Henry, "Why 'grammaticus'?"

The Number of Grammarians at Bordeaux

Thanks to Ausonius's *Professores*, we know the municipal teachers of Bordeaux better than those of any other fourth-century city, save Antioch; for the *grammatici*, even that exception need not be made. Accordingly, historians of late-antique education have often exploited Ausonius's information concerning curriculum or the function and social position of the teachers.[1]

Attempts to determine how many teachers there were and how they were organized have been nearly as common. For example, C. Jullian suggested (without argument) an arrangement that would accommodate four *grammatici* for Greek and Latin and two Latin *rhetores*,[2] a revision of figures he had earlier proposed.[3] More recently, R. Étienne has argued that there were seven or eight chairs of grammar and five chairs of rhetoric.[4]

Étienne's proposal, however, is difficult to accept. First, the figures appear too high on their face: there is no evidence that even Antioch could boast so many chairs of rhetoric,[5] and Libanius's experience at Nicomedia (*Or.* 1.48ff.) shows that that substantial city normally had only one public appointment; *Or.* 1.25, referring to 339/40, and *Or.* 2.14,

---

1. Apart from the use of the *Professores* by Marrou, *Histoire*[6], *passim*, see the discussions in Roger, *Enseignement* 4ff.; Haarhoff, *Schools* 104ff.; Jouai, *Magistraat* 32ff.; Favez, "École"; cf. also the works cited in Chap. 3 "Bordeaux."

2. *Histoire* 8.251 n. 5.

3. *Ausone* 66: six *grammatici* (Greek and Latin) and four *rhetores*; similarly Haarhoff, *Schools* 115; Bolgar, *Classical Heritage* 33. As will be suggested below, Jullian's later estimate for the *grammatici* may be close to the mark.

4. *Bordeaux* 239ff.

5. Cf. Wolf, *Schulwesen* 43f.; Petit, *Étudiants* 92f. The statement of Marrou, *Histoire*[6] 612 n. 13, that there were five municipal chairs at Antioch, gains no support from the texts he cites.

referring to 353, reveal that Athens, a major center of rhetorical study in the East, had only three.[6] Further, the implications of the figures make little sense. We should note especially that for the period covered by the *Professores*, roughly the first two-thirds of s.IV, continuously staffing the twelve or thirteen chairs Étienne posited would certainly have required more than the twenty-eight or twenty-nine teachers Ausonius names, given the rate of turnover that must have obtained because of premature death or for other reasons. The numbers can be made to work only if one assumes what was clearly not the case, that nearly every teacher's tenure was about thirty years long, like Ausonius's. Finally, the figures were reached by unsatisfactory means: e.g., to arrive at his figure for the chairs of rhetoric, Étienne merely assumed (*Bordeaux* 245) that all rhetoricians known to have taught at Bordeaux after 352/53 were active at the same time; a similar assumption underlay his calculations (ibid. 239) for the number of grammatical chairs; the grammarians Ammonius and Anastasius were arbitrarily omitted; and the functions of Crispus and Urbicus were misstated.

A. D. Booth has recently analyzed the question much more carefully and subtly.[7] According to Booth, the teaching corps of Bordeaux must have been far smaller than previously supposed, consisting simply of one Latin *rhetor*, one Latin *grammaticus*, and one Greek *grammaticus*. Much of his argument is persuasive, and I am prepared to believe that normally only one professor of rhetoric and one professor of Greek were active in the city.[8] But I think it unlikely that the city supported only one Latin *grammaticus* at all times. I can see three serious objections to Booth's analysis on this point.

First, as remarked above, Étienne's figures could make sense only on the clearly false assumption that nearly all the teachers whom Ausonius commemorated enjoyed tenures as long as his own; a basic assumption of Booth's analysis stands at the opposite extreme and is only slightly less difficult—that as a *grammaticus* Ausonius had a tenure roughly seven times longer than the average, and some four times longer than the longest tenure among the other teachers.[9] Although we know, for example, that Ausonius's nephew Herculanus died teaching at a very

6. For the dating of the reference in *Or.* 2.14, cf. Norman, *Autobiography* 154.

7. See Booth, "Academic Career." Although Alan Booth and I disagree about the Latin *grammatici*, I should emphasize that his discussion has placed the matter on an entirely new footing and has persuaded me to revise some of my views.

8. On the Greek *grammatici*, see below.

9. These calculations are based on the table in Booth, "Academic Career" 341, where Ausonius's tenure as *grammaticus* is dated "ca 339–ca 360." The average tenure of the other teachers tentatively dated there for the period ca. 316–ca. 366 is 3.1 years; the longest is that of Leontius ("ca 330–ca 335"). The results are not much altered if one includes Macrinus ("from before 315 to ca

young age (Part II no. 70), and although two Latin grammarians left their chairs at Bordeaux for positions elsewhere,[10] it seems *prima facie* unlikely that all the other Latin grammarians would have had such short tenures or, to look at it another way, that Ausonius would have held his chair as long as his six immediate predecessors together. The improbability appears still greater if one considers that the Latin grammarians' average tenure would have to have been less than half the rhetoricians';[11] one could explain this discrepancy only by assuming that the grammarians regularly began teaching much later than the rhetoricians or that they died much younger—both of which seem arbitrary—or that their professional, social, or geographic mobility was significantly greater, which is certainly not true.[12] Much the same difficulty arises if one notes that only five Greek grammarians[13] would have been active in the same period (from shortly before 315 until ca. 366) during which at least thirteen men must be supposed to have occupied the Latin chair. The burden of these improbabilities and incongruities is cumulative; in short, too many teachers must fit into too short a time if Bordeaux had only one Latin *grammaticus*.

Second, the squeeze gives a very unlikely shape to the careers of several grammarians, most notably of Nepotianus (Part II no. 105), whose beginnings as a *grammaticus* Booth must place ca. 362. By then Nepotianus could scarcely have been much less than sixty-seven years old: he cannot have been born much later than 295 (see Part II s.v.). To be sure, we find a late start in the profession in the case of Phoebicius, who immigrated to Bordeaux when already a *senex* and received a chair through the patronage of his son, probably the rhetorician Attius Patera (see Part II no. 122); but the like is highly improbable for Nepotianus, a lifelong resident of the city who rose from grammar to a chair of rhetoric and a provincial governorship—on Booth's reconstruction, he cannot have held the latter two posts before the age of seventy. A similar problem concerns Anastasius, a native and gramm. of Bordeaux whom *ambitio* drove to Poitiers when he was already *in senio* (cf. *Prof.* 10.52f., with Part II no. 11). Booth must date the move ca. 330 ("Academic Career" 341), but he

316"). Since he is supposed to have succeeded Thalassus ("before 315"), and since Ausonius (b. ca. 310) had a living memory of the latter (*Prof.* 12.1-3, 7-8; with Part II no. 148), the succession could not have occurred much before 315; Macrinus, too, must then be thought to have had a very short tenure.

10. Concordius and Anastasius; see Part II nos. 35, 11. Anastasius, however, left only *in senio*, according to *Prof.* 10.52f.; see below.

11. Average tenure for the *rhetores* is 6.75 years; see Booth's table, "Academic Career" 339.

12. See Chap. 3 pp. 104-5.

13. Corinthus, Spercheus, Menestheus, Citarius, Crispus; see Booth, "Academic Career" 341.

must also date the beginning of Anastasius's tenure in Bordeaux ca. 326, when presumably he was already in or on the verge of his dotage.

Third, there is a problem with Crispus and Urbicus (*Prof.* 21; see Part II nos. 40, 165), who Ausonius says taught both Greek and Latin. Booth must argue that the two did not "function in both capacities simultaneously" but taught serially—Crispus first teaching Greek, then Latin; Urbicus taking up the Greek chair Crispus vacated, then the Latin—on the grounds that "the *grammaticus Latinus* and the *grammaticus Graecus* appear as distinct teachers in Ausonius and other sources" ("Academic Career" 341f.). But that premise is not correct, since Ausonius himself gives evidence of a grammarian who taught both languages simultaneously at Trier ca. 376 (*Epist.* 13.26ff., with Part II no. 65). Further, nothing in *Prof.* 21 suggests the complicated sequence of appointments noted above: although Ausonius does set aside sections of the poem to praise the skills of each man individually (see Part II no. 40), a disinterested reading most naturally suggests that the two were exact contemporaries and colleagues, performing their duties at the same time.[14]

In sum, the belief that there was only one Latin *grammaticus* at Bordeaux involves too many difficulties; I suggest instead that there were ordinarily two such positions in the city. Before developing that suggestion, however, I would advise a mild agnosticism. The information Ausonius has given us, for all its fullness, is still less than we would like, and, worse, it may mislead: any analysis that aims at precision has set its foundations in quicksand. Only exceptionally can we draw any reliable conclusions about the chronology and tenure of the *grammatici*; at one extreme, Ausonius's comments on the early fourth-century teachers are extremely sketchy (see esp. *Prof.* 10 and 12); and his decision to commemorate only the dead (*Prof.* praef. 4; *Prof.* 25) almost certainly means that some teachers who began their activity in the 370s—perhaps even some who were Ausonius's colleagues in the 360s, before he went to Trier—have been omitted. As a result, and not surprisingly, we are best informed about the teachers who were active during the second third of s.IV, the time of Ausonius's tenure at Bordeaux, ca. 336–ca. 367. But even those data leave much to be desired: for example, as a rare piece of information concerning succession, we know that Acilius Glabrio became a *grammaticus* when Ausonius became a *rhetor*; but we have not the least idea who followed Glabrio—and he very likely died before 360 (see Part II no. 64).

The most that can safely be done is to categorize the *grammatici* according to the languages they taught and according to the two general periods

14. Note esp. *Prof.* 21.13, to Urbicus, *nam tu Crispo coniuncte tuo*; note also the resounding triple anaphora that rounds out the poem: vv. 25–28, *ambo . . . ambo . . . ambo.*

Table 1 The Grammarians of Bordeaux in the Fourth Century

Latin	Source	Greek	Source
		BEFORE AUSONIUS'S TENURE	
Ammonius	*Prof.* 10	Corinthus	*Prof.* 8
Anastasius[a]	*Prof.* 10	Spercheus	*Prof.* 8
Concordius[b]	*Prof.* 10		
Macrinus	*Prof.* 10		
Phoebicius	*Prof.* 10		
Sucuro	*Prof.* 10		
Thalassus	*Prof.* 12		
		DURING AUSONIUS'S TENURE	
Ausonius[c]		Menestheus	*Prof.* 8
Crispus[d]	*Prof.* 21	Citarius	*Prof.* 13
Acilius Glabrio[e]	*Prof.* 24	Crispus[d]	*Prof.* 21
Herculanus	*Prof.* 11; cf. *Par.* 17	Urbicus[d]	*Prof.* 21
Iucundus	*Prof.* 9		
Leontius Lascivus	*Prof.* 7		
Nepotianus[c]	*Prof.* 15		
Urbicus[d]	*Prof.* 21		

[a] Later at Poitiers		[d] Taught Latin and Greek	
[b] Later at another city		[e] Succeeded Ausonius	
[c] Later *rhetor*			

in which they can be placed, before and during Ausonius's stint as a teacher in the city.[15] This has been done in Table 1, which lists nineteen *grammatici* accounting for twenty-one chairs; Crispus and Urbicus must each be counted twice, once for Greek and once for Latin.[16] The chronological distinction is convenient and corresponds to the differences in detail found in the *Professores*. It should not, however, obscure the fact that some teachers—e.g., Nepotianus and Leontius Lascivus (both older contemporaries of Ausonius), Leontius's brother Iucundus, and Menestheus, and Citarius—were probably or possibly active in both periods, though they are all enrolled on the lower half of Table 1. Arguments for dating can be found in the entries for the individual *grammatici* in Part II and are not repeated here. The dates should not, in any event, be seriously controversial. The teachers in each section of Table 1 are listed alphabetically.

15. Cf. Étienne, *Bordeaux* 239; Booth, "Academic Career" 340f.
16. Victorius, the *subdoctor* or *proscholus* of Ausonius (*Prof.* 22; Part II no. 162), has been omitted, because he was not a *grammaticus*.

I do not believe that the evidence allows a thorough, precise reconstruction of concurrent and successive tenures. Nonetheless, for three
reasons I propose that there were ordinarily two Latin *grammatici* and
one Greek *grammaticus* holding chairs at Bordeaux.[17]

First, the fact that for the same general period Ausonius commemor-
ates fifteen *grammatici* for Latin but only six for Greek is a crude but
plausible index: the ratio of 2.5:1 suggests that at any given moment
there were two Latin teachers for one Greek. The ratio allows for some
variability in tenure, yet it does not require us to assume that the average
tenure of the Latin *grammatici* was drastically and inexplicably shorter
than that of Greek *grammatici* (see above).

Second, the presence of two Latin *grammatici* is implied by the distinction Ausonius appears to make between elementary instructors and
teachers at a more advanced level. Ausonius does not note the difference
in so many words in the *Professores*; but the distinct function of the latter
(correctly recognized but somewhat misleadingly called "de 'echte' grammatici" by Jouai, *Magistraat* 32) can be inferred from Ausonius's specific
mention of the former,[18] and especially from the careers of Ausonius
himself and of his nephew Heculanus. At *Epist.* 22.67–75, Ausonius recalls
his teaching career:[19]

> multos lactantibus annis
> ipse alui gremioque fovens et murmura solvens
> eripui tenerum blandis nutricibus aevum.
> 70 mox pueros molli monitu et formidine leni
> pellexi, ut mites peterent per acerba profectus,
> carpturi dulcem fructum radicis amarae.
> idem vesticipes motu iam puberis aevi
> ad mores artesque bonas fandique vigorem
> 75 produxi.

Since the passage clearly sketches the stages in his career, with the shifts
marked by *mox* and *idem*, and since vv. 73–75 clearly refer to his time as
rhetor, vv. 67–72 must refer to his time as *grammaticus*. Evidently Ausonius
began as a teacher of the youngest pupils—a teacher of the *elementa*, like

17. The adverb "ordinarily" requires qualification; see below.
18. Teachers of *elementa*: certainly Ammonius (*Prof.* 10.36–37) and Crispus
(*Prof.* 21.4–6); probably also Macrinus, who was Ausonius's first teacher (*Prof.*
10.11ff.). A few other cases offer grounds for speculation, but the evidence is too
skimpy to discuss here.
19. On the interpretation of this passage see Kaster, "Notes" 331f. and
nn. 28, 40, with Booth, "Elementary and Secondary Education" 6, 7f. (differently
"Academic Career" 332f.).

the others already noted—before going on to teach older, more advanced boys. A similar sequence can be deduced from what we are told of his nephew. While still very young, Herculanus was a *grammaticus* at Bordeaux (*Prof.* 11 tit.; cf. v. 3, Part II no. 70), yet Ausonius hoped that he would succeed to his own chair of grammar.[20] Since this implies a significant difference between their two positions, we should conclude that the young Herculanus taught the elements, with prospects for advancement, just as Ausonius, when a *grammaticus*, had moved on from elementary teaching to more advanced instruction before becoming a *rhetor*.

Third, a more general but no less relevant consideration: as a provincial capital and the seat of the *vicarius* of the southern Gallic diocese, Bordeaux was an important administrative center; it thus bears comparison with Trier or Milan, each of which apparently had at least two Latin grammarians in the late fourth century.[21] Even in Gaza, a city considerably less important than Bordeaux, τὸ κεφάλαιον ὅλον, the teaching corps of grammarians, at the end of the fifth century or the beginning of the sixth consisted of two γραμματικοί for Greek and one for Latin:[22] *mutatis mutandis*, Bordeaux could surely claim as much.

We should, therefore, be prepared to suppose that Bordeaux ordinarily had four *professores*: one Latin *rhetor*, one Greek *grammaticus*, and two Latin *grammatici*, the last two apparently with differentiated functions— one more *grammaticus* than Booth allowed; one less *grammaticus* and one less *rhetor* than Jullian suggested (n. 2 above). Yet "ordinarily" is a slippery notion, and a caveat should be added: it is necessary to remember that the appointment of *professores* depended on a number of factors—the availability of funds and of suitable candidates, the willingness of the town council to act, and the ability of a suitable candidate to marshal the necessary patronage—all of which together could produce variations in the size and composition of the teaching corps. For the *grammatici*, this might mean that at one moment there would be only one Latin grammarian; at another, conceivably, three. At another time there might be

20. *Prof.* 11.3. The hope was frustrated by Herculanus's early death (vv. 4–5; *Par.* 17.9), and Acilius Glabrio became Ausonius's successor (*Prof.* 24.6; Part II no. 64).

21. Trier: Auson. *Epist.* 13; with Part II nos. 65, 166, the former teaching Greek as well as Latin (see above). Milan: Part II nos. 159, 172. Contrast Gratian's law of 376 (*CTh* 13.3.11), which seems to provide for the appointment of one *rhetor* and one Latin and one Greek *grammaticus* in the *metropoles* of the northern Gallic diocese: although one may be tempted to regard that provision as a norm—so Booth, whose argument relies heavily on the analogy of that law, "Academic Career" 334 and esp. 340—it should rather be thought of as the minimum teaching corps required, which the imperial fisc in this case undertook to provide.

22. Procop. Gaz. *Ep.* 13.11ff., quoted at Part II no. 7.

two *grammatici* present, each of whom could teach both languages (so Crispus and Urbicus). It is best to keep such possible variations in mind and to avoid too rigid a scheme.

A final observation. Among the *grammatici*, some correlation between social and professional status is apparent, although the correspondences are not complete. Ausonius and Nepotianus, both of whom went on to become rhetoricians, and Acilius Glabrio, who succeeded to Ausonius's chair of grammar, certainly came from families that were more than a cut above that of at least one teacher of the elements, Crispus, who was of libertine birth; the name of another teacher of *elementa*, Ammonius, suggests that he was of foreign extraction and possibly of low local status. Yet if my discussion above is correct, Ausonius and his nephew Herculanus, the son of a leading *curialis*, would also have taught the elements; but Ausonius soon advanced (*mox*, *Epist.* 22.70), and Herculanus had his own prospects for advancement at the time of his death, at a very young age. Though social status by itself evidently did not determine at what level one began teaching, it may have been important in determining whether one progressed, either from the elementary to the advanced level in the grammarian's school, like Ausonius and, potentially, Herculanus, or from *grammaticus* to *rhetor*, like Ausonius and Nepotianus.

Geographical-Chronological List of Teachers

The list below includes every teacher entered in Part II whose place of activity is known or can reasonably be conjectured. The list begins with the two capital cities and then proceeds in the order of the *fasti* of provincial governors in *PLRE*, starting with Africa and then moving roughly from west to east through the major administrative districts of the empire. (Note that the dioceses of Gaul have not been distinguished and that no separate list has been made for the teachers of Alexandria.) The teachers in each section of the list are arranged chronologically, so far as our information allows; men who taught, e.g., in both Africa and Constantinople are entered in the two appropriate sections, with a parenthetical note concerning their prior or subsequent movements.

Most of the brief remarks that appear below should be self-explanatory. Note in particular that the language taught is mentioned only for Latin teachers in the East or for Greek teachers in the West. The *grammatici*, strictly so called, are not distinguished here from the other teachers—*magistri ludi*, διδάσκαλοι, *vel sim.*—included in the prosopography. References "s.v." are to Part II.

Name	Locality	Date	Comments
		ROME	
Marius Plotius Sacerdos		s.III 2/2?	
Aelius Donatus		s.IV med.	see s.v., no. 52: from Africa?
Anonymus 4		s.IV med.	from Africa
? Probus		s.IV	see s.v., no. 127: from Africa?

Name	Locality	Date	Comments
Crispinianus		s.IV 3/4	
Bonifatius		s.IV ex. / s.V init.	
Servius		s.IV ex. – s.V 1/3	
Phocas		s.IV ex. / s.V	
Deuterius		s.IV 2/2 / s.VI	
? Gorgonius		s.IV / s.VI	see s.v., no. 224: a teacher?
Anonymus 10		s.IV 2/2 / s.VI	
Anonymus 11		s.VI init.?	
? Anonymus 17		s.V ex. / s.VI init.	see s.v., no. 281: perhaps a fiction?

	CONSTANTINOPLE		
Nicocles		s.IV 2/3	from Sparta
? Acacius		355	on his location, see s.v., no. 1
Didymus		before 357	from Egypt; previously in Antioch
Evanthius		d. 358	Latin
Chrestus		358	Latin; from Africa
? Harpocration		358	more probably sophist than gramm.; from Egypt via Antioch
Ammonius		s.IV ex.	from Alexandria
Helladius		s.IV ex. – s.V 1/4	from Alexandria
Paulus		s.V init. (before 419)	Latin gramm. (probably); later Novatian bishop
Syrianus		s.V 1/4	
Theofilus		s.V 1/4	Latin
Horapollon		s.IV ex. / s.V 1/3	from Egypt
? Orion		s.V 1/4 – 1/2	from Alexandria; very doubtful for Constantinople; see s.v., no. 110
Dioscorius		s.V 2/4 – 2/2	from Myra (Lycia)
Orus		s.V 1/2 – 2/3	from Alexandria
Cledonius		s.V med. – 2/2?	Latin
? Hyperechius		s.V 3/4	see s.v., no. 79: from Alexandria

Name	Locality	Date	Comments
Pamprepius		476–78	to Constantinople? native of Panopolis; previously at Athens
? Theoctistus		s.V 2/2	Latin; see s.v., no. 149: at Constantinople?
Eugenius		s.V 2/2 / s.VI init.	from Augustopolis (Phrygia Salutaris)
Stephanus (no. 144)		s.V. ex. / s.VI 1/2	
Priscianus		s.V ex. / s.VI init.	Latin; from Caesarea (Mauretania Caesariensis?)
Urbanus (no. 164)		s.VI init.	Latin; formerly a student at Alexandria
Speciosus		s.VI 1/3	Latin gramm. or rhetorician; from Africa
Metrodorus (no. 101)		s.VI 1/3 – 1/2	from Tralles (Asia)
Ioannes Lydus		s.VI 2/4	Latin; simultaneously absentee *praefectianus* (see s.v., no. 92); from Philadelphia (Lycia)
? Eutyches		s.VI 1/2	Latin; activity conjectural but likely for Constantinople
? Damocharis		s.VI 2/3	native of Cos; probably active at Constantinople
Hermolaus		s.VI 2/3?	
Metrodorus		s.V / s.VI?	see s.v., no. 100: perhaps identical with Metrodorus from Tralles, above

Name	Locality	Date	Comments
AFRICA			
Flavius (no. 61) Victor	Cirta / Constantina (Numidia)	s.III ex. / s.IV init. s.IV 1/4 (by 303; still active 320)	later at Nicomedia
? Aelius Donatus		s.IV med.	see s.v., no. 52: later at Rome; from Africa?
Anonymus 4		s.IV med.	an African at Rome
? Probus		s.IV	see s.v., no 127: from Africa? to Rome?
Chrestus		before 358	from Africa; to Constantinople
Annius Namptoius	Thuburbo Maius (Africa Proconsularis)	361	
Aur. Augustinus	Thagaste	372/73	later rhetorician at Carthage, Rome, Milan
Nebridius		before 385	native of Africa; subdoctor at Milan
Maximus	Madaurus	s.IV 2/2–ex.	
Domitius Rufinus	Iomnium (Mauretania Caesariensis)	s.IV / s.V?	
Cresconius		s.V init.	
Felicianus	Carthage	s.V 2/2	
Iulianus Pomerius		s.V ex.	see s.v., no. 124: later at Arles; perhaps a rhetorician in Africa
Pompeius		s.V 2/2 / s.VI	
? Calbulus	at an episcopal see	s.V ex. / s.VI init.?	
Calcidius		s.V 2/2 / s.VI	
? Speciosus		s.VI 1/3	Latin gramm. or rhetorician; active at Constantinople

Name	Locality	Date	Comments
Faustus	Carthage?	s.VI init. – 1/2	
Fl. Cresconius Corippus		s.VI 1/2	later a *palatinus* at Constantinople

		SPAIN	
Fabius(?) Demetrius	Tarraco	s.III	

		GAUL	
L. Terentius Iulianus *signo* Concordius	Trier	s.III / s.IV	
Concordius	Bordeaux → another city	s.IV 1/3	
Phoebicius	Bordeaux	s.IV init.	from Bayeux
Sucuro	Bordeaux	s.IV init.	
Thalassus	Bordeaux	s.IV init.	
Corinthus	Bordeaux	s.IV 1/4	Greek
Spercheus	Bordeaux	s.IV 1/4	Greek
Macrinus	Bordeaux	s.IV 1/4	
Ammonius	Bordeaux	s.IV 1/3	
Anastasius	Bordeaux → Poitiers	s.IV 1/3	
Menestheus	Bordeaux	s.IV 2/4	Greek
Marcellus	Narbo	s.IV med.?	native of Bordeaux
Staphylius	Elimberris (mod. Auch; Novempopulana)	s.IV 1/2	gramm. or rhetorician, or both
Iucundus	Bordeaux	s.IV 2/4 or 2/3	
Leontius *signo* Lascivus	Bordeaux	s.IV 2/4 or 2/3	
Nepotianus	Bordeaux	s.IV 1/2 – 2/3	gramm. → rhetorician
Pomponius Maximus Herculanus	Bordeaux	s.IV 2/4	
Decimus Magnus Ausonius	Bordeaux	s.IV 2/3	gramm. → rhetorician

Name	Locality	Date	Comments
Victorius	Bordeaux	s.IV 2/3	*subdoctor sive proscholus*; later in Sicily and at Cumae
Acilius Glabrio	Bordeaux	s.IV med.	
Citarius	Bordeaux	s.IV 2/3	Greek; from Sicily, perhaps Syracuse
Crispus	Bordeaux	s.IV med.	Greek and Latin
Urbicus	Bordeaux	s.IV med.	Greek and Latin
Ursulus	Trier	376	
Harmonius	Trier	376	Greek and Latin
? Tetradius	Iculisma → Saintes?	s.IV 2/2	see s.v., no. 263: gramm., or rhetorician?
? Consentius	Narbo?	s.V 1/2?	see s.v., no. 203: probably not a gramm. by profession
? Hoënius	Arles?	s.V med.	see s.v., no. 233: teacher of Sidonius Apollinaris, perhaps a gramm.
? Agroecius		s.V 2/3 – 3/4?	see s.v., no. 181: rhetorician? → bishop of Sens?
Domitius	Clermont-Ferrand	s.V 3/4	
? Ioannes	The Auvergne?	ca. 476/80	see s.v., no. 80: gramm., or rhetorician?
? Hesperius	Clermont-Ferrand	s.V 2/2–ex.	see s.v., no. 229: gramm., or rhetorician?
Iulianus Pomerius	Arles	s.V ex. / s.VI init.	from Africa

ITALIA SUBURBICARIA

Name	Locality	Date	Comments
Citarius	Sicily (specifically, Syracuse?)	s. IV 2/3	Greek; later at Bordeaux
Melleus	Centum Cellae (Tuscia)	s.IV 2/2 / s.VI	

Name	Locality	Date	Comments
		ITALIA ANNONARIA	
Cassianus	Forum Cornelii	s.IV init.	
Fl. Simplicius		before 364	native of Emona (Venetia-Histria); not known to have taught there
Anonymus 5	Milan	384/86	*proscholus*
Nebridius	Milan	ca. 385	*subdoctor*; from Africa
Anonymus 6	Milan	384/86	
Verecundus	Milan	384–87	
Clamosus (no. 29)	Parentium (Histria)	s.IV 3/4 / s.V init.	
Clamosus (no. 30)	Parentium (Histria)	s.V med.	
Iunius Filargirius	Milan	not before s.V 1/4?	
Deuterius	Milan	s.VI init.	gramm. and rhetorician
Fl. Fortunatus	Aquileia	s.IV 2/2 / s.VI	
		EGYPT	
Lollianus *signo* Homoeus	Oxyrhynchus	253/60	
Paniscus	Panopolis?	s.III med.	for the location, see s.v., no. 243
Aur. Herodes	Karanis	299	
Anonymus ("The Elder") 14	Karanis	299	
Aur. Plution	Philoteris (Arsinoite nome)	300	
Sarapion	Oxyrhynchus	s.III ex. / s.IV init.	
Triphiodorus	Panopolis?	s.III / s.IV	for the location, see s.v., no. 157
Anonymus 13	Oxyrhynchus	s.III / s.IV	
Cabrias	Panopolis	dead by s.IV init.	probably identical with the following

Name	Locality	Date	Comments
Chabrias	Panopolis	dead by s.IV init.	probably identical with the preceding
Eutyches	Panopolis	dead by s.IV init.	
Theon	Panopolis	s.IV init.	
? Cleobulus		s.IV init.	from Egypt to Antioch; not known to have taught in Egypt
? Didymus		s.IV init.	from Egypt to Antioch and Constantinople; not known to have taught in Egypt
? Apollinarius		born not after 290; dead probably by 362	native of Alexandria who taught at Berytus and Laodicea; not known to have taught in Egypt
Anonymus 15 = Sosistratus	Arsinoite nome?	337	
? Eudaemon		s.IV 2/4–ex.	see s.v., no. 55: from Pelusium; received grammatical education in Egypt, not known to have taught there; much-traveled
? Harpocration		s.IV 2/4 – 2/3	more likely sophist than gramm.; native of Egypt who taught at Antioch and Constantinople; not known to have taught in Egypt
? Eudaemon		s.IV 2/4 – 2/3	more likely sophist than

Name	Locality	Date	Comments
			gramm.; native of Egypt who taught at Antioch and(?) Tarsus; not known to have taught in Egypt
? Diocles		s.IV 3/4	see s.v., no. 206, on his profession
Palladas	Alexandria	ca. 320? – s.IV ex.	
Ammonius	Alexandria	s.IV ex.	later at Constantinople
Helladius	Alexandria	s.IV ex.	later at Constantinople
Aur. Theodorus	Hermopolis	398	
Arethusius	Antinoopolis	s.IV	
Anonymus 16		s.IV?	
Theodosius (no. 151)	Alexandria	s.IV ex. / s.V init.	perhaps identical with the following
Theodosius (no. 152)	Alexandria	s.II ex. / s.V ex.	perhaps identical with the preceding
? Agathodaemon		s.IV ex. / s.V 1/3	see s.v., no. 3: conjectural for Egypt
? Ophelius		s.IV ex. / s.V 1/3	conjectural for Egypt: see s.v. Agathodaemon, no. 3
Horapollon	Alexandria and(?) elsewhere in Egypt	s.IV ex. / s.V 1/3	later in Constantinople; native of Phenebythis (Panopolite nome); for his career, see s.v., no. 77
Heraclammon	Hermopolis	s.IV ex. / s.V; not before 391	
Aur. Oursenouphius	Heracleopolite nome	411	

Name	Locality	Date	Comments
Hierax	Alexandria	s.V init.	
Orion	Alexandria	s.IV 1/4 – 1/2	native of Egyptian Thebes; see s.v., no. 110, for his teaching elsewhere
Ammonianus	Alexandria (probably)	s.V med.?	
? Orus		s.V 1/2 – 2/3	see s.v., no. 111: an Alexandrian at Constantinople; not known to have taught in Egypt
? Pamprepius		in Egypt from 440 until before late 472	see s.v., no. 114: from Panopolis; he taught in Athens and Constantinople but not, *ut vid.*, in Egypt
Asclepiades	Alexandria	s.IV 2/3 – 3/4	gramm. or philosopher, or both
? Hyperechius	Alexandria?	s.V 3/4	see s.v., no. 79: native of or teaching at Alexandria, or both; later at Constantinople?
Fl. Horapollon	Alexandria	s.V 3/3	native of Phenebythis (Panopolite nome)
Harpocras	Alexandria (probably)	s.V 3/3	
Fl. Her . . .	Hermopolis	s.V 2/2	
Fl. Pythiodorus	Hermopolis	s.V 2/2	
Anonymus 7	Hermopolis?	s.V 2/2	see s.v., no. 173, for location
? Romanus	Alexandria?	s.V ex. / s.VI init.	see s.v., no. 129, on location and date
? Hieronymus	Hermopolis	s.V 4/4 / s.VI 1/4	see s.v., no. 231: from Elusa, twice active in Egypt, the second time at

Name	Locality	Date	Comments
			Hermopolis; more likely sophist than gramm.
Stephanus	Alexandria	s.V 4/4 / s.VI 1/4	see s.v., no. 142: from Gaza?
? Stephanus	Alexandria?	519/38	see s.v., no. 143: location very un- certain
Aur. Cyrus	Antaeopolis	s.VI 1/2 (before 539)	
? Coluthus		*aet. incert.*: s.VI init.?	see s.v., no. 33: *loc. incert.*; prob- ably Egyptian, in view of his name
? Georgius		s.VI 1/2?	see s.v., no. 63: activity in Egypt very uncertain
Ioannes Philo- ponus	Alexandria	s.V ex. – s.VI 3/4	see s.v., no. 118, on his status as a gramm.
Anatolius	Alexandria	s.VI med.	
Ioannes (no. 84)	Alexandria?	before ca. 568	
? Serenus		s.IV / s.VI?	see s.v., no. 134, on place and date
Theodosius (no. 153)	Panopolis?	s.IV / s.VI	
Hesychius	Alexandria	s.V / s.VI	
Anonymus (-mi?) 8		s.V / s.VI	on the number of gramm., see s.v., no. 174
Anonymus 9	Aphrodito?	s.VI	

ASIANA

Name	Locality	Date	Comments
Aur. Trophimus	Altıntaş / Kurtköy	s.III 2/2 / s.IV	
? Dioscorius		s.V 2/4 – 2/2	see s.v., no. 48: native of Myra (Lycia), not known to have taught there; active at Constan- tinople

Name	Locality	Date	Comments
? Eugenius		s.V 2/2 / s.VI init.	see s.v., no. 56: native of Augustopolis (Phrygia Salutaris), not known to have taught there; active at Constantinople
? Diogenes	Cyzicus	s.IV / s.VI init.?	see s.v., no. 207, on his date and profession
Adamantius	Sardis?	before 580 (s.V ex. / s.VI init.?)	Latin
Martyrius	Sardis?	before 580 (s.VI 1/2–med.?)	Latin
Metrodorus (no. 101)	Tralles	s.VI 1/3 – 1/2	later at Constantinople
Damocharis		s.VI 2/3	see s.v., no. 42: native of Cos; probably active at Constantinople
? Theodoretus (no. 264)		*aet. incert.*: before ca. 568?	see s.v.: Smyrna or Philadelphia?

PONTICA

Name	Locality	Date	Comments
? Leontius	Nicomedia	s.III ex.	see s.v., no. 234, on his authenticity
? Babylas	Nicomedia	s.IV init.	see s.v., no. 192, on his authenticity
Flavius	Nicomedia	s.III ex. / s.IV init.	Latin; from Africa
? Acacius	Nicomedia?	355	on his location (more likely Constantinople), see s.v., no. 1
? Phalerius	Tavium (Galatia)	393	more likely rhetorician than gramm.

Name	Locality	Date	Comments
? Ioannes (no. 82)	Caesarea (Cappadocia? perhaps more likely Palaestina)	s.VI 1/4	gramm. and (or: later) presbyter
Anonymus 12	Syceon (Galatia I)	s.VI 2/3 – 3/4	
Philumenus	Mossyna / Epistraton (Galatia I)	s.VI 2/2	

MACEDONIA

Name	Locality	Date	Comments
Apollonius	Athens	260/68	
? Nicocles		s.IV 1/2 – 3/3	native of Sparta, not known to have taught there; active at Constantinople
? Philtatius	Athens	s.V init.	see s.v., no. 119, on his profession
Pamprepius	Athens	from before late 472 until May 476	see s.v., no. 114: native of Panopolis, apparently did not teach in Egypt; later active at Constantinople

ORIENS

Name	Locality	Date	Comments
Lupercus	Berytus (Phoenice)	born or *floruit* shortly before 268/70	
? Manippus or Marsippus	Carchar (Κασχάρης)	276/82	see s.v., no. 236: profession and authenticity doubtful
Anonymus 1	Anazarbus (Cilicia)	s.IV 1/3	
Apollinarius	Berytus (Phoenice) → Laodicea (Syria)	s.IV 1/2	native of Alexandria; not known to have taught there
Anonymus 2	Antioch (Syria)	ca. 329–34	

Name	Locality	Date	Comments
Didymus	Antioch (Syria)	s.IV 1/2	from Egypt; later at Constantinople
Cleobulus	Antioch (Syria)	s.IV 1/3 – 2/3	from Egypt
? Thespesius	Caesarea (Palaestina)	s.IV 2/3	see s.v., no. 268: more likely rhetorician than gramm.
Iulius	Antioch (Syria)	died 355/56	
Tiberinus	Antioch (Syria)	358	from Arabia
Alexander	Antioch (Syria) → Heliopolis (Phoenice)	s.IV 2/3	
Eudaemon	Elusa (Palaestina) → Antioch (Syria)	s.IV 2/4-ex.	from Pelusium; whether he was a gramm. or a rhetorician is not certain; on his profession and movements, see s.v., no. 55
? Harpocration	Antioch (Syria)	before 358	from Egypt, later at Constantinople; more likely sophist than gramm.
? Eudaemon	Antioch (Syria) →(?) Tarsus (Cilicia)	s.IV 2/4 – 2/3	from Egypt; on his profession and movements, see s.v., no. 210
Anonymus 3	Antioch (Syria)	s.IV 1/3 – 2/3	
Calliopius	Antioch (Syria)	s.IV 2/2	
Danaus	loc. incert., probably Oriens	s.IV 2/2	see s.v., no. 43, on his location
Diphilus	Palaestina	s.IV 3/3	see s.v., no. 49: not his province of origin
? Antiochus	Antioch (Syria)	s.IV ex.	see s.v., no. 184: gramm., or rhetorician?
? Orion		s.V 1/4 – 1/2	see s.v., no. 110: from Egypt;

Name	Locality	Date	Comments
			perhaps active in Caesarea (Palaestina?)
Alypius (no. 6)	Seleucia (Isauria)	s.V med.	
Olympius	Seleucia (Isauria)	s.V med.	probably identical with the following
? Solymius	Seleucia (Isauria)	s.V med.	see s.v., no. 259: teacher or student; probably identical with the preceding
Isocasius	Aegeae (Cilicia)	s.V 2/4 – 3/4	later a sophist at Antioch
Ioannes (no. 81)	*Antiochenae parochiae*	s.V 4/4	gramm. → presbyter
Alypius (no. 7)	Gaza (Palaestina) → Antioch (Syria)	s.V 4/4 / s.VI 1/4	
Stephanus (no. 141)	Gaza (Palaestina) → Antioch (Syria)	s.V 4/4 / s.VI 1/4	
Hierius	Gaza (Palaestina) → Antioch (Syria)	s.V 4/4 / s.VI 1/4	Latin
? Stephanus (no. 142)		s.V 4/4 / s.VI 1/4	from Gaza(?), not known to have taught there; active at Alexandria
? Hieronymus (no. 231)		s.V 4/4 / s.VI 1/4	from Elusa (Palaestina), not known to have taught there; twice active in Egypt; more likely sophist than gramm.
Rufinus	Antioch (Syria)	s.V med. / s.VI	Latin
Timotheus	Gaza (Palaestina)	s.V ex. / s.VI init.	
Sergius		s.VI init.	see s.v., no. 135: probably Oriens—Syria? Beroea?
Veronicianus	Antioch (Syria)	s.VI init.	

Name	Locality	Date	Comments
Ioannes	Caesarea (Palaes-tina?)	s.VI 1/4	gramm. and (or: later) presbyter; on his location, see s.v., no. 82
Ioannes (no. 83)	Gaza (Palaestina)	s.VI 1/2?	
? Georgius		s.VI 1/2?	see s.v., no. 63: *loc. incert.*
Arcadius	Antioch (Syria)	s.II ex. / s. VI med. (probably closer to the lat-ter *terminus* than to the former)	
Aetherius	Apamea (Osrhoene)	*aet. incert.*: prob-ably not before s.V ex. / s.VI init.	

This bibliography gives the full references for the secondary works noted in short form throughout the book. Articles in encyclopedias concerned with antiquity are not included, and the titles already noted in the list of abbreviations are not repeated here. Editions of primary sources are omitted unless an editor's substantive comments have been cited.

Abbott, F. F., and A. C. Johnson. *Municipal Administration in the Roman Empire*. Princeton, 1926.

Adams, J. N. *The Text and Language of a Vulgar Latin Chronicle*. Bulletin of the Institute of Classical Studies of the University of London, supplement 36. London, 1976.

Aistermann, J. *De M. Valerio Probo Berytio*. Bonn, 1910.

Alföldi, A. *A Conflict of Ideas in the Later Roman Empire: The Clash between the Senate and Valentinian I*. Oxford, 1952.

Alföldy, G. *Konsulat und Senatorenstand unter der Antoninen*. Antiquitas, 1. Reihe, 27. Bonn, 1977.

Alpers, K. *Das attizistische Lexikon des Oros: Untersuchung und kritische Ausgabe der Fragmente*. Sammlung griechischer und lateinischer Grammatiker, 4. Berlin and New York, 1981.

Anastasi, R. "Giorgio grammatico." *Sic. Gymn.* 20 (1967): 209–53.

Anderson, J. G. C., F. Cumont, and H. Grégoire, eds. *Studia Pontica*. Vol. 3:1, *Recueil des inscriptions grecques et latines du Pont et de l'Arménie*. Brussels, 1910.

Asmus, R. *Das Leben des Philosophen Isidoros von Damaskios aus Damaskos*. Die philosophische Bibliothek, 125. Leipzig, 1911.

——. "Pamprepios, ein byzantinischer Gelehrter und Staatsmann des 5. Jahrhunderts." *BZ* 22 (1913): 320–47.

——. "Zur Rekonstruktion von Damascius' Leben des Isidorus." *BZ* 18 (1909): 424–80.

Athanassiadi-Fowden, P. *Julian and Hellenism: An Intellectual Biography.* Oxford, 1981.

Auerbach, E. *Literary Language and Its Public in Late Latin Antiquity and in the Middle Ages.* Trans. R. Mannheim. Princeton, 1965.

Azéma, Y., ed. *Théodoret de Cyr. Correspondence.* 3 vols. Sources chrétiennes, vols. 40, 98, 111. Paris, 1955–65.

Bagnall, R. S., and P. J. Sijpesteijn. "Currency in the Fourth Century and the Date of *CPR* V 26." *ZPE* 24 (1977): 111–24.

Bagnall, R. S., and K. A. Worp. "Commodity Prices in P.Stras. 595." *ZPE* 27 (1977): 161–64.

Baldwin, B. "The Career of Corippus." *CQ* 28 (1978): 372–76.

———. "The Date of the *Cycle* of Agathias." *BZ* 73 (1980): 334–40.

———. "Four Problems in Agathias." *BZ* 70 (1977): 295–305.

———. "Some *addenda* to the Prosopography of the Later Roman Empire." *Historia* 25 (1976): 118–21; 31 (1982): 97–111.

———. *Suetonius.* Amsterdam, 1983.

Ballaira, G. "Sulla trattazione dell'iperbole in Diomede (*GL* 1,461,21–30 K.) ed in altri grammatici e retori latini e greci." In *Grammatici latini d'età imperiale: Miscellanea filologica*: 183–93. Pubblicazioni dell'Istituto di filologia classica e medievale dell'Università di Genova, 45. Genoa, 1976.

Bandy, A. C., ed. *Ioannes Lydus. On Powers, or The Magistracies of the Roman State.* Memoirs of the American Philosophical Society, 149. Philadelphia, 1982.

Bardy, G. *La question des langues dans l'Église ancienne.* Paris, 1948.

Barnes, T. D. *Constantine and Eusebius.* Cambridge, Mass., and London, 1981.

———. "Late Roman Prosopography: Between Theodosius and Justinian." *Phoenix* 37 (1983): 248–70.

———. "More Missing Names (A.D. 260–395)." *Phoenix* 27 (1973): 135–55.

Bartalucci, A. "Il 'Probus' di Giorgio Valla e il 'commentum vetustum' a Giovenale." *SIFC* 45 (1973): 233–57.

Barwick, K. "De Iunio Philargirio Vergilii interprete." *Commentationes philologae Ienenses* 8:2 (1909): 57–123.

———. *Remmius Palaemon und die römische Ars grammatica.* Philologus, supplement 15:2. Leipzig, 1922.

———. "Die sogenannte *Appendix Probi.*" *Hermes* 54 (1919): 409–22.

———. "Zur Geschichte und Rekonstruktion des Charisius-Textes." *Hermes* 59 (1924): 322–55, 420–29.

Bassignano, M. S. *Il flaminato nelle province romane dell'Africa.* Pubblicazioni dell'Istituto di storia antica dell'Università degli studi di Padova, 11. Rome, 1974.

Baynes, N. H. *Byzantine Studies and Other Essays.* London, 1955.

———. "The Early Life of Julian the Apostate." *JHS* 45 (1925): 251–54.

Bean, G. E. *Journeys in Northern Lycia 1965–1967*. Denkschriften der Österreichischen Akademie der Wissenschaften in Wien, philosophisch-historische Klasse, 104. Vienna, 1971.

Bean, G. E., and T. B. Mitford. *Journeys in Rough Cilicia 1964–1968*. Denkschriften der Österreichischen Akademie der Wissenschaften in Wien, philosophisch-historische Klasse, 102. Vienna, 1970.

Beckby, H., ed. *Anthologia Graeca*. 4 vols. Munich, 1957–58.

Bell, H. I. "An Egyptian Village in the Age of Justinian." *JHS* 64 (1944): 21–36.

Ben-David, J. "Organization, Social Control, and Cognitive Change in Science." In *Culture and Its Creators: Essays in Honor of Edward Shils*, ed. J. Ben-David and T. N. Clark: 244–65. Chicago, 1977.

Bergmann, A. A. "Zur Geschichte der socialen Stellung der Elementarlehrer und Grammatiker bei den Römern." Diss. Leipzig, 1877.

Bingen, J. "Note sur l'éphébie en Égypte romaine." *CdE* 45 (1970): 356.

Bischoff, B. "Ergänzungen zur Überlieferung des Paperinus/Papirius (Papirianus?)." *Beiträge zur Geschichte der deutschen Sprache und Literatur* (Tübingen) 100 (1978): 420–22.

Blank, D. *Ancient Philosophy and Grammar: The "Syntax" of Apollonius Dyscolus*. American Philological Association, American Classical Studies, 10. Chico, Calif., 1982.

Bledstein, B. J. *The Culture of Professionalism: The Middle Class and the Development of Higher Education in America*. New York, 1976.

Bloch, H. "The Pagan Revival in the West at the End of the Fourth Century." In *The Conflict between Paganism and Christianity in the Fourth Century*, ed. A. Momigliano: 193–218. Oxford, 1963.

Bodenheimer, F., and A. Rabinowitz, trans. *Timotheus of Gaza. On Animals* (Περὶ ζῴων). *Fragments of a Byzantine Paraphrase of an Animal-Book of the 5th Century A.D.* Travaux de l'Académie internationale d'histoire des sciences, 3. Paris and Leiden, 1949.

Boehm, W. *Johannes Philoponus, Grammatikos von Alexandrien (6. Jh. n. Chr.). Ausgewählte Schriften. Christliche Naturwissenschaft im Ausklang der Antike, Vorläufer der modernen Physik, Wissenschaft, und Bibel.* Munich, 1967.

Bolgar, R. R. *The Classical Heritage and Its Beneficiaries*. Cambridge, 1954.

Bonini, I. "Lo stile nei sermoni di Cesario di Arles." *Aevum* 36 (1962): 240–57.

Bonner, S. F. "The Edict of Gratian on the Remuneration of Teachers." *AJP* 86 (1965): 113–37.

———. *Education in Ancient Rome*. Berkeley and Los Angeles, 1977.

———. "The Teaching Profession in Ancient Rome." *PCA* 48 (1951): 29–30.

Booth, A. D. "The Academic Career of Ausonius." *Phoenix* 36 (1982): 329–43.

———. "The Appearance of the *schola grammatici*." *Hermes* 106 (1978): 117–25.

———. "A quel âge Libanius est-il entré à l'école du rhéteur?" *Byzantion* 53 (1983): 157–63.

———. "The Date of Jerome's Birth." *Phoenix* 33 (1979): 346–53.

———. "Elementary and Secondary Education in the Roman Empire." *Florilegium* 1 (1979): 1–14.

———. "The Image of the Professor in Ancient Society." *EMC* 20 (1976): 1–10.

———. "Litterator." *Hermes* 109 (1981): 371–78.

———. "Notes on Ausonius' *Professores*." *Phoenix* 32 (1978): 235–49.

———. "The Schooling of Slaves in First-Century Rome." *TAPA* 109 (1979): 11–19.

———. "Some Suspect Schoolmasters." *Florilegium* 3 (1981): 1–20.

Bouchery, H. *Themistius in Libanius' Brieven*. Antwerp, 1936.

Bower, E. W. "Some Technical Terms in Roman Education." *Hermes* 89 (1961): 462–77.

Bowersock, G. W. *Greek Sophists in the Roman Empire*. Oxford, 1969.

———. *Julian the Apostate*. Cambridge, Mass., 1978.

Bowie, E. L. "The Importance of Sophists." *YClS* 27 (1982): 29–59.

Bowra, C. M. "Palladas and Christianity." *PBA* 45 (1959): 255–67.

———. "Palladas and the Converted Olympians." *BZ* 53 (1960): 1–7.

———. "Palladas on Tyche." *CQ* 10 (1960): 118–28.

Bradford, A. S. *A Prosopography of the Lacedaemonians from the Death of Alexander the Great, 323 B.C., to the Sack of Sparta by Alaric, A.D. 396*. Vestigia, 27. Munich, 1977.

Braun, R., and J. Richer, eds. *L'empereur Julien* 1. Paris, 1978.

Brink, C. O., ed. *Horace on Poetry*. Vol. 2, *The Ars Poetica*. Cambridge, 1971.

Brock, S. P. "Some New Letters of the Patriarch Severos." In *Studia patristica* 12:1, ed. E. A. Livingstone: 17–24. Texte und Untersuchungen, 115. Berlin, 1975.

Brown, P. *Augustine of Hippo: A Biography*. Berkeley–Los Angeles–London, 1967.

———. *Religion and Society in the Age of Saint Augustine*. London, 1972.

———. *The World of Late Antiquity, A.D. 150–750*. London, 1971.

Browne, G. M. "Harpocration panegyrista." *Ill. Cl. Stud.* 2 (1977): 184–96.

———. "A Panegyrist from Panopolis." In *Proceedings of the Fourteenth International Congress of Papyrologists: Oxford, 24–31 July 1974*: 29–33. Greco-Roman Memoirs, 16. London, 1975.

Browning, R. *The Emperor Julian*. Berkeley–Los Angeles–London, 1976.

Brunt, P. A. "The Administration of Roman Egypt." *JRS* 65 (1975): 124–47.

_____. "The Romanization of the Local Ruling Classes in the Roman Empire." In *Assimilation et résistance à la culture gréco-romaine dans le monde ancien. Travaux du VIᵉ Congrès international d'études classiques*, ed. D. M. Pippidi: 161–73. Bucharest and Paris, 1968.

Brusin, G. "Nuove epigrafi cristiane di Aquileia." *RAC* 43 (1967): 33–47.

Bücheler, F. "Coniectanea." *RhM*, 3d ser., 37 (1882): 321–42.

Buckler, W. H., and W. M. Calder, eds. *Anatolian Studies Presented to Sir William Mitchell Ramsay*. Manchester–London–New York, 1923.

Buckler, W. H., W. M. Calder, and C. W. M. Cox. "Asia Minor, 1924: IV.—A Monument from the Upper Tembris Valley." *JRS* 17 (1927): 49–58.

Bühler, W., and C. Theodoridis. "Johannes von Damaskos *terminus post quem* für Choiroboskos." *BZ* 69 (1976): 397–401.

Burckas, V. "De Tib. Claudi Donati in Aeneida commentario." Diss. Jena, 1888.

Burton, G. P. "The *curator rei publicae*: Towards a Reappraisal." *Chiron* 9 (1979): 465–87.

_____. "Proconsuls, Assizes and the Administration of Justice under the Empire." *JRS* 65 (1975): 92–106.

Calder, W. M. "The Epigraphy of the Anatolian Heresies." In *Anatolian Studies Presented to Sir William Mitchell Ramsay*, ed. W. H. Buckler and W. M. Calder: 59–91. Manchester–London–New York, 1923.

Calderini, R. "Gli ἀγράμματοι nell'Egitto greco-romano." *Aegyptus* 30 (1950): 14–41.

Cameron, Alan. "The Authenticity of the Letters of St. Nilus of Ancyra." *GRBS* 17 (1976): 181–96.

_____. *Claudian: Poetry and Propaganda at the Court of Honorius*. Oxford, 1970.

_____. "The Date and Identity of Macrobius." *JRS* 56 (1966): 25–38.

_____. "The Date of Priscian's *De laude Anastasii*." *GRBS* 15 (1974): 313–16.

_____. "The Empress and the Poet: Paganism and Politics at the Court of Theodosius II." *YClS* 27 (1982): 217–89.

_____. "The Last Days of the Academy at Athens." *PCPS* 195 (1969): 7–29.

_____. "Macrobius, Avienus, and Avianus." *CQ* 17 (1967): 385–99.

_____. "Martianus and His First Editor." *CP* 81 (1986): 320–28.

_____. "Notes on Palladas." *CQ* 15 (1965): 215–29.

————. "Paganism and Literature in Late Fourth Century Rome." In *Christianisme et formes littéraires de l'antiquité tardive en Occident*, ed. M. Fuhrmann: 1–30. Entretiens sur l'antiquité classique, 23. Geneva, 1977.

————. "Palladas and Christian Polemic." *JRS* 55 (1965): 17–30.

————. "Palladas and the Fate of Gessius." *BZ* 57 (1964): 279–92.

————. "Palladas and the Nikai." *JHS* 84 (1964): 54–62.

————. "Roman School Fees." *CR* 15 (1965): 257–58.

————. "Wandering Poets: A Literary Movement in Byzantine Egypt." *Historia* 14 (1965): 470–509.

Cameron, Averil. *Agathias*. Oxford, 1970.

————. "Byzantine Africa—The Literary Evidence." In *Excavations at Carthage 1978 Conducted by the University of Michigan 7*, ed. J. H. Humphrey: 29–62. Ann Arbor, 1982.

————. "The Career of Corippus Again." *CQ* 30 (1980): 534–39.

————, ed. *Flavius Cresconius Corippus. In laudem Iustini Augusti minoris*. London, 1976.

Cameron, Averil, and Alan Cameron. "The *Cycle* of Agathias." *JHS* 86 (1966): 6–25.

————. "Further Thoughts on the 'Cycle' of Agathias." *JHS* 87 (1967): 131.

Campbell, B. "Who Were the 'Viri Militares'?" *JRS* 65 (1975): 11–31.

Caputo, G. "Flavius Népotianus, *comes et praeses provinciae Tripolitanae*." *REA* 53 (1951): 234–47.

Carney, T. F. *Bureaucracy in Traditional Society: Romano-Byzantine Bureaucracies Viewed from Within*. Lawrence, Kans., 1971.

della Casa, A. "Giulio Romano nella storia della grammatica latina." In J. Collart et al., *Varron, grammaire antique et stylistique latine*: 217–24. Publications de la Sorbonne, sér. "Études," 14. Paris, 1978.

————. "La 'grammatica' di Valerio Probo." In *Argentea aetas: In memoriam Entii V. Marmorale*: 139–60. Pubblicazioni dell'Istituto di filologia classica e medievale dell'Università di Genova, 37. Genoa, 1973.

Chadwick, H. *Early Christian Thought and the Classical Tradition*. Oxford, 1966.

————. *Priscillian of Avila: The Occult and the Charismatic in the Early Church*. Oxford, 1976.

Champlin, E. *Fronto and Antonine Rome*. Cambridge, Mass., and London, 1980.

Charneux, P. "Inscriptions d'Argos (suite)." *BCH* 80 (1956): 598–618.

Chastagnol, A. "Le sénateur Volusien et la conversion d'une famille de l'aristocratie romaine au Bas-Empire." *REA* 58 (1956): 241–53.

Chauvot, A. "Observations sur la date de l'*Éloge d'Anastase* de Priscien de Césarée." *Latomus* 36 (1977): 539–50.

Christes, J. *Bildung und Gesellschaft: Die Einschätzung der Bildung und ihrer Vermittler in der griechisch-römischen Antike.* Erträge der Forschung, 37. Darmstadt, 1975.

————. *Sklaven und Freigelassene als Grammatiker und Philologen im antiken Rom.* Forschungen zur antiken Sklaverei, 10. Wiesbaden, 1979.

Cipolla, C. M. *Literacy and Development in the West.* Baltimore, 1969.

Clark, T. N. *Prophets and Patrons: The French University and the Emergence of the Social Sciences.* Cambridge, Mass., 1973.

Clarke, M. L. *Higher Education in the Ancient World.* London, 1971.

————. "Juvenal 7.242–43." *CR* 23 (1973): 12.

Claude, D. *Die byzantinische Stadt im 6. Jahrhundert.* Byzantinisches Archiv, 13. Munich, 1969.

Claus, A. "Ο ΣΧΟΛΑΣΤΙΚΟΣ." Diss. Cologne, 1965.

Clausen, W. V. "Sabinus' MS of Persius." *Hermes* 91 (1963): 252–56.

Clover, F. M. "Carthage and the Vandals." In *Excavations at Carthage 1978 Conducted by the University of Michigan 7*, ed. J. H. Humphrey: 1–22. Ann Arbor, 1982.

Cohn, L. "Nicetae Serrarum Episcopi Rhythmi de marium, fluviorum, lacuum, montium, urbium, gentium, lapidum nominibus." *Neue Jahrbücher für Philologie und Pädogogik* 133 (1886): 649–66.

Coles, R. A. "More Papyri from the British Museum." *JEA* 53 (1967): 121–30.

Consbruch, M., ed. *Hephaestionis Enchiridion cum commentariis veteribus.* Stuttgart, 1971.

Coupry, J., and M. Feyel. "Inscriptions de Philippes." *BCH* 60 (1936): 37–58.

Courcelle, P. *Recherches sur les Confessions de Saint Augustin.* Paris, 1968.

Courtois, C., et al., eds. *Tablettes Albertini: Actes privés de l'époque vandale (fin du Ve siècle).* Paris, 1952.

Craig, J. D. *Jovialis and the Calliopian Text of Terence.* London and New York, 1927.

Crawford, M., and J. M. Reynolds. "The Aezani Copy of the Prices Edict." *ZPE* 34 (1979): 163–210.

Crum, W. E. "Colluthus, the Martyr and His Name." *BZ* 30 (1930): 323–27.

————. *Coptic Monuments.* Catalogue générale des antiquités égyptiennes du Musée du Caire, 4. Cairo, 1902.

Cupaiuolo, G. "Antiche edizioni del *De fabula* di Evanzio." *BStudLat.* 7 (1977): 42–51.

————. "Un *locus Vergilianus* nell'*Anthologia Latina*." *BStudLat.* 6 (1976): 37–53.

Cüppers, H., and W. Binsfeld. "Eine zweiseitig beschriftete Grabplatte aus der St.-Matthias-Basilika in Trier." *TZ* 35 (1972): 135–40.

Cybulla, K. *De Rufini Antiochensis commentariis*. Königsberg, 1907.

Dagron, G. "L'auteur des 'Actes' et des 'Miracles' de Sainte Thècle." *Anal. Boll.* 92 (1974): 5–11.

—⸻, ed. *Vie et miracles de Sainte Thècle*. Subsidia hagiographica, 62. Brussels, 1978.

Dagron, G., and J. Marcillet-Jaubert. "Inscriptions de Cilicie et d'Isaurie." *Belletin Türk Tarih Kurumu* 42 (1978): 373–420.

Dahlmann, H. *Kleine Schriften*. Collectanea, 19. Hildesheim and New York, 1970.

Daniel, R. W. "Liberal Education and Semiliteracy in Petronius." *ZPE* 40 (1980): 153–59.

Darrouzès, J. *Recherches sur les ὀφφίκια de l'Église byzantine*. Archive de l'Orient chrétien, 11. Paris, 1970.

Delatte, A. *Anecdota Atheniensia et alia* 2. Bibliothèque de la Faculté de philosophie et lettres de l'Université de Liège, 88. Liège, 1939.

Delatte, A., and P. Stroobant. "L'horoscope de Pamprépios, professeur et homme politique de Byzance." *Bulletin de la Classe des lettres et des sciences morales et politiques de l'Académie royale de Belgique*, 5th ser., 9 (1923): 58–76.

Delehaye, H. "Les deux saints Babylas." *Anal. Boll.* 19 (1900): 5–8.

—⸻. *Les passions des martyrs et les genres littéraires*. 2d ed. Subsidia hagiographica, 13B. Brussels, 1966.

De Nonno, M. "Frammenti misconosciuti di Plozio Sacerdote." *RFIC* 111 (1983): 385–421.

—⸻. ed. *La grammatica dell' "Anonymus Bobiensis" (GL I 533–565 Keil)*. Sussidi eruditi, 36. Rome, 1982.

De Rossi, G. B., ed. *Roma sotteranea cristiana*. 3 vols. Rome, 1864–77.

DeRuyt, F. "Note de vocabulaire virgilien: *somnia* et *insomnia*." *Latomus* 5 (1946): 245–48.

Devreesse, R. *Le patriarcat d'Antioche depuis la paix de l'Église jusqu'à la conquête arabe*. Paris, 1945.

Díaz de Bustamente, J. M. *Draconcio y sus carmina profana*. Monografías de la Universidad de Santiago de Compostela, 44. Santiago de Compostela, 1978.

Di Benedetto, V. "La Techne spuria." *ASNP*, 3d ser., 3:3–4 (1973): 797–814.

Dionisotti, A. C. "From Ausonius' Schooldays? A Schoolbook and Its Relations." *JRS* 72 (1982): 83–125.

—⸻. "Latin Grammar for Greeks and Goths." *JRS* 74 (1984): 202–8.

—⸻. "On Bede, Grammars, and Greek." *Revue Bénédictine* 92 (1982): 111–41.

Dodds, E. R. *Pagan and Christian in an Age of Anxiety: Some Aspects of Religious Experience from Marcus Aurelius to Constantine*. New York, 1965.

Dörner, F. K. *Bericht über eine Reise in Bithynien*. Denkschriften der Akademie der Wissenschaften in Wien, philosophisch-historische Klasse, 75:1. Vienna, 1952.

Downey, G. "Education in the Christian Roman Empire: Christian and Pagan Theories under Constantine and His Successors." *Speculum* 32 (1957): 48–61.

———. "John of Gaza and the Mosaic of Ge and Karpoi." In *Antioch-on-the-Orontes*, vol. 2, *The Excavations 1933–1936*, ed. R. Stillwell: 205–12. Princeton, 1938.

Duncan-Jones, R. P. "Age-Rounding in Greco-Roman Egypt." *ZPE* 33 (1979): 169–77.

———. "Age-Rounding, Illiteracy, and Social Differentiation in the Roman Empire." *Chiron* 7 (1977): 333–53.

———. *The Economy of the Roman Empire: Quantitative Studies*. Cambridge, 1974.

Eck, W. "Das Eindringen des Christentums in den Senatorenstand bis zu Konstantin d. Gr." *Chiron* 1 (1971): 381–406.

———. "Der Einfluss der konstantinischen Wende auf die Auswahl der Bischöfe im 4. und 5. Jahrhundert." *Chiron* 8 (1978): 561–85.

———. Review of *PLRE* I, by A. H. M. Jones, J. R. Martindale, and J. Morris. *Zephyrus* 23–24 (1972–73): 325–36.

Egenolff, P. *Die orthoepischen Stücke der byzantinischen Literatur*. Leipzig, 1887.

———. *Die orthographischen Stücke der byzantinischen Literatur*. Leipzig, 1888.

Esposito, M. "A Ninth-Century Commentary on Phocas." *CQ* 13 (1919): 166–69.

Étienne, R. *Bordeaux antique*. Bordeaux, 1962.

———. "La démographie de la famille d'Ausone." In *Études et chronique de démographie historique 1964*: 15–25. Paris, 1964.

Évrard, E. "Les convictions religieuses de Jean Philopon et la date de son commentaire aux 'Météorologiques.'" *Bulletin de la Classe des lettres et des sciences morales et politiques de l'Académie royale de Belgique*, 5th ser., 39 (1953): 299–357.

———. "La date de la naissance de Proclus le néoplatonicien." *AC* 29 (1960): 137–41.

Favez, C. "Une école gallo-romaine au IVᵉ siècle." *Latomus* 7 (1948): 223–33.

Feissel, D. "Notes d'épigraphie chrétienne (III)." *BCH* 102 (1978): 545–55.

———. "Notes d'épigraphie chrétienne (IV)." *BCH* 104 (1980): 459–75.

Ferrua, A. *Epigrammata Damasiana*. Paris, 1942.

———. "Nuove iscrizioni datate delle catacombe romane." *Epigraphica* 31 (1969): 181–204.

———. "Nuova regione catacombale presso S. Callisto." *RAC* 54 (1978): 167–225.

Festugière, A.-J. *Antioche païenne et chrétienne: Libanius, Chrysostome, et les moines de Syrie.* Paris, 1959.

Finch, C. E. "The Text of Sergii *De arte grammatica* in Codex Reg. Lat. 1587." In *Classical Studies Presented to Ben Edwin Perry*: 38–45. Illinois Studies in Language and Literature, 58. Urbana, 1969.

Finley, M. I. *The Use and Abuse of History.* New York, 1975.

Foerster, R., ed. *Libanius. Opera.* 12 vols. Leipzig, 1903–27. [Vols. 10–12 ed. E. Richtsteig.]

Fontaine, J. *Isidore de Séville et la culture classique dans l'Espagne wisigothique.* 2 vols. Paris, 1959.

Foraboschi, D. *Onomasticon alterum papyrologicum: Supplemento al "Namenbuch" di F. Preisigke.* Testi e documenti per lo studio dell'antichità, 16, serie papirologica, 2. Milan, 1967–71.

Forbes, C. A. *Teachers' Pay in Ancient Greece.* University of Nebraska Studies in the Humanities, 2. Lincoln, Nebr., 1942.

Fournier, P.-F. "Les noms de la ville." In E. Desforges et al., *Nouvelles recherches sur les origines de Clermont-Ferrand*: 548–71. Faculté des lettres et sciences humaines de l'Université de Clermont-Ferrand, Publications de l'Institut d'études du Massif Central, 5. Clermont-Ferrand, 1970.

Frantz, A. "Honors to a Librarian." *Hesperia* 35 (1966): 377–80.

Frei-Stolba, R. Review of *Personal Patronage under the Early Empire,* by R. P. Saller. *Gnomon* 55 (1983): 142–44.

Friedländer, L. *Roman Life and Manners under the Early Empire.* 7th ed. Trans. L. A. Magnus. 4 vols. London, 1907.

Friedländer, P. *Johannes von Gaza und Paulus Silentiarius: Kunstbeschreibungen justinianischer Zeit.* Leipzig, 1912.

Fuchs, H. "Die frühe christliche Kirche und die antike Bildung." In *Das frühe Christentum im römischen Staat,* ed. R. Klein: 33–46. Wege der Forschung, 267. Darmstadt, 1971.

Funaioli, G. *Esegesi virgiliana antica.* Milan, 1930.

Gabillon, A. "Romanianus, *alias* Cornelius: Du nouveau sur le bienfaiteur et l'ami de Saint Augustin." *REAug.* 24 (1978): 58–70.

Gager, J. G. "Moses and Alpha." *JTS* 20 (1969): 245–48.

Galland, C. *De Arcadii qui fertur libro de accentibus.* Strassburg, 1882.

Garnsey, P. "Aspects of the Decline of the Urban Aristocracy in the Empire." *ANRW* 2:1 (1974): 227–52.

———. *Social Status and Legal Privilege in the Roman Empire.* Oxford, 1970.

Garzya, A. "Per la tradizione manoscritta degli excerpta di Orione." *Le parole e le idee* 9 (1967): 216–21.

Garzya, A., and R. J. Loenertz, eds. *Procopii Gazaei epistolae et declamationes.* Studia patristica et Byzantina, 9. Ettal, 1963.

Gaudemet, J. *L'Église dans l'empire romain, IVe–Ve siècles.* Histoire du droit et des institutions de l'Église en Occident, 3. Paris, 1958.

Gelsomino, R. "Studi sulle fonti di Vibio Sequestre." *Helikon* 1 (1961): 645-60; 2 (1962): 131-61.

Gelzer, T. "Bemerkungen zur Sprache und Texte des Epikers Musaios." *MH* 24 (1967): 129-48; 25 (1968): 11-47.

Georgii, H. *Die antike Äneiskritik aus den Scholien und anderen Quellen.* Stuttgart, 1891.

————. "Zur Bestimmung der Zeit des Servius." *Philologus* 71 (1912): 518-26.

Gerlaud, B., ed. *Triphiodore. La prise d'Ilion.* Paris, 1982.

Gerstinger, H. *Pamprepios von Panopolis: Eidyllion auf die Tageszeiten und Enkomion auf den Archon Theagenes von Athen nebst Bruchstücken anderer epischer Dichtungen und zwei Briefe des Gregorios von Nazianz im Pap. Gr. Vindob. 29788A–C.* Sitzungsberichte der Akademie der Wissenschaften in Wien, philosophisch-historische Klasse, 208:3. Vienna and Leipzig, 1928.

Getty, R. J. "Insomnia in the Lexica." *AJP* 54 (1933): 1-28.

Gigon, O. *Die antike Kultur und das Christentum.* Gutersloh, 1966.

Gilliam, J. F. "A Student at Berytus in an Inscription from Pamphylia." *ZPE* 13 (1974): 147-50.

Glück, M. *Priscians Partitiones und ihre Stellung in der spätantiken Schule.* Hildesheim, 1967.

Gnilka, C. "Beobachtungen zum Claudiantext." In *Studien zur Literatur des Spätantike, Wolfgang Schmid zum 25. Jahrestag seiner Lehre in Bonn,* ed. C. Gnilka and W. Schetter: 45-90. Antiquitas, 1. Reihe, Abhandlungen zur alten Geschichte, 23. Bonn, 1975.

Golega, J. *Der homerische Psalter: Studien über die dem Apollinarios von Laodikeia zugeschriebene Psalmenparaphrase.* Studia patristica et Byzantina, 6. Ettal, 1960.

Goold, G. P. "Servius and the Helen Episode." *HSCP* 74 (1970): 101-68.

Gough, M. "Anazarbus." *Anat. Stud.* 2 (1952): 85-150.

Graff, H. "Mittheilung aus einer pariser Handschrift." *Bulletin de l'Académie impériale des sciences de St.-Pétersbourg* 7 (1864): 21-45.

Graindor, P. "Pamprépios (?) et Théagénès." *Byzantion* 4 (1927-28): 469-75.

Green, R. P. H. "Prosopographical Notes on the Family and Friends of Ausonius." *BICS* 25 (1978): 19-27.

Griffin, M. Review of *Greek Sophists in the Roman Empire,* by G. W. Bowersock. *JRS* 61 (1971): 278-80.

Griffiths, A. "Alcman's *Partheneion*: The Morning after the Night Before." *QUCC* 14 (1972): 7-30.

Grimal, P. "Les villas d'Ausone." *REA* 55 (1953): 113-25.

Grisart, A. "Valerius Probus de Beyrouth." *Helikon* 2 (1962): 379-414.

Grundmann, H. "Litteratus-illiteratus: Der Wandel einer Bildungsnorm von Altertum zum Mittelalter." *Archiv für Kulturgeschichte* 40 (1958): 1-65.

Gualandri, I. *Furtiva lectio: Studi su Sidonio Apollinare.* Testi e documenti per lo studio dell'antichità, 62. Milan, 1979.

Gudeman, A., ed. *P. Cornelii Taciti Dialogus de oratoribus.* 2d ed. Leipzig, 1914.

Guey, J. "Note sur Flavius Archontius Nilus et Flavius Népotianus." *REA* 53 (1951): 248–52.

Haarhoff, T. J. *Schools of Gaul: A Study of Pagan and Christian Education in the Last Century of the Western Empire.* Oxford, 1920.

von Haehling, R. *Die Religionszugehörigkeit der hohen Amtsträger des römischen Reiches seit Constantins I. Alleinherrschaft bis zum Ende der theodosianischen Dynastie.* Antiquitas, 3. Reihe, 23. Bonn, 1978.

Hagendahl, H. *Latin Fathers and the Classics.* Studia Graeca et Latina Gothoburgensia, 6. Göteborg, 1958.

————. *Von Tertullian zu Cassiodor: Die profane literarische Tradition in dem lateinischen christlichen Schrifttum.* Studia Graeca et Latina Gothoburgensia, 44. Göteborg, 1983.

Halkin, F. *Inédits byzantins d'Ochrida, Candie et Moscou.* Subsidia hagiographica, 38. Brussels, 1963.

————. "La passion inédite des saints Eustathe, Thespésius et Anatole." *Anal. Boll.* 93 (1975): 287–311.

de Halleux, A. "Le synode néochalcédonien d'Alexandrette (ca. 515) et l'Apologie pour Chalcédoine de Jean le Grammairien. A propos d'une édition récente." *RHE* 72 (1977): 593–600.

Happ, H. "Luxurius oder Luxorius? Ein Beitrag zur Lautgeschichte des spätlateinischen *u.*" *BN* 13 (1962): 243–57.

————. "Zur Lisorius-Frage." *Bulletin du Cange* 32 (1962): 189–225.

Hardy, B. C. "The Emperor Julian and His School Law." *Church History* 38 (1968): 131–43.

Harris, W. V. "Literacy and Epigraphy, I." *ZPE* 52 (1983): 87–111.

Haspels, G. H. E. *The Highlands of Phrygia.* Princeton, 1971.

Haupt, M. "Excerpta ex Timothei Gazaei libris de animalibus." *Hermes* 3 (1869): 1–30, 174.

Hauser-Meury, M. M. *Prosopographie zu den Schriften Gregors von Nazianz.* Theophaneia: Beiträge zur Religions- und Kirchengeschichte des Altertums, 13. Bonn, 1960.

Head, C. *The Emperor Julian.* Boston, 1976.

Headlam, W. *Herodas.* Cambridge, 1922.

Heberdey, R., and E. Kalinka. *Bericht über zwei Reisen im südwestlichen Kleinasien.* Denkschriften der Kaiserlichen Akademie der Wissenschaften in Wien, philosophisch-historische Classe, 45:1. Vienna, 1897.

Heinzelmann, M. "L'aristocratie et les évêchés entre Loire et Rhin jusqu'à la fin du VIIᵉ siècle." *Revue d'histoire de l'Église de France* 62 (1976): 75–90.

Heitsch, E. *Die griechische Dichterfragmente der römischen Kaiserzeit.* 2 vols. Abhandlungen der Akademie der Wissenschaften in Göttingen, philologisch-historische Klasse, 49, 58. Göttingen, 1961, 1964.

Helly, B., and J. Marcillet-Jaubert. "Remarques sur l'épigramme d'un medicin de Lambèse." *ZPE* 14 (1974): 252–56.

Helmer, S. *Der Neuchalkedonismus: Geschichte, Berechtigung und Bedeutung eines dogmengeschichtlichen Begriffes.* Bonn, 1962.

Henrichs, A. "Zwei Fragmente über die Erziehung (Antisthenes)." *ZPE* 1 (1967): 45–53.

Henry, D. P. "Why 'grammaticus'?" *Bulletin du Cange* 28 (1958): 165–80.

Heraeus, W. "Drei Fragmente eines Grammatikers Ovidius Naso?" *RhM*, 3d ser., 79 (1930): 391–405.

———. *Kleine Schriften.* Ed. J. B. Hofmann. Indogermanische Bibliothek, 3. Abteilung, Untersuchung 17. Heidelberg, 1937.

Hermann, T. "Johannes Philoponus als Monophysit." *ZNTW* 29 (1930): 209–64.

Herzog, R. "Urkunden zur Hochschulpolitik der römischen Kaiser." *Sitzungsberichte der Preussischen Akademie der Wissenschaften, philosophisch-historische Klasse,* Jahrgang 1935: 967–1019.

Hess, H. *The Canons of the Council of Sardica, A.D. 343: A Landmark in the Early Development of Canon Law.* Oxford, 1958.

Heussi, K. *Untersuchungen zu Nilus dem Asketen.* Texte und Untersuchungen, 42:2. Leipzig, 1917.

Hilgard, A., ed. *Excerpta ex libris Herodiani Technici.* Leipzig, 1887.

Hoffmann, O. *Die griechischen Dialekte in ihrem historischen Zusammenhange.* 3 vols. Göttingen, 1891–98.

Holford-Strevens, L. A. "Towards a Chronology of Aulus Gellius." *Latomus* 36 (1977): 93–109.

Holtz, L. "A l'école de Donat, de Saint Augustin à Bède." *Latomus* 36 (1977): 522–38.

———. *Donat et la tradition de l'enseignement grammatical: Étude sur l' "Ars Donati" et sa diffusion (IVe–IXe siècle) et édition critique.* Paris, 1981.

———. "Tradition et diffusion de l'oeuvre grammaticale de Pompée, commentateur de Donat." *RPh* 45 (1971): 48–83.

Holum, K. G. *Theodosian Empresses: Women and Imperial Dominion in Late Antiquity.* The Transformation of the Classical Heritage, 3. Berkeley–Los Angeles–London, 1982.

Honigmann, E., ed. *Le Synekdèmos d'Hiéroklès et l'opuscule géographique de George de Chypre.* Corpus Bruxellense historiae Byzantinae. Forma imperii Byzantini, fasc. 1. Brussels, 1939.

Hopfner, T. *Der Tierkult der alten Ägypter.* Denkschriften der Kaiserlichen Akademie der Wissenschaften in Wien, philosophisch-historische Klasse, 57:2. Vienna, 1914.

Hopkins, K. *Conquerors and Slaves*. Sociological Studies in Roman History, 1. Cambridge–New York–Melbourne–Sydney, 1978.

―――. "Elite Mobility in the Roman Empire." In *Studies in Ancient Society*, ed. M. I. Finley: 103–20. London, 1974.

―――. "Social Mobility in the Later Roman Empire: The Evidence of Ausonius." *CQ* 11 (1961): 239–49.

―――. "Structural Differentiation in Rome (200–31 B.C.): The Genesis of an Historical Bureaucratic Society." In *History and Social Anthropology*, ed. I. M. Lewis: 63–79. Association of Social Anthropologists, monograph 7. London–New York–Tavistock, 1968.

Hopkins, K., and J. M. Carter. "The Amount of the Corn Dole at Oxyrhynchus." *ZPE* 13 (1974): 195–96.

Hoppe, C. "De Tib. Claudio Donato Aeneidos interprete." Diss. Göttingen, 1891.

Hubert, R. P. M. "Isidore de Séville novateur? (*Origines*, I, xviii–xix)." *REL* 49 (1971): 290–313.

Huemer, J. "Die *Epitomae* des Grammatikers Virgilius Maro nach dem Fragmentum Vindobonense 19556." *Sitzungsberichte der Kaiserlichen Akademie der Wissenschaften in Wien, philosophisch-historische Classe* 99 (1882): 509–59.

Humphrey, J. H., ed. *Excavations at Carthage 1978 Conducted by the University of Michigan 7*. Ann Arbor, 1982.

Hunger, H. *Katalog der griechischen Handschriften der Österreichischen Nationalbibliothek*. Museion: Veröffentlichungen der Österreichischen Nationalbibliothek, n.s., 4. Reihe, Veröffentlichungen der Handschriftensammlung, 1. Vienna, 1961.

Hunt, E. D. *Holy Land Pilgrimages in the Later Roman Empire A.D. 312–460*. Oxford, 1982.

Iacopi, G. *Esplorazioni e studi in Paflagonia e Cappadocia: Relazione sulla seconda campagna esplorativa*. Rome, 1937.

Irmscher, J. "Alexandria, die christusliebende Stadt." *Bulletin de la Société d'archéologie copte* 19 (1970): 115–22.

―――. "Das Haus der Marina." In ΓΕΡΑΣ: *Studies Presented to G. Thomson on the Occasion of His 60th Birthday*, ed. L. Varcl and R. F. Willetts: 129–33. Prague, 1963.

―――. "Palladas." *Wissenschaftliche Zeitschrift der Humboldt-Universität zu Berlin, gesellschaft- und sprachwissenschaftliche Reihe* 6:3 (1956–57): 162–75.

―――. "Palladas-Probleme." *Wissenschaftliche Zeitschrift der Universität Rostock, gesellschaft- und sprachwissenschaftliche Reihe* 12 (1963): 235–39.

―――. "Palladas und Hypatia (zu Anthologia Palatina IX, 400)." In *Acta antiqua Philippopolitana: Studia historica et philologica. Actes de la VIe conférence internationale d'études classiques des pays socialistes*, ed. B. Gerov et al.: 313–18. Sofia, 1963.

Jachmann, G. *Die Geschichte des Terenztextes im Altertum.* Basel, 1924.

Jaeger, W. *Early Christianity and Greek Paideia.* London–Oxford–New York, 1961.

Jahn, O. "Die Subscriptionen in den Handschriften römischer Classiker." *Berichte über die Verhandlungen der Königlich-sächsischen Gesellschaft der Wissenschaften zu Leipzig, philologisch-historische Klasse* 3 (1851): 327–72.

Janson, T. *Latin Prose Prefaces: Studies in Literary Conventions.* Studia Latina Stockholmiensia, 13. Stockholm, 1964.

Jeep, L. "Die jetzige Gestalt der Grammatik des Charisius." *RhM,* 3d ser., 51 (1896): 401–40.

———. "Priscianus: Beiträge zur Überlieferungsgeschichte der römischen Literatur II." *Philologus* 68 (1909): 1–51.

———. *Zur Geschichte der Lehre von den Redetheilen bei den lateinischen Grammatikern.* Leipzig, 1893.

Jeudy, C. "L'*Ars de nomine et verbo* de Phocas, manuscrits et commentaires médiévaux." *Viator* 5 (1974): 61–156.

———. "Les manuscrits de l'*Ars de verbo* d'Eutyches et le commentaire de Rémi d'Auxerre." In *Mélanges Labande: Études de civilisation médiévale (IXe–XIIe siècles):* 421–36. Poitiers, 1974.

———. "La tradition manuscrite du *De aspiratione* attribué au grammairien Phocas." In *Hommages à André Boutemy,* ed. G. Cambier: 197–215. Collection Latomus, 145. Brussels, 1976.

Jocelyn, H. D. "The Annotations of M. Valerius Probus." *CQ* 34 (1984): 464–72.

———. "The Annotations of M. Valerius Probus (II)." *CQ* 35 (1985): 149–61.

———. "The Annotations of M. Valerius Probus, III: Some Virgilian Scholia." *CQ* 35 (1985): 466–74.

Johnson, A. C. *An Economic Survey of Ancient Rome.* Vol. 2, *Roman Egypt to the Reign of Diocletian.* Baltimore, 1936.

Jones, A. H. M. *The Roman Economy: Studies in Ancient Economic and Administrative History.* Ed. P. A. Brunt. Oxford, 1974.

———. "The Social Background of the Struggle between Paganism and Christianity." In *The Conflict between Paganism and Christianity in the Fourth Century,* ed. A. Momigliano: 17–37. Oxford, 1963.

Jones, C. P. "The Reliability of Philostratus." In *Approaches to the Second Sophistic: Papers Presented to the 105th Annual Meeting of the American Philological Association,* ed. G. W. Bowersock: 12–16. University Park, Pa., 1974.

———. *The Roman World of Dio Chrysostom.* Cambridge, Mass., and London, 1978.

———. "Two Epigrams from Nicomedia and Its Region." *ZPE* 21 (1976): 189–91.

Jouai, L. A. A. *De Magistraat Ausonius*. Nijmegen, 1938.

Jullian, C. *Ausone et Bordeaux: Études sur les derniers temps de la Gaule romaine*. Paris and Bordeaux, 1893.

_____. *Histoire de la Gaule*. 8 vols. Paris, 1908–20.

Kajanto, I. *Supernomina: A Study in Latin Epigraphy*. Societas scientiarum Fennica, Commentationes humanarum litterarum, 40:1. Helsinki, 1967.

Kalinka, E. "Das Palladas-Epigramm in Ephesos." *WS* 24 (1902): 292–95.

Kaster, R. A. "The Date of *FD* III,1.206." *ZPE* 51 (1983): 131–32.

_____. "The Echo of a Chaste Obscenity: Verg. *E*.VI.26 and Symm. *Ep*.VI.22.1." *AJP* 104 (1983): 395–97.

_____. "The Grammarian Palladas and the Friend of God: Magic and Patronage in Late Roman Alexandria." *ANRW*, Teil 3 (to appear).

_____. "Macrobius and Servius: *Verecundia* and the Grammarian's Function." *HSCP* 84 (1980): 219–62.

_____. "Notes on 'Primary' and 'Secondary' Schools in Late Antiquity." *TAPA* 113 (1983): 323–46.

_____. "P. Panop. 14.25." *ZPE* 51 (1983): 132–34.

_____. "A Reconsideration of 'Gratian's School-Law.'" *Hermes* 112 (1984): 100–114.

_____. "The Salaries of Libanius." *Chiron* 13 (1983): 37–59.

_____. "A Schoolboy's Burlesque from Cyrene?" *Mnemosyne* 37 (1984): 457–58.

_____. "Servius and *idonei auctores*." *AJP* 99 (1978): 181–209.

_____. "*Vie et miracles de Sainte Thècle* II.38: The Son(s) of Alypius." *Anal. Boll.* 101 (1983): 301–3.

_____. "The 'Wandering Poet' and the Governor." *Phoenix* 37 (1983): 152–58.

de Kat Eliassen, M. H. "Five Papyri from the Oslo Collection." *SO* 49 (1973): 39–56.

Keenan, J. G. "The Names Flavius and Aurelius as Status Designations in Later Roman Egypt." *ZPE* 11 (1973): 33–63; 13 (1974): 283–304.

Keil, H. *Analecta grammatica*. Halle, 1848.

_____. *De grammaticis quibusdam Latinis infimae aetatis commentatio*. Erlangen, 1868.

Kelly, J. N. D. *Jerome: His Life, Writings, and Controversies*. New York, 1975.

Kennedy, G. A. *Greek Rhetoric under Christian Emperors*. Princeton, 1983.

Keydell, R. "Palladas und das Christentum." *BZ* 50 (1957): 1–3.

Keylor, W. R. *Academy and Community: The Foundation of the French Historical Profession*. Cambridge, Mass., 1975.

Kinsey, T. E. "A Poor Schoolmaster?" *Mnemosyne* 32 (1979): 381.

Kirsch, W. "*Cura vatum*: Staat und Literatur in der lateinischen Spätantike." *Philologus* 124 (1980): 274–89.

Klein, R. "Kaiser Julians Rhetoren- und Unterrichtsgesetz." *Röm. Quartal-schrift* 76 (1981): 73–94.

_____. *Symmachus: Eine tragische Gestalt des ausgehenden Heidentums.* Darm-stadt, 1971.

Klingner, F. *Römische Geisteswelt.* 4th ed. Munich, 1961.

Knibbe, D. "*Quandocumque quis trium virum rei publicae constituendae* . . . : Ein neuer Text aus Ephesos." *ZPE* 44 (1981): 1–10.

Kopaček, T. A. "Curial Displacements and Flight in Later Fourth Century Cappadocia." *Historia* 23 (1974): 319–42.

Kost, K., ed. *Musaios. Hero und Leander: Einleitung, Text, Übersetzung und Kommentar.* Abhandlungen zur Kunst-, Musik- und Literaturwissen-schaft, 88. Bonn, 1971.

Koster, W. J. W. "De accentibus excerpta ex Choerobosco, Aetherio, Philopono, aliis." *Mnemosyne* 59 (1931): 132–64.

Kröhnert, O. *Canonesne poetarum scriptorum artificium per antiquitatem fuerunt?* Königsberg, 1897.

Kuch, H. ΦΙΛΟΛΟΓΟΣ *(philologus): Untersuchung eines Wortes von seinem ersten Auftreten in der Tradition bis zur ersten überlieferten lexikalischen Festle-gung.* Schriften der Deutschen Akademie der Wissenschaften zu Berlin, Sektion für Altertumswissenschaft, 48. Berlin, 1965.

_____. "Φιλόλογος in der Ἐκκλησιαστικὴ ἱστορία des Sozomenos." *Klio* 43–45 (1965): 337–43.

Kuhn, E. *Die städtische und bürgerliche Verfassung des römischen Reichs bis auf die Zeiten Justinians.* Parts 1, 2. Leipzig, 1864–65.

Kuijper, D. "Varia Dracontiana." Diss. Amsterdam, 1958.

Lacombrade, C. "Palladas d'Alexandrie ou les vicissitudes d'un professeur-poète à la fin du IVᵉ siècle." *AFLT (Pallas),* 1953: 17–26.

_____. *Synésios de Cyrène, hellène et chrétien.* Paris, 1951.

Laistner, M. L. W. *Christianity and Pagan Culture in the Later Roman Empire.* Ithaca, N.Y., 1951.

Lallemand, J. *L'administration civile de l'Égypte de l'avènement de Dioclétien à la création du diocèse (284–382): Contribution à l'étude des rapports entre l'Égypte et l'empire à la fin du IIIᵉ et au IVᵉ siècle.* Académie royale des sciences et lettres et des beaux-arts de Belgique, Classe des lettres et des sciences morales et politiques, Mémoires, 8°, 57:2. Brussels, 1964.

Lammert, F. "Der Grammatiker Hieronymus des Mittelalters." *PhW* 32 (1912): 1139–40.

Langhammer, W. *Die rechtliche und soziale Stellung der Magistratus municipales und der Decuriones in der Übergangsphase der Städte von sich selbstverwaltenden Gemeinden zu Vollzugsorganen des spätantiken Zwangsstaates (2.–4. Jahrhundert der römischen Kaiserzeit).* Wiesbaden, 1973.

Latte, K., ed. *Hesychii Alexandrini Lexicon.* Vols. 1, 2. Copenhagen, 1953–66.

Lauffer, S., ed. *Diokletians Preisedikt*. Texte und Kommentare, 5. Berlin, 1971.

Laum, B. *Das alexandrinische Akzentuationssystem, unter Zugrundelegung der theoretischen Lehren der Grammatiker und mit Heranziehung der praktischen Verwendung in der Papyri*. Studien zur Geschichte und Kultur des Altertums, Ergänzungsband 4. Paderborn, 1928.

Law, V. *The Insular Latin Grammarians*. Studies in Celtic History, 3. Woodbridge, Suffolk, 1982.

Lebek, W. D. "Das Begräbnis des Karrierjuristen (Bean-Mitford, Journeys in Rough Cilicia 1964–1968 Nr. 49)." *ZPE* 21 (1976): 39–41.

_____. *Verba prisca: Die Anfänge des Archaisierens in der lateinischen Beredsamkeit und Geschichtsschreibung*. Göttingen, 1970.

Lebon, J. *Le monophysisme sévérien: Étude historique, littéraire et théologique sur la résistance monophysite au Concile de Chalcédoine jusqu'à la constitution de l'Église jacobite*. Louvain, 1909.

Lehmann, P. "Reste und Spuren antiker Gelehrsamkeit in mittelalterlichen Texten." *Philologus* 83 (1928): 193–203.

Lehnert, G. "Griechisch-römische Rhetorik: Bericht über das Schrifttum der Jahre 1915–1925." *Burs. Jahresb*. 285 (1944–55): 5–211.

Leitzmann, H. *Apollinaris von Laodicea und seine Schule* 1. Tübingen, 1904.

Lemerle, P. *Le premier humanisme byzantin: Notes et remarques sur enseignement et culture à Byzance des origines au Xe siècle*. Paris, 1971.

Leo, F. "Die Überlieferungsgeschichte der terenzischen Komödien und der Commentar des Donatus." *RhM*, 3d ser., 38 (1883): 317–47.

Lepelley, C. *Les cités de l'Afrique romaine au Bas-Empire*. 2 vols. Paris, 1979–81.

Levy, H. L. "*To hexês* in Homeric Scholia and Servius' *ordo*." *TAPA* 100 (1969): 237–54.

Lewis, N. "Exemption from Liturgy in Roman Egypt." In *Atti dell'XI Congresso internazionale di papirologia*: 508–41. Milan, 1965.

_____. "The Recipients of the Oxyrhynchus Siteresion." *CdE* 49 (1974): 158–62.

Liebeschuetz, J. H. W. G. *Antioch: City and Imperial Administration in the Later Roman Empire*. Oxford, 1972.

Lindsay, W. M. "Notes on the Text of Terence." *CQ* 19 (1925): 28–36.

_____. "The Primary MS. of Probus *Inst. Art*." *AJP* 48 (1927): 231–34.

_____, ed. *Nonii Marcelli De conpendiosa doctrina libri XX*. 3 vols. Leipzig, 1903.

Livadaras, N. A. "Συμβολὴ εἰς τὸν καθαρισμὸν τῆς πατρότητος ἀποσπασμάτων ἀρχαίων Ἑλλήνων γραμματικῶν." *Athena* 72 (1971): 160–201.

Livrea, E. "Pamprepio ed il P. Vindob. 29788A–C." *ZPE* 25 (1977): 121–34.

————. "Per una nuova edizione critica di Trifiodoro." *RFIC* 104 (1976): 443–52.

Lloyd, R. B. "Republican Authors in Servius and the Scholia Danielis." *HSCP* 65 (1961): 291–341.

Löfstedt, B. "Miscellanea grammatica." *RCCM* 23 (1981): 159–64.

————, ed. *Ars Ambrosiana: Commentum anonymum in Donati Partes maiores.* CC SL 133C. Turnhout, 1982.

Löfstedt, E. *Late Latin.* Instituttet for sammenlignende kulturforskning, ser. A, Forelesninger, 25. Oslo and Cambridge, Mass., 1959.

Lossau, M. Review of *Priscians Partitiones und ihre Stellung in der spätantiken Schule,* by M. Glück. *Gnomon* 43 (1971): 167–70.

Loyen, A. "Bourg-sur-Gironde et les villas d'Ausone." *REA* 62 (1960): 113–26.

————. *Sidoine Apollinaire et l'esprit précieux en Gaule aux derniers jours de l'empire.* Paris, 1943.

————, ed. *Sidoine Apollinaire.* 3 vols. Paris, 1960–70.

Lucas, C. "Notes on the *Curatores Rei Publicae* of Roman Africa." *JRS* 30 (1940): 56–74.

Luck, G. "Palladas, Christian or Pagan?" *HSCP* 63 (1958): 455–71.

Ludwich, A. *De Ioanne Philopono grammatico.* Königsberg, 1889.

Luscher, A. *De Prisciani studiis Graecis.* Breslau, 1911.

Maas, P. Review of *Pamprepios von Panopolis,* by H. Gerstinger. *Gnomon* 5 (1929): 250–52.

McCail, R. C. "The *Cycle* of Agathias: New Identifications Scrutinized." *JHS* 89 (1969): 87–96.

————. "The Earthquake of A.D. 551 and the Birth-Date of Agathias." *GRBS* 8 (1967): 241–47.

————. "P. Gr. Vindob. 29788C: Hexameter Encomium to an Un-Named Emperor." *JHS* 98 (1978): 38–63.

McCrum, M., and A. G. Woodhead, eds. *Select Documents of the Principates of the Flavian Emperors.* Cambridge, 1961.

MacMullen, R. *Enemies of the Roman Order: Treason, Unrest, and Alienation in the Empire.* Cambridge, Mass., 1966.

————. "A Note on *sermo humilis.*" *JTS* 17 (1966): 108–12.

————. "Provincial Languages in the Roman Empire." *AJP* 87 (1966): 1–17.

————. "Roman Bureaucratese." *Traditio* 18 (1962): 364–78.

————. *Roman Government's Response to Crisis A.D. 235–337.* New Haven, 1976.

————. "Social Mobility and the Theodosian Code." *JRS* 54 (1964): 49–53.

Maehler, H. "Menander Rhetor and Alexander Claudius in a Papyrus Letter." *GRBS* 15 (1974): 305–12.

Mahdi, M. "Alfarabi against Philoponus." *JNES* 26 (1967): 233–60.

Mai, A. *Classicorum auctorum e Vaticanis codicibus editorum tomus V.* Rome, 1833.

Majer-Leonhard, E. ΑΓΡΑΜΜΑΤΟΙ. Frankfurt a.M., 1913.

Malcus, B. "Die Proconsuln von Asien von Diokletian bis Theodosius II." In *Opuscula Atheniensia* 7: 91–160. Skrifter utgivna av Svenska institutet i Athen, 4°, 12. Stockholm, 1967.

Manitius, M. *Geschichte der christlich-lateinischen Poesie, bis Mitte des 8. Jahrhunderts.* Stuttgart, 1891.

_____. *Geschichte der lateinischen Literatur des Mittelalters.* 3 vols. Handbuch der Altertumswissenschaft, 9:2. Munich, 1911–31.

_____. *Handschriften antiker Autoren in mittelalterlichen Bibliothekscatalogen.* Zentralblatt für Bibliothekswesen, Beiheft 67. Leipzig, 1935.

Marinone, N. *Elio Donato, Macrobio e Servio, commentatori di Vergilio.* Vercelli, 1946.

_____. "Per la cronologia di Servio." *AAT* 104 (1970): 181–211.

Mariotti, I., ed., *Marii Victorini Ars grammatica.* Florence, 1967.

Mariotti, S. "Luxorius e Lisorius." *RFIC* 92 (1964): 162–72.

Markus, R. W. "Paganism, Christianity and the Latin Classics in the Fourth Century." In *Latin Literature of the Fourth Century,* ed. J. W. Binns: 1–21. London, 1974.

Marquardt, J. *Das Privatleben der Römer.* 2nd ed. Handbuch der römischen Alterthümer, 7. Leipzig, 1886.

Marrou, H.-I. *Christiana tempora: Mélanges d'histoire, d'archéologie, d'épigraphie et de patristique.* Paris, 1978.

_____. *Histoire de l'éducation dans l'antiquité.* 6th ed. Paris, 1965.

_____. ΜΟΥΣΙΚΟΣ ΑΝΗΡ: *Étude sur les scènes de la vie intellectuelle figurant sur les monuments funéraires romains.* 2d ed. Rome, 1964.

_____. *Patristique et humanisme: Mélanges.* Patristica Sorbonensia, 9. Paris, 1976.

_____. *Saint Augustin et la fin de la culture antique.* Paris, 1937.

_____. *Saint Augustin et la fin de la culture antique: Retractatio.* Bibliothèque des Écoles françaises d'Athènes et de Rome, 145 bis. Paris, 1949.

_____. "La vie intellectuelle au forum de Trajan et au forum d'Auguste." *MEFRA* 49 (1932): 93–110.

Marshall, P. K. "Servius." In *Texts and Transmission,* ed. L. D. Reynolds: 385–88. Oxford, 1983.

Martin, H. "Jean Philopon et la controverse trithéiste du VIe siècle." In *Studia patristica* 5:3, ed. F. L. Cross: 519–25. Texte und Untersuchungen, 80. Berlin, 1962.

Martin, J., and P. Petit. *Libanios. Discours.* Vol. 1, *Autobiographie (Discours I).* Paris, 1979.

Martin, V. "Relevé topographique des immeubles d'une métropole (*P. Gen.* inv. 108)." *Recherches de papyrologie* 2 (1962): 37–73.

Martindale, J. R. "Prosopography of the Later Roman Empire: *Addenda et corrigenda* to Volume I." *Historia* 23 (1974): 246–52.

Maspéro, J. "Études sur les papyrus d'Aphrodité, II–V." *BIFAO* 7 (1910): 97–152.

———. "Horapollon et la fin du paganisme égyptien." *BIFAO* 11 (1913): 163–95.

Massa Positano, L., ed. *Enea di Gaza. Epistole.* 2d ed. Studi greci, 19. Naples, 1962.

Mastandrea, P. *Massimo di Madauros: Agostino, Epistulae 16 e 17.* Saggi e materiali universitari, 3. Padua, 1985.

Mathisen, R. W. "Hilarius, Germanus, and Lupus: The Aristocratic Background of the Chelidonius Affair." *Phoenix* 33 (1979): 160–69.

———. "Petronius, Hilarius, and Valerianus: Prosopographical Notes on the Conversion of the Roman Aristocracy." *Historia* 30 (1981): 106–12.

———. "*PLRE* II: Suggested *addenda* and *corrigenda*." *Historia* 31 (1982): 364–86.

Matranga, P. "Praefatio altera." In *Spicilegium Romanum*, ed. A. Mai, 4, xvii–xxxv. Rome, 1840.

Matthews, J. Review of *PLRE* I, by A. H. M. Jones, J. R. Martindale, and J. Morris. *CR* 24 (1974): 97–106.

———. *Western Aristocracies and Imperial Court A.D. 364–425.* Oxford, 1975.

Mazzarino, A. "Appunti sul metodo II. Intorno all'età e all'opera di Foca." *Helikon* 13–14 (1973–74): 505–27.

van der Meer, F. *Saint Augustin pasteur d'âmes* 2. Paris, 1955.

Mellor, R. ΘΕΑ 'ΡΩΜΗ: *The Worship of the Goddess Roma in the Greek World.* Hypomnemata, 42. Göttingen, 1975.

Merkelbach, R. "Analphabetische Klostervorsteher in Konstantinopel und Chalkedon." *ZPE* 39 (1980): 291–94.

———. "Ephesische Parerga (6): Fragment eines Epigramms auf Damocharis." *ZPE* 24 (1977): 255.

Micciarelli Collesi, A. M. "Nuovi 'excerpta' dall' 'etimologico' di Orione." *Byzantion* 40 (1970): 517–42.

———. "Per la tradizione manoscritta degli excerpta di Orione." *Bolletino della Badia greca di Grottaferrata* 24 (1970): 107–13.

Millar, F. *The Emperor in the Roman World (31 B.C. – A.D. 337).* Ithaca, N.Y., 1977.

———. "Local Culture in the Roman Empire: Libyan, Punic and Latin in Roman Africa." *JRS* 58 (1968): 126–34.

Milne, J. G. "The 'Philippus' Coin at Rome." *JRS* 30 (1940): 11–15.

Miltner, F. "Bericht über die österreichischen Ausgrabungen in Ephesos im Jahre 1957." *AAWW* 95 (1958): 79–89.

_____. "Vorläufiger Bericht über die Ausgrabungen in Ephesos." *JÖAI* 44 (1959), Beiblatt: 315–80.

Miltner, F., and H. Miltner. "Epigraphische Nachlese in Ankara." *JÖAI* 30 (1937), Beiblatt: 9–66.

Minio-Paluello, L. "The Text of the *Categoriae*: The Latin Tradition." *CQ* 39 (1945): 63–74.

Minitti Colonna, M. "De Musaeo." *Vichiana* 5 (1976): 62–86.

Mitchell, S. "R.E.C.A.M. Notes and Studies No. 1: Inscriptions of Ancyra." *Anat. Stud.* 27 (1977): 63–103.

Mitsos, M. T. "Ἐκ τοῦ Ἐπιγραφικοῦ Μουσείου." *Arch. Delt.* 20A (1965): 79–83.

Mócsy, A. "Die Unkenntnis des Lebensalters im römischen Reich." *AAntHung.* 14 (1966): 387–421.

Moeller, C. "Un représentant de la christologie néochalcédonienne au début du VIᵉ siècle en Orient: Nephalius d'Alexandrie." *RHE* 40 (1944–45): 73–140.

Mohrmann, C. *Études sur le latin des chrétiens* 3. Storia e letteratura, Raccolta di studi e testi, 103. Rome, 1965.

Molajoli, B. *La basilica eufrasiana di Parenzo.* 2d ed. Padua, 1943.

Mombritius, B. *Sanctuarium seu Vitae sanctorum.* 2d ed. 2 vols. Paris, 1910.

Momigliano, A. *Secondo contributo alla storia degli studi classici.* Rome, 1960.

_____, ed. *The Conflict between Paganism and Christianity in the Fourth Century.* Oxford, 1963.

Moretti, L. "Nuovi epigrammi greci di Roma." *Epigraphica* 37 (1975): 68–83.

Morosi, R. "L'*officium* del prefetto del pretorio nel VI secolo." *Rom. Barb.* 2 (1977): 103–48.

Müller, B. A. "Zu Stephanos Byzantios." *Hermes* 53 (1918): 337–57.

Müller, N. *Die jüdische Katacombe am Monteverde zu Rom: Der älteste bisher bekannt gewordene jüdische Friedhof des Abendlandes.* Leipzig, 1912.

Müller, N., and N. A. Bees. *Die Inschriften der jüdischen Katacombe am Monteverde zu Rom.* Leipzig, 1919.

Murgia, C. E. "The Date of Tacitus' *Dialogus.*" *HSCP* 84 (1980): 99–125.

_____. *Prolegomena to Servius 5: The Manuscripts.* University of California Publications in Classical Studies, 11. Berkeley and Los Angeles, 1975.

Naldini, M. *Il cristianesimo in Egitto: Lettere private nei papiri dei secoli II–IV.* Studi e testi di papirologia, 3. Florence, 1968.

Naumann, R., and F. Naumann. *Der Rundbau in Aezani.* Istanbuler Mitteilungen, Beiheft 10. Tübingen, 1973.

Neesen, L. "Die Entwicklung der Leistungen und Amter (*munera et honores*) im römischen Kaiserreich des zweiten bis vierten Jahrhunderts." *Historia* 30 (1981): 203–35.

Negri, A. M. "De codice Bononiensi 797." *RFIC* 87 (1959): 260–77.

Nellen, D. *Viri litterati: Gebildetes Beamtentum und spätrömisches Reich im Westen zwischen 284 und 395 nach Christus.* Bochumer historische Studien, Alte Geschichte, 2. Bochum, 1977.

Neugebauer, O., and H. B. van Hoesen, eds. and trans. *Greek Horoscopes.* Memoirs of the American Philosophical Society, 48. Philadelphia, 1959.

Nickau, K., ed. *Ammonius. De adfinium vocabulorum differentia.* Leipzig, 1966.

Nilsson, M. P. *Die hellenistische Schule.* Munich, 1955.

Nissen, T. J. *Die byzantinische Anakreonten.* Sitzungsberichte der Bayerischen Akademie der Wissenschaften, philosophisch-historische Abteilung, Jahrgang 1940, Heft 3. Munich, 1940.

Nixon, C. E. V. "Latin Panegyric in the Tetrarchic and Constantinian Period." In *History and Historians in Late Antiquity*, ed. B. Croke and A. M. Emmett: 88–99. Oxford and Elmsford, N.Y., 1983.

Nock, A. D. *Essays on Religion and the Ancient World.* Ed. Z. Stewart. 2 vols. Oxford, 1972.

———. "Orphism or Popular Philosophy?" *HTR* 33 (1940): 301–15.

Norman, A. F. "Gradations in Later Municipal Society." *JRS* 48 (1958): 79–85.

———. *Libanius' Autobiography (Oration I).* London–New York–Toronto, 1965.

———, ed. *Libanius. Selected Works.* Vol. 1, *The Julianic Orations.* Cambridge, Mass., and London, 1969.

Noske, G. "Quaestiones Pseudacroneae." Diss. Munich, 1969.

Novak, D. "Constantine and the Senate: An Early Phase of the Christianization of the Roman Aristocracy." *Anc. Soc.* 10 (1979): 271–310.

Nuchelmans, G. R. F. M. *Studien über φιλόλογος, φιλολογία, und φιλολογεῖν.* Amsterdam, 1950.

Nutton, V. "*Archiatri* and the Medical Profession in Antiquity." *PBSR* 32 (1977): 191–226.

———. "Two Notes on Immunities: *Digest* 27,1,6,10 and 11." *JRS* 61 (1971): 52–63.

O'Brien, M. B. *Titles of Address in Christian Latin Epistolography to 543 A.D.* Catholic University of America, Patristic Studies, 21. Washington, D.C., 1930.

O'Donnell, J. J. "Augustine's Classical Readings." *Rec. Aug.* 15 (1980): 144–75.

———. "The Career of Virius Nicomachus Flavianus." *Phoenix* 32 (1978): 129–43.

———. *Cassiodorus.* Berkeley–Los Angeles–London, 1979.

Ogilvie, R. M. *The Library of Lactantius.* Oxford, 1978.

Oguse, A. "Le papyrus grec de Strasbourg 364 + 16." *Aegyptus* 37 (1957): 77–88.

Osann, F. G. *Beiträge zur griechischen und römischen Litteraturgeschichte.* 2 vols. Darmstadt, 1835–39.

Pagallo, G. F. "Per una edizione critica del *De hypotheticis syllogismis* di Boezio." *IMU* 1 (1958): 69–104.

Page, D. L., ed. *Select Papyri.* Vol. 3, *Literary Papyri, Poetry.* Cambridge, Mass., and London, 1950.

Papadopulos-Kerameus, A. "Zur Geschichte der griechischen Etymologica." *Journal des Ministeriums der Volksaufklärung* (St. Petersburg), Sept. 1898: 115–33.

Pape, W., and G. Benseler. *Wörterbuch der griechischen Eigennamen.* 3d ed. 2 vols. Braunschweig, 1911.

Parsons, P. J. "Petitions and a Letter: The Grammarian's Complaint, 253–60 A.D." In *Collectanea Papyrologica: Texts Published in Honor of H. C. Youtie,* ed. A. E. Hanson, 2:409–46. Papyrologische Texte und Abhandlungen, 20. Bonn, 1976.

————. "A School-Book from the Sayce Collection." *ZPE* 6 (1970): 133–49.

Parsons, T. "Professions." In *International Encyclopedia of the Social Sciences,* ed. D. L. Sills, 12:536–47. New York and London, 1968.

Paschoud, F. *Roma aeterna: Études sur le patriotisme romain dans l'Occident latin à l'époque des grandes invasions.* Institut suisse de Rome. Rome, 1967.

Pasquali, G. *Storia della tradizione e critica del testo.* 2d ed. Florence, 1971.

Passalacqua, M. *I codici di Prisciano.* Sussidi eruditi, 29. Rome, 1978.

Pastorino, A., ed. *Opere di Decimo Magno Ausonio.* Turin, 1971.

Patlagean, E. *Pauvreté économique et pauvreté sociale à Byzance, 4e–7e siècles.* École des hautes études en sciences sociales, civilisations et sociétés, 48. Paris and La Haye, 1977.

Paton, W. R. "Simonides, Fr. 68, and a Fragment of Lupercus." *CR* 26 (1912): 9.

Pedersen, F. S. *Late Roman Public Professionalism.* Odense University Classical Studies, 9. Odense, 1976.

Pennisi, G. *Poeti e intellettuali nella Roma antica e tardantica: Catullo, Fulgenzio.* Reggio di Calabria, 1979.

Pesenti, G. "*Anecdota Latina.*" *RFIC* 45 (1917): 70–98.

Petit, P. *Les étudiants de Libanius.* Paris, 1956.

————. *Libanius et la vie municipale à Antioche au IVe siècle après J.-C.* Paris, 1955.

Pfligersdorffer, G. "Zur Frage nach dem Verfasser der pseudo-augustinischen Categoriae decem." *WS* 65 (1950–51): 131–37.

Picard, G. C. "D'Autun à Mactar: Universités et maisons de jeunes dans l'empire romain d'Occident." *Archéologie* 30 (1969): 15–21.

Pizzani, U., ed. *Fabio Planciade Fulgenzio. Definizione di parole antiche.* Scriptores Latini, 9. Rome, 1968.

Preisigke, F. *Namenbuch*. Heidelberg, 1922.

Pueschel, A. *De Vibii Sequestris libelli geographici fontibus et compositione*. Halle, 1907.

Quacquarelli, A. *Scuola e cultura dei primi secoli cristiani*. Brescia, 1974.

Quicherat, J. "Fragments inédits de littérature latine." *BECh* 2 (1840–41): 115–47.

Rabe, H. "Lexicon Messanense de iota ascripto." *RhM*, 3d ser., 47 (1892): 404–13.

——. "Die Listen griechischer Profanenschriftsteller." *RhM*, 3d ser., 65 (1910): 339–44.

——. "Nachtrag zum Lexicon Messanense de iota ascripto." *RhM*, 3d ser., 50 (1895): 148–52.

Ramsay, W. M. *The Cities and Bishoprics of Phrygia*. Oxford, 1895.

——. "Inscriptions of Cilicia, Cappadocia, and Pontus." *JPh* 11 (1882): 142–60.

Raubitschek, A. E. "Greek Inscriptions." *Hesperia* 35 (1966): 241–51.

——. "Phaidros and His Roman Pupils." *Hesperia* 18 (1949): 96–103.

Reeve, M. D. "Aelius Donatus." In *Texts and Transmission*, ed. L. D. Reynolds: 153–56. Oxford, 1983.

——. "Terence." In *Texts and Transmission*, ed. L. D. Reynolds: 412–20. Oxford, 1983.

——. "The Textual Tradition of Donatus' Commentary on Terence." *CP* 74 (1979): 310–26.

Reeve, M. D., and R. H. Rouse. "New Light on the Transmission of Donatus' *Commentum Terentii*." *Viator* 9 (1978): 235–49.

Reitzenstein, R. *Geschichte der griechischen Etymologika: Ein Beitrag zur Geschichte der Philologie in Alexandria und Byzanz*. Leipzig, 1897.

Rémondon, R. "À propos du papyrus d'Antinoé no. 38." *CdE* 32 (1957): 130–46.

——. "L'Égypte et la suprême résistance au christianisme (Vᵉ–VIIᵉ siècles)." *BIFAO* 51 (1952): 63–78.

Reynolds, L. D., ed. *Texts and Transmission: A Survey of the Latin Classics*. Oxford, 1983.

Ribbeck, O. *Prolegomena critica ad P. Vergilii Maronis opera maiora*. Leipzig, 1866.

Richard, M. "ΑΠΟ ΦΩΝΗΣ." *Byzantion* 20 (1950): 191–222.

——, ed. *Iohannis Caesariensis presbyteri et grammatici opera quae supersunt*. With an appendix by M. Aubineau. *CC SG* 1. Turnhout, 1977.

Riché, P. *Education and Culture in the Barbarian West from the Sixth through the Eighth Century*. Trans. J. J. Contreni. Columbia, S.C., 1976.

——. "La survivance des écoles publiques en Gaule au Vᵉ siècle." *Le moyen âge* 12 (1957): 421–36.

Richtsteig, E. "Einige Daten aus dem Leben Kaiser Julians." *PhW* 51 (1931): 428–32.

Ringer, F. K. *The Decline of the German Mandarins: The German Academic Community 1890–1933.* Cambridge, Mass., 1969.

———. *Education and Society in Modern Europe.* Bloomington and London, 1979.

Ritschl, F. W. *Opuscula philologica.* 5 vols. Leipzig, 1866–79.

Robert, L. *Collection Fröhner.* Vol. 1, *Inscriptions grecques.* Paris, 1936.

———. "Documents d'Asie Mineure." *BCH* 102 (1978): 395–543.

———. "Épigraphie et antiquités grecques." *ACF* 73 (1973–74): 473–92.

———. "Hellenica." *RPh* 13 (1939): 97–217.

———. *Hellenica.* 13 vols. Paris, 1940–65.

———. *Noms indigènes dans l'Asie Mineure gréco-romaine.* Bibliothèque archéologique et historique de l'Institut français d'archéologie d'Istanbul, 13. Paris, 1963.

———. "Un oracle gravé à Oinoanda." *CRAI,* 1971: 597–619.

Robert, L., and J. Robert. *La Carie: Histoire et géographie historique avec le recueil des inscriptions antiques.* Vol. 2, *Le plateau de Tablai et ses environs.* Paris, 1954.

Robins, R. H. *Ancient and Medieval Grammatical Theory in Europe.* London, 1951.

Roger, M. *L'enseignement des lettres classiques d'Ausone à Alcuin.* Paris, 1905.

Rosenblum, M. *Luxorius: A Latin Poet among the Vandals.* Records of Civilization: Sources and Studies, 62. New York, 1961.

Roueché, C. "A New Inscription from Aphrodisias and the Title πατὴρ τῆς πόλεως." *GRBS* 20 (1979): 173–85.

Rouse, R. H. "Charisius." In *Texts and Transmission,* ed. L. D. Reynolds: 50–53. Oxford, 1983.

Sabbadini, R. "Il commento di Donato a Terenzio." *SIFC* 2 (1894): 1–134.

———. "L'ortografia latina di Foca." *RFIC* 28 (1900): 529–44.

———. "Gli scolii Donatiani ai due primi atti dell'*Eunuco* di Terenzio." *SIFC* 3 (1895): 249–363.

———. "Spogli ambrosiani latini." *SIFC* 11 (1903): 165–85.

Saffrey, H.-D. "Le chrétien Jean Philopon et la survivance de l'école d'Alexandrie au VIᵉ siècle." *REG* 67 (1954): 396–410.

Şahin, S. "Neue Inschriften von der bithynischen Halbinsel." *ZPE* 18 (1975): 27–48.

Salamon, M. "Priscianus und sein Schülerkreis in Konstantinopel." *Philologus* 123 (1979): 91–96.

Saller, R. P. *Personal Patronage under the Early Empire.* Cambridge, 1982.

Santoro, A. *Esegeti virgiliani antichi: Donato, Macrobio, Servio.* Bari, 1946.

Sathas, K. N. Μεσαιωνικὴ Βιβλιοθήκη 1. Venice, 1872.

Savage, J. J. H. "The Manuscripts of Servius' Commentary on Virgil." *HSCP* 45 (1934): 157–204.

Schemmel, F. "Der Sophist Libanios als Schüler und Lehrer." *NJA* 20 (1907): 52–69.

Schillinger-Häfele, U. "Vierter Nachtrag zu *CIL* XIII und zweiter Nachtrag zu Fr. Vollmer, Inscriptiones Bavariae Romanae." *BRGK* 58 (1977): 447–603.

Schindel, U. *Die lateinischen Figurenlehren des 5. bis 7. Jahrhunderts und Donats Vergilkommentar.* Abhandlungen der Akademie der Wissenschaften in Göttingen, philologisch-historische Klasse, 91. Göttingen, 1975.

Schmidt, P. L. "Die Anfänge der institutionellen Rhetorik im Rom. Zur Vorgeschichte der augusteischen Rhetorenschulen." In *Monumentum Chiloniense: Studien zur augusteischen Zeit. Kieler Festschrift für Erich Burck zum 70. Geburtstag,* ed. E. Lefèvre: 183–216. Amsterdam, 1975.

Schopf, E. *Die konsonantischen Fernwirkungen: Fern-Dissimilation, Fern-Assimilation und Metathesis.* Forschungen zur griechischen und lateinischen Grammatik, 5. Göttingen, 1919.

Schubert, O. G. *Quaestionum de anthologia codicis Salmasiani pars I: De Luxorio.* Weimar, 1875.

Scivoletto, N. "La 'filologia' di Valerio Probo." *GIF* 12 (1959): 97–124.

Seeck, O. *Die Briefe des Libanius, zeitlich geordnet.* Texte und Untersuchungen, n.s., 15:1–2. Leipzig, 1906.

———. *Geschichte des Untergangs der antiken Welt.* 6 vols. in 12. Berlin, 1897–1921.

———. *Regesten der Kaiser und Päpste für die Jahre 311 bis 476 n. Chr.* Stuttgart, 1919.

Seitz, K. "Die Schule von Gaza: Eine literargeschichtliche Untersuchung." Diss. Heidelberg, 1892.

Ševčenko, I. "A Late Antique Epigram and the So-Called Elder Magistrate from Aphrodisias." In *Synthronon: Art et archéologie de la fin de l'antiquité et du moyen âge. Recueil d'études par André Grabar et un groupe de ses disciples*: 29–41. Bibliothèque des Cahiers archéologiques, 2. Paris, 1968.

———. "A Shadow Outline of Virtue: The Classical Heritage of Greek Christian Literature (Second to Seventh Century)." In *Age of Spirituality: A Symposium,* ed. K. Weitzmann: 53–73. New York and Princeton, 1980.

Siebenborn, E. *Die Lehre von der Sprachrichtigkeit und ihrer Kriterien: Studien zur antiken normativen Grammatik.* Studien zur antiken Philosophie, 5. Amsterdam, 1976.

Sievers, G. R. *Das Leben des Libanius.* Berlin, 1868.

Sijpesteijn, P. J. *Liste des gymnasiarques des métropoles de l'Égypte romaine.* Amsterdam, 1967.

————. "Some Remarks on *P.Oxy.* XVIII 2186." *CdE* 51 (1976): 141–45.

Sijpesteijn, P. J., and K. A. Worp. "Chronological Notes." *ZPE* 26 (1977): 267–86.

Snell, B. *The Discovery of the Mind: The Greek Origins of European Thought.* Trans. T. G. Rosenmeyer. New York, 1960.

Solignac, A. "Les fragments du *De natura animae* de Julien Pomère (fin du Vᵉ siècle)." *BLE* 75 (1974): 41–60.

Speck, P. *Die kaiserliche Universität von Konstantinopel: Präzisierungen zur Frage des höheren Schulwesens in Byzanz im 9. und 10. Jahrhundert.* Byzantinisches Archiv, 14. Munich, 1974.

————. Review of *Le premier humanisme byzantin*, by P. Lemerle. *BZ* 67 (1974): 385–93.

Spyridon of the Laura, and S. Eustratiades. *Catalogue of the Greek Manuscripts in the Library of the Laura on Mount Athos.* Harvard Theological Studies, 12. Cambridge, Mass., 1925.

Stache, U. J., ed. *Flavius Cresconius Corippus. In laudem Iustini Augusti minoris: Ein Kommentar.* Berlin, 1976.

Stanton, G. R. "Sophists and Philosophers: Problems of Classification." *AJP* 94 (1973): 350–64.

Stein, A. "Zur Abfassungszeit der Grammatik des Romanus." *Hermes* 63 (1928): 480–81.

Stein, E. *Histoire du Bas-Empire.* Ed. J.-R. Palanque. 2 vols. Paris, 1949–59.

————. "Kleine Beiträge zur römischen Geschichte." *Hermes* 52 (1917): 558–83.

Steinmetz, P. *Untersuchungen zur römischen Literatur des zweiten Jahrhunderts nach Christi Geburt.* Palingenesia, 16. Wiesbaden, 1982.

Stevens, C. E. *Sidonius Apollinaris and His Age.* Oxford, 1933.

Stroheker, K. F. *Der senatorische Adel im spätantiken Gallien.* Tübingen, 1948.

Sundwall, J. *Abhandlungen zur Geschichte des ausgehenden Römertums.* Helsinki, 1919.

Syme, R. " 'Donatus' and the Like." *Historia* 27 (1978): 588–603.

————. *Roman Papers* 3. Ed. A. R. Birley. Oxford, 1984.

————. *Tacitus.* 2 vols. Oxford, 1958.

Szidat, J. "Die Usurpation des Eugenius." *Historia* 28 (1979): 487–508.

Szilágyi, J. "Prices and Wages in the Western Provinces of the Roman Empire." *AAntHung.* 11 (1963): 325–89.

Szövérffy, J. *Weltliche Dichtungen des lateinische Mittelalters: Ein Handbuch.* Vol. 1, *Von den Anfängen bis zum Ende der Karolingerzeit.* Berlin, 1970.

Tannery, P. *Mémoires scientifiques* 1. Toulouse, 1912.

Theodoridis, C. *Die Fragmente des Grammatikers Philoxenos.* Sammlung griechischer und lateinischer Grammatiker, 2. Berlin and New York, 1976.

―――. "Der Hymnograph Klemens terminus post quem für Choiroboskos." *BZ* 73 (1980): 341–45.

Thierfelder, A., ed. *Philogelos*. Munich, 1968.

Thilo, G. "Beiträge zur Kritik der Scholiasten des Vergilius." *RhM*, 3d ser., 15 (1860): 119–52.

Thilo, G., and H. Hagen, eds. *Servii grammatici qui feruntur in Vergilii carmina Commentarii*. 3 vols. Leipzig, 1881–1902.

Thomas, E. *Essai sur Servius et son commentaire sur Virgile*. Paris, 1880.

Thomas, J. D. Review of *The Oxyrhynchus Papyri*, vol. 40, ed. J. R. Rea. *CR* 26 (1976): 110–12.

Thompson, H. A. "Athenian Twilight: A.D. 267–600." *JRS* 49 (1959): 61–72.

Tolkiehn, J. "'Apex Donati' bei Dosith. c.61,2." *WKPh* 31 (1914): 558–59.

―――. *Cominianus. Beiträge zur römischen Literaturgeschichte*. Leipzig, 1910.

―――. "Der Grammatiker Papirianus." *PhW* 51 (1931): 1563–64.

―――. "Der Kirchenvater Hieronymus als Donaterklärer." *PhW* 32 (1912): 766–67.

―――. "Die Lebenszeit des Grammatikers Charisius." *PhW* 30 (1910): 1054–55.

―――. "Noch einmal der Donatkommentar des Hieronymus." *PhW* 33 (1913): 447–48.

―――, ed. *Dosithei Ars grammatica*. Leipzig, 1913.

Townend, G. B. "Some Problems of Punctuation in the Latin Hexameter." *CQ* 19 (1969): 330–44.

Tsirpanlis, C. N. "John Lydos on the Imperial Administration." *Byzantion* 44 (1974): 479–501.

Turner, E. G. *Greek Papyri: An Introduction*. Princeton, 1968.

Uhlig, G. "Noch einmal EIEN und zum ersten Male ΘΕΟΔΩΡΗΤΟΥ ΠΕΡΙ ΠΝΕΥΜΑΤΩΝ." *Neue Jahrbücher für Philologie und Pädogogik* 121 (1880): 789–97.

Usener, H. *Kleine Schriften*. 4 vols. Leipzig, 1912–13.

―――. "Vier lateinische Grammatiker." *RhM*, 3d ser., 23 (1868): 490–507.

Ussani, V., Jr. *Insomnia: Saggi di critica semantica*. Rome, 1955.

Valckenaer, L. K. *Ammonius. De differentia adfinium vocabulorum*. 2d ed. Leipzig, 1822.

Vérilhac, A.-M. "La déesse ΦΥΣΙΣ dans une épigramme de Salamine de Chypre." *BCH* 96 (1972): 427–33.

Verzone, P. "Città ellenistiche e romane dell'Asia minore: Anazarbus." *Palladio* 7 (1957): 9–25.

Vian, F., ed. *Quintus de Smyrne. La suite d'Homère*. 3 vols. Paris, 1963–69.

Vollmer, F. "Textkritisches zu Statius." *RhM*, 3d ser., 51 (1896): 27–44.

Walden, J. W. H. *The Universities of Ancient Greece.* New York, 1909.

Wallace-Hadrill, A. *Suetonius: The Scholar and His "Caesars."* New Haven and London, 1983.

Warren, M. "On Five New Manuscripts of the Commentary of Donatus to Terence." *HSCP* 17 (1906): 31–42.

Weaver, P. R. C. "Social Mobility in the Early Roman Empire: The Evidence of the Imperial Freedmen and Slaves." In *Studies in Ancient Society,* ed. M. I. Finley: 121–40. London, 1974.

Wegener, E. P. "Some Oxford Papyri." *JEA* 23 (1977): 204–25.

Weil, H. "Vers pour la fête d'un poète grec du sixième siècle." *Revue critique d'histoire et de littérature* 9 (1870): 401–4.

Weinreich, O. Review of *Epigrammata Bobiensia,* vol. 2, ed. F. Munari. *Gnomon* 31 (1959): 239–50.

Weis, G. *Studia Anastasia* 1. Miscellanea Byzantina Monacensia, 4. Institut für Byzantinistik und neugriechische Philologie der Universität. Munich, 1965.

Weiss, P. "Die Abkürzungen ΓΒ und ΓΓ auf den spätkaiserzeitlichen Münzen von Tarsos und Anazarbos." *Chiron* 9 (1979): 545–52.

Weissengruber, F. "Augustins Wertung von Grammatik und Rhetorik im Traktat Contra Cresconium." *Hermes* 105 (1977): 101–24.

Weisshäupl, R. "Ephesische Latrinen-Inschriften." *JÖAI* 5 (1902), Beiblatt: 33–34.

Weisz, G. *The Emergence of Modern Universities in France, 1863–1914.* Princeton, 1982.

Wendel, C. "Späne II." *Hermes* 72 (1937): 346–51.

Wes, M. A. *Das Ende des Kaisertums im Westen des römischen Reichs.* Trans. K. E. Mittring. The Hague, 1967.

Wessely, C. *Ein Altersindizium im Philogelos.* Sitzungsberichte der Akademie der Wissenschaften in Wien, philosophisch-historische Klasse, 149:5. Vienna, 1905.

Wessner, P. "Bericht über die Erscheinungen auf dem Gebiete der lateinischen Grammatiker mit Einschluss der Scholienliteratur und Glossographie für die Jahre 1908–1920." *Burs. Jahresb.* 188 (1921): 34–254.

———. "Lucan, Statius und Juvenal bei den römischen Grammatikern." *PhW* 49 (1929): 296–303, 328–35.

———. Review of *Esegesi virgiliana antica,* by G. Funaioli. *PhW* 51 (1931): 206–9.

———. Review of *Die Geschichte des Terenztextes im Altertum,* by G. Jachmann. *Gnomon* 3 (1927): 339–47.

———, ed. "Fabii Planciadis Fulgentii expositio sermonum antiquorum." *Commentationes philologae Ienenses,* 6:2 (1899): 63–144.

Westerink, L. G., ed. *Anonymous Prolegomena to Platonic Philosophy.* Amsterdam, 1962.

Whittaker, C. R. "Inflation and Economy in the Fourth Century A.D." In *Imperial Revenue, Expenditures and Monetary Policy in the Fourth Century A.D.: The Fifth Oxford Symposium on Coinage and Monetary History,* ed. C. E. King: 1–22. BAR International Series, 76. Oxford, 1980.

Wieland, W. "Die Ewigkeit der Welt: Der Streit zwischen Iohannes Philoponus und Simplicius." In *Die Gegenwart der Griechen im neueren Denken. Festschrift für H.-G. Gadamer zum 60. Geburtstag:* 291–316. Tübingen, 1960.

Wifstrand, A. *Von Kallimachos zu Nonnos: Metrisch-stilistische Untersuchungen zur späteren griechischen Epik und zu verwandten Gedichtgattungen.* Skrifter utgivna av Vetenskaps societeten i Lund, 16. Lund, 1933.

Wightman, E. A. "Peasants and Potentates: An Investigation of Social Structures and Land Tenure in Roman Gaul." *AJAH* 3 (1978): 97–128.

Wilcken, U. "Urkunden-Referat." *APF* 11 (1935): 284–317.

Williams, R. D. "Servius, Commentator and Guide." *PVS* 6 (1966–67): 50–56.

Wilmanns, A. "Der Katalog der lorscher Klosterbibliothek aus dem zehnten Jahrhundert." *RhM,* 3d ser., 23 (1868): 385–410.

Wilson, N. G. *Scholars of Byzantium.* Baltimore, 1983.

———, ed. *St. Basil on the Value of Greek Literature.* London, 1975.

Wipszycka, E. "Un lecteur qui ne sait pas écrire ou un chrétien qui ne veut pas se souiller? (P.Oxy. XXXIII 2673)." *ZPE* 50 (1983): 117–21.

Wolf, P. *Vom Schulwesen der Spätantike: Studien zu Libanius.* Baden-Baden, 1952.

Wolska, W. *La topographie chrétienne de Cosmas Indicopleustès: Théologie et science au VIe siècle.* Bibliothèque byzantine, 3. Paris, 1962.

Woodward, A. M. "The Neocorate at Aegeae and Anazarbus in Cilicia." *NC* 3 (1963): 5–10.

Wormald, P. Review of *Western Aristocracies and Imperial Court A.D. 364–425,* by J. Matthews. *JRS* 66 (1976): 217–26.

Wouters, A. *The Grammatical Papyri from Graeco-Roman Egypt: Contributions to the Study of the "Ars grammatica" in Antiquity.* Brussels, 1979.

———. "P.Ant. 2.67: A Compendium of Herodian's ΠΕΡΙ ΚΑΘΟΛΙΚΗΣ ΠΡΟΣΩΔΙΑΣ, Book V." *OLP* 6–7 (1975–76): 601–13.

Youtie, H. C. "ΑΓΡΑΜΜΑΤΟΣ: An Aspect of Greek Society in Egypt." *HSCP* 75 (1971): 161–76.

———. "Because They Do Not Know Letters." *ZPE* 19 (1975): 101–8.

———. "Βραδέως γράφων: Between Literacy and Illiteracy." *GRBS* 12 (1971): 239–61.

———. "Pétaus, fils de Pétaus, ou le scribe qui ne savait pas écrire." *CdE* 41 (1966): 127–43.

———. "P. Gen. inv. 108 = SB VIII 9902." *ZPE* 7 (1971): 170–71.

———. *Scriptiunculae.* 2 vols. Amsterdam, 1973–75.

———. "ΥΠΟΓΡΑΦΕΥΣ: The Social Impact of Illiteracy in Graeco-Roman Egypt." *ZPE* 17 (1975): 201–21.

Zalateo, G. "Un nuovo significato della parola δοκιμασία." *Aegyptus* 37 (1957): 32–40.

Zetzel, J. E. G. *Latin Textual Criticism in Antiquity.* New York, 1981.

———. "Statilius Maximus and Ciceronian Studies in the Antonine Age." *BICS* 21 (1974): 107–23.

Ziegler, J. *Zur religiösen Haltung der Gegenkaiser im 4. Jahrhundert n. Chr.* Frankfurter Althistorische Studien, 4. Kallmünz, 1970.

Ziegler, R. "Münzen Kilikiens als Zeugnis kaiserlicher Getreidespenden." *JNG* 27 (1977): 29–67.

Zilliacus, H. "Anecdota Bodleiana." *JJP* 9–10 (1955–56): 127–34.

———. "Anredeformen (Nachträge zum RLAC)." *JAC* 7 (1964): 167–82.

———. *Untersuchungen zu den abstrakten Anredeformen und Höflichkeitstiteln im Griechischen.* Societas scientiarum Fennica, Commentationes humanarum litterarum, 15:3. Helsinki, 1949.

Zintzen, C., ed. *Damascii Vitae Isidori reliquiae.* Bibliotheca Graeca et Latina suppletiora, 1. Hildesheim, 1967.

INDEX

This index refers only to names and subjects found in Part I and the Appendixes. It does not cover Part II, but the individuals registered in the prosopography are here indicated by the numbers placed in parentheses after their names.

Designer: Janet Wood
Compositor: Eisenbrauns
Text: 10/12 Palatino
Display: Palatino
Printer: Braun-Brumfield, Inc.
Binder: Braun-Brumfield, Inc.